Cooking Light.

ANNUAL
RECIPES 2010

Oxmoor
House.

A Year at *Cooking Light*

At *Cooking Light,* our goal is, and always has been, to make healthy food taste great. This year, we tested thousands of recipes in order to bring you the best of the best. We also highlighted the latest research to help you make smart nutrition choices, featured the work and recipes of artisanal food producers and innovative restaurant chefs around the country to provide inspiration in your kitchen, and brought you more quick-and-easy recipes to better meet the needs of your busy lives.

◄ Mushroom Polenta Canapés (page 250) is one of the many recipes in the *Cooking Light* Join-the-Party Planning Kit that elevates a good party to stellar status.

▼ Our make-ahead strategies (page 249) ensure your party won't start without you.

Here are some of the year's highlights:

- In the January/February issue, we began the first of our **"Nutrition Essentials" series** (page 24), which looks at fad-free strategies to help you eat well in every sense of the word. We employed a team of experts—scientists, dietitians, chefs, and other culinary experts—to demystify the essentials of smart nutrition and turn research into easy, everyday food choices.
- The magazine's popular **"Cooking Class" series** focused this year on classic dishes, from casseroles (page 29) to basic mac 'n' cheese (page 272). Our Test Kitchens staff delight in preserving the delicious essence of traditional comfort-food recipes while converting them into modern, lighter dishes.
- Our annual **"Summer Cookbook"** (page 135) in the June issue got a small facelift when we brought you the season's finest offerings in a month-by-month guide. By choosing the top-rated recipes by month, you can experience the full flavors of summer produce as each fruit and vegetable is at its peak.
- In August, we shared **a taste of Greece** with you (page 192). The bright flavors of this Mediterranean cuisine lend themselves to entertaining. We offer a menu with an assortment of Greek-inspired small-plate dishes, including salads, skewers, spreads, and finger foods, that are especially fun and fitting in the hotter days of summer.
- The *Cooking Light* **Join-the-Party Planning Kit** (page 249) provides you with a variety of no-stress, make-ahead menus so you won't have to spend the whole night at the stove while your guests have all the fun.
- We began the holidays with our traditional, reader-favorite **"Holiday Cookbook"** (page 323) in November. Here, we include a variety of appetizers and drinks, entrées, sides, desserts, and tasty extras to ensure that you have all you need to make your holiday celebrations just right—from Thanksgiving to New Year's.

On behalf of all my colleagues at *Cooking Light*, I hope you enjoy this new edition of *Cooking Light Annual Recipes*. It's the happy result of a busy year in the kitchen!

Scott Mowbray
Editor

◀ This no-cook salsa highlights some of summer's freshest flavors (page 139).

▼ Experience the flavors of Greece with our menu of small-plate dishes (page 192).

Our Favorite Recipes

Not all recipes are created equal. At *Cooking Light,* only those that have passed muster with our Test Kitchens staff and food editors—not an easy crowd to please—make it onto the pages of our magazine. We rigorously test each recipe, often two or three times, to ensure that it's healthy, reliable, and tastes as good as it possibly can. So which of our recipes are our favorites? They're the dishes that are the most memorable. They're the ones readers keep calling and writing about, the ones our staff whip up for their own families and friends.

◀ **Mango-Agave Sorbet** *(page 75)*
This Mexican dessert is sweetened with agave nectar, which is found in the desert plant that is used to make tequila. Agave nectar has a low glycemic index, so it's better for people with blood sugar issues.

▼ **Seared Mahimahi with Edamame Succotash** *(page 27)*
At last, a recipe that demonstrates that proper portion size can be totally satisfying. Four-ounce portions of mahimahi are simply seasoned and quickly seared, then topped with a healthful mix of edamame, corn, and bell pepper.

◄ Stilton Burgers
(page 266)
The burger mixture gets great flavor and juiciness from just four simple ingredients. Tangy and pungent Stilton makes a tasty topping, and its strong flavor means you can use just a small amount, cutting down on saturated fat. You'll never go back to plain Cheddar.

▼ Lobster Américaine
(page 320)
Though the name means "American-style lobster," this recipe is actually a classic French preparation with a rich tomato-cream sauce. Lobster is usually a special-occasion splurge; it's well worth the cost and effort.

Our Favorite Recipes

▶ **Gingered Blueberry Shortcake** *(page 137)*
Blueberries signal the arrival of summer's sweetest days, and this dessert highlights them perfectly. Crumbly shortbread and homemade whipped cream elevate a simple berry to a memorably indulgent treat.

▼ **Pan-Fried Chicken** *(page 158)*
You thought fried chicken was off-limits in a healthy diet, didn't you? Frying in a thin layer of peanut oil yields the same crunchy crust and perfect juiciness as deep-frying with much less fat. Our breading, flavored with ginger, cinnamon, nutmeg, and paprika, is intriguingly different.

Fire-Seared Antipasto Platter (*page 143*)
Virtually anything can go on a platter like this. Throw whatever vegetables you've got on the grill, and pair with cheese, cured meats, condiments like capers and olives—the possibilities are endless.

Phyllo Pizza with Feta, Basil, and Tomatoes
(page 180)
Crispy, flaky layers of phyllo interspersed with cheese make the crust unique, and the fresh tomato and basil topping gives this pizza fresh summer flavor. It's a great way to show off your own garden or local farmers' market.

Our Favorite Recipes

◀ **Vanilla Bean Shortbread**
(page 111)
We swapped out half the butter for healthy-fat-rich canola oil, which makes these delicate cookies crispier without sacrificing their buttery richness.

▼ **Chicken with Dark Beer**
(page 30)
Similar to southern France's coq au vin, this northern French recipe simmers chicken in deeply flavored beer for tenderness and nice caramel flavor. Add in juniper berries and a little bit of gin for their fresh taste, plus yogurt for creamy texture, and you've got a recipe for a warming cold-weather meal.

Our Favorite Recipes

▶ **Roasted Banana Bars with Browned Butter–Pecan Frosting** *(page 46)* Roasted bananas, which add caramelized notes to these light-and-fluffy bars, pair well with a topping of tangy cream cheese icing and crunchy chopped pecans.

▼ **Ranch Steak Bruschetta Salad** *(page 46)* This recipe wowed us with its Southwestern flavor. A unique rub of cumin, chile powder, and coffee makes the steak stand out, while a simple horseradish-ranch dressing creates a kick.

Grilled Shrimp, Mango, and Avocado
(page 138)
Grilled shrimp skewers are pretty commonplace, but this dish features grilled mango and avocado wedges for something extra-special. The balance of creamy avocado, sweet-and-sour mango, and savory shrimp is mirrored by the Vietnamese-style dipping sauce, with its combination of sugar, tart lime juice, and pungent fish sauce.

Soy-Citrus Scallops with Soba Noodles *(page 101)* With quick-seared scallops over hearty soba noodles, this 20-minute meal is ideal for any night. The sweet-salty-sour-spicy marinade/sauce is what makes it a staff favorite.

Our Favorite Recipes

◄ **Charred Vegetable Salad** *(page 268)*
The naked flame of a grill does magical things to food that no other cooking method can quite recreate. A beautiful assortment of late-summer vegetables gains smoky, caramelized flavor and tenderness on the grill, so all that's needed is a supereasy herb vinaigrette to dress them.

▼ **Rainier Cherry Crumble** *(page 187)*
Rainier cherries are so sweet on their own that the filling for this crumble needs no extra sugar. The crunchy, nutty topping and warm, gooey filling blend for a delicious comforting dessert.

Aioli *(page 92)*

If you've never had homemade mayonnaise before, this aioli will be a revelation. Making it is nowhere near as hard as you think, and its wonderful garlicky flavor is miles above the jarred stuff. Prepare a batch, and try it in sandwiches, dips, dressings, sauces—you name it.

Our Favorite Recipes

◄ **Barley Risotto with Eggplant and Tomatoes** (*page 257*)
Trading Arborio rice for whole-grain barley not only boosts nutritional power but also keeps the familiar creamy, chewy texture of risotto. By changing up the vegetables and cheese, you can completely transform it for the season—try asparagus and an herbed chèvre in spring or butternut squash and blue cheese in fall.

▼ **Sautéed Sole with Browned Butter and Capers** (*page 198*)
As elegant as any restaurant offering, this recipe is unbelievably simple: Sauté the thin, flaky fillets for three minutes, then make a three-minute pan sauce that's rich with butter and bright with capers and lemon. Splurge on sole for a special meal, or substitute flounder, trout, or any flaky white fish for an everyday dinner.

Our Favorite Recipes

▶ **Chipotle Peanut Brittle** *(page 111)*
This candy balances smoky and spicy chipotle chile powder and salty peanuts with its sweetness to create an intriguing and satisfying snack. Break up a batch into individual servings to take to work for a midday recharge, or serve as an hors d'oeuvre at your next party.

Curried Beef Short Ribs *(page 67)*
Here's an international twist on a slow-cooker favorite: short ribs. Finished with lime juice and a little zest that lends a bright note, this rich, spicy dish pairs well with bold, fruit-forward, peppery red wines. Serve the saucy ribs over basmati rice with a side of bok choy for a hearty meal.

Black Bean Soup *(page 70)*
Fresh herbs, fiery serrano chile pepper, and aromatic cumin make this soup anything but boring. It cooks a long time to achieve its deep flavor, but thanks to the power of the slow cooker, you can spend five minutes assembling it in the morning and come home after work to a steaming bowl of thick, hearty soup.

Halibut with Citrus-Fennel Relish
(page 98)
Everything in this dish is so good for you—omega 3-rich halibut, vitamin C-rich citrus, antioxidant-rich fennel, and healthy fat-rich olive oil—and it tastes good, too. The eight-minute preparation yields an entrée with a great balance of sweetness, crunchy texture, and tender fish that has just 295 calories per serving.

Chicken Breasts Stuffed with Goat Cheese, Caramelized Spring Onions, and Thyme *(page 122)*
The delicate flavor of spring onions is ideal here, but if they're out of season you can use a sweet onion like a Vidalia to get the same effect. The creamy, sweet stuffing turns an otherwise plain chicken breast into something extra-special. You can also use this preparation with boneless pork chops.

Seared Figs and White Peaches with Balsamic Reduction *(page 144)*
A restaurant-quality dessert that will impress absolutely anyone, this one requires only eight ingredients and less than 10 minutes to make. Caramelizing the natural sugars in the fruit gives them rich flavor, an intense balsamic vinegar pan sauce mixed with creamy and tangy crème fraîche sets off the sweetness, and a sprinkle of pepper adds an unexpected surprise.

Bacon Mac *(page 273)*
A Cooking Class column revealed the secrets to light mac 'n' cheese that tastes as rich and indulgent as the original: a smooth slurry of milk and flour to thicken, and careful temperature control so the cheese melts just right. This creamy dish features lots of Cheddar and bacon but still comes in under 400 calories per serving.

Cinnamon Rolls *(page 307)*
The enormous cinnamon rolls at Chicago dining institution Ann Sather are legendary, though a bit out of control in the nutrition department. We captured their flavor but lightened them a bit by cutting down on the butter and using fat-free milk in place of whole.

Bucatini with Mushrooms *(page 291)*
A large assortment of mushrooms, including luxurious dried porcinis, is the key to the huge earthy flavor of this simple pasta dish. It's meatless, but you'd never know it with all the savory flavor of mushrooms, Parmesan, and truffle oil, plus the luscious texture of the sauce from a generous splash of cream.

Turnip-Parsnip Gratin *(page 344)*
The familiar potato has the ideal texture for gratins but doesn't offer much flavor of its own. Turnip and parsnip, however, provide sweet notes that match perfectly with the assertive Gruyère. The too-often-overlooked root veggies elevate a humble side to something elegant.

contents

©2009 by Oxmoor House, Inc.
Book Division of Southern Progress Corporation
P.O. Box 2262, Birmingham, Alabama 35201-2262

ISBN-13: 978-0-8487-3286-8
ISBN-10: 0-8487-3286-3

Printed in the United States of America
First printing 2009

Be sure to check with your health-care provider before making any changes in your diet.

Oxmoor House, Inc.
VP, Publishing Director: Jim Childs
Editorial Director: Susan Payne Dobbs
Brand Manager: Allison Long Lowery
Managing Editor: L. Amanda Owens

Cooking Light. Annual Recipes 2009
Editor: Rachel Quinlivan, R.D.
Photography Director: Jim Bathie
Senior Production Manager: Greg A. Amason

Contributors:
Designer: Carol Damsky
Copy Editor: Jacqueline B. Giovanelli
Proofreader: Norma Butterworth-McKittrick
Indexer: Mary Ann Laurens
Produce & Organics Buying Guide Editor: Georgia Dodge
Interns: Christine Taylor, Angela Valente

To order additional publications, call 1-800-765-6400.

For more books to enrich your life, visit **oxmoorhouse.com**

To search, savor, and share thousands of recipes, visit **myrecipes.com**

Cover: *Spaghetti with Tomato Sauce (page 72)*
Page 1: *Seared Figs and White Peaches with Balsamic Reduction (page 144)*

Cooking Light®

Editor: Scott Mowbray
Executive Editor: Billy R. Sims
Managing Editor: Maelynn Cheung
Deputy Editor: Phillip Rhodes
Senior Food Editor: Ann Taylor Pittman
Projects Editor: Mary Simpson Creel, M.S., R.D.
Associate Food Editors: Timothy Q. Cebula; Kathy Kitchens Downie, R.D.; Julianna Grimes
Associate Editors: Cindy Hatcher, Brandy Rushing
Test Kitchens Director: Vanessa T. Pruett
Assistant Test Kitchens Director: Tiffany Vickers
Senior Food Stylist: Kellie Gerber Kelley
Food Stylist: M. Kathleen Kanen
Test Kitchens Professionals: Mary Drennen Ankar, SaBrina Bone, Deb Wise
Art Director: Maya Metz Logue
Associate Art Directors: Fernande Bondarenko, J. Shay McNamee
Senior Designer: Brigette Mayer
Senior Photographer: Randy Mayor
Senior Photo Stylist: Cindy Barr
Photo Stylists: Jan Gautro, Leigh Ann Ross
Copy Chief: Maria Parker Hopkins
Assistant Copy Chief: Susan Roberts
Copy Editor: Johannah Gilman Paiva
Copy Researcher: Michelle Gibson Daniels
Production Manager: Liz Rhoades
Production Editor: Hazel R. Eddins
CookingLight.com Editor: Kim Cross
Administrative Coordinator: Carol D. Johnson
Editorial Assistant: Jason Horn
Intern: Cassandra Blohowiak

Weeknight Meal Makeovers

Our nutritious new versions of favorite boxed, take-out, and fast foods come in tasty, quick, family-friendly packages.

ANSWERING THE "WHAT'S FOR DINNER" QUESTION is something most of us face every night. For those of us who want to watch what we're eating, there are some healthful choices in take-out, as well as boxed and prepared meals from the market.

Yet an even more appealing selection is cooking these favorites yourself. That lets you balance time-saving convenience with fabulous taste and unbeatable nutrition.

Here we offer realistic weeknight options that come together fast. Ingredient lists are short, and the menus are ready in an hour or less (indeed, several are done in about 35 minutes). And when you start with high-quality ingredients, great flavor follows.

MEAL MAKEOVER MENU 1

[Time: 55 minutes]

Smothered Steak Burgers

Shoestring Fries with Garlicky Dijon Mayo

Beer or iced tea

Steak Burger

Fast-food version:
Serving size: 1 burger
Calories: 720
Fat: 42 grams
Sodium: 1,570 milligrams

Our version:
Serving size: 1 burger
Calories: 398
Fat: 12.9 grams
Sodium: 747 milligrams

QUICK & EASY

Smothered Steak Burgers

(pictured on page 210)

Sautéed mushrooms, steak sauce, and Worcestershire sauce create robust flavors in this knife-and-fork burger.

Cooking spray
2   tablespoons finely chopped shallots
1   garlic clove, minced
1   (8-ounce) package presliced button mushrooms
½   cup fat-free, less-sodium beef broth
1   tablespoon low-sodium steak sauce (such as Angostura)
1   teaspoon cornstarch
½   teaspoon freshly ground black pepper, divided
2   tablespoons ketchup
1   tablespoon Worcestershire sauce
1   pound ground sirloin
¼   teaspoon salt
4   green leaf lettuce leaves
4   (½-inch-thick) tomato slices
4   (2-ounce) Kaiser rolls, toasted

1 Heat a large nonstick skillet over medium heat. Coat pan with cooking spray. Add shallots and garlic to pan; cook 1 minute or until tender, stirring frequently. Increase heat to medium-high. Add mushrooms to pan; cook 10 minutes or until moisture evaporates, stirring occasionally. Combine broth, steak sauce, and cornstarch, stirring with a whisk. Add broth mixture to pan; bring to a boil. Cook 1 minute or until thickened, stirring constantly. Stir in ¼ teaspoon pepper. Remove mushroom mixture from pan; cover and keep warm. Wipe pan with paper towels.

2 Combine remaining ¼ teaspoon pepper, ketchup, and Worcestershire sauce in a large bowl, stirring with a whisk. Add beef to bowl; toss gently to combine. Shape beef mixture into 4 (½-inch-thick) patties; sprinkle evenly with salt.

3 Heat pan over medium-high heat. Coat pan with cooking spray. Add patties to pan; cook 4 minutes. Turn and cook 3 minutes or until desired degree of doneness. Place 1 lettuce leaf and 1 tomato slice on bottom half of each roll. Top each serving with 1 patty, about ¼ cup mushroom mixture, and top half of roll. Yield: 4 servings (serving size: 1 burger).

CALORIES 398; FAT 12.9g (sat 4.4g, mono 5.1g, poly 1.4g); PROTEIN 30.7g; CARB 38.4g; FIBER 1.9g; CHOL 41mg; IRON 4.9mg; SODIUM 747mg; CALC 79mg

French Fries

Fast-food version:
Serving size: 1 small order plus
    2 ketchup packets
Calories: 260
Fat: 11 grams
Sodium: 380 milligrams

Our version:
Serving size: 1 cup fries plus
    1 tablespoon sauce
Calories: 180
Fat: 7 grams
Sodium: 233 milligrams

Shoestring Fries with Garlicky Dijon Mayo

(pictured on page 210)

Cutting potatoes into thin strips, soaking them in hot water, and cooking at high heat makes for a crisp texture without much fat. Instead of ketchup, we enjoyed dipping the fries in this tangy sauce, a riff on aioli.

1 teaspoon sherry vinegar
1 large garlic clove, minced
3 tablespoons canola mayonnaise
1½ teaspoons whole-grain Dijon
    mustard
1 teaspoon chopped fresh parsley
1¼ pounds baking potatoes
1 tablespoon olive oil
¼ teaspoon kosher salt
    Cooking spray

❶ Preheat oven to 450°.
❷ Combine vinegar and garlic in a small bowl; let stand 5 minutes. Stir in mayonnaise, mustard, and parsley.
❸ Cut potatoes lengthwise into ¼-inch-thick slices; stack slices and cut lengthwise into ¼-inch-thick strips. Place in a large bowl; cover with hot water. Let stand 10 minutes. Drain potatoes; pat dry with paper towels. Combine potatoes, oil, and salt in a large bowl; toss gently to coat. Arrange potatoes in a single layer on a baking sheet coated with cooking spray. Bake at 450° for 35 minutes; carefully turn over and bake an additional 10 minutes or until lightly browned. Serve with sauce. Yield: 4 servings (serving size: about 1 cup fries and about 1 tablespoon sauce).

CALORIES 180; FAT 7g (sat 0.5g, mono 4.3g, poly 1.5g); PROTEIN 3.2g; CARB 26.2g; FIBER 1.9g; CHOL 0mg; IRON 1.3mg; SODIUM 233mg; CALC 21mg

---

MEAL MAKEOVER MENU 2

[Time: 30 minutes]

*Romaine salad
with shredded carrots*

Cajun Red Beans and Rice

Garlic breadsticks

Red Beans and Rice

Boxed version:
Serving size: 1½ cups (prepared with
    1.2 ounces chicken andouille sausage)
Calories: 429
Fat: 2.4 grams
Sodium: 2,562 milligrams

Our version:
Serving size: ¾ cup bean mixture
    plus ¾ cup rice
Calories: 336
Fat: 8.4 grams
Sodium: 698 milligrams

QUICK & EASY • MAKE AHEAD
Cajun Red Beans and Rice

Prechopped vegetables and canned beans keep this version of red beans and rice simple yet satisfying. Because this recipe begins with oil-sautéed aromatics, it contains more grams of fat per serving than its boxed counterpart—but the calories and sodium are significantly lower, and the taste is terrific.

2 tablespoons olive oil
2 (3-ounce) chicken andouille
    sausage links, chopped
1 (8-ounce) container prechopped
    onion, bell pepper, and celery mix
1½ teaspoons salt-free Cajun seasoning
¾ teaspoon salt
½ teaspoon dried oregano
2 garlic cloves, minced
1 (15-ounce) can red beans, rinsed
    and drained
¼ cup water
1 (14.5-ounce) can no-salt-added
    diced tomatoes, undrained
¼ teaspoon freshly ground black
    pepper
4 cups hot cooked long-grain rice

❶ Heat oil in a large nonstick skillet over medium-high heat. Add sausage and onion mix to pan; sauté 4 minutes. Add Cajun seasoning and next 3 ingredients to pan; cook 1 minute, stirring constantly. Partially mash beans with a fork. Add beans, ¼ cup water, and tomatoes to pan; bring to a boil. Reduce heat, and simmer 10 minutes or until thickened. Remove from heat; stir in pepper. Serve over rice. Yield: 5 servings (serving size: about ¾ cup bean mixture and about ¾ cup rice).

CALORIES 336; FAT 8.4g (sat 1.8g, mono 5.1g, poly 1.3g); PROTEIN 12.7g; CARB 51.6g; FIBER 5.9g; CHOL 36mg; IRON 3.3mg; SODIUM 698mg; CALC 90mg

[Time: 35 minutes]

*Mixed greens salad
with toasted pine nuts*

Double-Mushroom Pizza

Red grapes

Mushroom Pizza

Take-out version:
Serving size: 2 slices (thin crust)
Calories: 408
Fat: 16.2 grams
Sodium: 1,142 milligrams

Our version:
Serving size: 2 slices
Calories: 365
Fat: 12.3 grams
Sodium: 523 milligrams

QUICK & EASY
Double-Mushroom Pizza

  1 (10-ounce) whole wheat Italian
     thin pizza crust (such as Boboli)
     Cooking spray
1½ teaspoons olive oil, divided
  1 (8-ounce) package presliced
     cremini or button mushrooms
  1 (6-ounce) package presliced
     portobello mushrooms, chopped
1½ teaspoons chopped fresh thyme
  3 garlic cloves, minced
  ¾ cup 2% reduced-fat milk
  2 tablespoons all-purpose flour
  3 tablespoons grated Asiago cheese
  ¼ teaspoon black pepper
  1 large plum tomato, thinly sliced
  1 cup (4 ounces) shredded part-skim
     mozzarella cheese

❶ Preheat oven to 375°.
❷ Place pizza crust on a baking sheet
coated with cooking spray. Bake at 375°
for 5 minutes. Remove crust from oven
(do not turn oven off); set crust aside.

❸ Heat a large nonstick skillet over
medium-high heat. Coat pan with cooking spray; add 1 teaspoon oil to pan,
swirling to coat. Add mushrooms to pan;
sauté 8 minutes or until moisture evaporates. Stir in thyme; spoon mushroom
mixture into a bowl.
❹ Add remaining ½ teaspoon oil to pan,
and reduce heat to medium. Add garlic
to pan; cook 45 seconds. Combine milk
and flour in a small bowl, stirring well
with a whisk. Add milk mixture to pan;
cook 2 minutes or until thick, stirring
constantly. Add Asiago and pepper,
stirring until cheese melts.
❺ Spread sauce over crust, leaving a
½-inch border. Top evenly with mushroom mixture, tomato slices, and mozzarella. Bake at 375° for 10 minutes or until
cheese melts and begins to brown. Cut
pizza into 8 wedges. Yield: 4 servings
(serving size: 2 wedges).

CALORIES 365; FAT 12.3g (sat 6.4g, mono 4.4g, poly 0.4g);
PROTEIN 19.9g; CARB 11.1g; FIBER 7.5g; CHOL 24mg;
IRON 2mg; SODIUM 523mg; CALC 379mg

[Time: 35 minutes]

Chili Pasta with Beans

Steamed broccoli

Corn bread muffins

Chili Mac

Boxed version:
Serving size: 1⅓ cups (prepared with
    2 ounces ground sirloin)
Calories: 282
Fat: 6.4 grams
Sodium: 972 milligrams

Our version:
Serving size: 1⅓ cups
Calories: 294
Fat: 8 grams
Sodium: 644 milligrams

QUICK & EASY • MAKE AHEAD
Chili Pasta with Beans

Since this cooks in one skillet, prep and
cleanup are a snap. This dish is easy on
the budget, too, since it serves six using
less than a pound of meat. Top it off
with sliced green onions and a shower
of reduced-fat shredded Cheddar cheese.

  1 tablespoon canola oil
  ¾ cup chopped onion
  ¾ pound ground sirloin
  4 teaspoons chili powder
  1 teaspoon ground cumin
  1 teaspoon dried oregano
  2 cups water
  ¾ teaspoon salt
  6 ounces uncooked ruote (about
     2¼ cups uncooked wagon wheel–
     shaped pasta)
  1 (15-ounce) can no-salt-added pinto
     beans, rinsed and drained
  1 (14.5-ounce) can fire-roasted diced
     tomatoes with green chiles (such as
     Muir Glen), undrained
  1 (8-ounce) can no-salt-added tomato
     sauce

❶ Heat oil in a large nonstick skillet over
medium heat. Add onion and beef to
pan; cook 4 minutes or until onion is
tender and beef is browned, stirring to
crumble. Stir in chili powder, cumin,
and oregano; cook 1 minute. Stir in
2 cups water and remaining ingredients;
bring to a boil. Cover, reduce heat, and
simmer 18 minutes or until pasta is done.
Yield: 6 servings (serving size: about
1⅓ cups).

CALORIES 294; FAT 8g (sat 2.3g, mono 3.6g, poly 0.9g);
PROTEIN 18.8g; CARB 35.4g; FIBER 4.6g; CHOL 21mg;
IRON 3.7mg; SODIUM 644mg; CALC 59mg

[Time: 33 minutes]

Green tea

*Shrimp and Broccoli Fried Rice
with Toasted Almonds*

Sliced mango and kiwi

Shrimp Fried Rice

Take-out version:
Serving size: about 2 cups
Calories: 577
Fat: 20.5 grams
Sodium: Unavailable

Our version:
Serving size: 1¾ cups
Calories: 442
Fat: 12.6 grams
Sodium: 693 milligrams

QUICK & EASY

Shrimp and Broccoli Fried Rice with Toasted Almonds

Cooling rice in the freezer ensures the grains stay separate once stir-fried.

1¾ cups water, divided
1½ cups instant white rice (such as Minute Rice)
4 cups broccoli florets
1 large red bell pepper, chopped (about 1⅓ cups)
2 tablespoons roasted peanut oil, divided
1 teaspoon grated peeled fresh ginger
3 garlic cloves, minced
1¼ pounds large shrimp, peeled and deveined
½ cup fat-free, less-sodium chicken broth
3 tablespoons low-sodium soy sauce
1 teaspoon cornstarch
¼ cup sliced almonds, toasted
¼ cup chopped green onions

① Place 1½ cups water in a medium saucepan; bring to a boil. Add rice to pan; cover, reduce heat, and simmer 5 minutes. Remove pan from heat; let stand 5 minutes. Spoon rice into a 13 x 9–inch baking dish; place dish in freezer.
② Combine broccoli, bell pepper, and remaining ¼ cup water in a microwave-safe dish. Microwave at HIGH 5 minutes or until crisp-tender. Set aside.
③ Heat 1½ teaspoons oil in a large non-stick skillet over medium heat. Add ginger and garlic to pan; cook 1 minute, stirring frequently.
④ Increase heat to medium-high. Add shrimp to pan; cook 4 minutes or until shrimp are done. Remove shrimp mixture from pan. Remove rice from freezer.
⑤ Heat remaining 1½ tablespoons oil in pan over medium-high heat. Add rice to pan; cook 3 minutes or until thoroughly heated, stirring frequently. Combine broth, soy sauce, and cornstarch in a small bowl, stirring with a whisk. Stir broth mixture into rice. Add shrimp mixture and broccoli mixture to pan; cook 1½ minutes or until sauce thickens. Sprinkle with almonds and onions. Yield: 4 servings (serving size: about 1¾ cups).

CALORIES 442; FAT 12.6g (sat 1.9g, mono 5.4g, poly 4g); PROTEIN 37.5g; CARB 45.8g; FIBER 4.1g; CHOL 215mg; IRON 7mg; SODIUM 693mg; CALC 141mg

[Time: 25 minutes]

Hummus with carrot sticks

Falafel Pitas

*Greek yogurt with honey
and toasted walnuts*

Falafel Pita Sandwich

Take-out version:
Serving size: 1 sandwich (without cheese, sauce, or condiments)
Calories: 450
Fat: 10.4 grams
Sodium: 950 milligrams

Our version:
Serving size: 1 sandwich
Calories: 303
Fat: 10.8 grams
Sodium: 569 milligrams

QUICK & EASY

Falafel Pitas

If you don't have time to make the sauce, use commercial hummus thinned with lemon juice.

SAUCE:
1 cup 2% reduced-fat Greek yogurt
⅔ cup chopped peeled cucumber
1 teaspoon chopped fresh dill
1 garlic clove, minced
FALAFEL:
1 (15-ounce) can no-salt-added chickpeas (garbanzo beans)
¼ cup dry breadcrumbs
¼ cup finely chopped fresh parsley
3 tablespoons finely chopped red onion
1 teaspoon garlic salt
1 teaspoon ground coriander
1 teaspoon ground cumin
2 tablespoons olive oil

REMAINING INGREDIENTS:

- 2 (6-inch) whole wheat pitas, cut in half
- 2 cups shredded romaine lettuce
- 1 cup chopped plum tomato
- ⅔ cup thinly sliced peeled cucumber
- ¼ cup thinly sliced red onion

1 To prepare sauce, combine first 4 ingredients; set aside.

2 To prepare falafel, drain chickpeas in a colander over a bowl; reserve liquid. Place chickpeas, 3 tablespoons liquid (discard remaining liquid), breadcrumbs, and next 5 ingredients in a food processor; process until minced. Divide chickpea mixture into 8 equal portions, shaping each into a ½-inch-thick patty.

3 Heat oil in a large nonstick skillet over medium-high heat. Add patties to pan; cook 3 minutes on each side or until golden brown. Spread about ¼ cup sauce into each pita half. Fill each pita half with ½ cup lettuce, ¼ cup tomato, about 2 tablespoons sliced cucumber, 1 tablespoon sliced onion, and 2 patties. Yield: 4 servings (serving size: 1 stuffed pita).

CALORIES 303; FAT 10.8g (sat 2.2g, mono 5.4g, poly 1.8g); PROTEIN 14.4g; CARB 40.6g; FIBER 7.4g; CHOL 3mg; IRON 3.3mg; SODIUM 569mg; CALC 133mg

> Cooking at home, you control what goes into your dinner so you can monitor fat, sodium, and calories.

MEAL MAKEOVER MENU 7

[Time: 50 minutes]

Buttermilk Oven-Fried Chicken with Coleslaw

Dinner rolls

Fried Chicken with Coleslaw

Fast-food version:
Serving size: 1 chicken breast half plus 1 side order of coleslaw
Calories: 540
Fat: 31 grams
Sodium: 1,290 milligrams

Our version:
Serving size: 1 chicken breast half plus ¾ cup coleslaw
Calories: 342
Fat: 8.8 grams
Sodium: 672 milligrams

QUICK & EASY
Buttermilk Oven-Fried Chicken with Coleslaw

Look for cracker meal on the baking aisle. If you can't find it, make your own by pulsing 10 saltine crackers in a food processor until they're finely ground.

COLESLAW:
- 4 cups packaged cabbage-and-carrot coleslaw
- 3 tablespoons fat-free mayonnaise
- 1½ teaspoons sugar
- ½ teaspoon celery seeds
- 1½ teaspoons cider vinegar
- ⅛ teaspoon salt

CHICKEN:
- 1 cup low-fat buttermilk
- 4 (8-ounce) bone-in chicken breast halves, skinned
- ⅓ cup all-purpose flour
- ⅓ cup cracker meal
- ½ teaspoon salt
- ½ teaspoon black pepper
- 2 tablespoons butter

1 To prepare coleslaw, combine first 6 ingredients; toss to coat. Cover and chill.

2 Preheat oven to 425°.

3 To prepare chicken, combine buttermilk and chicken in a shallow dish, turning to coat.

4 Combine flour and cracker meal in a shallow dish. Transfer chicken from buttermilk to a work surface. Sprinkle chicken evenly with ½ teaspoon salt and pepper. Working with one chicken breast half at a time, dredge chicken in flour mixture, shaking off excess; set aside. Repeat procedure with remaining chicken and flour mixture.

5 Melt butter in a large ovenproof nonstick skillet over medium-high heat. Add chicken to pan, meat side down; cook 4 minutes or until golden brown. Turn chicken over, and bake at 425° for 32 minutes or until a thermometer registers 165°. Serve with coleslaw. Yield: 4 servings (serving size: 1 chicken breast half and ¾ cup slaw).

CALORIES 342; FAT 8.8g (sat 4.5g, mono 2.2g, poly 0.8g); PROTEIN 45.1g; CARB 18.5g; FIBER 2.6g; CHOL 123mg; IRON 2.3mg; SODIUM 672mg; CALC 95mg

9 Nutrition Essentials

A sneak peek at our series: fad-free strategies to make your diet its best ever

YOU HAVE ACCESS to more nutrition information than ever—from magazines to the Internet, newspapers, and television. When you add to that the hype about fad diets, the resulting information overload creates more confusion than clarity.

"Many people are still uncertain about what they should eat and think good nutrition is complicated," says Senior Food Editor Ann Taylor Pittman. "Even *Cooking Light* readers, who are more well versed in good nutrition than most, come to us with questions about everything from what constitutes a healthful fat to how to work more whole grains into their diet."

In this and other stories throughout the year, we will demystify the essentials of smart nutrition. First, we've identified the nine most important nutrition issues that influence the way we eat. And we've assembled a panel of top authorities in the nutrition, public health, culinary, and food-marketing fields to help guide us in translating complex science into real-world information you can use. We'll share their strategies for bringing smart nutrition to your plate.

MAKE AHEAD

Frisée Salad with Persimmons, Dates, and Almonds

1½ cups thinly sliced leek (about 1 large), divided
3 tablespoons water
2 tablespoons white wine vinegar
1 teaspoon extra-virgin olive oil
½ teaspoon kosher salt
1 ripe Fuyu persimmon, peeled and chopped (about 7 ounces)
6 cups frisée or bagged mâche salad greens
3 cups peeled and thinly sliced quartered ripe Fuyu persimmons (about 3)
3 tablespoons sliced almonds, toasted
8 pitted dates, chopped (about ¼ cup)

❶ Place 1 tablespoon leek in blender. Place 3 tablespoons water and next 4 ingredients in blender; process until smooth.
❷ Combine frisée and remaining leek in a large bowl, and toss with dressing.

Place 1 cup frisée mixture on each of 8 plates. Top each serving with about ⅓ cup sliced persimmon, about 1 teaspoon almonds, and 1½ teaspoons dates. Yield: 8 servings.

CALORIES 157; FAT 2g (sat 0.2g, mono 1.2g, poly 0.5g); PROTEIN 2.2g; CARB 37g; FIBER 6g; CHOL 0mg; IRON 1.2mg; SODIUM 134mg; CALC 57mg

MAKE AHEAD

Dijon Mustard Chicken Fricassee

¼ cup Dijon mustard
¼ cup chopped fresh parsley, divided
1 tablespoon chopped fresh thyme, divided
3 pounds chicken pieces, skinned
¼ teaspoon salt
¼ teaspoon freshly ground black pepper
1 tablespoon olive oil
1½ cups chopped onion (about 1 large)
3 garlic cloves, minced
1 cup dry white wine
1 cup fat-free, less-sodium chicken broth

❶ Combine mustard, 1 tablespoon parsley, 1½ teaspoons thyme, and chicken in a large zip-top plastic bag; toss well to coat. Chill 8 hours or overnight.
❷ Remove chicken from bag, and discard marinade. Sprinkle chicken with salt and pepper. Heat oil in a large Dutch oven over medium-high heat. Add chicken to pan, and cook 5 minutes on each side or until browned. Remove from pan.
❸ Add onion to pan; sauté 5 minutes or until tender, stirring frequently. Add garlic to pan; sauté 1 minute, stirring constantly. Stir in wine and broth, scraping pan to loosen browned bits. Stir in 1 tablespoon parsley and remaining 1½ teaspoons thyme. Return chicken to pan. Cover, reduce heat, and simmer 25 minutes or until chicken is done. Remove chicken with a slotted spoon. Keep warm.
❹ Cook sauce, uncovered, over medium heat 4 minutes or until slightly thick. Pour sauce over chicken, and sprinkle with remaining 2 tablespoons parsley. Yield: 4 servings (serving size: about 5 ounces chicken and ½ cup sauce).

CALORIES 244; FAT 10.6g (sat 2.4g, mono 5.2g, poly 2g); PROTEIN 28.2g; CARB 7.8g; FIBER 1.5g; CHOL 80mg; IRON 2.1mg; SODIUM 527mg; CALC 44mg

MAKE AHEAD

Almond-Cranberry Corn Bread

Nut meals can replace up to one-fourth of the all-purpose flour in baked goods.

3 ounces all-purpose flour (about ⅔ cup)
⅔ cup yellow cornmeal
⅔ cup almond meal
⅓ cup sugar
1 teaspoon baking powder
½ teaspoon baking soda
½ teaspoon salt
1½ tablespoons canola oil
1½ tablespoons sliced almonds
¾ cup fat-free buttermilk
½ cup dried cranberries
2 large egg whites
Cooking spray

Meet Our Advisors

Efisio Farris

Born and raised in Sardinia, Chef Efisio Farris has introduced his homeland's healthful cuisine to American diners through his restaurants, Arcodoro and Pomodoro in Dallas and Arcodoro in Houston, www.gourmetsardinia.com, and his new book, *Sweet Myrtle and Bitter Honey: The Mediterranean Flavors of Sardinia.*

Dan Buettner

Dan Buettner is *The New York Times* best-selling author of *The Blue Zones: Lessons for Living Longer from the People Who've Lived the Longest.* Buettner is an internationally recognized explorer who founded Blue Zones (www.bluezones. com), a project that researches the world's best practices in health and longevity and shares that information to help people live longer, better.

Robert Schueller

Robert Schueller (aka Produce Guy) is director of public relations for Melissa's (www.melissas.com), the nation's largest exotic produce supplier. He has introduced specialty items in *Melissa's Great Book of Produce* and the forthcoming *Produce Book.*

Raghavan Iyer

Born in Mumbai, Raghavan Iyer is a cookbook author and culinary teacher whose adventures at the stove began in his mother's kitchen. He is a two-time James Beard Award finalist, and the International Association of Culinary Professionals named Iyer 2004's Teacher of the Year.

Heather Bauer, RD

Heather Bauer, RD, author of *The Wall Street Diet,* specializes in the connections between eating habits, metabolism, and lifestyle. She offers private diet and nutrition counseling through her New York City–based nutrition practice, Nu-Train.

Walter Willett, MD, PhD

Chair of the Department of Nutrition at the Harvard School of Public Health, Willett oversees several landmark epidemiological studies, including the Nurses Health Study and the Health Professionals Follow-Up Study. Willett served on the advisory board for the 2005 USDA's Dietary Guidelines for Americans.

Liz Neumark

Liz Neumark is the founder of Great Performances, a cuisine and event planning company in New York City. Her company specializes in creating local menus using ingredients from within a 100-mile radius of a client's event. Great Performances also owns the Katchkie Farm in upstate New York, which specializes in organically grown produce.

Marion Nestle, PhD, MPH

Marion Nestle is the Paulette Goddard Professor of Nutrition, Food Studies, and Public Health at New York University. Her research focuses on the scientific, social, cultural, and economic factors that influence the development, implementation, and acceptance of federal dietary guidance policies. Her most recent book is *What to Eat.*

Tory McPhail

Tory McPhail is executive chef at the legendary Commander's Palace in New Orleans. He has worked with the Oschner Clinic in New Orleans to develop healthful dishes for the restaurant's menu.

Joanne Weir

Longtime *Cooking Light* contributor Chef Joanne Weir is a San Francisco–based cookbook author, teacher, and host of a PBS culinary series. Her books include *Wine Country Cooking, From Tapas to Meze,* and *Weir Cooking in the City.*

Deborah Madison

New Mexico–based cookbook author Deborah Madison is a frequent contributor to *Cooking Light.* As the author of *Local Flavors* and *Vegetarian Suppers,* she advocated for fresh, local, seasonal fare long before it became a trend.

Laurent Gras

As the executive chef/partner at Chicago's L2O seafood restaurant, Chef Laurent Gras applies his French training to a cornucopia of global ingredients sourced from artisanal purveyors. He's had a lifelong connection to food, growing up in Antibes, France, where his family had a small olive orchard.

Greg Drescher

Greg Drescher is executive director of strategic initiatives at the Culinary Institute of America's Worlds of Healthy Flavors program. Before joining the CIA, Drescher was cofounder and program chairman of Oldways Preservation and Exchange Trust.

---

❶ Preheat oven to 400°.

❷ Weigh or lightly spoon flour into dry measuring cups; level with a knife. Combine flour and next 6 ingredients in a large bowl.

❸ Heat oil in a small skillet over high heat. Add almonds to pan, and cook 2 minutes or until lightly toasted, stirring frequently. Strain oil through a fine sieve into flour mixture. Set aside 1 tablespoon almonds. Add remaining $1\frac{1}{2}$ teaspoons almonds to flour mixture. Combine buttermilk, cranberries, and egg whites, and add to flour mixture, stirring until well blended.

❹ Spoon batter into an 8-inch cast-iron skillet coated with cooking spray. Sprinkle reserved 1 tablespoon toasted almonds over top of batter. Bake bread at 400° for 20 minutes or until a wooden pick inserted in center comes out clean. Cool in pan 10 minutes on a wire rack. Yield: 12 servings (serving size: 1 wedge).

CALORIES 149; FAT 5.4g (sat 0.4g, mono 3.3g, poly 1.4g); PROTEIN 4g; CARB 21.9g; FIBER 1.9g; CHOL 0mg; IRON 0.5mg; SODIUM 218mg; CALC 45mg

Top 9 Nutrition Principles

1 Eat Smart, Be Fit, and Live Longer.

Dan Buettner, one of our panel of experts for the Nutrition Essentials series, has studied communities he calls Blue Zones where people live to the age of 100 at a much higher rate than the general population. **What you can do:** Eat a predominately plant-based diet that offers a balance of healthful fats; a variety of vitamins, minerals, and antioxidants; and quality sources of protein that are low in saturated fat, which is linked to elevated rates of cardiovascular disease. Other keys among Blue Zone groups: Make meals a family event, and perform daily exercise to help keep weight in check.

2 Eat Carbs That Satisfy.

The type of carbohydrate consumed is most important, says Walter Willett, MD, PhD, one of our panel experts. Eventually, all carbohydrates turn to sugar in our bodies. These sugars give us the energy needed to perform tasks—from breathing to bicep curls.

However, some carbohydrates convert to sugar more quickly than others, so focus on complex carbohydrates, the more slowly digested kind found in whole grains, legumes, and vegetables. They help you feel full and satisfied after a meal. **What you can do:** Whole grains, in particular, are a superior carbohydrate choice. The USDA recommends three servings daily in the current Dietary Guidelines.

3 Boost Your Nutrient Power.

Choose "nutrient-dense" foods—those inherently rich in vitamins, minerals, and nutrients without additional calories. The idea is to choose foods that offer the most nutritional bang for the caloric buck, such as fat-free milk, which has the same nutrients—protein, calcium, vitamins A and D—with less calories than whole milk. **How to do it:** Substitute nutrient-rich foods for some ingredients in a recipe to boost the nutrition profile.

4 Save Room for Treats.

Any way of eating that doesn't include the occasional indulgence is unsustainable. Even the current version of the USDA Dietary Guidelines allows goodies. If the rest of your diet includes smart options like fat-free milk, lean cuts of beef, plus plenty of produce and whole grains, you'll have room for these so-called "discretionary calories" to enjoy as you wish. **How to do it:** The key is to make even your discretionary calories nutritionally sound. Enjoy nutrient-dense options like nuts or make hot chocolate with unsweetened cocoa and fat-free milk.

5 Be Savvy About Salt.

Sodium plays a key role in muscle function and maintaining the body's fluid balance, but it's easy to consume too much. Over time, excess sodium can increase the risk of heart disease and stroke.

The USDA recommends no more than 2,300 milligrams of sodium daily for adults under age 50—the amount in one teaspoon of salt. But most Americans consume an extra 2,000 to 4,000mg daily. **How to do it:** Focus on fresh, whole foods. They may naturally contain some sodium, but not nearly as much as many processed foods. When you do use processed foods, look for no- or reduced-sodium versions to help avoid adding extra sodium.

6 Eat to Sustain You— and the Planet.

It's easy to become bogged down in the many issues dealing with how food affects the environment, and choosing among them can be confusing. You can't do it all, so pick the issues that matter to you.

Many experts agree that consuming a diet rich in a wide variety of plant foods is a smart first step toward sustainability. The simple reason: Fruits, vegetables, and grains require fewer resources to produce. **How to do it:** Place as much emphasis on produce-based side dishes as on meat entrées.

7 Beware of Portion Distortion.

We've all seen what appears to be a single-serve packaged snack, only to discover the label indicates it actually yields two servings. This can lead to overeating. **How to do it:** Portion control is easy to practice in your own kitchen. When buying fish, have it cut into 6-ounce portions. When cooking with ingredients that aren't already portioned or plating finished dishes, pay close attention to measurements. Use tools like measuring cups or kitchen scales to help you identify the correct amount. You'll soon begin to automatically recognize a proper portion.

8 Choose Premium Protein.

Protein helps you feel fuller longer. That's good news when it comes to managing your appetite. However, protein sources differ in their nutritional makeup, so you must also factor fat to make the best choice. **How to do it:** For most meals, choose a protein that offers the most of the nutrient for the least saturated fat. Plant-based proteins, like beans and lentils, come with little fat and plentiful vitamins and minerals. Nuts are generally rich in beneficial unsaturated fats. Animal proteins contain varying levels and types.

9 Sort the Latest Facts on Fat.

You'll notice we no longer include percentage of calories from fat per serving. We're making this adjustment in light of findings from large-scale studies that found the type of fat is more important to heart health than a particular food's ratio of calories from fat and replacing a portion of total calories with unsaturated fats may help protect against heart disease. **How to do it:** Look beyond the total fat in a given food. Read the label to check the amounts of mono- and polyunsaturated fats it contains. These figures should be higher than those for saturated and trans fats, which are linked to heart disease.

Mixed Vegetable and Rice Pilaf

A *biryani,* an Indian rice-based dish, is an ideal way to improve nutrition by augmenting the grain with vegetables.

- 1½ teaspoons cumin seeds, divided
- 2 tablespoons canola oil
- ¼ teaspoon coriander seeds
- ¼ teaspoon black peppercorns
- ¼ teaspoon freshly ground black pepper
- 4 green cardamom pods
- 3 whole cloves
- 2 dried red chiles
- 1 bay leaf
- 1 cup sliced red onion
- ⅓ cup finely chopped carrot
- 1¼ teaspoons kosher salt, divided
- ½ pound green beans, trimmed and cut into ¾-inch pieces (2 cups)
- 1 cup uncooked basmati rice
- ½ teaspoon ground turmeric
- ¾ pound red potatoes, cut into 1-inch pieces
- 2 cups water
- ¼ teaspoon garam masala
- ¾ cup frozen green peas

① Place 1 teaspoon cumin seeds in a small skillet over medium-high heat, and cook 2 minutes or until toasted, stirring occasionally. Remove from pan, and cool completely. Place toasted cumin seeds in a spice or coffee grinder, and process until finely ground. Set aside. **②** Heat oil in a Dutch oven over medium-high heat. Add remaining ½ teaspoon cumin seeds, coriander seeds, and next 6 ingredients to pan. Cook 2 minutes or until cumin browns, stirring frequently. Add onion, carrot, 1 teaspoon salt, and green beans, and cook 2 minutes, stirring occasionally. Stir in rice, turmeric, and potatoes. Add 2 cups water; bring mixture to a boil. Stir in remaining ¼ teaspoon salt, ground cumin seeds, and garam masala. Cover, reduce heat, and simmer 15 minutes or until rice is tender and liquid is absorbed. Remove from heat, and stir in peas. Cover and let mixture stand 5 minutes. Discard bay leaf. Yield: 7 servings (serving size: 1 cup).

CALORIES 170; FAT 4.7g (sat 0.4g, mono 2.5g, poly 1.5g); PROTEIN 4.3g; CARB 28.7g; FIBER 4.3g; CHOL 0mg; IRON 2.1mg; SODIUM 359mg; CALC 31mg

STAFF FAVORITE
Seared Mahimahi with Edamame Succotash

Using frozen vegetables allows you to measure out precisely what you need.

SUCCOTASH:
- 1 medium red bell pepper
- ¼ cup finely chopped green onions
- 2 teaspoons chopped fresh thyme
- 2 teaspoons rice wine vinegar
- 2 teaspoons fresh lime juice
- 2 teaspoons olive oil
- ¼ teaspoon salt
- ¼ teaspoon ground red pepper
- 2 garlic cloves, minced
- 1⅓ cups frozen corn kernels, thawed
- ½ cup frozen shelled edamame (green soybeans), thawed

MAHIMAHI:
- 1 teaspoon olive oil
- Cooking spray
- 4 (6-ounce) mahimahi or other firm white fish fillets
- ⅛ teaspoon salt
- ⅛ teaspoon freshly ground black pepper

① Preheat broiler. **②** To prepare succotash, cut bell pepper in half lengthwise; discard seeds and membranes. Place pepper halves, skins side up, on a foil-lined baking sheet; flatten with hand. Broil 15 minutes or until blackened. Place in a zip-top plastic bag; seal. Let stand 10 minutes. Peel and finely chop. Combine pepper, onions, and next 7 ingredients, tossing to combine. **③** Combine corn and edamame in a small microwave-safe bowl; cover with water. Microwave at HIGH 2 minutes; drain. Add corn mixture to bell pepper mixture; toss to combine. **④** To prepare mahimahi, heat 1 teaspoon oil in a large nonstick skillet coated with cooking spray over medium-high heat. Sprinkle both sides of fish with ⅛ teaspoon salt and ⅛ teaspoon black pepper. Add fish to pan; cook 4 minutes on each side or until fish flakes easily when tested with a fork. Serve with succotash. Yield: 4 servings (serving size: 1 fillet and ½ cup succotash).

CALORIES 379; FAT 9.4g (sat 1.5g, mono 5.5g, poly 1.6g); PROTEIN 35.8g; CARB 41.2g; FIBER 8g; CHOL 52mg; IRON 3.7mg; SODIUM 537mg; CALC 84mg

Crispy Tofu Pad Thai

Plant-based proteins like tofu and peanuts are abundant sources of protein.

- 1 (12.3-ounce) package reduced-fat, firm tofu, drained
- 1 tablespoon cornstarch
- 6 ounces flat uncooked rice noodles
- ½ cup ketchup
- 2 tablespoons sugar
- 2 tablespoons fish sauce
- 1 tablespoon Sriracha (hot chile sauce, such as Huy Fong)
- 2 tablespoons canola oil, divided
- 2 large eggs, lightly beaten
- 1 large egg white, lightly beaten
- ½ cup chopped green onions
- 2 tablespoons chopped fresh cilantro
- 2 tablespoons unsalted, dry-roasted peanuts, chopped
- 4 lime wedges

1 Place tofu on several layers of paper towels; cover with additional paper towels. Let stand 30 minutes, pressing down occasionally. Cut tofu into ½-inch cubes, and toss with cornstarch.
2 Prepare noodles according to package directions, omitting salt and fat. Drain well; set aside.
3 Combine ketchup and next 3 ingredients. Heat 1 tablespoon oil in a nonstick skillet over medium-high heat. Add tofu to pan; sauté 7 minutes or until golden. Remove tofu from pan.
4 Heat 1 teaspoon oil in pan. Add eggs and egg white; cook 30 seconds, stirring constantly. Remove from pan. Heat remaining 2 teaspoons oil in pan. Add noodles; cook 3 minutes. Stir in ketchup mixture; cook 30 seconds. Add egg mixture; cook 1 minute, stirring often. Remove from heat; stir in onions and cilantro. Place 1 cup noodle mixture on each of 4 plates. Top each with ½ cup tofu and 1½ teaspoons peanuts. Serve with lime wedges. Yield: 4 servings.

CALORIES 419; FAT 14.4g (sat 1.7g, mono 6.8g, poly 3.5g); PROTEIN 15.4g; CARB 57.5g; FIBER 2.8g; CHOL 106mg; IRON 3.3mg; SODIUM 845mg; CALC 374mg

---

MAKE AHEAD
Muesli with Cranberries and Flaxseed

Muesli, the German word for "mixture," typically refers to a breakfast cereal of grains, dried fruit, and nuts. A hearty breakfast like this—full of heart-healthy fats, whole grains, calcium and protein-rich yogurt, and dried fruits—will help you stay full all morning.

- 2 cups regular oats
- ½ cup dried cranberries
- ⅓ cup wheat germ
- ⅓ cup ground flaxseed
- ¼ cup maple syrup
- ½ teaspoon ground cinnamon
- ½ teaspoon vanilla extract
- 3 cups 1% low-fat milk
- 3 tablespoons slivered almonds, toasted
- 3 tablespoons chopped pecans, toasted
- 3 tablespoons pumpkinseed kernels, toasted
- 3 cups plain fat-free yogurt
- 2 tablespoons maple syrup

1 Combine first 7 ingredients in a large bowl; pour milk over mixture, stirring to combine. Cover and chill 3 hours or overnight.
2 Combine nuts and pumpkinseed kernels in a small bowl. Spoon ¾ cup oat mixture into each of 6 bowls. Top each serving with ½ cup yogurt; sprinkle each serving with 1½ tablespoons nut mixture, and drizzle with 1 teaspoon maple syrup. Yield: 6 servings.

CALORIES 421; FAT 12.4g (sat 2.2g, mono 4.8g, poly 4.3g); PROTEIN 19.5g; CARB 62.4g; FIBER 6.6g; CHOL 7mg; IRON 3.5mg; SODIUM 162mg; CALC 457mg

---

Sweet Potato–Pecan Burgers with Caramelized Onions

Choose breads labeled 100 percent whole wheat or whole grain to make sure you're getting their benefits. Nuts add healthful unsaturated fats and filling protein to this tasty vegetarian sandwich.

ONIONS:
- 1 teaspoon canola oil
- 3 cups sliced onion
- 2 tablespoons balsamic vinegar
- 1 teaspoon sugar
- ⅛ teaspoon salt

BURGERS:
- 2½ cups (½-inch) cubed peeled sweet potato
- Cooking spray
- 2½ cups chopped onion
- 3 garlic cloves
- 1 cup regular oats
- 1½ teaspoons ground cumin
- ¾ teaspoon salt
- ¼ teaspoon pepper
- ½ cup chopped pecans, toasted
- 1 tablespoon canola oil, divided
- 6 Boston lettuce leaves
- 6 (1½-ounce) 100% whole wheat or whole-grain buns
- 6 tablespoons chili sauce

1 To prepare onions, heat 1 teaspoon oil in a large nonstick skillet over medium-high heat. Add sliced onion to pan; sauté 12 minutes or until browned, stirring occasionally. Stir in vinegar, sugar, and ⅛ teaspoon salt; cook 30 seconds or until vinegar is absorbed. Remove onion mixture from pan; keep warm. Wipe pan dry with a paper towel.
2 To prepare burgers, place potato in a large saucepan; cover with water. Bring to a boil. Reduce heat, and simmer 15 minutes or until tender; drain.
3 Heat large nonstick skillet over medium-high heat. Coat pan with cooking spray. Add chopped onion and garlic to pan; sauté 5 minutes or until tender.
4 Place potato, chopped onion mixture, oats, and next 3 ingredients in a food

processor; process until smooth. Place potato mixture in a large bowl; stir in nuts. Divide potato mixture into 6 equal portions, shaping each into a ¹/₂-inch-thick patty.

⑤ Wipe pan dry with a paper towel. Heat 1¹/₂ teaspoons oil in pan over medium-high heat. Add 3 patties to pan; cook 4 minutes or until browned. Carefully turn patties over; cook 3 minutes or until browned. Remove from pan; keep warm. Repeat procedure with remaining 1¹/₂ teaspoons oil and 3 patties. Place lettuce leaves and patties on bottom halves of buns; top each patty with 1 tablespoon chili sauce, about 3 tablespoons onion mixture, and top halves of buns. Yield: 6 servings (serving size: 1 burger).

CALORIES 376; FAT 12.3g (sat 0.9g, mono 5.8g, poly 3.2g); PROTEIN 11.3g; CARB 59g; FIBER 7.9g; CHOL 0mg; IRON 3.4mg; SODIUM 785mg; CALC 89mg

QUICK & EASY
Mango Lassi

Choose low-fat or fat-free dairy products to keep saturated fat in check while delivering healthful calcium, potassium, and vitamin D. This sweet Indian-style, smoothie-like drink is a blend of fresh mango, tangy Greek yogurt, and milk.

- 1 cup chopped fresh mango
- 1½ tablespoons sugar
- 1½ cups fat-free plain Greek yogurt
- ½ cup 1% low-fat milk
- 2 teaspoons chopped pistachios
  Dash of ground cardamom (optional)

① Combine mango and sugar in a blender; process until pureed. Add yogurt and milk; process until smooth. Serve with pistachios; sprinkle with cardamom, if desired. Yield: 3 servings (serving size: 1 cup lassi and about ¹/₂ teaspoon pistachios).

CALORIES 137; FAT 1.4g (sat 0.4g, mono 0.6g, poly 0.3g); PROTEIN 7g; CARB 27.5g; FIBER 1.2g; CHOL 4mg; IRON 0.2mg; SODIUM 89mg; CALC 207mg

Classic Casseroles

An explanation of why cooks have always loved these comforting, hearty standbys

CASSEROLES HAVE BEEN BELOVED FOR SO LONG that they predate written history. From the time people began to cook in clay pots, these humble dishes have been a staple in the cuisines of most cultures.

Whatever the cuisine, casseroles are a cook's dream. Most recipes call for inexpensive cuts of meat, and the results are satisfying meals that require little more than bread or pasta to soak up the sauce. The recipes included here are complete with sauces or broths, which keep the dishes moist and flavorful, and they can all be cooked ahead and reheated.

MAKE AHEAD
White Winter Vegetable Stew (*Soupe Savoyarde*)

This warming stew hails from the French Alps. Although the recipe calls for Cheddar, Gruyère or domestic Swiss cheese can take its place. The cheese adds a rich flavor and melts into the stew, thickening it slightly. Other root vegetables such as parsnips, kohlrabi, or fennel can be added to vary the flavors. Make the stew up to 24 hours ahead and refrigerate. Reheat it just before serving as the toast broils.

- 1 baking potato, cut into (¹/₂-inch) cubes (about 1 pound)
- 2 tablespoons butter
- 1½ cups chopped onion
- 3 cups thinly sliced leek (about 3 large)
- ¾ teaspoon salt
- ¼ teaspoon freshly ground black pepper
- 2 turnips, peeled and cut into (¹/₂-inch) cubes
- 1 small celery root, peeled and cut into (¹/₂-inch) cubes
- 2 cups water
- 2 cups whole milk
- 8 (1-ounce) slices French bread
- 8 (¹/₂-ounce) slices sharp white Cheddar cheese

① Place potato in a medium bowl; cover with cold water to 1 inch above potato. Set aside.

② Melt butter in a large Dutch oven over medium heat. Add onion to pan, and cook 7 minutes or until soft but not browned, stirring occasionally. Add leek and next 4 ingredients to pan. Place a sheet of aluminum foil directly over vegetable mixture. Cover, reduce heat to low, and cook 15 minutes or until vegetables are tender. Discard foil.

③ Drain potatoes; add to pan. Stir in 2 cups water. Cover and simmer 20 minutes or until vegetables are tender, stirring occasionally.

④ Heat milk in a small, heavy saucepan over medium heat to 180° or until tiny bubbles form around edges (do not boil). Gradually stir hot milk into vegetable mixture, stirring constantly. Remove from heat. Taste and adjust seasoning, if desired.

⑤ Preheat broiler.

⑥ Place bread slices in a single layer on a baking sheet. Broil 1 minute or until toasted. Place 1 bread slice in each of 8 bowls; top each bread slice with 1 cheese slice. Ladle 1¹/₄ cups stew into each bowl. Yield: 8 servings.

CALORIES 311; FAT 10.5g (sat 6.2, mono 2.7g, poly 0.8g); PROTEIN 12g; CARB 43.6g; FIBER 4.9g; CHOL 29mg; IRON 2.7mg; SODIUM 640mg; CALC 278mg

How to Make Braised Casseroles

Essential to success with this type of recipe is long, slow cooking. This not only marries the flavors, but the moist heat also penetrates and tenderizes inexpensive cuts of meats that would otherwise remain tough. Ideal candidates are large cuts, such as lamb shanks, a whole brisket, or pork roasts, such as Boston butt. When braising, add flavorful liquid to partially cover the food, cover the pot, and cook until the meat is fork-tender.

A. Use a large deep skillet so the heat is diffused and food cooks evenly. The diameter of the base should be about three times the height of the sides. If it's too shallow, moisture will evaporate easily and the food can dry out as it cooks. Check periodically, and if the liquid dips too far down, top it off. Start with large pieces of meat. Here we're using bone-in chicken pieces because they take longer to cook than boneless. Season and brown the meat in the skillet so you can dissolve the flavorful bits left behind in the bottom of the pan when it is deglazed.

B. Begin to build flavor in the dish by adding vegetables, spices, and herbs. Add hearty ingredients like tough root vegetables, spices, and dried herbs to the skillet early, and allow them to cook and flavor the dish. It's best to garnish with delicate chopped fresh herbs just before serving.

C. Create a bouquet garni by wrapping ingredients such as sprigs of fresh herbs, peppercorns, or bay leaves in cheesecloth. Place the bundle in the skillet to infuse the cooking liquid and meat as the dish simmers.

D. To achieve the best results, partially submerge the meat in a flavorful liquid as it cooks. Broth, milk, cream, cider, beer, wine, or spirits are all good options. Plain water is also useful in casseroles—"stock from the tap," an old chef used to say with a wink as he added water to almost cover.

Chicken with Dark Beer (*Coq à la Bière*)

Cooks in the south of France like their chicken cooked in wine, but those in the north go for the caramel intensity of dark beer laced with plenty of onions.

- 3 tablespoons all-purpose flour
- ½ teaspoon salt
- ¼ teaspoon freshly ground black pepper
- 2 bone-in chicken breast halves, skinned
- 2 bone-in chicken thighs, skinned
- 2 chicken drumsticks, skinned
- 2 tablespoons butter
- 1 tablespoon canola oil
- 3 tablespoons dry gin
- ¾ cup chopped celery
- ¾ cup chopped peeled carrot
- ½ cup chopped shallots (about 3 medium)
- 3 juniper berries, crushed
- 1 (8-ounce) package mushrooms, halved
- 3 sprigs fresh thyme
- 3 sprigs fresh flat-leaf parsley
- 1 bay leaf
- 1 cup dark beer
- ¼ cup whole-milk Greek-style yogurt
- 2 teaspoons white wine vinegar
- 1 tablespoon chopped fresh flat-leaf parsley

1 Combine first 3 ingredients; sprinkle evenly over both sides of chicken. Heat butter and oil in a large deep skillet over medium-high heat. Add chicken to pan; sauté 5 minutes on each side or until browned. Remove pan from heat. Pour gin into one side of pan; return pan to heat. Ignite gin with a long match; let flames die down. Remove chicken from pan; keep warm.

2 Add celery and next 3 ingredients to pan; sauté 5 minutes or until vegetables are tender, stirring occasionally. Add mushrooms. Place thyme, parsley, and bay leaf on a double layer of cheesecloth. Gather edges of cheesecloth together; tie securely. Add cheesecloth bag to pan. Return chicken to pan, nestling into vegetable mixture. Stir in beer; bring to a simmer. Cover, reduce heat, and simmer 45 minutes or until a thermometer inserted in meaty parts of chicken registers 160°. (Breasts may cook more quickly. Check them after 35 minutes, and remove when done; keep warm.)

③ Discard cheesecloth bag. Remove chicken from pan; keep warm. Place pan over medium heat; stir in yogurt. Cook 1 minute or until thoroughly heated (do not boil because yogurt can curdle). Remove from heat; stir in vinegar. Taste and adjust seasoning, if desired. Place 1 chicken breast half or 1 drumstick and 1 thigh on each of 4 plates; top each serving with about ³⁄₄ cup sauce and vegetable mixture. Sprinkle with chopped parsley. Yield: 4 servings.

CALORIES 370; FAT 16g (sat 6.6g, mono 5g, poly 3g); PROTEIN 30.8g; CARB 15.1g; FIBER 1.4g; CHOL 103mg; IRON 2mg; SODIUM 465mg; CALC 55mg

MAKE AHEAD

Gratin of Belgian Endive with Bacon (*Gratin d'Endives Ardennaise*)

Serve this dish as a hearty appetizer or side dish. If you prefer, double the serving size to yield four entrée portions. As endive leaves age, they curl and turn bitter, so be sure to choose plump, white, firm heads, and store them in a dark, cool place.

- 8 heads Belgian endive, trimmed and halved
- 1 teaspoon sugar
- ½ teaspoon salt, divided
- ½ teaspoon black pepper, divided
- 2 cups 2% reduced-fat milk, divided
- 1.1 ounces all-purpose flour (about ¼ cup)
- 1 tablespoon butter
- Dash of grated fresh nutmeg
- Cooking spray
- 2 slices center-cut bacon, cooked and crumbled
- ½ cup (2 ounces) shredded Gruyère cheese

① Preheat oven to 375°.

② Sprinkle endive evenly with sugar, ¼ teaspoon salt, and ¼ teaspoon pepper. Arrange endive halves, cut sides down, on a foil-lined baking sheet; cover with foil. Bake at 375° for 20 minutes or until endive is tender when pierced with a fork, turning after 15 minutes.

③ Increase oven temperature to 400°.

④ Cook 1³⁄₄ cups milk in a heavy saucepan over medium-high heat to 180° or until tiny bubbles form around edge (do not boil). To make a slurry, weigh or lightly spoon flour into a dry measuring cup; level with a knife. Stir flour into remaining ¼ cup milk, whisking until well blended. Stir slurry, remaining ¼ teaspoon salt, and remaining ¼ teaspoon pepper into hot milk; bring to a boil, stirring constantly with a whisk. Reduce heat to medium, and simmer 2 minutes or until sauce thickens. Remove from heat; add butter and nutmeg, stirring until blended. Taste and adjust seasoning, if desired.

⑤ Arrange endive in a 13 x 9–inch shallow casserole dish coated with cooking spray; sprinkle evenly with bacon. Pour sauce over endive; top with cheese. Bake at 400° for 20 minutes or until browned and bubbly. Yield: 8 servings (serving size: 2 endive halves and about ¼ cup sauce).

CALORIES 120; FAT 5.8g (sat 3.3g, mono 1.8g, poly 0.4g); PROTEIN 6.6g; CARB 11.2g; FIBER 3.6g; CHOL 18mg; IRON 0.5mg; SODIUM 263mg; CALC 179mg

---

How to Make a Gratin

Gratins are a subcategory of casseroles because they're baked in a shallow dish (not more than three inches deep), also called a "gratin," that allows for maximum surface area exposure. The ingredients often consist of vegetables covered with sauce and topped with breadcrumbs or cheese. Finally, the dish is baked or broiled until the top is golden. No matter what ingredients are arranged beneath, "gratin" actually refers to the golden brown topping.

A. Layer the vegetables in a shallow dish. Endive, potatoes, squash, tomatoes, eggplant, and a variety of vegetables work well in this preparation.

B. Separately make a sauce, and spread it over the top. Or you can simply add liquid, such as milk, cream, broth, or a combination, to the dish.

How to Make Cassoulet

A dish with humble beginnings in southwestern France's Languedoc region, cassoulet was originally tasty peasant fare made with white beans and a variety of meats, such as pork, lamb, duck, or goose. Today you find this hearty offering on French bistro menus in Paris and around the world. Traditional recipes can take a few days to prepare, but this version, done in a matter of hours, delivers the same rich flavor.

A. The classic Toulouse-style cassoulet directs you to prepare a lamb stew enriched with pork, bacon, sausage, and duck. Here we take a similar approach, beginning with rendering bacon and using the fat to brown lamb and duck separately in the casserole. Remove each, and set aside. Lightly brown the onion in the rich, meaty drippings to build on the flavor. Then stir in the tomato sauce. Return the meats to the pot, and bake until they're cooked and tender.

B. Traditional recipes begin with fresh or dried beans, but to save time, we use canned beans. Layer the beans, bacon, and meat mixture in the casserole so all of the elements simmer together to develop a rich, cohesive flavor.

C. The final step is to create a golden crust as the cassoulet bakes by sprinkling the mixture with dry breadcrumbs before the final baking.

D. The finished dish is a hearty, rich casserole with a crusty, browned top.

Cassoulet

Cassoulet serves a large gathering, and leftovers reheat well. Spicy precooked Italian sausage or Polish kielbasa are a close match to the lively garlic sausage from southwestern France traditionally used in this dish. Cassoulet can be prepared two days ahead and refrigerated; top with breadcrumbs and finish cooking it in the oven before serving.

- ¼ cup salt
- 6 (8-ounce) duck leg quarters
- 1½ tablespoons canola oil
- 4 thick-cut bacon slices, sliced crosswise into (½-inch-thick) strips
- 1 (¾-pound) boneless leg of lamb, trimmed and cut into (1-inch) cubes
- 1½ cups chopped onion
- ¼ teaspoon freshly ground black pepper
- ¼ cup no-salt-added tomato puree
- 3 garlic cloves, minced
- 2 cups fat-free, less-sodium chicken broth
- 2 cups water
- 4 (15-ounce) cans organic Great Northern beans, drained
- 8 ounces cooked spicy Italian sausage, diagonally sliced
- ¼ cup dry breadcrumbs

❶ Rub salt evenly over duck; cover and refrigerate 30 minutes.

❷ Heat oil in a large Dutch oven over medium heat. Add bacon to pan; cook 7 minutes or until crisp, stirring occasionally. Remove bacon from pan using a slotted spoon; set aside. Increase heat to medium-high. Add lamb to drippings in pan; cook 8 minutes, turning to brown on all sides. Remove lamb from pan, and set aside.

❸ Preheat oven to 300°.

❹ Rinse duck with cold water; pat dry with paper towels. Add half of duck, skin sides down, to pan; cook over medium heat 15 minutes or until golden brown. Turn duck over, and cook 10 minutes or until browned and fat under skin is melted. Remove duck from pan. Repeat procedure with remaining duck, reserving 1 tablespoon duck fat in pan; set duck aside. Add onion and pepper to pan; cook 7 minutes or until lightly browned, stirring occasionally. Stir in tomato puree and garlic; cook 1 minute. Return lamb to pan. Nestle duck into lamb mixture; add broth and 2 cups water. Cover and bake at 300° for 2½ hours or until lamb and duck are very tender. Remove duck from pan; let stand until tepid. Remove skin from duck; discard. Cut duck legs in half through joint. Return duck to lamb mixture. Taste and adjust seasoning, if desired.

5 Increase oven temperature to 375°.

6 Stir 2 cans of beans into lamb mixture. Add bacon and sausage; top mixture with remaining 2 cans of beans. Sprinkle breadcrumbs evenly over top. Cover and cook 1 hour and 10 minutes. Uncover and cook an additional 20 minutes or until browned and bubbly. Yield: 12 servings (serving size: 1 drumstick or thigh and about ¾ cup bean mixture).

CALORIES 323; FAT 14.4g (sat 4.6g, mono 4.4g, poly 1.2g); PROTEIN 27.1g; CARB 20g; FIBER 7.1g; CHOL 79mg; IRON 2.9mg; SODIUM 821mg; CALC 88mg

WINE NOTE: Traditionally, a rustic red from the south of France—a wine with the requisite meatiness and earthiness to mirror the duck and beans—is served with cassoulet. Try the Perrin & Fils Gigondas "La Gille" 2005 (Gigondas, France), $28, which is seductively earthy and has wonderful flavors of cherry jam.

With the right techniques, humble ingredients create a stellar dish worthy of entertaining.

MAKE AHEAD • FREEZABLE
Triple Red Pork Stew
(Ragout Pebronata)

Red wine, red peppers, and tomatoes join in this glorious Mediterranean mélange. Pasta or polenta would be welcome accompaniments. Prepare this stew up to three days ahead, refrigerate, and reheat to serve. You can also freeze it for up to a month.

- ¾ teaspoon salt, divided
- ½ teaspoon black pepper, divided
- 2 pounds boneless pork shoulder (Boston butt), trimmed and cut into (2-inch) cubes
- 2 tablespoons canola oil, divided
- 2 tablespoons all-purpose flour
- 3 cups shiraz or other hearty red wine, divided
- 1 (14-ounce) can fat-free, less-sodium beef broth
- 3 tablespoons olive oil, divided
- 1½ cups chopped onion
- 4 garlic cloves, chopped
- 3 pounds tomatoes, peeled, seeded, and cut in strips (about 4½ cups)
- 3 sprigs fresh flat-leaf parsley
- 3 springs fresh thyme
- 1 bay leaf
- 2 red bell peppers, cut into thin strips
- 4 cups hot cooked rigatoni pasta

1 Preheat oven to 350°.

2 Combine ½ teaspoon salt and ¼ teaspoon black pepper; sprinkle evenly over pork. Heat 1 tablespoon canola oil in a large Dutch oven over high heat. Add half of pork to pan; sauté 4 minutes, turning to brown on all sides. Remove pork from pan; keep warm. Repeat procedure with remaining 1 tablespoon canola oil and pork. Reduce heat to medium. Add flour to pan; sauté 1 minute or until flour browns, stirring constantly. Add 2 cups wine to pan; bring to a boil, scraping pan to loosen browned bits. Return pork to pan. Stir in broth; bring to a boil.

3 Cover and bake at 350° for 1½ hours or until pork crushes easily between your finger and thumb, stirring occasionally. Cool slightly. Remove pork from broth mixture using a slotted spoon. Bring broth mixture to a boil over high heat; cook until reduced to 1½ cups (about 15 minutes). Return pork to broth mixture, and cook 2 minutes or until thoroughly heated.

4 Heat 1½ tablespoons olive oil in large skillet over medium heat. Add onion to pan; sauté 5 minutes or until starting to brown, stirring frequently. Stir in garlic, and sauté 1 minute. Add remaining ¼ teaspoon salt, remaining ¼ teaspoon black pepper, tomatoes, and next 3 ingredients; bring to a simmer. Cook 30 minutes or until the mixture is thick, stirring occasionally.

5 Heat remaining 1½ tablespoons olive oil in a large skillet over medium heat. Add bell peppers to pan; sauté 10 minutes or until wilted, stirring frequently. Increase heat to high. Add remaining 1 cup wine, and bring to a boil. Cook until reduced by half (about 7 minutes). Add tomato mixture to bell pepper mixture. Reduce heat, and simmer 10 minutes or until thick, stirring occasionally. Discard parsley, thyme, and bay leaf. Stir sauce into pork mixture, and simmer an additional 10 minutes so flavors blend. Taste and adjust seasoning, if desired. Serve over pasta. Yield: 8 servings (serving size: ½ cup pasta and about ¾ cup pork mixture).

CALORIES 543; FAT 21.9g (sat 4.8g, mono 12g, poly 3.4g); PROTEIN 39.1g; CARB 48.3g; FIBER 5.9g; CHOL 98mg; IRON 4.7mg; SODIUM 567mg; CALC 65mg

Provençal Cod Steaks with Wilted Lettuce and Tomato

Braised lettuce is a tasty garnish for fish, protecting it from drying out and adding an unusual touch of green. The fish is surrounded by layers of onion, tomato, and lettuce, and then topped with lettuce leaves instead of a lid. Any firm fish can substitute for cod. Prepare up to two hours ahead, and serve at room temperature, if you wish.

- 6 (6-ounce) cod fillets
- 3 tablespoons red wine vinegar
- 3 tablespoons water
- 1 lemon
- 1 (12-ounce) head romaine lettuce, trimmed
- 3 cups peeled, seeded, and chopped tomato (about 2 pounds)
- 2 cups coarsely chopped onion
- 3 garlic cloves, minced
- Cooking spray
- 1 teaspoon salt, divided
- ½ teaspoon freshly ground black pepper, divided
- ¼ cup extra-virgin olive oil

❶ Place fillets in a shallow dish. Combine vinegar and 3 tablespoons water; drizzle over fillets. Cover and refrigerate 30 minutes.
❷ Carefully cut rind and white pithy part from lemon using a small knife. Cut lemon crosswise into thin slices; discard seeds. Reserve 6 whole lettuce leaves; coarsely shred remaining lettuce.
❸ Preheat oven to 325°.
❹ Layer about 2 cups shredded lettuce, 1½ cups tomato, 1 cup onion, 1½ teaspoons garlic, and half of lemon slices in a 13 x 9-inch casserole dish coated with cooking spray. Sprinkle vegetable mixture with ¼ teaspoon salt and ⅛ teaspoon pepper. Place fillets on top of vegetable mixture. Sprinkle fish evenly with ½ teaspoon salt and ¼ teaspoon pepper. Repeat layers with remaining chopped lettuce,

tomato, onion, garlic, and lemon slices. Sprinkle with remaining ¼ teaspoon salt and ⅛ teaspoon pepper. Top with reserved whole lettuce leaves; drizzle with oil.
❺ Bake at 325° for 20 minutes or until fish flakes easily when tested with a fork or until desired degree of doneness. Remove whole lettuce leaves and fillets from pan; keep warm. Return vegetables to oven. Bake an additional 20 minutes or until vegetables are tender. Place 1 whole lettuce leaf on each of 6 plates; top each serving with 1 fillet. Spoon about 1 cup vegetable mixture over each fillet. Yield: 6 servings.

CALORIES 269; FAT 10.4g (sat 1.5g, mono 6.8g, poly 1.4g); PROTEIN 29.6g; CARB 14.5g; FIBER 3.8g; CHOL 65mg; IRON 1.8mg; SODIUM 502mg; CALC 77mg

Big Night Menu
serves 10

This Italian-accented menu feeds a crowd. Make the beef up to three days ahead; then reheat and serve.

Milanese Braised Beef

Creamy polenta

Combine 3½ cups 2% reduced-fat milk; 1¼ cups fat-free, less-sodium chicken broth; and 1 teaspoon salt in a large saucepan; bring to a boil. Gradually add 1¼ cups instant polenta, stirring constantly with a whisk. Cook over medium heat 15 minutes or until thick, stirring frequently. Remove from heat; stir in ¾ cup (3 ounces) grated fresh Parmigiano-Reggiano cheese and ¼ cup mascarpone cheese. Serve immediately.

Garden salad

Milanese Braised Beef

This Italian recipe features the classic pairing of red wine with beef. A juicy stewing cut, such as chuck or top round, is slowly roasted in the casserole pot with wine and a few seasonings until tender. The added vegetables make this a complete meal. The flavor only gets better with time, so cook ahead, if you prefer, and store up to three days in the refrigerator before serving.

- 3 tablespoons all-purpose flour
- 1¼ teaspoons salt, divided
- ½ teaspoon freshly ground black pepper, divided
- ½ teaspoon ground cinnamon
- ⅛ teaspoon ground cloves
- 1 (3-pound) boneless chuck roast, trimmed
- 1 cup (¼-inch) cubed pancetta (about 4 ounces)
- 3 garlic cloves, sliced
- 1 tablespoon canola oil
- 1 tablespoon butter
- 1½ cups chopped onion
- 2 cups Chianti
- 1¼ cups fat-free, less-sodium beef broth
- 3 sprigs fresh basil
- 3 sprigs fresh marjoram
- 1 bay leaf
- 4 carrots, peeled and diagonally cut into (⅜-inch-thick) slices (about 12 ounces)
- 6 parsnips, peeled and diagonally cut into (⅜-inch-thick) slices (about 1½ pounds)
- ¼ cup water
- 1 tablespoon cornstarch

❶ Preheat oven to 300°.
❷ Combine flour, ¼ teaspoon salt, ¼ teaspoon pepper, cinnamon, and cloves, stirring well. Make several small slits on outside of roast with a paring knife; stuff with pancetta and garlic slices. Roll roast; secure at 1-inch intervals with twine. Sprinkle roast with

remaining 1 teaspoon salt and ¼ teaspoon pepper. Coat surface of roast with flour mixture, patting with your hands so it adheres.

❸ Heat oil and butter in a large Dutch oven over medium heat. Add roast to pan; cook 15 minutes, turning to brown on all sides. Add onion to pan around roast; cook 5 minutes or until browned. Stir in wine and broth. Place basil, marjoram, and bay leaf on a double layer of cheesecloth. Gather edges of cloth together; tie securely. Add cheesecloth bag to pan; bring to a boil. Cover and bake at 300° for 2½ hours, turning roast every 45 minutes. Nestle carrots and parsnips in pan; bake 1 additional hour or until roast is tender enough to cut with a spoon.

❹ Transfer roast and vegetables to a platter. Discard twine; keep beef and vegetables warm. Strain wine mixture through a sieve into a large bowl; discard cheesecloth bag. Return wine mixture to pan; bring to a boil. Cook 10 minutes. Combine ¼ cup water and cornstarch in small bowl, stirring with a whisk. Add cornstarch mixture to pan, and bring to a boil. Cook 1 minute, stirring constantly. Remove from heat. Taste and adjust seasoning, if desired. Serve with roast and vegeables. Yield: 10 servings (serving size: 2½ ounces beef, ½ cup vegetables, and ⅓ cup sauce).

CALORIES 462; FAT 18.4g (sat 6.9g, mono 7.6g, poly 1.7g); PROTEIN 45.9g; CARB 26.4g; FIBER 3.4g; CHOL 140mg; IRON 5.8mg; SODIUM 797mg; CALC 68mg

WINE NOTE: Pinot noir is a nice match for this classic casserole because the dish incorporates many flavors found in pinot (cinnamon, cloves, black pepper, and bay), plus the wine's hint of cherry is a sumptuous contrast to the savoriness of all those slow-cooked beefy flavors. An excellent pinot: Cambria "Julia's Vineyard" Pinot Noir 2006 ($24) from California's Santa Maria Valley.

Chinese New Year

Join a top Chinese-Canadian cook as he rings in the Year of the Ox with a delicious menu featuring symbolic recipes.

CHINESE NEW YEAR MARKS NOT ONLY A NEW BEGINNING but also the start of huge multicourse feasts. Large groups of family and friends gather to imbibe and eat sumptuous meals of special dishes considered auspicious because they represent wealth, luck, happiness, and long life—everything we all hope for in a new year. This year we'll observe the start of the Year of the Ox, January 26, and the fun will continue for two weeks.

CHINESE NEW YEAR MENU

(Serves 8)

Stir-Fried Shrimp with Garlic and Chile Sauce

Long Life Noodles

Stir-Fried Bok Choy and Lettuce with Mushrooms

Chinese Potstickers

Spicy Sweet-and-Sour Chicken

Salt-Baked Chicken

Pickled Spiced Cucumber, Carrots, and Daikon

Double Mango Pudding

Green tea

Assorted beers and wines

MAKE AHEAD
Pickled Spiced Cucumber, Carrots, and Daikon

The golden carrots represent prosperity in this spicy-hot, make-ahead condiment.

- 2 cups (1-inch) chopped peeled English cucumber (about 1 cucumber)
- 2 cups (½-inch) diced peeled daikon radish
- 1 cup (½-inch) diced peeled carrot
- 4 teaspoons coarse sea salt, divided
- 5 tablespoons sugar
- 6 tablespoons rice vinegar
- 1 teaspoon chili oil
- 3 Sichuan peppercorns, coarsely crushed
- 1 Thai chile, minced

❶ Combine first 3 ingredients in a large bowl. Add 2 teaspoons salt; toss well. Let stand 20 minutes. Transfer vegetable mixture to a colander. Rinse well with cold water; drain well.
❷ Combine remaining 2 teaspoons salt, sugar, and remaining ingredients in a large bowl. Add vegetable mixture; stir well. Transfer to an airtight container, and refrigerate at least 2 days before serving. Yield: 16 servings (serving size: about 2½ tablespoons).

CALORIES 26; FAT 0.4g (sat 0.1g, mono 0.1g, poly 0.2g); PROTEIN 0.3g; CARB 5.7g; FIBER 0.6g; CHOL 0mg; IRON 0.1mg; SODIUM 296mg; CALC 9mg

Prep Note

Stir-fried fare is best served hot from the pan, so as the host, expect to spend time in the kitchen. You can streamline the work, however, by chopping and slicing vegetables, cleaning shrimp, and combining sauces earlier in the day. Several dishes in our menu, like Double Mango Pudding, Chinese Potstickers, and Pickled Spiced Cucumber, Carrots, and Daikon, are meant to be prepared ahead of time—an arrangement that makes sense when you're having a party.

QUICK & EASY

Stir-Fried Shrimp with Garlic and Chile Sauce

A platter of succulent stir-fried orange-pink shrimp symbolizes gold coins (wealth) and good fortune for the coming year. Order fresh shrimp from the seafood counter; have it peeled and deveined while you shop for the rest of the menu.

- ½ cup fat-free, less-sodium chicken broth
- 2 teaspoons cornstarch
- 1 teaspoon sugar
- 2 teaspoons Shaoxing (Chinese rice wine) or dry sherry
- 2 teaspoons low-sodium soy sauce
- ¼ teaspoon white pepper
- 1 tablespoon canola oil
- 1½ pounds large shrimp, peeled and deveined
- 2 tablespoons minced garlic
- 1½ teaspoons minced peeled fresh ginger
- 1 jalapeño pepper, seeded and finely chopped
- ½ cup (1-inch) slices green onions
- ½ teaspoon dark sesame oil
- Cilantro sprigs (optional)

1 Combine first 6 ingredients in a small bowl, stirring with a whisk.
2 Heat a wok or large skillet over high heat. Add canola oil to pan. Add shrimp to pan; stir-fry 1 minute or until shrimp begin to turn pink. Add garlic, ginger, and jalapeño; stir-fry 1 minute. Stir in broth mixture; cook 1 minute or until shrimp are done and sauce is thickened, stirring constantly. Remove from heat; stir in onions and sesame oil. Garnish with cilantro sprigs, if desired. Yield: 8 servings (serving size: ½ cup).

CALORIES 120; FAT 3.5g (sat 0.5g, mono 1.4g, poly 1.2g); PROTEIN 17.7g; CARB 3.4g; FIBER 0.3g; CHOL 129mg; IRON 2.2mg; SODIUM 200mg; CALC 53mg

QUICK & EASY

Stir-Fried Bok Choy and Lettuce with Mushrooms

The lettuce represents growing wealth for the coming year as the Cantonese word for lettuce is *saang choy*, which sounds like "increasing fortune."

- 1 cup boiling water
- 8 dried shiitake mushrooms (about 2 ounces)
- 2 tablespoons low-sodium soy sauce
- 1 tablespoon Shaoxing (Chinese rice wine) or dry sherry
- ½ teaspoon sugar
- 4 teaspoons canola oil, divided
- 1 teaspoon minced peeled fresh ginger
- ½ cup fat-free, less-sodium chicken broth
- 2 tablespoons oyster sauce
- ½ teaspoon cornstarch
- 2 medium garlic cloves, thinly sliced
- 8 heads baby bok choy, halved lengthwise
- 1 medium head romaine lettuce, cut crosswise into 1-inch pieces (about 8 cups)

1 Combine 1 cup boiling water and mushrooms in a bowl; cover and let stand 20 minutes. Drain mushrooms in a colander over a bowl, reserving liquid. Rinse mushrooms. Remove and discard stems; cut each cap into quarters. Set aside.
2 Combine soy sauce, wine, and sugar in a small bowl, stirring with a whisk.
3 Heat a small saucepan over medium-high heat. Add 1 teaspoon oil and ginger to pan; sauté 30 seconds. Add reserved mushrooms; sauté 1 minute. Add reserved mushroom liquid and broth; bring to a boil. Cover, reduce heat, and simmer 20 minutes.
4 Combine oyster sauce and cornstarch in a small bowl, stirring with a whisk; stir into mushroom mixture. Bring to a boil, stirring constantly. Cook 1 minute or until thickened. Remove from heat; keep warm.
5 Heat a wok or large skillet over high heat. Add remaining 1 tablespoon oil to pan. Add garlic; stir-fry 10 seconds. Add bok choy; stir-fry 2 minutes or until bok choy begins to soften. Add lettuce; stir-fry 2 minutes or until lettuce wilts. Stir in mushroom mixture and soy sauce mixture; cook 3 minutes or until bok choy is tender. Yield: 8 servings (serving size: about ⅔ cup).

CALORIES 105; FAT 3.4g (sat 0.3g, mono 1.5g, poly 1.2g); PROTEIN 7.7g; CARB 15.5g; FIBER 5.9g; CHOL 0mg; IRON 4.1mg; SODIUM 468mg; CALC 463mg

Salt-Baked Chicken

Traditionally, this recipe uses a whole chicken, marinated, wrapped in lotus leaves, immersed in a bed of hot rock salt in a wok, and cooked on a stovetop. The modern convenience of an oven makes it much easier to control the cooking temperature. Allowing the chicken to stand at room temperature for an hour before cooking creates succulent results.

- 2½ cups boiling water
- 1 (1 x 2-inch) strip dried tangerine peel
- 1 (4.5- to 5-pound) roasting chicken
- 5½ teaspoons coarse sea salt, divided
- ¼ cup finely chopped shallots
- 2 tablespoons minced ginger
- 2 tablespoons Shaoxing (Chinese rice wine) or dry sherry
- 1 tablespoon low-sodium soy sauce
- 1½ teaspoons sesame oil
- 1 teaspoon honey
- 2 green onions, cut into 1-inch pieces
- Cooking spray

❶ Combine 2½ cups boiling water and tangerine peel in a bowl; cover and let stand 30 minutes. Drain in a colander over a bowl, reserving liquid.

❷ Remove and discard giblets and neck from chicken. Trim excess fat. Starting at neck cavity, loosen skin from breast and drumsticks by inserting fingers, gently pushing between skin and meat. Rub 1 tablespoon salt under skin; let stand 5 minutes. Rinse chicken under cold water; pat dry with paper towels. Place chicken on rack of a roasting pan; let stand 1 hour at room temperature.

❸ Preheat oven to 425°.

❹ Transfer chicken to a work surface. Combine remaining 2½ teaspoons salt, shallots, and next 5 ingredients in a small bowl. Rub 3 tablespoons shallot mixture inside cavity of chicken. Place onions and tangerine peel inside cavity. Rub remaining shallot mixture under loosened skin.

❺ Place chicken, breast side up, on rack of a roasting pan coated with cooking spray. Pour reserved tangerine soaking liquid into a shallow roasting pan; place rack in pan. Bake at 425° for 1 hour or until a meat thermometer registers 165° and skin has turned a dark golden brown color. Let stand 15 minutes. Discard skin, and slice. Yield: 8 servings (serving size: 3 ounces).

CALORIES 171; FAT 4.4g (sat 1g, mono 1.4g, poly 1.2g); PROTEIN 26.8g; CARB 2.5g; FIBER 0.3g; CHOL 85mg; IRON 1.6mg; SODIUM 885mg; CALC 21mg

Year of the Ox

Chinese astrology is portrayed by 12 animal signs, each with its own symbolism and characteristics. Every New Year ushers in a new sign. Unlike the traditional January 1st New Year in the West, the start of Chinese New Year changes depending on the Chinese lunar calendar. In 2009, the Year of the Ox began on January 26, and people born under this sign are said to be honest, reliable, hardworking, pragmatic, and tolerant, with sound financial judgment.

Spicy Sweet-and-Sour Chicken

This home-style sweet-and-sour chicken has a lighter, fresher-tasting sauce than typical restaurant versions.

    4   teaspoons cornstarch, divided
    5   teaspoons low-sodium soy sauce, divided
    1   teaspoon minced peeled fresh ginger
    1   teaspoon dark soy sauce
    1   teaspoon Shaoxing (Chinese rice wine) or dry sherry
    ⅛   teaspoon white pepper
    2   garlic cloves, minced
    1   pound skinless, boneless chicken breast, cut into 2 x ½-inch-thick pieces
    ½   cup fat-free, less-sodium chicken broth
    1   tablespoon brown sugar
    3   tablespoons ketchup
    2½ tablespoons rice vinegar
    2   teaspoons chile paste
    1   teaspoon dark sesame oil
    1   tablespoon canola oil, divided
    1   cup (½-inch) diced onion
    1   cup (½-inch) diced green bell pepper
    1   cup (½-inch) diced medium red bell pepper
    ½   cup (1-inch) slices green onions
    1   cup (½-inch) diced fresh pineapple

❶ Combine 2 teaspoons cornstarch, 2 teaspoons low-sodium soy sauce, and next 5 ingredients in a medium bowl. Add chicken; stir well to coat. Set aside.

❷ Combine broth, remaining 2 teaspoons cornstarch, brown sugar, remaining 1 tablespoon low-sodium soy sauce, ketchup, and next 3 ingredients.

❸ Heat ½ teaspoon canola oil in a large skillet over medium-high heat. Add diced onion, bell peppers, and green onions to pan; sauté 4 minutes or until crisp-tender. Transfer to a bowl.

❹ Heat remaining 2½ teaspoons canola oil in pan. Add chicken mixture to pan, and spread in an even layer; cook, without stirring, 1 minute. Sauté an additional 3 minutes or until chicken is done.

❺ Return vegetable mixture to pan. Add soy sauce mixture and pineapple, stirring well to combine. Bring to a boil; cook 1 minute or until thickened, stirring constantly. Yield: 8 servings (serving size: about ⅔ cup).

CALORIES 132; FAT 3.8g (sat 0.6g, mono 1.7g, poly 1.1g); PROTEIN 12.7g; CARB 12.2g; FIBER 1.4g; CHOL 31mg; IRON 0.9mg; SODIUM 304mg; CALC 26mg

MAKE AHEAD
Double Mango Pudding

Orange mangoes symbolize gold and riches. Prepare and chill pudding the night before. Whip the cream just before serving.

    3   mangoes, peeled and divided
    2¼ cups water, divided
    ½   cup sugar
    1   tablespoon unflavored gelatin
    ¼   cup whipping cream

❶ Coarsely chop 2 mangoes. Dice remaining mango.

❷ Combine coarsely chopped mangoes and ¼ cup water in a blender; process until smooth. Press puree through a fine sieve over a bowl; discard solids.

❸ Bring ¾ cup water to a boil in a medium saucepan. Add sugar to pan, stirring until dissolved. Remove from heat. Stir in remaining 1¼ cups water. Sprinkle gelatin over water in saucepan; let stand 1 minute. Add mango puree, stirring with a whisk. Pour mixture evenly into each of 8 (6-ounce) ramekins or custard cups. Cover and chill overnight or until set. Top evenly with diced mango.

❹ Place cream in a medium bowl; beat with a mixer at high speed until stiff peaks form. Serve with pudding. Yield: 8 servings (serving size: 1 ramekin and 1 tablespoon whipped cream).

CALORIES 127; FAT 3g (sat 1.8g, mono 0.9g, poly 0.1g); PROTEIN 1.3g; CARB 25.9g; FIBER 1.4g; CHOL 10mg; IRON 0.1mg; SODIUM 8mg; CALC 15mg

New Year Pantry

You'll need a few ingredients to lend your celebration authentic flavor. You can find many of these items in large supermarkets, and all of them in an Asian grocery. We also offer suggestions for substitutions, where applicable.

• **Sesame oil.** You'll find two varieties: light, which has subtle flavor and a high smoke point that makes it ideal for stir-frying, and dark, which has a nutty flavor and aroma and is typically used to finish a dish or a dipping sauce.

• **Dried mushrooms.** We used readily available shiitake mushrooms (also called Chinese black mushrooms) for recipe testing. But try any variety or combination of Asian dried mushrooms, such as wood ear, cloud ear, and Chinese black.

• **Shaoxing.** This fermented rice wine (pronounced shaow-SHEEN) is produced in northern China. If you pick up a bottle labeled "Shaoxing Cooking Wine," know that it might contain added salt, so you may need to cut back on salt in the recipe. Substitute dry sherry in a pinch.

• **Chinese black vinegar.** This assertively flavored rice vinegar is often used in stir-fries. Substitute balsamic vinegar.

• **Hoisin sauce.** Made from soybeans, sugar, garlic, Chinese five-spice powder, and chiles, this thick sauce lends sweet flavor and a reddish hue to stir-fries and other dishes.

• **Oyster sauce.** Redolent with the briny essence of oysters, this smoky-sweet sauce has a thick texture and dark-brown color. It is used in noodle dishes and stir-fries.

• **Soy sauce.** Made from fermented soybeans and roasted wheat or barley, this condiment lends a meaty saltiness to Asian fare. We call for low-sodium soy sauce to keep sodium in check, along with dark soy sauce, which has richer flavor and color.

MAKE AHEAD • FREEZABLE

Chinese Potstickers

Variations of these dumplings are popular throughout China. In northern China they are served in the hours between the old and new year. These potstickers may take some time to prepare, but gather a few friends to help assemble them. Cook two dozen for your party, and freeze the extras for future snacks or meals. Simply pop the extra, uncooked dumplings in a heavy-duty zip-top plastic bag.

DUMPLINGS:

- 3 cups chopped napa (Chinese) cabbage (about 4 ounces)
- 4 dried shiitake mushrooms (about 1½ ounces)
- ¼ cup finely chopped green onions
- 2 tablespoons plus 1 teaspoon cornstarch, divided
- 1½ teaspoons minced peeled fresh ginger
- 1 teaspoon sugar
- 1½ teaspoons oyster sauce
- ⅛ teaspoon white pepper
- 5 ounces lean ground pork
- 5 ounces ground chicken breast
- 1 large egg white
- 48 gyoza skins
- ¼ cup canola oil, divided
- 1⅓ cups water, divided

SAUCE:

- 3 tablespoons finely chopped peeled fresh ginger
- 2 tablespoons minced green onions
- 3 tablespoons dark soy sauce
- 6 tablespoons low-sodium soy sauce
- 3 tablespoons Chinese black vinegar or balsamic vinegar
- 2 tablespoons Shaoxing (Chinese cooking wine) or dry sherry
- 2 teaspoons chile puree with garlic sauce
- 2 teaspoons dark sesame oil

❶ To prepare dumplings, cook cabbage in boiling water 1 minute or until tender. Drain and rinse with cold water; drain. Cool; chop.

❷ Place mushrooms in a small bowl; cover with boiling water. Cover and let stand 30 minutes or until tender. Drain mushrooms; chop.

❸ Combine cabbage, mushrooms, ¼ cup green onions, 2 tablespoons cornstarch, and next 7 ingredients in a large bowl. Cover and refrigerate 4 hours.

❹ Working with 1 gyoza skin at a time (cover remaining gyoza skins to prevent drying), spoon 2 teaspoons pork mixture into center of each skin. Moisten edges of gyoza skin with water. Fold in half, pinching edges together to seal. Place dumpling, seam side up, on a baking sheet sprinkled with remaining 1 teaspoon cornstarch (cover loosely with a towel to prevent drying). Repeat procedure with remaining gyoza skins and filling.

❺ Heat 1 tablespoon canola oil in a large nonstick skillet over medium-high heat. Add 12 dumplings to pan; cook 3 minutes. Add ⅓ cup water. Reduce heat, and simmer 3 minutes or until water evaporates. Repeat procedure with remaining canola oil, dumplings, and water.

❻ To prepare sauce, combine 3 tablespoons chopped ginger and remaining ingredients in a small bowl. Serve sauce with dumplings. Yield: 16 servings (serving size: 3 dumplings and about 1 tablespoon sauce).

CALORIES 132; FAT 5.1g (sat 0.7g, mono 2.3g, poly 1.3g); PROTEIN 6.5g; CARB 14.7g; FIBER 1g; CHOL 15mg; IRON 0.8mg; SODIUM 511mg; CALC 23mg

Long Life Noodles

Any type of noodle is a must at Chinese New Year. However, long noodles represent a long unbroken life (so cutting them into shorter strands would symbolically shorten your life). Pull out your largest skillet or wok because this recipe creates a full pan.

- 1 pound fresh Asian-style wheat noodles
- 1½ tablespoons Shaoxing (Chinese rice wine) or dry sherry
- 1½ teaspoons hoisin sauce
- ½ teaspoon cornstarch
- 6 ounces boneless pork tenderloin cut into 2 x ¼-inch julienne strips
- 3 tablespoons dark soy sauce
- 2 tablespoons oyster sauce
- 1 tablespoon low-sodium soy sauce
- ½ teaspoon sugar
- 2 tablespoons canola oil, divided
- 3 cups chopped napa (Chinese) cabbage
- ½ teaspoon minced garlic
- 1¼ cups (1-inch) slices green onions

❶ Cook noodles according to package directions, omitting fat and salt. Drain and rinse with cold water; drain. Set aside.

❷ Combine wine, hoisin sauce, and cornstarch in a small bowl, stirring with a whisk. Add pork; stir to coat. Cover and let stand 10 minutes.

❸ Combine dark soy sauce and next 3 ingredients in a small bowl, stirring with a whisk; set mixture aside.

❹ Heat 1 teaspoon oil in a wok or large skillet over high heat. Add cabbage to pan; stir-fry 2 minutes. Transfer cabbage to a bowl.

❺ Heat 2 teaspoons oil in pan. Add garlic; stir-fry 10 seconds or until fragrant. Add pork mixture; stir-fry 3 minutes or until done. Add pork mixture to bowl with cabbage.

❻ Wipe pan clean with paper towels, and return to heat. Heat remaining 1 tablespoon oil. Add reserved noodles; stir-fry 1 minute. Add onions and soy sauce mixture to pan, and stir-fry 1 minute. Add pork mixture; stir to combine. Cook 1 minute or until hot. Yield: 8 servings (serving size: about ¾ cup).

CALORIES 164; FAT 5g (sat 0.5g, mono 2.4g, poly 1.2g); PROTEIN 9.3g; CARB 19.6g; FIBER 0.8g; CHOL 14mg; IRON 0.6mg; SODIUM 550mg; CALC 36mg

Noodles

A noodle dish is crucial to your New Year celebration since long pasta represents a long life. You'll often find several types of dried Asian noodles at supermarkets, and all manner of dried and fresh varieties at Asian groceries. Just follow the package directions for cooking the noodles before adding them to a stir-fry. Sturdy wheat noodles with added egg, such as *e-fu*, lo mein, or Shanghai-style noodles, are good candidates.

> The New Year's Eve meal is the most important Chinese celebration. Each family incorporates foods that have special meanings, and the dinner usually consists of eight or nine dishes since both numbers are considered lucky.

TECHNIQUE

Savory Quick Breads

Round out your next meal with these simple loaves, scones, and popovers. They stir together and bake in about an hour.

Savory quick breads—excellent accompaniments to soups, salads, and main dishes—are simple to make, requiring only that you measure ingredients precisely and mix lightly. We share recipes for three types of quick breads here.

Quick bread **loaves** are the most straightforward—simply combine the dry ingredients, add the wet, mix, and scrape the batter into a loaf pan.

When preparing **scones**, cut chilled butter into the dry ingredients until the mixture resembles coarse meal. The small bits of flour-coated butter will melt during baking, yielding a tender, flaky scone. Avoid overworking the butter or your scones will come out crumbly and dry.

Unlike quick bread loaves and scones, **popovers** don't have a leavening agent such as baking soda or baking powder. Instead, their high proportion of liquid helps the batter rise. Allow the milk and egg mixture to stand at room temperature for 30 minutes before adding the dry ingredients. In addition, preheat the pan before adding the batter, which will cause it to immediately begin to rise. Use a popover pan if you have one. Otherwise, a standard muffin tin will suffice, but bake the popovers about five minutes less than you would in a popover pan.

Quick breads taste best right after they're baked, so plan to prepare them no more than a few hours before serving. The wonderful aroma of freshly baked bread will waft through the kitchen, and the tender bread that emerges from the oven will be a welcome addition to your meal.

Pumpkin-Parmesan Scones

Canned pumpkin puree makes these scones moist and tender, and it imbues them with the antioxidant beta-carotene. Pumpkinseed kernels add nutty crunch. Serve with a hearty soup or stew.

6.75 ounces all-purpose flour (about 1½ cups)
2.38 ounces whole wheat flour (about ½ cup)
   2 teaspoons baking powder
   ½ teaspoon baking soda
   ½ teaspoon salt
   ¼ cup chilled butter, cut into small pieces
   ½ cup canned pumpkin
   ½ cup fat-free plain yogurt
   2 large egg whites, divided
   2 tablespoons grated fresh Parmesan cheese
   1 tablespoon pumpkinseed kernels

❶ Preheat oven to 400°.
❷ Weigh or lightly spoon flours into dry measuring cups; level with a knife. Combine flours, baking powder, baking soda, and salt in a large bowl; cut in butter with a pastry blender or 2 knives until mixture resembles coarse meal. Combine pumpkin, yogurt, and 1 egg white, stirring with a whisk. Add to flour mixture; stir just until moist.
❸ Turn dough out onto a lightly floured surface; knead lightly 4 times with floured hands. Pat dough into an 8-inch circle on a baking sheet lined with parchment paper. Cut dough into 12 wedges, cutting into but not through dough. Brush remaining 1 egg white over top of dough. Sprinkle dough with cheese and pumpkinseeds, pressing lightly to adhere. Bake at 400° for 20 minutes or until golden. Slice scones along score lines with a serrated knife. Serve warm. Yield: 12 servings (serving size: 1 wedge).

CALORIES 129; FAT 4.9g (sat 2.7g, mono 1.2g, poly 0.5g); PROTEIN 4.4g; CARB 17.6g; FIBER 1.4g; CHOL 11mg; IRON 1.3mg; SODIUM 253mg; CALC 83mg

Parsley-Lemon-Garlic Popovers

The Italian garnish known as gremolata—made of parsley, lemon rind, and garlic—provides the basis for these tasty popovers. Try them with beef tenderloin or pot roast.

   1 cup 2% reduced-fat milk
   2 large egg whites
   1 large egg
2.75 ounces all-purpose flour (about ⅔ cup)
1.5 ounces whole wheat flour (about ⅓ cup)
   ¼ teaspoon salt
   ¼ cup finely chopped fresh flat-leaf parsley
   1 teaspoon grated lemon rind
   1 large garlic clove, minced
      Cooking spray
   2 teaspoons butter, melted

❶ Combine first 3 ingredients in a medium bowl, stirring with a whisk until blended. Let stand 30 minutes.
❷ Preheat oven to 375°.
❸ Weigh or lightly spoon flours into dry measuring cups; level with a knife. Combine flours and salt, stirring with a whisk. Gradually add flour mixture to milk mixture, stirring well with a whisk. Stir in parsley, rind, and garlic.
❹ Coat 6 popover cups with cooking spray; brush butter evenly among cups to coat. Place popover cups in a 375° oven for 5 minutes. Divide batter evenly among prepared popover cups. Bake at 375° for 40 minutes or until golden. Serve immediately. Yield: 6 servings (serving size: 1 popover).

CALORIES 124; FAT 3.2g (sat 1.6g, mono 0.9g, poly 0.3g); PROTEIN 6.1g; CARB 17.9g; FIBER 1.3g; CHOL 42mg; IRON 1.3mg; SODIUM 160mg; CALC 64mg

Kalamata Olive Bread with Oregano

A Greek salad and Pork Chops Oreganata (page 50) go well with this fragrant loaf, though simply buttered slices will also satisfy.

   1 tablespoon olive oil
   1 cup finely chopped onion
   9 ounces all-purpose flour (about 2 cups)
   1 teaspoon baking soda
   ½ teaspoon salt
   1 cup low-fat buttermilk
   2 tablespoons butter, melted
   2 large egg whites
   ¼ cup pitted kalamata olives, chopped
   1 tablespoon chopped fresh oregano
      Cooking spray

❶ Preheat oven to 350°.
❷ Heat oil in a large nonstick skillet over medium-high heat. Add onion to pan; sauté 3 minutes or until onion is tender. Set aside.
❸ Weigh or lightly spoon flour into dry measuring cups; level with a knife. Combine flour, baking soda, and salt in a large bowl; make a well in center of mixture. Combine buttermilk, butter, and egg whites, stirring with a whisk. Add buttermilk mixture to flour mixture, stirring just until moist. Fold in onion, olives, and oregano.
❹ Spread batter into an 8 x 4-inch loaf pan coated with cooking spray. Bake at 350° for 45 minutes or until a wooden pick inserted in center comes out clean. Cool 10 minutes in pan on a wire rack; remove from pan. Cool completely on wire rack. Yield: 12 servings (serving size: 1 slice).

CALORIES 133; FAT 4.6g (sat 1.8g, mono 2.2g, poly 0.4g); PROTEIN 3.8g; CARB 18.8g; FIBER 0.8g; CHOL 7mg; IRON 1mg; SODIUM 302mg; CALC 39mg

Parmesan Popovers

Classic popovers are moist on the inside, crispy on the outside. We've added a crunchy top layer of Parmesan. If you don't have the cheese on hand, simply omit it for a more traditional version.

- 1 cup 2% reduced-fat milk
- 2 large egg whites
- 1 large egg
- 2.75 ounces all-purpose flour (about ⅔ cup)
- 1.5 ounces whole wheat flour (about ⅓ cup)
- ¼ teaspoon salt
- Cooking spray
- 2 teaspoons butter, melted
- ¼ cup (1 ounce) grated fresh Parmesan cheese

1 Combine first 3 ingredients in a medium bowl, stirring with a whisk until blended. Let stand 30 minutes.
2 Preheat oven to 375°.
3 Weigh or lightly spoon flours into dry measuring cups; level with a knife. Combine flours and salt, stirring with a whisk. Gradually add flour mixture to milk mixture, stirring well with a whisk.
4 Coat 6 popover cups with cooking spray; brush butter evenly among cups to coat. Place popover cups in a 375° oven for 5 minutes. Divide batter evenly among prepared popover cups. Sprinkle evenly with cheese. Bake at 375° for 40 minutes or until golden. Serve immediately. Yield: 6 servings (serving size: 1 popover).

CALORIES 143; FAT 4.5g (sat 2.3g, mono 0.9g, poly 0.3g); PROTEIN 8g; CARB 17.5g; FIBER 1.2g; CHOL 45mg; IRON 1.1mg; SODIUM 243mg; CALC 127mg

Buttermilk Quick Bread

Savory flavor, tender texture, and a crunchy crust make this bread a good all-purpose accompaniment.

- 9 ounces all-purpose flour (about 2 cups)
- 2 tablespoons sugar
- 1 teaspoon baking soda
- ½ teaspoon salt
- 1½ cups low-fat buttermilk
- ¼ cup butter, melted
- 2 large egg whites
- Cooking spray

1 Preheat oven to 350°.
2 (A) Weigh or lightly spoon flour into dry measuring cups, and level with a knife. Combine flour and next 3 ingredients in a large bowl; (B) make a well in center of mixture. Combine buttermilk, butter, and egg whites, stirring with a spoon. (C) Add to flour mixture, (D) stirring just until moist.
3 Spread batter into an 8 x 4–inch loaf pan coated with cooking spray. Bake at 350° for 45 minutes or until a wooden pick inserted in center comes out clean. Cool 10 minutes in pan on a wire rack; remove from pan. Cool completely on wire rack. Yield: 12 servings (serving size: 1 slice).

CALORIES 137; FAT 4.6g (sat 2.8g, mono 1.2g, poly 0.3g); PROTEIN 4.1g; CARB 19.7g; FIBER 0.6g; CHOL 12mg; IRON 1mg; SODIUM 266mg; CALC 48mg

A

B

C

D

Black Pepper–Sage Popovers

These savory popovers go well with roast chicken or turkey. Vary them by substituting finely chopped fresh marjoram or thyme for sage.

- 1 cup 2% reduced-fat milk
- 1 tablespoon finely chopped fresh sage
- 2 large egg whites
- 1 large egg
- 2.75 ounces all-purpose flour (about ⅔ cup)
- 1.5 ounces whole wheat flour (about ⅓ cup)
- ¼ teaspoon salt
- ⅛ teaspoon coarsely ground black pepper
  Cooking spray
- 2 teaspoons butter, melted

1 Combine first 4 ingredients in a medium bowl, stirring with a whisk until blended. Let stand 30 minutes.
2 Preheat oven to 375°.
3 Weigh or lightly spoon flours into dry measuring cups; level with a knife. Combine flours, salt, and pepper, stirring with a whisk. Gradually add flour mixture to milk mixture, stirring well with a whisk.
4 Coat 6 popover cups with cooking spray, and brush melted butter evenly among cups to coat. Place popover cups in a 375° oven for 5 minutes. Divide batter evenly among prepared popover cups. Bake at 375° for 40 minutes or until golden. Serve immediately. Yield: 6 servings (serving size: 1 popover).

CALORIES 123; FAT 3.2g (sat 1.6g, mono 0.9g, poly 0.3g); PROTEIN 6g; CARB 17.6g; FIBER 1.2g; CHOL 42mg; IRON 1.1mg; SODIUM 257mg; CALC 61mg

QUICK & EASY
Yogurt Scones

These scones are terrific with chili, or you can split them in half lengthwise and serve with sloppy joe sauce.

- 6.75 ounces all-purpose flour (about 1½ cups)
- 2.38 ounces whole wheat flour (about ½ cup)
- 1 tablespoon sugar
- 2 teaspoons baking powder
- ½ teaspoon baking soda
- ½ teaspoon salt
- ¼ cup chilled butter, cut into small pieces
- ½ cup thinly sliced green onions
- ¾ cup fat-free plain yogurt
- 1 large egg white

1 Preheat oven to 425°.
2 Weigh or lightly spoon flours into dry measuring cups; level with a knife. Combine flours and next 4 ingredients in a large bowl; cut in butter with a pastry blender or 2 knives until mixture resembles coarse meal. Stir in onions. Combine yogurt and egg white, stirring with a whisk. Add to flour mixture, stirring just until moist (dough will be sticky).
3 Turn dough out onto a lightly floured surface; knead lightly 4 times with floured hands. Pat dough into an 8-inch circle on a baking sheet lined with parchment paper. Cut dough into 12 wedges, cutting into but not through dough. Bake at 425° for 15 minutes or until golden. Serve warm. Yield: 12 servings (serving size: 1 wedge).

CALORIES 121; FAT 4g (sat 2.4g, mono 1g, poly 0.3g); PROTEIN 3.3g; CARB 18.3g; FIBER 1.1g; CHOL 10mg; IRON 1.1mg; SODIUM 273mg; CALC 72mg

INSPIRED VEGETARIAN
Culinary Crossroad

A tasty blend of North African, Arabic, Spanish, and French influences, Moroccan food satisfies a craving for the exotic.

Morocco's long history is reflected in its food. The country is situated on the North African shores of the Mediterranean and incorporates the rugged Atlas Mountains. Nomadic North African Berbers created the basis of the country's lush and varied cuisine. But a raft of foreign influences flavors Moroccan cuisine, as well.

A centuries-old penchant for Persian sweet-and-sour cooking styles still persists, and ingredients like saffron, nuts, pickled lemons, and pomegranates are staples of the Moroccan larder. These Arabic foods and Spanish culinary hallmarks, such as olives, olive oils, herbs, peppers, and salt, were introduced to Moroccan cooks in the 15th century, when the Spanish Inquisition drove Spanish Muslims and Jews to Morocco.

The French colonized North Africa from the late 1800s through 1956; their legacy is seen in the trendy restaurants of the country's cities, such as Fez and Marrakesh. Urban chefs embrace a "Nouvelle Marocaine" style in which French techniques and flavors meld with native recipes.

One constant in Moroccan food is delicious vegetarian fare. Our recipes use winter produce, nuts, chickpeas, lentils, and couscous to deliver authentic tastes with ingredients you'll find in any large supermarket.

Ras el Hanout

The blend's Arabic name means "head" or "top of the shop," and variations can contain up to 27 different spices, depending on the recipe.

- 2½ teaspoons kosher salt
- 2 teaspoons ground cumin
- 2 teaspoons ground ginger
- 2 teaspoons freshly ground black pepper
- 1½ teaspoons ground cinnamon
- 1 teaspoon ground coriander
- 1 teaspoon ground red pepper
- 1 teaspoon ground allspice
- 1 teaspoon saffron threads, crushed
- ½ teaspoon ground cloves
- ¼ teaspoon freshly ground nutmeg

❶ Combine all ingredients in a small bowl. Store in an airtight container for up to 1 month. Yield: ¼ cup (serving size: ¼ teaspoon).

CALORIES 2; FAT 0.1g (sat 0g, mono 0g, poly 0g); PROTEIN 0.1g; CARB 0.3g; FIBER 0.1g; CHOL 0mg; IRON 0.1mg; SODIUM 98mg; CALC 3mg

Moroccan Country Bread (Khubz Maghrebi)

Though best eaten the day it's made, you can also freeze the bread for up to one month; thaw at room temperature, wrap in foil, and reheat at 300° for 15 minutes.

- 1½ packages dry yeast (about 1 tablespoon)
- 2½ cups warm water (100° to 110°)
- 31.5 ounces all-purpose flour (about 7 cups) plus 2 teaspoons, divided
- 2 teaspoons kosher salt
- Cooking spray
- 1 tablespoon extra-virgin olive oil

❶ Dissolve yeast in 2½ cups warm water in a large bowl. Weigh or lightly spoon flour into dry measuring cups; level with a knife. Stir salt into yeast mixture. Gradually stir in 7 cups flour, one cup at a time; beat with a mixer at medium speed until dough forms a ball. Turn dough out onto a lightly floured surface; shape dough into a 12-inch log. Divide dough into 3 pieces; shape each piece into a (4-inch) dome-shaped loaf. Place loaves on a baking sheet lightly covered with flour; dust tops lightly with 2 teaspoons flour, and lightly coat with cooking spray. Cover and let rise in a warm place (85°), free from drafts, 1 hour or until doubled in size. (Gently press two fingers into dough. If indentation remains, dough has risen enough.)
❷ Position oven rack in lower third of oven. Preheat oven to 350°.
❸ Uncover loaves, and brush each with 1 teaspoon oil. Bake at 350° for 30 minutes or until bread sounds hollow when tapped (bread doesn't brown). Remove from oven; cool on wire racks. Yield: 24 servings (serving size: ⅛ of a loaf).

CALORIES 139; FAT 0.9g (sat 0.1g, mono 0.5g, poly 0.2g); PROTEIN 4g; CARB 28g; FIBER 1.1g; CHOL 0mg; IRON 1.8mg; SODIUM 161mg; CALC 6mg

Orange and Olive Salad (S'lata Botukan wa Zaytoon)

Salads are a key part of Moroccan meals; several salads with various fruits or vegetables may be on the table at lunch or dinner. To prepare ahead, refrigerate the orange mixture and juice mixture separately. Bring to room temperature and toss before serving.

- 4 oranges, peeled
- ½ cup green olives, pitted and halved (such as picholine or cerignola)
- ¼ cup finely chopped fresh cilantro
- ¼ teaspoon kosher salt
- ¼ teaspoon freshly ground black pepper
- 2½ tablespoons fresh lemon juice
- 1½ tablespoons olive oil
- 1 teaspoon orange-flower water
- Dash of sugar

❶ Cut each orange crosswise into 5 slices. Place orange slices in a bowl; toss with olives and cilantro. Sprinkle with salt and pepper.
❷ Combine juice and remaining ingredients; stir with a whisk. Pour over salad; toss gently to combine. Yield: 6 servings (serving size: about ⅔ cup).

CALORIES 77; FAT 5.1g (sat 0.5g, mono 3.7g, poly 0.8g); PROTEIN 0.6g; CARB 8.5g; FIBER 1.5g; CHOL 0mg; IRON 0.1mg; SODIUM 259mg; CALC 25mg

Ramadan Soup (Harira)

Harira's hearty, rich flavors, abundant protein, and sultry seasonings translate well into a vegetarian interpretation with chickpeas and lima beans.

- 2 cups water
- 2 cups organic vegetable broth (such as Emeril's)
- 1¾ cups diced yellow onion
- ½ cup dried lentils
- ½ cup organic no-salt-added tomato puree (such as Muir Glen)
- ¾ teaspoon kosher salt
- ¼ teaspoon saffron threads, crushed
- ⅛ teaspoon freshly ground black pepper
- ½ cup frozen lima beans, thawed
- ⅓ cup finely chopped celery
- ¼ cup coarsely chopped fresh cilantro
- ¼ cup coarsely chopped fresh parsley
- 1 teaspoon tomato paste
- 1 (15-ounce) can chickpeas (garbanzo beans), rinsed and drained
- 8 lemon wedges

❶ Place first 8 ingredients in a large saucepan; bring to a boil. Cover, reduce heat, and simmer 20 minutes. Stir in beans and next 5 ingredients; bring to a boil. Cover, reduce heat, and simmer 20 minutes or until vegetables are tender. Serve with lemon wedges. Yield: 8 servings (serving size: ¾ cup soup and 1 lemon wedge).

CALORIES 211; FAT 1.6g (sat 0.1g, mono 0.5g, poly 0.9g); PROTEIN 12g; CARB 39.5g; FIBER 9.8g; CHOL 0mg; IRON 3.9mg; SODIUM 593mg; CALC 60mg

Vegetable Tagine with Preserved Lemons (*Tajine bil Khodar wa Limoon Mikhali*)

The hearty stews known as tagines are named after the conical clay vessels they're cooked in, though ours is made in a Dutch oven. Preserved lemons imbue the stew with sour saltiness. You'll find them at Middle Eastern markets, or make your own. Serve the tagine over quick-cooking couscous.

        2   preserved lemons, in water, divided
        1   teaspoon extra-virgin olive oil
    2⅓   cups finely chopped yellow onion (about 2)
        2   cups boiling organic vegetable broth (such as Emeril's)
        1   cup hot water
        1   teaspoon Ras el Hanout (page 43)
        ¼   teaspoon kosher salt
        1   pound carrots, peeled and chopped into 1-inch pieces
        ½   pound turnips, peeled and chopped into 1-inch pieces
        ½   pound Yukon gold potatoes, peeled and cut into 1½-inch chunks
        ½   pound sweet potatoes, peeled and cut into 1½-inch chunks
        1   (2-inch) cinnamon stick
        1   (9-ounce) package frozen artichoke hearts, thawed

1 Dice 1 lemon into ¼-inch pieces; set aside. Slice remaining lemon into ¼-inch-thick slices; set aside.
2 Heat oil in a large Dutch oven over medium heat. Add onion to pan; sauté 5 minutes or until soft. Add broth and next 8 ingredients; bring to a boil. Cover, reduce heat, and simmer 30 minutes or until vegetables are tender. Add diced lemon and artichokes to pan; simmer 5 minutes. Discard cinnamon stick. Garnish with lemon slices. Yield: 6 servings (serving size: 1⅓ cups).

CALORIES 155; FAT 1.7g (sat 0.2g, mono 0.6g, poly 0.2g); PROTEIN 4.3g; CARB 32.2g; FIBER 8.4g; CHOL 0mg; IRON 1.2mg; SODIUM 532mg; CALC 89mg

---

Soup and Sandwich Menu
serves 8

If you can't find kasseri cheese, halloumi melts just as tastily.

Moroccan Pumpkin Soup

Warm pear and cheese sandwiches

Place 1 (½-ounce) slice kasseri cheese on each of 16 (1-ounce) slices whole-grain bread. Place bread in a single layer on a baking sheet; broil 2 minutes or until golden. Peel, core, and thinly slice 3 ripe pears; divide pear slices evenly among 8 bread slices. Place 10 cups mixed salad greens in a large bowl. Combine ¼ cup thinly sliced shallot, 1 tablespoon red wine vinegar, 1½ teaspoons Dijon mustard, ½ teaspoon salt, and ¼ teaspoon freshly ground black pepper. Slowly add 3 table-spoons extra-virgin olive oil, stirring constantly with a whisk. Drizzle dressing over greens, and toss to coat. Top each serving with about ½ cup greens mixture, 1 tablespoon roasted pumpkin seeds, and remaining bread slices.

Orange segments

Moroccan Pumpkin Soup (*Chorbat al qara'a*)

While fresh pumpkin is more traditional in this recipe, butternut squash is easy to prepare and a good alternative.

    3½   cups (1-inch) cubed peeled fresh pumpkin or butternut squash (about 1¼ pounds)
        2   cups organic vegetable broth (such as Emeril's)
    1¾   cups diced yellow onion
        1   cup water
        1   teaspoon Ras el Hanout (page 43)
        ¾   teaspoon kosher salt
        ½   teaspoon ground coriander
        ½   cup whole milk
        1   tablespoon butter
        8   teaspoons plain yogurt
        ¼   cup chopped fresh cilantro

1 Combine first 7 ingredients in a large saucepan; bring to a boil. Cover, reduce heat, and simmer 10 minutes or until vegetables are tender.
2 Place half of squash mixture in a blender. Remove center piece of blender lid (to allow steam to escape); secure blender lid on blender. Place a clean towel over opening in blender lid (to avoid splatters). Blend until smooth. Pour pureed mixture into a large bowl. Repeat procedure with remaining squash mixture. Return pureed mixture to pan over low heat. Add milk and butter to pan; cook 3 minutes or until thoroughly heated. Serve with yogurt and cilantro. Yield: 8 servings (serving size: about ⅔ cup soup, 1 teaspoon yogurt, and 1½ teaspoons cilantro).

CALORIES 91; FAT 2.3g (sat 1.3g, mono 0.6g, poly 0.1g); PROTEIN 2.2g; CARB 17.4g; FIBER 2.8g; CHOL 6mg; IRON 0.9mg; SODIUM 392mg; CALC 84mg

---

Roasted Vegetable Couscous with Chickpeas and Onion–Pine Nut Topping (*Al Cuscus bil Khodar al-mausim*)

(pictured on page 211)

This entrée is crowned with a slightly sweet sauté of onions, raisins, buttery pine nuts, and honey.

COUSCOUS:

        5   cups diced peeled sweet potato (about 1½ pounds)
        2   cups (½-inch) diced peeled parsnips (about 10 ounces)
    1½   tablespoons extra-virgin olive oil
        1   teaspoon Ras el Hanout (page 43)
        3   carrots, peeled and cut crosswise into 2-inch pieces (about 9 ounces)
        1   teaspoon kosher salt, divided
    1¼   cups organic vegetable broth (such as Emeril's)
        1   cup uncooked couscous
        1   (15-ounce) can no-salt-added chickpeas (garbanzo beans), rinsed and drained

TOPPING:

- 1 tablespoon olive oil
- 1 yellow onion, cut into ¼-inch-thick slices, separated into rings
- ¼ cup pine nuts
- ¼ cup raisins
- 1 teaspoon ground cinnamon
- 1 tablespoon honey

1 Preheat oven to 450°.

2 To prepare couscous, combine first 5 ingredients in a large bowl; stir in ½ teaspoon salt. Place potato mixture on a baking sheet. Bake at 450° for 30 minutes or until vegetables are tender, stirring occasionally.

3 Bring broth to a boil in a medium saucepan. Stir in couscous and remaining ½ teaspoon salt. Remove from heat; cover and let stand 10 minutes. Fluff with a fork; gently stir in chickpeas. Keep warm.

4 To prepare topping, heat 1 tablespoon oil in a medium skillet over medium heat. Add onion to pan, and cook 12 minutes or until tender and golden brown, stirring occasionally. Add pine nuts and raisins; cook 2 minutes. Stir in cinnamon; cook 30 seconds. Stir in honey, and remove from heat.

5 Mound couscous in the middle of a serving platter. Place roasted vegetables around base of couscous. Arrange 5 carrots vertically around couscous; spoon topping over top of couscous. Yield: 6 servings (serving size: about ¾ cup vegetables, about ⅔ cup couscous, and 2 tablespoons topping).

CALORIES 520; FAT 13.7g (sat 1.5g, mono 7.4g, poly 3.8g); PROTEIN 11.7g; CARB 90.5g; FIBER 13.9g; CHOL 0mg; IRON 3.5mg; SODIUM 688mg; CALC 135mg

Triumphs at the Table

The grand-prize and category winners create delectable dishes at the fourth annual *Cooking Light* Ultimate Reader Recipe Contest.

THE FOURTH ANNUAL *Cooking Light* Ultimate Reader Recipe Contest captured the attention of home cooks from across the country, who submitted their best original recipes to compete for a $20,000 grand prize. Participants created light dishes in one of four categories: starters and drinks, family dinners, side salads and side dishes, and desserts. Qualifying recipes had to incorporate one of 10 products from this year's sponsors: Al Fresco Sausage, Annie's Naturals Dressings/Marinades, Birds Eye Frozen Vegetables, Bush's Best Beans, Eggland's Best Eggs, Kerrygold Cheeses and Butters from Ireland, Nakano Seasoned Rice Vinegar, Newman's Own Pasta Sauce, Stacy's Pita Chips, and Swanson Broth.

Our food staff reviewed more than 3,000 recipe entries to select the top contenders and chose 12 finalists, three in each category. The recipes met our staff's standards for taste, appearance, nutritional content, and mainstream appeal, as well as appropriate use of the sponsor product. Then the finalists traveled to our Test Kitchens in Birmingham, Alabama, to prepare their recipes for a judging panel of independent food professionals, who selected the top dishes. Four category winners each took home $5,000, and the grand-prize winner was awarded $20,000, plus a $5,000 category prize to donate to her charity of choice.

Spicy Black Bean Hummus

Category Winner—Starters and Drinks
"I created this recipe three years ago based on a popular appetizer my friends ordered at a pizzeria in Greenville, South Carolina. I researched the ingredients and added my own variations to suit my preference for spicy flavors. I received glowing feedback from my husband and friends, and now I keep this recipe on hand for parties and tailgates."

—Maureen Redmond, Easley, South Carolina

- 1 garlic clove, peeled
- 2 tablespoons fresh lemon juice
- 1 tablespoon tahini (roasted sesame seed paste)
- 1 teaspoon ground cumin
- ¼ teaspoon salt
- 1 (15-ounce) can black beans, rinsed and drained
- 1 small jalapeño pepper, chopped (about 2 tablespoons)
- Dash of crushed red pepper
- 2 teaspoons extra-virgin olive oil
- Dash of ground red pepper
- 1 (6-ounce) bag pita chips

1 Place garlic in a food processor; process until finely chopped. Add lemon juice and next 6 ingredients; process until smooth. Spoon bean mixture into a medium bowl, and drizzle with oil. Sprinkle with ground red pepper. Serve with pita chips. Yield: 8 servings (serving size: about 2½ tablespoons hummus and 4 chips).

CALORIES 148; FAT 6.2g (sat 0.7g, mono 1.2g, poly 0.6g); PROTEIN 4.5g; CARB 20.6g; FIBER 3.5g; CHOL 0mg; IRON 1.7mg; SODIUM 381mg; CALC 16mg

Braised Baby Artichokes

Category Winner—Sides and Salads

"I simply love the taste of this unique little vegetable. The recipe has a bit of lemony tang, and I opt for a Vidalia onion to complement that flavor."

—Nikki LoRé, Rochester, New York

6   cups water
2   tablespoons fresh lemon juice, divided
12 baby artichokes (about 1½ pounds)
1   large Vidalia or other sweet onion, peeled and quartered
1   cup fat-free, less-sodium chicken broth
¼   cup extra-virgin olive oil
1   teaspoon dried marjoram
1   teaspoon freshly ground black pepper
½   teaspoon salt
2   garlic cloves, peeled

❶ Combine 6 cups water and 1 table-spoon juice in a large bowl. Working with 1 artichoke at a time, cut off stem of artichoke to within 1 inch of base; peel stem. Remove bottom leaves and tough outer leaves from artichoke, leaving tender heart and bottom. Trim about 1 inch from top of artichoke. Place artichoke in lemon water. Repeat procedure with remaining artichokes. Drain and set aside.
❷ Place onion in center of a Dutch oven. Arrange artichokes in a single layer around onion. Add broth and remaining ingredients to pan; bring to a boil. Cover, reduce heat, and simmer 18 minutes or just until onion is tender (artichokes will be very tender). Stir in remaining 1 tablespoon juice. Remove artichokes and onion from pan with a slotted spoon; set aside, and keep warm. Bring broth mixture to a boil; cook 4 minutes or until slightly thickened. Pour sauce over artichoke mixture. Yield: 4 servings (serving size: 3 artichokes and 1 onion quarter).

CALORIES 198; FAT 14.1g (sat 2g, mono 10g, poly 2g); PROTEIN 5.3g; CARB 18.5g; FIBER 7.8g; CHOL 0mg; IRON 0.3mg; SODIUM 565mg; CALC 17mg

Ranch Steak Bruschetta Salad

Grand Prize Winner
Category Winner—Family Dinners

"My family loves steak, so I wanted to make a version of one of our favorite Southwestern dishes that was lighter, healthier, packed with flavor, and not drenched in heavy sauce or loaded with salty seasonings."

—Devon Delaney, Princeton, New Jersey

SALAD DRESSING:
6   tablespoons ranch dressing
1½ tablespoons prepared horseradish
STEAKS:
1   tablespoon freshly ground black pepper
2   teaspoons ground coffee
1½ teaspoons ground cumin
1½ teaspoons ancho chile powder
4   (4-ounce) beef tenderloin steaks, trimmed (1 inch thick)
Cooking spray
REMAINING INGREDIENTS:
¼   cup chopped shallots
¼   cup chopped fresh basil
¼   cup chopped bottled roasted red bell peppers
1   tablespoon fresh lemon juice
12 cherry tomatoes, halved
6   cups loosely packed arugula
12 (1-ounce) slices French bread, toasted

❶ To prepare salad dressing, combine ranch dressing and horseradish in a small bowl; cover and chill.
❷ To prepare steaks, combine black pepper and next 3 ingredients. Rub both sides of steaks with pepper mixture, and let stand 10 minutes.
❸ Heat a nonstick grill pan over medium heat. Coat steaks with cooking spray. Add steaks to pan; cook 3 minutes on each side or until desired degree of doneness. Remove steaks from pan; let stand 7 minutes.
❹ Combine shallots and next 4 ingredients in a small bowl; toss well.
❺ Arrange 1 cup arugula on each of 6 serving plates, and top each serving with 2 toast slices. Cut each steak diagonally across grain into thin slices. Divide steak slices evenly among toast slices; top each serving with about 2 tablespoons tomato mixture. Drizzle each serving with about 1 tablespoon salad dressing. Serve immediately. Yield: 6 servings.

CALORIES 384; FAT 13.2g (sat 3g, mono 2g, poly 0.8g); PROTEIN 25.3g; CARB 41.4g; FIBER 3.4g; CHOL 55mg; IRON 4.2mg; SODIUM 565mg; CALC 88mg

Roasted Banana Bars with Browned Butter–Pecan Frosting

Category Winner—Desserts

"I have been baking banana bars with my mother since I was old enough to stir the batter, so I was pleased when I was able to lighten them for my family and still maintain the original flavor. I browned butter in a saucepan to enhance its richness, thus eliminating the need for full-fat cream cheese. This is a great way to use ripe, speckled bananas."

—Lindsay Weiss, Overland Park, Kansas

BARS:
2   cups sliced ripe banana (about 3 medium)
⅓   cup packed dark brown sugar
1   tablespoon butter, chilled and cut into small pieces
9   ounces cake flour (about 2¼ cups)
¾   teaspoon baking soda
½   teaspoon baking powder
¼   cup nonfat buttermilk
1   teaspoon vanilla extract
½   cup butter, softened
1¼   cups granulated sugar
2   large eggs
Baking spray with flour

FROSTING:

- ¼ cup butter
- 2 cups powdered sugar
- ⅓ cup (3 ounces) ⅓-less-fat cream cheese, softened
- 1 teaspoon vanilla extract
- ¼ cup chopped pecans, toasted

① Preheat oven to 400°.

② To prepare bars, combine first 3 ingredients in an 8-inch square baking dish. Bake at 400° for 35 minutes, stirring after 17 minutes. Cool slightly.

③ Reduce oven temperature to 375°.

④ Weigh or lightly spoon cake flour into dry measuring cups; level with a knife. Combine 9 ounces (about 2¼ cups) flour, soda, and baking powder in a medium bowl. Combine banana mixture, buttermilk, and 1 teaspoon vanilla in another medium bowl. Place ½ cup butter and granulated sugar in a large bowl; beat with a mixer at medium speed until well blended. Add eggs to granulated sugar mixture; mix well. Add flour mixture to sugar mixture alternating with banana mixture, beginning and ending with flour mixture.

⑤ Pour batter into a 13 x 9-inch baking pan coated with baking spray. Bake at 375° for 20 minutes or until a wooden pick inserted in center comes out clean. Cool completely in pan on a wire rack.

⑥ To prepare frosting, melt ¼ cup butter in a small saucepan over medium heat; cook 4 minutes or until lightly browned. Cool slightly. Combine browned butter, powdered sugar, cream cheese, and 1 teaspoon vanilla in a medium bowl; beat with a mixer until smooth. Spread frosting over cooled bars. Sprinkle with pecans. Yield: 2 dozen (serving size: 1 bar).

CALORIES 221; FAT 8.4g (sat 4.7g, mono 2.3g, poly 0.6g); PROTEIN 2.3g; CARB 35.1g; FIBER 0.6g; CHOL 39mg; IRON 1mg; SODIUM 117mg; CALC 23mg

Tips from the Finalists

"Take a dish you love and try to revamp it using bold flavors."

—Devon Delaney, grand prize winner and category winner, family dinners

"Don't be discouraged if you prepare a recipe and it isn't an instant success. I can't tell you how many times I've messed up a dish. You become a better cook learning from your failures."

—Lindsay Weiss, category winner, desserts

"Submit an original dish you make all the time for the people you love. That way you know how the dish behaves and what to expect from it. There's an emotional story behind a good recipe."

—Emily Almaguer, finalist, family dinners

"Trust your own instincts, and use flavors with which you are familiar."

—Lisa Richardson, finalist, starters and drinks

"Prepare some of the past winning recipes so you have an idea of what the judges are looking for."

—Catherine McMichael, finalist, side salads and side dishes

Dinner Tonight

Meals to suit your schedule, from flank steak to Thai-style shrimp soup to Greek-inspired pork chops

QUICK & EASY

Quick Barbecue Flank Steak

·····················20 minutes

Try this with coleslaw and Texas toast. For the toast, combine 1 tablespoon softened butter and 1 minced garlic clove; spread on 4 (1½-ounce) slices toasted sourdough bread.

- 1 cup barbecue sauce
- ¼ cup fresh lemon juice
- 1 tablespoon prepared mustard
- 1½ teaspoons celery seeds
- ¼ teaspoon hot sauce
- 2 garlic cloves, minced
- 1 (1-pound) flank steak, trimmed
- Cooking spray

① Preheat broiler.

② Combine first 6 ingredients in a large bowl; add steak, turning to coat. Remove steak from sauce, reserving sauce mixture. Place steak on a broiler pan coated with cooking spray; broil 6 minutes on each side or until desired degree of doneness. Let stand 5 minutes. Cut steak diagonally across grain into thin slices.

③ While steak stands, bring sauce mixture to a boil in a saucepan over high heat. Reduce heat, and cook 5 minutes. Serve with steak. Yield: 4 servings (serving size: 3 ounces steak and ¼ cup sauce).

CALORIES 234; FAT 10.1g (sat 3.9g, mono 4.1g, poly 0.8g); PROTEIN 24.6g; CARB 10.4g; FIBER 1.1g; CHOL 57mg; IRON 3.2mg; SODIUM 625mg; CALC 38mg

Chicken with Southwestern Salsa

......................................*20 minutes*

Serve with a mixed green salad. For the dressing, combine ¼ cup fresh lime juice, 1 tablespoon sugar, 2 tablespoons olive oil, ¼ teaspoon salt, and ¼ teaspoon cumin in a large bowl. Add 6 cups torn romaine lettuce, ½ cup thinly sliced red onion, and ¼ cup diced avocado; toss gently to combine.

- 1 tablespoon canola oil, divided
- 1 teaspoon ground cumin, divided
- ¾ teaspoon ground coriander, divided
- ½ teaspoon salt
- ¼ teaspoon black pepper
- ⅛ teaspoon ground red pepper
- 4 (6-ounce) skinless, boneless chicken breast halves
- ½ cup prechopped onion
- 1 teaspoon bottled minced garlic
- ⅓ cup chopped plum tomato
- ¼ cup chopped fresh cilantro
- 2 tablespoons fresh lime juice
- 1 (15½-ounce) can black beans, rinsed and drained
- 1 (8¾-ounce) can no-salt-added whole kernel corn, drained

❶ Heat 2 teaspoons oil in a large nonstick skillet over medium-high heat. Combine ½ teaspoon cumin, ½ teaspoon coriander, salt, black pepper, and red pepper; sprinkle mixture evenly over chicken. Add chicken to pan; cook 7 minutes on each side or until done.
❷ While chicken cooks, heat remaining 1 teaspoon oil in a small skillet over medium-high heat. Add onion to pan; sauté 1 minute. Add garlic; sauté 30 seconds. Transfer onion mixture to a bowl; add remaining ½ teaspoon cumin, remaining ¼ teaspoon coriander, tomato, and remaining ingredients to onion mixture, tossing well. Yield: 4 servings (serving size: 1 chicken breast half and ¾ cup salsa).

CALORIES 317; FAT 8.7g (sat 1.4g, mono 3.5g, poly 1.9g); PROTEIN 39g; CARB 24.4g; FIBER 5.2g; CHOL 94mg; IRON 2.2mg; SODIUM 705mg; CALC 50mg

Grilled Turkey and Ham Sandwiches

......................................*20 minutes*

Enjoy with carrot sticks and tomato soup. Heat 1 teaspoon olive oil in a medium saucepan over medium-high heat. Add 2 teaspoons bottled minced garlic to pan, and sauté 1 minute. Add 2 (14.5-ounce) cans undrained diced tomatoes; 1 (14-ounce) can fat-free, less-sodium chicken broth; 1 tablespoon balsamic vinegar; and ½ teaspoon black pepper. Reduce heat, and simmer 10 minutes, stirring occasionally. Garnish with chopped parsley, if desired.

Prep tip: Assemble and cook the sandwiches while the soup simmers.

- 1 tablespoon light mayonnaise
- 1 teaspoon Dijon mustard
- 8 (1-ounce) slices country white bread
- 4 (1-ounce) slices deli, lower-salt turkey breast
- 4 (½-ounce) slices deli, lower-salt ham
- 4 (½-ounce) slices reduced-fat Cheddar cheese
- 8 (¼-inch-thick) slices tomato
- Cooking spray

❶ Combine mayonnaise and mustard in a small bowl. Spread about 1 teaspoon mayonnaise mixture over 1 side of each of 4 bread slices. Top each slice with 1 turkey slice, 1 ham slice, 1 cheese slice, and 2 tomato slices. Top with remaining bread slices.
❷ Heat a large nonstick skillet over medium heat. Coat pan with cooking spray. Add sandwiches to pan; cook 4 minutes or until lightly browned. Turn sandwiches over; cook 2 minutes or until cheese melts. Yield: 4 sandwiches (serving size: 1 sandwich).

CALORIES 237; FAT 5.8g (sat 1.8g, mono 0.9g, poly 0.9g); PROTEIN 18.4g; CARB 29.1g; FIBER 0.4g; CHOL 28mg; IRON 1.1mg; SODIUM 781mg; CALC 166mg

Filet Mignon with Arugula Salad

......................................*20 minutes*

Arugula, a peppery salad green, makes a tasty bed for pan-seared steak. Asiago garlic bread is a fitting accompaniment. Combine 1 tablespoon olive oil and 1 minced garlic clove; brush evenly over 4 (1-inch-thick) French bread slices. Top each bread slice with 1 tablespoon grated Asiago cheese. Broil 2 minutes or until cheese melts and bread is toasted.

- Cooking spray
- 4 (4-ounce) beef tenderloin steaks, trimmed
- ½ teaspoon salt, divided
- ¼ teaspoon black pepper, divided
- 2 teaspoons butter
- ½ cup prechopped red onion
- 1 (8-ounce) package presliced cremini mushrooms
- 2 tablespoons fresh lemon juice
- 1 (5-ounce) bag baby arugula

❶ Heat a large nonstick skillet over medium-high heat. Coat pan with cooking spray. Sprinkle beef with ¼ teaspoon salt and ⅛ teaspoon pepper. Add beef to pan; cook 4 minutes on each side or until desired degree of doneness. Remove beef from pan; keep warm.
❷ Melt butter in pan; coat pan with cooking spray. Add remaining ¼ teaspoon salt, remaining ⅛ teaspoon pepper, red onion, and mushrooms to pan; sauté 4 minutes or until mushrooms release their liquid. Combine juice and arugula in a large bowl. Add mushroom mixture to arugula mixture; toss gently to combine. Arrange 1½ cups salad mixture on each of 4 plates; top each serving with 1 steak. Yield: 4 servings.

CALORIES 191; FAT 8.9g (sat 3.8g, mono 3.1g, poly 0.5g); PROTEIN 20.5g; CARB 7g; FIBER 1.8g; CHOL 59mg; IRON 3.3mg; SODIUM 349mg; CALC 72mg

Chicken Biryani
30 minutes

Serve with a salad of thinly sliced cucumber and plum tomato wedges topped with a yogurt dressing. Combine ⅓ cup plain low-fat yogurt, 1 tablespoon chopped green onions, 1 teaspoon fresh lemon juice, ¼ teaspoon ground cumin, ⅛ teaspoon salt, and a dash of ground red pepper.

- 2 teaspoons canola oil
- 1 pound skinless, boneless chicken breast, cut into 1-inch pieces
- 1 cup chopped onion (about 1 medium onion)
- 1 jalapeño pepper, seeded and minced
- 1 teaspoon minced fresh ginger
- 1½ teaspoons garam masala
- ¾ teaspoon ground cumin
- ½ teaspoon salt
- 2 garlic cloves, minced
- 2 cups chopped plum tomato (about 2 tomatoes)
- 1 cup uncooked basmati rice
- ⅓ cup golden raisins
- 1 (14-ounce) can fat-free, less-sodium chicken broth
- ¼ cup chopped fresh cilantro
- ¼ cup sliced almonds
- 4 lime wedges

① Heat oil in a large nonstick skillet over medium-high heat. Add chicken to pan; sauté 3 minutes. Add onion and jalapeño; sauté 3 minutes. Add ginger and next 4 ingredients; sauté 30 seconds. Add tomato and next 3 ingredients; bring to a boil. Cover, reduce heat, and simmer 15 minutes or until rice is tender. Stir in cilantro. Sprinkle with almonds; serve with lime wedges. Yield: 4 servings (serving size: 1½ cups rice mixture, 1 tablespoon almonds, and 1 lime wedge).

CALORIES 437; FAT 9.1g (sat 1.4g, mono 4.6g, poly 2.3g); PROTEIN 29.8g; CARB 63.2g; FIBER 4.5g; CHOL 66mg; IRON 3.4mg; SODIUM 555mg; CALC 58mg

Country Captain Chicken
30 minutes

Both South Carolina and Georgia lay claim to this Southern classic, which may have been brought to America by a ship's captain ferrying spices from the Far East. Rice is a traditional side dish. To make it fast, cook 1 (3½-ounce) bag boil-in-bag rice, omitting salt and fat; stir in ¼ teaspoon salt and ¼ teaspoon black pepper. Top each serving with 1 tablespoon bottled mango chutney.

- 1 tablespoon curry powder
- ¼ teaspoon salt
- ¼ teaspoon black pepper
- 1 pound skinless, boneless chicken breast, cut into ¾-inch pieces
- 1½ tablespoons olive oil
- 2½ cups vertically sliced onion (about 2 medium)
- ¾ cup thinly sliced green bell pepper (about 1 medium)
- 2 garlic cloves, minced
- ⅔ cup fat-free, less-sodium chicken broth
- ¼ cup dried currants
- 2 tablespoons chopped fresh thyme, divided
- 1 (14.5-ounce) can diced tomatoes with jalapeño, undrained
- ½ cup sliced almonds, toasted

① Combine first 3 ingredients. Sprinkle chicken with curry mixture.
② Heat oil in a large nonstick skillet over medium-high heat. Add chicken mixture to pan; sauté 5 minutes. Add onion, bell pepper, and garlic; sauté 3 minutes. Add broth, currants, 1 tablespoon thyme, and tomatoes; bring to a boil. Reduce heat, and simmer 5 minutes. Stir in remaining 1 tablespoon thyme, and cook 1 minute. Sprinkle with almonds. Yield: 4 servings (serving size: 1½ cups chicken mixture and 1 tablespoon almonds).

CALORIES 314; FAT 11.2g (sat 1.4g, mono 7g, poly 1.9g); PROTEIN 30.5g; CARB 23.2g; FIBER 4.6g; CHOL 66mg; IRON 2.6mg; SODIUM 683mg; CALC 86mg

Brown Butter Gnocchi with Spinach and Pine Nuts
30 minutes

Prepare a quick salad to accompany the gnocchi. Combine 1 tablespoon fresh lemon juice, 1 tablespoon extra-virgin olive oil, 1 teaspoon brown sugar, ½ teaspoon freshly ground black pepper, and ⅛ teaspoon salt in a large bowl; stir with a whisk. Add 6 cups gourmet salad mix to bowl; toss gently to coat. Sauvignon blanc will pair enticingly with this dish.

- 1 (16-ounce) package vacuum-packed gnocchi (such as Vigo)
- 2 tablespoons butter
- 2 tablespoons pine nuts
- 2 garlic cloves, minced
- 1 (10-ounce) package fresh spinach, torn
- ¼ teaspoon salt
- ¼ teaspoon freshly ground black pepper
- ¼ cup (1 ounce) finely shredded Parmesan cheese

① Cook gnocchi according to package directions, omitting salt and fat; drain.
② Heat butter in a large nonstick skillet over medium heat. Add pine nuts to pan; cook 3 minutes or until butter and nuts are lightly browned, stirring constantly. Add garlic to pan; cook 1 minute. Add gnocchi and spinach to pan; cook 1 minute or until spinach wilts, stirring constantly. Stir in salt and pepper. Sprinkle with Parmesan cheese. Yield: 4 servings (serving size: 1 cup gnocchi mixture and 1 tablespoon cheese).

CALORIES 289; FAT 10.8g (sat 5.1g, mono 2.9g, poly 1.8g); PROTEIN 9.5g; CARB 40.3g; FIBER 1.8g; CHOL 20mg; IRON 2.2mg; SODIUM 877mg; CALC 164mg

Thai Hot and Sour Soup with Shrimp

······················*30 minutes*

Stir-fry a batch of ginger snow peas to serve with the soup. Heat 1½ teaspoons dark sesame oil in a large nonstick skillet over medium-high heat. Add 3 cups trimmed snow peas and 1 teaspoon bottled minced fresh ginger to pan; sauté 3 minutes. Stir in 2 tablespoons low-sodium soy sauce and ½ teaspoon black pepper. Shrimp chips, available at Asian groceries and in the Asian foods aisle at some supermarkets, are a crunchy way to round out the meal.
Smart substitution: If you can't find kaffir lime leaves, use three long strips of lime rind.

   6 cups fat-free, less-sodium chicken broth
   4 kaffir lime leaves
   1 (4-inch) lemongrass stalk, halved and crushed
   ½ habanero chile pepper, minced
   1 cup thinly sliced shiitake mushrooms (about 2 ounces)
   ½ pound large shrimp, peeled and deveined
   ¼ cup fresh lime juice
   2 teaspoons fish sauce
   1 medium tomato, cut into wedges
   2 green onions, thinly sliced (about ½ cup)
   1 cup light coconut milk
   2 tablespoons chopped fresh cilantro

❶ Combine first 4 ingredients in a large saucepan; bring to a boil. Cook 5 minutes. Add mushrooms and shrimp to pan; cook 3 minutes or until shrimp are done. Add juice and next 3 ingredients; cook 2 minutes. Remove from heat; stir in coconut milk and cilantro. Discard lemongrass stalk and lime leaves. Yield: 4 servings (serving size: 2 cups).

CALORIES 135; FAT 4.4g (sat 3.1g, mono 0.3g, poly 0.5g); PROTEIN 16.6g; CARB 8.4g; FIBER 2.2g; CHOL 86mg; IRON 2.7mg; SODIUM 838 mg; CALC 63mg

Ancho Chile–Beef Fajitas with Mango

······················*40 minutes*

Ground ancho chiles add subtle, earthy heat. If you prefer more spice, substitute chipotle chile powder. To prepare a guacamole side dish, combine ¾ cup chopped avocado, 1 tablespoon finely chopped red onion, 2 teaspoons chopped fresh cilantro, 1½ teaspoons fresh lemon juice, ¼ teaspoon salt, and ⅛ teaspoon ground red pepper, mashing to desired consistency. Serve immediately with baked tortilla chips.
Quick tip: Look for bottled mango slices in the refrigerated section of the produce department.

   1 teaspoon fresh lime juice
   ¾ teaspoon ground ancho chile powder
   ½ teaspoon Worcestershire sauce
   ¼ teaspoon ground cumin
   1 (8-ounce) beef tenderloin, trimmed and cut into ¼-inch-thick strips
   1 teaspoon olive oil
   ½ cup thinly sliced sweet onion
   ½ cup thinly sliced red bell pepper
   ½ cup thinly sliced green bell pepper
   ½ cup thinly sliced mango
   1 plum tomato, coarsely chopped
   2 teaspoons low-sodium soy sauce
   1 tablespoon chopped fresh cilantro
   4 (6-inch) fat-free flour tortillas
   2 tablespoons prepared salsa
   2 tablespoons reduced-fat sour cream

❶ Combine first 4 ingredients in a medium bowl. Add beef; toss well.
❷ Heat oil in a large nonstick skillet over medium-high heat. Add onion and bell peppers to pan; sauté 4 minutes or until onion is almost tender, stirring occasionally. Add mango and tomato to pan; sauté 1 minute. Add beef mixture; sauté 2 minutes or until desired degree of doneness, stirring occasionally. Add soy sauce; cook 15 seconds. Remove from heat; stir in cilantro.

❸ Heat tortillas according to package directions. Place 2 tortillas on each of 2 plates; top each tortilla with about ¾ cup beef mixture. Top each tortilla with 1½ teaspoons prepared salsa and 1½ teaspoons sour cream. Yield: 2 servings.

CALORIES 450; FAT 12.9g (sat 3.9g, mono 4.7g, poly 0.7g); PROTEIN 30.6g; CARB 54.6g; FIBER 5.2g; CHOL 68mg; IRON 2.3mg; SODIUM 930mg; CALC 86mg

Pork Chops Oreganata

······················*40 minutes*

While the pork marinates, you can prepare a warm bulgur salad. Combine 3 cups hot cooked bulgur and 5 ounces baby spinach; cover and let stand 15 minutes or until spinach wilts. Stir in 1 cup halved cherry tomatoes, 3 tablespoons fresh lemon juice, 2 tablespoons extra-virgin olive oil, ½ teaspoon salt, and ¼ teaspoon black pepper. Sprinkle with ¼ cup (1 ounce) crumbled feta cheese.

   1 tablespoon extra-virgin olive oil
   2 teaspoons grated lemon rind
   2 tablespoons fresh lemon juice
   1 teaspoon chopped fresh oregano
   3 garlic cloves, minced
   4 (4-ounce) boneless pork chops
   ½ teaspoon kosher salt
   ¼ teaspoon freshly ground black pepper
      Cooking spray

❶ Combine first 5 ingredients in an 11 x 7-inch baking dish. Add pork, turning to coat. Let pork stand 30 minutes, turning occasionally.
❷ Preheat broiler.
❸ Remove pork from baking dish; discard marinade. Sprinkle pork evenly with salt and pepper. Place pork on a broiler pan coated with cooking spray. Broil 4 minutes on each side or until done. Yield: 4 servings (serving size: 1 chop).

CALORIES 168; FAT 6g (sat 1.9g, mono 2.7g, poly 0.5g); PROTEIN 26.5g; CARB 0.2g; FIBER 0g; CHOL 78mg; IRON 1.1mg; SODIUM 283mg; CALC 16mg

Cornmeal-Crusted Tilapia with Tomatillo Salsa

·················*40 minutes*

Roasted potatoes go well with the fish. Toss 6 cups quartered red potatoes with 1 tablespoon olive oil and ½ teaspoon kosher salt. Arrange potato mixture in an even layer on a baking sheet, and bake at 400° for 40 minutes or until tender, turning once. Toss potatoes with ¼ cup chopped fresh flat-leaf parsley. Add steamed green beans to round out the plate.

SALSA:
- ½ cup fresh cilantro leaves
- ½ cup chopped onion
- 1 tablespoon fresh lime juice
- 2 serrano chiles, seeded and chopped
- 1 (11-ounce) can tomatillos, drained
- 1 garlic clove, minced

FISH:
- ¼ cup all-purpose flour
- ¼ cup cornmeal
- 1 tablespoon water
- 1 large egg white
- 4 (6-ounce) tilapia fillets
- ¾ teaspoon salt
- ½ teaspoon chili powder
- 1 tablespoon olive oil

1 To prepare salsa, combine first 6 ingredients in a blender; process until smooth. Set aside.

2 To prepare fish, combine flour and cornmeal in a shallow dish. Combine 1 tablespoon water and egg white in a shallow dish, stirring well. Sprinkle both sides of fish evenly with salt and chili powder. Heat oil in a large nonstick skillet over medium-high heat. Dip fish in egg mixture; dredge in flour mixture. Add fish to pan; cook 2½ minutes on each side or until fish flakes easily when tested with a fork or until desired degree of doneness. Serve with salsa. Yield: 4 servings (serving size: 1 fillet and about ¼ cup salsa).

CALORIES 252; FAT 7.1g (sat 1.2g, mono 3.3g, poly 1.9g); PROTEIN 28.9g; CARB 18.5g; FIBER 3g; CHOL 64mg; IRON 2.2mg; SODIUM 659mg; CALC 32mg

Superlative Swag Bars

Our editor in chief requests a slimmed-down version of a North Carolina inn's decadent treat.

While on vacation last year, Mary Kay Culpepper, editor in chief of *Cooking Light*, stayed at The Swag Country Inn in Waynesville, North Carolina, adjacent to the edge of the Great Smoky Mountains National Park. She loved hiking on the inn's winding trails, and each day Managing Chef Shawn McCoy and his staff packed guests' knapsacks with a hearty picnic lunch, including the chewy, peanut-buttery Swag Bar. Culpepper and her fellow visitors at the inn were enchanted by the bar's combination of creamy and crunchy textures. Like many guests before, she wanted to re-create the treat as a souvenir of her trip, and the inn's owner, Deener Matthews, happily shared the recipe. But once Culpepper saw the indulgent ingredients, she asked Associate Food Editor Kathy Kitchens Downie, RD, to develop a more healthful version so she could enjoy memories of her Smoky Mountain getaway anytime.

While the sugar, corn syrup, and peanut butter in the original recipe created a pleasingly chewy texture, they were also responsible for 132 calories in each serving. We slightly reduced the amounts of these components to cut about 27 calories per bar. We trimmed the overall amount of cereal and substituted a whole-grain variety to slightly boost the nutrition and drop another 24 calories and 70 milligrams of sodium per serving. The original's eight ounces of semisweet chocolate chips created a generous layer of chocolaty goodness—and added calories and fat—atop the bars. We cut back to two ounces and switched to dark chocolate, which typically has a bit less sugar than the semisweet variety and more intense chocolate flavor, so the smaller amount has more impact. We also added 1½ cups of heart-healthy peanuts to carry the nutty flavor and offer more crunch. The total fat remains the same—9.2 grams—but the overall fat profile is better with the peanuts' healthful unsaturated fats.

serving size: 1 bar		
	before	after
CALORIES PER SERVING	196	155
SATURATED FAT	2.6g	1.9g

Swag Bars

These no-bake bars come together quickly with common pantry ingredients. Make sure the cereal is well crushed (try packing it in a sealed zip-top plastic bag and using a rolling pin) so it incorporates into the peanut butter mixture.

- 1¾ cups creamy peanut butter
- ¾ cup sugar
- ¾ cup light-colored corn syrup
- 1½ cups (6 ounces) chopped lightly salted, dry-roasted peanuts
- 3½ cups (4 ounces) whole-grain flaked cereal (such as Total), finely crushed
- Cooking spray
- ⅓ cup (2 ounces) chopped dark chocolate

1 Combine first 3 ingredients in a heavy saucepan over medium-high heat. Cook 4 minutes or just until mixture begins to boil, stirring constantly. Remove from heat; stir in peanuts and cereal. Spread mixture evenly into a 13 x 9-inch baking pan coated with cooking spray.

2 Place chocolate in a small microwave-safe bowl. Microwave at HIGH 1 minute or until chocolate melts, stirring every 20 seconds. Drizzle chocolate evenly over peanut mixture. Score into 36 bars while warm. Yield: 36 servings (serving size: 1 bar).

CALORIES 155; FAT 9.2g (sat 1.9g, mono 4.2g, poly 2.5g); PROTEIN 4.5g; CARB 16.2g; FIBER 1.5g; CHOL 0mg; IRON 2.3mg; SODIUM 121mg; CALC 113mg

Smoky Slow Cooker Chili

A barbecue expert, former Test Kitchens Professional Mike Wilson knows a thing or two about pork and smoke. He uses both elements to concoct a robust slow cooker chili with Mexican flair. (He also shares directions for cooking it on the stove.)

Wilson's best advice: Follow your instincts. "I figured tossing an inexpensive smoked ham hock into the chili would add smoke flavor to the whole pot, but I didn't want it to overwhelm the dish," he explains. So the hock is cooked and then discarded—leaving behind that woodsiness with little fat or sodium. Fresh tomatillos and a spritz of lime " add a little tartness to balance the smokiness," Wilson says.

> "I figured tossing an inexpensive smoked ham hock into the chili would add smoke flavor to the whole pot, but I didn't want it to overwhelm the dish."
>
> —Mike Wilson, former Test Kitchens Professional

STAFF FAVORITE • MAKE AHEAD

Smoky Slow Cooker Chili

(pictured on page 209)

Pork shoulder is usually sold in weights greater than a pound. Ask your butcher to trim off the amount you need, or look for pork shoulder steaks. Serve with corn bread.

Cooking spray
- 1 pound ground pork
- 1 pound boneless pork shoulder, cut into ½-inch pieces
- 3 cups chopped onion
- 1¾ cups chopped green bell pepper
- 3 garlic cloves, minced
- 3 tablespoons tomato paste
- 1 cup lager-style beer (such as Budweiser)
- ½ teaspoon salt, divided
- 3 tablespoons chili powder
- 1 tablespoon ground cumin
- 2 teaspoons dried oregano
- ¾ teaspoon freshly ground black pepper
- 6 tomatillos, quartered
- 2 bay leaves
- 2 (14½-ounce) cans plum tomatoes, undrained and chopped
- 1 (15-ounce) can no-salt-added pinto beans, drained
- 1 (7¾-ounce) can Mexican hot-style tomato sauce (such as El Paso)
- 1 smoked ham hock (about 8 ounces)
- 1½ tablespoons sugar
- ½ cup finely chopped cilantro
- ½ cup finely chopped green onions
- ½ cup (2 ounces) crumbled queso fresco
- 8 lime wedges

1 Heat a large nonstick skillet over medium-high heat. Coat pan with cooking spray. Add ground pork to pan; cook 5 minutes or until browned, stirring to slightly crumble. Drain well. Transfer pork to an electric slow cooker.
2 Recoat pan with cooking spray. Add pork shoulder; cook 5 minutes or until lightly browned, turning occasionally. Transfer pork to slow cooker.
3 Recoat pan with cooking spray. Add onion and bell pepper; sauté 8 minutes, stirring frequently. Add garlic; sauté 1 minute. Add tomato paste; cook 1 minute, stirring constantly. Stir in beer; cook 1 minute. Transfer onion mixture to slow cooker. Add ¼ teaspoon salt, chili powder, and next 9 ingredients to slow cooker. Cover and cook on HIGH 5 hours or until meat is tender. Remove bay leaves and ham hock; discard. Stir in remaining ¼ teaspoon salt and sugar. Ladle about 1⅓ cups chili into each of 8 bowls; top each serving with 1 tablespoon cilantro, 1 tablespoon green onions, and 1 tablespoon cheese. Serve each serving with 1 lime wedge. Yield: 8 servings.

NOTE: You can also cook the chili in a slow cooker on LOW for 8 hours. For cooking chili on the stovetop, use a total of 12 ounces beer and simmer, covered, for 2½ to 3 hours or until pork shoulder is tender.

CALORIES 354; FAT 14.2g (sat 5.1g, mono 5.9g, poly 1.4g); PROTEIN 28.5g; CARB 26.4g; FIBER 6.8g; CHOL 82mg; IRON 3.8mg; SODIUM 645mg; CALC 108mg

Keeping It Simple

Take five ingredients, make fabulous food—it's that easy. Just follow our tips.

DELICIOUS DISHES DON'T NECESSARILY REQUIRE A LONG LIST of ingredients or lots of time in the kitchen. In the following recipes, we demonstrate that plenty of great entrées, from pastas and goulash to sandwiches, can be made with just five ingredients (not counting salt, pepper, water, or cooking spray) and a minimum of fuss.

Simple Tip

Splurge on quality. In this dish, a fine extra-virgin olive oil helps the salsa shine. One special ingredient—say artisan bread, a special sausage, or a robust cheese—can add rich flavor to an otherwise ordinary sandwich, casserole, or pasta. While quality ingredients are important in every recipe, they really stand out in a simple dish.

QUICK & EASY
Roasted Tilapia with Orange-Parsley Salsa

All parts of the orange—juice, rind, and pulp—flavor the quickly cooked fish. Substitute brown, basmati, or jasmine rice, if you prefer.

  3 oranges (about 1 pound)
 ¼ cup chopped fresh parsley, divided
  2 tablespoons extra-virgin olive oil, divided
 ¾ teaspoon salt, divided
  4 (6-ounce) tilapia fillets
 ½ teaspoon freshly ground black pepper, divided
  2 cups hot cooked instant white rice

❶ Grate 2 teaspoons orange rind. Peel and section oranges over a bowl, reserving 2 tablespoons juice. Chop sections. Combine rind, chopped orange, 2 tablespoons parsley, 5 teaspoons oil, and ¼ teaspoon salt in a bowl; toss well.
❷ Preheat oven to 400°.
❸ Sprinkle fish evenly with ¼ teaspoon salt and ¼ teaspoon pepper. Place fish in an ovenproof skillet coated with remaining 1 teaspoon oil. Bake at 400° for 14 minutes or until fish flakes easily when tested with a fork or until desired degree of doneness.
❹ Combine 2 tablespoons reserved juice, remaining 2 tablespoons parsley, remaining ¼ teaspoon salt, remaining ¼ teaspoon pepper, and rice. Spoon ½ cup rice onto each of 4 plates; top each with 1 fillet and ¼ cup salsa. Yield: 4 servings.

CALORIES 423; FAT 12.1g (sat 2.6g, mono 6.7g, poly 2.1g); PROTEIN 47.4g; CARB 32.7g; FIBER 3g; CHOL 97mg; IRON 3mg; SODIUM 543mg; CALC 76mg

Simple Tip

Stock the pantry with flavor boosters. In this recipe, salsa verde adds zip. Commercial spice rubs and special condiments, such as chutneys, salsas, and peanut sauce, can add great taste with minimal effort.

QUICK & EASY
Goat Cheese and Roasted Corn Quesadillas

  1 cup fresh corn kernels (about 1 large ear)
 ⅔ cup (5 ounces) goat cheese, softened
  8 (6-inch) corn tortillas
 ¼ cup chopped green onions (about 1 green onion)
 10 tablespoons bottled salsa verde, divided
     Cooking spray

❶ Heat a large nonstick skillet over medium-high heat. Add corn; sauté 2 minutes or until browned. Place corn in a small bowl. Add goat cheese to corn; stir until well blended. Divide corn mixture evenly among 4 tortillas; spread to within ¼ inch of sides. Sprinkle each tortilla with 1 tablespoon green onions. Drizzle each with 1½ teaspoons salsa; top with remaining 4 tortillas.
❷ Heat pan over medium-high heat. Coat pan with cooking spray. Place 2 quesadillas in pan; cook 1½ minutes on each side or until golden. Remove from pan; keep warm. Wipe pan clean with paper towels; recoat with cooking spray. Repeat procedure with remaining quesadillas. Cut each quesadilla into 4 wedges. Serve with remaining 8 tablespoons salsa. Yield: 4 servings (serving size: 4 wedges and 2 tablespoons salsa).

CALORIES 223; FAT 8.9g (sat 5.2g, mono 1.8g, poly 0.9g); PROTEIN 9.9g; CARB 28.6g; FIBER 3.2g; CHOL 16mg; IRON 1mg; SODIUM 266mg; CALC 75mg

Simple Tip

Use herbs. Add a fresh herb, even something as simple and versatile as chives or chopped parsley, to the mix in this chicken stuffing; it will brighten the look and taste of the entire dish.

QUICK & EASY
Almond-Stuffed Chicken
(pictured on page 213)

Toast the almonds in a skillet before you cook the chicken, and you'll have just one pan to clean. Serve with couscous and haricots verts.

- ⅓ cup light garlic-and-herbs spreadable cheese (such as Boursin light)
- ¼ cup slivered almonds, toasted, coarsely chopped, and divided
- 3 tablespoons chopped fresh parsley, divided
- 4 (6-ounce) skinless, boneless chicken breast halves
- ½ teaspoon salt
- ¼ teaspoon freshly ground black pepper
- 1½ teaspoons butter

❶ Combine spreadable cheese, 3 tablespoons almonds, and 2 tablespoons parsley in a small bowl. Set aside.
❷ Cut a horizontal slit through thickest portion of each breast half to form a pocket. Stuff 1½ tablespoons almond mixture into each pocket; secure each pocket with a wooden pick. Sprinkle chicken with salt and pepper.
❸ Heat butter in a large nonstick skillet over medium heat. Add chicken to pan; cook 6 minutes on each side or until done. Remove from pan; cover and let stand 2 minutes. Top chicken with remaining 1 tablespoon chopped almonds and remaining 1 tablespoon parsley. Yield: 4 servings.

CALORIES 288; FAT 12.7g (sat 4.3g, mono 4.5g, poly 1.8g); PROTEIN 37.5g; CARB 3.9g; FIBER 0.9g; CHOL 111mg; IRON 1.7mg; SODIUM 496mg; CALC 109mg

Simple Tip

Get the most flavor. Use cooking techniques that intensify the taste of foods. Roasting the tomatoes for this dish boosts their sweetness and helps make the dish shine. The same principle applies to the sautéed tomato paste and roasted peppers in Sausage and Roasted Pepper Pasta (page 56).

QUICK & EASY
Tomato-Ricotta Spaghetti

Roasting tomatoes intensifies their sweetness. We also tested this recipe with grated Parmigiano-Reggiano—it's a splurge that makes the difference.

- 2 pints cherry tomatoes, halved (about 4 cups)
- 5 teaspoons extra-virgin olive oil, divided
- ½ teaspoon salt, divided
- 8 ounces uncooked spaghetti
- ⅓ cup chopped fresh basil
- ¼ teaspoon freshly ground black pepper
- ½ cup (2 ounces) ricotta salata cheese, crumbled

❶ Preheat oven to 400°.
❷ Place tomatoes on a foil-lined baking sheet. Drizzle with 1 teaspoon oil; sprinkle with ⅛ teaspoon salt. Bake at 400° for 20 minutes or until tomatoes collapse.
❸ Cook pasta according to package directions, omitting salt and fat. Drain pasta in a colander over a bowl, reserving ⅓ cup cooking liquid. Return pasta and reserved liquid to pan; stir in tomatoes, remaining 4 teaspoons oil, remaining ⅜ teaspoon salt, basil, pepper, and cheese. Toss well. Serve immediately. Yield: 4 servings (serving size: 1¼ cups).

CALORIES 314; FAT 8.4g (sat 1.8g, mono 4.7g, poly 1.4g); PROTEIN 10.5g; CARB 50.3g; FIBER 3.6g; CHOL 5mg; IRON 2.7mg; SODIUM 331mg; CALC 66mg

Simple Tip

Use precut vegetable mixtures. Fresh or frozen, blends of bell peppers and onions or Asian vegetables count as one ingredient on the shopping list but add variety to dishes like fajitas, stir-fries, and soups.

QUICK & EASY
Paprika Pork

Assorted colors of fresh peppers and paprika turn bottled marinara into a rich Hungarian goulash-style sauce.

- Cooking spray
- 3 cups prechopped multicolored bell peppers
- 1 (1-pound) pork tenderloin, trimmed and cut into 1-inch pieces
- ½ teaspoon salt, divided
- ½ teaspoon freshly ground black pepper, divided
- 4 teaspoons paprika
- 1½ cups red wine pasta sauce
- 1 cup water
- 3 cups hot cooked medium egg noodles (about 2½ cups uncooked pasta)

❶ Heat a large saucepan over medium-high heat. Coat pan with cooking spray. Add bell peppers to pan; sauté 5 minutes or until tender. Remove from pan.
❷ Coat pan with cooking spray. Sprinkle pork with ¼ teaspoon salt and ¼ teaspoon black pepper. Add pork to pan; cook 4 minutes, browning on all sides. Stir in paprika; cook 1 minute. Add pasta sauce, 1 cup water, and bell peppers; bring to a boil. Reduce heat, and simmer 25 minutes or until meat is tender, stirring occasionally. Stir in remaining ¼ teaspoon salt and ¼ teaspoon black pepper; cook 1 minute. Serve over egg noodles. Yield: 4 servings (serving size: about 1 cup pork mixture and ¾ cup noodles).

CALORIES 396; FAT 8.5g (sat 2g, mono 2.5g, poly 1.4g); PROTEIN 32g; CARB 48.8g; FIBER 6.6g; CHOL 109mg; IRON 4.9mg; SODIUM 666mg; CALC 116mg

QUICK & EASY

Lemon-Salmon Salad Sandwiches

Look for salmon in pouches in the canned fish section of the supermarket. A hearty white bread has sufficient heft to stand up to the sandwich filling. Slices from a bakery artisan loaf would dress up the sandwich even more.

- 1 large lemon
- ¼ cup light mayonnaise
- ½ teaspoon freshly ground black pepper
- 2 (7-ounce) packages salmon
- ¾ cup thinly sliced cucumber
- 8 (1-ounce) slices white bread

1 Finely grate 1 teaspoon lemon rind; squeeze 3 tablespoons juice from lemon over a medium bowl. Add rind, mayonnaise, and pepper to bowl; stir well. Let stand 5 minutes. Add salmon to bowl; stir until well blended.
2 Layer cucumber evenly over 4 bread slices; top each with about ½ cup salmon mixture. Top with remaining 4 bread slices. Yield: 4 servings (serving size: 1 sandwich).

CALORIES 362; FAT 12.7g (sat 1.9g, mono 5.6g, poly 3.9g); PROTEIN 34g; CARB 29.4g; FIBER 0.3g; CHOL 74mg; IRON 2.9mg; SODIUM 850mg; CALC 87mg

Hearty Weeknight Supper Menu

serves 4

Roasted Brussels sprouts retain a crisp-tender texture and gain caramelized flavor from browned edges. Choose boil-in-bag brown rice if you're in a hurry; it cooks in about 10 minutes.

Balsamic Pork with Shallots

Roasted Brussels sprouts

Cut 1 pound trimmed Brussels sprouts in half lengthwise. Combine Brussels sprouts, 2 tablespoons melted butter, ½ teaspoon salt, and ¼ teaspoon freshly ground black pepper on a jelly-roll pan. Bake at 425° for 15 minutes or until browned and tender. Remove from oven. Sprinkle with 1 teaspoon grated lemon rind; toss to combine.

Brown rice

Pinot noir

Vanilla low-fat ice cream with caramel sauce and toasted slivered almonds

Our strategy is simple: Focus on quality ingredients, take a few judicious shortcuts, and rely on secret weapons from the pantry.

QUICK & EASY

Balsamic Pork with Shallots

This dish is reminiscent of bistro-style steak with shallot sauce. Serve with rice, egg noodles, or roasted potatoes.

- 5 teaspoons olive oil, divided
- 1 (1-pound) pork tenderloin, trimmed and cut crosswise into (½-inch-thick) slices
- ½ teaspoon salt, divided
- ½ teaspoon freshly ground black pepper, divided
- 2¼ cups thinly sliced shallots (about 8)
- 1 garlic clove, minced
- ½ cup water
- 2 tablespoons balsamic vinegar

1 Heat 1 teaspoon oil in a large nonstick skillet over medium-high heat. Sprinkle pork with ¼ teaspoon salt and ¼ teaspoon pepper. Add pork to pan; cook 3 minutes on each side or until done. Remove from pan, and keep warm.
2 Add remaining 4 teaspoons oil to pan; reduce heat to medium. Add shallots to pan; cook 10 minutes or until tender, stirring occasionally. Add garlic; cook 2 minutes. Stir in ½ cup water and vinegar; simmer 6 minutes. Stir in remaining ¼ teaspoon salt and remaining ¼ teaspoon pepper. Spoon shallot mixture over pork. Serve immediately. Yield: 4 servings (serving size: 3 ounces pork and ¼ cup shallot mixture).

CALORIES 260; FAT 9.6g (sat 2.1g, mono 5.9g, poly 1.1g); PROTEIN 26.2g; CARB 16.9g; FIBER 0.7g; CHOL 74mg; IRON 2.6mg; SODIUM 365mg; CALC 44mg

Sausage and Roasted Pepper Pasta

- 4 medium bell peppers (about 1½ pounds)
- 8 ounces uncooked penne pasta
- 12 ounces hot turkey Italian sausage
- 2 tablespoons tomato paste
- ¼ teaspoon freshly ground black pepper
- ⅛ teaspoon salt
- ¼ cup (1 ounce) grated fresh Parmigiano-Reggiano cheese

1 Preheat broiler.

2 Cut bell peppers in half lengthwise; discard seeds and membranes. Place pepper halves, skin sides up, on a foil-lined baking sheet; flatten with hand. Broil 10 minutes or until thoroughly blackened. Place bell peppers in a zip-top plastic bag; seal. Let stand 15 minutes. Peel; discard skins. Chop and set aside.

3 Cook pasta according to package directions, omitting salt and fat. Drain in a colander over a bowl, reserving 1 cup cooking liquid; keep warm.

4 Heat a large nonstick skillet over medium-high heat. Remove casings from sausage. Add sausage to pan, and cook 8 minutes or until browned, stirring to crumble. Add bell peppers to pan. Move sausage mixture to outside edges of pan, leaving an open space in center. Add tomato paste to open space in pan; cook 1 minute, stirring constantly. Stir tomato paste into sausage mixture. Stir in pasta and reserved cooking liquid; cook 3 minutes or until thoroughly heated. Stir in black pepper and salt. Sprinkle with cheese. Yield: 4 servings (serving size: 1½ cups pasta mixture and 1 tablespoon cheese).

CALORIES 430; FAT 11.5g (sat 3.7g, mono 4.4g, poly 1.3g); PROTEIN 28.9g; CARB 52.4g; FIBER 4.4g; CHOL 79mg; IRON 4.4mg; SODIUM 894mg; CALC 79mg

May You Live To Be 100

In Sardinia—where the expression and experience are common—and in other places where people live long, family, food, and lifestyle make a difference.

EFISIO FARRIS IMMIGRATED TO AMERICA from his native Orosei, Sardinia, more than 20 years ago. When he moved to Dallas and opened his first restaurant, Pomodoro, it was the only Sardinian-influenced restaurant in America at the time. Since then, Farris has made it his mission to bring a bit of the island's lifestyle to American diners.

"People ask me, 'Why did you leave Sardinia?' I tell them I never left—I brought Sardinia with me," he says. At first, when Sardinian ingredients were scarce in this country, Farris traveled home and toted them back in his suitcase. Now he shares the island's food through an import business called Gourmet Sardinia, cooking classes, and a cookbook, *Sweet Myrtle and Bitter Honey*, plus restaurants in Dallas and Houston.

As it happened, he was onto something big. Located off the western coast of Italy, Sardinia is the second largest island in the Mediterranean, boasting nearly 1,100 miles of shoreline and a bounty of wild and cultivated fare. Sardinia's people also live long, making the island what *National Geographic* and *Cooking Light* Nutrition Essentials Advisory Panel member Dan Buettner have identified as a Blue Zone—one of those rare places in the world (along with Okinawa, Japan; Seventh Day Adventists in Loma Linda, California; and Costa Rica's Nicoya Peninsula) where people often live past 100. It's so common that islanders have an expression in the native dialect, Sardo: *A Chent'Annos* ("May you live to be 100").

This would have come as no surprise to Farris's grandfather, Mannoi Nicola, who lived to 107. "My grandfather would say he lived the same way forever," he recalls. That way included specific qualities Sardinia shares with other Blue Zone communities: close family and community relationships, plenty of socializing, nearly constant moderate physical activity, and a largely plant-based diet (see "Keys to a Long Life," page 57).

Tomato-Poached Eggs with Sardinian Music Bread (Ovos kin Tomate e Casu)

You'll find variations of this dish throughout Sardinia, but four ingredients all cooks keep on hand are pane carasau, tomatoes, pecorino Sardo (a sheep's-milk cheese), and eggs.

    2   tablespoons extra-virgin olive oil
    ⅓   cup sliced green onions
    2   garlic cloves, minced
    ½   teaspoon kosher salt, divided
    ½   teaspoon freshly ground black
        pepper, divided
    2   (14.5-ounce) cans whole plum
        tomatoes, undrained and coarsely
        chopped (such as San Marzano)
    4   large eggs
    4   sheets pane carasau (Sardinian
        music bread), each broken into
        4 wedges
    ½   cup (2 ounces) finely grated aged
        pecorino Sardo
    2   tablespoons chopped fresh basil

❶ Heat oil in a large skillet over medium heat. Add onions and garlic to pan; cook 3 minutes or until fragrant, stirring often. Stir in ¼ teaspoon salt, ¼ teaspoon pepper, and tomatoes; bring to a boil. Reduce heat, and simmer 15 minutes, stirring occasionally.
❷ Reduce heat to low. Working with 1 egg at a time, crack eggs over tomato mixture, about 1 inch apart in pan. Sprinkle eggs with remaining ¼ teaspoon salt and ¼ teaspoon pepper. Cover and cook 5 minutes or until desired degree of doneness. Remove from heat.
❸ Arrange 4 wedges pane carasau on each of 4 plates; spoon ¾ cup tomato sauce over each serving. Top each serving with 1 egg, and sprinkle with 2 tablespoons grated cheese. Top each serving with 1½ teaspoons chopped fresh basil. Yield: 4 servings.

CALORIES 474; FAT 17.1g (sat 5g, mono 8g, poly 1.6g); PROTEIN 21.7g; CARB 61.2g; FIBER 8.3g; CHOL 226mg; IRON 6.8mg; SODIUM 836mg; CALC 267mg

---

QUICK & EASY
Zucchini with Peppermint (Curcurica kin Menta)

Ricotta salata is a firm cheese common on the island. *Salata* means salty; the process for making the cheese involves salting traditional soft ricotta and aging it until it's firm. Purchase pane carasau (Sardinian music bread), a paper-thin flatbread, from GourmetSardinia (www.gourmetsardinia.com).

    1½ tablespoons extra-virgin olive oil
    1   tablespoon finely chopped green
        onion tops
    5   cups cubed zucchini (about
        2 pounds)
    1   tablespoon chopped fresh
        flat-leaf parsley
    ¼   teaspoon sea salt
    2   tablespoons torn mint leaves
    6   tablespoons freshly crumbled
        ricotta salata cheese
    2   sheets pane carasau (Sardinian
        music bread), each broken into
        3 pieces
    Mint sprigs (optional)

❶ Heat oil in a large nonstick skillet over medium-high heat. Add onions to pan; sauté 1 minute, stirring frequently. Add zucchini, parsley, and salt. Reduce heat to medium-low, and cook 20 minutes or until zucchini is tender, stirring frequently. Add torn mint; cook 1 minute. Sprinkle with cheese; serve over pane carasau. Garnish with mint sprigs, if desired. Yield: 6 servings (serving size: ½ cup zucchini mixture, 1 tablespoon cheese, and ⅓ sheet pane carasau).

CALORIES 160; FAT 5.4g (sat 1.3g, mono 2.9g, poly 0.5g); PROTEIN 6.8g; CARB 23.1g; FIBER 3.8g; CHOL 5mg; IRON 2.1mg; SODIUM 152mg; CALC 77mg

---

Keys to a Long Life

Sardinia is one of four regions identified as a Blue Zone by *National Geographic* and *Cooking Light* Nutrition Essentials Advisory Panel member Dan Buettner. Blue Zones are areas where residents reach the age of 100 at high rates and enjoy unusually active golden years.

Buettner and a team of researchers have studied Sardinians, among others, to uncover the lifestyle factors that contribute to their longevity. Their findings, partially funded by *National Geographic* and the National Institute on Aging, are in the recently published *The Blue Zones: Lessons for Living Longer from the People Who've Lived the Longest*.

Residents of Sardinia have a number of qualities that contribute to their long lives, and Buettner believes anyone can adopt the lifestyle characteristics uncovered by his research. Among the traditional Sardinian habits that can translate to modern American life:

• **Walk—a lot.** Sardinian shepherds log many miles following their flocks to pasture. Try to cover at least five to six miles a day.
• **Consume a plant-based diet.** For centuries, fava beans and bread, along with foraged plants and cheese, formed the basis of the Sardinian diet. Meat was only an occasional treat.
• **Drink to your health.** A daily glass or two of red wine offers healthful flavonoids. Sardinian wines made with Cannonau grapes, which are particularly antioxidant rich, are available in the United States.
• **Spend time with family.** All the centenarians Buettner interviewed named family as their top priority. All but one were cared for by family members.
• **Laugh at adversity.** Sardinians are known for their sardonic wit, which they share with everyone.

Pork Chops with Fava Beans
(Porcu kin Ava Frisca)

1¼ cups shelled fava beans (about 2½ pounds unshelled)
1 cup pearl onions
1 tablespoon extra-virgin olive oil
4 (8-ounce) bone-in center-cut pork chops, trimmed
1 teaspoon sea salt, divided
1 cup dry white wine
2 teaspoons chopped fresh thyme
¼ teaspoon black pepper
4 garlic cloves, crushed
3 fresh myrtle leaves, coarsely crushed
¾ cup water
2 tablespoons chopped fresh parsley
1 tablespoon chopped fresh basil

❶ Cook fava beans in boiling water 1 minute. Drain and rinse with cold water; drain. Remove and discard tough outer skins from beans. Cook onions in boiling water 1 minute. Drain and rinse with cold water; drain. Pinch stem end of each onion; discard peels. Combine beans and onions; set aside.
❷ Heat oil in a large nonstick skillet over medium-high heat. Sprinkle pork with ¼ teaspoon salt. Add pork to pan; cook 2 minutes on each side or until browned. Remove pork from pan. Stir in ¼ teaspoon salt, wine, and next 4 ingredients; cook 1 minute, scraping pan to loosen browned bits. Return pork to pan. Reduce heat, and cook 4 minutes; turn pork occasionally.
❸ Add bean mixture, remaining ½ teaspoon salt, ¾ cup water, parsley, and basil to pan. Cover and cook 12 minutes. Remove pork from pan. Bring bean mixture to a boil; cook until reduced to 2 cups (about 4 minutes). Discard myrtle. Serve bean mixture with pork chops. Yield: 4 servings (serving size: 1 pork chop and ½ cup bean mixture).

CALORIES 463; FAT 13.8g (sat 4.1g, mono 6.9g, poly 1.4g); PROTEIN 47.7g; CARB 36.7g; FIBER 12g; CHOL 98mg; IRON 5.2mg; SODIUM 668mg; CALC 103mg

Risotto-Style Fregula with Mushrooms, Abbamele, and Goat Cheese (Fregula kin Antunna e Crapinu)

Fregula is a small, toasted semolina pasta. Israeli couscous is a more readily available stand-in; you can also substitute buckwheat honey for abbamele.

2¼ cups fat-free, less-sodium chicken broth
1 cup water
1 tablespoon olive oil
8 ounces wild mushrooms
⅓ cup chopped shallots
1¼ cups uncooked fregula
¾ teaspoon kosher salt
¼ cup dry white wine
¼ cup finely chopped fresh chives
¼ cup (2 ounces) goat cheese
1 tablespoon abbamele, divided
3 tablespoons chopped walnuts, toasted

❶ Combine broth and 1 cup water in a saucepan over medium heat; bring to a simmer. Heat oil in a large skillet over medium heat. Add mushrooms; cook 5 minutes or until moisture evaporates. Add shallots; cook 4 minutes, stirring frequently. Add fregula and salt; cook 1 minute, stirring constantly. Stir in wine; cook 30 seconds or until liquid is nearly absorbed, stirring constantly.
❷ Set aside ¼ cup broth mixture; cover and keep warm. Add remaining broth mixture, ½ cup at a time, to pan, stirring constantly until each portion of broth is absorbed before adding the next (about 15 minutes total). Remove from heat.
❸ Stir in reserved ¼ cup broth mixture, chives, goat cheese, and 1½ teaspoons abbamele. Sprinkle with walnuts. Drizzle each serving with ¼ teaspoon abbamele. Serve immediately. Yield: 6 servings (serving size: ½ cup fregula mixture and 1½ teaspoons walnuts).

CALORIES 235; FAT 7.2g (sat 1.9g, mono 2.6g, poly 1.8g); PROTEIN 8.6g; CARB 30.2g; FIBER 1.5g; CHOL 4mg; IRON 1.2mg; SODIUM 419mg; CALC 34mg

Recipe Contest Finalists

Here are four more delicious finalist recipes from the fourth annual *Cooking Light* Ultimate Reader Recipe Contest.

From a sweet carrot soup to yeasty potato rolls to chocolaty biscotti, these dishes integrate enjoyable flavor combinations and straightforward preparation techniques.

MAKE AHEAD • FREEZABLE
Deep Dark Chocolate Biscotti
(pictured on page 211)

Category Finalist—Desserts
"Whole wheat flour, flaxseed, and almonds add fiber and antioxidants."
—Linda Rogers, Manistee, Michigan

9.5 ounces whole wheat flour (about 2 cups)
2 tablespoons flaxseed
½ teaspoon baking soda
¼ teaspoon salt
⅓ cup granulated sugar
⅓ cup packed dark brown sugar
2 large egg whites
1 large egg
1½ teaspoons vanilla extract
⅔ cup dark chocolate chips
¾ cup unsalted almonds

❶ Preheat oven to 350°.
❷ Weigh or lightly spoon flour into dry measuring cups; level with a knife. Combine flour and next 3 ingredients in a bowl, stirring with a whisk. Combine granulated sugar and next 3 ingredients in a bowl; beat with a mixer at high speed 2 minutes. Add vanilla; mix well. Add flour mixture to egg mixture; stir until combined. Fold in chocolate and almonds. Divide dough into 3 equal portions. Roll each portion into a 6-inch-long roll. Arrange rolls 3 inches apart

on a baking sheet lined with parchment paper. Pat to a 1-inch thickness. Bake at 350° for 28 minutes or until firm.

❸ Remove rolls from baking sheet; cool 10 minutes on a wire rack. Cut rolls diagonally into 30 (½-inch) slices. Place, cut sides down, on baking sheet. Reduce oven temperature to 325°; bake 7 minutes. Turn cookies over; bake 7 minutes (cookies will be slightly soft in center but will harden as they cool). Remove from baking sheet; cool on wire rack. Yield: 2½ dozen (serving size: 1 biscotto).

CALORIES 94; FAT 3.5g (sat 0.9g, mono 1.7g, poly 0.7g); PROTEIN 2.7g; CARB 14.4g; FIBER 1.9g; CHOL 7mg; IRON 0.7mg; SODIUM 49mg; CALC 18mg

MAKE AHEAD • FREEZABLE
Creamy Carrot Soup

Category Finalist—Starters and Drinks
"I prepared this soup for my parents, who watch my daughter one afternoon a week. They absolutely loved its velvety sweetness. Garnish with shredded carrot and fresh mint."

—Lisa Richardson,
Glendale, California

  1   tablespoon extra-virgin olive oil
  1¾ cups chopped Vidalia or other sweet onion
  2   pounds carrots, cut into ½-inch pieces
  1   teaspoon fine sea salt
  ½   teaspoon freshly ground black pepper
      Dash of ground ginger
  2   cups water
  2   cups fat-free, less-sodium chicken broth
  2   tablespoons heavy cream, divided

❶ Heat oil in a large Dutch oven over medium heat. Add onion and carrots to pan; cook 10 minutes, stirring frequently. Stir in salt, pepper, and ginger.
❷ Add 2 cups water and broth to pan; bring to a boil. Cover, reduce heat, and simmer 25 minutes or until carrots are tender. Remove from heat; cool.

❸ Place half of carrot mixture and 1 tablespoon cream in a food processor or blender; process 20 seconds or until smooth. Pour pureed mixture into a large bowl. Repeat procedure with remaining carrot mixture and 1 tablespoon cream. Return mixture to pan, and cook over medium heat until thoroughly heated. Yield: 4 servings (serving size: 1½ cups).

CALORIES 180; FAT 6.9g (sat 2.3g, mono 3.3g, poly 0.9g); PROTEIN 3.6g; CARB 28.7g; FIBER 7.6g; CHOL 10mg; IRON 0.9mg; SODIUM 963mg; CALC 97mg

STAFF FAVORITE • MAKE AHEAD
FREEZABLE
Monday Morning Potato Rolls and Bread

Category Finalist—Sides and Salads
"I make a fairly traditional Sunday meal of chicken and potatoes for my family. I hated to see the leftovers go to waste, so I used the mashed potatoes to create these delicious rolls. I experimented with 10 variations before settling on this version. My kids and husband love the rolls so much that they never last until Tuesday!"

—Catherine McMichael,
Saginaw, Michigan

  1   cup mashed cooked peeled baking potatoes (about 8 ounces)
  1   cup fat-free milk
  3   tablespoons honey
  2   tablespoons butter
21.4   ounces bread flour (about 4½ cups), divided
  2½   teaspoons dry yeast
  1½   teaspoons sea salt
  2   large eggs
  1   teaspoon olive oil
       Cooking spray

❶ Combine first 4 ingredients in a microwave-safe bowl. Microwave at HIGH for 2 minutes or until mixture is 110°. Stir with a whisk until smooth.
❷ Weigh or lightly spoon flour into dry measuring cups; level with a knife. Combine 6.75 ounces (about 1½ cups) flour, yeast, and salt in a large mixing bowl.

Add potato mixture to flour mixture, stirring with a fork until combined. Add eggs; stir until combined.
❸ Add 9 ounces (about 2 cups) flour to potato mixture; stir until a soft dough forms. Turn dough out onto a floured surface. Knead until smooth and elastic (about 10 minutes); add enough of remaining 1 cup flour, 1 tablespoon at a time, to prevent dough from sticking to hands (dough will feel sticky).
❹ Place dough in a large bowl coated with olive oil, turning to coat top. Cover and let rise in a warm place (85°), free from drafts, 1 hour or until doubled in size. (Gently press two fingers into dough. If indentation remains, dough has risen enough.) Punch dough down; cover and let rest 5 minutes.
❺ Divide dough in half. Working with 1 portion (cover remaining dough to prevent drying), roll portion into a 14 x 7–inch rectangle on a floured surface. Roll up rectangle tightly, starting with a short edge, pressing firmly to eliminate air pockets; pinch seam and ends to seal. Place loaf, seam side down, in an 8 x 4–inch loaf pan coated with cooking spray.
❻ Shape remaining portion into 9 portions, and shape each into a ball. Place balls in an 8-inch square baking dish coated with cooking spray. Coat top of loaf and rolls with cooking spray. Cover and let rise in a warm place (85°), free from drafts, 30 minutes or until doubled in size. (Gently press two fingers into dough. If the indentation remains, dough has risen enough.)
❼ Preheat oven to 350°.
❽ Bake at 350° for 30 minutes or until tops of rolls are browned and loaf sounds hollow when tapped on the bottom. Remove from pans; cool on wire racks. Yield: 18 servings (serving size: 1 roll or one-ninth of loaf).

CALORIES 168; FAT 2.8g (sat 1.1g, mono 0.8g, poly 0.4g); PROTEIN 5.7g; CARB 30.1g; FIBER 1.1g; CHOL 28mg; IRON 1.8mg; SODIUM 207mg; CALC 24mg

Hidden Rainbow Albondigas

Category Finalist—Family Dinners
"When I met my husband three years ago, he suggested I try cooking *albondigas,* a traditional Mexican soup with meatballs and vegetables. His mother taught me how to prepare her authentic version. My children wouldn't eat chunks of vegetables, so I needed to re-create the dish. Now I take pleasure in knowing that my children are eating a colorful dish of 'hidden' vegetables."

—Emily Almaguer,
Fort Worth, Texas

1 tablespoon olive oil
1 (16-ounce) bag frozen pepper stir-fry (such as Birds Eye)
¾ cup diced carrot
2 (14.5-ounce) cans diced tomatoes, drained
1 (4-ounce) can chopped green chiles, drained
2 (32-ounce) cartons fat-free, less-sodium chicken broth
1 (32-ounce) carton fat-free, less-sodium beef broth
1 pound skinless, boneless chicken breast, cut into ½-inch pieces
1 (1-pound) pork tenderloin, trimmed and cut into ½-inch pieces
1½ cups shredded yellow squash
1 cup fresh cilantro sprigs
¾ cup uncooked long-grain white rice, divided
½ cup chopped sweet onion
1 teaspoon salt, divided
1 teaspoon freshly ground black pepper, divided
1 large egg
2 tablespoons fresh lime juice

❶ Heat oil in a large Dutch oven over medium-high heat. Add pepper stir-fry to pan; cook 5 minutes, stirring occasionally. Add carrot; sauté 5 minutes. Stir in tomatoes and next 3 ingredients; bring to a boil. Reduce heat, and simmer 15 minutes or until carrot is tender.

❷ Place one-third of broth mixture in a blender. Remove center piece of blender lid (to allow steam to escape); secure lid on blender. Place a clean towel over opening in blender lid (to avoid splatters). Blend until smooth; pour into a large bowl. Repeat procedure with remaining broth mixture. Return to pan.

❸ Place chicken, pork, squash, cilantro, ¼ cup rice, onion, ½ teaspoon salt, ½ teaspoon black pepper, and egg in a food processor; process 30 seconds or until blended. Bring broth mixture to a boil. Drop meat mixture by rounded tablespoonfuls (about 45 meatballs) into broth mixture. Add remaining ½ cup rice to pan; reduce heat, and simmer 45 minutes or until meatballs are done. Stir in remaining ½ teaspoon salt and ½ teaspoon black pepper. Stir in juice. Yield: 12 servings (serving size: about 1½ cups).

CALORIES 184; FAT 3.5g (sat 0.9g, mono 1.7g, poly 0.5g); PROTEIN 20.8g; CARB 16.2g; FIBER 2g; CHOL 64mg; IRON 1.6mg; SODIUM 790mg; CALC 26mg

TEST KITCHENS SECRETS
Fresh Whole Wheat Pitas

Test Kitchens Professional SaBrina Bone says it's worth the effort to prepare homemade pitas because they're tasty, nutritious, and unparalleled for sandwiches. She shares three tips to guarantee delicious and healthful loaves.

First, "Keep as much air in the dough as possible," she says. Don't punch down the dough after it rises, and gently roll dough into discs to achieve an airy result. Second, get the oven really hot to create airy steam in the slightly sticky dough as it bakes. And third, with the bread's nutrition profile in mind, Bone incorporated white whole wheat flour, a whole-grain flour milled from hard white wheat. Its lighter color and flavor work well in these pitas and other whole wheat baked goods where tenderness is key.

Fresh Whole Wheat Pitas

1 tablespoon sugar
1 package dry yeast (about 2¼ teaspoons)
1 cup plus 2 tablespoons warm water (100° to 110°)
10 ounces bread flour (about 2¼ cups)
4.75 ounces white whole wheat flour (about 1 cup), divided
2 tablespoons 2% Greek-style yogurt (such as Fage)
1 tablespoon extra-virgin olive oil
¾ teaspoon salt
Olive oil cooking spray

❶ Dissolve sugar and yeast in 1 cup plus 2 tablespoons warm water in a large bowl; let stand 5 minutes. Weigh or lightly spoon flours into dry measuring cups; level with a knife. Add bread flour, 3 ounces (about ¾ cup) whole wheat flour, yogurt, oil, and salt to yeast mixture; beat with a mixer at medium speed until smooth. Turn dough out onto a floured surface. Knead dough until smooth and elastic (about 10 minutes); add enough of remaining whole wheat flour, 1 tablespoon at a time, to prevent dough from sticking to hands (dough will feel sticky). Place dough in a large bowl coated with cooking spray, turning to coat top. Cover and let rise in a warm place (85°), free from drafts, 45 minutes or until doubled in size.

❷ Position oven rack on lowest shelf.

❸ Preheat oven to 500°.

❹ Divide dough into 8 portions. Working with 1 portion at a time, gently roll each portion into a 5½-inch circle. Place 4 dough circles on each of 2 baking sheets heavily coated with cooking spray. Bake, 1 sheet at a time, at 500° for 8 minutes or until puffed and browned. Cool on a wire rack. Yield: 8 servings (serving size: 1 pita).

CALORIES 211; FAT 2.9g (sat 0.4g, mono 1.5g, poly 0.4g); PROTEIN 7g; CARB 39.9g; FIBER 3.1g; CHOL 0mg; IRON 2.5mg; SODIUM 225mg; CALC 11mg

Lunch to Go

With our creative, make-ahead recipes, you can have a midday meal that you'll look forward to enjoying.

TAKING YOUR LUNCH TO WORK SAVES YOU MONEY, and when you start with fresh ingredients, you'll enjoy a more healthful meal as well. With just a little organization and a few supplies— such as an insulated bag and serving-sized containers—your lunch box options will be invitingly inspired.

QUICK & EASY • MAKE AHEAD
Tabbouleh with Chicken and Red Pepper

If you're making the mixture a few hours or more in advance, store the cucumber and tomato separately and add them close to serving time to keep the salad at its best. Serve with Lemony Hummus with Spicy Whole Wheat Pita Chips (page 62) for a Middle Eastern–themed light lunch.

- ½ cup uncooked bulgur
- ½ cup boiling water
- 1½ cups diced plum tomato
- ¾ cup shredded cooked chicken breast
- ¾ cup minced fresh flat-leaf parsley
- ½ cup finely chopped red bell pepper
- ½ cup diced English cucumber
- ¼ cup minced fresh mint
- 1½ tablespoons fresh lemon juice
- 1 tablespoon extra-virgin olive oil
- ½ teaspoon salt
- ¼ teaspoon freshly ground black pepper

❶ Combine bulgur and ½ cup boiling water in a large bowl. Cover and let stand 15 minutes or until bulgur is tender. Drain well; return bulgur to bowl. Cool.
❷ Add tomato and remaining ingredients; toss well. Yield: 4 servings (serving size: 1¼ cups).

CALORIES 150; FAT 4.7g (sat 0.8g, mono 2.9g, poly 0.7g); PROTEIN 11.2g; CARB 16.9g; FIBER 4.5g; CHOL 22mg; IRON 1.6mg; SODIUM 326mg; CALC 33mg

MAKE AHEAD
Barley and Beef Soup

Make this soup the night before to allow time for its flavors to develop. Pour hot servings into a thermos to take for lunch, or reheat individual portions in the microwave as needed. Serve the soup with crusty bread, crackers, or Spicy Whole Wheat Pita Chips (page 62).

- Cooking spray
- 2 cups chopped onion (about 1 large)
- 1 pound chuck steak, trimmed and cut into ½-inch cubes
- 1½ cups chopped peeled carrot (about 4)
- 1 cup chopped celery (about 4 stalks)
- 5 garlic cloves, minced
- 1 cup uncooked pearl barley
- 5 cups fat-free, less-sodium beef broth
- 2 cups water
- ½ cup no-salt-added tomato puree
- ½ teaspoon kosher salt
- ¼ teaspoon freshly ground black pepper
- 2 bay leaves

❶ Heat a large Dutch oven over medium heat. Coat pan with cooking spray. Add onion and beef to pan; cook 10 minutes or until onion is tender and beef is browned, stirring occasionally. Add carrot and celery to pan; cook 5 minutes, stirring occasionally. Stir in garlic; cook 30 seconds. Stir in barley and remaining ingredients, and bring to a boil. Cover, reduce heat, and simmer 40 minutes or until barley is done and vegetables are tender. Discard bay leaves. Yield: 6 servings (serving size: about 1¾ cups).

CALORIES 275; FAT 5g (sat 1.6g, mono 2.3g, poly 0.5g); PROTEIN 21.8g; CARB 36g; FIBER 8g; CHOL 43mg; IRON 3.1mg; SODIUM 649mg; CALC 57mg

---

Four Tasty Takeaways

Make dishes ahead when possible. Barley and Beef Soup (at left), like many soups and stews, improves with time; make it the night before. Lemony Hummus (page 62), too, will grow better as its ingredients marry.

Keep it separate. To prevent soggy sandwiches, pack separate zip-top bags of tomato slices, lettuce, and bread, and then assemble the sandwiches just before serving. Similarly, don't dress leafy salads until you're ready to eat. Salt will draw moisture out of watery ingredients, so add items such as tomatoes and cucumbers to a grain salad at the last minute for the best results.

Put leftovers to good use. Consider applying extras from dinner to the next day's lunch. Slice leftover chicken or beef, and serve it on top of pasta or salad greens, mix it into a grain salad (see Tabbouleh with Chicken and Red Pepper, at left), or make it into a sandwich. Chop extra grilled vegetables and add them to soups, salads, or sandwiches.

Stay safe. Keep cold food cold (below 40°) and hot food hot (above 140°) as it travels. Use insulated lunch bags, coolers, thermoses, ice bags, and frozen gel packs to help with temperature control. If reheating items in a microwave, the United States Department of Agriculture recommends they reach 165° and are served steaming hot.

Tuna Pan Bagnat

A favorite in southern France, *pan bagnat* (pan ban-YAH) means "bathed bread." The bread in this sandwich is meant to absorb some liquid from the filling, so it's fine to assemble it entirely ahead of time. Serve with potato salad, pasta salad, or baked chips.

- ⅓ cup finely chopped red onion
- 2 tablespoons chopped pitted niçoise olives
- 1 tablespoon fresh lemon juice
- ¼ teaspoon kosher salt
- ¼ teaspoon freshly ground black pepper
- 1 (6-ounce) can premium tuna, packed in oil, drained
- 1 hard-cooked large egg, chopped
- ¼ cup thinly sliced fresh basil
- 2 teaspoons extra-virgin olive oil
- 1 (8-ounce) whole wheat French bread baguette
- 1 garlic clove, halved
- 1 cup thinly sliced plum tomato (about 1)

① Combine first 7 ingredients in a medium bowl. Combine basil and oil; stir with a whisk. Cut bread in half horizontally. Hollow out top and bottom halves of bread, leaving a 1-inch-thick shell; reserve torn bread for another use. Rub cut sides of garlic clove over cut sides of bread; discard garlic. Drizzle basil mixture evenly over cut sides of bread. Spoon tuna mixture on bottom half of baguette. Arrange tomato slices over tuna mixture. Cover with top half of baguette. Wrap filled baguette in plastic wrap, and let stand 20 minutes. Cut filled baguette into 4 (3-inch) equal portions. Yield: 4 servings (serving size: 1 sandwich).

CALORIES 248; FAT 9.3g (sat 1.4g, mono 4.6g, poly 2g); PROTEIN 14.5g; CARB 26.3g; FIBER 2.2g; CHOL 63mg; IRON 2mg; SODIUM 589mg; CALC 84mg

Lemony Hummus with Spicy Whole Wheat Pita Chips

This dish makes a wholesome accompaniment for sandwiches and salads. Keep extra pita chips stored in an airtight container for up to three days.

HUMMUS:

- 3 tablespoons fresh lemon juice
- 3 tablespoons water
- 2 tablespoons tahini (sesame seed paste)
- 1 teaspoon ground cumin
- 2 teaspoons extra-virgin olive oil
- ½ teaspoon minced garlic
- ¼ teaspoon salt
- 1 (15½-ounce) can chickpeas (garbanzo beans), rinsed and drained

CHIPS:

- 2 teaspoons ground cumin
- 1 teaspoon paprika
- ½ teaspoon kosher salt
- ¼ teaspoon ground red pepper
- 6 mini whole-wheat pitas, split in half horizontally
- Cooking spray

① Preheat oven to 350°.
② To prepare hummus, place first 8 ingredients in a food processor; process until smooth.
③ To prepare chips, combine 2 teaspoons cumin and next 3 ingredients. Cut each pita half into 4 wedges. Arrange pita wedges on a baking sheet. Lightly coat pita with cooking spray. Sprinkle cumin mixture evenly over pita. Bake at 350° for 10 minutes or until crisp. Serve with hummus. Yield: 8 servings (serving size: 3½ tablespoons hummus and 6 chips).

CALORIES 132; FAT 4g (sat 0.5g, mono 1.8g, poly 1.3g); PROTEIN 4.9g; CARB 20.9g; FIBER 3.4g; CHOL 0mg; IRON 1.5mg; SODIUM 345mg; CALC 38mg

Dinner Tonight

From down-home tastes to simple international classics, these quick-fix meals will fit your hectic work schedule or busy home life.

Lemon Pepper Shrimp Scampi

························*20 minutes*

Sautéed asparagus makes a fine accompaniment for this entrée. Heat 2 teaspoons olive oil in a large nonstick skillet over medium-high heat. Add 1 pound trimmed asparagus spears; sauté 4 minutes. Sprinkle with ¼ teaspoon salt and ⅛ teaspoon black pepper.

- 1 cup uncooked orzo
- 2 tablespoons chopped fresh parsley
- ½ teaspoon salt, divided
- 7 teaspoons unsalted butter, divided
- 1½ pounds peeled and deveined jumbo shrimp
- 2 teaspoons bottled minced garlic
- 2 tablespoons fresh lemon juice
- ¼ teaspoon black pepper

① Cook orzo according to package directions, omitting salt and fat; drain. Place orzo in a medium bowl. Stir in parsley and ¼ teaspoon salt; cover and keep warm.
② While orzo cooks, melt 1 tablespoon butter in a large nonstick skillet over medium-high heat. Sprinkle shrimp with remaining ¼ teaspoon salt. Add half of shrimp to pan; sauté 2 minutes or until almost done. Transfer shrimp to a plate. Melt 1 teaspoon butter in pan. Add remaining shrimp to pan; sauté 2 minutes or until almost done. Transfer to plate.
③ Melt remaining 1 tablespoon butter in pan. Add garlic to pan; cook 30 seconds, stirring constantly. Stir in shrimp, juice,

and pepper; cook 1 minute or until shrimp are done. Yield: 4 servings (serving size: ½ cup orzo mixture and about 7 shrimp).

CALORIES 403; FAT 10.4g (sat 4.8g, mono 2.2g, poly 1.4g); PROTEIN 40.1g; CARB 34.7g; FIBER 1.7g; CHOL 276mg; IRON 4.3mg; SODIUM 549mg; CALC 97mg

QUICK & EASY

Flank Steak with Cucumber-Pepperoncini Relish

··20 minutes

Pepperoncini peppers are yellow, wrinkled, and slightly spicy; we use both the chopped pickled pepper and pickling liquid to flavor the crunchy relish. Serve with soft pita wedges and a simple dill-garlic yogurt dip. Combine ⅔ cup plain 2% reduced-fat Greek-style yogurt (such as Fage), 2 teaspoons chopped fresh dill, 1½ teaspoons fresh lemon juice, 1 teaspoon bottled minced garlic, ⅛ teaspoon salt, and a dash of ground red pepper.

- 1 (1-pound) flank steak, trimmed
- 1 tablespoon bottled minced garlic
- ½ teaspoon salt
- ¼ teaspoon black pepper
- Cooking spray
- 1 tablespoon pickled pepperoncini pepper pickling liquid
- 1 tablespoon extra-virgin olive oil
- ½ teaspoon Dijon mustard
- 1 pickled pepperoncini pepper, chopped
- 2 tablespoons chopped fresh flat-leaf parsley
- 2 tablespoons crumbled feta cheese
- ½ English cucumber, quartered lengthwise and sliced (about 1 cup)

❶ Preheat broiler.
❷ Sprinkle both sides of flank steak evenly with garlic, salt, and ¼ teaspoon black pepper. Place steak on a broiler pan coated with cooking spray; broil steak 5 minutes on each side or until desired degree of doneness. Place steak on a cutting board; cover and let stand 5 minutes. Uncover; cut steak diagonally across grain into thin slices.
❸ Combine pepperoncini pickling liquid, oil, and mustard in a medium bowl, stirring well with a whisk. Add chopped pepperoncini pepper and next 3 ingredients to oil mixture in bowl; toss well to combine. Serve steak with relish. Yield: 4 servings (serving size: 3 ounces steak and ¼ cup relish).

CALORIES 219; FAT 11.1g (sat 3.8g, mono 5.2g, poly 0.6g); PROTEIN 24.9g; CARB 2.4g; FIBER 0.6g; CHOL 46mg; IRON 1.7mg; SODIUM 459mg; CALC 43mg

QUICK & EASY

Pan-Grilled Thai Tuna Salad

···20 minutes

Precut matchstick carrots and bottled fresh orange sections save time. Try this salad with a side of crunchy rice crackers. Prepare a refreshing dessert to follow the spicy dish. Spoon ½ cup coconut sorbet into each of 2 dessert bowls; top each serving with 2 tablespoons diced peeled mango and 1 tablespoon toasted flaked sweetened coconut.

- Cooking spray
- 2 (6-ounce) Yellowfin tuna steaks (about 1 inch thick)
- ¼ teaspoon salt
- ⅛ teaspoon black pepper
- 4 cups thinly sliced napa (Chinese) cabbage
- 1 cup thinly sliced cucumber
- ½ cup matchstick-cut carrots
- ⅓ cup presliced red onion
- 1 navel orange, sectioned and chopped
- 1 tablespoon sugar
- 2 tablespoons chopped fresh cilantro
- 2 tablespoons fresh lime juice
- 2 tablespoons rice vinegar
- ½ teaspoon dark sesame oil
- ¼ teaspoon sambal oelek (ground fresh chile paste) or Sriracha (hot chile sauce, such as Huy Fong)

❶ Heat a grill pan over medium-high heat. Coat pan with cooking spray. Sprinkle fish evenly with salt and pepper. Add fish to pan; cook 2 minutes on each side or until desired degree of doneness. Transfer to a cutting board.
❷ Combine cabbage and next 4 ingredients in a large bowl. Combine sugar and remaining ingredients in a small bowl, stirring well with a whisk. Reserve 1 tablespoon dressing. Drizzle remaining dressing over salad; toss gently to coat. Divide salad mixture evenly between 2 plates. Cut each tuna steak across the grain into ¼-inch slices; arrange over salad mixture. Drizzle 1½ teaspoons reserved dressing over each serving. Yield: 2 servings.

CALORIES 307; FAT 3g (sat 0.6g, mono 0.8g, poly 1g); PROTEIN 41.8g; CARB 28.4g; FIBER 5.2g; CHOL 74mg; IRON 1.6mg; SODIUM 398mg; CALC 201mg

QUICK & EASY

Seared Scallops with Warm Tuscan Beans

··20 minutes

For the best sear, pat scallops dry with paper towels before seasoning and cooking. Grilled garlic bread is great for dipping into the brothy beans.

- 2 tablespoons olive oil, divided
- 1½ pounds sea scallops
- ¼ teaspoon salt
- 1 cup prechopped onion
- ⅛ teaspoon crushed red pepper
- 2 garlic cloves, minced
- ¼ cup dry white wine
- 1 cup fat-free, less-sodium chicken broth
- 1 (19-ounce) can cannellini beans or other white beans, rinsed and drained
- 1 (6-ounce) package fresh baby spinach
- 2 tablespoons chopped fresh basil

❶ Heat 1 tablespoon oil in a large non-stick skillet over medium-high heat.

Continued

Sprinkle scallops evenly with salt. Add scallops to pan; cook 2 minutes on each side or until done. Remove scallops from pan; keep warm.

2 Add remaining 1 tablespoon oil and onion to pan; sauté 2 minutes. Add pepper and garlic; cook 20 seconds, stirring constantly. Stir in wine; cook 1 minute or until most of liquid evaporates. Stir in broth and beans; cook 2 minutes. Add spinach; cook 1 minute or until spinach wilts. Remove from heat; stir in basil. Yield: 4 servings (serving size: about 4 ounces scallops and ¾ cup bean mixture).

CALORIES 314; FAT 8.7g (sat 1.2g, mono 5.1g, poly 1.8g); PROTEIN 33.7g; CARB 24.8g; FIBER 6.1g; CHOL 56mg; IRON 3.2mg; SODIUM 781mg; CALC 112mg

QUICK & EASY

Halibut with Coconut–Red Curry Sauce

· ·*30 minutes*

A bed of seasoned rice with bok choy soaks up the sauce. Combine 1½ cups water and ¾ cup basmati rice in a medium saucepan; bring to a boil. Cover, reduce heat, and simmer 12 minutes. Stir in 2 cups chopped baby bok choy; cover and cook 8 minutes or until liquid is absorbed. Combine 1½ tablespoons low-sodium soy sauce, 1 tablespoon fresh lime juice, ½ teaspoon sugar, and ½ teaspoon dark sesame oil; stir into rice mixture.

- 2 teaspoons canola oil, divided
- 4 (6-ounce) halibut fillets
- 1 cup chopped onion
- ½ cup chopped green onions
- 1 tablespoon grated peeled fresh ginger
- 1 cup light coconut milk
- 1 tablespoon sugar
- 1 tablespoon fish sauce
- ¾ teaspoon red curry paste
- ½ teaspoon ground coriander
- 1 tablespoon chopped fresh basil
- 2 teaspoons fresh lime juice

1 Heat 1 teaspoon oil in a large nonstick skillet over medium-high heat. Add fish

to pan; cook 5 minutes on each side or until fish flakes easily when tested with a fork or until desired degree of doneness. Remove fish from pan; keep warm.

2 Add remaining 1 teaspoon oil to pan. Add onion, green onions, and ginger; sauté 2 minutes. Stir in coconut milk and next 4 ingredients. Bring to a boil; cook 1 minute. Remove from heat. Stir in basil and juice. Yield: 4 servings (serving size: 1 fillet and about ⅓ cup sauce).

CALORIES 278; FAT 9.3g (sat 3.6g, mono 2.7g, poly 2g); PROTEIN 37.1g; CARB 10.9g; FIBER 1.1g; CHOL 54mg; IRON 2mg; SODIUM 475mg; CALC 102mg

QUICK & EASY

Spicy Asian Noodles with Chicken

· ·*30 minutes*

Add a snow pea sauté to complete the meal. Heat 2 teaspoons canola oil in a large nonstick skillet over medium-high heat. Add 2 minced garlic cloves; sauté 15 seconds. Add 2 cups trimmed snow peas and 1 cup drained sliced water chestnuts; sauté 3 minutes or until crisp-tender. Remove from heat; stir in 1 tablespoon low-sodium soy sauce.

- 1 tablespoon dark sesame oil, divided
- 1 tablespoon grated peeled fresh ginger
- 2 garlic cloves, minced
- 2 cups chopped roasted skinless, boneless chicken breasts
- ½ cup chopped green onions
- ¼ cup chopped fresh cilantro
- 3 tablespoons low-sodium soy sauce
- 2 tablespoons rice vinegar
- 2 tablespoons hoisin sauce
- 2 teaspoons sambal oelek (ground fresh chile paste)
- 1 (6.75-ounce) package thin rice sticks (rice-flour noodles)
- 2 tablespoons chopped dry-roasted peanuts

1 Heat 2 teaspoons oil in a small skillet over medium-high heat. Add ginger and

garlic to pan; cook 45 seconds, stirring constantly. Place in a large bowl. Stir in remaining 1 teaspoon oil, chicken, and next 6 ingredients.

2 Cook noodles according to package directions. Drain and rinse under cold water; drain. Cut noodles into smaller pieces. Add noodles to bowl; toss well to coat. Sprinkle with peanuts. Yield: 4 servings (serving size: 1¾ cups).

CALORIES 381; FAT 8.1g (sat 1.5g, mono 3.2g, poly 2.7g); PROTEIN 27.5g; CARB 47.1g; FIBER 2.3g; CHOL 60mg; IRON 3.1mg; SODIUM 614mg; CALC 55mg

QUICK & EASY

Fiesta Chicken Tacos with Mango and Jicama Salad

· ·*30 minutes*

Try this with a side of chipotle refritos. Combine 1 tablespoon fresh lime juice, 1 teaspoon minced canned chipotle chile in adobo sauce, 1 (16-ounce) can refried beans, and 1 minced garlic clove in a saucepan. Cook over medium heat 5 minutes or until thoroughly heated. Sprinkle with 2 teaspoons chopped fresh cilantro.

SALAD:

- ¾ cup (3-inch) julienne-cut peeled jicama
- ½ cup sliced peeled ripe mango
- ¼ cup presliced red onion
- 1 tablespoon fresh lime juice
- ½ teaspoon sugar
- 1½ teaspoons chopped fresh cilantro
- ¼ teaspoon salt
- Dash of black pepper

TACOS:

- 1 tablespoon olive oil, divided
- 1 pound skinless, boneless chicken breast, cut into thin strips
- ½ teaspoon chili powder
- ½ teaspoon ground cumin
- ⅛ teaspoon ground chipotle chile pepper
- 1 cup presliced red bell pepper
- 1 cup presliced red onion
- ¼ teaspoon salt
- 8 (6-inch) corn tortillas
- 1 cup mixed salad greens

❶ To prepare salad, combine first 8 ingredients.

❷ To prepare tacos, heat 2 teaspoons oil in a large nonstick skillet over medium-high heat. Sprinkle chicken evenly with chili powder, cumin, and chipotle chile pepper. Add chicken mixture to pan, and sauté 3 minutes. Remove from pan.

❸ Heat remaining 1 teaspoon oil in pan. Add bell pepper and 1 cup onion; cook 3 minutes or until crisp-tender. Return chicken mixture to pan; cook 2 minutes or until chicken is done. Sprinkle with ¼ teaspoon salt.

❹ Heat tortillas according to package directions. Arrange 2 tablespoons mixed greens, about ⅓ cup chicken mixture, and about 2 tablespoons salad in each tortilla; fold over. Yield: 4 servings (serving size: 2 tacos).

CALORIES 320; FAT 6.4g (sat 1.1g, mono 3.2g, poly 1.3g); PROTEIN 30.4g; CARB 36.1g; FIBER 5.8g; CHOL 66mg; IRON 2.2mg; SODIUM 471mg; CALC 129mg

QUICK & EASY
Spiced Pork Chops with Apple Chutney
••••••••••••••••••••••••••••••*30 minutes*

Slender haricots verts complement this entrée. Heat 2 teaspoons olive oil in a large nonstick skillet over medium-high heat. Add 12 ounces haricots verts to pan; cook 3 minutes, stirring occasionally. Stir in ¼ teaspoon salt, ⅛ teaspoon black pepper, and 2 thinly sliced garlic cloves; cook 5 minutes or until garlic is lightly browned.

CHUTNEY:
- 1 tablespoon butter
- 5 cups (¼-inch) cubed peeled apple (about 3 apples)
- ¼ cup dried cranberries
- 3 tablespoons brown sugar
- 3 tablespoons cider vinegar
- 2 teaspoons minced peeled fresh ginger
- ¼ teaspoon salt
- ¼ teaspoon dry mustard
- ⅛ teaspoon ground allspice

PORK:
- ¾ teaspoon ground chipotle chile pepper
- ½ teaspoon salt
- ½ teaspoon garlic powder
- ½ teaspoon ground coriander
- ¼ teaspoon black pepper
- 4 (4-ounce) boneless center-cut pork loin chops, trimmed
- Cooking spray

❶ To prepare chutney, melt butter in a nonstick skillet over medium-high heat. Add apple; sauté 4 minutes or until lightly browned. Add cranberries and next 6 ingredients; bring to a boil. Reduce heat, and simmer 8 minutes or until apples are tender; stir occasionally.

❷ To prepare pork, while chutney simmers, heat a grill pan over medium-high heat. Combine chipotle chile pepper and next 4 ingredients; sprinkle over pork. Coat grill pan with cooking spray. Add pork to pan; cook 4 minutes on each side or until done. Serve with chutney. Yield: 4 servings (serving size: 1 chop and about ⅓ cup chutney).

CALORIES 321; FAT 9.6g (sat 4.2g, mono 3.6g, poly 0.7g); PROTEIN 24.4g; CARB 34.6g; FIBER 2.4g; CHOL 72mg; IRON 1.1mg; SODIUM 520mg; CALC 45mg

QUICK & EASY
Speedy Cioppino
••••••••••••••••••••••••*40 minutes*

The bright taste of a lemon-dressed salad goes well with the seafood stew. Combine 1½ tablespoons fresh lemon juice, 1 tablespoon extra-virgin olive oil, ½ teaspoon Dijon mustard, ½ teaspoon sugar, ¼ teaspoon salt, ⅛ teaspoon black pepper, and 1 minced garlic clove, stirring with a whisk. Combine 6 cups gourmet salad greens, 1 cup halved cherry tomatoes, and ½ cup slivered red onion. Drizzle dressing over salad; toss gently to coat.

- 1 tablespoon olive oil
- 1½ cups (1-inch) cubed red potatoes (about 8 ounces)
- 1 cup prechopped onion
- ½ cup finely chopped fennel bulb
- 1 tablespoon bottled minced garlic
- ½ teaspoon dried oregano
- ⅛ teaspoon saffron threads, crushed
- 1 cup dry white wine
- 1 (14.5-ounce) can petite-cut diced tomatoes, undrained
- 1 (8-ounce) bottle clam juice
- 1½ pounds mussels (about 40), scrubbed and debearded
- ½ pound peeled and deveined large shrimp
- 1 (8-ounce) cod fillet
- 2 tablespoons chopped fresh basil

❶ Heat oil in a Dutch oven over medium-high heat. Add potatoes and next 5 ingredients; sauté 5 minutes or until vegetables start to soften. Stir in wine, tomatoes, and clam juice; bring to a boil. Cover and cook 15 minutes.

❷ Add mussels, shrimp, and cod to pan; cover and cook 6 minutes or until cod is done and mussel shells open. Discard any unopened shells. Stir gently to break cod into chunks. Sprinkle with basil. Yield: 4 servings (serving size: about 1¾ cups stew and about 10 mussels).

CALORIES 311; FAT 7.2g (sat 1.2g, mono 3.2g, poly 1.5g); PROTEIN 36.5g; CARB 24.4g; FIBER 3.8g; CHOL 140mg; IRON 7mg; SODIUM 674mg; CALC 122mg

Fennel-Rubbed Pork with Shallot-Pomegranate Reduction

··································· *40 minutes*

Crush fennel seeds in a small bowl, pressing down firmly with the back of a spoon using a back-and-forth motion. Serve this dish with walnut couscous. Heat 1 teaspoon olive oil in a saucepan over medium-high heat. Add ½ cup chopped onion; sauté 3 minutes. Add 1¼ cups water, ½ teaspoon salt, and ⅛ teaspoon black pepper; bring to a boil. Stir in 1 cup couscous. Remove from heat; cover and let stand 5 minutes. Fluff with a fork. Sprinkle with 3 tablespoons toasted chopped walnuts and 2 tablespoons chopped fresh parsley.

SAUCE:

- 1½ cups pomegranate juice
- ½ cup orange juice
- ⅓ cup chopped shallots
- 3 tablespoons sugar
- 4 teaspoons chilled butter, cut into small pieces
- 1 tablespoon red wine vinegar
- ¼ teaspoon salt

PORK:

- ¾ teaspoon fennel seeds, crushed
- ½ teaspoon garlic powder
- ½ teaspoon ground cumin
- ¼ teaspoon salt
- ¼ teaspoon black pepper
- 1 (1-pound) pork tenderloin, trimmed
- 1 teaspoon olive oil

① Preheat oven to 450°.
② To prepare sauce, combine first 4 ingredients in a saucepan; bring to a boil. Cook until reduced to ½ cup (about 18 minutes). Remove from heat. Gradually add butter; stir with a whisk until blended. Stir in vinegar and ¼ teaspoon salt.
③ To prepare pork, while sauce reduces, combine fennel seeds and next 4 ingredients; rub over pork. Heat oil in a large ovenproof skillet over medium-high heat. Add pork; cook 2 minutes on each side or until browned. Place skillet in oven. Bake at 450° for 18 minutes or until a thermometer registers 155° (slightly pink). Let stand 5 minutes; cut into ¼-inch slices. Serve with sauce. Yield: 4 servings (serving size: 3 ounces pork and about 2 tablespoons sauce).

CALORIES 302; FAT 10g (sat 4.3g, mono 3.9g, poly 0.7g); PROTEIN 23.9g; CARB 28.6g; FIBER 0.5g; CHOL 75mg; IRON 1.7mg; SODIUM 381mg; CALC 37mg

Tex-Mex Calzones

··································· *40 minutes*

For one less thing to cook, use 2 cups chopped leftover chicken in place of ground turkey. Toss together a black bean salad to go with these family-friendly turnovers. Combine 1 (15-ounce) can rinsed and drained black beans, 1 cup quartered cherry tomatoes, ½ cup chopped red onion, ¼ cup chopped celery, 2 tablespoons fresh lime juice, 2 tablespoons chopped fresh cilantro, and 1 tablespoon olive oil in a medium bowl; toss well to coat.

- 8 ounces ground turkey breast
- ½ cup chopped onion
- ½ cup chopped green bell pepper
- ½ cup chopped red bell pepper
- ¾ teaspoon ground cumin
- ½ teaspoon chili powder
- 2 garlic cloves, minced
- ½ cup fat-free fire-roasted salsa verde
- 1 (11-ounce) can refrigerated thin-crust pizza dough
- ¾ cup (3 ounces) preshredded Mexican blend cheese
  Cooking spray
- ¼ cup fat-free sour cream

① Preheat oven to 425°.
② Heat a large nonstick skillet over medium-high heat. Add ground turkey to pan; cook 3 minutes, stirring to crumble. Add onion and next 5 ingredients to pan; cook 4 minutes or until vegetables are crisp-tender, stirring mixture occasionally. Remove turkey mixture from heat; stir in salsa.
③ Unroll dough; divide into 4 equal portions. Roll each portion into a 6 x 4–inch rectangle. Working with 1 rectangle at a time, spoon about ½ cup turkey mixture onto one side of dough. Top with 3 tablespoons cheese; fold dough over turkey mixture, and press edges together with a fork to seal. Place on a baking sheet coated with cooking spray. Repeat procedure with remaining dough and turkey mixture. Bake at 425° for 12 minutes or until browned. Serve with sour cream. Yield: 4 servings (serving size: 1 calzone and 1 tablespoon sour cream).

CALORIES 416; FAT 14.1g (sat 6.1g, mono 4.9g, poly 1.6g); PROTEIN 25.7g; CARB 46.2g; FIBER 2.5g; CHOL 44mg; IRON 2.5mg; SODIUM 771mg; CALC 195mg

A home-cooked meal can be on the table in 20, 30, or 40 minutes with these quick-fix recipes.

Go Slow

Don't let the rush for dinner prevent you from enjoying family and food. Turn to the slow cooker to prepare dishes that simmer to perfection all day, producing supper without a fuss.

SLOW-COOKER DISHES ARE AN IDEAL OPTION for busy folks. Chop and brown a few ingredients, place them in the cooker, and set the controls. Enticing aromas fill the house throughout the day, and come dinnertime, just lift the top and serve.

Slow cookers have recently experienced a surge in popularity. Time-pressed cooks use slow cookers to transform tough, inexpensive cuts of meat into succulent meals with minimal effort. Our collection of recipes featuring international tastes proves the slow cooker delivers delicious results that suit the modern global palate.

STAFF FAVORITE • MAKE AHEAD
Curried Beef Short Ribs

Finishing this dish with lime zest and juice brightens its rich flavors.

2 teaspoons canola oil
2 pounds beef short ribs, trimmed
1½ teaspoons kosher salt, divided
¼ teaspoon freshly ground black pepper, divided
⅓ cup minced shallots
3 tablespoons minced garlic
3 tablespoons minced peeled fresh ginger
¼ cup water
2 tablespoons red curry paste
¼ cup light coconut milk
1 tablespoon sugar
1 tablespoon fish sauce
1 teaspoon grated lime rind
1 tablespoon fresh lime juice
4 cups hot cooked basmati rice

❶ Heat oil in a large nonstick skillet over medium-high heat. Sprinkle ribs with ¾ teaspoon salt and ⅛ teaspoon pepper. Add half of ribs to pan; cook 2 minutes on each side or until browned. Place ribs in an electric slow cooker. Repeat procedure with remaining ribs.
❷ Add shallots, garlic, and ginger to pan; sauté 2 minutes. Stir in ¼ cup water and curry paste; cook 1 minute. Stir in coconut milk, sugar, and fish sauce. Add coconut milk mixture to cooker. Cover and cook on LOW 6 hours.
❸ Remove ribs from cooker; keep warm. Strain cooking liquid through a colander over a bowl; discard solids. Place a zip-top plastic bag inside a 2-cup glass measure. Pour cooking liquid into bag; let stand 10 minutes (fat will rise to top). Seal bag; carefully snip off 1 bottom corner of bag. Drain drippings into a small bowl, stopping before fat layer reaches opening; discard fat. Stir in remaining ¾ teaspoon salt, remaining ⅛ teaspoon pepper, rind, and juice. Shred rib meat with 2 forks; discard bones. Serve sauce over ribs and rice. Yield: 6 servings (serving size: about 3 ounces ribs, ⅔ cup rice, and about 2½ tablespoons sauce).

CALORIES 410; FAT 16.1g (sat 6.5g, mono 7g, poly 0.9g); PROTEIN 27g; CARB 37.1g; FIBER 0.7g; CHOL 70mg; IRON 4.1mg; SODIUM 841mg; CALC 24mg

WINE NOTE: The intense flavor of this dish will overwhelm most wines. Reach for a fruit-forward red like Planeta La Segreta Rosso 2007 ($15). This Sicilian blend has big flavors that can handle rich curry sauce, while the wine adds its own complementary peppery, Asian spice note.

MAKE AHEAD
Chicken Thighs with Olives and Tomato Sauce

Add capers along with the olives, parsley, and seasoning for a more briny flavor, if you like. The parsley goes in last to keep its flavor and color intense.

12 chicken thighs (about 4 pounds), skinned
1 teaspoon kosher salt, divided
¼ teaspoon freshly ground black pepper, divided
1 teaspoon olive oil
1½ tablespoons minced garlic
¼ cup dry white wine
3 tablespoons tomato paste
2 to 3 teaspoons crushed red pepper
1 (28-ounce) can diced tomatoes, drained
¼ cup sliced pitted kalamata olives
2 tablespoons chopped fresh flat-leaf parsley

❶ Sprinkle chicken with ½ teaspoon salt and ⅛ teaspoon black pepper. Heat oil in a large skillet over medium-high heat. Add chicken to pan; cook 2 minutes on each side or until browned. Place chicken in an electric slow cooker. Add garlic to pan, and sauté 30 seconds, stirring constantly. Add wine, scraping pan to loosen browned bits; cook 30 seconds. Place wine mixture in cooker. Add tomato paste, red pepper, and tomatoes to cooker. Cover and cook on HIGH 4 hours. Stir in remaining ½ teaspoon salt, remaining ⅛ teaspoon pepper, olives, and parsley. Yield: 6 servings (serving size: 2 chicken thighs and about ⅓ cup sauce).

CALORIES 270; FAT 12.9g (sat 3.3g, mono 5.6g, poly 2.8g); PROTEIN 29.1g; CARB 8.7g; FIBER 2.2g; CHOL 99mg; IRON 2.4mg; SODIUM 658mg; CALC 44mg

For Best Slow-Cooker Results

Brown is better. Strictly speaking, meat doesn't need to be browned before it's added to the slow cooker, but it's a step we find worth the effort. The caramelized surface of the meat will lend rich flavor to the finished dish. And meat dredged in flour before browning will add body to the sauce (as in Provençal Beef Stew, page 69). Ground meat should always be browned and drained before going into the slow cooker; otherwise, it may clump and add grease to the dish.

Spice judiciously. Whole spices and dried herbs like cinnamon sticks, bay leaves, caraway seeds, and peppercorns will give intense flavor to a dish that cooks for several hours, so be careful not to overdo them. Chopped fresh herbs such as parsley remain vibrant if you stir them in near the end or when the dish is finished.

Don't break it. Dairy products, particularly fat-free or reduced-fat items, will curdle if simmered for too long. To keep these ingredients from breaking, add them to the dish near the end of the cooking time.

Use less liquid. Because the slow cooker generates steam that doesn't escape, there will be more liquid in the food when it's finished cooking than when it started. If you create or adapt a recipe for the slow cooker, decrease (by as much as half) the amount of liquid you normally use in the dish.

High or low? Use the HIGH setting if you need to cook a more tender cut of meat relatively quickly. But for tougher cuts, it's best to use the LOW setting and cook longer to allow time for the meat to become tender. Generally, cooker temperatures range from 170° to 280°.

No peeking. Don't be tempted to lift the lid until the dish is done. The steam generated during slow cooking is part of the cooking medium. Opening the lid will release this steam and increase cooking time. Moreover, when you lift the lid, temperatures can drop into the "danger zone" (between 40° and 140°) where bacteria multiply rapidly.

Account for variables. Our Test Kitchens professionals have found that some slow cookers—particularly some newer models—cook hotter than others. In one instance, liquid imperceptibly evaporated from the cooker, leaving far less sauce than when the same dish was prepared in a different model. Because not all slow cookers are created equal, don't rely on the stated cook time for a recipe until you know how your cooker performs.

Stay safe. Don't add frozen food to the slow cooker or use the cooker to defrost food—always defrost in the refrigerator or microwave. In a cooker, thawing food will linger too long between 40° and 140°, leaving it vulnerable to bacterial contamination. For the same reason, don't reheat food in the cooker.

Slow cookers are a boon to busy cooks because they do most of the work for you.

MAKE-AHEAD
Zinfandel-Braised Leg of Lamb

Reducing the wine before placing it in the slow cooker gives the dish a more rounded flavor.

1   (2½-pound) boneless leg of lamb
1   teaspoon kosher salt, divided
1   teaspoon freshly ground black pepper, divided
1   tablespoon all-purpose flour
2   teaspoons olive oil
1   tablespoon juniper berries, crushed
1   teaspoon whole allspice, crushed
6   garlic cloves, sliced
1   cup zinfandel or other light red wine
1   teaspoon dried basil
2   bay leaves
6   cups hot cooked egg noodles (about 4¾ cups uncooked pasta)

1 Unroll lamb; trim fat. Sprinkle evenly with ¹/₂ teaspoon salt and ¹/₂ teaspoon pepper. Reroll lamb; secure at 1-inch intervals with twine. Sprinkle evenly with flour. Heat oil in a nonstick skillet over medium-high heat. Add lamb to pan; cook 6 minutes, turning to brown on all sides. Place lamb in an electric slow cooker. Add juniper berries, allspice, and garlic to pan; cook over medium heat 2 minutes or until garlic is lightly browned. Add wine to pan, scraping pan to loosen browned bits; cook until reduced to ¹/₂ cup (about 3 minutes). Scrape wine mixture into cooker; add basil and bay leaves. Cover and cook on LOW 8 hours or until lamb is tender.

2 Remove lamb from cooker; keep warm. Strain cooking liquid through a sieve into a bowl; discard solids. Add remaining ¹/₂ teaspoon salt and remaining ¹/₂ teaspoon pepper to cooking liquid; stir. Remove twine from lamb, and discard. Break lamb into chunks with 2 forks. Serve lamb and cooking liquid over egg noodles. Yield: 6 servings (serving size: 3 ounces lamb, ¹/₄ cup sauce, and 1 cup noodles).

CALORIES 481; FAT 14.3g (sat 4.2g, mono 6.2g, poly 1.7g); PROTEIN 42.2g; CARB 43.4g; FIBER 2.4g; CHOL 155mg; IRON 5.4mg; SODIUM 408mg; CALC 46mg

MAKE AHEAD

Asian-Spiced Veal Shanks

- 1 tablespoon canola oil
- 6 (8-ounce) veal shanks, trimmed
- 1 teaspoon kosher salt, divided
- ¹/₂ teaspoon freshly ground black pepper, divided
- 1¹/₂ cups (1-inch) slices green onions
- 3 tablespoons sliced peeled ginger
- 8 garlic cloves, crushed
- 1 star anise
- ¹/₄ cup rice wine vinegar
- 2 tablespoons water
- 2 tablespoons sugar
- 1 teaspoon grated orange rind
- 2 tablespoons fresh orange juice
- 2 tablespoons low-sodium soy sauce
- ¹/₂ teaspoon crushed red pepper

1 Heat oil in a large nonstick skillet over medium-high heat. Sprinkle veal with ¹/₂ teaspoon salt and ¹/₄ teaspoon black pepper. Add 3 shanks to pan; cook 2¹/₂ minutes on each side or until browned. Place veal in an electric slow cooker. Repeat procedure with remaining 3 shanks.

2 Reduce heat to medium. Add onions and next 3 ingredients to pan; cook 3 minutes. Add vinegar and 2 tablespoons water; cook 1 minute or until liquid almost evaporates. Place ginger mixture in cooker. Combine sugar and remaining ingredients; add to cooker. Cover and cook on LOW 8 hours or until veal is tender.

3 Remove veal from cooker; keep warm. Strain cooking liquid through a fine sieve over a bowl; discard solids. Place a zip-top plastic bag inside a 2-cup glass measure. Pour cooking liquid into bag; let stand 10 minutes (fat will rise to top). Seal bag; carefully snip off 1 bottom corner of bag. Drain drippings into a medium bowl, stopping before fat layer reaches opening; discard fat. Stir in remaining ¹/₂ teaspoon salt and remaining ¹/₄ teaspoon black pepper. Remove veal from bones, and shred meat with 2 forks. Discard bones. Serve veal with cooking liquid. Yield: 6 servings (serving size: about 3 ounces veal and ¹/₄ cup sauce).

CALORIES 217; FAT 6.3g (sat 1.2g, mono 2.8g, poly 1.1g); PROTEIN 29.7g; CARB 9g; FIBER 0.9g; CHOL 112mg; IRON 1.7mg; SODIUM 532mg; CALC 59mg

MAKE AHEAD

Provençal Beef Stew

Chuck roast, a tough cut of meat, grows tender in the slow cooker. Serve this rustic stew with crusty bread and red wine—perhaps a Côtes du Rhône or Chateauneuf-du-Pâpe from southern France.

- 2 teaspoons olive oil
- 1¹/₂ pounds boneless chuck roast, trimmed and cut into 1-inch cubes
- 1¹/₂ teaspoons kosher salt, divided
- ¹/₂ teaspoon freshly ground black pepper, divided
- 2 tablespoons all-purpose flour
- 2 medium onions, each cut into 8 wedges
- 8 garlic cloves, crushed
- ¹/₄ cup dry red wine
- 1 cup fat-free, less-sodium beef broth
- 2 tablespoons tomato paste
- 3 bay leaves
- 3 fresh thyme sprigs
- 1 (14.5-ounce) can diced tomatoes, drained
- 3 cups (1-inch) slices zucchini
- 2 cups (1-inch) slices carrots

1 Heat oil in a large nonstick skillet over medium-high heat. Sprinkle beef with ¹/₂ teaspoon salt and ¹/₄ teaspoon pepper; dredge in flour. Add beef to pan; sauté 2 minutes, browning on all sides. Place beef in an electric slow cooker. Add onions and garlic to pan; sauté 5 minutes. Add wine to pan, scraping pan to loosen browned bits. Place onion mixture in cooker. Add broth and next 4 ingredients to cooker; top with zucchini and carrots. Cover and cook on LOW 8 hours or until beef is tender. Stir in remaining 1 teaspoon salt and remaining ¹/₄ teaspoon pepper. Discard bay leaves and thyme sprigs. Yield: 6 servings (serving size: 1¹/₃ cups).

CALORIES 271; FAT 8.9g (sat 2.8g, mono 4.1g, poly 0.6g); PROTEIN 31.1g; CARB 16.5g; FIBER 3.5g; CHOL 86mg; IRON 4.2mg; SODIUM 739mg; CALC 57mg

MAKE-AHEAD
Black Bean Soup

Cumin and fiery serrano chile infuse this simple soup as it cooks, and a dollop of sour cream provides a refreshing contrast to the spicy flavors. For less heat, seed the chile first or use a milder pepper, such as jalapeño. You can also omit the chile altogether, if you prefer.

- 1 pound dried black beans
- 4 cups fat-free, less-sodium chicken broth
- 2 cups chopped onion
- 1 cup water
- 1 tablespoon ground cumin
- 3 bay leaves
- 1 serrano chile, finely chopped
- 2 tablespoons fresh lime juice
- 1 teaspoon kosher salt
- ¼ cup chopped fresh cilantro
- 3 tablespoons reduced-fat sour cream
- Cilantro sprigs (optional)

1 Sort and wash beans; place in a large bowl. Cover with water to 2 inches above beans; cover and let stand 8 hours. Drain.

2 Combine beans, broth, and next 5 ingredients in an electric slow cooker. Cover and cook on LOW 10 hours. Discard bay leaves. Stir in juice and salt. Ladle 1½ cups soup into each of 6 bowls; sprinkle each with 2 teaspoons chopped cilantro. Top each serving with 1½ teaspoons sour cream. Garnish with cilantro sprigs, if desired. Yield: 6 servings.

CALORIES 288; FAT 2.3g (sat 0.9g, mono 0.4g, poly 0.5g); PROTEIN 18.5g; CARB 50g; FIBER 17.5g; CHOL 3mg; IRON 4.6mg; SODIUM 581mg; CALC 87mg

Pasta Made Easy

Prepare authentic—and perennially satisfying—Italian entrées with our tips and dinner ideas.

MOST OF US ASSOCIATE PASTA WITH ITALY. No surprise since Italians consume more pasta than anyone else and serve it at most meals as a first course (*primo piatto*). The following recipes offer American-style entrée portions, but you can simply reduce the serving size if you prefer to serve a first course. Either way, it's easy to cook classic Italian pasta dishes at home.

Classic Pasta Dough

Italians use soft wheat flour to make fresh pasta. We tested the recipe with soft wheat flour and all-purpose flour and tasted them side by side, and we much prefer the soft wheat version—it gives the pasta a silkier texture. Order Italian-style flour from www.kingarthurflour.com, or look for Italian 00 flour at gourmet or on-line stores. Use this dough to make Ravioli with Herbed Ricotta Filling (page 73).

- 5.6 ounces soft wheat flour (about 1¼ cups)
- ⅛ teaspoon fine sea salt
- 2 large eggs

1 Weigh or lightly spoon flour into dry measuring cups; level with a knife. Place flour, salt, and eggs in a food processor; pulse 10 times or until mixture is crumbly (dough will not form a ball). Turn dough out onto a lightly floured surface; knead until smooth and elastic (about 4 minutes). Shape dough into a disc; wrap with plastic wrap. Let dough stand at room temperature 20 minutes.

2 Unwrap dough. Divide dough into 8 equal portions. Working with 1 portion at a time (keep remaining dough covered to prevent drying), pass dough through pasta rollers of a pasta machine on the widest setting. Fold dough in half crosswise; fold in half again. Pass dough through rollers again. Move width gauge to next setting; pass pasta through rollers. Continue moving width gauge to narrower settings; pass dough through rollers once at each setting to form 8 (15 x 3-inch) pasta strips. Lay strips flat on a lightly floured surface; cover. Repeat procedure with remaining dough portions. Yield: 4 servings (serving size: 2 ounces uncooked pasta).

CALORIES 178; FAT 2.9g (sat 0.8g, mono 1g, poly 0.3g); PROTEIN 6.9g; CARB 30.2g; FIBER 0.2g; CHOL 106mg; IRON 0.9mg; SODIUM 107mg; CALC 21mg

---

Pasta Pronto

Hand or machine? A pasta machine, called for in step two of the recipe at left, yields pasta with smooth exterior surfaces. Hand-cranked Italian pasta machines are easy and satisfying to use. You can find them at kitchenware and department stores for about $30. Some stand mixers and food processors also have attachments for rolling pastas.

Make It Fresh: Pasta

In Emilia-Romagna, Italy, the dough is classically made with soft wheat flour and whole fresh eggs. Purists in the province prefer pasta doughs that have been rolled out on a wooden board to those rolled out with a machine, saying that sauce clings much better to the hand-rolled variety.

1. Place flour, salt, and eggs in a food processor, and process until combined and crumbly—the mixture won't form a ball.

2. Transfer to a lightly floured surface, and knead several minutes to form a soft dough. Then shape dough into a disc, wrap it tightly with plastic wrap, and allow it to rest for 20 minutes.

3. Divide dough into equal portions. Pass each portion through rollers with width gauge on the widest setting to stretch pasta. Fold dough in half crosswise; fold in half again. Pass dough through rollers again. Move width gauge to next setting; pass pasta through rollers. Continue moving width gauge to narrower settings; pass dough through rollers once at each setting to form pasta sheets.

Bucatini alla Carbonara

Bucatini is hollow spaghetti; *guanciale* (gwahn-CHAY-lay) is cured pork.

- ¼ pound guanciale, chopped
- 6 quarts water
- 1 tablespoon fine sea salt
- 12 ounces uncooked bucatini (long hollow pasta)
- ¾ cup (3 ounces) grated pecorino Romano cheese, divided
- ¼ teaspoon freshly ground black pepper
- 3 large eggs, lightly beaten

1 Heat a large skillet over medium-high heat. Add guanciale; cook until crisp, stirring frequently. Remove from heat. **2** Bring 6 quarts water and salt to a boil in an 8-quart pot. Add pasta to pot; stir. Cover; return water to a boil. Uncover and cook 10 minutes or until almost al dente. Drain pasta in a colander over a bowl, reserving ½ cup cooking water. **3** Combine ¼ cup reserved cooking water, ½ cup cheese, and remaining ingredients in a bowl, stirring well. Add egg mixture and pasta to guanciale. Place pan over low heat. Cook 5 minutes or until sauce thickens and pasta is al dente, tossing constantly. (Do not overcook or sauce will curdle.) Remove from heat. Stir in remaining ¼ cup reserved cooking water; toss to combine. Place about 1 cup pasta mixture on each of 6 plates; top each serving with 2 teaspoons remaining cheese. Yield: 6 servings.

CALORIES 363; FAT 12.8g (sat 5.8g, mono 4.9g, poly 1.4g); PROTEIN 17.2g; CARB 43.1g; FIBER 1.9g; CHOL 132mg; IRON 2.4mg; SODIUM 637mg; CALC 159mg

Make It Fresh: Tomato Sauce

Fresh tomato sauce is a staple in Italy, where it's usually served with spaghetti. Although the sauce tastes rich and delicious, it takes only about 30 minutes to prepare. See recipe at right.

1. To peel tomatoes, core and cut a small X through the skin on the bottom of tomatoes with a sharp knife. Place them in boiling water for about 30 seconds or just until skins begin to peel back. Quickly remove tomatoes from pan, and plunge them into ice water. Drain and remove skins. Cut each tomato in half lengthwise, and squeeze the juices and seeds into a colander over a bowl. Reserve tomato juices, and discard seeds. Finely chop tomatoes.

2. Heat extra-virgin olive oil in a large skillet over medium heat. Add garlic, and cook just until it begins to brown lightly, taking care not to burn it.

3. Add tomatoes and reserved juices, and cook until almost all of the liquid evaporates. Finish cooking the pasta with the sauce, which should be in a skillet large enough to combine the two and allow for tossing. Add enough of the pasta cooking water to the sauce to give the dish a creamy texture and marry the sauce to the pasta.

QUICK & EASY
Spaghetti with Tomato Sauce
(pictured on page 212)

> 1½ pounds plum tomatoes, peeled and halved lengthwise
> 3   tablespoons extra-virgin olive oil, divided
> 2   garlic cloves, minced
> 2   tablespoons plus ½ teaspoon fine sea salt, divided
> ¼   teaspoon crushed red pepper
> 6   quarts water
> 12 ounces uncooked spaghetti
> ¼   cup minced fresh basil
> 6   tablespoons grated fresh Parmigiano-Reggiano cheese

❶ Squeeze juice and seeds from tomato halves into a fine-mesh sieve over a bowl, reserving juices; discard seeds. Finely chop tomatoes.

❷ Heat 2 tablespoons oil in a large nonstick skillet over medium heat. Add garlic to pan; cook 30 seconds or just until garlic begins to brown, stirring constantly. Add tomatoes, reserved juices, ½ teaspoon salt, and pepper. Increase heat to medium-high; cook 15 minutes or until liquid almost evaporates, stirring occasionally.

❸ Bring 6 quarts water and remaining 2 tablespoons salt to a boil in an 8-quart pot. Add pasta to pot; stir. Cover; return water to a boil. Uncover and cook 8 minutes or until pasta is almost al dente. Drain pasta in a colander over a bowl, reserving ½ cup cooking water.

❹ Add hot pasta and reserved cooking water to tomato mixture. Cook 5 minutes or until sauce is thick and pasta is al dente, tossing to combine. Remove from heat. Sprinkle with basil; toss. Place 1 cup pasta mixture on each of 6 plates. Drizzle each serving with ½ teaspoon remaining oil; sprinkle each with 1 tablespoon cheese. Yield: 6 servings.

CALORIES 313; FAT 9.5g (sat 2.1g, mono 5.6g, poly 1.5g); PROTEIN 10.3g; CARB 47g; FIBER 3.2g; CHOL 4mg; IRON 2.3mg; SODIUM 576mg; CALC 83mg

MAKE AHEAD
Ravioli with Herbed Ricotta Filling

You can shape the pasta and freeze it up to a month before cooking.

RAVIOLI:

- ¾ cup (6 ounces) whole-milk ricotta cheese
- ¼ cup (1 ounce) grated fresh Parmigiano-Reggiano cheese
- 2 tablespoons finely chopped fresh basil
- ½ teaspoon grated lemon rind
- ¼ teaspoon freshly ground black pepper
- 1 large egg
- Classic Pasta Dough (page 70)
- 6 quarts water
- 2 tablespoons fine sea salt

SAUCE:

- 2 tablespoons extra-virgin olive oil
- 2 garlic cloves, minced
- ¼ cup chopped fresh basil
- ¼ cup (1 ounce) shaved fresh Parmigiano-Reggiano cheese

1 To prepare ravioli, place ricotta in a cheesecloth-lined colander, and drain 30 minutes. Combine ricotta, ¼ cup Parmigiano-Reggiano, and next 4 ingredients, stirring until well combined.

2 Place 1 (15 x 3–inch) Classic Pasta Dough sheet on a lightly floured surface. Spoon 1½ teaspoons filling mixture 1½ inches from left edge in center of sheet. Spoon 1½ teaspoons filling mixture at 3-inch intervals along length of sheet. Moisten edges and in between each filling portion with water, and place 1 (15 x 3–inch) pasta sheet on top, pressing to seal. Cut pasta sheet crosswise into 5 (3 x 3–inch) ravioli, trimming edges with a sharp knife or pastry wheel. Place ravioli on a lightly floured baking sheet (cover with a damp towel to prevent drying). Repeat procedure with remaining

Make It Fresh: Ravioli

1. Lay one pasta sheet on a flat, lightly floured work surface. Spoon the filling at 3-inch intervals along the length of the sheet, leaving plenty of space on all sides.

2. Use a pastry brush or your fingers to moisten the edges and the space between the filling portions on each pasta sheet with water. Place a second pasta sheet over filling, pressing edges to seal.

3. Use a sharp knife or a pasta wheel to cut the sheets crosswise into ravioli. Serve with a delicate sauce, and allow the pasta to be the star.

pasta sheets and filling mixture to form 20 ravioli.

3 Bring 6 quarts water and salt to a boil in an 8-quart pot. Add half of ravioli to pot; cook 1½ minutes or until no longer translucent. Remove ravioli from water with a slotted spoon. Repeat procedure with remaining ravioli.

4 To prepare sauce, heat oil in a large skillet over low heat. Add garlic to pan; cook 6 minutes or until garlic is tender. Remove from heat. Place 5 ravioli in each of 4 shallow bowls; drizzle each serving with 1½ teaspoons garlic oil. Top each serving with 1 tablespoon basil and 1 tablespoon shaved Parmigiano-Reggiano. Serve immediately. Yield: 4 servings.

CALORIES 394; FAT 20.5g (sat 8.1g, mono 9.1g, poly 1.6g); PROTEIN 19g; CARB 33g; FIBER 0.4g; CHOL 193mg; IRON 1.6mg; SODIUM 731mg; CALC 283mg

Make It Fresh: Ragù alla Bolognese

1. Begin by sautéing the aromatic ingredients. The sauce acquires deep flavor as you cook the ingredients slowly over medium heat, which brings the natural sweetness forward while neutralizing the bite of the onion.

2. Some recipes call for finely minced cuts of tough meat, such as beef chuck or pork shoulder. For convenience, we use a mixture of ground meats. The next step in a ragù is to add a flavorful liquid, such as wine or broth, and reduce it.

3. Last is to add liquid, usually milk or cream, along with a sachet of spices and fresh herbs, and simmer the sauce slowly until the meats are tender and the flavors meld.

Tagliatelle alla Bolognese

Meat-based pasta sauces are popular throughout Italy. The most prominent, ragù alla Bolognese, originated in the northern city of Bologna.

- 2 ounces pancetta, finely minced
- 2 cups finely chopped onion (about 1 large)
- 1 cup finely chopped celery (about 2 stalks)
- ¾ cup finely chopped carrot
- 12 ounces ground veal
- 12 ounces ground pork
- 4 teaspoons fine sea salt, divided
- ½ teaspoon freshly ground black pepper
- ½ cup white wine
- 2 tablespoons tomato paste
- 5 sprigs fresh flat-leaf parsley
- 3 whole cloves
- 2 allspice berries
- 1 fresh thyme sprig
- 1¾ cups whole milk
- 6 quarts water
- 12 ounces uncooked tagliatelle or fettuccine
- 6 tablespoons chopped fresh flat-leaf parsley

1 Heat a large Dutch oven over medium heat. Add pancetta to pan, and cook 2 minutes, stirring occasionally. Add onion, celery, and carrot; cook 10 minutes or until tender, stirring occasionally. Add veal, pork, 1 teaspoon salt, and pepper; cook 5 minutes or until browned, stirring to crumble. Stir in wine. Cook 3 minutes or until liquid almost evaporates, stirring occasionally. Stir in tomato paste. Reduce heat to medium-low.

2 Place 5 parsley sprigs and next 3 ingredients on a double layer of cheesecloth. Gather edges of cheesecloth together; tie securely. Add cheesecloth bag and milk to pan; bring to a simmer. Simmer on low heat 1 hour or until thick, stirring occasionally. Discard cheesecloth bag.

3 Bring 6 quarts water and remaining 1 tablespoon salt to a boil in an 8-quart pot. Add pasta to pot; stir. Cover; return water to a boil. Uncover and cook 8 minutes or until al dente. Drain. Place 1 cup pasta in each of 6 shallow bowls; spoon about ¾ cup sauce over each serving. Sprinkle each with 1 tablespoon chopped parsley. Yield: 6 servings.

CALORIES 551; FAT 22.2g (sat 9g, mono 8.9g, poly 1.9g); PROTEIN 33g; CARB 53.8g; FIBER 3.6g; CHOL 101mg; IRON 3.4mg; SODIUM 839mg; CALC 136mg

QUICK & EASY

Fettuccine with Olive Oil, Garlic, and Red Pepper

- ¼ cup extra-virgin olive oil, divided
- 3 garlic cloves, minced
- 1 tablespoon minced fresh parsley
- ¼ teaspoon crushed red pepper
- 6 quarts water
- 1 tablespoon plus ¼ teaspoon fine sea salt, divided
- 12 ounces uncooked fettuccine

1 Heat 2 tablespoons oil in a large skillet over medium heat. Add garlic; cook 30 seconds or just until garlic begins to brown, stirring frequently. Stir in parsley and pepper. Remove from heat.
2 Bring 6 quarts water and 1 tablespoon salt to a boil in an 8-quart pot. Add pasta to pot; stir. Cover; return water to a boil. Uncover and cook 8 minutes or until almost al dente. Drain pasta in a colander over a bowl, reserving ½ cup cooking water. Add hot pasta, reserved cooking water, and remaining ¼ teaspoon salt to garlic mixture. Increase heat to medium-high; cook 2 minutes or until pasta is al dente, tossing to combine. Place 1 cup pasta mixture on each of 6 plates; drizzle each serving with 1 teaspoon remaining oil. Yield: 6 servings.

CALORIES 293; FAT 10.2g (sat 1.5g, mono 6.8g, poly 1.7g); PROTEIN 7.5g; CARB 42.9g; FIBER 1.9g; CHOL 0mg; IRON 1.9mg; SODIUM 238mg; CALC 16mg

5 Food Trends to Try

Incorporate some of the new ingredients, dishes, and techniques that have the affection of food lovers nationwide into your meals.

AT THE FOUR-STAR CHICAGO RESTAURANT ALINEA, Chef Grant Achatz pairs lamb and pistachios with the "floral pepperiness" of allspice. He infuses water with ground allspice, adds vinegar, and thickens the mixture with *agar* (a seaweed-derived starch used for gelling foods to be served hot). He makes an accompanying allspice gastrique, and seasons the meat with allspice, clove, black pepper, nutmeg, cinnamon, and salt.

While most home cooks aren't going to make allspice and sherry vinegar puddings thickened with agar, they will increasingly pair meats with sweet spices like allspice and nutmeg as this and other ideas migrate from high-end restaurants to home kitchens.

Chef Dave Cruz of the restaurant Ad Hoc in Yountville, California, proudly talks about his heirloom bean dishes, such as those made with the Black Calypso beans from Steve Sando's nearby Rancho Gordo. Then he sighs and says, "But I guess everybody is using these now." Indeed, heirloom beans are another ingredient that is quickly moving from the chef's kitchen to the home.

These and other foods, flavors, and techniques explored here are girded by three common ideas converging to define our food culture: a global perspective; an imperative for eating foods that are flavorful, economical, and healthful; and a concern for the earth and the plants and animals we raise for food.

STAFF FAVORITE • MAKE AHEAD FREEZABLE

Mango-Agave Sorbet

The Mexican pedigree of this dessert makes it a fitting way to end a dinner of Hidden Rainbow Albondigas (page 60). Because tequila also comes from the agave plant, it fits naturally here; we use silver, or clear, tequila to keep the mango color vibrant. Dress up scoops with lime rind curls, if desired.

- 4 cups cubed peeled ripe mango (about 3 pounds)
- ½ cup fresh orange juice (about 3 oranges)
- ⅓ cup fresh lime juice (about 3 limes)
- ⅓ cup tequila
- ¾ cup light agave nectar
- ⅓ cup water

1 Place first 4 ingredients in a food processor; process until smooth. Pour mixture into a bowl, and stir in agave nectar and ⅓ cup water. Cover and chill 2 hours.
2 Pour mixture into freezer can of an ice-cream freezer; freeze according to manufacturer's instructions. Spoon sorbet into a freezer-safe container; cover and freeze 8 hours or until firm. Yield: 8 servings (serving size: ½ cup).

CALORIES 233; FAT 0.5g (sat 0.1g, mono 0.2g, poly 0.1g); PROTEIN 1g; CARB 55.4g; FIBER 3.1g; CHOL 0mg; IRON 0.3mg; SODIUM 4mg; CALC 20mg

Top 5 Food Trends

1 Chaat

Chaat (CHOT) refers to Indian street food—a variety of small snack plates—often defined by a balance of spicy and acidic, salty and sweet, and soft and crunchy components. The idea of small plates featuring the vibrant tastes of northern and western India is starting to take hold in the United States. Indeed, attendees of last fall's food festival in San Francisco hosted by Slow Food Nation—itself a trendsetting group—sampled dishes served by the Bay Area's popular Vik's Chaat Corner.

"The skills required to produce most chaats are relatively minimal, mostly chopping and mixing," explains Krishnendu Ray, assistant professor of food studies at New York University. "Chaats carry lively, fresh flavors, overflowing with chiles, cilantro, coconut, and tamarind. The concept works easily for hurried Americans."

Ray suggests novices begin with a neutral base, such as boiled cubed potatoes, and toss them with vibrant accents like chopped spring onions, mint, cilantro, lime, and tamarind sauce. You could also try a salad of avocados, strawberries, plums, cucumbers, and pineapples with a squeeze of lemon or lime and a sprinkling of chaat masala, a zesty blend of spices (available in Indian and Asian markets and specialty stores).

2 Heritage Meats

Heritage meats—derived from old strains of rare breeds of livestock—and grass-fed meats are becoming increasingly available at butcher shops and grocers. They fetch a higher price than typical meats yet have a growing list of advocates.

"I believe there are compelling environmental and ethical reasons for choosing humanely raised and heritage animals. But for chefs and home cooks, there's a simpler imperative: taste," says Dan Barber, chef and owner of the Stone Barn restaurants in Manhattan and Westchester County, New York. "Whether ensuring an animal's access to the outdoors or preserving an endangered breed, I think good animal husbandry doesn't just raise living standards and make for happier animals. It makes for more delicious food."

Barber adds that heritage breeds of livestock often have better intramuscular marbling, which also enhances taste. Herbed Heritage Pork Loin with White Wine Reduction (page 79) and Grass-Fed Beef Tenderloin Steaks with Sautéed Mushrooms (page 77) capitalize on the meat's robust taste.

3 Agave Nectar

Agave nectar, made from the sap of the same desert plant essential to tequila, has been used for thousands of years in central Mexico. It became widely available to home cooks in the mid-1990s, and its unrefined sweetness appeals to a broadening audience.

"It is a great alternative to table sugar," says Ania Catalano, a Connecticut caterer and author of *Baking with Agave Nectar*. "Because it's low glycemic, it's a better choice for people who have blood sugar issues."

Agave nectar is available at health food stores, specialty grocers, and natural foods aisles of supermarkets. It costs about $2 per cup.

With the texture of honey, it comes in three varieties—amber, light, and raw. Light is neutral-flavored, while amber and raw have a faint maple taste. Because the nectar is more intensely sweet than table sugar, Catalano recommends replacing sugar with 75 percent equivalent volume of agave nectar for foods such as cakes, cookies, pies, and frozen desserts.

4 Allspice & Nutmeg

It may be easy for American cooks to relegate allspice and nutmeg to desserts and beverages. But in kitchens elsewhere, these spices are critical to a wide array of dishes, from Jamaican jerk sauces to Irish corned beef, and from Chinese stir-fries to Italian gnocchi. Exposure to world cuisines is encouraging cooks in the United States to experiment with spices. "Allspice is great with game," says David Myers, owner/chef of Los Angeles restaurants Sona, Comme Ça, and Boule. "It adds complex spice notes that round out the sharper flavor points in these meats without making itself known the way cinnamon can.

"As for nutmeg, the tiniest amount grated into gnocchi lends a subtle flavor that you don't necessarily recognize but you know if it's not there."

We find the warm, slightly sweet taste of nutmeg enhances our Spice-Rubbed Pork Tenderloin (page 77) and Asian-Marinated Flank Steak (page 78), and that both nutmeg and allspice—freshly grated, ideally—pair well in general with duck, game, and deeply flavored cuts of beef and pork.

5 Heirloom Beans

Why are time-honored varieties of beans finding fresh favor in home kitchens? "I think heirlooms taste better," says Steve Sando, whose Rancho Gordo in Napa, California, grows and sells nearly 30 varieties of distinctive beans. "Runner beans tend to be buttery. Christmas limas have a distinct chestnut taste, and the bean broth is beefy. Some types are like potatoes in texture; others are creamy. They are not bred for uniform growth, uniform size, or disease resistance. They've been saved [from extinction] because they taste good."

What's more, Sando says his and other growers' methods are good for the soil. "The beans are initially cleaned right in the fields by the combines, and the pods go back into the soil as green manure," he says. We used heirloom beans in Borlotti Minestone (page 78) and Anasazi and Black Bean Chili (page 79).

Grass-Fed Beef Tenderloin Steaks with Sautéed Mushrooms

At taste testing, we found that grass-fed beef's mineral-like flavor is enhanced by grilling.

- 1 tablespoon extra-virgin olive oil
- 4 shallots, peeled and quartered
- 2 teaspoons chopped fresh thyme
- 1/8 teaspoon salt
- 1/8 teaspoon crushed red pepper
- 3 (4-ounce) packages presliced exotic mushroom blend (such as shiitake, cremini, and oyster)
- 2 garlic cloves, minced
- 1/4 cup Madeira wine or dry sherry
- 1 tablespoon low-sodium soy sauce
- 2 tablespoons chopped fresh parsley
- Cooking spray
- 4 (4-ounce) grass-fed beef tenderloin steaks, trimmed (about 1 inch thick)
- 1/2 teaspoon salt
- 1/4 teaspoon freshly ground black pepper

❶ Heat oil in a large nonstick skillet over medium-high heat. Add shallots; sauté 3 minutes or until lightly browned. Add thyme and next 3 ingredients; sauté 6 minutes or until lightly browned. Add garlic; sauté 2 minutes. Stir in wine and soy sauce; cook 15 seconds or until liquid almost evaporates. Stir in parsley; cover and set aside.

❷ Heat a grill pan over medium-high heat. Coat pan with cooking spray. Sprinkle steaks with 1/2 teaspoon salt and black pepper. Add steaks to pan; cook 3 minutes on each side or until desired degree of doneness. Let stand 5 minutes. Serve with mushroom mixture. Yield: 4 servings (serving size: 1 steak and 1/2 cup mushroom mixture).

CALORIES 212; FAT 7.6g (sat 2g, mono 4g, poly 0.5g); PROTEIN 26.3g; CARB 11.7g; FIBER 1g; CHOL 60mg; IRON 4.5mg; SODIUM 576mg; CALC 17mg

WINE NOTE: To contrast the leanness of grass-fed beef, serve it with a full-bodied, soft red. Many varietals would work, but cabernet sauvignon's structure and depth have a special affinity with beef. Try the Geyser Peak Cabernet Sauvignon 2005 from the Alexander Valley of California. It's a steal at $18.

Pork Tenderloin with Salty-Sweet Glaze

Amber agave nectar lends a light maple note. Tamari is a condiment reminiscent of soy sauce, which makes an acceptable substitute.

- 1/4 cup amber agave nectar
- 1 tablespoon chopped green onions
- 1 tablespoon reduced-sodium tamari
- 2 teaspoons grated peeled fresh ginger
- 1 garlic clove, minced
- 1½ tablespoons seasoned rice vinegar, divided
- Cooking spray
- 1 (1-pound) pork tenderloin, trimmed
- 1 teaspoon water
- Dash of ground red pepper

❶ Preheat oven to 350°.

❷ Combine first 5 ingredients in a small saucepan; stir in 1 tablespoon vinegar. Bring to a boil over medium-high heat. Cook until reduced to 1/4 cup (about 3 minutes). Reserve 2 tablespoons agave mixture; set aside. Keep remaining 2 tablespoons mixture warm in pan.

❸ Heat a large ovenproof nonstick skillet over medium-high heat. Coat pan with cooking spray. Add pork to pan; cook 5 minutes, browning on all sides.

❹ Bake at 350° for 10 minutes. Brush pork with 2 tablespoons reserved agave mixture. Bake an additional 5 minutes or until a thermometer registers 155° (slightly pink). Let stand 5 minutes.

❺ Add remaining 1½ teaspoons vinegar, 1 teaspoon water, and red pepper to remaining 2 tablespoons agave mixture in saucepan. Cut pork crosswise into 1/2-inch slices. Drizzle glaze over pork. Yield: 4 servings (serving size: 3 ounces pork and about 2 teaspoons glaze).

CALORIES 208; FAT 3.9g (sat 1.3g, mono 1.8g, poly 0.4g); PROTEIN 23.9g; CARB 17.9g; FIBER 0.1g; CHOL 74mg; IRON 1.4mg; SODIUM 344mg; CALC 8mg

Spice-Rubbed Pork Tenderloin

Allspice, nutmeg, and cinnamon—a combination often found in cold-weather baked goods—accent the savory rub mixture. Turn the pork frequently in the pan so the spices don't burn and grow bitter.

- 1 teaspoon sugar
- 1 teaspoon garlic powder
- 3/4 teaspoon salt
- 1/2 teaspoon freshly ground allspice
- 1/2 teaspoon ground cumin
- 1/4 teaspoon dried thyme
- 1/4 teaspoon freshly ground nutmeg
- 1/4 teaspoon ground cinnamon
- 1/8 teaspoon ground red pepper
- 1 (1-pound) pork tenderloin, trimmed
- 2 teaspoons olive oil

❶ Preheat oven to 350°.

❷ Combine first 9 ingredients; rub over pork. Let stand 20 minutes. Heat oil in a medium ovenproof skillet over medium-high heat. Add pork to pan; cook 4 minutes, browning on all sides.

❸ Bake at 350° for 15 minutes or until a thermometer registers 155° (slightly pink), turning after 7 minutes. Let stand 10 minutes. Cut pork crosswise into 1/2-inch-thick slices. Yield: 4 servings (serving size: 3 ounces pork).

CALORIES 166; FAT 6.3g (sat 1.7g, mono 3.4g, poly 0.7g); PROTEIN 24g; CARB 2.1g; FIBER 0.5g; CHOL 74mg; IRON 1.7mg; SODIUM 500mg; CALC 13mg

Asian-Marinated Flank Steak

The warmth of nutmeg helps round out the sweet, salty, and tangy marinade. Try it with grass-fed flank steak, if available. Serve this dish with steamed sugar snap peas and rice or soba noodles.

- 3 tablespoons hoisin sauce
- 2 tablespoons water
- 2 tablespoons rice vinegar
- 1 tablespoon low-sodium soy sauce
- 2 teaspoons grated peeled fresh ginger
- 1 teaspoon dark sesame oil
- ¼ teaspoon freshly grated nutmeg
- ⅛ teaspoon crushed red pepper
- 2 garlic cloves, minced
- 1 (1-pound) flank steak, trimmed
  Cooking spray

❶ Combine first 9 ingredients in a small bowl. Reserve ¼ cup hoisin mixture; spoon remaining mixture into a large zip-top plastic bag. Add steak to bag; seal and marinate in refrigerator 24 hours, turning bag occasionally. Remove steak from bag; discard marinade.
❷ Prepare grill or grill pan to medium-high heat.
❸ Place steak on grill rack coated with cooking spray; grill 4 minutes on each side or until desired degree of doneness. Let stand 5 minutes. Cut steak diagonally across grain into thin slices. Serve with reserved ¼ cup sauce. Yield: 4 servings (serving size: 3 ounces steak and 1 tablespoon sauce).

CALORIES 194; FAT 7.1g (sat 2.6g, mono 2.8g, poly 0.9g); PROTEIN 24.5g; CARB 6.4g; FIBER 0.5g; CHOL 37mg; IRON 1.7mg; SODIUM 378mg; CALC 25mg

Borlotti Minestrone

Borlotti beans—the Italian variety of cranberry beans—can be ordered from www.ranchogordo.com, among other online retailers.

- 1¼ cups dried borlotti beans (about ½ pound)
- ½ cup coarsely chopped bacon (about 6 slices)
- 1 cup chopped onion (about 1 small)
- 1 cup chopped fennel bulb
- ¾ cup chopped carrot (about 2 carrots)
- ¾ cup chopped celery (about 2 stalks)
- 1 teaspoon dried basil
- 3 garlic cloves, minced
- 2 cups chopped zucchini (about 2 medium)
- 6 cups chopped kale
- 3 cups water
- 2 tablespoons tomato paste
- 2 (14-ounce) cans fat-free, less-sodium chicken broth
- 1 (14.5-ounce) can petite-diced tomatoes, undrained
- ¼ teaspoon salt
- ¼ teaspoon crushed red pepper
- ½ cup (2 ounces) grated fresh Parmigiano-Reggiano cheese

❶ Sort and wash beans; place in a large bowl. Cover with water to 2 inches above beans; cover and let stand 8 hours or overnight. Drain beans.
❷ Place beans in a large saucepan, and cover with water to 3 inches above beans; bring to a boil. Reduce heat; simmer 1½ hours or until tender. Drain.
❸ Heat a large Dutch oven over medium-high heat. Add bacon to pan; cook 6 minutes or until crisp, stirring frequently. Add onion and next 5 ingredients, and sauté 4 minutes. Add zucchini; sauté 3 minutes. Add kale; sauté 2 minutes or until kale wilts. Add 3 cups water and next 3 ingredients; bring to a boil. Cover, reduce heat, and simmer 30 minutes. Add beans; simmer, uncovered, 30 minutes. Stir in salt and pepper. Ladle soup into bowls; sprinkle each serving with cheese. Yield: 8 servings (serving size: 1¼ cups soup and 1 tablespoon cheese).

CALORIES 224; FAT 5.7g (sat 2.4g, mono 2.1g, poly 0.9g); PROTEIN 14.9g; CARB 31.6g; FIBER 10.7g; CHOL 12mg; IRON 3mg; SODIUM 662mg; CALC 199mg

Pepper Pancakes with Fresh Cilantro Chutney

- 2¼ cups loosely packed fresh cilantro leaves (about 1¼ ounces)
- ¼ cup mint leaves, torn
- 2 tablespoons chopped green onions
- 2 teaspoons fresh lime juice
- 1 teaspoon canola oil
- ½ teaspoon sugar
- 1 small garlic clove, quartered
  Cooking spray
- ½ cup finely chopped red bell pepper
- ¼ cup finely chopped onion
- 2 teaspoons finely chopped seeded serrano chile (about 1 chile)
- 4 ounces chickpea (garbanzo bean) flour (about 1 cup)
- 1½ ounces semolina or pasta flour (about ¼ cup)
- ¾ teaspoon salt
- ½ teaspoon ground cumin
- ½ teaspoon fennel seeds, crushed
- 1 cup water
- 1½ teaspoons canola oil, divided
- 6 tablespoons plain fat-free yogurt

❶ Place first 7 ingredients in a food processor; pulse 4 times or until chopped.
❷ Heat a large nonstick skillet over medium heat. Coat pan with cooking spray. Add bell pepper and ¼ cup onion; cook 4 minutes, stirring frequently. Add serrano; cook 1 minute. Place bell pepper mixture in a large bowl. Weigh or lightly spoon flours into dry measuring cups; level with a knife. Add flours, salt, cumin, and fennel seeds to bell pepper mixture. Stir in 1 cup water, and let stand 3 minutes.
❸ Heat ½ teaspoon oil in pan over medium heat. Pour ⅓ cup batter per pancake

into pan; spread batter into 2 (5-inch) circles. Cook 2 minutes or until tops are covered with bubbles and edges look cooked. Flip pancakes; cook 2 minutes or until bottoms are lightly browned. Repeat procedure twice with remaining oil and batter. Serve with chutney and yogurt. Yield: 6 servings (serving size: 1 pancake, about 2 teaspoons chutney, and 1 tablespoon yogurt).

CALORIES 114; FAT 3.1g (sat 0.2g, mono 1.2g, poly 0.6g); PROTEIN 4.8g; CARB 17.5g; FIBER 1.7g; CHOL 0mg; IRON 1.7mg; SODIUM 309mg; CALC 49mg

Herbed Heritage Pork Loin with White Wine Reduction

We find Berkshire pork tender and juicy yet milder than the more robust Duroc. Both varieties are forgiving—partly because of their even marbling, the meat remains succulent even if slightly overcooked.

- 1 teaspoon salt
- ½ teaspoon ground coriander
- ½ teaspoon freshly ground black pepper
- 1 (3-pound) boneless heritage pork loin, trimmed (such as Berkshire or Duroc)
- 2 tablespoons chopped fresh parsley
- 1 tablespoon chopped fresh rosemary
- 1 tablespoon chopped fresh oregano
- 1 tablespoon chopped fresh sage
- 2 teaspoons chopped fresh thyme
- 1 teaspoon olive oil
- Cooking spray
- ½ cup finely chopped shallots
- ⅔ cup dry white wine
- 1 cup fat-free, less-sodium chicken broth
- ¼ cup fresh orange juice (about 1 large orange)

1 Preheat oven to 425°.
2 Sprinkle first 3 ingredients over pork. Combine parsley and next 4 ingredients; rub over pork.
3 Heat oil in a large nonstick skillet over medium-high heat. Add pork to pan; cook 7 minutes, browning on all sides.

Place pork in a shallow roasting pan or broiler pan coated with cooking spray. Bake at 425° for 35 minutes or until a thermometer registers 155° (slightly pink). Remove pork to a cutting board. Cover loosely with foil; let stand 10 minutes.
4 Place roasting pan over medium heat. Add shallots to pan; cook 2 minutes. Add wine, scraping pan to loosen browned bits; bring to a boil. Cook until mixture is reduced to ⅓ cup (about 3 minutes). Add broth and juice; cook until mixture is reduced to ¾ cup (about 8 minutes). Serve sauce with pork. Yield: 12 servings (serving size: 3 ounces pork and 1 tablespoon sauce).

CALORIES 212; FAT 11.9g (sat 4.4g, mono 5.3g, poly 1.1g); PROTEIN 22.8g; CARB 2.1g; FIBER 0.1g; CHOL 68mg; IRON 1.1mg; SODIUM 290mg; CALC 32mg

---

Chili Night Menu
serves 8

This simple menu is ideal for casual gatherings where you can set up a buffet. To spice up the corn bread, leave the seeds in the jalapeño.

Anasazi and Black Bean Chili

Southwest Corn Bread

Combine 1 (8½-ounce package) corn muffin mix (such as Jiffy) and ½ teaspoon ground cumin in a medium bowl. Combine ⅓ cup 2% reduced-fat milk, 2 tablespoons finely chopped seeded jalapeño pepper, and 1 large egg, stirring with a whisk. Add milk mixture to muffin mix mixture; stir in ½ cup reduced-fat shredded Mexican-blend cheese. Spoon into an 8-inch square baking pan coated with cooking spray. Bake at 400° for 25 minutes or until a wooden pick inserted in center comes out clean.

Romaine and tomato salad
Mexican amber beer
Orange sections sprinkled with grated toasted coconut

Anasazi and Black Bean Chili

Slightly sweet red-and-white Anasazis contrast with robust black beans in flavor and color. You can substitute pintos for the Anasazi beans, if you prefer.

- 1¼ cups dried Anasazi beans (about ½ pound)
- 1¼ cups dried black (turtle) beans (about ½ pound)
- Cooking spray
- 2 cups chopped onion
- 1 cup chopped red bell pepper
- 1 cup chopped green bell pepper
- ½ cup chopped poblano pepper
- 2 teaspoons minced seeded serrano chile
- 4 garlic cloves, minced
- 2 cups fat-free, less-sodium chicken broth
- 1 tablespoon ground cumin
- 1 tablespoon chili powder
- 2 teaspoons dried oregano
- ¼ teaspoon ground allspice
- 3 (14.5-ounce) cans diced tomatoes, undrained
- 1⅓ cups chopped Spanish chorizo sausage (about 2 links)
- Fat-free sour cream (optional)
- Chopped onion (optional)

1 Sort and wash Anasazi beans; place in a large bowl. Cover with water to 2 inches above beans. Repeat procedure with black beans. Cover and let stand 8 hours or overnight. Drain separately.
2 Place Anasazi beans in a large saucepan; cover with water to 3 inches above beans. Bring to a boil. Reduce heat; simmer 50 minutes or until tender. Drain. Repeat procedure with black beans.
3 Heat a large Dutch oven over medium-high heat. Coat pan with cooking spray. Add onion and next 5 ingredients; sauté 6 minutes or until tender. Add beans, broth, and next 5 ingredients; bring to a boil. Cover, reduce heat, and simmer

Continued

15 minutes. Stir in chorizo; simmer 15 minutes. Serve with sour cream and chopped onion, if desired. Yield: 8 servings (serving size: 1½ cups chili).

CALORIES 367; FAT 9.9g (sat 3.4g, mono 4.3g, poly 0.9g); PROTEIN 19.4g; CARB 52.2g; FIBER 15.6g; CHOL 20mg; IRON 7.3mg; SODIUM 635mg; CALC 277mg

BEER NOTE: A Mexican dark lager, like Negra Modelo ($8/6-pack), offers a heartiness that makes it ideal with chili. This beer's chocolate flavors are perfect with smoky beans, while a touch of caramel sweetness provides a balance for spicy sausage and chiles.

QUICK & EASY
Bhel Puri

Look for puffed rice and *sev* at Indian markets; you can substitute chow mein noodles for sev. Find chutneys on the supermarket's international aisle.

- 2 cups (½-inch) cubed peeled baking potato
- 4 cups Indian puffed rice
- 1 cup chopped seeded plum tomato
- ½ cup finely chopped red onion
- ½ cup chopped peeled ripe mango
- ¼ cup sev (fine Indian noodles)
- ¼ cup chopped fresh cilantro
- 3 tablespoons tamarind-date chutney
- 1 tablespoon mint chutney
- 2 teaspoons finely chopped seeded serrano chile (about 1 chile)

❶ Place potato in a medium saucepan; cover with water. Bring to a boil; cook 8 minutes or until tender. Drain; cool. ❷ Combine potato and remaining ingredients in a large bowl; toss well. Serve immediately. Yield: 6 servings (serving size: about 1 cup).

CALORIES 165; FAT 1.1g (sat 0.2g, mono 0.3g, poly 0.5g); PROTEIN 3.5g; CARB 36g; FIBER 2g; CHOL 0mg; IRON 1mg; SODIUM 16mg; CALC 21mg

LIGHTEN UP
Better Broccoli and Chicken Noodle Soup

We rescue a Georgia accounting teacher's favorite childhood comfort food.

A childhood favorite, Broccoli and Chicken Noodle Soup, is a weeknight go-to for Amanda Farmer of Bishop, Georgia. She received the recipe from her mother, Brenda Geiger, and wanted to give it to a friend for a cookbook project. Yet Farmer felt some guilt. Several ingredients contributed to the soup's heavy nutritional report card: processed cheese, butter, whole milk, and half-and-half add a hefty amount of fat. Its canned cream of mushroom soup, regular chicken broth, and processed cheese added significant sodium.

"I know it's high in calories and fat, and I want a healthier recipe that's still satisfying," she wrote with her request to *Cooking Light* for an overdue makeover of the recipe.

serving size: 1 cup		
	before	after
CALORIES PER SERVING	534	317
FAT	33g	12.3g
SATURATED FAT	18.6g	6.8g
SODIUM	1,289mg	723mg

STAFF FAVORITE
Broccoli and Chicken Noodle Soup
(pictured on page 213)

If the broccoli florets are large, break them into pieces at the stalk instead of chopping them; they'll cook more quickly. Count on having dinner on the table in about 40 minutes, and serve this soup immediately for the best results. If you wait, you'll find it gets thicker with time. If you have leftovers, you'll want to thin the soup with chicken broth or milk to the desired consistency.

Cooking spray
- 2 cups chopped onion
- 1 cup presliced mushrooms
- 1 garlic clove, minced
- 3 tablespoons butter
- 1.1 ounces all-purpose flour (about ¼ cup)
- 4 cups 1% low-fat milk
- 1 (14-ounce) can fat-free, less-sodium chicken broth
- 4 ounces uncooked vermicelli, broken into 2-inch pieces
- 2 cups (8 ounces) shredded light processed cheese (such as Velveeta Light)
- 4 cups (1-inch) cubed cooked chicken breast
- 3 cups small broccoli florets (8 ounces)
- 1 cup half-and-half
- 1 teaspoon freshly ground black pepper
- ¾ teaspoon salt

❶ Heat a Dutch oven over medium-high heat. Coat pan with cooking spray. Add onion, mushrooms, and garlic to pan; sauté 5 minutes or until liquid evaporates, stirring occasionally. Reduce heat to medium; add butter to mushroom mixture, stirring until butter melts. Sprinkle mushroom mixture with flour; cook 2 minutes, stirring occasionally. Gradually add milk and broth, stirring constantly with a whisk; bring to a boil. Reduce heat to medium-low; cook 10 minutes or until slightly thick, stirring constantly. Add pasta to pan; cook 10 minutes. Add cheese to pan, and stir until cheese melts. Add chicken and remaining ingredients to pan; cook 5 minutes or until broccoli is tender and soup is thoroughly heated. Yield: 10 servings (serving size: 1 cup).

CALORIES 317; FAT 12.3g (sat 6.8g, mono 2.9g, poly 0.9g); PROTEIN 27.5g; CARB 23.8g; FIBER 1.9g; CHOL 74mg; IRON 1.6mg; SODIUM 723mg; CALC 179mg

Make It Fast & Make It Fresh

Five entrées ready in less than 30 minutes

QUICK & EASY

Cilantro-Lime Chicken with Avocado Salsa

(pictured on page 216)

Fresh: Just-squeezed citrus brightens the taste of boneless, skinless chicken breasts and adds zip to the simple salsa.
Fast: A three-minute dip into a pungent marinade is all that's needed to deliver big flavor to chicken breasts. Serve with saffron rice.

CHICKEN:

- 2 tablespoons minced fresh cilantro
- 2½ tablespoons fresh lime juice
- 1½ tablespoons olive oil
- 4 (6-ounce) boneless, skinless chicken breast halves
- ¼ teaspoon salt
- Cooking spray

SALSA:

- 1 cup chopped plum tomato (about 2)
- 2 tablespoons finely chopped onion
- 2 teaspoons fresh lime juice
- ¼ teaspoon salt
- ⅛ teaspoon freshly ground black pepper
- 1 avocado, peeled and finely chopped

❶ To prepare chicken, combine first 4 ingredients in a large bowl; toss and let stand 3 minutes. Remove chicken from marinade; discard marinade. Sprinkle chicken evenly with ¼ teaspoon salt. Heat a grill pan over medium-high heat. Coat pan with cooking spray. Add chicken to pan, and cook 6 minutes on each side or until done.
❷ To prepare salsa, combine tomato and next 4 ingredients in a medium bowl. Add avocado; stir gently to combine. Serve salsa over chicken. Yield: 4 servings (serving size: 1 chicken breast half and about ¼ cup salsa).

CALORIES 289; FAT 13.2g (sat 2.4g, mono 7.5g, poly 1.9g); PROTEIN 35.6g; CARB 6.6g; FIBER 3.6g; CHOL 94mg; IRON 1.6mg; SODIUM 383mg; CALC 29mg

QUICK & EASY

Salmon with Maple-Lemon Glaze

Fresh: Finish the fish under the broiler to caramelize the glaze. Serve with roasted potato wedges and peas.
Fast: Common pantry ingredients create a sweet-tangy glaze for rich salmon fillets. It's also tasty with pork tenderloin or boneless, skinless chicken thighs.

- 2 tablespoons fresh lemon juice
- 2 tablespoons maple syrup
- 1 tablespoon cider vinegar
- 1 tablespoon canola oil
- 4 (6-ounce) skinless salmon fillets
- ½ teaspoon salt
- ¼ teaspoon freshly ground black pepper
- Cooking spray

❶ Preheat broiler.
❷ Combine first 4 ingredients in a large zip-top plastic bag. Add fish to bag; seal. Refrigerate 10 minutes, turning bag once.
❸ Remove fish from bag, reserving marinade. Place marinade in a microwave-safe bowl. Microwave at HIGH 1 minute.
❹ Heat a large ovenproof nonstick skillet over medium-high heat. Coat pan with cooking spray. Sprinkle fish evenly with salt and pepper. Add fish to pan; cook 3 minutes. Turn fish over. Brush marinade evenly over fish. Broil 3 minutes or until fish flakes easily when tested with a fork or until desired degree of doneness. Yield: 4 servings (serving size: 1 fillet).

CALORIES 287; FAT 14g (sat 2.7g, mono 6.7g, poly 3.6g); PROTEIN 31g; CARB 7.5g; FIBER 0.1g; CHOL 80mg; IRON 0.7mg; SODIUM 363mg; CALC 23mg

10 Tips to Make It Fast

1. Use a food processor or mini chopper to quickly chop, slice, or shred onions, potatoes, celery, or carrots.
2. When cooking in a skillet, allow the pan to preheat while you season the food to go in it.
3. Lean, healthful cuts such as flank steak and pork tenderloin cook in less than 30 minutes.
4. To save prep time, purchase precut vegetables and packaged prewashed salad greens.
5. Choose portion-sized boneless cuts—chicken breasts or thighs, pork chops, or fish fillets.
6. Think ahead. Grill more chicken breasts than you need, and freeze the rest for later.
7. In general, when you're in a hurry, stick to sautéing and broiling instead of roasting or braising.
8. After sautéing chicken or pork in a skillet, deglaze the pan with chicken broth or other liquid for an easy sauce. (See "Pan Sauces," page 93.)
9. Turn to quick-cooking starches for go-to sides: couscous, egg noodles, and polenta.
10. Start longer tasks first, and complete shorter ones in the meantime.

10 Tips to Make It Fresh

1. A sprinkling of chopped fresh herbs or a squeeze of citrus enlivens just about any dish.

2. Many farmers' markets open in the spring, so take advantage of their local offerings.

3. Ask your fishmonger what seafood is in season, has arrived recently, and hasn't been frozen.

4. Create your own low-sodium convenience products: Cook and freeze dried beans or roast bell peppers when you have extra time.

5. Minimally processed chicken, beef, and pork have pure taste and minimal salt.

6. Combine fresh vegetables with starches for intriguing side dishes—cubed zucchini stirred into rice, for example.

7. Start a container garden of herbs or tomatoes on your patio or windowsill.

8. Most spring produce fares best when it is cooked only a few minutes, leaving its crisp snap intact.

9. Shop once or twice a week for fresh meats or fish to keep quality high.

10. Eating a variety of colorful produce leads to a healthful diet, so fill your plate with more fruits and veggies.

QUICK & EASY • MAKE AHEAD

Potato, Chicken, and Fresh Pea Salad

Fresh: Spring ingredients, such as fingerling potatoes and sugar snap peas, transform rotisserie chicken into a pretty one-dish meal befitting the season.
Fast: Serve warm, at room temperature, or chilled for maximum versatility. Leftovers make an easy and satisfying lunch.

- 1 pound fingerling potatoes, cut crosswise into 1-inch pieces
- 2 cups fresh sugar snap peas
- 2 cups chopped boneless, skinless rotisserie chicken breast
- ½ cup finely chopped red bell pepper
- ½ cup finely chopped red onion
- 2 tablespoons extra-virgin olive oil
- 2 tablespoons white wine vinegar
- 1 tablespoon fresh lemon juice
- 1 tablespoon Dijon mustard
- 1 teaspoon minced fresh tarragon
- 1 teaspoon salt
- ½ teaspoon freshly ground black pepper
- 1 garlic clove, minced

1 Place potatoes in a large saucepan; cover with cold water. Bring to a boil. Reduce heat, and simmer 10 minutes or until almost tender. Add peas; cook 2 minutes or until peas are crisp-tender. Drain; place vegetables in a large bowl. Add chicken, bell pepper, and onion.
2 Combine oil and remaining ingredients, stirring with a whisk. Drizzle over salad; toss gently to combine. Yield: 4 servings (serving size: about 1½ cups).

CALORIES 316; FAT 9.3g (sat 1.7g, mono 5.8g, poly 1.3g); PROTEIN 26.4g; CARB 29.2g; FIBER 3.6g; CHOL 60mg; IRON 2.4mg; SODIUM 680mg; CALC 50mg

---

QUICK & EASY

Seared Scallops with Roasted Tomatoes

Fresh: Serve on fettuccine tossed with extra-virgin olive oil and grated lemon rind.
Fast: Use a cast-iron skillet to create a brown crust on the scallops and cook them in a flash; broiling tomatoes intensifies their sweetness with minimal effort.

- 3 cups grape tomatoes
- Cooking spray
- ½ teaspoon kosher salt, divided
- ½ teaspoon freshly ground black pepper, divided
- 1 tablespoon olive oil
- 1½ pounds sea scallops
- 2 tablespoons thinly sliced fresh basil

1 Preheat broiler.
2 Arrange tomatoes in a single layer in a shallow roasting pan; lightly coat tomatoes with cooking spray. Sprinkle tomatoes with ¼ teaspoon salt and ¼ teaspoon pepper; toss well to coat. Broil 10 minutes or until tomatoes begin to brown, stirring occasionally.
3 While tomatoes cook, heat oil in a large cast-iron skillet over medium-high heat. Pat scallops dry; sprinkle both sides of scallops with remaining ¼ teaspoon salt and remaining ¼ teaspoon pepper. Add scallops to skillet; cook 2 minutes on each side or until desired degree of doneness. Serve scallops with tomatoes; sprinkle with basil. Yield: 4 servings (serving size: about 4½ ounces scallops, about ⅓ cup tomatoes, and 1½ teaspoons basil).

CALORIES 204; FAT 5.1g (sat 0.7g, mono 2.6g, poly 1g); PROTEIN 29.6g; CARB 9.4g; FIBER 1.4g; CHOL 56mg; IRON 1.1mg; SODIUM 519mg; CALC 49mg

Chicken and Feta Tabbouleh
(pictured on page 217)

Fresh: Delicious when eaten right away, the flavors in this one-bowl meal stand up admirably when it's prepared ahead—making this a good take-to-work lunch. Serve with toasted pita wedges or flat-bread.

Fast: For a speedier version, use pre-chopped onions, precrumbled cheese, and presliced cooked chicken breast.

- ¾ cup uncooked bulgur
- 1 cup boiling water
- 2 cups chopped boneless, skinless rotisserie chicken breast
- 1 cup chopped plum tomato
- 1 cup chopped English cucumber
- ¾ cup chopped fresh parsley
- ½ cup (2 ounces) crumbled feta cheese
- ⅓ cup finely chopped green onions
- ¼ cup chopped fresh mint
- 2 tablespoons fresh lemon juice
- 1 tablespoon extra-virgin olive oil
- 1 teaspoon bottled minced garlic
- ¼ teaspoon salt
- ¼ teaspoon ground cumin
- ¼ teaspoon black pepper

1 Place bulgur in a medium bowl, and cover with 1 cup boiling water. Let stand 15 minutes or until liquid is absorbed. **2** Combine chicken and remaining ingredients in a large bowl. Add bulgur to chicken mixture; toss gently to combine. Yield: 4 servings (serving size: 1½ cups).

CALORIES 296; FAT 9.5g (sat 3.4g, mono 4.1g, poly 1.2g); PROTEIN 28.2g; CARB 25.6g; FIBER 6.4g; CHOL 72mg; IRON 2.7mg; SODIUM 344mg; CALC 128mg

Ecofriendly Ways to Choose & Prepare Food Deliciously

Raw Spring Vegetable Salad with Goat Cheese

Here a simple dressing coats crisp shavings of raw carrots and radishes.

- 2 medium carrots
- ¼ cup thinly sliced spring onion
- 1 (8-ounce) bunch radishes with tops
- 1 tablespoon thinly sliced fresh basil
- 2 tablespoons fresh lemon juice
- 1 tablespoon extra-virgin olive oil
- ¼ teaspoon fine sea salt
- ¼ teaspoon freshly ground black pepper
- 1 (4-ounce) package goat cheese, cut into 8 slices

1 Shave carrots into ribbons with a vegetable peeler to measure 2 cups. Combine carrots and onion in a large bowl. **2** Wash radishes and radish greens thoroughly; drain and pat dry. Cut radishes into thin slices to equal 1¾ cups; thinly slice radish greens to equal 1 cup. Add radishes, radish greens, basil, and next 4 ingredients to carrot mixture; toss gently to coat. **3** Arrange goat cheese on a serving platter; top with salad. Serve immediately. Yield: 4 servings (serving size: 2 cheese slices and about 1 cup salad).

CALORIES 132; FAT 9.5g (sat 4.6g, mono 3.8g, poly 0.6g); PROTEIN 6.2g; CARB 6.4g; FIBER 2g; CHOL 13mg; IRON 1.1mg; SODIUM 309mg; CALC 73mg

Strawberries in Meyer Lemon Syrup

Meyer lemons have sweeter, more aromatic juice than regular lemons. To ensure the dessert doesn't get too tart if substituting regular lemon juice, begin with 2 tablespoons juice, and taste; add more juice if desired. Garnish with fresh mint sprigs.

- 4 cups quartered small strawberries
- ¼ cup fresh Meyer lemon juice
- ¼ cup sugar
- ¼ cup whipping cream

1 Place first 3 ingredients in a large bowl; toss gently to coat. Cover and chill 20 minutes. **2** Place cream in a medium bowl; stir constantly with a whisk until soft peaks form. Serve whipped cream with berry mixture. Yield: 4 servings (serving size: 1 cup berry mixture and 2 tablespoons whipped cream).

CALORIES 157; FAT 6g (sat 3.5g, mono 1.7g, poly 0.5g); PROTEIN 1.5g; CARB 27g; FIBER 3.4g; CHOL 20mg; IRON 0.7mg; SODIUM 7mg; CALC 37mg

Potato and Greens Torta

A potato ricer gives the torta the most desirable texture; they're inexpensive (as little as $10) and produce the creamiest mashed potatoes.

1½ pounds small Yukon gold potatoes
3½ teaspoons fine sea salt, divided
1 tablespoon extra-virgin olive oil
3 garlic cloves, minced
4 cups torn romaine lettuce
2 cups packed fresh spinach leaves
2 cups packed arugula leaves
½ cup 2% reduced-fat milk
½ cup (2 ounces) shredded fontina cheese
2 large eggs, lightly beaten
Cooking spray
3 tablespoons dry breadcrumbs
¼ cup (1 ounce) grated fresh pecorino Romano cheese

❶ Preheat oven to 375°.
❷ Place potatoes and 1 tablespoon salt in a large saucepan; cover with water. Bring to a boil. Reduce heat; simmer 15 minutes or until tender. Drain, and cool slightly. Peel potatoes; discard peels. Press cooked potatoes through a ricer into a large bowl.
❸ Heat oil in a large nonstick skillet over medium heat. Add garlic; cook 2 minutes, stirring frequently. Stir in romaine, spinach, and arugula; cook 1 minute or until greens wilt, tossing frequently. Remove greens from pan; finely chop.
❹ Add greens, milk, fontina, eggs, and remaining ½ teaspoon salt to potatoes; stir well to combine. Coat a 9-inch pie plate with cooking spray; dust with breadcrumbs. Add potato mixture to prepared dish. Bake at 375° for 25 minutes. Remove from oven; sprinkle with pecorino. Let stand 10 minutes before serving. Yield: 6 servings (serving size: 1 wedge).

CALORIES 214; FAT 9.1g (sat 3.8g, mono 3.6g, poly 0.9g); PROTEIN 10.3g; CARB 24.2g; FIBER 3.2g; CHOL 88mg; IRON 2.1mg; SODIUM 520mg; CALC 189mg

QUICK & EASY
Tuna Scaloppine with Onion, Mint, and Almond Topping

The topping would also make a fine accompaniment for grilled or sautéed chicken breasts.

¼ cup finely chopped almonds
¼ cup fresh tangerine juice
2 tablespoons finely chopped red onion
2 tablespoons finely chopped fresh mint
1 tablespoon extra-virgin olive oil
½ teaspoon finely chopped fennel seeds
½ teaspoon fine sea salt, divided
½ teaspoon freshly ground black pepper, divided
4 (6-ounce) sushi-grade Shiro/ Magura Yellowfin tuna steaks, each split in half horizontally
Cooking spray

❶ Combine first 6 ingredients in a small bowl; stir in ¼ teaspoon salt and ¼ teaspoon pepper.
❷ Sprinkle fish evenly with remaining ¼ teaspoon salt and remaining ¼ teaspoon pepper. Heat a large nonstick skillet over medium-high heat. Coat pan with cooking spray. Add 4 fish slices; cook 1 minute on each side or until desired degree of doneness. Repeat procedure with remaining fish. Serve with almond mixture. Yield: 4 servings (serving size: 2 fish slices and 2 tablespoons almond mixture).

CALORIES 277; FAT 9.7g (sat 1.2g, mono 5.7g, poly 2g); PROTEIN 42g; CARB 4.2g; FIBER 1.3g; CHOL 77mg; IRON 1.8mg; SODIUM 354mg; CALC 58mg

Pasta with Artichokes and Fresh Ricotta

4 cups water
3 tablespoons fresh lemon juice
4 medium artichokes
3 tablespoons extra-virgin olive oil, divided
2 tablespoons chopped fresh garlic
¾ teaspoon fine sea salt, divided
3 cups uncooked penne rigate pasta (about 12 ounces tube-shaped pasta)
¼ cup chopped fresh flat-leaf parsley
½ teaspoon freshly ground black pepper
½ cup fresh whole-milk ricotta cheese
¾ cup (3 ounces) shaved fresh Parmigiano-Reggiano cheese

❶ Combine 4 cups water and juice. Cut off stem of each artichoke to within 1 inch of base; peel stem. Remove bottom leaves and tough outer leaves, leaving tender heart and bottom. Cut each artichoke in half lengthwise. Remove fuzzy thistle from bottom with a spoon. Thinly slice each artichoke heart; place in lemon water. Drain.
❷ Heat 2 tablespoons oil in a large skillet over medium heat. Add garlic to pan, and cook 1 minute. Add artichokes and ¼ teaspoon salt; cover and cook 10 minutes or until artichokes are tender, stirring occasionally.
❸ Cook pasta according to package directions, omitting salt and fat. Drain pasta in a colander over a bowl, reserving ½ cup cooking liquid. Combine remaining 1 tablespoon oil, remaining ½ teaspoon salt, artichoke mixture, pasta, reserved cooking liquid, parsley, and pepper in a large bowl, tossing to combine. Add ricotta in spoonfuls, stirring gently to combine. Spoon 1⅓ cups pasta mixture into each of 6 bowls; top each serving with 2 tablespoons Parmigiano-Reggiano. Yield: 6 servings.

CALORIES 403; FAT 14.1g (sat 5.2g, mono 6.8g, poly 0.9g); PROTEIN 18.2g; CARB 53.5g; FIBER 6.6g; CHOL 20mg; IRON 3.4mg; SODIUM 617mg; CALC 268mg

Fresh Asparagus with Anchovy-Butter Crostini

The butter has a pronounced anchovy taste; use one to two fillets if you prefer more subtlety.

- 16 (½-inch-thick) slices French bread baguette
- 2 tablespoons unsalted butter, softened
- 2 tablespoons minced fresh flat-leaf parsley
- 2 teaspoons fresh lemon juice
- 3 canned anchovy fillets, drained and finely chopped
- 1 pound thin asparagus spears, trimmed
- ⅛ teaspoon fine sea salt
- 4 lemon wedges

1 Preheat oven to 350°.

2 Arrange bread in a single layer on a baking sheet. Bake at 350° for 6 minutes or until toasted. Combine butter, and next 3 ingredients; spread about ½ teaspoon butter mixture evenly over each bread slice.

3 Steam asparagus, covered, 3 minutes or until crisp-tender. Drain and rinse with cold water; drain. Pat asparagus dry with paper towels. Divide asparagus evenly among each of 4 salad plates; sprinkle evenly with salt. Arrange 4 crostini and 1 lemon wedge on each plate. Yield: 4 servings.

CALORIES 161; FAT 6.1g (sat 3.7g, mono 1.6g, poly 0.4g); PROTEIN 6g; CARB 21.8g; FIBER 2.9g; CHOL 18mg; IRON 3.6mg; SODIUM 370mg; CALC 39mg

Ecofriendly Food Choices

1 Opt For Local Sources.

Eating locally grown foods helps support local economies, cuts down on food miles (the distance food has to travel from farm to processing site to market), and promotes fresh, seasonal produce.

Identifying the options is sometimes as easy as reading the sign above the food, but other times it requires investigation. For example, comparing two handfuls of fresh peas, you can often distinguish the locally grown by their admittedly less-than-perfect appearance from the factory farmed "hyper-green" ones. "Factory-raised produce tends to be uniform," says Liz Solms, founder of Philadelphia-based Sweet Pea Nourishment.

Another option: Ask. Simply talking with the people at your local farmers' market who sell food can influence your decision.

2 Enjoy Foods In Season.

By purchasing and preparing food in the season when it grows naturally—asparagus in spring, tomatoes in summer—you're more likely to eat locally. You're more likely to eat well, too; seasonal fruits and vegetables are at their peak of freshness and flavor.

Eating seasonally sounds great for the summer, but what about winter? Is it strictly dinners of root vegetables and cabbage?

"It's not all or nothing," says Sean Buchanan, executive chef at Solstice restaurant at Stowe Mountain Lodge, Vermont. He emphasizes seasonal cuisine whenever possible, but "we don't stop serving salad for the winter. If something is not produced here, or out of season, we make compromises."

3 Eat More Plant-Based Foods.

"When you eat meat, you consume more resources than with vegetables," says Kate Heyhoe, author of *Cooking Green: Reducing Your Carbon Footprint in the Kitchen the New Green Basics Way*. Animal protein production requires eight times the fossil fuel energy of plant protein. Heyhoe's suggestion is not to eliminate meat from your diet, but to stretch portions and add grains and nuts that will satisfy your appetite for protein or to occasionally enjoy meatless meals.

4 Make Smart Seafood Choices.

Selecting sustainable fish requires more details than most other foods.

"Fisheries are dynamic and change from year to year, so the source is harder to pin down than that of fresh fruits or vegetables," explains Brad Ack, regional director for the Marine Stewardship Council (MSC).

The MSC has identified 38 fisheries that meet its criteria for sustainability, and 88 more are undergoing certification. Look for the blue-and-white MSC certification stickers on your seafood, including that sold at large grocery stores like Whole Foods Market and Wal-Mart.

5 Take Small Steps.

Is it possible to have a kitchen that is 100 percent "sustainable"? Probably not, and that's OK. Sustainability is a big idea, and it's best achieved in small steps. Much the way recycling bottles has become a way of life for many, so has the occasional vegetarian dinner. As with any change, each small step you take leads toward success.

Peas and Tender Lettuce with Mint Butter

- 2 tablespoons chopped fresh mint
- 2 tablespoons unsalted butter, softened
- 3 tablespoons water
- ½ teaspoon fine sea salt
- 2 cups shelled fresh green peas (about 2 pounds unshelled peas)
- 4 cups shredded romaine lettuce

① Combine mint and butter in a small bowl; set aside.
② Bring 3 tablespoons water and salt to a boil in a saucepan. Add peas to pan; cover, reduce heat, and simmer 5 minutes. Top peas with lettuce; cover and cook 1 to 2 minutes or until lettuce wilts. Remove from heat; stir in butter mixture. Serve immediately. Yield: 4 servings (serving size: ¾ cup).

CALORIES 130; FAT 6.2g (sat 3.7g, mono 1.5g, poly 0.5g); PROTEIN 5.5g; CARB 14.4g; FIBER 5.6g; CHOL 15mg; IRON 1.9mg; SODIUM 298mg; CALC 44mg

---

Season's Bounty Menu
serves 4

Shrimp Salad with Blood Oranges and Slivered Fennel

Minted pea soup

Add 2 cups fresh English peas, 1 tablespoon sugar, and 1 teaspoon salt to 2 quarts boiling water; cook 5 minutes or until tender. Drain; rinse with cold water. Drain. Place peas, 2 cups fat-free, less-sodium chicken broth, and ½ teaspoon salt in a blender; puree until smooth. Strain mixture through a sieve over a bowl, pressing mixture through sieve with a wooden spoon; discard solids. Garnish each serving with 1 teaspoon chopped fresh mint leaves and freshly ground black pepper.

Sparkling water

Fresh strawberries with crème fraîche

Shrimp Salad with Blood Oranges and Slivered Fennel

U.S.-farmed or wild shrimp are a good sustainable seafood choice. For pretty slivers of fennel, use a mandoline to slice the bulb.

- ¼ cup fresh blood orange juice (about 1 orange)
- 1 tablespoon fresh lemon juice
- 2 tablespoons extra-virgin olive oil, divided
- ½ teaspoon sea salt, divided
- ¼ teaspoon freshly ground black pepper
- 24 jumbo shrimp, peeled and deveined (about 1½ pounds)
- Cooking spray
- 3 blood oranges, peeled and cut crosswise into thin slices
- 2 cups thinly sliced fennel bulb (about 1 small)
- Chopped fennel fronds (optional)

① Combine orange juice, lemon juice, 1½ tablespoons oil, ¼ teaspoon salt, and pepper, stirring well with a whisk.
② Prepare grill to medium-high heat.
③ Combine shrimp, remaining 1½ teaspoons oil, and remaining ¼ teaspoon salt; toss to coat. Thread 4 shrimp onto each of 6 (12-inch) skewers. Place skewers on a grill rack coated with cooking spray, and grill 3 minutes on each side or until done. Remove shrimp from skewers; keep warm.
④ Divide orange slices evenly among 4 plates; top each serving with ½ cup fennel and 6 shrimp. Drizzle 1 tablespoon dressing over each serving. Sprinkle with fennel fronds, if desired. Serve immediately. Yield: 4 servings.

CALORIES 329; FAT 9.8g (sat 1.5g, mono 5.4g, poly 1.9g); PROTEIN 36.3g; CARB 22.2g; FIBER 4.9g; CHOL 259mg; IRON 4.6mg; SODIUM 570mg; CALC 178mg

---

Watercress Salad with Eggs and Chive-Caper Vinaigrette

If you're lucky enough to have access to fresh farm eggs, they'll make for a stellar dish.

- 1 tablespoon finely chopped fresh chives
- 1 tablespoon chopped capers
- 1½ tablespoons extra-virgin olive oil
- 1 teaspoon Dijon mustard
- 1 teaspoon champagne or white wine vinegar
- 6 cups trimmed watercress
- 4 hard-cooked large eggs, quartered
- ¼ teaspoon fine sea salt
- ¼ teaspoon freshly ground black pepper

① Combine first 5 ingredients in a small bowl, stirring with a whisk.
② Place watercress in a large bowl. Drizzle half of vinaigrette over watercress; toss gently to coat.
③ Divide watercress mixture evenly among 4 salad plates; top each serving with 4 egg quarters. Drizzle salads evenly with remaining vinaigrette; sprinkle evenly with salt and pepper. Yield: 4 servings.

CALORIES 124; FAT 10.1g (sat 2.3g, mono 5.6g, poly 1.2g); PROTEIN 7.6g; CARB 1.4g; FIBER 0.4g; CHOL 212mg; IRON 1.1mg; SODIUM 309mg; CALC 90mg

Ecofriendly Kitchen Tips From the Pros

Be frugal. "Frugality is a trait that can help any kitchen become more sustainable," says *Cooking Light* Food Editor Ann Taylor Pittman. Examples: Save poultry and beef bones for use when making stocks. Use day-old bread you might otherwise throw away to make bread pudding.

Compost food waste. "Most people can reduce their post-consumer waste by about 20 percent by composting," says Executive Chef Sean Buchanan of Solstice restaurant in Vermont. Bonus points if you use the compost to nurture homegrown herbs and vegetables.

Use your microwave. A microwave effectively uses 57.5 percent of its energy to heat food. Compare that to a gas cooktop, which uses only 7.1 percent. "When heating water for tea, consider heating it in the microwave rather than boiling it on the stovetop," Pittman says.

Make the most of appliances. Use your appliances to cook once and eat twice, Buchanan says. For example, if you're planning to grill four chicken breasts for dinner one night, add an additional breast or two, and use the leftovers to make a simple chicken salad for lunch the next day.

Consider the toaster oven when making meals for one or two, suggests Eric Ripert, executive chef and co-owner of Le Bernardin in New York City. The oven's small size means it heats quickly, using less energy. Ripert uses his toaster oven to cook dishes such as broiled red snapper fillets and caramelized mango.

Keep the refrigerator door closed. Every time you open it, warm air rushes in, then the compressor starts working to readjust the temperature, using energy. Take another cue from Ripert: "Try to get everything you need to prepare your meal in one trip."

Easy-on-the-Cook Easter Brunch

Sit down to delicate spring fare with this festive meal. It's simple to prepare, thanks to our make-ahead plan.

EASTER BRUNCH MENU
(serves 8)

*make-ahead

Prosciutto and Melon Salad with Cantaloupe Vinaigrette
*make the vinaigrette and slice the melons a day ahead

Ginger and Thyme–Brined Pork Loin
*brine the pork and prepare the glaze the day before

Potato and Leek Cakes with Blue Cheese Sauce
*prepare the sauce a day in advance

Sautéed green beans

Riesling

Glazed Lemon-Blueberry Poppy Seed Bundt Cake
*bake up to a day before the brunch

Coffee, tea

Prosciutto and Melon Salad with Cantaloupe Vinaigrette

A fresh interpretation of the classic Italian antipasto of melon and prosciutto, this recipe adds arugula to the mix. Ripe cubed cantaloupe ensures a smooth dressing. Prepare vinaigrette a day in advance, and refrigerate.

1 cup (½-inch) cubed cantaloupe
2 tablespoons rice vinegar
4 teaspoons canola oil
1 teaspoon sugar
¼ teaspoon salt
12 cups arugula leaves
1 medium honeydew melon, peeled, seeded, and cut into 24 slices
1 medium cantaloupe, peeled, seeded, and cut into 24 slices
8 very thin slices prosciutto (about 4 ounces)
½ teaspoon freshly ground black pepper

❶ Place first 5 ingredients in a food processor; process until smooth.
❷ Place 1½ cups arugula on each of 8 salad plates. Top each serving with 3 honeydew slices, 3 cantaloupe slices, and 1 prosciutto slice. Drizzle each serving with about 1 tablespoon dressing; sprinkle evenly with pepper. Yield: 8 servings.

CALORIES 110; FAT 4.1g (sat 0.7g, mono 2g, poly 1.1g); PROTEIN 5g; CARB 15.2g; FIBER 1.1g; CHOL 8mg; IRON 1mg; SODIUM 321mg; CALC 61mg

Ginger and Thyme–Brined Pork Loin

Marinating for a day in brine infuses the loin with subtle sweetness and makes the meat juicy.

1 cup chopped fresh thyme sprigs
2 cups water
½ cup ginger preserves (such as Dundee)
3 tablespoons kosher salt
1 (2-pound) boneless pork loin roast, trimmed
1 teaspoon freshly ground black pepper
Cooking spray
1 tablespoon ginger preserves
1 teaspoon chopped fresh thyme

❶ Combine first 4 ingredients in a large bowl, stirring with a whisk until salt

Continued

dissolves. Pour thyme mixture into a large zip-top plastic bag. Add pork to bag; seal. Marinate in refrigerator 24 hours, turning occasionally.

② Preheat oven to 425°.

③ Remove pork from bag; discard marinade. Pat pork dry with a paper towel. Rub pork with pepper. Place pork on rack of a roasting pan coated with cooking spray. Combine 1 tablespoon preserves and 1 teaspoon thyme in a small bowl. Place rack with pork in pan. Bake at 425° for 25 minutes. Reduce heat to 325° (do not remove pork from oven); bake 30 minutes. Brush preserves mixture over pork; bake an additional 5 minutes or until a thermometer registers 155° (slightly pink). Place pork on a platter; let stand 15 minutes before cutting into ½-inch slices. Yield: 8 servings (serving size: 3 ounces pork).

CALORIES 172; FAT 6g (sat 2.1g, mono 2.7g, poly 0.7g); PROTEIN 24.8g; CARB 3.2g; FIBER 0.1g; CHOL 62mg; IRON 0.9mg; SODIUM 396mg; CALC 30mg

Potato and Leek Cakes with Blue Cheese Sauce

Leeks lend a delicate flavor to these potato cakes, and the creamy topping provides a cool, savory contrast.

SAUCE:
- 1 cup fat-free sour cream
- 1 cup (4 ounces) crumbled blue cheese
- 2 tablespoons chopped fresh chives
- ½ teaspoon minced garlic
- ¼ teaspoon freshly ground black pepper
- ⅛ teaspoon salt

CAKES:
- Cooking spray
- 1 cup diced leek
- 6 cups shredded peeled baking potato (about 2 pounds)
- 3 tablespoons all-purpose flour
- ½ teaspoon salt
- ½ teaspoon freshly ground black pepper
- 2 large eggs, lightly beaten

① To prepare sauce, combine first 6 ingredients in a bowl, stirring well. Cover and chill.

② To prepare cakes, heat a large nonstick skillet over medium-high heat. Coat pan with cooking spray. Add leek to pan; sauté 3 minutes or until tender. Place leek in a large bowl. Wipe pan with paper towels.

③ Place potato in a sieve; gently squeeze potato to remove excess moisture. Add potato, flour, and remaining ingredients to leek in bowl; stir well. Return pan to medium-high heat. Recoat pan with cooking spray. Divide potato mixture into 16 equal portions, shaping each into a ¼-inch-thick patty. Add 8 patties to pan; cook 5 minutes on each side or until golden. Repeat procedure with remaining 8 patties. Serve with sauce. Yield: 8 servings (serving size: 2 cakes and ¼ cup sauce).

CALORIES 222; FAT 5.5g (sat 3.1g, mono 1.6g, poly 0.4g); PROTEIN 8.4g; CARB 33.9g; FIBER 2.1g; CHOL 69mg; IRON 1.1mg; SODIUM 448mg; CALC 136mg

MAKE AHEAD

Glazed Lemon-Blueberry Poppy Seed Bundt Cake

Garnish with fresh blueberries and ribbons of lemon rind.

CAKE:
- Cooking spray
- 1½ tablespoons dry breadcrumbs
- 1¾ cups granulated sugar
- ¾ cup butter, softened
- 4 large eggs
- 13¾ ounces all-purpose flour (about 3 cups)
- 1 tablespoon baking powder
- 1 tablespoon poppy seeds
- ½ teaspoon baking soda
- ½ teaspoon salt
- 1½ cups fresh blueberries
- ¾ cup nonfat buttermilk
- ⅓ cup fresh lemon juice (about 3 lemons)
- 1 teaspoon vanilla extract
- 1 teaspoon lemon extract

GLAZE:
- 1 cup powdered sugar
- 1 tablespoon nonfat buttermilk
- 1 tablespoon fresh lemon juice

① Preheat oven to 350°.

② To prepare cake, coat a 12-cup Bundt pan with cooking spray, and dust with breadcrumbs.

③ Combine granulated sugar and butter in a large bowl; beat with a mixer at medium speed until light and fluffy (about 5 minutes). Add eggs, one at a time, beating well after each addition. Weigh or lightly spoon flour into dry measuring cups; level with a knife. Combine flour and next 4 ingredients; stir with a whisk. Add blueberries to flour mixture; toss to coat. Combine ¾ cup buttermilk and next 3 ingredients. Add flour mixture and buttermilk mixture alternately to sugar mixture, beginning and ending with flour mixture. Pour batter into prepared pan.

④ Bake at 350° for 45 minutes or until a wooden pick inserted in center comes out clean. Cool pan on a wire rack 10 minutes. Remove cake from pan; cool on rack.

⑤ To prepare glaze, place powdered sugar in a small bowl; add 1 tablespoon buttermilk and 1 tablespoon juice, stirring with a whisk until combined. Pour glaze over warm cake; cool completely. Yield: 16 servings (serving size: 1 slice).

CALORIES 304; FAT 9.8g (sat 5.7g, mono 2.7g, poly 0.7g); PROTEIN 4.7g; CARB 49.6g; FIBER 1g; CHOL 68mg; IRON 1.5mg; SODIUM 300mg; CALC 85mg

Sauces Made Simple

Learn the building blocks of making superb sauces that elevate the most humble dishes.

Step By Step: Emulsified Sauces

Hollandaise, vinaigrette, and mayonnaise are examples of emulsified sauces that require the combining of insoluble liquids, such as oil and vinegar. To do so, it's necessary to create an emulsion by suspending the acid in the fat. Here's how:

1. Although it's possible to emulsify by adding oil to juice or vinegar drop-by-drop and stirring with a whisk, you'll achieve a more stable emulsion if you add mustard or egg yolk to the mixture.

2. Gradually add butter or oil to the base of the sauce, stirring constantly with a whisk.

3. Remember, the more fat added to an emulsified sauce, the thicker it becomes. For example, mayonnaise requires more oil than vinaigrette.

Hollandaise Sauce

A silky, buttery sauce, Hollandaise transforms simple dishes into something special. Hollandaise sauce is great with steamed vegetables, fish, and poached eggs. Serve Béarnaise with lean grilled or sautéed fish, poultry, filet mignon, or other foods low in saturated fat.

- ½ cup unsalted butter
- 2 large egg yolks
- 2 tablespoons cold water
- 1 tablespoon fresh lemon juice
- ⅛ teaspoon salt

1 Place butter in a small saucepan over medium-low heat; cook 5 minutes or until completely melted. Carefully skim solids off top with a spoon; discard solids. Slowly pour remaining butter out of pan, leaving remaining solids in pan; discard solids.

2 Combine egg yolks and 2 tablespoons water in a small saucepan, stirring with a whisk until foamy. Place pan over medium heat, stirring constantly until mixture thickens slightly. Gradually add ¼ cup clarified butter, about 1 tablespoon at a time, stirring with a whisk until each addition is incorporated and mixture is thick. Reserve remaining clarified butter for another use.

3 Stir juice and salt into butter mixture, whisking until blended. Yield: about ⅔ cup (serving size: about 1 tablespoon).

CALORIES 63; FAT 6.5g (sat 3.9g, mono 0.4g, poly 0.1g); PROTEIN 0.5g; CARB 0.3g; FIBER 0g; CHOL 57mg; IRON 0.1mg; SODIUM 31mg; CALC 5mg

---

BÉARNAISE SAUCE:

Prepare recipe through step 2. Omit juice. Combine 3 tablespoons dry white wine, 3 tablespoons white wine vinegar, 1½ tablespoons minced shallots, and 3 tarragon sprigs in a heavy saucepan; bring to a simmer. Cook until reduced to 2 tablespoons. Strain through a sieve into butter mixture. Stir in salt, ⅛ teaspoon black pepper, and ½ teaspoon chopped fresh tarragon. Yield: about ⅔ cup (serving size: about 1 tablespoon).

CALORIES 63; FAT 6.5g (sat 3.9g, mono 0.4g, poly 0.1g); PROTEIN 0.5g; CARB 0.2g; FIBER 0g; CHOL 57mg; IRON 0.1mg; SODIUM 32mg; CALC 5mg

---

Red Wine Reduction Sauce (*Marchand du Vin*)

(pictured on page 215)

This sauce is great for beef steaks, veal, venison tenderloin, or duck breast. If you make homemade demi-glace, freeze the leftovers in ice cube trays, and use it to enrich sauces or stews.

- 1 cup full-bodied red wine (such as cabernet sauvignon)
- ¼ cup finely chopped shallots
- 2 tablespoons Beef Demi-Glace (recipe on page 90)
- 3 thyme sprigs
- 1 bay leaf
- 2 tablespoons chilled unsalted butter, cut into small pieces
- ⅛ teaspoon salt
- ⅛ teaspoon freshly ground black pepper

1 Combine first 5 ingredients in a small saucepan; bring to a boil. Cook until reduced to 3 tablespoons (about 10 minutes). Strain mixture through a sieve over a bowl; discard solids. Add butter, stirring constantly until smooth. Stir in salt and pepper. Yield: 4 servings (serving size: about 1 tablespoon).

CALORIES 129; FAT 7g (sat 4.1g, mono 2.1g, poly 0.3g); PROTEIN 3.2g; CARB 2.9g; FIBER 0.3g; CHOL 25mg; IRON 0.8mg; SODIUM 119mg; CALC 13mg

2 tablespoons tomato paste
2½ pounds meaty beef bones
   (such as oxtail)
Cooking spray
3 quarts cold water, divided
3 cups coarsely chopped yellow onion
1½ cups coarsely chopped celery
1 cup coarsely chopped carrot
12 black peppercorns
10 flat-leaf parsley sprigs
3 thyme sprigs
2 bay leaves

1 Preheat oven to 400°.

2 Brush tomato paste evenly over beef bones. Place bones in a shallow roasting pan coated with cooking spray. Bake at 400° for 40 minutes or until slightly charred, turning after 20 minutes.

3 Place bones in a large stockpot. Carefully add 2 cups cold water to roasting pan, scraping pan to loosen browned bits. Pour liquid from pan into stockpot. Add onion and remaining ingredients to pot. Add remaining 10 cups cold water; bring to a boil. Reduce heat, and simmer 2 hours; skim surface occasionally, discarding foam.

4 Strain stock through a fine sieve lined with cheesecloth into a large bowl; discard solids. Cool to room temperature. Cover and chill 8 hours or overnight.

5 Skim solidified fat from surface of stock; discard fat. Place stock in a large saucepan; bring to a boil. Reduce heat, and simmer until syrupy and reduced to 6 tablespoons (about 1 hour and 15 minutes), skimming foam from surface as needed. Yield: 6 tablespoons (serving size: 1 tablespoon).

CALORIES 55; FAT 2.6g (sat 1.1g, mono 1.2g, poly 0.1g); PROTEIN 6.2g; CARB 2.2g; FIBER 0.5g; CHOL 21mg; IRON 1mg; SODIUM 83mg; CALC 10mg

Step By Step: Reduction Sauces

Marchand du Vin and demi-glace are both reduction sauces. To make them, you concentrate the flavors by evaporating most of the liquid. Here's an example:

1. To make beef demi-glace, brush tomato paste on meaty beef bones, and roast them to maximize their flavor. Add the roasted bones, aromatic ingredients, and cold water to a stockpot. Simmer the mixture over low heat, skimming the surface as necessary.

2. Strain the stock, and cool to room temperature. Cover and refrigerate until thoroughly chilled. Skim solidified fat from the surface.

3. Return stock to a pan, and bring to a boil. Lower heat, and reduce stock until it's syrupy.

Step By Step: Starch-Thickened Sauces

Béchamel and velouté are two examples of starch-thickened sauces. Here are instructions on how to make them:

1. Béchamel and velouté, both known as white sauces, are based on blond roux. To make a blond roux, heat the fat—usually butter—gently, so it doesn't brown. Although it's not always necessary, you may add onion or other aromatic ingredients to the pan at this point. Then sprinkle flour (or other starch) into pan, stirring constantly. Be sure to cook flour for at least a minute to eliminate any raw taste.

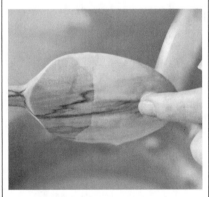

2. Gradually add liquid to flour mixture in pan, stirring constantly with a whisk until smooth. Simmer the sauce until it is thick enough to coat the back of a spoon. Strain the sauce through a sieve to remove any solids or lumps, and serve immediately.

Béchamel Sauce

Contemporary Béchamel recipes essentially consist of milk that is thickened with roux (a combination of butter and flour). Use it on crepes, vegetables, chicken, beef, or casseroles.

- 2 tablespoons unsalted butter
- ¼ cup finely chopped onion
- 1 tablespoon all-purpose flour
- 1½ cups whole milk
- ¼ teaspoon salt
  Dash of freshly ground white pepper
  Freshly grated nutmeg (optional)

❶ Place butter in a small saucepan over medium-low heat; cook until butter melts, stirring occasionally. Add onion to pan; cook 10 minutes or until tender (do not brown), stirring occasionally. Sprinkle flour over onion; cook 2 minutes, stirring constantly.
❷ Gradually add milk to flour mixture, stirring constantly with a whisk until smooth; bring to a simmer. Simmer 10 minutes or until thickened, stirring frequently. Strain mixture through a fine sieve over a bowl; discard solids.
❸ Stir in salt, pepper, and nutmeg, if desired. Serve immediately. Yield: 1⅓ cups (serving size: about 2½ tablespoons).

CALORIES 56; FAT 4.3g (sat 2.7g, mono 1.1g, poly 0.2g); PROTEIN 1.6g; CARB 2.8g; FIBER 0g; CHOL 12mg; IRON 0.1mg; SODIUM 92mg; CALC 53mg

MORNAY SAUCE:
Prepare Béchamel Sauce. Wipe pan clean with paper towels. Return Béchamel Sauce to pan, and place over medium-low heat. Add ½ cup (2 ounces) shredded Gruyère cheese, stirring until smooth. Serve immediately. Yield: 1½ cups (serving size: about 2½ tablespoons).

CALORIES 67; FAT 5.2g (sat 3.1g, mono 1.4g, poly 0.3g); PROTEIN 2.9g; CARB 2.3g; FIBER 0g; CHOL 16mg; IRON 0.1mg; SODIUM 92mg; CALC 97mg

Velouté Sauce

Since this recipe is simply broth thickened with roux, homemade stock yields the best results. If you don't have the time to make your own, purchase stock from gourmet stores or specialty markets. Substitute fish broth or clam juice for the chicken stock to serve with fish or seafood. If you prefer a sauce that has more body and flavor, just continue simmering it until it's slightly thicker and reduced to about 1 cup. Use it on whole chicken, grilled chicken breasts, or roasted pork loin.

- 1 tablespoon unsalted butter
- 1½ tablespoons all-purpose flour
- 1¾ cups chicken stock
- ¼ teaspoon salt
- ⅛ teaspoon freshly ground black pepper

❶ Melt butter in a small saucepan over medium heat. Add flour to pan, and cook 3 minutes, stirring frequently with a whisk. Gradually add stock, stirring with a whisk until smooth, and bring to a simmer. Simmer 10 minutes, stirring occasionally until slightly thick, and stir in salt and pepper. Yield: 1⅓ cups (serving size: about 3½ tablespoons).

CALORIES 26; FAT 2.1g (sat 1.3g, mono 0.6g, poly 0.1g); PROTEIN 0.4g; CARB 1.8g; FIBER 0.1g; CHOL 5mg; IRON 0.1mg; SODIUM 284mg; CALC 3mg

Balancing Act

Even rich, buttery sauces, such as béarnaise or beurre blanc, have a place in a healthy diet. Just think strategically about the foods with which you pair them. Choose steamed vegetables, fish, shellfish, or other lean meats to keep total saturated fat within reasonable limits. For example, 3 ounces of cooked lean filet mignon steak topped with one serving of our Béarnaise Sauce (page 89) contains 6.4 grams of saturated fat, well within a healthy range for an entrée.

Aioli

Aioli is simply mayonnaise with the addition of minced fresh garlic. Use it on sandwiches, or as a dip, spread, or dressing. There are almost an infinite number of variations—curry, saffron, or cooked mushroom.

- 1 teaspoon fresh lemon juice
- ½ teaspoon Dijon mustard
- 2 large pasteurized egg yolks
- ¾ cup canola oil
- ¼ teaspoon salt
- ⅛ teaspoon freshly ground black pepper
- 1 garlic clove, minced

❶ Combine first 3 ingredients in a medium bowl, stirring well with a whisk. Gradually add oil, about 1 tablespoon at a time, stirring with a whisk until each addition is incorporated and mixture is thick. Stir in salt, pepper, and garlic. Yield: 1 cup (serving size: about 2½ teaspoons).

CALORIES 80; FAT 8.8g (sat 0.8g, mono 5.1g, poly 2.6g); PROTEIN 0.3g; CARB 0.2g; FIBER 0g; CHOL 20mg; IRON 0.1mg; SODIUM 31mg; CALC 2mg

Morel Mayonnaise

Dried morel mushrooms add meaty flavor to this mayonnaise. You can substitute your favorite dried mushrooms, if necessary. It's great on roast beef, sandwiches, steak, and salads.

- 1 teaspoon fresh lemon juice
- ½ teaspoon Dijon mustard
- 2 large pasteurized egg yolks
- ¾ cup canola oil
- ¼ teaspoon salt
- ⅛ teaspoon freshly ground black pepper
- ½ ounce dried morel mushrooms
- ½ cup boiling water

❶ Combine first 3 ingredients in a medium bowl, stirring well with a whisk. Gradually add oil, about 1 tablespoon at a time, stirring with a whisk until each addition is incorporated and mixture is thick. Stir in salt and pepper.
❷ Combine morel mushrooms and ½ cup boiling water in a small bowl; cover and let stand 15 minutes. Drain mushrooms in a colander over a bowl, reserving solids and liquid. Strain reserved liquid through a fine sieve over a small saucepan; bring liquid to a boil. Cook until reduced to 1 tablespoon (about 5 minutes); cool completely. Finely chop mushrooms. Stir reduced liquid and mushrooms into mayonnaise mixture. Cover and chill at least 4 hours. Yield: 1¼ cups (serving size: about 1 tablespoon).

CALORIES 82; FAT 8.8g (sat 0.8g, mono 5.1g, poly 2.6g); PROTEIN 0.4g; CARB 0.5g; FIBER 0g; CHOL 20mg; IRON 0.2mg; SODIUM 31mg; CALC 2mg

Step By Step: Mayonnaise

Another example of an emulsified sauce, mayonnaise becomes thicker as you begin to incorporate more oil. Here's how to make it:

1. The secret to success when making mayonnaise is to start the emulsion quickly. A combination of egg yolks and Dijon mustard is the key to a great finished sauce.

2. Add the oil to the mayonnaise mixture drop by drop in the beginning. Once the emulsion is formed, add about 1 tablespoon at a time, whisking constantly until each addition is fully incorporated.

Beurre Blanc

Although this is one of the simplest sauces to prepare, the flavor is tangy and rich. Take care to add the butter bit by bit, stirring constantly with a whisk until each addition is completely incorporated. Use it on fish, shellfish, chicken, or pork chops.

- ¼ cup dry white wine
- 1½ tablespoons white wine vinegar
- 1½ tablespoons minced shallots
- ½ teaspoon whole black peppercorns
- 6 tablespoons unsalted butter, chilled and cut into small pieces
- ⅛ teaspoon salt
- Dash of freshly ground white pepper

① Combine first 4 ingredients in a small saucepan; bring to a boil. Cook until reduced to 2 tablespoons (about 4½ minutes). Reduce heat to low. Add chilled butter, 2 pieces at a time, stirring with a whisk after each addition until butter is fully incorporated. Strain mixture through a fine sieve over a bowl; discard solids. Add salt and pepper. Yield: about ½ cup (serving size: about 1 tablespoon).

CALORIES 82; FAT 8.5g (sat 5.4g, mono 2.2g, poly 0.3g); PROTEIN 0.1g; CARB 0.2g; FIBER 0g; CHOL 23mg; IRON 0mg; SODIUM 75mg; CALC 3mg

White Sauce

Use this variation on Béchamel on pasta and pork.

- 2 tablespoons unsalted butter
- 3 tablespoons finely chopped onion
- 3 tablespoons finely chopped celery
- 3 tablespoons finely chopped carrot
- 2 tablespoons finely chopped prosciutto
- 1 tablespoon all-purpose flour
- 1½ cups whole milk
- 3 flat-leaf parsley sprigs
- 3 thyme sprigs
- 1 bay leaf
- ¼ teaspoon salt
- Dash of freshly ground white pepper
- Freshly grated nutmeg (optional)

① Place butter in a small saucepan over medium-low heat. Add onion and next 3 ingredients to pan, and cook 10 minutes (do not brown), stirring occasionally. Sprinkle flour over onion mixture, and cook 2 minutes, stirring constantly. ② Gradually add milk to flour mixture, stirring with a whisk until smooth. Add herbs and bay leaf; bring to a simmer. Simmer 10 minutes or until thickened, stirring frequently. Strain mixture through a fine sieve over a bowl; discard solids. Stir in salt, pepper, and nutmeg, if desired. Yield: about 1⅓ cups (serving size: about 2½ tablespoons).

CALORIES 56; FAT 4.3g (sat 2.7g, mono 1.1g, poly 0.2g); PROTEIN 1.7g; CARB 2.8g; FIBER 0g; CHOL 12mg; IRON 0.1mg; SODIUM 95mg; CALC 53mg

Pan Sauces

These simple sauces incorporate naturally occurring pan juices or tasty browned bits that are left behind in the cooking pan. Try one of these ideas listed below, or add your favorite herbs or spices to make your own creation.

Pan sauce for sautéed chicken breast: Add ⅓ cup apple juice to drippings in pan; cook over medium-high heat for 3 minutes or until mixture is reduced to ¼ cup. Stir in 1 teaspoon cider vinegar and 1 (14-ounce) can fat-free, less-sodium chicken broth. Cook for 8 minutes or until reduced to ¼ cup. Stir in 1 tablespoon butter.

Pan gravy for roast chicken: Heat drippings from a roast chicken in bottom of roasting pan over medium-high heat; add ¼ cup white wine, stirring with a whisk. Cook 2 minutes; stir in 1½ cups fat-free, less-sodium chicken broth; 1½ cups sliced shiitake mushroom caps; and 3 large thyme sprigs. Combine ¼ cup broth with 2 teaspoons all-purpose flour, stirring with a whisk until smooth. Stir flour mixture into wine mixture; bring to a boil. Cook 1 minute or until mixture thickens. Stir in ⅛ teaspoon freshly ground black pepper. Makes about 1½ cups.

Mustard pan sauce for roast pork tenderloin: Heat pan drippings from roast pork tenderloin in roasting pan over medium-high heat. Stir in 1 cup fat-free, less-sodium chicken broth; 1 teaspoon Dijon mustard; and ½ teaspoon chopped fresh thyme. Bring to a boil. Cook 8 minutes or until reduced to ⅓ cup. Stir in 1 teaspoon cold butter.

Fixes for Broken Sauces

Even when made properly, sauces can be delicate. Occasionally, the elements separate, resulting in a broken sauce with a curdled appearance. Depending on the sauce, there's often a remedy.

Beurre blanc can be rescued by placing about 1 or 2 tablespoons of heavy cream in a saucepan and reducing it by half. Reduce heat to low, and slowly whisk the separated beurre blanc into the cream to stabilize the sauce.

Mayonnaise can be saved by placing an additional egg yolk and mustard in a large bowl and whisking until it's pale and frothy. Then slowly add the broken sauce, whisking constantly until thick.

Vinaigrette will form a stronger emulsion if you whisk the broken mixture into a bit more mustard or an egg yolk.

Béchamel and other starch-thickened sauces can be repaired by whisking the broken sauce into a new roux.

Cheese Course

Like many artisanal food producers, this owner of an acclaimed creamery learns how to balance quality and quantity.

The story of the Fromagerie Belle Chèvre near the town of Elkmont, Alabama, parallels that of a number of America's artisanal food makers. Since its beginnings in 1989, the label has earned the kind of cult status that puts small artisans on the map. It has won scores of American Cheese Society awards, starred at a White House dinner, and procured a spot on the shelves of the nation's top cheese shops. But because of its limited production, Belle Chèvre didn't find wide acclaim or distribution right away.

An energetic former technology entrepreneur with a passion for food, Tasia Malakasis purchased Belle Chèvre two years ago from its founder, the talented cheesemaker Liz Parnell, and has since taken steps to grow the company. The 37-year-old Huntsville, Alabama, native had long considered a career in food.

One weekend in 2000, while trolling the shelves at boutique food purveyor Dean & DeLuca, she discovered Belle Chèvre. "I couldn't believe it when I picked up that cheese," she says. "The creamery was 15 miles from where I grew up. It was fateful."

Malakasis began to dream of ownership of Belle Chèvre and pursued Parnell over the next several years. She eventually talked her way into a brief meeting and then an apprenticeship, taking every messy job Parnell threw at her, from scrubbing down the holding tank to rolling cheeses in ash. Most importantly, she got along with the small staff, which includes three generations of one family. Parnell soon saw that Malakasis's association with the creamery "was meant to be." So Parnell accepted Malakasis's offer to purchase the creamery.

"I was at a crossroads," recalls Parnell. "My cheese business either had to grow or just sit there on the vine, and I really didn't want to put a lot more energy or money into it."

In her first year of ownership, with Parnell working as a consultant, Malakasis detailed a plan to help the business grow. The result: Sales in 2007 increased by 75 percent over the previous year to a new high.

But her plans don't stop there. "There is so much more I'd like to do here," says Malakasis, surveying her small domain. "I'd love to grow all my own herbs for our *herbes de Provence*. I'd love to make a Greek-style yogurt. And of course I'll eventually have to build a new creamery—one that a delivery truck can actually drive up to."

QUICK & EASY
Goat Cheese Grits

The addition of goat cheese makes this traditional Southern side dish smooth and satisfying. Garnish with an extra sprig of fresh parsley.

- 4 cups water
- 1 cup uncooked quick-cooking grits
- ¾ teaspoon salt
- ½ cup (4 ounces) goat cheese
- 2 teaspoons finely chopped fresh parsley
- 1 teaspoon finely chopped fresh basil
- ¼ teaspoon freshly ground black pepper

1 Bring 4 cups water to a boil in a medium saucepan. Gradually add grits and salt to pan, stirring constantly with a whisk. Reduce heat, and simmer 5 minutes or until thick, stirring occasionally. Remove from heat; stir in cheese and remaining ingredients. Yield: 10 servings (serving size: about ½ cup).

CALORIES 99; FAT 3.6g (sat 2.4g, mono 0.8g, poly 0.2g); PROTEIN 3.8g; CARB 12.8g; FIBER 0.3g; CHOL 9mg; IRON 0.8mg; SODIUM 237mg; CALC 38mg

QUICK & EASY
Berry Salad with Goat Cheese Dressing

Buttermilk and cheese offer a tangy counterpoint to the sweet berries.

- 2 tablespoons Champagne vinegar
- 2 tablespoons fat-free buttermilk
- 2 tablespoons honey
- 2 teaspoons Dijon mustard
- ¼ teaspoon salt
- ⅛ teaspoon freshly ground black pepper
- 1 (3-ounce) package soft goat cheese
- 6 cups torn romaine lettuce
- 2 cups trimmed arugula
- ¾ cup fresh blueberries
- ¾ cup fresh raspberries
- ½ cup hulled fresh strawberries

❶ Place first 7 ingredients in a blender or food processor; process until smooth. Combine romaine and remaining ingredients in a large bowl. Drizzle goat cheese mixture over lettuce mixture; toss gently to coat. Serve immediately. Yield: 8 servings (serving size: 1 cup).

CALORIES 112; FAT 4.7g (sat 3g, mono 1g, poly 0.3g); PROTEIN 4.6g; CARB 14.8g; FIBER 3g; CHOL 11mg; IRON 1.2mg; SODIUM 196mg; CALC 86mg

Warm Potato and Goat Cheese Salad

Thick, rich goat's milk fromage blanc (fresh soft goat cheese) combines with sour cream for the basis of a creamy dressing that stands in for mayonnaise.

2½ pounds cubed peeled Yukon gold potatoes
¼ cup dry white wine
½ teaspoon salt
½ teaspoon freshly ground black pepper
⅓ cup finely chopped onion
½ cup chopped fresh flat-leaf parsley
1 (3-ounce) package goat cheese
½ cup goat's milk fromage blanc
¼ cup light sour cream
¼ cup red wine vinegar
2 tablespoons chopped fresh tarragon
2 tablespoons extra-virgin olive oil
1 teaspoon Dijon mustard
1 garlic clove, minced

❶ Place potatoes in a large saucepan; cover with water. Bring to a boil. Reduce heat; simmer 15 minutes or until tender. Drain. Combine warm potatoes, wine, salt, and pepper in a large bowl; toss gently. Add onion, parsley, and goat cheese. Combine fromage blanc and remaining ingredients, stirring with a whisk until smooth. Add fromage blanc mixture to potato mixture; toss gently to coat. Yield: 12 servings (serving size: ⅔ cup).

CALORIES 159; FAT 6.9g (sat 2g, mono 2.3g, poly 0.3g); PROTEIN 5.5g; CARB 18.4g; FIBER 1.3g; CHOL 7mg; IRON 1.1mg; SODIUM 180mg; CALC 29mg

MAKE AHEAD

Asparagus, Green Onion, and Goat Cheese Quiche

The shell is a basic pâte brisée dough, which yields a flaky, buttery-tasting crust. It comes together quickly in the food processor, and the rolling out instructions in step 3 are absolutely foolproof. Make this dish up to two days ahead, and serve it warm or at room temperature. Since oven times vary, check the quiche for doneness after about 25 minutes.

CRUST:
3.9 ounces all-purpose flour (about ¾ cup plus 2 tablespoons)
¼ teaspoon salt
¼ cup chilled butter, cut into small pieces
1 tablespoon ice water
Cooking spray

FILLING:
2 tablespoons butter
12 ounces asparagus, chopped
½ teaspoon salt, divided
¼ teaspoon freshly ground black pepper, divided
1 cup sliced green onions
4 ounces soft goat cheese, crumbled
3 large eggs
1 large egg yolk
¾ cup 2% reduced-fat milk
Dash of grated fresh nutmeg

❶ To prepare crust, weigh or lightly spoon flour into dry measuring cups; level with a knife. Place flour and ¼ teaspoon salt in a food processor; pulse 2 times or until combined. Add ¼ cup chilled butter; pulse 4 times or until mixture resembles coarse meal. With processor on, add ice water through food chute, processing just until combined (do not form a ball).

❷ Preheat oven to 425°.

❸ Press dough gently into a 4-inch circle on plastic wrap. Cover and chill 20 minutes. Slightly overlap 2 sheets of plastic wrap on a slightly damp surface. Unwrap and place chilled dough on plastic wrap.

Cover with 2 additional sheets of overlapping plastic wrap. Roll dough, still covered, into an 11-inch circle. Place dough in freezer 5 minutes or until plastic wrap can be easily removed.

❹ Remove 2 sheets of plastic wrap; let stand 1 minute or until pliable. Fit dough, plastic-wrap side up, into a 9-inch pie plate lightly coated with cooking spray. Remove remaining plastic wrap. Press dough into bottom and up sides of pan; fold edges under and flute. Line pastry with foil; place pie weights or dried beans on foil. Bake at 425° for 15 minutes or until lightly browned. Remove weights and foil. Reduce oven temperature to 350°. Bake crust an additional 5 minutes or until pastry is golden. Remove pan from oven, and cool on a wire rack.

❺ To prepare filling, melt 2 tablespoons butter in a large skillet over medium-high heat. Add asparagus to pan. Sprinkle ¼ teaspoon salt and ⅛ teaspoon pepper over asparagus; sauté 8 minutes or until crisp-tender, stirring frequently. Add onions; sauté 2 minutes or until asparagus just begins to brown. Remove from heat. Spoon asparagus mixture into prepared shell in an even layer. Arrange goat cheese in an even layer over asparagus mixture.

❻ Combine eggs, egg yolk, and milk. Stir in remaining ¼ teaspoon salt, remaining ⅛ teaspoon pepper, and nutmeg. Pour custard into pie plate. Bake at 350° for 30 minutes or until quiche is almost set in center. Remove from oven, and cool 5 minutes on a wire rack before slicing. Yield: 8 servings (serving size: 1 wedge).

CALORIES 222; FAT 14.4g (sat 8.5g, mono 4g, poly 0.8g); PROTEIN 8.5g; CARB 14.2g; FIBER 1.8g; CHOL 136mg; IRON 2.5mg; SODIUM 378mg; CALC 83mg

Grilled Turkey Burgers with Goat Cheese Spread

A small amount of pungent goat cheese flavors the creamy spread. Double the spread, and use it on grilled chicken or turkey sandwiches.

- 2 teaspoons grated lemon rind
- ½ teaspoon salt
- 2 garlic cloves, minced
- 1 pound ground turkey breast
- 1 (10-ounce) package frozen chopped spinach, thawed and drained
- 1 large egg white
- ¼ teaspoon freshly ground black pepper, divided
  Cooking spray
- ½ cup 2% reduced-fat Greek-style yogurt (such as Fage)
- ¼ cup (1 ounce) crumbled goat cheese
- 2 tablespoons chopped fresh flat-leaf parsley
- 1 tablespoon chopped fresh oregano
- 1 tablespoon chopped fresh mint
- 6 (2-ounce) whole-wheat hamburger buns, toasted
- 6 green leaf lettuce leaves
- 6 (⅛-inch-thick) slices red onion

1 Combine first 6 ingredients and ⅛ teaspoon pepper in a large bowl, mixing gently. Divide turkey mixture into 6 equal portions, shaping each into a ¼-inch-thick patty. Heat a grill pan over medium-high heat. Coat pan with cooking spray. Add patties to pan; cook 8 minutes on each side or until done. **2** Combine remaining ⅛ teaspoon pepper, yogurt, and next 4 ingredients in a bowl, stirring well. Spread 1½ tablespoons yogurt mixture on the bottom half of each bun; top each serving with 1 lettuce leaf, 1 onion slice, and 1 patty. Place top half of bun on each serving. Yield: 6 servings (serving size: 1 burger).

CALORIES 269; FAT 5.7g (sat 2.2g, mono 1g, poly 1.4g); PROTEIN 23.9g; CARB 33.9g; FIBER 6.2g; CHOL 28mg; IRON 3mg; SODIUM 588mg; CALC 182mg

Take a Field Trip

Chefs and farmers are hosting alfresco meals to showcase local fare. We bring their recipes home to you. Be inspired!

JOIN A TREND growing in fields across America. The subtle but profound grassroots movement to encourage people to buy locally produced food is blossoming in new ways. For example, instead of waiting for spring produce to arrive at the farmers' market, Outstanding in the Field founder Jim Denevan goes directly to the source. And he takes about 130 lucky diners with him for five-course meals prepared by top chefs amid the rolling fields of some of the finest farms in North America and Europe.

Celebrating its 10th year, Outstanding in the Field strives to connect people to the origins of their food and the people who produce it. The dinners—which start at $180 per person—are the culmination of an afternoon adventure during which guests are led on a tour of the farm as the farmer answers their questions and points out its unique features.

"You know how you're not supposed to go to the supermarket when you're hungry? By the time we sit down to eat, our diners have been literally surrounded by their dinner all day, and they're ready for it," Denevan says.

Outstanding in the Field is one of several organizations nationwide to offer meals like this throughout the growing season. The events embody the larger farm-to-table movement, which has spurred interest in eating and purchasing food locally. Whether they're held in city restaurants with visiting farmers or amid blooming orchards with visiting chefs, these dinners offer folks great local produce and a deeper appreciation for the origins of their food.

Arugula and Celery Salad with Lemon-Anchovy Dressing

Plate & Pitchfork in Portland, Oregon, organizes farm dinners that often feature this delightfully simple salad. It's great with grilled tuna. You can serve the leftover dressing over pasta, steamed new potatoes, or grilled chicken.

- 6 cups baby arugula leaves
- ½ cup diagonally cut celery
- ¼ cup almonds, toasted and chopped
- ¼ cup fresh flat-leaf parsley leaves
- ⅛ teaspoon kosher salt
- ⅛ teaspoon freshly ground black pepper
- ⅓ cup Lemon-Anchovy Dressing
- ¼ cup (1 ounce) shaved Parmigiano-Reggiano cheese

1 Combine first 6 ingredients in a large bowl. Add ⅓ cup Lemon-Anchovy Dressing; toss gently to coat. Sprinkle with cheese. Serve immediately. Yield: 4 servings (serving size: 1 cup).

CALORIES 125; FAT 10.2g (sat 1.9g, mono 6.2g, poly 1.8g); PROTEIN 5.1g; CARB 5g; FIBER 2.2g; CHOL 4mg; IRON 1.2mg; SODIUM 325mg; CALC 155mg

LEMON-ANCHOVY DRESSING:
- 2 tablespoons fresh flat-leaf parsley leaves
- 3 tablespoons water
- 2 tablespoons fresh lemon juice
- 1½ teaspoons Dijon mustard
- ½ teaspoon salt
- 3 garlic cloves
- 1 canned anchovy fillet, rinsed
- 3 tablespoons extra-virgin olive oil

❶ Place first 7 ingredients in a blender; process until smooth. With blender on, slowly add oil. Process until blended. Yield: ²/₃ cup (serving size: 4 teaspoons).

NOTE: Store in an airtight container in refrigerator up to one week.

CALORIES 50; FAT 5.3g (sat 0.7g, mono 3.8g, poly 0.8g); PROTEIN 0.3g; CARB 1g; FIBER 0.1g; CHOL 0mg; IRON 0.1mg; SODIUM 189mg; CALC 5mg

WINE NOTE: Arugula, celery, and lemons all contain green flavors. A wine that works well with this trio—and won't be undone by the anchovies—is the outrageously fresh Sauvignon Republic 2007 from the Russian River Valley of California ($18).

MAKE AHEAD
Panzanella

Jim Denevan of Outstanding in the Field prepares this salad to showcase specialty varieties of vegetables.

  8 ounces ciabatta, cut into 1-inch cubes
  2 orange bell peppers (about 1 pound)
  2 cups sliced radicchio (about 4 ounces)
  2 tablespoons capers
  1 pound cherry tomatoes, halved
  1 medium cucumber, halved lengthwise, seeded, and sliced
  3 tablespoons red wine vinegar
  1½ teaspoons finely chopped canned anchovy fillets
  ½ teaspoon honey
  ¼ teaspoon salt
  ¼ teaspoon freshly ground black pepper
  ¼ cup extra-virgin olive oil
  ¼ cup torn fresh basil leaves

❶ Preheat oven to 350°.
❷ Place bread on a jelly-roll pan. Bake at 350° for 10 minutes or until crisp, stirring occasionally.
❸ Preheat broiler.
❹ Cut bell peppers in half lengthwise; discard seeds and membranes. Place pepper halves, skin sides up, on a foil-lined baking sheet; flatten with hand. Broil 10 minutes or until blackened. Place in a heavy-duty zip-top plastic bag; seal. Let stand 10 minutes. Peel; cut into 1-inch pieces.
❺ Combine bread, bell peppers, and next 4 ingredients in a large bowl. Combine vinegar and next 4 ingredients in a small bowl. Gradually add oil, stirring with a whisk. Pour over bread mixture; toss.
❻ Let stand 20 minutes or just until bread begins to soften. Sprinkle with basil. Yield: 10 servings (serving size: about 1 cup).

CALORIES 136; FAT 6.8g (sat 1g, mono 4.8g, poly 0.8g); PROTEIN 3.5g; CARB 16.6g; FIBER 1.7g; CHOL 2mg; IRON 1.2mg; SODIUM 349mg; CALC 17mg

Lamb Shoulder Braised with Spring Vegetables, Green Herbs, and White Wine

This recipe from Dinners at the Farm in Connecticut combines spring produce with lamb.

  1½ tablespoons butter
  4 cups chopped onion (about 1 pound)
  6 garlic cloves, crushed
  2 pounds lamb shoulder, trimmed and cut into 1½-inch pieces
  3 cups fruity white wine (such as riesling)
  1 teaspoon salt
  ½ teaspoon freshly ground black pepper
  1 tablespoon chopped fresh oregano
  1 tablespoon chopped fresh flat-leaf parsley
  2 teaspoons chopped fresh rosemary
  ½ pound small red potatoes, halved
  ½ pound turnips, peeled and cut into 1-inch cubes
  ½ pound carrots, peeled and cut into 1-inch pieces
  ½ pound asparagus, trimmed and cut into 2-inch pieces

❶ Melt butter in a Dutch oven over medium-high heat. Add onion to pan; sauté 4 minutes. Add garlic, and sauté 1 minute. Spoon onion mixture into a large bowl. Add half of lamb to pan; sauté 4 minutes or until browned. Remove from pan; add to onion mixture. Repeat procedure with remaining lamb.
❷ Add wine to pan, scraping pan to loosen browned bits. Return lamb mixture to pan; add salt and pepper. Combine oregano, parsley, and rosemary. Add half of herb mixture to pan; bring to a boil. Cover, reduce heat, and simmer 1½ hours or until lamb is tender. Add potatoes, turnips, and carrots to pan. Cover and cook 40 minutes or until tender. Add asparagus; cook 5 minutes or until asparagus is tender. Stir in remaining herb mixture. Yield: 8 servings (serving size: 1¼ cups).

CALORIES 325; FAT 12.6g (sat 5.3g, mono 4.7g, poly 1.1g); PROTEIN 34.3g; CARB 17.2g; FIBER 3.6g; CHOL 110mg; IRON 4.2mg; SODIUM 448mg; CALC 75mg

WINE NOTE: This succulent lamb shoulder surrounded by roasted root vegetables is fantastic with an earthy pinot noir. Try one that's rich and full bodied to mirror the richness of the lamb. Talley Pinot Noir 2006 from California's Arroyo Grande Valley ($36) is sensational.

"Farmers know their stuff when it comes to good food and good cooking."

—Jim Denevan of Outstanding in the Field

Halibut with Citrus-Fennel Relish

Farm-inspired menus are a specialty of City Catering Company in Seattle. This dish takes advantage of fresh produce, as well as halibut, which is in season in the spring. You can use all orange or a combination of orange and grapefruit. Blood oranges would also make a lovely choice.

- 4 (6-ounce) halibut fillets
- ¾ teaspoon salt, divided
- ¾ teaspoon freshly ground black pepper, divided
- 2 tablespoons extra-virgin olive oil, divided
- 1¼ cups shaved fennel bulb (about ½ bulb)
- 1¼ cups coarsely chopped orange sections (about 2 oranges)
- 1 tablespoon chopped fennel fronds

❶ Sprinkle fish with ½ teaspoon salt and ½ teaspoon pepper. Heat 1 tablespoon oil in a large nonstick skillet over medium-high heat. Add fish to pan; cook 4 minutes on each side or until fish flakes easily with a fork or until desired degree of doneness.

❷ Combine fennel, orange, fennel frond, remaining 1 tablespoon oil, remaining ¼ teaspoon salt, and remaining ¼ teaspoon pepper; toss gently. Serve with fish. Yield: 4 servings (serving size: about 1 fillet and about ½ cup fennel mixture).

CALORIES 295; FAT 11g (sat 1.5g, mono 6.7g, poly 1.9g); PROTEIN 36.3g; CARB 12.9g; FIBER 4.5g; CHOL 54mg; IRON 1.9mg; SODIUM 543mg; CALC 126mg

Spring Asparagus Risotto

Clif Holt, chef-owner of Little Savannah in Birmingham, Alabama, prepares this classic risotto for harvest dinners at Jones Valley Urban Farm. For a vegetarian entrée, use vegetable broth.

- 4 cups (1-inch) slices asparagus (about 1½ pounds), divided
- 3 cups fat-free, less-sodium chicken broth, divided
- 1½ cups water
- 1 tablespoon butter
- 2 cups chopped onion (about 1 large)
- 2 cups uncooked Arborio rice or other medium-grain rice
- ½ cup dry white wine
- 1 cup (4 ounces) grated fresh Parmigiano-Reggiano cheese, divided
- ¼ cup heavy whipping cream
- 1 teaspoon salt
- ½ teaspoon freshly ground black pepper

❶ Place 1 cup asparagus and 1 cup broth in a blender; puree until smooth. Combine puree, remaining 2 cups broth, and 1½ cups water in a medium saucepan; bring to a simmer (do not boil). Keep warm over low heat.

❷ Melt butter in a large heavy saucepan over medium heat. Add onion to pan; cook 8 minutes or until tender, stirring occasionally. Stir in rice; cook 1 minute, stirring constantly. Stir in wine; cook 2 minutes or until liquid is nearly absorbed, stirring constantly. Add ½ cup broth mixture; cook 2 minutes or until liquid is nearly absorbed, stirring constantly. Add remaining broth mixture, ½ cup at a time, stirring constantly until each portion of broth mixture is absorbed before adding the next (about 30 minutes total). Stir in remaining 3 cups asparagus; cook 2 minutes.

❸ Stir in ¾ cup cheese and next 3 ingredients. Transfer risotto to a bowl. Serve with remaining ¼ cup cheese. Yield:

8 servings (serving size: 1¼ cups risotto and 1½ teaspoons cheese).

CALORIES 283; FAT 7.7g (sat 4.4g, mono 2g, poly 0.3g); PROTEIN 10.5g; CARB 44g; FIBER 4.1g; CHOL 23mg; IRON 2.2mg; SODIUM 634mg; CALC 144mg

Soy-Sesame Kale

City Catering Company in Seattle likes to use dinosaur kale—also called lacinato kale, *cavolo nero*, and black kale—in this speedy side dish.

- 3 tablespoons low-sodium soy sauce
- 3 tablespoons mirin (sweet rice wine)
- 1 tablespoon rice vinegar
- 1 tablespoon dark sesame oil
- 2 teaspoons minced peeled fresh ginger
- 3 garlic cloves, minced
- 1½ pounds dinosaur kale, trimmed and cut into 2-inch pieces
  Cooking spray

❶ Combine first 6 ingredients in a large bowl, stirring with a whisk. Add kale; toss to coat. Heat a large nonstick skillet over medium-high heat. Coat pan with cooking spray. Add half of kale mixture to pan; sauté 4 minutes or until wilted and tender. Transfer to a bowl. Repeat procedure with remaining kale mixture. Yield: 8 servings (serving size: ¾ cup).

CALORIES 59; FAT 2.1g (sat 0.3g, mono 0.8g, poly 0.9g); PROTEIN 2.2g; CARB 8g; FIBER 1.1g; CHOL 0mg; IRON 1.1mg; SODIUM 248mg; CALC 74mg

Roasted Asparagus Salad with Pecorino, Lemon, and Olive Oil

Classic spring flavors of asparagus, egg, and lemon combine in this salad from Dinners at the Farm. You can use Parmesan cheese in place of pecorino, if you prefer.

- 2 pounds asparagus, trimmed
- 3 tablespoons extra-virgin olive oil, divided
- ½ teaspoon fine sea salt, divided
- ½ teaspoon freshly ground black pepper, divided
- 6 cups torn Boston lettuce (about 2 small heads)
- 2 large hard-cooked eggs, each cut into 6 slices
- 2 tablespoons fresh lemon juice
- ¼ cup (1 ounce) shaved fresh pecorino Romano cheese

1 Preheat oven to 450°.

2 Place asparagus on a large jelly-roll pan. Drizzle with 1 tablespoon oil, and sprinkle with ¼ teaspoon salt and ¼ teaspoon pepper; toss well. Arrange asparagus in a single layer on pan. Bake at 450° for 8 minutes or until crisp-tender, tossing once. Cool slightly.

3 Arrange lettuce on a large platter. Top with asparagus and egg slices. Combine remaining 2 tablespoons oil, juice, remaining ¼ teaspoon salt, and remaining ¼ teaspoon pepper, stirring with a whisk. Drizzle over asparagus and lettuce. Top with cheese. Serve immediately. Yield: 6 servings (serving size: 1 cup lettuce, about 8 asparagus spears, 2 egg slices, 2 teaspoons dressing, and 2 teaspoons cheese).

CALORIES 150; FAT 10.3g (sat 2.4g, mono 5.7g, poly 1.4g); PROTEIN 7.6g; CARB 8.2g; FIBER 3.9g; CHOL 74mg; IRON 4.1mg; SODIUM 296mg; CALC 107mg

Pasta Dinner Menu
serves 6

Linguine with Arugula Pesto

Radish and pea salad with citrus vinaigrette

Place 3 cups sugar snap peas and 1 teaspoon salt in 2 quarts boiling water; cook 4 minutes or until crisp-tender. Drain; rinse with cold water. Drain. Combine peas, 1 cup thinly sliced radish, 2 tablespoons chopped fresh mint, 2 tablespoons chopped fresh flat-leaf parsley, ½ teaspoon salt, and ¼ teaspoon freshly ground black pepper; toss. Combine 2 tablespoons fresh lemon juice, ½ teaspoon orange rind, and ½ teaspoon Dijon mustard, stirring well with a whisk. Gradually add 3 tablespoons extra-virgin olive oil, stirring well until each addition is incorporated; toss with pea mixture.

Sauvignon blanc

Amaretti cookies and coffee

Linguine with Arugula Pesto

The chefs at Connecticut's Dinners at the Farm prefer to use Sylvetta arugula, a variety that is quite peppery; standard arugula will work fine in this recipe, too.

- 12 ounces uncooked linguine
- 1 tablespoon pine nuts, toasted
- 1 garlic clove, crushed
- 2 cups loosely packed arugula
- 2 cups loosely packed basil leaves
- 2 tablespoons extra-virgin olive oil
- 2 teaspoons fresh lemon juice
- ¾ teaspoon salt
- ¼ teaspoon black pepper
- 6 tablespoons grated fresh pecorino Romano cheese

1 Cook pasta according to package directions, omitting salt and fat. Drain in a colander over a bowl, reserving ½ cup cooking liquid. Place pasta in a large serving bowl.

2 Place nuts and garlic in a food processor; process until minced. Add arugula and next 5 ingredients, and process until well combined.

3 Add arugula mixture and reserved cooking liquid to pasta in serving bowl; toss well to coat. Serve with cheese. Yield: 6 servings (serving size: 1⅓ cups pasta and 1 tablespoon cheese).

CALORIES 291; FAT 8.3g (sat 2g, mono 4.2g, poly 1.7g); PROTEIN 10.2g; CARB 44g; FIBER 2.6g; CHOL 7mg; IRON 1.4mg; SODIUM 376mg; CALC 113mg

Bring the Farm Dinner Home

1. Host a U-pick potluck. Find local growers and suppliers at www.pickyourown.org and www.localharvest.org, and then invite friends to choose a nearby farm where they can find the raw ingredients and inspiration for a dish.

2. Source local ingredients. Farmers sell boxes of produce by subscription directly to buyers through Community Supported Agriculture programs (CSAs), supplying home cooks with all the makings for their own farm-to-table meals (learn more at www.localharvest.org/csa). You can also buy produce directly from producers at farmers' markets, and get cooking suggestions from the farmers who know those ingredients best.

3. Grow your guest list. Invite your favorite farmer, sausage maker, or cheese maker from your farmers' market to be a guest speaker. Extend the invitation to neighbors, fellow cooks, and local food groups while lifting your hosting load by following the tips at www.sustainabletable.org/getinvolved/buildcommunity/host.html.

Dinner Tonight

From down-home tastes to simple international classics, these 11 quick-fix meals will easily fit your busy schedule.

QUICK & EASY
Mediterranean Turkey Burgers

··*30 minutes*

Prepare a spicy and creamy tzatziki sauce to spread on the burgers or to serve on the side for dipping. Combine ½ cup plain low-fat, Greek-style yogurt; ¼ cup finely chopped seeded cucumber; ¼ teaspoon salt; and ⅛ teaspoon ground red pepper. Serve with sliced bell pepper and celery sticks.

- ½ cup panko (Japanese breadcrumbs)
- ¼ cup (1 ounce) crumbled feta cheese
- 1 tablespoon minced red onion
- 2 tablespoons commercial pesto
- ¼ teaspoon salt
- ¼ teaspoon freshly ground black pepper
- 1 pound ground turkey breast
- 1 garlic clove, minced
- Cooking spray
- 2 cups arugula
- 2 (6-inch) whole wheat pitas, toasted and halved

❶ Combine first 8 ingredients in a bowl; mix until combined. Divide panko mixture into 4 portions, shaping each into a ½-inch-thick oval patty.
❷ Heat a nonstick grill pan over medium-high heat. Coat pan with cooking spray. Add patties to pan; cook 6 minutes on each side or until done. Place 1 patty and ½ cup arugula in each pita half. Yield: 4 servings (serving size: 1 stuffed pita half).

CALORIES 303; FAT 8.8g (sat 2.9g, mono 4.1g, poly 0.8g); PROTEIN 33g; CARB 24.3g; FIBER 3g; CHOL 56mg; IRON 1.9mg; SODIUM 595mg; CALC 101mg

---

Choice Ingredient: Arugula

- **Learn:** This aromatic, leafy green (sometimes called rocket, roquette, or rucola) is a member of the same botanical family as watercress, cabbage, and broccoli. It's low in calories (a cup contains a mere five) and rich in lutein and vitamin A.
- **Taste:** Arugula's flavor is often likened to peppery mustard, making it somewhat stronger than most lettuces, so it's often mixed with other greens.
- **Purchase:** You'll find arugula as loose leaves in bins or bags. Sometimes it's bundled with stems attached. Either way, look for firm, fresh, uniformly green leaves without yellow or brown spots.
- **Store:** Arugula is highly perishable and will only last about two days after purchase. Store in the refrigerator, inside a perforated plastic bag or wrapped in moist paper towels. Rinse thoroughly and dry before using.
- **Use:** Most often used as a salad green, arugula boosts flavor and pairs well with vinaigrettes. It can also be wilted like spinach and served as a healthful side dish. You can even use arugula in place of basil to make a peppery pesto.

QUICK & EASY
Chicken, Cashew, and Red Pepper Stir-Fry

··*30 minutes*

This dish balances salty, sweet, tangy, and spicy ingredients. Spoon it alongside a quick rice pilaf. Cook 1 (10-ounce) package frozen white rice (such as Birds Eye SteamFresh) according to package directions. Combine cooked rice, 2 tablespoons drained chopped water chestnuts, ½ teaspoon crushed red pepper, ¼ teaspoon salt, and ¼ teaspoon freshly ground black pepper. If you have it, use bottled minced garlic to shave prep time.

- 3¾ teaspoons cornstarch, divided
- 2 tablespoons low-sodium soy sauce, divided
- 2 teaspoons dry sherry
- 1 teaspoon rice wine vinegar
- ¾ teaspoon sugar
- ½ teaspoon hot pepper sauce (such as Tabasco)
- 1 pound chicken breast tenders, cut lengthwise into thin strips
- ½ cup coarsely chopped unsalted cashews
- 2 tablespoons canola oil
- 2 cups julienne-cut red bell pepper (about 1 large)
- 1 teaspoon minced garlic
- ½ teaspoon minced peeled fresh ginger
- 3 tablespoons thinly sliced green onions

❶ Combine 1 teaspoon cornstarch, 1 tablespoon soy sauce, and next 4 ingredients in a small bowl; stir with a whisk.
❷ Combine remaining 2¾ teaspoons cornstarch, remaining 1 tablespoon soy sauce, and chicken in a medium bowl; toss well to coat.
❸ Heat a large nonstick skillet over medium-high heat. Add cashews to pan; cook 3 minutes or until lightly toasted, stirring frequently. Remove from pan.
❹ Add oil to pan, swirling to coat. Add chicken mixture to pan; sauté 2 minutes or until lightly browned. Remove chicken from pan; place in a bowl. Add bell pepper to pan; sauté 2 minutes. Add garlic and ginger; cook 30 seconds. Add chicken and cornstarch mixture to pan; cook 1 minute or until sauce is slightly thick. Sprinkle with cashews and green onions. Yield: 4 servings (serving size: 1 cup).

CALORIES 324; FAT 16.6g (sat 2.5g, mono 9.2g, poly 3.8g); PROTEIN 30g; CARB 13.5g; FIBER 2g; CHOL 66mg; IRON 2.4mg; SODIUM 350mg; CALC 33mg

Orange-Glazed Salmon Fillets with Rosemary

20 minutes

Serve with seasoned haricots verts. Cook 1 pound haricots verts in boiling water 3 minutes or until crisp-tender. Drain; rinse with cold water. Pat dry. Combine with ⅓ cup chopped roasted red bell pepper and ¼ cup toasted pine nuts. Combine 2 tablespoons red wine vinegar, ⅛ teaspoon salt, ⅛ teaspoon pepper, and ⅛ teaspoon dry mustard. Toss with bean mixture.

- 4 (6-ounce) salmon fillets (1 inch thick)
- ½ teaspoon kosher salt
- ¼ teaspoon freshly ground black pepper
- Cooking spray
- 2 tablespoons minced shallots
- ¼ cup dry white wine
- ½ teaspoon chopped fresh rosemary
- ¾ cup fresh orange juice (about 2 oranges)
- 1 tablespoon maple syrup

❶ Sprinkle fillets evenly with salt and pepper. Heat a large nonstick skillet over medium-high heat. Coat pan with cooking spray. Add fillets; cook 2 minutes on each side or until fish flakes easily when tested with a fork or until desired degree of doneness. Remove from pan.
❷ Recoat pan with cooking spray. Add shallots; sauté 30 seconds. Stir in wine and rosemary; cook 30 seconds or until liquid almost evaporates. Add juice and syrup; bring to a boil, and cook 1 minute. Return fillets to pan; cook 1 minute on each side or until thoroughly heated. Yield: 4 servings (serving size: 1 fillet and 1½ tablespoons sauce).

CALORIES 226; FAT 5.6g (sat 1.4g, mono 2g, poly 1.7g); PROTEIN 30.4g; CARB 9.5g; FIBER 0.2g; CHOL 70mg; IRON 1.1mg; SODIUM 311mg; CALC 70mg

Chipotle Sloppy Joes

20 minutes

Plate with a simple slaw. Combine ⅓ cup canola-based mayonnaise, 1½ teaspoons sugar, ½ teaspoon freshly ground black pepper, ¼ teaspoon salt, and ¼ teaspoon dry mustard in a large bowl; stir with a whisk. Add 3 cups packaged cabbage-and-carrot coleslaw, tossing well to combine.

- Cooking spray
- 2½ cups presliced Vidalia or other sweet onion
- 1 (7-ounce) can chipotle chiles in adobo sauce
- 1 pound ground sirloin
- ½ cup prechopped green bell pepper
- 2 tablespoons tomato paste
- 1 teaspoon kosher salt
- ½ teaspoon ground cumin
- 1 (8-ounce) can no-salt-added tomato sauce
- 5 (1½-ounce) hamburger buns, toasted

❶ Heat a small nonstick skillet over medium-high heat. Coat pan with cooking spray. Add onion; cover and cook 8 minutes or until golden brown, stirring frequently. Remove from heat; set aside.
❷ Remove 1 teaspoon adobo sauce from can; set aside. Remove 1 chipotle chile from can; chop and set aside. Reserve remaining chiles and adobo sauce for another use.
❸ Heat a large nonstick skillet over medium-high heat. Coat pan with cooking spray. Add beef to pan; cook 4 minutes or until browned, stirring to crumble. Add bell pepper; sauté 2 minutes. Stir in chopped chipotle chile, adobo sauce, tomato paste, and next 3 ingredients; cook 3 minutes, stirring occasionally. Spoon ½ cup beef mixture over bottom half of each bun; top evenly with onions and top half of bun. Yield: 5 servings (serving size: 1 sandwich).

CALORIES 273; FAT 6.1g (sat 2.1g, mono 2.1g, poly 1.3g); PROTEIN 23.3g; CARB 32.1g; FIBER 3.4g; CHOL 48mg; IRON 3.7mg; SODIUM 724mg; CALC 84mg

Soy-Citrus Scallops with Soba Noodles

20 minutes

Steamed peas with vinaigrette round out the plate. Steam 1 cup snow peas and 1 cup trimmed sugar snap peas, covered, 3 minutes or until crisp-tender. Combine with ⅓ cup thinly sliced radishes. Combine 1 tablespoon rice vinegar, 1 tablespoon soy sauce, 2 teaspoons canola oil, 1½ teaspoons mirin, ¼ teaspoon black pepper, and ⅛ teaspoon kosher salt; stir with a whisk. Pour over peas mixture; toss.

- 3 tablespoons low-sodium soy sauce
- 1 tablespoon fresh orange juice
- 1 tablespoon rice vinegar
- 1 tablespoon honey
- ½ teaspoon bottled ground fresh ginger
- ¼ teaspoon chili garlic sauce
- 1 tablespoon dark sesame oil, divided
- 1 pound large sea scallops
- 4 cups hot cooked soba (about 6 ounces uncooked buckwheat noodles)
- ⅛ teaspoon salt
- ¼ cup thinly sliced green onions

❶ Combine first 6 ingredients and 1 teaspoon oil in a shallow baking dish; add scallops to dish in a single layer. Marinate 4 minutes on each side.
❷ Heat remaining 2 teaspoons oil in a large skillet over medium-high heat. Remove scallops from dish, reserving marinade. Add scallops to pan; sauté 1 minute on each side or until almost done. Remove scallops from pan; keep warm. Place remaining marinade in pan; bring to a boil. Return scallops to pan; cook 1 minute. Toss noodles with salt and green onions. Place 1 cup noodle mixture on each of 4 plates. Top each serving with about 3 scallops; drizzle with 1 tablespoon sauce. Yield: 4 servings.

CALORIES 315; FAT 4.5g (sat 0.6g, mono 1.5g, poly 1.5g); PROTEIN 28g; CARB 42.7g; FIBER 1.9g; CHOL 37mg; IRON 1.3mg; SODIUM 653mg; CALC 41mg

Peppery Monterey Jack Pasta Salad

······································*20 minutes*

Acini di pepe [ah-CHEE-nee dee-PAY-pay] are tiny pasta rounds resembling peppercorns. Use ditalini (very short tube-shaped macaroni) or any other small pasta shape if you can't find acini di pepe in your supermarket. Serve with Asiago breadsticks. Combine ½ cup grated Asiago cheese, 1 tablespoon sesame seeds, and 1 teaspoon freshly ground black pepper in a small bowl. Separate 1 (7-ounce) can refrigerated breadstick dough to form 8 sticks; roll each breadstick in cheese mixture. Bake according to package directions. Freeze leftover baked breadsticks, completely cooled and tightly wrapped, for up to one month.

  6 ounces uncooked acini di pepe pasta (about 1 cup)
2¼ cups diced plum tomato (about 14 ounces)
  ⅓ cup capers, rinsed and drained
  ¼ cup finely chopped red onion
  ¼ cup sliced pickled banana peppers
  ¼ cup chopped fresh parsley
  2 tablespoons cider vinegar
  1 tablespoon extra-virgin olive oil
  ½ teaspoon dried oregano
  ⅛ teaspoon salt
  2 ounces Monterey Jack cheese, cut into ¼-inch cubes
  1 (16-ounce) can navy beans, rinsed and drained
  1 ounce salami, chopped
  1 garlic clove, minced

❶ Cook pasta according to package directions, omitting salt and fat. Drain.
❷ Combine tomato and remaining ingredients in a large bowl. Add pasta to tomato mixture, tossing well to combine. Yield: 4 servings (serving size: about 1½ cups).

CALORIES 371; FAT 11.6g (sat 4.7g, mono 5.3g, poly 1.4g); PROTEIN 16.6g; CARB 51.7g; FIBER 6.3g; CHOL 21mg; IRON 3.5mg; SODIUM 919mg; CALC 164mg

Hoisin Flank Steak with Asian Cucumber Salad

······································*30 minutes*

Spiced wonton chips that bake while the steak rests are an easy accompaniment. Thaw 8 wonton wrappers, if frozen. Cut wrappers in half diagonally; brush tops of wrappers evenly with 2 teaspoons dark sesame oil. Combine ¼ teaspoon Chinese five-spice powder and ⅛ teaspoon salt in a small bowl. Sprinkle wrappers evenly with five-spice powder mixture. Bake at 450° for 3 minutes or just until crisp.

  3 tablespoons hoisin sauce
  1 teaspoon bottled ground fresh ginger
  ½ teaspoon grated orange rind
  1 (1-pound) flank steak, trimmed
Cooking spray
  2 cups thinly sliced seeded peeled cucumber
  ¼ cup thinly vertically sliced red onion
  ¼ cup matchstick-cut carrot
  1 tablespoon sugar
  1 tablespoon chopped fresh cilantro
  2 tablespoons fresh lime juice
  2 teaspoons fish sauce
  ⅛ teaspoon salt

❶ Preheat broiler.
❷ Combine first 3 ingredients in a small bowl. Brush steak with half of hoisin mixture. Place steak on a broiler pan coated with cooking spray. Broil 6 minutes. Turn steak over, and brush with remaining hoisin mixture. Broil 6 minutes or until desired degree of doneness. Place steak on a cutting board; let stand 5 minutes.
❸ Combine cucumber and remaining ingredients in a bowl; toss to combine. Cut steak diagonally across grain into thin slices. Serve with cucumber salad. Yield: 4 servings (serving size: 3 ounces steak and ½ cup salad).

CALORIES 213; FAT 7.7g (sat 2.9g, mono 2.8g, poly 0.3g); PROTEIN 24.6g; CARB 11.5g; FIBER 0.7g; CHOL 38mg; IRON 1.7mg; SODIUM 501mg; CALC 30mg

Southwest Shrimp and Corn Chowder

······································*30 minutes*

Quesadillas are an easy side. Heat a large nonstick skillet over medium-high heat. Coat pan with cooking spray. Place 2 (6-inch) flour tortillas in pan. Top each tortilla with 2½ tablespoons preshredded reduced-fat Mexican blend cheese, 1½ tablespoons chopped green onions, and 1 tablespoon chopped pickled jalapeño peppers. Cook 1 minute or just until cheese melts and tortilla is toasted. Top each with 1 tortilla. Flip quesadillas; cook 30 seconds. Cut each quesadilla into 6 wedges, and serve with a small bowl of salsa.

  2 tablespoons butter
  1 cup chopped green onions
  ½ cup chopped red bell pepper
  2 tablespoons finely chopped serrano chile (about 1 small)
  1 (4.5-ounce) can chopped green chiles, undrained
  3 tablespoons all-purpose flour
1½ cups 2% reduced-fat milk
1½ cups fat-free, less-sodium chicken broth
1½ cups frozen Southern-style hash brown potatoes, diced and thawed
  ½ teaspoon salt
  ½ teaspoon ground cumin
  1 (15.25-ounce) can whole-kernel corn with red and green peppers, drained
  1 pound peeled and deveined small shrimp
  2 tablespoons chopped fresh cilantro

❶ Melt butter in a large Dutch oven over medium-high heat. Add onions, bell pepper, and serrano chile to pan; sauté 2 minutes or until tender. Add canned chiles to pan; cook 1 minute. Add flour to pan; cook 1 minute, stirring constantly. Stir in milk and next 5 ingredients; bring to a boil. Cook 5 minutes or until slightly thick. Stir in shrimp; cook 1 minute or until shrimp are done. Remove from heat; stir in cilantro. Yield: 6 servings (serving size: about 1 cup).

CALORIES 212; FAT 6.7g (sat 3.4g, mono 1.5g, poly 0.7g); PROTEIN 19.3g; CARB 18.3g; FIBER 2.2g; CHOL 130mg; IRON 2.5mg; SODIUM 702mg; CALC 131mg

QUICK & EASY

Roasted Pork Tenderloin with Orange and Red Onion Salsa

· ·*40 minutes*

For a hearty side, cook 1 (10-ounce) package frozen long-grain brown rice according to package directions. Combine cooked rice, 1 cup rinsed and drained canned black beans, 1 tablespoon chopped fresh cilantro, ¼ teaspoon salt, ¼ teaspoon ground cumin, and ⅛ teaspoon chili powder.

  1 tablespoon canola oil
  1 (1-pound) pork tenderloin, trimmed
  ½ teaspoon salt, divided
  ½ teaspoon black pepper, divided
  1 cup coarsely chopped orange sections (about 2 oranges)
  ½ cup diced red onion
  ¼ cup chopped fresh cilantro
  2 tablespoons fresh lime juice
  2 teaspoons minced seeded jalapeño pepper
  1 teaspoon minced garlic

❶ Preheat oven to 450°.
❷ Heat oil in a large ovenproof skillet over medium-high heat. Sprinkle pork evenly with ¼ teaspoon salt and ¼ teaspoon black pepper. Add pork to pan; cook 2 minutes on each side or until lightly browned. Transfer pan to oven. Bake at 450° for 17 minutes or until a thermometer registers 160°. Let stand 5 minutes; cut across grain into ½-inch-thick slices.
❸ Combine remaining ¼ teaspoon salt, remaining ¼ teaspoon black pepper, oranges, and remaining ingredients. Serve salsa with pork. Yield: 4 servings (serving size: 3 ounces pork and about ¼ cup salsa).

CALORIES 220; FAT 8.5g (sat 2g, mono 4.1g, poly 1.5g); PROTEIN 23.6g; CARB 13.6g; FIBER 4g; CHOL 65mg; IRON 1.5mg; SODIUM 342mg; CALC 44mg

QUICK & EASY

Herbed Stuffed Chicken Breasts

· ·*40 minutes*

Prepare roasted asparagus as a bright partner for this dish. Combine ¼ teaspoon salt, ¼ teaspoon freshly ground black pepper, and 1 pound trimmed asparagus on a jelly-roll pan coated with cooking spray; toss gently. Bake at 400° for 10 minutes or until asparagus is crisp-tender. Place asparagus in a large bowl; toss with 1 tablespoon butter and 1 tablespoon chopped fresh chives. Complete the meal with a sliced baguette and a glass of white wine.

  ¼ cup (2 ounces) goat cheese
  ½ teaspoon chopped fresh rosemary
  2 ounces Canadian bacon, finely chopped
  4 (6-ounce) skinless, boneless chicken breasts
  ¼ teaspoon salt
  ¼ teaspoon freshly ground black pepper
    Cooking spray

❶ Preheat oven to 400°.
❷ Combine first 3 ingredients in a small bowl. Cut a horizontal slit through thickest portion of each chicken breast half to form a pocket. Stuff about 3 tablespoons cheese mixture into each pocket; close opening with a wooden pick. Sprinkle chicken evenly with salt and pepper.
❸ Heat a large cast-iron skillet over medium-high heat. Coat pan with cooking spray. Add chicken to pan; cook 4 minutes. Turn chicken over; place pan in oven. Bake at 400° for 25 minutes or until chicken is done. Let stand 5 minutes. Discard wooden picks. Cut chicken diagonally into ½-inch-thick slices. Serve with pan juices. Yield: 4 servings (serving size: 1 chicken breast half and about 1 tablespoon pan juices).

CALORIES 302; FAT 13.5g (sat 5.1g, mono 4.8g, poly 2.2g); PROTEIN 42.1g; CARB 0.5g; FIBER 0g; CHOL 116mg; IRON 1.7mg; SODIUM 486mg; CALC 40mg

QUICK & EASY

Baked Shrimp with Feta

· ·*40 minutes*

(pictured on page 214)

Orzo accented with fresh herbs completes this meal. Cook 1 cup orzo pasta according to package directions, omitting salt and fat. Drain; toss orzo with ¼ cup chopped fresh basil, 2 tablespoons chopped fresh parsley, 1 tablespoon extra-virgin olive oil, ½ teaspoon salt, and ¼ teaspoon freshly ground black pepper.

  1 tablespoon fresh lemon juice
  1½ pounds large shrimp, peeled and deveined
    Cooking spray
  1 teaspoon olive oil
  ½ cup prechopped onion
  1 garlic clove, minced
  2 tablespoons bottled clam juice
  1 tablespoon white wine
  ½ teaspoon dried oregano
  ¼ teaspoon black pepper
  1 (14.5-ounce) can diced tomatoes, drained
  ½ cup (2 ounces) crumbled feta cheese
  2 tablespoons chopped fresh flat-leaf parsley

❶ Preheat oven to 450°.
❷ Combine lemon juice and shrimp in a large bowl; toss well. Heat a large nonstick skillet over medium-high heat. Coat pan with cooking spray. Add oil to pan, swirling to coat. Add onion to pan; sauté 1 minute. Add garlic; sauté 1 minute. Add clam juice and next 4 ingredients; bring to a boil. Reduce heat, and simmer 5 minutes. Stir in shrimp mixture. Place mixture in an 11 x 7-inch baking dish coated with cooking spray. Sprinkle cheese evenly over mixture. Bake at 450° for 12 minutes or until shrimp are done and cheese melts. Sprinkle with parsley; serve immediately. Yield: 4 servings (serving size: 1 cup).

CALORIES 253; FAT 7.1g (sat 2.8g, mono 1.9g, poly 1.4g); PROTEIN 37.5g; CARB 8.1g; FIBER 1.6g; CHOL 271mg; IRON 4.7mg; SODIUM 516mg; CALC 182mg

Butterscotch Bars

Sweet success: "I like this healthier version of my favorite Butterscotch Bars."

Carol Bischoff, a retired college administrator from Deer Isle, Maine, has always had a sweet tooth. She says these rich butterscotch bars, with a buttery crust and gooey-nutty center, are irresistible. When family visits, they look forward to the box of the bars Bischoff leaves in the guest rooms. But she and her husband now have goals to stay fit and eat more healthfully, and after trying the recipe using heart-healthy canola oil in place of some of the butter, she wasn't happy with the results. So Bischoff sent the recipe to *Cooking Light* for a nutritional makeover.

Plenty of butter, butterscotch chips, sweetened condensed milk, and walnuts contributed to the hefty 223 calories per serving for this bar cookie. One sweet bar had 5 grams of saturated fat per serving, about one-third the daily allotment per American Heart Association diet recommendations.

We started with the middle layer, which needed the most work. First, we swapped fat-free sweetened condensed milk for the regular version to maintain sweetness and richness with fewer calories. Then we reduced the amount of butterscotch chips by a third and omitted 2 tablespoons butter in this part of the recipe without compromising flavor or texture. These three changes trimmed 42 calories and 2½ grams of fat (nearly 2 grams saturated) per serving. We also slightly tweaked the base layer, which serves double-duty as the crumb topping. Eliminating 3 tablespoons of butter and ½ cup brown sugar shaved 20 calories and 1 gram of fat per bar. Lastly, we used fewer walnuts (which are heart-healthy) and finely chopped and toasted them to extend their flavor and crunch. This cut another 10 calories and about 1 gram of fat.

serving size: 1 bar		
	before	after
CALORIES PER SERVING	223	148
TOTAL FAT	18.2g	5.1g
SATURATED FAT	5.4g	2.7g

STAFF FAVORITE • MAKE AHEAD
Butterscotch Bars
(pictured on page 220)

A small square of these rich bars is enough to satisfy a dessert craving. The flour and oats mixture is somewhat dry after combining, but it serves as both a solid base for the soft butterscotch chip layer and a crumbly, streusel-like topping.

- 1 cup packed brown sugar
- 5 tablespoons butter, melted
- 1 teaspoon vanilla extract
- 1 large egg, lightly beaten
- 9 ounces all-purpose flour (about 2 cups)
- 2½ cups quick-cooking oats
- ½ teaspoon salt
- ½ teaspoon baking soda
- Cooking spray
- ¾ cup fat-free sweetened condensed milk
- 1¼ cups butterscotch morsels (about 8 ounces)
- ⅛ teaspoon salt
- ½ cup finely chopped walnuts, toasted

1 Preheat oven to 350°.

2 Combine sugar and butter in a large bowl. Stir in vanilla and egg. Weigh or lightly spoon flour into dry measuring cups; level with a knife. Combine flour and next 3 ingredients in a bowl. Add oat mixture to sugar mixture; stir with a fork until combined (mixture will be crumbly). Place 3 cups oat mixture into bottom of a 13 x 9-inch baking pan coated with cooking spray; press into bottom of pan. Set aside.

3 Place sweetened condensed milk, butterscotch morsels, and ⅛ teaspoon salt in a microwave-safe bowl; microwave at HIGH 1 minute or until butterscotch morsels melt, stirring every 20 seconds. Stir in walnuts. Scrape mixture into pan, spreading evenly over crust. Sprinkle evenly with remaining oat mixture, gently pressing into butterscotch mixture. Bake at 350° for 30 minutes or until topping is golden brown. Place pan on a cooling rack; run a knife around outside edge. Cool completely. Yield: 36 servings (serving size: 1 bar).

CALORIES 148; FAT 5.1g (sat 2.7g, mono 0.9g, poly 1.1g); PROTEIN 2.6g; CARB 23.4g; FIBER 0.8g; CHOL 11mg; IRON 0.8mg; SODIUM 87mg; CALC 31mg

"There were many excellent changes, and I like this healthier version of my longtime dessert favorite."

—Carol Bischoff
Deer Isle, Maine

Recipe Contest Finalists

Here are more finalist entries from the 2008 annual *Cooking Light* Ultimate Reader Recipe Contest.

In this chapter we complete our series featuring the finalists and their recipes from four categories: starters and drinks, family dinners, side salads and side dishes, and desserts. You'll also learn tips and suggestions from the contestants for re-creating their dishes.

MAKE AHEAD

Black-Eyed Pea Salad

Category Finalist—Sides and Salads
"Organic tomatoes bring the best flavor to this vegetarian dish. I pick them straight from my garden, but you can substitute canned diced tomatoes."

—Judy Holder, Elk City, Oklahoma

½   teaspoon fine sea salt
1   garlic clove, minced
¼   cup rice wine vinegar
2   tablespoons roasted garlic extra-virgin olive oil (such as Consorzio)
1   teaspoon ground cumin
3   cups chopped peeled tomato (about 2 large)
½   cup finely chopped onion
2   tablespoons chopped fresh cilantro
1   (15-ounce) can black-eyed peas, rinsed and drained
1   jalapeño pepper, seeded and minced
1   (6-ounce) bag baked pita chips

❶ Combine salt and garlic in a medium bowl; mash with a fork until a paste consistency. Add vinegar, oil, and cumin, stirring with a whisk. Add tomato and next 4 ingredients; toss well. Serve with pita chips. Yield: 6 servings (serving size: about ³/₄ cup salad and 1 ounce chips).

CALORIES 228; FAT 10.1g (sat 1.2g, mono 6.4g, poly 2g); PROTEIN 5.5g; CARB 30.6g; FIBER 4.6g; CHOL 0mg; IRON 2mg; SODIUM 573mg; CALC 12mg

Italian Tomato Tart

Category Finalist—Starters and Drinks
"The beauty of this dish is you can make it year-round; however, it's great in the spring and summer, when fresh basil is plentiful. I use kitchen shears to chop the fresh basil."

—Sherry Ricci, Mendon, New York

CRUST:

1   (10-ounce) package frozen long-grain brown rice (such as Birds Eye SteamFresh)
2   tablespoons commercial pesto
1   tablespoon grated fresh Parmesan cheese
1   large egg
Cooking spray

FILLING:

½   cup fat-free milk
½   cup egg substitute
¼   teaspoon salt
⅛   teaspoon freshly ground black pepper
Dash of ground red pepper
1   large egg
¾   cup (3 ounces) shredded part-skim mozzarella cheese
1   ounce prosciutto, cut into thin strips (about ¼ cup)
3   small plum tomatoes, thinly sliced
1   tablespoon chopped fresh basil

❶ Preheat oven to 350°.
❷ To prepare crust, cook rice according to package directions. Combine cooked rice, pesto, Parmesan cheese, and 1 egg; firmly press mixture into bottom and up sides of a 9-inch pie plate coated with cooking spray. Bake at 350° for 15 minutes. Remove dish from oven.
❸ Increase oven temperature to 400°.
❹ To prepare filling, combine milk and next 5 ingredients in a bowl; stir with a whisk.
❺ Sprinkle half of mozzarella and half of prosciutto into bottom of prepared crust. Top with half of tomato slices. Repeat procedure with remaining mozzarella, prosciutto, and tomatoes. Pour milk mixture over tomatoes; bake at 400° for 10 minutes. Reduce oven temperature to 325° (do not remove tart from oven); bake an additional 35 minutes or until set. Cool 10 minutes before serving. Sprinkle with basil. Cut into wedges. Yield: 4 servings (serving size: 1 wedge).

CALORIES 279; FAT 13.9g (sat 4.8g, mono 4.8g, poly 1.4g); PROTEIN 18.5g; CARB 19.3g; FIBER 1.8g; CHOL 127mg; IRON 2mg; SODIUM 542mg; CALC 289mg

MAKE AHEAD • FREEZABLE

Garden Harvest Cake

Category Finalist—Desserts
"Zucchini, carrot, and apples add moisture and flavor, eliminating the need for excess butter and oil. This simple cake only takes about 10 minutes to prepare the batter."

—Jennifer Dunklee, Medford, Massachusetts

4.5   ounces all-purpose flour (about 1 cup)
¾   cup sugar
2   teaspoons ground cinnamon
1   teaspoon baking soda
¼   teaspoon salt
½   cup grated peeled Granny Smith apple (about 1 medium)
½   cup grated carrot (about 1 medium)
½   cup shredded zucchini
¼   cup chopped walnuts, toasted
¼   cup canola oil
¼   cup nonfat buttermilk
2   large eggs
Cooking spray

❶ Preheat oven to 350°.
❷ Weigh or lightly spoon flour into a dry measuring cup; level with a knife. Combine flour and next 4 ingredients in a large bowl, stirring with a whisk. Add apple and next 3 ingredients to flour mixture; toss well. Combine oil, buttermilk, and eggs in a small bowl, stirring with a whisk. Add egg mixture to flour mixture, stirring just until combined. Spoon batter into an 8 x 4-inch loaf pan coated with cooking spray. Bake at 350° for 50 minutes
Continued

or until a wooden pick inserted in center comes out clean. Cool 10 minutes in pan on a wire rack; remove cake from pan. Cool completely on wire rack before slicing. Yield: 9 servings (serving size: 1 slice).

CALORIES 223; FAT 9.7g (sat 1g, mono 4.4g, poly 3.6g); PROTEIN 3.8g; CARB 31.4g; FIBER 1.3g; CHOL 47mg; IRON 1.2mg; SODIUM 233mg; CALC 30mg

FREEZABLE
Sausage-Stuffed Manicotti

Category Finalist—Family Dinners
"I developed this recipe many years ago. Since then, I've lightened it with turkey sausage, and I use smaller amounts of flavorful cheeses, where a little goes a long way. This dish requires some time, but it's well worth the effort."

—Beverly O'Ferrall, Linkwood, Maryland

- 10 uncooked manicotti
  Cooking spray
- 1 pound sweet turkey Italian sausage
- 1½ cups chopped onion
- 1 cup chopped green bell pepper
- 2 tablespoons butter
- 2 tablespoons all-purpose flour
- 2 cups fat-free milk
- ⅛ teaspoon black pepper
- 1½ cups (6 ounces) shredded part-skim mozzarella cheese
- 2 cups tomato-basil pasta sauce (such as Newman's Own)
- ¼ cup (1 ounce) grated fresh Parmesan cheese

❶ Cook pasta according to package directions, omitting salt and fat.
❷ Heat a large nonstick skillet over medium-high heat. Coat pan with cooking spray. Remove casings from sausage. Add sausage to pan; cook 5 minutes or until browned, stirring to crumble. Add onion and bell pepper to pan; sauté 5 minutes or until tender.
❸ Melt butter in a medium saucepan over medium heat. Stir in flour; cook 2 minutes, stirring constantly with a whisk. Remove from heat; gradually add milk, stirring with a whisk. Return pan to heat; bring to a boil. Cook 6 minutes or until thickened, stirring constantly with a whisk. Remove from heat; stir in black pepper. Add ½ cup milk mixture to sausage mixture; stir well.
❹ Preheat oven to 350°.
❺ Spoon about ⅓ cup sausage mixture into each manicotti; arrange manicotti in a single layer in a 13 x 9-inch baking dish coated with cooking spray. Sprinkle mozzarella over manicotti; spread remaining milk mixture evenly over mozzarella. Top milk mixture with pasta sauce, spreading to cover. Sprinkle with Parmesan. Bake at 350° for 35 minutes or until bubbly. Yield: 10 servings (serving size: 1 stuffed manicotti).

CALORIES 292; FAT 11.5g (sat 4.9g, mono 3.5g, poly 1.8g); PROTEIN 19.6g; CARB 25.8g; FIBER 1.4g; CHOL 57mg; IRON 1.8mg; SODIUM 719mg; CALC 193mg

TEST KITCHENS SECRETS
Herbed Passover Rolls

How to make Passover rolls as light as air.

This recipe was created by *Cooking Light* Test Kitchens Professional Deb Wise with Passover in mind. Yet the rolls' savory flavor would be welcome at any dinner, any time of year. Because Jewish dietary restrictions forbid chemical leavening compounds, like baking powder or soda, at a Passover meal, Wise devised this recipe using the classic French technique for *pâte à choux* (literally, "short paste," which is the foundation for cream puffs and éclairs). A liquid mixture is heated on the stovetop, and flour (or, in this case, matzo meal) is stirred in until the dough becomes smooth and pulls away from the sides of the saucepan. Then eggs, which help the dough rise, are added one at a time with the help of a mixer. The result is light-as-can-be rolls with a nice exterior crunch and pillowy interior.

STAFF FAVORITE • MAKE AHEAD FREEZABLE
Herbed Passover Rolls

(pictured on page 214)

To make ahead, cool rolls completely and freeze for up to one month. Use leftover matzo meal as a binder for meatballs or meat loaf, or to bread chicken or fish for pan-frying.

- 1¼ cups water
- ⅓ cup canola oil
- 1 tablespoon sugar
- 1 teaspoon kosher salt
- 2 cups matzo meal
- 4 large eggs
- 1 tablespoon chopped fresh chives
- 2 teaspoons finely chopped fresh thyme

❶ Preheat oven to 375°.
❷ Cover a large, heavy baking sheet with parchment paper.
❸ Combine first 4 ingredients in a medium saucepan over medium-high heat; bring to a boil. Reduce heat to low; add matzo meal, stirring well with a wooden spoon until mixture pulls away from sides of pan (about 30 seconds). Remove from heat; place dough in bowl of a stand mixer. Cool slightly. Add eggs, 1 at a time, beating at low speed with paddle attachment until well combined and scraping sides and bottom of bowl after each egg. Stir in chives and thyme.
❹ With moistened fingers, shape about ¼ cupfuls of dough into 12 mounds and place 2 inches apart onto prepared pan. Bake at 375° for 55 minutes or until browned and crisp. Cool on a wire rack. Yield: 12 servings (serving size: 1 roll).

CALORIES 134; FAT 8g (sat 1g, mono 4.3g, poly 2.1g); PROTEIN 3.8g; CARB 12.5g; FIBER 0.6g; CHOL 71mg; IRON 1mg; SODIUM 181mg; CALC 13mg

The Sweet Taste of May

Because the time is ripe at berry patches all around the country, just-picked strawberries star in seven irresistible recipes.

KIDS LIKE TWO-YEAR-OLD TEAGAN EISENRING are a familiar sight at Berry Patch Farms in Brighton, Colorado. She gawks in amazement at the rows of ripe, juicy organic strawberries on her first trip to the farm. Teagan stoops to pluck her first berry from a row of plants in the pick-it-yourself strawberry patch, then pauses to take a bite. Her eyes grow wide, her brow furrows in concentration, and bright red juice dribbles down her chin. She plucks another, then another.

This wholehearted sampling of the merchandise is fine with farm owners Tim and Claudia Ferrell. In fact, they encourage customers to taste before they pick. Although strawberries are common to other parts of the country, the Ferrells think theirs are made sweeter by the cool Colorado temperatures and the farm's rich soil. They claim that once you taste a fresh ripe berry from their 40-acre farm, you'll keep coming back year after year.

Because the Ferrells farm organically, it's labor intensive, but they say they wouldn't have it any other way. Over the 10 years the Ferrells have worked this farm, their business has grown. The six acres dedicated to strawberries are a draw for loyal customers, but they also grow and sell you-pick flowers and other crops on the remaining acreage. Satisfied customers return each year to sample the candy onions, Swiss chard, kale, and lettuces, as well as the sweet strawberries.

Consequently, kids such as Teagan can be part of a working farm for a day. The Ferrells feel it's good for little ones to see first-hand how things grow and that food doesn't just materialize in grocery stores. "This farm isn't just for Tim and me," Claudia says. "It's ours to share."

MAKE AHEAD
Strawberry Cordial Jam

Keep this refrigerated for up to one month.

- 6 cups chopped strawberries (about 1½ pounds)
- 1 cup sugar
- 3 tablespoons crème de cassis (black currant–flavored liqueur)
- 1 tablespoon water
- ⅛ teaspoon ground cinnamon
- ⅛ teaspoon ground cardamom

❶ Combine all ingredients in a medium saucepan over medium-high heat; bring to a boil. Reduce heat, and simmer until reduced to 2 cups (about 1 hour and 10 minutes), stirring occasionally. Cool completely; cover and chill 8 hours. Yield: 16 servings (serving size: 2 tablespoons).

CALORIES 73; FAT 0.2g (sat 0g, mono 0g, poly 0.1g); PROTEIN 0.3g; CARB 16.8g; FIBER 0.2g; CHOL 0mg; IRON 0.2mg; SODIUM 1mg; CALC 6mg

QUICK & EASY
Strawberry, Pistachio, and Goat Cheese Pizza

This dish is a refreshing departure from traditional pizza. Substitute your favorite soft cheese or greens.

- 1 (12-ounce) prebaked pizza crust (such as Mama Mary's)
- ⅓ cup (3 ounces) crumbled goat cheese
- 1 cup sliced strawberries
- 1 cup trimmed watercress
- ½ teaspoon extra-virgin olive oil
- ½ teaspoon fresh lemon juice
- Dash of salt
- Dash of freshly ground black pepper
- ¼ cup (1 ounce) shaved fresh Parmigiano-Reggiano cheese
- 3 tablespoons shelled dry-roasted pistachios, chopped

❶ Preheat oven to 425°.
❷ Place crust on a baking sheet. Bake at 425° for 8 minutes. Remove from oven; arrange goat cheese evenly over crust.
❸ Combine strawberries and next 5 ingredients; toss gently to coat. Arrange strawberry mixture evenly over goat cheese. Sprinkle pizza with Parmigiano-Reggiano and nuts. Cut into 12 wedges. Serve immediately. Yield: 6 servings (serving size: 2 wedges).

CALORIES 273; FAT 12.4g (sat 4g, mono 3.3g, poly 4.1g); PROTEIN 10.7g; CARB 30.9g; FIBER 1.9g; CHOL 10mg; IRON 2.5mg; SODIUM 348mg; CALC 154mg

Strawberry Layer Cake

You can use fresh orange juice instead of Grand Marnier in the frosting.

CAKE:

- 1¼ cups sliced ripe strawberries
- 10 ounces all-purpose flour (about 2¼ cups)
- 2¼ teaspoons baking powder
- ¼ teaspoon salt
- 1½ cups granulated sugar
- ½ cup butter, softened
- 2 large eggs
- 2 large egg whites
- ¾ cup low-fat buttermilk
- ¼ teaspoon red food coloring
- Cooking spray

FROSTING:

- ⅓ cup (3 ounces) ⅓-less-fat cream cheese
- ⅓ cup butter, softened
- 2 tablespoons Grand Marnier (orange-flavored liqueur)
- 3 cups powdered sugar
- 12 whole strawberries (optional)

❶ Preheat oven to 350°.

❷ To prepare cake, place strawberries in a food processor; process until smooth.

❸ Weigh or lightly spoon flour into dry measuring cups; level with a knife. Combine flour, baking powder, and salt, stirring with a whisk. Place granulated sugar and ½ cup butter in a large bowl; beat with a mixer at medium speed until well blended. Add eggs, one at a time, beating well after each addition. Beat in egg whites. Add flour mixture and buttermilk alternately to sugar mixture, beginning and ending with flour mixture. Add pureed strawberries and food coloring; beat just until blended.

❹ Divide batter between 2 (8-inch) round cake pans coated with cooking spray. Bake at 350° for 30 minutes or until a wooden pick inserted in center comes out clean. Cool in pans on a wire rack for 10 minutes. Remove from pans; cool completely on wire racks.

❺ To prepare frosting, place cream cheese, ⅓ cup butter, and liqueur in a medium bowl; beat with a mixer at medium speed until blended. Gradually add powdered sugar, and beat just until blended.

❻ Place 1 cake layer on a plate; spread with ½ cup frosting. Top with remaining cake layer. Spread remaining frosting over top and sides of cake. Cut 1 whole strawberry into thin slices, cutting to, but not through, the stem end. Fan strawberry on top of cake just before serving, if desired. Cut remaining 11 strawberries in half. Garnish cake with strawberry halves, if desired. Yield: 16 servings (serving size: 1 slice).

CALORIES 346; FAT 11.3g (sat 6.9g, mono 2.8g, poly 0.6g); PROTEIN 4.2g; CARB 57.5g; FIBER 0.7g; CHOL 55mg; IRON 1.1mg; SODIUM 226mg; CALC 70mg

Gorgonzola-Stuffed Chicken Breasts with Strawberry Gastrique

Gastrique is the French term for a thick, syrupy reduction sauce made from sugar, vinegar, and, often, fruit. Chicken broth balances its sweet-tart flavor. We loved the pungent Gorgonzola cheese here, but you might substitute your favorite blue cheese.

SAUCE:

- 1 cup chopped strawberries
- ½ cup sugar
- ½ cup sherry vinegar
- ⅓ cup fat-free, less-sodium chicken broth
- ¼ teaspoon ground coriander

CHICKEN:

- ¼ cup (1 ounce) crumbled Gorgonzola cheese
- 2 teaspoons fresh thyme leaves
- 2 ounces prosciutto, chopped
- 4 (6-ounce) skinless, boneless chicken breast halves
- Cooking spray
- ⅛ teaspoon salt
- ⅛ teaspoon freshly ground black pepper

❶ To prepare sauce, place strawberries in a small, heavy saucepan; partially mash with a fork. Stir in sugar and next 3 ingredients; bring to a boil. Reduce heat, and simmer until reduced to ⅔ cup (about 30 minutes), stirring occasionally. Strain mixture through a sieve over a bowl; discard solids.

❷ To prepare chicken, combine cheese, thyme, and prosciutto in a bowl. Cut a horizontal slit through thickest portion of each chicken breast half to form a pocket; spoon 3 tablespoons cheese mixture into each pocket.

❸ Heat a large nonstick skillet over medium heat. Coat pan with cooking spray. Sprinkle both sides of chicken evenly with salt and pepper. Add chicken to pan; cook 5 minutes or until browned. Turn chicken over; cook 4 minutes or until done. Serve with sauce. Yield: 4 servings (serving size: 1 chicken breast half and about 2 tablespoons sauce).

CALORIES 340; FAT 10.6g (sat 4g, mono 3.4g, poly 1.8g); PROTEIN 32.5g; CARB 27.9g; FIBER 1g; CHOL 92mg; IRON 1.4mg; SODIUM 479mg; CALC 60mg

WINE NOTE: If you haven't tasted Soave in awhile, it's time to get reacquainted with this northern Italian white. Quality examples like Inama Vin Soave 2006 ($15) have the body to handle fish or white meats, like this dish. Soave's generous acidity can match the vinegary gastrique, while the herbal and citrus nuances lift the coriander.

Berry-Lemon Shortcakes

- 4 cups sliced strawberries
- ¼ cup plus 2 teaspoons powdered sugar, divided
- 1½ teaspoons fresh lemon juice
- 5½ ounces all-purpose flour (about 1¼ cups)
- ⅓ cup granulated sugar
- 1 tablespoon poppy seeds
- 1 teaspoon baking powder
- ¼ teaspoon baking soda
- ⅛ teaspoon salt
- 2 tablespoons chilled butter, cut into small pieces
- ½ cup fat-free buttermilk
- 1 teaspoon turbinado sugar
- Cooking spray
- ¼ cup whipping cream

① Place strawberries, ¼ cup powdered sugar, and juice in a small bowl; toss.
② Preheat oven to 425°.
③ Weigh or lightly spoon flour into dry measuring cups; level with a knife. Combine flour and next 5 ingredients in a large bowl, stirring well with a whisk. Cut in butter with a pastry blender or two knives until mixture resembles coarse meal. Add buttermilk, stirring just until moist.
④ Turn dough out onto a lightly floured surface; knead one or two times until well blended. Pat dough into a 6 x 4-inch rectangle. Cut dough into 6 (2-inch) squares; sprinkle evenly with turbinado sugar. Place squares 1 inch apart on a baking sheet coated with cooking spray. Bake at 425° for 13 minutes; cool on rack.
⑤ Place whipping cream in a bowl; beat with a mixer at high speed until soft peaks form. Add remaining 2 teaspoons powdered sugar. Continue beating until stiff peaks form. Split shortcakes in half crosswise. Place 1 bottom half of cake on each of 6 plates; top each serving with ½ cup strawberry mixture. Spoon 1½ tablespoons whipped cream over each serving. Place 1 top half of cake over each serving. Yield: 6 servings.

CALORIES 281; FAT 8.7g (sat 4.8g, mono 2.2g, poly 1g); PROTEIN 4.7g; CARB 47.9g; FIBER 3.1g; CHOL 24mg; IRON 1.9mg; SODIUM 236mg; CALC 120mg

QUICK & EASY
Strawberry-Avocado Salsa

Serve this sweet and savory salsa with roast chicken, sautéed fish, or grilled pork tenderloin. You can also enjoy it as a snack with baked tortilla chips.

- 1 cup finely chopped strawberries
- ¼ cup finely chopped peeled avocado
- 2 tablespoons finely chopped red onion
- 2 tablespoons chopped fresh cilantro
- ½ teaspoon grated lime rind
- 2 tablespoons fresh lime juice
- 2 teaspoons finely chopped seeded jalapeño pepper
- ¼ teaspoon sugar

① Combine all ingredients in a medium bowl; toss gently. Serve immediately. Yield: 4 servings (serving size: ¼ cup).

CALORIES 34; FAT 1.6g (sat 0.2g, mono 0.9g, poly 0.3g); PROTEIN 0.6g; CARB 5.4g; FIBER 1.5g; CHOL 0mg; IRON 0.3mg; SODIUM 2mg; CALC 11mg

Strawberry Bellini

The original version of this cocktail hails from Harry's Bar in Venice. Our rendition substitutes strawberries for the traditional peaches. You can prepare the strawberry base up to one day ahead. Make sure to give it another spin in the blender just before mixing the cocktails.

- 6 cups sliced strawberries
- ¼ cup powdered sugar
- 2 tablespoons brandy
- 3 cups prosecco or other sparkling wine
- 6 large strawberries

① Place first 3 ingredients in a blender. Let stand 10 minutes. Process until smooth; chill.
② Place ¼ cup strawberry mixture in each of 6 glasses. Add ½ cup prosecco to each serving; stir to blend. Garnish each serving with 1 large strawberry. Yield: 6 servings.

CALORIES 176; FAT 0.7g (sat 0g, mono 0.1g, poly 0.3g); PROTEIN 1.2g; CARB 21.1g; FIBER 3.7g; CHOL 0mg; IRON 0.8mg; SODIUM 2mg; CALC 29mg

Strawberries benefit from organic practices since they absorb chemicals, if exposed.

Good News for Good Fats

Palate and heart, rejoice: Emerging research shows some fats have powerful health benefits. Our recipes explore this tasty development.

WHETHER IT'S A FRUITY OLIVE OIL drizzled over a salad, slices of avocado tucked into a sandwich, or buttery pine nuts tossed with pasta, ingredients with fats round out flavors and add satisfying textures to dishes. Now a growing body of research cites certain fats—the unsaturated ones found in many plants and fish—as health promoters, too. These fats may offer protection against heart disease, stroke, inflammation, and type 2 diabetes.

"What's important for health and preventing disease is the type of fat, not the percent of calories from fat," says Meir Stampfer, MD, DPH, Harvard Medical School professor of medicine.

Because of this shift, we have changed the nutritional policy of *Cooking Light:* We no longer publish the percentage of calories from fat in the nutrition analysis of recipes. Instead, we emphasize prudent amounts of beneficial fats while keeping unhealthful saturated fats in check. This allows for fresh flavors and new techniques in our recipes.

"Our recipes employ healthful fats to best effect," says *Cooking Light* Associate Food Editor Kathy Kitchens Downie, RD.

"The total fat values for some recipes may seem high at first glance," she says. "But if you look at the whole picture from the analysis, you'll see that you're getting a healthy balance."

In many cases, the fat grams in these recipes come from good-for-you poly- and monounsaturated varieties. Yet even the saturated fat—from main dishes to cookies—should fit easily into a day's allotment. (The American Heart Association and the Dietary Guidelines for Americans suggest aiming for 15 grams or 22 grams of saturated fat daily, respectively.)

Vegetable oils, avocados, or nuts and seeds may derive 85 to 100 percent of their calories from fat, but they can—and should—be part of a nutritious, balanced diet. "Focusing on percent of calories from fat, without distinction of type of fat, may do more harm than good by continuing to oversimplify the dietary advice," says Stampfer.

"All fats contain more than twice the calories per gram than protein or carbohydrate," says Downie. So bearing this in mind, *Cooking Light* will continue to offer recipes with sound portion sizes and appropriate calories for the serving. As always, we will evaluate each recipe's total nutrition package. And since our recipes typically don't use processed foods or ingredients that harbor artificial trans fats, most would contribute trace amounts—if any.

QUICK & EASY
Arugula and Pear Salad with Toasted Walnuts

"Splurge on a high-quality olive oil because of the superior flavors it offers to this simple salad," says *Cooking Light* Advisory Panelist and Chef Efisio Farris.

- 1 tablespoon minced shallots
- 2 tablespoons extra-virgin olive oil
- 2 teaspoons white wine vinegar
- ¼ teaspoon salt
- ¼ teaspoon Dijon mustard
- ⅛ teaspoon freshly ground black pepper
- 6 cups baby arugula leaves
- 2 Bosc pears, thinly sliced
- ¼ cup chopped walnuts, toasted

❶ Combine first 6 ingredients in a large bowl; stir with a whisk. Add arugula and pears to bowl; toss to coat. Place about 1½ cups salad on each of 4 plates; sprinkle each serving with 1 tablespoon walnuts. Yield: 4 servings.

CALORIES 168; FAT 12.5g (sat 1.5g, mono 5.7g, poly 4.6g); PROTEIN 2.5g; CARB 15.1g; FIBER 3g; CHOL 0mg; IRON 0.7mg; SODIUM 164mg; CALC 106mg

Oil-Poached Salmon with Fresh Cucumber Salad

When the *Cooking Light* Test Kitchens made this restaurant favorite, we discovered that the fish absorbed just 2 tablespoons of the oil. To ensure even cooking, prepare the fillets in a similar shape, and make sure the oil's temperature returns to and stays at 150° after the fish is added.

SALMON:
- 5 cups olive oil
- ½ cup fresh basil leaves
- 1 large lemon, thinly sliced
- 4 garlic cloves, crushed
- 4 (6-ounce) skinless salmon fillets (about 1 inch thick)
- ¼ teaspoon salt
- ⅛ teaspoon freshly ground black pepper

1 large English cucumber, peeled
   and thinly diagonally sliced (about
   2 cups)
¼ teaspoon salt, divided
¼ teaspoon freshly ground black
   pepper, divided
2 tablespoons fresh lemon juice
1 tablespoon chopped fresh basil
   Fresh basil leaves (optional)

❶ To prepare salmon, clip a kitchen thermometer onto side of a 10-inch skillet.
Add first 4 ingredients to pan; heat to
150°. Add fish to oil; cook for 12 minutes
or until desired degree of doneness.
Remove fish from oil; place on paper
towels to drain. Sprinkle with ¼ teaspoon salt and ⅛ teaspoon pepper.
❷ Toss cucumber with ⅛ teaspoon salt
and ⅛ teaspoon pepper; set aside.
❸ Combine juice, chopped basil, remaining ⅛ teaspoon salt, and remaining ⅛
teaspoon pepper in a small bowl; drizzle
over fish. Serve with cucumber salad.
Garnish with basil leaves, if desired.
Yield: 4 servings (serving size: 1 fillet,
½ cup cucumber salad, and 1 tablespoon
dressing).

CALORIES 231; FAT 11.9g (sat 1.8g, mono 6.3g, poly 2.9g);
PROTEIN 28.1g; CARB 2.1g; FIBER 0.5g; CHOL 73mg;
IRON 1.2mg; SODIUM 390mg; CALC 29mg

Fat Findings

Three common-sense steps can help
you incorporate good-for-you fats into
your diet.
1. Substitute good-for-you fats from
plant-based foods for animal-based
fats, when possible. For example,
use canola oil in place of butter for
sautéing vegetables.
2. Enjoy sensible portions of lean cuts
of beef and pork as well as low-fat dairy
to keep saturated fats in check.
**3. Employ nuts, seeds, olives, and
flavorful oils** with beneficial fats as a
garnish instead of a main ingredient to
manage calories.

STAFF FAVORITE ▪ MAKE AHEAD
Vanilla Bean Shortbread

"This half-oil, half-butter version yields
a crisper, more delicate cookie," says
Cooking Light Advisory Panelist Greg
Drescher of the Culinary Institute of
America. Make up to five days in advance,
and store in an airtight container.

   Cooking spray
9 ounces all-purpose flour (about
   2 cups)
¼ cup cornstarch
¼ teaspoon salt
½ cup butter, softened
½ cup canola oil
½ cup sugar
1 vanilla bean, split lengthwise

❶ Preheat oven to 350°.
❷ Line bottom and sides of a 13 x 9–inch
baking pan with foil; coat foil with cooking spray, and set aside.
❸ Weigh or lightly spoon flour into dry
measuring cups; level with a knife. Combine flour, cornstarch, and salt in a large
bowl; stir with a whisk.
❹ Place butter in a medium bowl; beat
with a mixer at medium speed 2 minutes
or until light and fluffy. Add oil; beat
with a mixer at medium speed 3 minutes
or until well blended. Gradually add
sugar, beating well. Scrape seeds from
vanilla bean, and add seeds to butter
mixture; discard bean. Add flour mixture, beating at low speed just until
blended. Spoon dough into prepared pan.
Place a sheet of heavy-duty plastic wrap
over dough; press to an even thickness.
Discard plastic wrap. Bake at 350° for
30 minutes or until edges are lightly
browned. Cool in pan 5 minutes on a wire
rack; cut into 32 pieces. Carefully lift foil
from pan; cool squares completely on a
wire rack. Yield: 32 servings (serving size:
1 piece).

CALORIES 101; FAT 6.4g (sat 2.1g, mono 2.8g, poly 1.2g);
PROTEIN 0.9g; CARB 10.1g; FIBER 0.2g; CHOL 8mg;
IRON 0.4mg; SODIUM 39mg; CALC 2mg

QUICK & EASY ▪ MAKE AHEAD
Chipotle Peanut Brittle

This smoky-sweet brittle is a great snack;
substitute pecans or almonds, if you prefer.

    Cooking spray
1   cup sugar
1   cup light-colored corn syrup
1   tablespoon butter
1   (11.5-ounce) container salted,
    dry-roasted peanuts
1½ teaspoons baking soda
1   teaspoon chipotle chile powder

❶ Line a large baking sheet with parchment paper; coat paper with cooking
spray.
❷ Combine sugar, corn syrup, and butter
in a large, heavy saucepan over medium
heat. Cook 18 minutes or until a candy
thermometer registers 275°, stirring
frequently. Add peanuts; cook 3 minutes
or until a candy thermometer registers
295°, stirring constantly. Remove from
heat; stir in baking soda and chile
powder. (The baking soda will cause
mixture to bubble and become opaque.)
❸ Quickly pour mixture onto prepared
pan; cover with a sheet of parchment
paper. Using a rolling pin, quickly roll
mixture to an even thickness. Discard
top parchment sheet. Cool mixture completely; break into pieces. Store in an
airtight container. Yield: 28 servings
(serving size: 1 ounce).

CALORIES 133; FAT 6.2g (sat 1.1g, mono 3g, poly 1.9g);
PROTEIN 2.8g; CARB 18.7g; FIBER 1g; CHOL 1mg;
IRON 0.3mg; SODIUM 173mg; CALC 8mg

A prudent serving of beef tenderloin keeps the saturated fat in check in this sandwich. Try it with a dollop of heart-healthy mayo.

Steak and Fennel Sandwiches

(pictured on page 221)

If you're keeping track of fat grams, this hefty sandwich provides about one-third of your day's needs. We suggest using a jarred canola-based mayonnaise if you would rather purchase the condiment instead of preparing it yourself.

½ teaspoon ground fennel seeds
½ teaspoon salt
¼ teaspoon ground cumin
¼ teaspoon freshly ground black pepper
4 teaspoons olive oil, divided
3 cups thinly sliced fennel bulb (about 1 bulb)
4 (4-ounce) beef tenderloin steaks, trimmed (1 inch thick)
8 teaspoons Homemade Mayonnaise (page 113)
8 (1-ounce) slices ciabatta, lightly toasted
1 cup arugula

❶ Combine first 4 ingredients in a small bowl.

❷ Heat 2 teaspoons oil in a large nonstick skillet over medium-high heat. Add ½ teaspoon spice mixture and fennel; sauté 15 minutes or until fennel is tender and lightly browned, stirring frequently. Transfer to a bowl; wipe pan clean with paper towels.

❸ Heat remaining 2 teaspoons oil in pan; sprinkle steaks evenly with remaining spice mixture. Add steaks to pan; cook 4 minutes on each side or until desired degree of doneness. Remove from pan; let stand 10 minutes. Thinly slice steaks.

❹ To prepare sandwiches, spread 2 teaspoons Homemade Mayonnaise onto each of 4 bread slices. Top each with one-fourth of beef, one-fourth of fennel, and ¼ cup arugula. Top with remaining 4 bread slices. Yield: 4 servings (serving size: 1 sandwich).

CALORIES 475; FAT 23.6g (sat 4.2g, mono 13.5g, poly 3.8g); PROTEIN 30.7g; CARB 36.4g; FIBER 3.4g; CHOL 79mg; IRON 4.2mg; SODIUM 794mg; CALC 70mg

Homemade Mayonnaise

"All good cooking is about flavor, and that's why fresh mayonnaise is worth the effort. It's inexpensive, easy to make, and tastes spectacular," says Tory McPhail, advisory panelist and chef at Commander's Palace in New Orleans. Refrigerate any leftover mayonnaise; it will be good for another four to five days.

- 1 tablespoon fresh lemon juice
- ½ teaspoon Dijon mustard
- ⅛ teaspoon salt
- 1 large pasteurized egg
- ¾ cup canola oil

❶ Place first 4 ingredients in a blender; process until smooth. With blender on, gradually pour in oil; process until smooth and completely blended. Yield: ¾ cup (serving size: 2 teaspoons).

CALORIES 87; FAT 9.6g (sat 0.8g, mono 5.6g, poly 2.8g); PROTEIN 0.4g; CARB 0.1g; FIBER 0g; CHOL 12mg; IRON 0.1mg; SODIUM 24mg; CALC 2mg

---

Mayonnaise 101

Cooking Light Advisory Panelist Chef Tory McPhail gives these tips for making mayonnaise:

1. Start with room-temperature ingredients.
2. Use a fresh, high-quality oil for the best flavor and emulsifying properties.
3. Blend just until the mixture becomes smooth and creamy (not too stiff).
4. If the mayonnaise breaks (oil will puddle on the surface), add a little ice water while processing, and the mayonnaise should come back together.
5. After chilling, you can whisk in a few drops of ice water to re-emulsify the mixture.

Coconut-Crusted Chicken with Cashew-Curry Sauce

Besides their abundant monounsaturated fat, cashews also contribute a pleasing crunch to the sauce. The chicken and sauce gain a flavor and texture lift with flaked coconut and light coconut milk.

CHICKEN:

- 4 (6-ounce) skinless, boneless chicken breast halves
- ½ teaspoon salt
- 2 tablespoons cornstarch
- ¼ teaspoon ground red pepper
- ¾ cup panko (Japanese breadcrumbs)
- ½ cup flaked unsweetened coconut
- 1 large egg white, lightly beaten
- 2 teaspoons canola oil

SAUCE:

- ¾ cup light coconut milk
- 2 teaspoons sugar
- 1 teaspoon red curry paste
- ½ teaspoon cornstarch
- 1 teaspoon canola oil
- ¼ cup finely chopped shallots
- 1 tablespoon minced peeled fresh ginger
- 2 garlic cloves, minced
- ⅓ cup chopped dry-roasted cashews
- 1 tablespoon fresh lime juice
- 2 teaspoons fish sauce
- 4 lime wedges (optional)
- 4 fresh cilantro sprigs (optional)

❶ Preheat oven to 400°.
❷ To prepare chicken, sprinkle chicken evenly with ½ teaspoon salt. Combine 2 tablespoons cornstarch and red pepper in a large zip-top plastic bag. Combine panko and flaked coconut in a shallow dish. Place egg white in another shallow dish. Add chicken to bag; seal and shake well to coat evenly. Remove from bag; discard remaining cornstarch mixture. Dip 1 chicken breast half in egg white; dredge in panko mixture. Repeat procedure with remaining 3 chicken breast halves, egg white, and panko mixture.
❸ Heat 2 teaspoons oil in a large ovenproof nonstick skillet over medium-high heat. Add chicken to pan; cook 2 minutes on each side or until lightly browned. Place skillet in oven. Bake at 400° for 8 minutes or until done.
❹ To prepare sauce, combine coconut milk and next 3 ingredients in a small bowl. Heat 1 teaspoon oil in a large saucepan over medium heat. Add shallots, ginger, and garlic to pan; cook 1 minute, stirring frequently. Add coconut milk mixture; bring to a boil. Cook 1 minute or just until slightly thick, stirring constantly. Remove from heat; stir in cashews, juice, and fish sauce. Garnish each serving with 1 lime wedge and 1 cilantro sprig, if desired. Yield: 4 servings (serving size: 1 chicken breast half and 3 tablespoons sauce).

CALORIES 376; FAT 15.4g (sat 5.8g, mono 5.8g, poly 2.4g); PROTEIN 43.8g; CARB 15.4g; FIBER 1.1g; CHOL 99mg; IRON 2.4mg; SODIUM 772mg; CALC 34mg

---

Spinach-Chive Pesto

Pine nuts and olive oil contribute unsaturated fats, while salty cheese renders a small amount of saturated fat. "This pesto would be great to flavor scrambled eggs," says *Cooking Light* Advisory Panelist Amy Myrdal Miller, MS, RD.

- 1 cup baby spinach leaves
- ¼ cup pine nuts, toasted
- ¼ cup (1 ounce) grated fresh Parmigiano-Reggiano cheese
- 2 tablespoons extra-virgin olive oil
- 2 teaspoons fresh lemon juice
- ¼ teaspoon salt
- 1 garlic clove, chopped
- 1 (1-ounce) package fresh chives, chopped (about ¾ cup)

❶ Place all ingredients in a food processor; process until finely chopped, scraping sides. Yield: about ½ cup (serving size: 1 tablespoon).

CALORIES 72; FAT 7.2g (sat 1.2g, mono 3.5g, poly 2g); PROTEIN 1.8g; CARB 1.2g; FIBER 0.4g; CHOL 2mg; IRON 0.4mg; SODIUM 115mg; CALC 37mg

Flavor Fiesta Menu

serves 4

An easy grilled entrée is at the heart of a dinner that celebrates Cinco de Mayo *con mucho gusto.*

Grilled Flank Steak with Avocado Relish

Black beans and rice

Melt 1 tablespoon butter in a medium saucepan over medium-high heat. Add ¼ cup chopped shallots and 1 teaspoon minced garlic; sauté 3 minutes, stirring frequently. Add ⅔ cup uncooked long-grain white rice; sauté 1 minute. Add 1⅓ cups fat-free, less-sodium chicken broth and ¼ teaspoon ground cumin. Bring to a boil; cook 20 minutes or until liquid is absorbed. Remove from heat; stir in 2 tablespoons chopped fresh cilantro and 1 (15-ounce) can black beans, rinsed and drained.

Mango wedges
Mexican beer
Flan

Grilled Flank Steak with Avocado Relish

A little fruity avocado oil and fresh avocado (both full of good-for-you fats) boost flavor in relatively lean flank steak. If you don't have avocado oil, use any type of fruity olive oil, like an Italian extra-virgin variety. This recipe also works well in a grill pan over medium-high heat.

> 2 teaspoons grated lime rind, divided
> 4 teaspoons avocado oil or fruity extra-virgin olive oil, divided
> ½ teaspoon salt, divided
> ⅛ teaspoon freshly ground black pepper
> 1 garlic clove, minced
> 1 (1-pound) flank steak, trimmed
> Cooking spray
> 1 cup diced peeled avocado
> ½ cup chopped plum tomato
> 2 tablespoons chopped red onion
> 1 tablespoon fresh lime juice
> 2 teaspoons finely chopped seeded jalapeño pepper (about 1 small)
> 4 lime wedges

① Combine 1 teaspoon rind, 2 teaspoons oil, ¼ teaspoon salt, black pepper, and garlic in a small bowl.
② Score a diamond pattern on both sides of steak. Rub both sides of steak with oil mixture. Cover and refrigerate 2 hours.
③ Prepare grill to medium-high heat.
④ Place steak on a grill rack coated with cooking spray; grill 6 minutes on each side or until desired degree of doneness. Let stand 5 minutes. Cut steak diagonally across grain into thin slices.
⑤ Combine remaining 1 teaspoon rind, remaining 2 teaspoons oil, remaining ¼ teaspoon salt, diced avocado, and next 4 ingredients in a small bowl. Serve sliced steak with relish and lime wedges. Yield: 4 servings (serving size: 3 ounces steak, about ⅓ cup relish, and 1 lime wedge).

CALORIES 283; FAT 17.7g (sat 4.1g, mono 10g, poly 1.7g); PROTEIN 25g; CARB 6.4g; FIBER 3.5g; CHOL 42mg; IRON 1.9mg; SODIUM 349mg; CALC 28mg

MAKE AHEAD • FREEZABLE
Maple and Walnut Quick Bread

Walnuts are a good source of polyunsaturated fats, and they add great texture to recipes. Walnut oil in the batter underscores the nutty flavor in this walnut-topped loaf.

> 5.8 ounces all-purpose flour (about 1¼ cups)
> 3.3 ounces whole-wheat flour (about ¾ cup)
> ½ cup sugar
> 2 teaspoons baking powder
> ½ teaspoon baking soda
> ½ teaspoon salt
> 1 cup low-fat buttermilk
> ⅓ cup maple syrup
> ¼ cup walnut oil
> 1 large egg
> ½ teaspoon vanilla extract
> Cooking spray
> ⅓ cup finely chopped walnuts, toasted

① Preheat oven to 350°.
② Weigh or lightly spoon flours into dry measuring cups; level with a knife. Combine flours, sugar, and next 3 ingredients in a large bowl; make a well in center of mixture. Combine buttermilk and next 3 ingredients in a bowl; add to flour mixture, stirring just until moist. Stir in vanilla. Spoon batter into an 8 x 4-inch loaf pan coated with cooking spray. Sprinkle with walnuts. Bake at 350° for 50 minutes or until a wooden pick inserted in center comes out clean. Cool in pan 10 minutes on a wire rack; remove from pan. Cool completely on wire rack. Yield: 1 loaf/14 servings (serving size: 1 slice).

CALORIES 178; FAT 6.5g (sat 0.8g, mono 1.4g, poly 3.9g); PROTEIN 3.6g; CARB 27.5g; FIBER 1.3g; CHOL 16mg; IRON 1.1mg; SODIUM 224mg; CALC 73mg

Dinner Tonight

Our 11 delicious entrée recipes and side dish suggestions help you put supper—from broiled snapper to grilled kebabs—on the table in a flash.

QUICK & EASY
Ancho-Rubbed Flank Steak
······················ *20 minutes*

Roasted, simply seasoned potato wedges and a tartly dressed salad topped with smoky bacon complement this satisfying main dish. Combine 1 tablespoon cider vinegar, 1 teaspoon Dijon mustard, ¼ teaspoon salt, and ¼ teaspoon freshly ground black pepper in a large bowl; stir well with a whisk. Gradually add 2 tablespoons olive oil to vinegar mixture, stirring constantly with a whisk. Add 6 cups arugula and 1 cup halved cherry tomatoes to dressing in bowl; toss well to coat. Sprinkle 2 cooked and crumbled bacon slices evenly over salad.

- ½ teaspoon kosher salt
- ½ teaspoon brown sugar
- ½ teaspoon ground ancho chile powder
- ¼ teaspoon ground cumin
- Dash of freshly ground black pepper
- 1 (1-pound) flank steak, trimmed
- 2 teaspoons olive oil

❶ Combine first 5 ingredients in a small bowl; rub evenly over both sides of steak.
❷ Heat oil in a large skillet over medium-high heat. Add steak; cook 3 minutes on each side or until desired degree of doneness. Let stand 5 minutes; cut steak diagonally across grain into thin slices. Yield: 4 servings (serving size: 3 ounces).

CALORIES 175; FAT 7.8g (sat 2.6g, mono 3.8g, poly 0.5g); PROTEIN 23.8g; CARB 0.8g; FIBER 0.1g; CHOL 37mg; IRON 1.5mg; SODIUM 286mg; CALC 19mg

QUICK & EASY
Snapper with Basil-Mint Sauce
······················ *20 minutes*

Serve with jasmine rice and sautéed green beans. Heat 1 teaspoon olive oil in a large skillet over medium-high heat. Add ¼ cup chopped onion; sauté 3 minutes. Stir in 1 pound trimmed, halved green beans; sauté 5 minutes. Stir in ¼ cup water; cover and cook 2 minutes. Stir in 1 tablespoon low-sodium soy sauce.

- 4 (6-ounce) snapper fillets
- Cooking spray
- ¼ teaspoon salt
- ⅛ teaspoon freshly ground black pepper
- 1 cup fresh basil leaves
- ¼ cup fresh mint leaves
- 2 tablespoons chopped seeded jalapeño pepper
- 2 tablespoons olive oil
- 2 tablespoons water
- 2 teaspoons fresh lime juice
- ⅛ teaspoon salt
- 1 garlic clove, chopped

❶ Preheat broiler.
❷ Arrange fish in a single layer on a broiler pan lightly coated with cooking spray. Sprinkle fish with ¼ teaspoon salt and pepper. Broil 6 minutes or until fish flakes easily when tested with a fork or until desired degree of doneness.
❸ Place basil and remaining ingredients in a food processor; process 1 minute or until smooth. Serve with fish. Yield: 4 servings (serving size: 1 fillet and about 1 tablespoon sauce).

CALORIES 237; FAT 9.1g (sat 1.4g, mono 5.4g, poly 1.6g); PROTEIN 35.3g; CARB 1.4g; FIBER 0.7g; CHOL 63mg; IRON 0.8mg; SODIUM 328mg; CALC 77mg

QUICK & EASY
Chicken and Strawberry Salad
······················ *20 minutes*

(pictured on page 218)

Pair this simple, no-cook meal with toasted buttery baguette slices. Broil 8 (½-inch) slices French bread baguette 1½ minutes. Turn slices over; brush evenly with 2 tablespoons melted butter. Broil 1½ minutes or until lightly browned.

DRESSING:
- 1 tablespoon sugar
- 2 tablespoons red wine vinegar
- 1 tablespoon water
- ⅛ teaspoon salt
- ⅛ teaspoon freshly ground black pepper
- 2 tablespoons extra-virgin olive oil

SALAD:
- 4 cups torn romaine lettuce
- 4 cups arugula
- 2 cups quartered strawberries
- ⅓ cup vertically sliced red onion
- 12 ounces skinless, boneless rotisserie chicken breast, sliced
- 2 tablespoons unsalted cashews, halved
- ½ cup (2 ounces) crumbled blue cheese

❶ To prepare dressing, combine first 5 ingredients in a small bowl. Gradually drizzle in oil, stirring constantly with a whisk.
❷ To prepare salad, combine romaine and next 4 ingredients in a bowl; toss gently. Place about 2 cups chicken mixture on each of 4 plates. Top each serving with 1½ teaspoons cashews and 2 tablespoons cheese. Drizzle about 4 teaspoons dressing over each serving. Yield: 4 servings.

CALORIES 333; FAT 16.4g (sat 4.9g, mono 8.3g, poly 2.1g); PROTEIN 32g; CARB 14.8g; FIBER 3.5g; CHOL 83mg; IRON 2.5mg; SODIUM 347mg; CALC 156mg

Broiled Salmon with Peppercorn-Lime Rub
·························*20 minutes*

(pictured on page 219)

Try a fresh, quick, and satisfying quinoa-vegetable salad with your broiled fish. Combine 1¼ cups fat-free, less-sodium chicken broth and ¾ cup uncooked quinoa in a medium saucepan; bring mixture to a boil. Cover and simmer 12 minutes or until liquid is almost absorbed. Stir in 1½ cups chopped zucchini and ½ cup chopped red bell pepper. Cover and cook 5 minutes or until liquid is absorbed. Remove from heat. Stir in 2 tablespoons chopped fresh chives, 2 teaspoons extra-virgin olive oil, ¼ teaspoon salt, and ¼ teaspoon freshly ground black pepper.

- 4 (6-ounce) salmon fillets (about ¾ inch thick)
- Cooking spray
- 2 teaspoons grated lime rind
- ½ teaspoon kosher salt
- ½ teaspoon cracked black pepper
- 1 garlic clove, minced
- Lime wedges (optional)

❶ Preheat broiler.
❷ Place fish, skin sides down, on a broiler pan coated with cooking spray. Combine rind and next 3 ingredients; sprinkle over fish. Broil 7 minutes or until fish flakes easily when tested with a fork or until desired degree of doneness. Serve with lime wedges, if desired. Yield: 4 servings (serving size: 1 fillet).

CALORIES 318; FAT 18.5g (sat 3.7g, mono 6.6g, poly 6.7g); PROTEIN 34.1g; CARB 2.2g; FIBER 0.6g; CHOL 100mg; IRON 0.8mg; SODIUM 336mg; CALC 28mg

Fresh Salmon-Cilantro Burgers
·························*30 minutes*

A spinach salad with a sweet, slightly spicy Asian-influenced dressing makes a tasty accompaniment. Combine 2 tablespoons hoisin sauce, 1 tablespoon rice vinegar, 2 teaspoons canola oil, 2 teaspoons water, and ¼ teaspoon chile paste in a large bowl; stir well with a whisk. Add half of 1 (5-ounce) package baby spinach, ½ cup yellow bell pepper strips, and ¼ cup thinly sliced red onion to bowl; toss to coat.

- ¼ cup reduced-fat mayonnaise
- 1 tablespoon chopped fresh cilantro
- 1 tablespoon fresh lime juice
- ⅛ teaspoon salt
- ⅛ teaspoon freshly ground black pepper
- 1 (1-pound) salmon fillet, skinned and cut into 1-inch pieces
- ¼ cup dry breadcrumbs
- 2 tablespoons fresh cilantro leaves
- 2 tablespoons chopped green onions
- 1 tablespoon chopped seeded jalapeño pepper
- 2 tablespoons fresh lime juice
- ½ teaspoon salt
- ¼ teaspoon freshly ground black pepper
- Cooking spray
- 4 (1½-ounce) hamburger buns with sesame seeds, toasted
- 12 (¼-inch-thick) slices English cucumber
- 4 leaf lettuce leaves

❶ Combine first 5 ingredients in a small bowl; cover and chill.
❷ Place salmon in a food processor; pulse until coarsely chopped. Add breadcrumbs and next 6 ingredients; pulse 4 times or until well blended. Divide salmon mixture into 4 equal portions, shaping each into a ¾-inch-thick patty.
❸ Heat a grill pan over medium-high heat. Coat pan with cooking spray. Add patties to pan; cook 2 minutes. Carefully turn patties over, and cook 2 minutes or until done.
❹ Spread about 1 tablespoon mayonnaise mixture over bottom half of each bun. Top each serving with 1 salmon patty, 3 cucumber slices, 1 lettuce leaf, and top half of bun. Yield: 4 servings (serving size: 1 burger).

CALORIES 341; FAT 11.5g (sat 2g, mono 2.9g, poly 4.9g); PROTEIN 31.6g; CARB 30.9g; FIBER 1.8g; CHOL 66mg; IRON 2.2mg; SODIUM 816mg; CALC 67mg

Chicken and Cashews
·························*30 minutes*

Precut vegetables will shave even more time off this dish. Pair this entrée with a simple rice pilaf. Heat 1 tablespoon canola oil in a large saucepan over medium-high heat. Add ½ cup chopped onion and 2 teaspoons grated peeled fresh ginger to pan; sauté 2 minutes. Stir in 1 cup water, ½ cup long-grain rice, and ¼ teaspoon salt; bring to a boil. Cover, reduce heat, and simmer 12 minutes or until liquid is absorbed. Remove from heat; stir in 2 tablespoons chopped fresh cilantro.

- 3 tablespoons low-sodium soy sauce, divided
- 2 tablespoons dry sherry
- 4 teaspoons cornstarch, divided
- 1 pound skinless, boneless chicken breast, cut into bite-sized pieces
- ½ cup fat-free, less-sodium chicken broth
- 2 tablespoons oyster sauce
- 1 tablespoon honey
- 2 teaspoons sesame oil, divided
- ¾ cup chopped onion
- ½ cup chopped celery
- ½ cup chopped red bell pepper
- 1 tablespoon grated peeled fresh ginger
- 2 garlic cloves, minced
- ½ cup chopped green onions (about 3 green onions)
- ¼ cup chopped unsalted dry-roasted cashews

① Combine 1 tablespoon soy sauce, sherry, 2 teaspoons cornstarch, and chicken in a large bowl; toss well to coat. Combine remaining 2 tablespoons soy sauce, remaining 2 teaspoons cornstarch, broth, oyster sauce, and honey in a small bowl.

② Heat 1 teaspoon oil in a large nonstick skillet over medium-high heat. Add chicken mixture to pan; sauté 3 minutes. Remove from pan. Heat remaining 1 teaspoon oil in pan. Add onion, celery, and bell pepper to pan; sauté 2 minutes. Add ginger and garlic; sauté 1 minute. Return chicken mixture to pan; sauté 1 minute. Stir in broth mixture. Bring to a boil; cook 1 minute, stirring constantly. Remove from heat. Sprinkle with green onions and cashews. Yield: 4 servings (serving size: about 3/4 cup).

CALORIES 257; FAT 9g (sat 1.9g, mono 4.2g, poly 2.3g); PROTEIN 26g; CARB 17g; FIBER 1.9g; CHOL 63mg; IRON 2mg; SODIUM 584mg; CALC 45mg

QUICK & EASY

Spiced Lamb and Vegetable Kebabs with Cilantro-Mint Sauce

··*40 minutes*

For dessert, try mango-cardamom sauce over ice cream. Place 1 chopped peeled ripe mango, 2 tablespoons fresh lime juice, and 1/8 teaspoon ground cardamom in a food processor; process until smooth.

KEBABS:

1½ teaspoons ground cumin
1½ teaspoons ground coriander
 2 teaspoons grated peeled fresh ginger
 2 teaspoons canola oil
 ½ teaspoon salt
 2 garlic cloves, minced
 1 (1-pound) boneless leg of lamb, trimmed and cut into 1-inch pieces
16 cherry tomatoes
16 (2-inch) pieces yellow bell peppers
16 (½-inch) wedges red onion
 Cooking spray

SAUCE:

 ½ cup fresh cilantro leaves
 ¼ cup fresh mint leaves
 2 tablespoons chopped green onions
 2 tablespoons water
 1 tablespoon canola oil
 1 tablespoon fresh lime juice
 ¼ teaspoon ground cumin
 ⅛ teaspoon salt
 1 garlic clove, chopped
 1 small jalapeño pepper, seeded and minced

① Prepare grill to medium-high heat.
② To prepare kebabs, combine first 6 ingredients in a large bowl; add lamb, tossing to coat. Thread lamb, tomatoes, bell pepper, and onion alternately onto each of 8 (8-inch) skewers. Place kebabs on a grill rack coated with cooking spray; grill 10 minutes or until desired degree of doneness, turning occasionally.
③ To prepare sauce, place cilantro and remaining ingredients in a blender; process until smooth. Serve with kebabs. Yield: 4 servings (serving size: 2 kebabs and 1 tablespoon sauce).

CALORIES 256; FAT 13.3g (sat 3.4g, mono 6.6g, poly 1.8g); PROTEIN 24.9g; CARB 9.4g; FIBER 2.6g; CHOL 76mg; IRON 2.9mg; SODIUM 442mg; CALC 38mg

QUICK & EASY

Greek Shrimp and Asparagus Risotto

·······································*40 minutes*

If you don't have fresh dill on hand, chopped fresh flat-leaf parsley or chives would also work well in this dish. Balance the plate with a lively fennel salad. Combine 2 tablespoons fresh lemon juice, 1 tablespoon olive oil, ¼ teaspoon salt, ¼ teaspoon crushed fennel seeds, and ⅛ teaspoon freshly ground black pepper in a large bowl. Add 6 cups torn romaine lettuce and 1 cup thinly sliced fennel bulb; toss well to coat.

 3 cups fat-free, less-sodium chicken broth
 1 cup water
 2 teaspoons olive oil
2¾ cups chopped Vidalia or other sweet onion (about 2 medium)
 1 cup Arborio rice
 2 garlic cloves, minced
1¾ cups (½-inch) slices asparagus (about 8 ounces)
 1 pound peeled and deveined medium shrimp, cut into 1-inch pieces
 ½ cup (2 ounces) crumbled feta cheese
 1 tablespoon chopped fresh dill
 2 tablespoons fresh lemon juice
 ¼ teaspoon salt
 ⅛ teaspoon freshly ground black pepper

① Bring broth and 1 cup water to a simmer in a medium saucepan (do not boil). Keep warm over low heat.
② Heat oil in a large saucepan over medium-high heat. Add onion to pan; sauté 5 minutes or until tender. Stir in rice and garlic; sauté 1 minute. Add broth mixture, ½ cup at a time, stirring constantly until each portion of broth is absorbed before adding the next (about 30 minutes total).
③ Stir in asparagus and shrimp, and cook 5 minutes or until shrimp are done, stirring constantly. Remove from heat, and stir in cheese and remaining ingredients. Yield: 4 servings (serving size: 1½ cups risotto).

CALORIES 426; FAT 8.9g (sat 3.6g, mono 2.8g, poly 1.2g); PROTEIN 33g; CARB 53.5g; FIBER 5.1g; CHOL 189mg; IRON 4.5mg; SODIUM 868mg; CALC 194mg

Ginger Beef Salad with Miso Vinaigrette

·····································*40 minutes*

Serve with soba noodles. For dessert, heat ¼ cup sugar, ¼ cup torn mint, and ¼ cup water until sugar melts. Strain; cool. Stir in 4 cups halved strawberries.

- 1 (1-pound) flank steak, trimmed
- 2 tablespoons minced peeled fresh ginger
- ¼ teaspoon salt
- 2 garlic cloves, minced

Cooking spray

- 2 tablespoons chopped fresh cilantro
- 2 tablespoons white miso (soybean paste)
- 2 tablespoons water
- 2 tablespoons rice vinegar
- 1 tablespoon canola oil
- 2 teaspoons grated peeled fresh ginger
- ½ teaspoon chile paste with garlic
- 6 cups torn Bibb lettuce (about 3 small heads)
- ¾ cup thinly sliced yellow bell pepper
- ¼ cup thinly sliced red onion
- ½ English cucumber, halved lengthwise and sliced

1 Preheat broiler.
2 Sprinkle steak evenly with ginger, salt, and garlic. Place on a broiler pan coated with cooking spray; broil 6 minutes on each side or until desired degree of doneness. Let stand 5 minutes. Cut steak diagonally across grain into thin slices.
3 Combine cilantro and next 6 ingredients in a small bowl, stirring with a whisk. Combine lettuce and remaining ingredients in a large bowl. Drizzle half of miso mixture over lettuce mixture; toss to coat.
4 Place 1½ cups lettuce mixture on each of 4 plates. Top each with 3 ounces steak and miso mixture. Yield: 4 servings.

CALORIES 282; FAT 9.3g (sat 2.6g, mono 4.3g, poly 1.4g); PROTEIN 26.9g; CARB 22.9g; FIBER 3g; CHOL 37mg; IRON 3.2mg; SODIUM 708mg; CALC 57mg

Grilled Cumin Chicken with Fresh Tomatillo Sauce

·····································*40 minutes*

Serve chipotle rice with this dish. Combine 1 cup long-grain rice and 2 cups fat-free, less-sodium chicken broth in a medium saucepan; bring to a boil. Cover, reduce heat, and simmer 15 minutes or until liquid is absorbed. Stir in ¼ cup thinly sliced green onions and ½ teaspoon minced chipotle chile, canned in adobo sauce.

- 2 teaspoons olive oil
- ½ teaspoon ground cumin
- ⅛ teaspoon freshly ground black pepper
- 2 garlic cloves, minced
- 4 (6-ounce) skinless, boneless chicken breast halves
- ½ pound tomatillos
- ½ cup fat-free, less-sodium chicken broth
- ¼ cup fresh cilantro leaves
- ¼ cup chopped green onions
- 2 tablespoons fresh lime juice
- ½ teaspoon sugar
- ¼ teaspoon salt
- 1 garlic clove, chopped
- 1 jalapeño pepper, seeded and chopped
- ¼ teaspoon salt

Cooking spray

1 Prepare grill to medium-high heat.
2 Combine first 4 ingredients in a large zip-top plastic bag. Add chicken to bag; seal and let stand 15 minutes.
3 Discard husks and stems from tomatillos. Combine tomatillos and broth in a small saucepan over medium-high heat; cover and cook 8 minutes. Drain and cool slightly. Place tomatillos, cilantro, and next 6 ingredients in a food processor; process until smooth.
4 Remove chicken from bag; discard marinade. Sprinkle chicken evenly with ¼ teaspoon salt. Place on a grill rack coated with cooking spray; grill 6 minutes on each side or until chicken is done. Serve with tomatillo sauce. Yield: 4 servings (serving size: 1 chicken breast half and about 5 tablespoons sauce).

CALORIES 237; FAT 5.1g (sat 1g, mono 2.3g, poly 1g); PROTEIN 40.4g; CARB 6g; FIBER 1.5g; CHOL 99mg; IRON 1.9mg; SODIUM 465mg; CALC 35mg

Grilled Steak with Caper-Herb Sauce

·····································*30 minutes*

Bring the steak to room temperature before grilling so it cooks quickly and evenly. Serve with grilled garlic bread. Grill 4 slices French bread 2 minutes on each side or until browned. Brush each slice with 1 teaspoon olive oil; rub with halved garlic clove.

- 1 (1-pound) boneless sirloin steak
- ¼ teaspoon salt
- ¼ teaspoon freshly ground black pepper

Cooking spray

- 1 cup fresh flat-leaf parsley leaves
- 1 cup basil leaves
- 2 tablespoons thinly sliced green onions
- 2 tablespoons extra-virgin olive oil
- 2 tablespoons fat-free, less-sodium chicken broth
- 1 tablespoon capers
- 1 tablespoon fresh lemon juice
- 1 garlic clove, chopped
- 1 canned anchovy fillet, chopped

1 Prepare grill to medium-high heat.
2 Sprinkle steak with salt and pepper. Place steak on a grill rack coated with cooking spray; grill 6 minutes on each side. Let stand 10 minutes.
3 Place parsley and remaining ingredients in a food processor; process until blended. Cut steak diagonally across grain into thin slices. Serve with sauce. Yield: 4 servings (serving size: 3 ounces steak and about 1 tablespoon sauce).

CALORIES 194; FAT 13g (sat 3.2g, mono 7.3g, poly 1.2g); PROTEIN 16.3g; CARB 2.4g; FIBER 1.1g; CHOL 42mg; IRON 3.5mg; SODIUM 295mg; CALC 45mg

Chicken & Spring Veggies

Add tender fresh produce to your favorite cuts of chicken. These eight recipes deliver all the flavor of the season.

Roast Chicken with Smashed New Potatoes and Garlicky Jus

An hour and a half of (mostly hands-off) cooking time yields a Sunday classic.

CHICKEN:

Cooking spray
1 lemon, thinly sliced
1 (4-pound) whole chicken
¼ teaspoon salt
¼ teaspoon freshly ground black pepper
4 sprigs fresh rosemary
1 whole garlic head
1 cup dry white wine
1 (14-ounce) can fat-free, less-sodium chicken broth
1 tablespoon butter

POTATOES:

16 new potatoes, unpeeled (about 2 pounds)
⅓ cup fat-free milk
2 tablespoons chopped fresh chives
1 tablespoon extra-virgin olive oil
1 tablespoon white wine vinegar
¼ teaspoon salt
¼ teaspoon freshly ground black pepper

❶ To prepare chicken, heat a large non-stick skillet over medium-high heat. Coat pan with cooking spray. Add lemon to pan; sauté 5 minutes or until lightly browned, turning occasionally. Remove from pan; cool.

❷ Preheat oven to 400°.

❸ Remove and discard giblets from chicken; trim excess fat. Starting at neck cavity, loosen skin from breast and drumsticks by inserting fingers, gently pushing between skin and meat. Combine ¼ teaspoon salt and ¼ teaspoon pepper; rub salt mixture under loosened skin. Insert lemon slices in a single layer under loosened skin. Place rosemary inside body cavity. Lift wing tips up and over back; tuck under chicken. Place chicken on a roasting pan coated with cooking spray. Lightly coat chicken with cooking spray. Remove white papery skin from garlic head (do not peel or separate cloves). Place garlic head in pan.

❹ Bake at 400° for 15 minutes. Reduce oven temperature to 350° (do not remove chicken from oven); bake an additional 1 hour or until a thermometer inserted in meaty part of thigh registers 165°. Remove chicken from pan; let stand 10 minutes. Remove skin; discard. Loosely cover chicken; keep warm.

❺ Remove garlic from pan; set aside. Place a zip-top plastic bag inside a 2-cup glass measure. Pour drippings into bag; let stand 10 minutes (fat will rise to top). Seal bag; carefully snip off 1 bottom corner of bag. Drain drippings back into pan, stopping before fat layer reaches opening; discard fat.

❻ Separate garlic cloves; squeeze to extract pulp. Place pan over medium-high heat. Stir in garlic pulp, wine, and broth; bring to a boil, scraping pan to loosen browned bits. Cook 10 minutes or until sauce is slightly thick. Remove from heat; stir in butter.

❼ To prepare potatoes, place potatoes in a saucepan; cover with water. Bring to a boil. Reduce heat, and simmer 20 minutes or until very tender; drain. Return potatoes to pan. Mash with a potato masher to desired consistency. Add milk and remaining ingredients; stir until combined. Serve chicken with gravy and potatoes. Yield: 4 servings (serving size: 4 ounces chicken, about ¼ cup gravy, and 1 cup potatoes).

CALORIES 533; FAT 12.7g (sat 3.9g, mono 5.2g, poly 2.1g); PROTEIN 54.9g; CARB 46.3g; FIBER 3.7g; CHOL 158mg; IRON 5mg; SODIUM 673mg; CALC 79mg

Produce Tip

The term **new potato** refers to any thin-skinned potato harvested in early spring while the plant is still thriving, regardless of its skin color or variety. (Fully mature potatoes are harvested after the plant dies.) If you can't find true new potatoes, use small red- or white-skinned potatoes.

Braised Chicken with Baby Vegetables and Peas

Look for a whole chicken, cut up. If you prefer the fuller flavor of dark meat, use four chicken leg quarters instead.

- 2 tablespoons butter, divided
- 2 bone-in chicken breast halves, skinned
- 2 bone-in chicken thighs, skinned
- 2 chicken drumsticks, skinned
- ½ teaspoon salt
- ¼ teaspoon freshly ground black pepper
- 2 (14-ounce) cans fat-free, less-sodium chicken broth
- 1 cup dry white wine
- ½ teaspoon chopped fresh thyme
- 12 baby turnips, peeled (about 8 ounces)
- 12 baby carrots, peeled (about 8 ounces)
- 12 pearl onions, peeled (about 8 ounces)
- 6 fresh flat-leaf parsley sprigs
- 2 bay leaves
- 2 tablespoons all-purpose flour
- ¾ cup fresh green peas
- 2 tablespoons chopped fresh flat-leaf parsley

❶ Melt 1 tablespoon butter in a Dutch oven over medium-high heat. Sprinkle chicken evenly with salt and pepper. Add chicken to pan; sauté 5 minutes on each side or until browned. Remove from pan.
❷ Add broth to pan; cook 1 minute, scraping pan to loosen browned bits. Add wine and next 6 ingredients; stir. Add chicken to pan, nestling into vegetable mixture; bring to a boil. Cover, reduce heat, and simmer 20 minutes or until chicken is done. Discard parsley sprigs and bay leaves. Remove chicken and vegetables from pan.
❸ Place a zip-top plastic bag inside a 2-cup glass measure. Pour cooking liquid into bag; let stand 10 minutes (fat will rise to top). Seal bag; carefully snip off 1 bottom corner of bag. Drain cooking liquid back into pan, stopping before fat layer reaches opening; discard fat. Bring liquid to a boil; cook until reduced to 1½ cups (about 5 minutes).
❹ Melt remaining 1 tablespoon butter in a small skillet. Add flour, stirring until smooth. Add flour mixture to cooking liquid; cook 2 minutes or until slightly thick, stirring constantly. Return chicken and vegetable mixture to pan; stir in peas. Cook 3 minutes or until thoroughly heated. Garnish with chopped parsley. Yield: 4 servings (serving size: ¾ cup vegetables, ⅓ cup sauce, 1 chicken breast half or 1 chicken thigh and 1 drumstick, and 1½ teaspoons parsley).

CALORIES 324; FAT 11.4g (sat 5.1g, mono 3.4g, poly 1.5g); PROTEIN 32.6g; CARB 22.1g; FIBER 5.2g; CHOL 100mg; IRON 3.3mg; SODIUM 818mg; CALC 89mg

QUICK & EASY
Chicken Breasts with Mushroom Sauce

Butter and whipping cream add a wonderful lushness to this savory pan gravy, which features fresh morel and button mushrooms.

- 6 (6-ounce) skinless, boneless chicken breast halves
- 3 tablespoons butter, divided
- ½ teaspoon salt
- ¼ teaspoon freshly ground black pepper
- 4 ounces morel mushrooms
- 4 ounces button mushrooms, thinly sliced
- 2 cups fat-free, less-sodium chicken broth
- ¼ cup whipping cream
- 4½ cups hot cooked egg noodles
  Fresh flat-leaf parsley sprigs (optional)

❶ Place each chicken breast half between 2 sheets of heavy-duty plastic wrap; flatten to ¼-inch thickness using a meat mallet or small heavy skillet. Heat 2 teaspoons butter in a large nonstick skillet over medium heat. Sprinkle chicken evenly with salt and pepper. Add 2 breast halves to pan, and cook 3 minutes on each side or until done. Repeat procedure twice with 4 teaspoons butter and remaining chicken. Keep warm.
❷ Melt remaining 1 tablespoon butter in pan over medium-high heat. Add mushrooms to pan; sauté 5 minutes or until moisture evaporates, stirring frequently. Remove mushroom mixture from pan. Add broth to pan; bring to a boil, scraping pan to loosen browned bits. Cook until reduced to 1 cup (about 5 minutes). Return mushroom mixture to pan. Stir in cream; cook 2 minutes or until slightly thick, stirring occasionally.
❸ Place ¾ cup egg noodles on each of 6 plates. Cut each chicken breast half into 1-inch-thick strips. Top each serving with 1 chicken breast half and about ⅓ cup mushroom mixture. Garnish each serving with parsley sprigs, if desired. Yield: 6 servings.

CALORIES 452; FAT 14.2g (sat 7g, mono 3.8g, poly 1.6g); PROTEIN 47g; CARB 32.2g; FIBER 2.2g; CHOL 162mg; IRON 3.4mg; SODIUM 489mg; CALC 49mg

Produce Tip

Distinctive **morel mushrooms** grace this dish with their nutty, woodsy flavor and unique texture. Because of their sponge-like crevices, wash them well to remove dirt. If you can't find fresh morels, look for one ounce dried, then rehydrate them in hot water before adding to the sauce.

Oven-Roasted Chicken Breasts with Artichokes and Toasted Breadcrumbs

If you can't find baby artichokes, use six large globe artichokes instead and cook them a bit longer, just until tender.

5	quarts water, divided
⅓	cup kosher salt
6	bone-in chicken breast halves, skinned
¼	cup fresh lemon juice
18	baby artichokes
2	tablespoons olive oil, divided
¼	teaspoon freshly ground black pepper
1	tablespoon canola oil
1	cup dry white wine
1	(14-ounce) can fat-free, less-sodium chicken broth
1½	ounces French bread baguette
2	tablespoons chopped fresh flat-leaf parsley

1 Combine 3 quarts water and salt in a Dutch oven, stirring until salt dissolves. Add chicken to salt mixture. Cover and refrigerate 2 hours.

2 Combine remaining 2 quarts water and juice. Cut off stem of each artichoke to within 1 inch of base; peel stem. Remove bottom leaves and tough outer leaves, leaving tender heart and bottom. Cut each artichoke in half lengthwise; place in lemon water.

3 Heat 1 tablespoon olive oil in a large skillet over medium-high heat. Drain artichokes; pat dry. Add artichokes to pan. Cover and cook 10 minutes or until tender. Uncover and cook an additional 5 minutes or until browned, stirring frequently. Keep warm.

4 Preheat oven to 450°.

5 Remove chicken from salt mixture; discard salt mixture. Pat chicken dry; sprinkle evenly with pepper.

6 Heat canola oil in a large ovenproof skillet over medium-high heat. Wrap handle of pan with foil. Add chicken to pan, meat sides down; sauté 1 minute.

Bake at 450° for 10 minutes. Turn chicken over; bake an additional 12 minutes or until done. Keep warm.

7 Place a zip-top plastic bag inside a 2-cup glass measure. Pour drippings into bag; let stand 10 minutes (fat will rise to top). Seal bag; carefully snip off 1 bottom corner of bag. Drain drippings back into pan, stopping before fat layer reaches opening; discard fat.

8 Add wine to drippings in pan; bring to a boil, scraping pan to loosen browned bits. Reduce heat, and simmer until reduced to 1 cup (about 5 minutes). Add broth to pan; simmer until reduced to 1½ cups (about 10 minutes).

9 Reduce oven temperature to 350°. Place bread in food processor; pulse 10 times or until coarse crumbs measure 1 cup. Combine remaining 1 tablespoon olive oil and breadcrumbs in a bowl; toss to coat. Arrange crumbs in a single layer on a baking sheet; bake at 350° for 5 minutes or until golden. Add parsley; toss to combine. Serve chicken with artichokes and sauce. Top with breadcrumbs. Serve immediately. Yield: 6 servings (serving size: 1 chicken breast half, 6 artichoke halves, ¼ cup sauce, and about 2½ tablespoons breadcrumbs).

CALORIES 293; FAT 10.5g (sat 1.8g, mono 5.8g, poly 2.2g); PROTEIN 32.5g; CARB 19.3g; FIBER 7.5g; CHOL 73mg; IRON 3.2mg; SODIUM 835mg; CALC 82mg

Produce Tip

Contrary to popular belief, **baby artichokes** are not immature. In fact, they are fully grown but simply positioned low on the stalk. Choose ones that are olive green with tightly closed leaves. Because they have a tendency to discolor, place them in acidulated water after cutting.

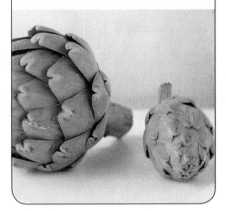

STAFF FAVORITE

Chicken Thighs with Lemon, Olives, and Artichokes

Be sure to zest the lemon before cutting and juicing it for this tangy recipe.

1½	tablespoons olive oil
12	bone-in chicken thighs (about 3 pounds), skinned
7	cups water, divided
2½	cups finely chopped onion
¼	cup chopped fresh flat-leaf parsley
1	teaspoon paprika
1	teaspoon ground cumin
½	teaspoon salt
¼	teaspoon saffron threads, crushed
¼	teaspoon freshly ground black pepper
5	garlic cloves, minced
10	tablespoons fresh lemon juice, divided
12	baby artichokes
2	teaspoons grated lemon rind
¾	cup kalamata olives, pitted
6	fresh cilantro sprigs (optional)
3	cups hot cooked couscous

Continued

① Heat oil in a large Dutch oven over medium-high heat. Add chicken to pan; sauté 4 minutes on each side or until browned. Add 3 cups water, onion, and next 7 ingredients to pan; bring to a boil. Reduce heat, and simmer 25 minutes.

② Combine remaining 4 cups water and ¼ cup juice. Cut off stem of each artichoke to within 1 inch of base; peel stem. Remove bottom leaves and tough outer leaves, leaving tender heart and bottom. Cut each artichoke in half lengthwise; place in lemon water.

③ Drain artichokes; pat dry. Add artichokes, remaining 6 tablespoons juice, and rind to chicken mixture. Cover and cook 20 minutes or until artichokes are tender. Remove chicken and artichokes with a slotted spoon.

④ Bring liquid to a boil; cook, uncovered, until reduced by half (about 15 minutes). Return chicken and artichokes to pan, and stir in olives. Reduce heat, and simmer 3 minutes or until thoroughly heated. Garnish with cilantro sprigs, if desired. Serve with couscous. Yield: 6 servings (serving size: 2 chicken thighs, ⅔ cup artichoke mixture, and ½ cup couscous).

CALORIES 429; FAT 15.2g (sat 2.7g, mono 8.7g, poly 2.6g); PROTEIN 35.4g; CARB 39.6g; FIBER 9.2g; CHOL 115mg; IRON 4mg; SODIUM 810mg; CALC 104mg

Produce Tip

Room-temperature **lemons** with smooth, glossy skin (as opposed to bumpy rinds) produce the most juice.

Chicken Skewers with Fava Bean and Mint Salad

Plate with a side of fluffy couscous.

2 cups shelled fava beans (about 4 pounds unshelled)
¼ cup extra-virgin olive oil, divided
1 teaspoon grated lemon rind
2 tablespoons fresh lemon juice
2 tablespoons chopped fresh mint
¾ teaspoon salt, divided
½ teaspoon freshly ground black pepper, divided
1¾ pounds skinless, boneless chicken breast halves, cut into (1-inch) pieces
Cooking spray
6 lemon wedges (optional)
Fresh mint sprigs (optional)

① Prepare grill to medium-high heat.
② Cook fava beans in boiling water for 1 minute or until tender. Drain and rinse with cold water; drain. Remove tough outer skins from beans; discard skins.
③ Combine 3 tablespoons oil, rind, juice, chopped mint, ¼ teaspoon salt, and ¼ teaspoon pepper in a medium bowl. Add fava beans to oil mixture; toss to coat.
④ Thread chicken evenly onto 12 (8-inch) skewers. Brush chicken with remaining 1 tablespoon oil; sprinkle evenly with remaining ½ teaspoon salt and ¼ teaspoon pepper. Place skewers on grill rack coated with cooking spray; grill 8 minutes or until done, turning once. Serve with fava bean mixture. Garnish with lemon wedges and mint sprigs, if desired. Yield: 6 servings (serving size: 2 skewers and ⅓ cup fava bean mixture).

CALORIES 447; FAT 13.8g (sat 2.3g, mono 7.8g, poly 2.8g); PROTEIN 43.3g; CARB 52.4g; FIBER 0.1g; CHOL 55mg; IRON 5.3mg; SODIUM 416mg; CALC 121mg

WINE NOTE: Mirror the flavors in this dish with a wine that's crisp and has green flavors of its own. A New Zealand sauvignon blanc is just the ticket. Try Babich 2007 from Marlborough, New Zealand, about $14.

Produce Tip

Open **fava bean** pods to remove the beans. As the recipe directs, you also need to cook the beans briefly in boiling water, and then peel off their tough outer skins.

Chicken Breasts Stuffed with Goat Cheese, Caramelized Spring Onions, and Thyme

1½ teaspoons olive oil
1⅓ cups thinly sliced spring onions (about 1 pound)
¾ teaspoon salt, divided
¼ teaspoon freshly ground black pepper
¾ cup (3 ounces) crumbled goat cheese
1 tablespoon chopped fresh flat-leaf parsley
1 tablespoon fat-free milk
1½ teaspoons chopped fresh thyme
6 (6-ounce) skinless, boneless chicken breast halves
Cooking spray
½ cup dry white wine
1 cup fat-free, less-sodium chicken broth

① Heat oil in a large skillet over medium heat. Add onions, ¼ teaspoon salt, and pepper to pan; cook 12 minutes, stirring frequently. Cover, reduce heat, and cook

8 minutes, stirring occasionally. Uncover and cook 5 minutes or until golden, stirring occasionally. Cool slightly. Combine onion mixture, ¼ teaspoon salt, cheese, and next 3 ingredients in a small bowl, stirring with a fork.

❷ Cut a horizontal slit through thickest portion of each chicken breast half to form a pocket; stuff 1½ tablespoons cheese mixture into each pocket. Sprinkle chicken evenly with remaining ¼ teaspoon salt.

❸ Return pan to medium-high heat. Coat pan with cooking spray. Add chicken to pan; sauté 5 minutes; turn chicken over. Cover, reduce heat, and cook 10 minutes or until chicken is done. Remove chicken from pan; let stand 10 minutes. Add wine to pan; bring to a boil, scraping pan to loosen browned bits. Cook until reduced by half (about 2 minutes). Add broth, and cook until reduced to ¼ cup (about 9 minutes). Serve with chicken. Yield: 6 servings (serving size: 1 chicken breast half and 2 teaspoons sauce).

CALORIES 274; FAT 9.5g (sat 4.3g, mono 3.2g, poly 1.2g); PROTEIN 39.3g; CARB 6.6g; FIBER 2.2g; CHOL 105mg; IRON 2.8mg; SODIUM 530mg; CALC 123mg

Produce Tip

Spring onions look like oversized green onions. Since they're picked before full maturity, they have a milder flavor than pungent full-grown onions. Look for spring onions at farmers' markets or in the produce section of major supermarkets. If you can't find them, substitute leeks.

Chicken Scaloppine with Sugar Snap Pea, Asparagus, and Lemon Salad

Scaloppine are chicken breasts pounded thin; they cook to perfection in four minutes. The crisp salad comes together quickly, too, which makes this a great dinner for a busy night.

- 3 cups julienne-cut trimmed sugar snap peas (about 1 pound)
- 2 cups (1-inch) slices asparagus (about 1 pound)
- 6 (6-ounce) skinless, boneless chicken breast halves
- ¾ teaspoon salt, divided
- ½ teaspoon freshly ground black pepper
- Cooking spray
- 1 cup fat-free, less-sodium chicken broth
- ⅓ cup dry white wine
- 1 tablespoon butter
- 1 tablespoon chopped fresh mint
- 2½ tablespoons extra-virgin olive oil
- 1 teaspoon grated lemon rind
- 1½ tablespoons fresh lemon juice
- 6 lemon wedges

❶ Steam peas and asparagus, covered, 4 minutes or until crisp-tender. Rinse pea mixture with cold water; drain. Chill.

❷ Place each chicken breast half between 2 sheets of heavy-duty plastic wrap; pound to ¼-inch thickness using a meat mallet or small heavy skillet. Sprinkle chicken evenly with ½ teaspoon salt and pepper. Heat a large nonstick skillet over medium-high heat. Coat pan with cooking spray. Add 2 breast halves to pan; sauté 2 minutes on each side or until done. Repeat procedure twice with remaining chicken. Remove chicken from pan, and keep warm. Add broth and wine to pan; bring to a boil, scraping pan to loosen browned bits. Cook until reduced to ½ cup (about 5 minutes). Remove from heat; stir in butter.

❸ Combine remaining ¼ teaspoon salt, mint, and next 3 ingredients, stirring well with a whisk. Drizzle oil mixture over pea mixture; toss gently to coat. Serve pea mixture with chicken and sauce. Garnish with lemon wedges. Yield: 6 servings (serving size: 1 chicken breast half, about 1 cup pea mixture, 4 teaspoons sauce, and 1 lemon wedge).

CALORIES 315; FAT 10g (sat 2.6g, mono 5.2g, poly 1.4g); PROTEIN 43.3g; CARB 10.3g; FIBER 3.7g; CHOL 104mg; IRON 4.1mg; SODIUM 495mg; CALC 98mg

Produce Tips

Asparagus: Look for stalks with deep green or purplish tips that are tightly closed and not slick. Remove the fibrous ends by bending each stalk until it snaps; the tough part will break off naturally.

Sugar Snap Peas: These peas are crunchy and sweet. Choose plump, crisp pods, and refrigerate them for up to three days.

Inspired Salad From Hawaii

Your most delicious creations, from a terrific garden salad to dishes whipped up from pantry and fridge staples

Living on Kona, Hawaii's big island, is paradise for Maureen Nibecker, and anyone else who craves fresh produce. She tends herbs and vegetables in her garden and picks bananas, papayas, Tahitian limes, avocados, and cherries from her in-laws' farm.

Nibecker has always loved to cook, but her hobby took off when she moved from her native California two years ago. She now lives in the small town of Honokaa, a place she describes as having "one stop sign," so cooking at home is a must. Since many staples have to be shipped to Hawaii and are more expensive than they'd be on the mainland, Nibecker turns to the farm and garden at dinnertime.

This salad was inspired by a dish at one of her favorite restaurants in nearby Hilo. "It was a basic iceberg lettuce and tomato salad with an Asian-spiced peanut dressing," she recalls. She updated it with baby salad greens and added fresh herbs, bean sprouts, onions, and carrots. "I also developed my own peanut dressing and was delighted by its taste. Everything is so much better when you make it yourself with fresh ingredients," she concludes.

Thai Salad with Peanut Dressing

"These ingredients reflect the types of food my family enjoys year-round—fresh herbs and vegetables from our garden and local farmers. Sometimes we add chopped cooked chicken or my husband's fresh fish catch of the day for a main dish."

—Maureen Nibecker, Honokaa, Hawaii

DRESSING:

- 3 tablespoons water
- 2 tablespoons rice wine vinegar
- 1 tablespoon chopped green onions
- 1 tablespoon reduced-fat peanut butter
- 1 tablespoon low-sodium soy sauce
- 1 teaspoon grated peeled fresh ginger
- 1 teaspoon Sriracha (hot chile sauce, such as Huy Fong)
- 1 teaspoon dark sesame oil
- 2 teaspoons dry-roasted peanuts

SALAD:

- 2 cups mixed baby salad greens
- ½ cup fresh bean sprouts
- 2 tablespoons vertically sliced red onion
- 2 tablespoons fresh mint leaves
- 2 tablespoons fresh cilantro leaves
- 6 baby carrots, peeled
- 4 cherry tomatoes, quartered

❶ To prepare dressing, place first 8 ingredients in a blender; cover and process until smooth. Add peanuts, and process 10 seconds.

❷ To prepare salad, divide greens and remaining ingredients evenly between 2 serving plates. Drizzle each salad with ¼ cup dressing. Yield: 2 servings.

CALORIES 160; FAT 8.2g (sat 1.4g, mono 3.6g, poly 2.8g); PROTEIN 6.4g; CARB 18.4g; FIBER 4.6g; CHOL 0mg; IRON 2.1mg; SODIUM 554mg; CALC 68mg

Excellent-for-Entertaining Menu
serves 6

Fresh Herb–Marinated Lamb Tenderloin Kebabs

Green beans with feta

Steam 1 pound trimmed green beans 5 minutes or until crisp-tender. Combine beans and ⅓ cup thinly sliced red onion in a large bowl. Add 3 tablespoons extra-virgin olive oil, ½ teaspoon salt, and ¼ teaspoon freshly ground black pepper; toss to coat. Top with ⅔ cup coarsely chopped toasted walnuts and ½ cup (2 ounces) crumbled feta cheese.

Couscous
Iced mint tea
Lemon sorbet

Fresh Herb–Marinated Lamb Tenderloin Kebabs

"My family enjoys lamb, so I was delighted to discover lamb tenderloin at the supermarket. The butcher explained it's a perfect cut to slice and thread onto skewers. It has a wonderful flavor, and like beef and pork tenderloin, it's a lean and versatile choice. I like to serve these with roasted asparagus, broccoli, or cauliflower and either quinoa or toasted brown rice with saffron."

—Florence Gardner, Greenville, South Carolina

- ¼ cup fresh lemon juice
- 3 tablespoons chopped fresh mint
- 3 tablespoons chopped fresh rosemary
- 3 tablespoons chopped fresh oregano
- 3 tablespoons chopped fresh thyme
- 2 tablespoons olive oil
- 2 tablespoons honey
- 1 tablespoon Dijon mustard
- 1 teaspoon salt
- 1 teaspoon freshly ground black pepper
- 3 garlic cloves, minced
- 1½ pounds lamb tenderloin, cut into 2-inch pieces

① Preheat grill to medium-high heat.
② Combine all ingredients except lamb in a large zip-top plastic bag. Add lamb to bag; seal and marinate in refrigerator 30 minutes.
③ Remove lamb from bag; discard marinade. Thread lamb pieces evenly onto 12 (10-inch) skewers. Grill 2 minutes on each side or until desired degree of doneness. Yield: 6 servings (serving size: 2 skewers).

CALORIES 221; FAT 10.7g (sat 3.4g, mono 5.4g, poly 0.8g); PROTEIN 25.6g; CARB 4.1g; FIBER 0.4g; CHOL 81mg; IRON 1.9mg; SODIUM 299mg; CALC 24mg

Spinach Risotto with Shrimp and Goat Cheese

"When one of my favorite restaurants closed, I developed my own version of their renowned seafood risotto. I think spinach adds great flavor and boosts the nutritional value."

—Brandy Jamison-Neth,
Denver, Colorado

Cooking spray
1 pound large shrimp, peeled and deveined
1 tablespoon olive oil
1½ cups chopped onion (about 1 medium)
2 garlic cloves, minced
1 cup uncooked Arborio or other medium-grain rice
¾ cup dry white wine
4 cups fat-free, less-sodium chicken broth
¼ cup chopped fresh cilantro
Dash of saffron threads
1 (10-ounce) package frozen chopped spinach, thawed, drained, and squeezed dry
½ cup (2 ounces) crumbled goat cheese

① Heat a large nonstick skillet over medium-high heat. Coat pan with cooking spray. Add shrimp to pan; sauté 4 minutes or until done. Remove shrimp from pan; set aside and keep warm.

② Heat oil in pan over medium heat. Add onion to pan; cook 5 minutes. Add garlic; cook 1 minute. Add rice; cook 1 minute, stirring constantly. Stir in wine; cook 4 minutes or until liquid is nearly absorbed, stirring constantly.
③ Add broth, ½ cup at a time, stirring constantly until each portion of broth is absorbed before adding next (about 25 minutes total). Stir in cilantro, saffron, and spinach with last ½ cup broth. Add shrimp and cheese, stirring to combine. Serve immediately. Yield: 4 servings (serving size: 1½ cups).

CALORIES 444; FAT 11.7g (sat 4.6g, mono 4g, poly 1.4g); PROTEIN 37.2g; CARB 48.3g; FIBER 5.9g; CHOL 187mg; IRON 5.4mg; SODIUM 662mg; CALC 326mg

MAKE AHEAD • FREEZABLE
Limelight Blueberry Muffins

"Lime adds a little tartness that complements the sweetness of the fresh blueberries."

—Jenna Baldwin,
Mesa, Arizona

7.9 ounces all-purpose flour (about 1¾ cups)
1 cup sugar
2 teaspoons baking powder
¼ teaspoon salt
½ cup light sour cream
⅓ cup canola oil
1 teaspoon grated lime rind
2 tablespoons fresh lime juice
1 teaspoon vanilla extract
2 large egg whites
1 large egg
1 (6-ounce) container plain low-fat yogurt
Cooking spray
1 cup fresh blueberries

① Preheat oven to 350°.
② Weigh or lightly spoon flour into dry measuring cups; level with a knife. Combine flour and next 3 ingredients in a large bowl; make a well in center of mixture.

③ Combine sour cream and next 7 ingredients in a bowl; stir with a whisk. Add sour cream mixture to flour mixture; stir just until moist. Spoon batter evenly into 12 muffin cups coated with cooking spray. Sprinkle blueberries evenly over muffins. Bake at 350° for 25 minutes or until muffins spring back when touched lightly in center. Cool in pans 10 minutes on a wire rack. Serve warm or at room temperature. Yield: 12 muffins (serving size: 1 muffin).

CALORIES 225; FAT 7.7g (sat 1.3g, mono 3.8g, poly 1.9g); PROTEIN 4.7g; CARB 34.5g; FIBER 0.8g; CHOL 19mg; IRON 1.1mg; SODIUM 166mg; CALC 74mg

MAKE AHEAD
Mango Chutney

"I created this from ingredients I had in my refrigerator and pantry to use as a condiment on turkey burgers."

—Whitney Miller,
Poplarville, Mississippi

1½ cups cubed peeled ripe mango (about 1 medium)
⅓ cup chopped yellow onion
⅓ cup chopped red bell pepper
⅓ cup golden raisins
¼ cup water
3 tablespoons brown sugar
2 tablespoons fresh lime juice
2 teaspoons diced jalapeño pepper
1 teaspoon white vinegar
1 teaspoon balsamic vinegar
¼ teaspoon ground ginger
⅛ teaspoon salt
⅛ teaspoon black pepper
1 garlic clove, minced

① Combine all ingredients in a saucepan. Cook over medium heat 30 minutes or until thick, stirring occasionally. Remove from heat; mash with a potato masher until desired consistency. Cool completely. Store in an airtight container in refrigerator for up to 2 days. Yield: 1¼ cups (serving size: 2 tablespoons).

CALORIES 35; FAT 0.1g (sat 0g, mono 0g, poly 0.1g); PROTEIN 0.5g; CARB 8.9g; FIBER 0.8g; CHOL 0mg; IRON 0.3mg; SODIUM 33mg; CALC 11mg

Lightened Enchiladas

A cheesy chicken casserole is revamped to meet a Texas reader's health goals.

"My son-in-law, Marc, is from a traditional Mexican family, and we're Italian," said Anna Marie "Rie" Lotti, a life insurance broker from Katy, Texas. "This is a dish we all love because it's cheesy and good," Lotti says of Cheesy Chicken Enchiladas, a recipe that's been in her family for two decades. Lotti notes their lifestyle has changed a lot since she started making the casserole: Both she and her husband, Tom, keep tabs on sodium, saturated fat, and calories since Tom was diagnosed with type 2 diabetes a few years ago. "I'm glad my daughter, Dawn, sent the recipe to *Cooking Light* for a makeover," she says.

Plenty of cheese and sour cream, as well as canned cream of chicken soup, contributed to the hefty 773 calories per serving of this filling entrée. Plus, the soup and abundant 2 pounds of cheese added to the dish's sodium content.

The Solution:

• **Cheese:** Using half the amount of cheese and opting for a reduced-fat Mexican blend in the filling cut 149 calories, 13.4 grams of fat (8.4 grams saturated), and 126 milligrams of sodium per serving.

• **Topping:** We topped the casserole with one-fourth the original amount of cheese and employed a sharp reduced-fat Cheddar to trim 97 calories, 8.3 grams of fat (5.2 grams saturated), and 134 milligrams of sodium per serving.

• **Sour cream:** In place of 2 cups of the full-fat sour cream, we used a combination of 1²/₃ cups low-fat plain yogurt and ¹/₃ cup butter to shave 29 calories and about 4 grams of fat (2.4 grams saturated) per serving.

• **Canned soup:** We substituted a reduced-fat, reduced-sodium version of canned cream of chicken soup for a savings of 1.5 grams of fat and 102 milligrams of sodium per serving.

• **Tortillas:** Instead of frying the tortillas in oil, we brushed them with a prudent 1 tablespoon canola oil to keep fat and calories in check and pan-toasted them.

"The family thoroughly enjoyed the new version of the enchiladas," says Lotti. "The tortillas were tender, and the filling was flavorful and creamy with extra onion and garlic and the combined sour cream and butter."

serving size: 1 enchilada		
	before	after
CALORIES PER SERVING	773	454
TOTAL FAT	53.4g	20.3g
SATURATED FAT	27.9g	10.4g
SODIUM	1,096mg	757mg

Cheesy Chicken Enchiladas

Serve with a salad of fresh mango, jicama, and shredded lettuce topped with a lime vinaigrette.

2½ cups chopped cooked chicken breast
2 cups (8 ounces) preshredded reduced-fat 4-cheese Mexican blend cheese
1²/₃ cups plain low-fat yogurt
¹/₃ cup butter, melted
¼ cup chopped onion
1 teaspoon minced garlic
¼ teaspoon freshly ground black pepper
1 (10¾-ounce) can condensed reduced-fat, reduced-sodium cream of chicken soup (such as Healthy Request), undiluted
1 (4.5-ounce) can chopped green chiles, drained
8 (8-inch) flour tortillas
1 tablespoon canola oil
Cooking spray
½ cup (2 ounces) finely shredded reduced-fat sharp Cheddar cheese
¼ cup chopped green onions

❶ Preheat oven to 350°.
❷ Combine first 9 ingredients in a large bowl. Remove 1 cup chicken mixture; set mixture aside.
❸ Heat a large skillet over medium-high heat. Working with 1 tortilla at a time, brush oil over both sides of tortilla. Add tortilla to pan; cook 5 seconds on each side or until toasted and soft. Remove from pan; arrange ½ cup chicken mixture down center of tortilla. Roll jelly-roll style; place filled tortilla, seam side down, in a 13 x 9–inch baking dish coated with cooking spray. Repeat procedure with remaining 7 tortillas, remaining oil, and remaining chicken mixture. Spread reserved 1 cup chicken mixture evenly over enchiladas. Cover and bake at 350° for 20 minutes. Uncover; sprinkle evenly with Cheddar cheese and green onions; bake an additional 5 minutes or until cheese melts. Yield: 8 servings (serving size: 1 enchilada).

CALORIES 454; FAT 20.3g (sat 10.4g, mono 6.7g, poly 1.5g); PROTEIN 30.8g; CARB 36.6g; FIBER 2.2g; CHOL 73mg; IRON 2.3mg; SODIUM 757mg; CALC 347mg

WINE NOTE: Just as a crunchy green salad with mango will complement Cheesy Chicken Enchiladas, so too will a crisp, tropical fruit-filled California chardonnay, like Kali Hart Vineyard Chardonnay 2007 ($17). With its medium body and lively acidity, this white wine slices through creamy dairy products, like cheese and yogurt. A shot of citrus flavor and a nice bit of lingering sweetness also give it the ability to balance spicy chiles.

Eggs Exactly Right

Learn indispensable techniques for cooking with this essential ingredient.

EGGS ARE ECONOMICAL and may just be the world's most versatile food. Their neutral taste makes them a good vehicle for an array of flavors. And because they coagulate when cooked, they do work that no other ingredient can perform, binding foods like custard and providing structure in countless other recipes. Eggs also fit conveniently into a healthful diet. Here you'll learn six simple ways to prepare tasty egg dishes that go beyond breakfast or brunch and also happen to be good for you.

QUICK & EASY
Wild Mushroom Omelet

Use a mix of seasonal varieties or your favorite mushrooms to fill this classic French-style omelet. If your pan becomes too hot and the eggs begin to set too quickly, simply lift the pan off the heat to slow the cooking as you stir. Garnish with fresh flat-leaf parsley sprigs for a pretty presentation, and serve with fresh fruit.

- 2 tablespoons finely chopped shallots
- 2 tablespoons water
- 2 ounces wild mushrooms, coarsely chopped
- 1 tablespoon chopped fresh flat-leaf parsley
- 1 teaspoon fresh lemon juice
- ⅛ teaspoon salt
- 1 tablespoon butter, divided
- 4 large eggs, divided
- ¼ teaspoon salt, divided
- ⅛ teaspoon ground white pepper, divided

1 Combine first 3 ingredients in a small skillet over medium-high heat; bring to a simmer. Cook 3 minutes or until water evaporates and mushrooms are tender, stirring occasionally. Remove from heat. Stir in parsley, lemon juice, and ⅛ teaspoon salt.

2 Melt 1½ teaspoons butter in an 8-inch skillet over medium-high heat. Place 2 eggs in a small bowl. Add ⅛ teaspoon salt and a dash of pepper, stirring with a whisk until eggs are frothy. Pour egg mixture into pan, and stir briskly with a heatproof spatula for about 10 seconds or until egg starts to thicken. Quickly pull egg that sets at sides of pan to center with spatula, tipping pan to pour uncooked egg to sides. Continue this procedure 10 to 15 seconds or until almost no runny egg remains. Remove pan from heat; arrange half of mushroom mixture (about 1½ tablespoons) over omelet in pan. Run spatula around edges and under omelet to loosen it from pan. To fold the omelet, hold pan handle with one hand and tip pan away from you. Give the handle a sharp tap with your other hand so top edge of omelet flips over, or fold edge over with a fork. Slide omelet from pan onto a plate, rolling it as it slides, so it lands folded in three with the seam underneath. Tuck in sides of omelet to neaten it. Repeat procedure with remaining 1½ teaspoons butter, 2 eggs, ⅛ teaspoon salt, dash of pepper, and 1½ tablespoons mushroom mixture. Yield: 2 servings (serving size: 1 omelet).

CALORIES 210; FAT 15.7g (sat 6.7g, mono 5.3g, poly 1.6g); PROTEIN 13.7g; CARB 4.1g; FIBER 0.3g; CHOL 438mg; IRON 2.2mg; SODIUM 588mg; CALC 67mg

Step By Step: How to Make an Omelet

1. Melt butter in a hot pan, and add whisked eggs. Working quickly, stir the egg that coagulates around the sides back into the runny, uncooked center. Continue cooking and stirring as you tip the pan, allowing the uncooked egg to run out to the sides. Repeat this procedure until eggs are cooked to desired consistency.

2. Sprinkle filling over the omelet. Remove pan from heat. Run the spatula around edges and under the omelet to loosen it from the pan.

3. Hold the pan over a plate, and tip it up and away, sliding omelet from pan onto the plate, rolling it as it slides. Serve immediately.

Eggs in Overcoats

Here we stuff scrambled eggs into their shells for a fancy presentation, though it is optional. For a silky texture, stop cooking eggs when they resemble thickened custard with small curds as the eggs will continue to thicken in the pan's heat. If you don't have an egg topper for Step 1, tap the top of each egg with kitchen shears to create a small opening, and then snip away a portion of the top part of the shell.

- 6 large eggs
- 2 teaspoons chilled butter, cut into small pieces
- ¼ teaspoon salt
- ⅛ teaspoon freshly ground black pepper
- 2 teaspoons crème fraîche
- 2 teaspoons caviar

① Using an egg topper, carefully cut a lid from each egg. Empty eggs into a bowl, reserving 4 shells. Bring a small pan of water to a boil. Rinse reserved egg shells; carefully lower them into the boiling water. Simmer 3 minutes. Remove shells, and let them dry upside down on a towel.

② Combine butter and eggs in a medium nonstick saucepan over medium-high heat, stirring eggs constantly with a flexible heatproof spatula or wooden spoon until they start to thicken (about 3 minutes). Eggs will start to coagulate suddenly, often around sides or base of pan. Lift pan off heat, and stir rapidly so that any cooked egg dissolves back into liquid part, stirring for about 30 seconds. Return pan to heat; cook about 3 minutes or until eggs thicken slightly, stirring constantly. Remove pan from heat, and stir 30 seconds. Continue placing eggs over heat for about 3-minute intervals and removing for 30 seconds, stirring constantly until desired degree of doneness (repeat procedure about 5 times total). Sprinkle eggs evenly with salt and pepper.

③ Divide egg mixture evenly, and carefully spoon into 4 prepared egg shells. Top each serving with ½ teaspoon crème fraîche and ½ teaspoon caviar. Set eggs in egg cups, and serve immediately. Yield: 4 servings (serving size: about 1½ eggs, ½ teaspoon crème fraîche, and ½ teaspoon caviar).

CALORIES 134; FAT 10.3g (sat 4.1g, mono 3.4g, poly 1.1g); PROTEIN 9.7g; CARB 0.7g; FIBER 0g; CHOL 329mg; IRON 1.5mg; SODIUM 264mg; CALC 42mg

Step By Step:
How to Scramble Eggs

1. Combine butter and eggs in a saucepan over medium-high heat.

2. Stir eggs constantly, and cook the mixture about 3 minutes or until it starts to thicken slightly. Remove pan from heat, and continue stirring about 30 seconds. Return pan to heat. Keep an eye on the heat. If the pan becomes too hot and the eggs start to seize, remove pan from heat, stirring constantly to fold the melted butter and cooked eggs back into the uncooked mixture.

3. Continue cooking briefly and removing pan from the heat, stirring constantly, until eggs are almost set and still appear moist. Sprinkle eggs with salt and pepper.

Poached Eggs with Buttery Multigrain Toast

The eggs can be poached ahead and stored in cold water in the refrigerator. If you do so, be sure to undercook them slightly. Warm them in hot water before serving.

- 1 tablespoon white vinegar
- 4 large eggs
- 2 tablespoons butter, softened
- 4 (1½-ounce) slices multigrain bread
- 2 cups baby arugula
- ¼ teaspoon salt
- ¼ teaspoon freshly ground black pepper

① Preheat broiler.
② In a (12-inch) skillet, bring a 2-inch layer of water (about 4 cups) to a low boil with vinegar. Break an egg into a bubbling area so the bubbles spin the egg and set the white around the yolks. Add remaining eggs; turn down heat and poach them so they scarcely bubble for 3 minutes or until desired degree of doneness. To test them, lift an egg with a slotted spoon and press with your fingertip: The white should be set with the yolk still soft. Transfer eggs to a bowl of warm water. Trim strings from edges of each egg with kitchen shears, if desired.
③ Spread 1½ teaspoons butter over each bread slice. Place bread slices in a single layer on a heavy baking sheet; broil 3 minutes or until golden. Place 1 toasted bread slice on each of 4 plates; top each serving with ½ cup arugula and 1 egg. Sprinkle evenly with salt and pepper, and serve immediately. Yield: 4 servings.

CALORIES 231; FAT 12.3g (sat 5.5g, mono 4g, poly 1.3g); PROTEIN 10.9g; CARB 20.6g; FIBER 2.9g; CHOL 227mg; IRON 2.6mg; SODIUM 468mg; CALC 83mg

Step By Step:
How to Poach Eggs

1. Add a little vinegar to the poaching water to help the egg whites set quickly, and bring the mixture to a low boil. Add eggs to the pan, and cook 3 minutes or until whites are just set but yolks are still runny.

2. Carefully lift eggs from pan with a slotted spoon.

3. If desired, neaten edges with kitchen shears. Season eggs, and serve.

Crab Salad–Stuffed Eggs

For best results, slice the radishes as thinly as possible. If you have a mandoline, this is the time to use it, but you can also slice them by hand (small ones are easiest to cut by hand). Chill the radishes and lemon juice at least 30 minutes, and keep in mind that the longer you chill them, the pinker they'll become.

2 cups thinly sliced radishes (about 1 pound)
1 tablespoon fresh lemon juice, divided
½ teaspoon salt, divided
8 large eggs
¼ teaspoon freshly ground black pepper
2 tablespoons extra-virgin olive oil
3 tablespoons plain Greek-style fat-free yogurt
1 cup lump crabmeat, drained and shell pieces removed (about 5 ounces)
¼ cup finely chopped celery (about 3 medium stalks)
1 teaspoon dry mustard
24 butter lettuce leaves

❶ Combine radishes, 2 teaspoons juice, and ¼ teaspoon salt in a bowl; toss. Cover and chill at least 30 minutes.
❷ Place eggs in a medium saucepan, and cover with cold water to 1 inch above eggs; bring to a boil. Reduce heat, and simmer 10 minutes. Place eggs in ice water, and cool completely. Gently crack eggshells; peel under cold running water. Cut each egg in half lengthwise. Remove yolks. Press yolks through a sieve into a bowl. Set aside 1 tablespoon yolks. Combine remaining 1 teaspoon juice, remaining yolks, remaining ¼ teaspoon salt, and pepper in a bowl; gradually add oil, stirring well with a whisk until oil is incorporated. Stir in yogurt. Add crabmeat, celery, and mustard; stir gently until combined. Taste crab filling and adjust seasoning, if necessary.

❸ Arrange a fan of 3 lettuce leaves on each of 8 plates. Cut a thin slice from bottom of each egg white half to help them sit flat. Pile crab filling evenly into egg white halves. Place 2 egg white halves on each plate to one side of lettuce. Sprinkle reserved 1 tablespoon yolk over egg white halves. Arrange ¼ cup radish mixture on other side of each serving. Yield: 8 servings.

CALORIES 140; FAT 9.1g (sat 2.1g, mono 4.4g, poly 1.1g); PROTEIN 11.5g; CARB 4g; FIBER 1.3g; CHOL 237mg; IRON 2mg; SODIUM 411mg; CALC 72mg

Step By Step:
How to Hard-Boil Eggs

1. To hard-boil, place eggs in a saucepan, and cover with cold water. Bring water to a boil quickly over medium-high heat.
2. As soon as the water boils, reduce heat, and simmer 10 minutes. Transfer eggs to a bowl of ice water until cooled completely. Peel shell from egg; yolks should be bright yellow.

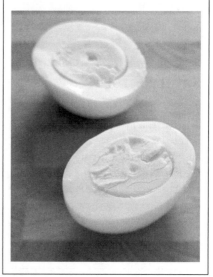

Step By Step:
How to Soft-Boil Eggs

1. To soft-boil, bring water to a boil. Lower eggs into boiling water, cover pan, and remove from heat. Let stand 6 minutes.
2. Transfer eggs to ice water until completely cooled.
3. Soft-boiled eggs have molten yolks with whites that are just set, so carefully peel shell from egg, taking care not to puncture the delicate center.

Safety First

Some uncooked eggs may carry salmonella bacteria. In recipes where eggs are not cooked to 160°, a temperature that destroys bacteria, use pasteurized eggs. (People at risk, such as the elderly, infants, and those with weakened immune systems, should avoid such recipes.) As a precaution, eggs should always be stored in the refrigerator. And always wash your hands thoroughly after handling raw eggs.

Soup and Salad Menu
serves 6

This light yet satisfying meal is ideal for an alfresco luncheon. Though the recipe calls for the soup to be chilled, it's also good hot or at room temperature.

Summer Caesar Salad

Asparagus soup

Cut 1½ pounds asparagus into 1-inch pieces. Bring 3 cups fat-free, less-sodium chicken broth to a boil in a medium saucepan. Add asparagus to broth; cook 2 minutes or until tender. Remove asparagus with a slotted spoon; place in a large bowl of ice water. Drain. Cool broth to room temperature. Place broth, asparagus, ¼ teaspoon salt, and ¼ teaspoon black pepper in a blender; process until smooth. Cover and chill. Divide soup evenly among 6 bowls. Top each serving with 1 teaspoon crème fraîche or light sour cream and ½ teaspoon chopped fresh chives.

Sauvignon blanc
Raspberries topped with whipped cream

STAFF FAVORITE
Summer Caesar Salad

- ¼ cup extra-virgin olive oil, divided
- 1 garlic clove, halved lengthwise and divided
- 5 cups (½-inch) cubed day-old French bread baguette (about 6 ounces)
- 4 large pasteurized eggs
- 2 tablespoons fresh lemon juice
- 1 teaspoon water
- ½ teaspoon Worcestershire sauce
- 4 canned anchovy fillets, chopped
- 10 cups arugula
- ⅔ cup fresh mint leaves, torn
- ¼ teaspoon freshly ground black pepper
- ⅛ teaspoon salt
- ¼ cup (1 ounce) grated fresh Parmigiano-Reggiano cheese

❶ Preheat oven to 350°.
❷ Heat 1 tablespoon oil in a large ovenproof skillet over medium heat. Add 1 garlic half to pan; cook 1 minute. Add bread cubes; toss to coat. Bake at 350° for 10 minutes or until browned, stirring occasionally.
❸ Place eggs in a medium saucepan. Cover with cold water to 1 inch above eggs. Remove eggs from pan; bring water to a boil. Using a spoon, gently lower eggs into boiling water. Cover saucepan, remove from heat, and let stand 6 minutes. Place eggs in a bowl of ice water, and cool completely. Gently crack eggshells, and peel over a large bowl, pouring yolks into bowl. Coarsely chop egg whites. Discard eggshells.
❹ Mince remaining garlic. Add minced garlic, lemon juice, and next 3 ingredients to yolks; mash with a fork to form a paste. Gradually add remaining 3 tablespoons oil, 1 tablespoon at a time, stirring well with a whisk until each addition is incorporated and mixture emulsifies and thickens slightly. Add chopped egg whites, croutons, arugula, and mint to dressing. Sprinkle evenly with pepper and salt; toss gently. Sprinkle with cheese. Serve immediately. Yield: 6 servings (serving size: 1⅓ cups).

CALORIES 249; FAT 14.5g (sat 3.1g, mono 8.1g, poly 1.7g); PROTEIN 11.5g; CARB 19.9g; FIBER 1.5g; CHOL 149mg; IRON 2.6mg; SODIUM 595mg; CALC 165mg

Step By Step:
How to Bake Eggs

1. Break eggs into ramekins or custard cups over garnishes such as caramelized onions and croutons (as in Summer Caesar Salad at left), or directly into the cups.
2. Spoon a little cream directly over the tops of eggs to prevent them from drying out and becoming tough during cooking.
3. Since timing is critical, keep an eye on the eggs, and pull them from the oven before they're completely set as they'll continue cooking for a minute or two after you remove them from the oven.

Baked Eggs en Cocotte with Onions

Cooking spray
4 (1-ounce) slices French-style country bread, cut into (½-inch) cubes
1⅓ cups thinly sliced onion
½ teaspoon salt, divided
¼ teaspoon ground white pepper, divided
2 tablespoons water
6 large eggs
¼ cup half-and-half
Fresh flat-leaf parsley sprigs

① Preheat oven to 350°.
② Lightly coat 6 (8-ounce) ramekins with cooking spray. Spread bread cubes in an even layer on a baking sheet, and lightly coat with cooking spray. Bake at 350° for 10 minutes or until bread is crisp and lightly browned, stirring after 5 minutes.
③ Heat a small skillet over medium heat. Coat pan with cooking spray. Add onion, ¼ teaspoon salt, and ⅛ teaspoon pepper to pan; cook 10 minutes or until onion is tender. Increase heat to medium-high. Stir in 2 tablespoons water; cook 5 minutes or until golden brown, stirring frequently. Divide onion among prepared ramekins; top with croutons. Sprinkle remaining ¼ teaspoon salt and remaining ⅛ teaspoon pepper evenly over croutons.
④ Carefully break 1 egg into each ramekin on top of croutons; drizzle 2 teaspoons half-and-half over each egg. Arrange ramekins in a roasting pan lined with a dish towel (to anchor them in the pan). Pour boiling water halfway up sides of ramekins to make a water bath. Bake at 350° for 15 minutes or until whites are almost set. They should be slightly underdone as they will continue cooking in the hot dishes when you take them from the oven. Garnish with flat-leaf parsley sprigs, if desired. Yield: 6 servings (serving size: 1 ramekin).

CALORIES 163; FAT 6.7g (sat 2.3g, mono 1.9g, poly 0.7g); PROTEIN 8.9g; CARB 16.9g; FIBER 1.7g; CHOL 215mg; IRON 1.6mg; SODIUM 393mg; CALC 64mg

---

Step By Step: How to Bake Custard

Moist, gentle heat and perfect timing are the keys to creamy custards.
1. Cook in a water bath. Place ramekins on a towel in a baking pan; add boiling water until water comes about halfway up the sides of the ramekins.
2. Bake custard until almost set. To test for doneness, shake the container gently; the filling should be almost set but still wobble in the center as it will continue to cook after being pulled from the oven.

Mussel Flans with Herb Dressing

FLANS:
36 medium mussels (about 1½ pounds), scrubbed and debearded
½ cup dry white wine
¼ cup chopped shallots
1 garlic clove, chopped
⅛ teaspoon crushed saffron threads
1 (1-ounce) slice white bread, torn
⅓ cup heavy whipping cream
4 large eggs
Cooking spray

HERB DRESSING:
2 tablespoons white wine vinegar
⅛ teaspoon salt
¼ teaspoon black pepper
¼ cup extra-virgin olive oil
1 tablespoon chopped fresh chives
2 teaspoons chopped fresh tarragon
6 (1-ounce) slices white bread, toasted

① To prepare flans, rinse mussels with cold water; drain. Discard any broken or open shells that do not close when tapped on counter. Set mussels aside.
② Combine wine, shallots, and garlic in a large Dutch oven; bring to a simmer. Cook 1 minute. Add mussels to pan. Cover, increase heat to high, and cook 5 minutes or just until mussels open; discard any unopened shells. Remove from heat, and cool 5 minutes. Using a slotted spoon, remove mussels from pan, reserving cooking liquid. Remove meat from mussels; discard shells. Set aside.
③ Preheat oven to 350°.
④ Strain cooking liquid through a cheesecloth-lined sieve into a small saucepan; discard solids. Add saffron to cooking liquid; bring to a boil. Remove from heat. Add torn bread to saffron mixture. Let stand 5 minutes.
⑤ Set aside 6 mussels for garnish; chill. Pull off and discard rubbery rings from remaining mussels. Combine mussels, saffron mixture, and cream in a food processor; process 1 minute or until smooth. Place eggs in a large bowl; stir with a whisk until just frothy. Add mussel mixture to eggs; stir until combined.
⑥ Cut parchment paper to fit in bottom of each of 6 (6-ounce) ramekins. Line ramekins with parchment rounds; coat with cooking spray. Divide mussel mixture evenly among prepared ramekins. Place ramekins in a 13 x 9-inch baking pan lined with a dish towel (to anchor them in pan). Pour boiling water halfway up sides of ramekins. Bake at 350° for 20 minutes or until centers are just set. A slight wobble in center is fine. Remove flans from pan; cool on a wire rack to room temperature.
⑦ To prepare dressing, combine vinegar, salt, and pepper in a small bowl. Gradually add olive oil, 1 tablespoon at a time, stirring well with a whisk until each addition is incorporated and dressing emulsifies and thickens slightly. Whisk in chives and tarragon.
⑧ Cut toasted bread into rounds using a cutter slightly larger than ramekins (or rim of a clean, dry ramekin can be used). Working with one flan at a time, run a sharp knife around edge of flan and carefully invert onto a toast round; discard parchment. Set flan, toast side down, onto a plate. Repeat with remaining flans and toast. Place 1 reserved mussel on top of each flan; drizzle each serving with 1½ tablespoons dressing. Yield: 6 servings.

CALORIES 372; FAT 20.7g (sat 6g, mono 10g, poly 2.7g); PROTEIN 20.5g; CARB 21.8g; FIBER 0.8g; CHOL 191mg; IRON 6.4mg; SODIUM 626mg; CALC 107mg

Grilled Lunch for a Perfect Day

A glorious afternoon and the company of friends and family set the stage for a memorable meal to savor outdoors.

QUICK & EASY
Prosciutto-Melon Bites with Lime Drizzle

(pictured on page 221)

- 16 (1-inch) cubes cantaloupe
- 16 (1-inch) cubes honeydew melon
- 16 (¼-ounce) very thin slices prosciutto, cut in half lengthwise
- 1 tablespoon fresh lime juice
- 2 teaspoons extra-virgin olive oil
- ¼ teaspoon crushed red pepper
- 2 tablespoons thinly sliced fresh mint

❶ Wrap each cantaloupe cube and each honeydew cube with ½ prosciutto slice.

Thread 1 wrapped cantaloupe cube and 1 wrapped honeydew cube onto each of 16 (4-inch) skewers. Arrange on a platter. ❷ Combine juice, oil, and pepper, stirring with a whisk; drizzle evenly over skewers. Sprinkle evenly with mint. Yield: 8 servings (serving size: 2 skewers).

CALORIES 61; FAT 3g (sat 0.8g, mono 1.7g, poly 0.5g); PROTEIN 4.2g; CARB 5g; FIBER 0.3g; CHOL 13mg; IRON 0.3mg; SODIUM 282mg; CALC 5mg

MAKE AHEAD
Grilled Pizza with Asparagus and Caramelized Onion

- 1 tablespoon extra-virgin olive oil, divided
- 2 cups thinly vertically sliced onion
- 2 cups (2-inch) slices asparagus (about ½ pound)
- 1 tablespoon thinly sliced ready-to-use sun-dried tomatoes
- ⅛ teaspoon salt
- 1 (8-ounce) portion fresh pizza dough
- ¾ cup (3 ounces) shredded fontina cheese
- 1½ teaspoons fresh oregano leaves
- ¼ teaspoon freshly ground black pepper

❶ Prepare grill to medium-high heat. ❷ Heat 2 teaspoons oil in a large nonstick skillet over medium-high heat. Add onion to pan; sauté 5 minutes. Reduce heat to medium-low; cook 5 minutes or until browned. Add asparagus to pan; cook 5 minutes or until asparagus is crisp-tender. Stir in tomatoes and salt.

❸ Roll dough into a 12-inch circle on a lightly floured surface; brush each side of dough with ½ teaspoon remaining oil. ❹ Place dough on a grill rack; grill 1½ minutes or until crust bubbles and is well marked. Reduce grill heat to low; turn dough over. Arrange onion mixture over crust; sprinkle evenly with cheese. Cover and grill over low heat 3½ minutes or until cheese melts; remove pizza from grill. Sprinkle with oregano and black pepper. Yield: 8 servings (serving size: 1 slice).

CALORIES 152; FAT 5.8g (sat 2.3g, mono 2.2g, poly 0.9g); PROTEIN 6.3g; CARB 19.4g; FIBER 1.7g; CHOL 12mg; IRON 1.7mg; SODIUM 314mg; CALC 74mg

Haricots Verts Salad

- 1½ tablespoons extra-virgin olive oil
- 2 garlic cloves, minced
- 3 tablespoons pine nuts, toasted and divided
- 2 tablespoons red wine vinegar
- ½ teaspoon kosher salt, divided
- ½ teaspoon black pepper
- 16 large basil leaves (about ½ cup)
- 1½ pounds haricots verts
- 3 tablespoons chopped ready-to-use sun-dried tomatoes

❶ Heat oil and garlic in a small skillet over medium heat; cook 2 minutes, stirring occasionally. Remove from heat; cool slightly. Place garlic mixture, 1 tablespoon nuts, vinegar, ¼ teaspoon salt, pepper, and basil in a food processor; pulse until well combined. ❷ Cook beans in boiling water 4 minutes or until crisp-tender; drain. Rinse under cold water; drain. Place in a large bowl. Add basil mixture and remaining ¼ teaspoon salt; toss to coat. Sprinkle with 2 tablespoons nuts and tomatoes. Yield: 8 servings (serving size: about ¾ cup).

CALORIES 76; FAT 4.9g (sat 0.5g, mono 2.5g, poly 1.4g); PROTEIN 2.3g; CARB 7.6g; FIBER 3.3g; CHOL 0mg; IRON 1.3mg; SODIUM 150mg; CALC 40mg

Grilled Halibut with Three-Pepper Relish

RELISH:

1 yellow bell pepper, quartered
1 red bell pepper, quartered
1 orange bell pepper, quartered
Cooking spray
2 tablespoons chopped fresh parsley
2 tablespoons chopped capers
1 tablespoon olive oil
1 tablespoon balsamic vinegar
¼ teaspoon kosher salt
¼ teaspoon black pepper
1 garlic clove, minced

FISH:

1 tablespoon olive oil
8 (6-ounce) skinless halibut fillets
2 teaspoons chopped fresh thyme
¾ teaspoon kosher salt
½ teaspoon freshly ground black pepper

1 Prepare grill to medium-high heat.
2 To prepare relish, coat bell pepper pieces with cooking spray. Place pieces on a grill rack; grill 3 minutes on each side or until lightly charred. Remove from grill; cool slightly. Coarsely chop bell pepper pieces. Combine chopped bell peppers, parsley, and next 6 ingredients; set aside.
3 To prepare fish, brush 1 tablespoon oil evenly over fish. Sprinkle fish evenly with thyme, ¾ teaspoon salt, and ½ teaspoon black pepper. Place fish on grill rack; grill 4 minutes on each side or until fish flakes easily when tested with a fork or until desired degree of doneness. Serve with relish. Yield: 8 servings (serving size: 1 fillet and ¼ cup relish).

CALORIES 224; FAT 7.3g (sat 1g, mono 3.7g, poly 1.6g); PROTEIN 34.6g; CARB 3.5g; FIBER 1.1g; CHOL 52mg; IRON 1.8mg; SODIUM 392mg; CALC 85mg

WINE NOTE: This dish begs for a good sauvignon blanc. Bell peppers, herbs, and capers all have bold flavors ranging from fresh green to herbal to briny. A good sauvignon will mirror all the green flavors here and provide a crisp counterpoint to the subtle flavor of the fish. Try the Kunde Sauvignon Blanc 2007 from the Sonoma Valley (about $16).

QUICK & EASY ▪ MAKE AHEAD

Italian Grilled Zucchini and Red Onion

This simple side dish is tastiest at room temperature, so it's an ideal make-ahead. Any leftovers would be good the next day for lunch with couscous.

1 tablespoon olive oil
4 (½-inch-thick) slices red onion (about 1 large)
2 pounds small zucchini, cut lengthwise into (¼-inch-thick) slices
½ teaspoon kosher salt, divided
½ teaspoon freshly ground black pepper, divided
2 tablespoons red wine vinegar
⅓ cup (about 1½ ounces) shaved fresh Parmigiano-Reggiano cheese
2 tablespoons thinly sliced fresh mint

1 Prepare grill to medium-high heat.
2 Combine first 3 ingredients in a large bowl. Sprinkle zucchini mixture with ¼ teaspoon salt and ¼ teaspoon pepper; toss gently to coat. Arrange vegetables in a single layer on a grill rack; grill 4 minutes on each side or until zucchini is tender and vegetables are well marked. Remove zucchini from grill; reduce grill heat to medium-low. Grill onion an additional 5 minutes or until tender. Combine zucchini, onion, and vinegar in a large bowl, tossing to coat. Sprinkle with remaining ¼ teaspoon salt, remaining ¼ teaspoon pepper, cheese, and mint. Yield: 8 servings (serving size: about ¾ cup).

CALORIES 63; FAT 3.3g (sat 1.2g, mono 1.7g, poly 0.3g); PROTEIN 3.5g; CARB 5.9g; FIBER 1.6g; CHOL 4mg; IRON 0.6mg; SODIUM 215mg; CALC 86mg

Party Timeline

With some smart planning, you can have most of the work done before guests arrive.

Up to 1 week ahead:
• Make the sorbet.

Up to 2 days ahead:
• Make and refrigerate relish for halibut.
• Blanch haricots verts and toast nuts for salad.

The day before:
• Prepare onion mixture and shred cheese for pizza.
• Cube melon.

2 hours before dinner:
• Bring pizza dough to room temperature.
• Assemble melon skewers; refrigerate on serving platter. Make drizzle.

1 hour before:
• Light the grill.
• Roll out pizza dough.
• Take relish out of refrigerator, and allow it to come to room temperature.
• Spoon sorbet into dessert bowls, and keep in freezer.

30 minutes before:
• Grill zucchini and red onion, and finish with seasonings.
• Make dressing for salad, and toss.

As guests arrive:
• Pour drizzle over melon skewers.
• Grill pizza.

Just before serving:
• Grill halibut.

Limoncello-Mint Sorbet with Fresh Blackberries

(pictured on page 219)

Limoncello, the citrusy Italian liqueur, brightens this sorbet. It's nice to have a bottle on hand to splash with soda in a spritzer or macerate with fruit for a quick dessert.

    2   cups water
 1⅓   cups sugar
    ½   cup limoncello
    1   cup fresh lemon juice (about
         6 large lemons)
    ½   cup chopped fresh mint
    2   cups blackberries
         Lemon slices (optional)

1 Combine first 3 ingredients in a saucepan over medium-high heat; bring to a boil, stirring until sugar dissolves. Remove from heat; add lemon juice and mint. Cover and chill.

2 Strain juice mixture through a sieve into a bowl; discard solids. Pour mixture into freezer can of an ice-cream freezer; freeze according to manufacturer's instructions. Spoon sorbet into a freezer-safe container; cover and freeze 1 hour or until firm. Serve with blackberries; garnish with lemon slices, if desired. Yield: 8 servings (serving size: about ½ cup sorbet and ¼ cup berries).

CALORIES 184; FAT 0.2g (sat 0g, mono 0g, poly 0.1g); PROTEIN 0.6g; CARB 39.3g; FIBER 2g; CHOL 0mg; IRON 0.2mg; SODIUM 1mg; CALC 13mg

Coconut Cupcakes with Lime Buttercream Frosting

We love these cupcakes' coconut flavor and are intrigued by the ingredient that provides a delicate crumb: It's potato starch, says the developer, former *Cooking Light* Test Kitchens Professional Kathleen Kanen.

Texture suffers when you lighten cakes by using less butter and sugar. Mild-flavored potato starch is a fine powder that ensures a moist, light result in baked goods. (Make sure you purchase potato *starch*, however. Kanen says potato *flour* is heavier and denser.)

Kanen's further advice: Employ the creaming method, a technique that starts by beating butter and sugar together to incorporate plenty of air in the batter. Eggs go in next, then the dry flour mixture is added alternately with liquid to retain the beaten-in air. In these cupcakes, it works like a charm. Make a batch—and don't skip the luscious frosting. We promise you'll be pleased.

MAKE AHEAD • FREEZABLE
Coconut Cupcakes with Lime Buttercream Frosting

Look for potato starch in the supermarket baking aisle. Use lemon rind and fresh lemon juice in place of the lime for a variation.

CUPCAKES:
         Cooking spray
 4.5   ounces all-purpose flour (about
         1 cup)
    3   tablespoons potato starch
    1   teaspoon baking powder
    ½   teaspoon salt
    ¾   cup granulated sugar
    2   tablespoons butter, softened
    1   large egg
    1   large egg white
 ⅔   cup fat-free milk
    2   tablespoons flaked sweetened
         coconut
    ½   teaspoon vanilla extract
FROSTING:
    3   tablespoons butter, softened
    1   teaspoon half-and-half
    ½   teaspoon grated lime rind
    1   tablespoon fresh lime juice
 4.75 ounces powdered sugar, sifted
         (about 1⅓ cups)

1 Preheat oven to 350°.

2 To prepare cupcakes, place 2 muffin cup liners in each of 12 muffin cups; coat liners with cooking spray.

3 Weigh or lightly spoon flour into a dry measuring cup; level with a knife. Combine flour and next 3 ingredients in a small bowl; stir with a whisk.

4 Combine ¾ cup sugar and 2 tablespoons butter in a large bowl; beat with a mixer at medium speed until blended (mixture will be consistency of damp sand). Add egg and egg white, one at a time, beating well after each addition. Add flour mixture and milk alternately to egg mixture, beginning and ending with flour mixture. Fold in coconut and vanilla.

5 Spoon batter evenly into prepared muffin cups. Bake at 350° for 18 minutes or until cupcakes spring back when touched lightly in center. Cool in pan 2 minutes; remove from pan. Cool completely on a wire rack.

6 To prepare frosting, combine 3 tablespoons butter and next 3 ingredients in a medium bowl; beat with a mixer at medium speed until smooth. Gradually add powdered sugar, beating just until smooth. Spread about 2½ teaspoons frosting onto each cupcake. Yield: 12 servings (serving size: 1 cupcake).

CALORIES 196; FAT 5.6g (sat 3.4g, mono 1.4g, poly 0.3g); PROTEIN 2.5g; CARB 34.8g; FIBER 0.3g; CHOL 31mg; IRON 0.7mg; SODIUM 179mg; CALC 52mg

Summer Cookbook

Celebrate the season's finest offerings with this month-by-month guide, complete with top-rated recipes and shopping, storage, and preparation tips.

June

Welcome summer with these refreshing dishes—from exciting sides to a fruit-filled dessert.

STAFF FAVORITE ▪ MAKE AHEAD
Raspberry-Rhubarb Pie

Refrigerated pie dough makes preparing this tasty dessert a snap. Cornstarch and tapioca ensure a velvety filling by thickening the fruit juices.

- 2 tablespoons uncooked quick-cooking tapioca
- 4½ cups fresh raspberries (about 24 ounces)
- 3½ cups chopped fresh rhubarb (about 6 stalks)
- 1 cup packed brown sugar
- ¼ cup cornstarch
- 2 tablespoons crème de cassis (black currant–flavored liqueur)
- ⅛ teaspoon salt
- ½ (15-ounce) package refrigerated pie dough (such as Pillsbury)
- Cooking spray
- 6 tablespoons all-purpose flour
- ¼ cup sliced almonds
- 2 tablespoons brown sugar
- 2 tablespoons chilled butter, cut into small pieces
- ¼ teaspoon almond extract
- ⅛ teaspoon salt

1. Preheat oven to 350°.
2. Place tapioca in a spice or coffee grinder; process until finely ground. Combine tapioca, raspberries, and next 5 ingredients in a bowl; toss well. Let raspberry mixture stand 10 minutes; stir to combine.
3. Roll 1 (9-inch) dough portion into an 11-inch circle. Fit dough into a 9-inch pie plate coated with cooking spray, draping excess dough over edges. Spoon raspberry mixture and any remaining liquid into dough. Fold edges under; flute. Bake at 350° for 40 minutes.
4. While pie bakes, place flour and remaining ingredients in a food processor; pulse 10 times or until mixture resembles coarse crumbs.
5. Increase oven temperature to 375°.
6. Sprinkle topping evenly over pie. Bake at 375° for 15 minutes or until topping is golden brown and filling is thick and bubbly. Cool completely on a wire rack. Yield: 12 servings (serving size: 1 wedge).

CALORIES 248; FAT 7.9g (sat 3g, mono 3.4g, poly 0.5g); PROTEIN 2g; CARB 43.3g; FIBER 4g; CHOL 7mg; IRON 1.1mg; SODIUM 146mg; CALC 65mg

Storage Tip

Raspberries & Rhubarb Raspberries are highly perishable, so refrigerate no more than 3 days. Spray berries with water and drain on paper towels before use.

Trim and discard rhubarb leaves, and wash stalks just before using. There's no need to peel.

Cooking Tip

Field Peas Generally, fresher peas will be very tender; they may not need to cook quite as long as a recipe recommends.

QUICK & EASY
Cooked Field Peas

Use this simple recipe as a template, varying the fresh herbs used here or by adding a pinch of ground red pepper, if desired. This dish makes a grand side to corn bread and grilled pork.

- 3 cups fresh, shelled pink-eyed peas (or other field pea variety)
- 4 cups cold water
- 2 tablespoons chopped onion
- ½ teaspoon kosher salt
- ⅛ teaspoon freshly ground black pepper
- 1 fresh thyme sprig
- 1 small garlic clove, crushed

1. Sort and wash peas; place in a medium saucepan. Add 4 cups cold water and remaining ingredients to pan; bring to a boil. Partially cover, reduce heat, and simmer 30 minutes or until tender; skim surface occasionally, discarding solids. Drain; discard thyme and garlic. Yield: 6 servings (serving size: about ½ cup).

CALORIES 86; FAT 0.3g (sat 0.1g, mono 0g, poly 0.1g); PROTEIN 5.2g; CARB 16.2g; FIBER 4.5g; CHOL 0mg; IRON 1.2mg; SODIUM 62mg; CALC 20mg

Arugula Salad with Chicken and Apricots

2 (6-ounce) skinless, boneless chicken breast halves
1 tablespoon minced fresh parsley
2 teaspoons minced fresh tarragon
½ teaspoon salt, divided
¼ teaspoon freshly ground black pepper
   Cooking spray
3 tablespoons olive oil
4 teaspoons white wine vinegar
   Dash of freshly ground black pepper
4 cups baby arugula
4 cups gourmet salad greens
3 apricots (about 8 ounces), pitted and thinly sliced
⅓ cup thinly vertically sliced red onion

❶ Prepare grill to medium-high heat.
❷ Place chicken between 2 sheets of heavy-duty plastic wrap; pound each piece to ½-inch thickness using a meat mallet or small heavy skillet. Sprinkle chicken with parsley, tarragon, ¼ teaspoon salt, and ¼ teaspoon pepper.
❸ Place chicken on grill rack coated with cooking spray; grill 4 minutes on each side or until done. Transfer to a plate; cool to room temperature.
❹ Combine oil, vinegar, remaining ¼ teaspoon salt, and dash of pepper in a small bowl, stirring with a whisk.
❺ Combine arugula and remaining ingredients in a large bowl. Pour vinaigrette over arugula mixture; toss well to coat. Place about 2 cups arugula mixture on each of 4 plates. Cut chicken breast halves crosswise into thin slices; top each serving evenly with chicken. Serve immediately. Yield: 4 servings.

CALORIES 243; FAT 12.9g (sat 2.1g, mono 8.3g, poly 1.7g); PROTEIN 22.2g; CARB 10.1g; FIBER 2.9g; CHOL 54mg; IRON 2.1mg; SODIUM 364mg; CALC 86mg

WINE NOTE: In this salad, arugula's peppery bite is nicely balanced by fragrant herbs, sweet apricots, and grilled chicken. A great wine with a complexly flavored salad like this is pinot gris from Oregon. It has a fresh, clean feel and a creamy, fruity flavor. Two favorites: Lemelson Tikka's Run and Chehalem, both 2007 from the Willamette Valley, and both $19.

Beetroot Gratin

Serve with grilled steak or pork.

2 pounds beets
2 tablespoons water
   Cooking spray
½ cup (2 ounces) crumbled Roquefort cheese
¾ teaspoon black pepper
½ teaspoon kosher salt
1 tablespoon sherry vinegar
½ cup half-and-half
½ cup Italian-seasoned panko (Japanese breadcrumbs)

❶ Preheat oven to 375°.
❷ Leave root and 1-inch stem on beets; scrub with a brush. Reserve beet greens. Wrap beets and 2 tablespoons water in foil. Bake at 375° for 1 hour or until tender. Trim off beet roots; rub off skins. Cut beets into ¼-inch slices.
❸ Cook reserved greens in boiling water 2 minutes; drain. Rinse with cold water; drain and pat dry. Coarsely chop, reserving ¾ cup greens; reserve remaining greens for another use.
❹ Arrange half of beets in a single layer in an 11 x 7–inch baking dish coated with cooking spray. Sprinkle with half the cheese, black pepper, salt, and sherry vinegar. Repeat procedure with remaining beets, cheese, black pepper, salt, and sherry vinegar. Spread greens evenly on top of beet mixture. Pour half-and-half evenly over greens; top evenly with panko. Bake at 375° for 25 minutes or until beets are tender. Yield: 6 servings (serving size: about 1 cup).

CALORIES 128; FAT 5.4g (sat 3.2g, mono 0.8g, poly 0.1g); PROTEIN 5g; CARB 16g; FIBER 3.6g; CHOL 15mg; IRON 1.1mg; SODIUM 422mg; CALC 89mg

MAKE AHEAD
Macerated Berries with Whipped Cream

Use any combination of the best-quality berries you can find to prepare this simple recipe that showcases the finest fresh summer fruit.

4   cups sliced strawberries
2½ cups blueberries
2½ tablespoons torn fresh mint
3½ tablespoons honey
2½ tablespoons Grand Marnier (orange-flavored liqueur)
¾   teaspoon balsamic vinegar
¼   cup heavy whipping cream, chilled
1   tablespoon powdered sugar
3   tablespoons chopped dry-roasted pistachios
    Mint sprigs (optional)

❶ Combine first 6 ingredients in a bowl. Cover and let stand at room temperature 1 hour.
❷ Place cream and sugar in a small bowl; beat with a mixer at high speed until stiff peaks form. Spoon over strawberry mixture; sprinkle with pistachios. Garnish with mint sprigs, if desired. Serve immediately. Yield: 8 servings (serving size: about ⅔ cup berry mixture, about 1 tablespoon whipped cream, and about 1 teaspoon pistachios).

CALORIES 145; FAT 4.5g (sat 1.9g, mono 1.6g, poly 0.7g); PROTEIN 1.7g; CARB 24.4g; FIBER 3.1g; CHOL 10mg; IRON 0.7mg; SODIUM 5.1mg; CALC 26mg

MAKE AHEAD
Potato Salad with Herbs and Grilled Summer Squash

(pictured on page 222)

A cornichon is the French version of a gherkin. You'll find these small, tart pickles in gourmet grocery stores; otherwise, gherkins will work just fine. You may substitute 1 tablespoon drained capers for the pickles. Make up to two hours ahead.

SALAD:

- 2 pounds small red potatoes
- ¾ pound yellow squash, cut lengthwise into ½-inch slices
- Cooking spray
- ¼ teaspoon kosher salt
- ⅛ teaspoon freshly ground black pepper

DRESSING:

- ⅓ cup chopped fresh chives
- 3 tablespoons chopped fresh parsley
- 2 tablespoons chopped fresh basil
- 1 tablespoon chopped fresh tarragon
- ¼ teaspoon grated lemon rind
- 3 tablespoons fresh lemon juice
- 2 tablespoons water
- 2 tablespoons extra-virgin olive oil
- 2 tablespoons finely chopped cornichons
- ¼ teaspoon kosher salt
- ⅛ teaspoon freshly ground black pepper

1 Prepare grill to medium-high heat.
2 To prepare salad, place potatoes in a large saucepan; cover with water. Bring to a boil. Reduce heat, and simmer 18 minutes or until tender. Drain; cut potatoes into quarters, and place in a large bowl. Set aside.

3 Lightly coat squash with cooking spray. Sprinkle evenly with ¼ teaspoon salt and ⅛ teaspoon pepper. Place squash on grill rack; grill 2 minutes on each side or until browned and tender. Remove squash from heat, and add to potatoes.
4 To prepare dressing, combine chives and remaining ingredients in a small bowl; stir with a whisk. Pour dressing over potato mixture, tossing gently to combine. Serve salad warm or chilled. Yield: 6 servings (serving size: 1 cup).

CALORIES 160; FAT 5g (sat 0.8g, mono 3.4g, poly 0.8g); PROTEIN 3.8g; CARB 27g; FIBER 3.4g; CHOL 0mg; IRON 1.5mg; SODIUM 206mg; CALC 33mg

QUICK & EASY
Strawberry-Basil Salad with Balsamic Vinaigrette

This may sound like a surprising salad combination, but these two summertime stars—fresh basil and strawberries—pair deliciously well in a pretty first course.

- 3 tablespoons olive oil
- 3 tablespoons balsamic vinegar
- ½ teaspoon salt
- ⅛ teaspoon freshly ground black pepper
- 8 cups torn romaine lettuce
- 2 cups sliced strawberries (1 pound)
- ½ cup vertically sliced Vidalia or other sweet onion
- ¼ cup torn fresh basil

1 Combine first 4 ingredients in a large bowl; stir well with a whisk. Add lettuce and remaining ingredients; toss gently to coat. Serve salad immediately. Yield: 6 servings (serving size: 1½ cups).

CALORIES 102; FAT 7.2g (sat 1g, mono 5g, poly 0.9g); PROTEIN 1.5g; CARB 9.1g; FIBER 2.9g; CHOL 0mg; IRON 1.1mg; SODIUM 206mg; CALC 41mg

July

The heart of the summer brings a bounty of ripe produce. We put it to use in fresh dishes simple enough for every day.

MAKE AHEAD
Gingered Blueberry Shortcake

Sweet, juicy, peak-season berries make this dish shine. For convenience, make the berry mixture, whipped cream, and shortcakes in advance, then assemble just before serving. Prepare the berry mixture and whipped cream earlier in the day, and refrigerate; bring berry mixture to room temperature or warm slightly in a pan before serving. Make the shortcakes as time permits, freeze them, then defrost at room temperature when ready to serve.

- 4 cups blueberries
- 3 tablespoons granulated sugar
- 1 tablespoon fresh lime juice
- 9 ounces all-purpose flour (about 2 cups)
- 1 tablespoon baking powder
- ½ teaspoon salt
- 6 tablespoons chilled butter, cut into small pieces
- 3 tablespoons minced crystallized ginger
- ¾ cup 2% reduced-fat milk
- 1 large egg white
- 1 tablespoon water
- 1 tablespoon turbinado sugar or granulated sugar
- ⅓ cup heavy whipping cream
- 2 tablespoons powdered sugar

Continued

❶ Preheat oven to 400°.

❷ Combine first 3 ingredients in a medium saucepan over medium-low heat; cook 3 minutes or until berries begin to pop, stirring frequently. Set aside.

❸ Weigh or lightly spoon flour into dry measuring cups; level with a knife. Place flour, baking powder, and salt in a food processor; pulse 3 times to combine. Add butter and ginger to processor; pulse until mixture resembles coarse meal. Place mixture in a large bowl; add milk, stirring just until moist. Turn mixture out onto a lightly floured surface. Press mixture into a 7-inch circle; cut into 8 wedges. Place wedges 1 inch apart on a baking sheet. Combine egg white and 1 tablespoon water in a small bowl. Lightly brush tops of wedges with egg white mixture; sprinkle evenly with turbinado sugar. Bake at 400° for 20 minutes or until golden brown. Cool on a wire rack.

❹ Place cream in a medium bowl; beat with a mixer at medium speed until soft peaks form. Add powdered sugar, beating until stiff peaks form. Split shortcakes in half horizontally; spoon $1/3$ cup berry mixture over each bottom half. Top each with $1^{1}/_{2}$ tablespoons whipped cream; cover with shortcake tops. Yield: 8 servings (serving size: 1 shortcake).

CALORIES 319; FAT 12.8g (sat 8g, mono 3.4g, poly 0.6g); PROTEIN 5.4g; CARB 47g; FIBER 2.6g; CHOL 38mg; IRON 2.2mg; SODIUM 415mg; CALC 149mg

Storage Tip

Fresh Herbs To extend the life of herbs, wrap them gently in a damp paper towel, seal in a zip-top plastic bag, and store in the refrigerator.

QUICK & EASY • MAKE AHEAD

Lemon Verbena Gimlet Cocktails

(pictured on page 224)

Bruising, or partially crushing, the verbena helps draw out its essential oils. Substitute vodka for gin, if you prefer. If you make this ahead, stir in club soda just before serving so the drink stays fizzy.

- 1 cup water
- ¼ cup sugar
- ¼ cup torn fresh lemon verbena leaves
- ¾ cup dry gin
- ¾ cup club soda, chilled
- ¼ cup fresh lime juice (about 2 limes)
- Lemon verbena sprigs (optional)
- Lime slices (optional)

❶ Combine 1 cup water and sugar in a small saucepan. Rub torn verbena to bruise; add to pan. Bring sugar mixture to a boil, stirring gently as needed to dissolve sugar evenly; cook 30 seconds. Remove from heat; cool completely. Strain mixture through a sieve over a bowl; discard solids.

❷ Combine sugar mixture, gin, soda, and juice. Serve over ice. Garnish with verbena sprigs and lime slices, if desired. Yield: 4 servings (serving size: about $1/2$ cup).

CALORIES 157; FAT 0g; PROTEIN 0.1g; CARB 13.9g; FIBER 0.1g; CHOL 0mg; IRON 0mg; SODIUM 10mg; CALC 5mg

Buying Tip

Mangoes Select mangoes that are sweetly fragrant at their stem end, yield slightly to gentle pressure, and have smooth, unblemished, yellow and blushed red skin.

STAFF FAVORITE

Grilled Shrimp, Mango, and Avocado

This dish features a Vietnamese-style sauce known as "nuoc cham" [noo-ahk CHAHM] that traditionally includes fish sauce, lime juice, chiles, and sugar. Your avocados should be ripe but still slightly firm so they'll slice easily and not break apart as they grill. Leaving the skin on helps them maintain their shape—remove skin before serving, if you like.

- ¾ cup water
- 1 tablespoon sugar
- 6 tablespoons fresh lime juice (about 3 limes)
- 2½ tablespoons fish sauce
- 1 garlic clove, minced
- 1 tablespoon finely grated carrot
- 1 tablespoon thinly sliced serrano chile (about 1 chile)
- 36 large shrimp (about 2 pounds)
- Cooking spray
- 2 ripe unpeeled avocados, halved
- 2 peeled mangoes, each cut into 6 wedges
- 12 lime wedges
- 6 large Bibb lettuce leaves
- Chopped fresh cilantro (optional)

❶ Combine first 5 ingredients in a small bowl. Reserve $3/4$ cup juice mixture. Stir carrot and chile into remaining $1/2$ cup juice mixture, and set aside.

❷ Peel shrimp, leaving tails intact. Starting at tail end, butterfly each shrimp, cutting to, but not through, back side of shrimp. Combine reserved $3/4$ cup juice mixture and shrimp in a large bowl, tossing to coat; cover and marinate in refrigerator 1 hour, tossing occasionally. Remove shrimp from bowl, reserving marinade.

❸ Prepare grill to medium-high heat.

❹ Place reserved marinade in a small saucepan; bring to a boil. Reduce heat, and simmer 5 minutes. Cool slightly.

❺ Thread 3 shrimp onto each of 12 (10-inch) skewers. Place shrimp on a grill rack coated with cooking spray. Grill shrimp 2½ minutes on each side or until done, basting frequently with cooked marinade.

❻ Cut 3 avocado halves in half lengthwise; peel and dice remaining avocado half. Brush cooked marinade over mango and avocado wedges; coat with cooking spray. Arrange in a single layer on grill rack coated with cooking spray. Coat lime wedges with cooking spray; place on grill rack. Grill fruit 2 minutes on each side or until marked but not soft, basting frequently with marinade.

❼ Place 1 lettuce leaf on each of 6 salad plates; top each leaf with 2 mango slices, 2 lime wedges, and 1 avocado wedge. Place 2 skewers on each plate; sprinkle evenly with diced avocado. Sprinkle with cilantro, if desired. Serve with carrot mixture. Yield: 6 servings.

CALORIES 324; FAT 11.8g (sat 1.8g, mono 6.1g, poly 2.1g); PROTEIN 33.1g; CARB 23.7g; FIBER 5.9g; CHOL 230mg; IRON 4.5mg; SODIUM 811mg; CALC 109mg

Cooking Tip

Stone Fruits Stone fruits such as plums, nectarines, and cherries lend themselves nicely not only to desserts, but also savory dishes. They pair particularly well with grilled and roasted meats.

Cherry and Lemon-Ricotta Gratin

This rustic dessert is served in a skillet for a homey presentation. Use cherry or raspberry liqueur if crème de cassis is not available.

  1 tablespoon grated lemon rind
  1 (15-ounce) carton part-skim ricotta cheese
  1 tablespoon fresh lemon juice
  1 tablespoon crème de cassis (black currant-flavored liqueur)
  ¼ teaspoon black pepper
  6 tablespoons sugar, divided
1½ pounds sweet cherries, pitted
  ⅛ teaspoon salt
  2 large egg whites
  3 tablespoons sliced almonds, toasted

❶ Combine rind and ricotta in a medium bowl; set aside.

❷ Combine juice, liqueur, and pepper in a small bowl. Sprinkle 3 tablespoons sugar evenly in a 12-inch ovenproof skillet over medium-high heat; cook 2 minutes or until sugar starts to melt. Add cherries to pan; cook 2 minutes without stirring. Pour liqueur mixture over cherries; cook 2 minutes or until mixture thickens.

❸ Preheat broiler.

❹ Combine remaining 3 tablespoons sugar, salt, and egg whites in the top of a double boiler; place over simmering water. Cook 2 minutes or until a thermometer registers 140°, stirring constantly with a whisk. Remove from heat, and beat with a mixer at high speed until stiff peaks form. Fold one-fourth of egg white mixture into ricotta mixture until blended; fold in remaining egg white mixture. Spoon ricotta mixture evenly over cherries using ¼-cup measure. Broil 3 minutes or until topping is browned. Top evenly with almonds. Yield: 8 servings.

CALORIES 194; FAT 6.2g (sat 2.9g, mono 2.2g, poly 0.7g); PROTEIN 8.5g; CARB 27.7g; FIBER 2.3g; CHOL 16mg; IRON 0.7mg; SODIUM 117mg; CALC 165mg

MAKE AHEAD
Plum Preserves

  6 cups sliced ripe plums (about 3 pounds)
2¼ cups sugar
  ½ cup water
  2 tablespoons fresh lemon juice
  1 (4-inch) cinnamon stick

❶ Combine plums and sugar in a large bowl; cover and let stand at room temperature 8 hours.

❷ Combine plum mixture and remaining ingredients in a Dutch oven; bring to a boil. Cover, reduce heat to medium-low, and simmer 15 minutes.

❸ Uncover and cook over medium heat until reduced to 5 cups (about 1 hour), stirring and mashing fruit occasionally. Pour into a large bowl; cool completely. Discard cinnamon stick. Cover and refrigerate up to 2 weeks. Yield: 5 cups (serving size: 2 tablespoons).

CALORIES 60; FAT 0g; PROTEIN 0.2g; CARB 15.6g; FIBER 0.5g; CHOL 0mg; IRON 0.1mg; SODIUM 0mg; CALC 0mg

QUICK & EASY • MAKE AHEAD
Nectarine and Radish Salsa

Serve this no-cook condiment with grilled chicken, pork, or fish. Or use as a topping for grilled bread or a dip for toasted tortilla wedges.

2¼ cups (¼-inch) diced nectarines
1½ cups radishes, halved lengthwise and thinly sliced
  ½ cup chopped cucumber
  ¼ cup finely chopped red onion
  1 tablespoon fresh lime juice
  2 teaspoons chopped fresh cilantro
1½ teaspoons sugar
  ¼ teaspoon salt

❶ Combine all ingredients in a medium bowl; toss well. Let stand 30 minutes. Yield: 4 cups (serving size: ⅓ cup).

CALORIES 18; FAT 0.1g (sat 0g, mono 0g, poly 0.1g); PROTEIN 0.5g; CARB 4.3g; FIBER 0.8g; CHOL 0mg; IRON 0.1mg; SODIUM 55mg; CALC 7mg

Plum and Crème Fraîche Sorbet

Similar to sour cream, though less tangy and thicker, crème fraîche is available in gourmet markets and specialty stores.

4½ cups chopped ripe plums
(about 2 pounds)
1¼ cups sugar
½ cup crème fraîche

❶ Combine plums and sugar in a large bowl; toss well to coat. Let mixture stand at room temperature 1 hour.
❷ Place plum mixture in a food processor or blender; process until smooth. Press mixture through a fine sieve over a large bowl; discard solids. Add crème fraîche, stirring with a whisk until blended. Cover and chill. Pour mixture into the freezer can of an ice-cream freezer; freeze according to manufacturer's instructions. Spoon sorbet into a freezer-safe container; cover sorbet, and freeze 1 hour or until firm. Yield: 8 servings (serving size: about ½ cup).

CALORIES 231; FAT 5.8g (sat 3.3g, mono 1.9g, poly 0.2g); PROTEIN 1.3g; CARB 45g; FIBER 1.6g; CHOL 14mg; IRON 0.1mg; SODIUM 5mg; CALC 5mg

Buying Tip

Snap Beans The freshest snap beans will break—or snap—in half when the ends are bent toward the center.

Three Bean Farmers' Market Stew

This hearty vegetable-based dish makes a meal on its own, though you can stir in shredded precooked chicken in the end, if you like. Use all green beans if Romano and yellow wax beans are unavailable.

STEW:

3 slices center-cut bacon, thinly sliced
3 garlic cloves, crushed
¼ teaspoon crushed red pepper
6 ounces (1-inch) cut Romano beans
6 ounces (1-inch) cut green beans
6 ounces (1-inch) cut yellow wax beans
¼ teaspoon kosher salt
3 cups diced plum tomato (about 5 tomatoes)
1½ cups fat-free, less-sodium chicken broth
2 teaspoons chopped fresh rosemary
¼ teaspoon freshly ground black pepper
½ cup (2 ounces) grated Parmigiano-Reggiano cheese, divided

CROSTINI:

1 teaspoon olive oil
8 (½-inch-thick) slices diagonally cut French bread baguette
1 garlic clove, halved
½ teaspoon chopped fresh rosemary

❶ To prepare stew, cook bacon in a Dutch oven over medium heat until crisp. Remove bacon from pan, and set aside.
❷ Add garlic to drippings in pan; cook 2 minutes or until lightly browned, stirring frequently. Add red pepper; cook 20 seconds, stirring frequently. Add beans and salt; cook 3 minutes, stirring frequently. Stir in tomato; cook 1 minute, stirring occasionally. Stir in broth, rosemary, and black pepper; bring to a boil.

Cover, reduce heat, and simmer 30 minutes or until beans are tender. Stir in ¼ cup cheese.
❸ Preheat oven to 425°.
❹ To prepare crostini, brush oil evenly over cut sides of bread; rub bread with cut sides of garlic. Sprinkle one side of each piece of bread evenly with rosemary. Arrange slices on a baking sheet. Bake at 425° for 10 minutes or until lightly browned.
❺ Ladle 1¼ cups soup into each of 4 bowls. Sprinkle each serving with 1 tablespoon cheese; serve each with 2 crostini. Yield: 4 servings.

CALORIES 243; FAT 8.9g (sat 3.9g, mono 1.7g, poly 0.5g); PROTEIN 12.8g; CARB 31.3g; FIBER 6.6g; CHOL 16mg; IRON 3.1mg; SODIUM 783mg; CALC 205mg

Casual Entertaining Menu
serves 6

This menu lends itself to an easy outdoor gathering since you can do some of the work ahead. Make the blackberry sauce in advance, but stir the butter in after reheating. Serve the couscous warm or at room temperature. Purchase biscotti from your favorite bakery.

Grilled Pork with Blackberry-Sage Sauce

Pistachio-cherry couscous

Bring 1½ cups fat-free, less-sodium chicken broth and ½ teaspoon salt to a boil in a medium saucepan. Stir in 1½ cups uncooked couscous and ½ cup dried cherries. Remove from heat, cover, and let stand 5 minutes. Uncover; fluff with a fork. Stir in ⅓ cup coarsely chopped pistachios, 2 tablespoons chopped green onions, 1 tablespoon extra-virgin olive oil, and 1 teaspoon grated lemon rind.

Steamed haricots verts
Red zinfandel
Chocolate biscotti

Grilled Pork with Blackberry-Sage Sauce

If your blackberries are particularly sweet or tart, adjust the amount of sugar in the sauce accordingly by a half teaspoon or so to find the right balance.

Cooking spray
2 tablespoons minced shallots
3 cups fresh blackberries (about 1 pound)
½ teaspoon chopped fresh sage
1 (14-ounce) can fat-free, less-sodium chicken broth
2 tablespoons balsamic vinegar
1½ teaspoons sugar
1 tablespoon butter
¾ teaspoon kosher salt, divided
1 teaspoon black pepper
1 (1½-pound) pork tenderloin, trimmed
Sage sprigs (optional)

❶ Prepare grill to medium heat.
❷ Heat a medium saucepan over medium heat. Coat pan with cooking spray. Add shallots to pan; cook 3 minutes or until tender, stirring occasionally. Add blackberries, sage, and broth; bring to a boil. Reduce heat, and simmer 20 minutes or until blackberries break down. Press blackberry mixture through a fine sieve over a bowl; discard solids. Return liquid to pan. Stir in vinegar and sugar; bring to a boil. Cook until reduced to ¾ cup (about 9 minutes), and remove from heat. Stir in butter and ¼ teaspoon salt, stirring until butter melts. Keep warm.
❸ Sprinkle remaining ½ teaspoon salt and pepper over pork. Place pork on grill rack coated with cooking spray; cover and grill 20 minutes or until a thermometer registers 155° (slightly pink), turning pork occasionally. Let stand 10 minutes. Cut crosswise into ¼-inch-thick slices. Serve with blackberry sauce; garnish with sage sprigs, if desired. Yield: 6 servings (serving size: about 3 ounces pork and 2 tablespoons sauce).

CALORIES 199; FAT 6.1g (sat 2.6g, mono 2.3g, poly 0.7g); PROTEIN 25.3g; CARB 10g; FIBER 4g; CHOL 79mg; IRON 2mg; SODIUM 439mg; CALC 32mg

Miso Grilled Cucumbers

These distinctive cukes make a choice side for grilled poultry, beef, and fish. Look for miso in large supermarkets and Asian markets. You'll find mirin in your supermarket's international section.

¼ cup white miso (soybean paste)
1 tablespoon fresh lime juice
1 tablespoon mirin (sweet rice wine)
1 teaspoon dark sesame oil
6 medium pickling cucumbers (about 2¼ pounds), quartered lengthwise
Cooking spray
1 teaspoon sesame seeds, toasted
¼ teaspoon freshly ground black pepper

❶ Combine first 4 ingredients in a large bowl, stirring with a whisk. Add cucumbers to bowl, tossing to coat. Cover and marinate in refrigerator 1½ hours.
❷ Prepare grill to medium-high heat.
❸ Remove cucumbers from bowl, reserving marinade. Arrange cucumbers in a single layer on grill rack coated with cooking spray; grill 2 minutes, brushing cucumbers with reserved marinade. Turn cucumbers over, and grill 3 minutes or until browned, brushing with reserved marinade.
❹ Sprinkle cucumbers with sesame seeds and pepper. Serve immediately. Yield: 6 servings (serving size: 4 cucumber spears).

CALORIES 54; FAT 1g (sat 0.1g, mono 0.3g, poly 0.3g); PROTEIN 3.8g; CARB 8.6g; FIBER 3.8g; CHOL 0mg; IRON 2.1mg; SODIUM 360mg; CALC 35mg

August

Flavors of the month range from sweet Maine lobsters to fiery chiles of all shapes and hues.

Lobster Rolls

(pictured on page 224)

The lobster roll is an affordable way to stretch and enjoy this premium ingredient. The humble hot dog bun is traditional here, an important component that won't upstage the star. You can make the mayo-based lobster filling up to a day ahead and keep it refrigerated until just before serving.

5 tablespoons canola mayonnaise
¼ cup finely chopped celery
3 tablespoons minced onion
2 tablespoons whole milk Greek-style yogurt (such as Fage)
1½ teaspoons chopped fresh dill
½ teaspoon kosher salt
⅛ teaspoon ground red pepper
1 pound cooked lobster meat, cut into bite-sized pieces (about 3 [1½-pound] lobsters)
2 tablespoons butter, melted
8 (1½-ounce) hot dog buns
8 Bibb lettuce leaves

Continued

① Combine first 7 ingredients in a medium bowl, stirring well. Add lobster to mayonnaise mixture; toss. Cover and chill 1 hour.

② Brush butter evenly over cut sides of buns. Heat a large skillet over medium-high heat. Place buns, cut sides down, in pan; cook 2 minutes or until toasted. Line each bun with 1 lettuce leaf; top with ⅓ cup lobster mixture. Yield: 8 servings (serving size: 1 sandwich).

CALORIES 272; FAT 12.3g (sat 3.3g, mono 5.1g, poly 2.9g); PROTEIN 16.3g; CARB 22.9g; FIBER 1.2g; CHOL 52mg; IRON 1.9mg; SODIUM 629mg; CALC 105mg

Storage Tip

Corn Buy and store corn in the husk; remove (or pull husks back) just before cooking. Keep refrigerated for 3 to 5 days; if the silks turn dull or dark, the corn is past its prime.

QUICK & EASY

Spicy Braised Clams with Sausage and Corn

Briny littleneck clams are balanced with spicy jalapeño peppers and sweet summer corn in this delightful summer stew. Serve with a tossed green salad and crusty French bread.

- 1 teaspoon olive oil
- 8 ounces turkey Italian sausage
- 3 garlic cloves, thinly sliced
- 1 thinly sliced seeded jalapeño pepper
- ½ cup dry white wine
- 3 cups chopped fresh plum tomato (about 4 tomatoes)
- 2 tablespoons chopped fresh oregano
- 2 tablespoons chopped fresh basil, divided
- ⅛ teaspoon kosher salt
- ½ teaspoon freshly ground black pepper
- 1½ cups fresh corn kernels (about 2 ears)
- 1½ pounds littleneck clams

① Heat oil in a large Dutch oven over medium heat. Remove casings from sausage. Add sausage to pan; cook 4 minutes, stirring to crumble. Add garlic and jalapeño; cook 1 minute, stirring frequently. Add wine; cook 2 minutes or until liquid almost evaporates, scraping pan to loosen browned bits. Stir in tomato, oregano, 1 tablespoon basil, salt, and black pepper; bring mixture to a simmer. Cover and cook 10 minutes, stirring occasionally. Stir in corn; cover and cook 2 minutes.

② Increase heat to medium-high; stir in clams. Cover and cook 5 minutes or until clams open; discard any unopened shells. Place about 7 clams and ¾ cup sausage mixture in each of 4 bowls. Sprinkle each serving with ¾ teaspoon basil. Yield: 4 servings.

CALORIES 237; FAT 8.3g (sat 2g, mono 3.2g, poly 2.5g); PROTEIN 20.4g; CARB 23.1g; FIBER 3.7g; CHOL 65mg; IRON 9mg; SODIUM 516mg; CALC 51mg

MAKE AHEAD

Roasted Corn, Pepper, and Tomato Chowder

Grilling the vegetables heightens their sweetness, and blue cheese provides a pungent counterpoint in this soup. Substitute crumbled goat cheese or feta, if you prefer.

- 3 red bell peppers, halved and seeded
- 3 ears shucked corn
- 1½ pounds tomatoes, halved, seeded, and peeled (about 4)
- 2 tablespoons extra-virgin olive oil
- 4 cups chopped onion (about 2 medium)
- 3 (14-ounce) cans fat-free, less-sodium chicken broth
- ¼ teaspoon salt
- ¼ teaspoon freshly ground black pepper
- ¼ cup (1 ounce) crumbled blue cheese
- 2 tablespoons chopped fresh chives

① Prepare grill to medium-high heat.

② Arrange bell peppers, skin sides down, and corn in a single layer on a grill rack; grill 5 minutes, turning corn occasionally. Add tomatoes; grill an additional 5 minutes or until vegetables are slightly charred. Remove from heat; cool 10 minutes. Coarsely chop tomatoes and bell peppers; place in a medium bowl. Cut kernels from ears of corn; add to tomato mixture.

③ Heat oil in a large Dutch oven over medium heat. Add onion; cook 7 minutes or until tender, stirring occasionally. Stir in tomato mixture; cook 3 minutes, stirring occasionally. Increase heat to high, and stir in broth. Bring to a boil. Reduce heat, and simmer 30 minutes or until vegetables are tender. Cool 20 minutes.

④ Place one-third of tomato mixture in a blender; process until smooth. Place pureed mixture in a large bowl. Repeat procedure twice with remaining tomato mixture. Wipe pan clean with paper towels. Press tomato mixture through a sieve into pan; discard solids. Place pan over medium heat; cook until thoroughly heated. Stir in salt and black pepper. Ladle about 1½ cups soup into each of 6 bowls; top each serving with 2 teaspoons cheese and 1 teaspoon chives. Yield: 6 servings.

CALORIES 155; FAT 7.2g (sat 1.7g, mono 3.9g, poly 1.2g); PROTEIN 5.4g; CARB 21g; FIBER 4.4g; CHOL 4mg; IRON 1.1mg; SODIUM 620mg; CALC 45mg

MAKE AHEAD
Fire-Seared Antipasto Platter

More of a game plan than a set recipe, this dish lends itself to an assortment of ingredients you may have on hand. For example, if you can't find capocollo—cured sausage similar to salami—substitute salami or pepperoni. Serve the platter while the vegetables are warm or at room temperature.

DRESSING:

- 6 tablespoons fresh lemon juice
- 3 tablespoons balsamic vinegar
- 2 teaspoons extra-virgin olive oil
- ¼ teaspoon kosher salt
- 2 garlic cloves, minced

VEGETABLES:

- 3 plum tomatoes, halved
- 2 red bell peppers, quartered and seeded
- 2 yellow bell peppers, quartered and seeded
- 2 zucchini, cut lengthwise into ½-inch-thick slices
- 1 red onion, cut into ½-inch-thick slices
- 1 (1½-pound) eggplant, cut crosswise into ½-inch-thick slices
- Cooking spray

GARNISHES:

- 4 ounces prosciutto, thinly sliced
- 1 ounce capocollo, thinly sliced
- 2 ounces fresh mozzarella cheese, thinly sliced
- 2 tablespoons chopped fresh basil
- 2 teaspoons capers
- 6 green olives, sliced
- ⅛ teaspoon kosher salt

① Prepare grill to medium-high heat.
② To prepare dressing, combine first 5 ingredients in a bowl, stirring with a whisk.
③ To prepare vegetables, brush ¼ cup dressing evenly over tomatoes, peppers, zucchini, onion, and eggplant. Place vegetables on a grill rack coated with cooking spray; grill 5 minutes on each side or until lightly charred. Arrange vegetables on a platter; brush with remaining dressing. Arrange prosciutto, capocollo, and cheese on platter. Sprinkle platter with basil and remaining ingredients. Yield: 4 servings (serving size: about 4 ounces eggplant, 1 tomato half, 2 bell pepper halves, ½ zucchini, ¼ onion, 1 ounce prosciutto, ¼ ounce capocollo, ½ ounce mozzarella, 1½ teaspoons basil, ½ teaspoon capers, 1½ olives, and 1 tablespoon marinade).

CALORIES 291; FAT 13.2g (sat 4.6g, mono 5.5g, poly 1.6g); PROTEIN 15.6g; CARB 32g; FIBER 10.1g; CHOL 36mg; IRON 2.3mg; SODIUM 986mg; CALC 147mg

WINE NOTE: Easygoing tannins make northern Italy's Valpolicella the go-to red wine for cured meats. Without the use of oak, Tenuta Sant'Antonio Nanfré Valpolicella 2007 ($13) lets its fruit flavors shine. The cherry flavors and earthy notes meld beautifully with the charred vegetables.

Watermelon Salad with Pickled Onions and Feta

The sharpness of pickled onions offers a pleasing contrast to crisp, juicy watermelon and salty, creamy feta cheese.

- 1 cup vertically sliced red onion
- ¼ cup red wine vinegar
- ¼ teaspoon kosher salt
- 1½ tablespoons white balsamic vinegar
- 1 tablespoon extra-virgin olive oil
- ¼ teaspoon freshly ground black pepper
- 2½ cups cubed seedless watermelon
- 1 small cucumber, halved lengthwise and thinly sliced (about 1 cup)
- ¼ cup (1 ounce) crumbled feta cheese
- 2 tablespoons chopped fresh mint
- 2 tablespoons chopped fresh basil

① Combine first 3 ingredients in a small bowl, and let stand 30 minutes. Drain.
② Combine balsamic vinegar, oil, and pepper in a large bowl; stir well with a whisk. Add onion mixture, watermelon, and cucumber; toss gently to coat. Arrange watermelon mixture on a platter. Top with cheese, mint, and basil. Yield: 6 servings (serving size: ⅔ cup).

CALORIES 77; FAT 3.9g (sat 1.3g, mono 2g, poly 0.4g); PROTEIN 1.9g; CARB 9.8g; FIBER 1.2g; CHOL 6mg; IRON 0.4mg; SODIUM 152mg; CALC 51mg

Cool Honeydew-Mint Soup

A refreshing tangy-sweet soup is a nice
way to conclude an outdoor summer meal
of grilled chicken or fish. Just a bit of salt
heightens the flavor of all the ingredients.
If your honeydew melons need sweeten-
ing, add extra honey.

- 1 (2-pound) honeydew melon,
  peeled, seeded, and cut into 1-inch
  pieces, divided
- ¼ cup loosely packed fresh mint leaves
- ¼ cup fresh lime juice (about
  3 limes)
- 1 tablespoon honey
- ⅛ teaspoon salt
- 6 thin lime slices (optional)
- 6 thinly sliced fresh mint leaves
  (optional)

❶ Place 1 cup honeydew melon, ¼ cup
loosely packed fresh mint leaves, juice,
and honey in a blender; process until
smooth. Add remaining melon and salt;
process until smooth. Transfer melon
mixture to a bowl; cover and chill at least
1 hour. Ladle about ¾ cup soup into each
of 6 bowls; garnish each serving with 1
thin lime slice and 1 thinly sliced mint
leaf, if desired. Yield: 6 servings.

CALORIES 68; FAT 0.2g (sat 0.1g, mono 0g, poly 0.1g);
PROTEIN 0.9g; CARB 17.7g; FIBER 1.3g; CHOL 0mg;
IRON 0.3mg; SODIUM 77mg; CALC 13mg

Seared Figs and White Peaches with Balsamic Reduction

Ripe figs and peaches have naturally high
levels of sugar, which means they'll caramelize beautifully without additional
sugar or copious amounts of fat. This
simple yet elegant dessert is a great way
to maintain the texture and floral flavors
of these delicate fruits. Toasted whole
black peppercorns add an interesting
savory flavor to this dish.

- 1 teaspoon black peppercorns
- 2 teaspoons butter, divided
- 2 teaspoons chopped fresh thyme,
  divided
- 4 firm ripe white peaches (about
  1¾ pounds), halved and pitted
- 8 firm ripe Black Mission figs,
  halved lengthwise (about 1
  pound)
- ⅓ cup balsamic vinegar
- ⅓ cup crème fraîche
- ⅛ teaspoon salt

❶ Cook peppercorns in a small skillet
over medium heat 6 minutes or until
fragrant and toasted. Cool. Place peppercorns in a heavy-duty zip-top plastic bag;
seal. Crush peppercorns with a meat
mallet or rolling pin; set aside.
❷ Melt 1 teaspoon butter in a large
skillet over medium-high heat; stir in
1 teaspoon thyme. Add peaches, cut sides
down, to pan. Cook 2 minutes or until
browned. Remove from pan. Place 1
peach half, cut sides up, on each of 8
plates. Melt remaining 1 teaspoon butter
in pan; stir in remaining 1 teaspoon

thyme. Add figs, cut sides down, to pan;
cook 2 minutes or until browned. Place 2
fig halves on each plate.
❸ Add vinegar to pan; cook over medium-
low heat until reduced to 3 tablespoons
(about 3 minutes). Cool slightly. Spoon
about 2 teaspoons crème fraîche into
center of each peach half; drizzle about
1 teaspoon vinegar over each serving.
Sprinkle each serving with about ⅛ teaspoon pepper. Sprinkle evenly with salt.
Yield: 8 servings.

CALORIES 133; FAT 4.8g (sat 2.8g, mono 0.4g, poly 0.2g);
PROTEIN 1.6g; CARB 22.4g; FIBER 3.2g; CHOL 12mg;
IRON 0.6mg; SODIUM 50mg; CALC 32mg

Fig and Sour Cream Ice Cream

We tested this recipe using Brown Turkey
figs. Their subtle coppery skin won't
discolor the cream as it churns. The ice
cream will be very soft served fresh out
of the churn. If you drain the liquid, repack
with ice and salt, cover, and ripen the ice
cream, it should set up.

- 2 cups coarsely chopped fresh figs
- ¾ cup sugar, divided
- 1 teaspoon fresh lemon juice
- ⅛ teaspoon salt, divided
- 2½ cups whole milk
- 4 large egg yolks
- 1 cup reduced-fat sour cream
- 1 teaspoon vanilla extract

❶ Combine figs, 2 tablespoons sugar,
juice, and a dash of salt. Cover and
chill.
❷ Cook milk in a heavy saucepan over
medium-high heat to 180° or until tiny
bubbles form around edge (do not boil).
Remove from heat.

3 Combine remaining 10 tablespoons sugar, remaining dash of salt, and egg yolks in a bowl, stirring with a whisk. Gradually add half of hot milk to egg mixture, stirring constantly with a whisk. Return milk mixture to pan; cook over medium-low heat 5 minutes or until a thermometer registers 160°, stirring constantly. Place pan in an ice-filled bowl; cool custard mixture, stirring occasionally. Stir in sour cream and vanilla. Cover and chill.

4 Pour custard mixture into freezer can of an ice-cream freezer; freeze according to manufacturer's instructions. Stop machine and remove lid. Add fig mixture to freezer can. Replace lid; restart ice-cream freezer, and freeze 5 minutes or until set. Carefully drain liquid from bucket; repack bucket with ice and salt. Cover with kitchen towels; ripen at least 1 hour. Yield: 8 servings (serving size: 2/3 cup).

CALORIES 243; FAT 8.7g (sat 4.7g, mono 2.8g, poly 0.6g); PROTEIN 6.1g; CARB 35g; FIBER 1.5g; CHOL 120mg; IRON 0.4mg; SODIUM 91mg; CALC 159mg

Storage Tip

Chiles If you're a fan of spicy foods, use chiles with the seeds intact. To tame the heat, remove seeds and membranes. It's also advisable to wear latex gloves while chopping hot peppers. The oils are hard to wash off your fingers.

Grilled Pepper Poppers

The three-cheese filling is a nice complement for the spicy peppers. You can also use a milder chile, such as a cherry pepper. Shredded Cheddar cheese can take the place of Parmesan, if you like.

- ½ cup (4 ounces) soft goat cheese
- ½ cup (4 ounces) fat-free cream cheese, softened
- ½ cup (2 ounces) grated fresh Parmesan cheese
- ½ cup finely chopped seeded tomato
- 2 tablespoons thinly sliced green onions
- 2 tablespoons chopped fresh sage
- ½ teaspoon kosher salt
- 16 jalapeño peppers, halved lengthwise and seeded (about 1½ pounds)
  Cooking spray
- 2 tablespoons chopped fresh cilantro

1 Prepare grill to medium-high heat.
2 Combine first 7 ingredients in a bowl, stirring well. Spoon about 2 teaspoons cheese mixture into each pepper half. Place pepper halves, cheese sides up, on a grill rack coated with cooking spray. Grill peppers 5 minutes or until bottoms of peppers are charred and cheese mixture is lightly browned. Carefully place peppers on a serving platter. Sprinkle with cilantro. Yield: 16 servings (serving size: 2 pepper halves).

CALORIES 84; FAT 4.8g (sat 3.1g, mono 1.2g, poly 0.2g); PROTEIN 7.1g; CARB 3.5g; FIBER 0.9g; CHOL 11mg; IRON 0.6mg; SODIUM 334mg; CALC 117mg

Oatmeal Cookie–Peach Cobbler

You can make this in individual ramekins with one dollop of dough on top of each. The baking time remains the same.

TOPPING:
- ½ cup granulated sugar
- ½ cup packed brown sugar
- ½ cup butter, softened
- 2 teaspoons vanilla extract
- 1 large egg
- 4.5 ounces all-purpose flour (about 1 cup)
- 1 cup old-fashioned rolled oats
- ½ teaspoon baking powder
- ½ teaspoon salt

FILLING:
- 11 cups sliced peeled peaches (about 5 pounds)
- ⅓ cup granulated sugar
- 2 tablespoons all-purpose flour
- 2 tablespoons fresh lemon juice
  Cooking spray

1 Preheat oven to 350°.
2 To prepare topping, place first 3 ingredients in a large bowl; beat with a mixer at medium speed until light and fluffy. Add vanilla and egg; beat well. Weigh or lightly spoon 1 cup flour into a dry measuring cup; level with a knife. Combine 1 cup flour, oats, baking powder, and salt; stir with a whisk. Add flour mixture to sugar mixture; beat at low speed until blended. Cover and chill 30 minutes.
3 To prepare filling, combine peaches and next 3 ingredients in a bowl; toss to coat. Spoon mixture into a 13 x 9–inch baking dish coated with cooking spray. Dollop 12 mounds of chilled dough over peach mixture at even intervals. Bake at 350° for 40 minutes or until lightly browned and bubbly. Yield: 12 servings (serving size: about 1 cup).

CALORIES 307; FAT 9.1g (sat 5.1g, mono 2.4g, poly 0.7g); PROTEIN 4.5g; CARB 54.1g; FIBER 3.8g; CHOL 38mg; IRON 1.6mg; SODIUM 177mg; CALC 43mg

September

As summer winds down, heartier fare bridges the gap to fall.

Tomato Flatbread with Goat Cheese

(pictured on page 223)

Serve with salad for a light lunch, or offer as an appetizer at your next outdoor party. Choose different colors of tomatoes for the most striking presentation.

  1 package dry yeast (about 2¼ teaspoons)
 ¾ cup warm water (100° to 110°)
11.25 ounces all-purpose flour (about 2½ cups)
 1¼ teaspoons salt
 ½ teaspoon freshly ground black pepper
  2 tablespoons olive oil
Cooking spray
  3 medium heirloom tomatoes, cut into ⅛-inch-thick slices (about 1¼ pounds)
  1 cup (4 ounces) crumbled goat cheese
  1 tablespoon chopped fresh chives
  1 tablespoon chopped fresh parsley
  8 fresh basil leaves
Freshly ground black pepper (optional)

① Dissolve yeast in ¾ cup warm water in a bowl; let stand 5 minutes or until bubbly. Weigh or lightly spoon flour into dry measuring cups; level with a knife. Combine flour, salt, and ½ teaspoon pepper in a large bowl; make a well in center of mixture. Add yeast mixture to flour mixture; stir just until moist. Add oil; stir until a dough forms. Turn dough out onto a lightly floured surface. Knead until smooth and elastic (about 10 minutes). Place dough in a bowl coated with cooking spray, turning to coat top. Cover and let rise in a warm place (85°), free from drafts, 1 hour or until doubled in size. (Press two fingers into dough. If indentation remains, dough has risen enough.)

② Punch dough down; cover and let rest 5 minutes. Roll dough into a 16 x 11–inch rectangle; place dough on a jelly-roll pan coated with cooking spray. Cover and let rise 1 hour or until doubled in size.
③ While dough rises, arrange tomato slices in a single layer on several layers of paper towels; cover with additional paper towels. Lightly press down occasionally.
④ Preheat oven to 375°.
⑤ Arrange tomato slices over dough. Sprinkle evenly with cheese. Bake at 375° for 28 minutes or until lightly browned. Remove flatbread from pan; cool 5 minutes on a wire rack. Sprinkle with chives and parsley. Arrange basil over flatbread; sprinkle with additional pepper, if desired. Yield: 12 servings (serving size: 1 piece).

CALORIES 160; FAT 5.5g (sat 2.3g, mono 2.3g, poly 0.5g); PROTEIN 5.4g; CARB 22.2g; FIBER 1.4g; CHOL 7mg; IRON 1.7mg; SODIUM 298mg; CALC 38mg

Tex-Mex Fiesta Menu
serves 4

Grilled Flank Steak Soft Tacos with Avocado-Lime Salsa

Smoky refried beans

Cook 2 slices applewood-smoked bacon in a medium skillet over medium heat until crisp. Remove bacon from pan, reserving drippings. Crumble bacon; set aside. Add ½ cup chopped onion and 2 minced garlic cloves to drippings in pan; cook 5 minutes or until tender, stirring occasionally. Stir in ⅓ cup fat-free, less-sodium chicken broth and 1 (15-ounce) can drained and rinsed pinto beans; mash with a potato masher to desired consistency. Cook until thoroughly heated, stirring occasionally. Sprinkle with bacon and 1 tablespoon chopped fresh cilantro.

Blue corn tortilla chips

Mexican beer

Vanilla low-fat ice cream with cinnamon and store-bought dulce de leche

Grilled Flank Steak Soft Tacos with Avocado-Lime Salsa

STEAK:
  1 tablespoon chili powder
  2 teaspoons grated lime rind
 ½ teaspoon salt
 ½ teaspoon chipotle chile powder
 ¼ teaspoon freshly ground black pepper
  1 (1-pound) flank steak, trimmed
Cooking spray

SALSA:
  1 cup diced peeled avocado
 ¾ cup finely chopped tomato
 ⅓ cup finely chopped Vidalia or other sweet onion
 ¼ cup chopped fresh cilantro
 ½ teaspoon grated lime rind
  2 tablespoons fresh lime juice
 ¼ teaspoon salt
 ¼ teaspoon hot pepper sauce (such as Tabasco)

REMAINING INGREDIENTS:
  8 (6-inch) corn tortillas
  2 cups very thinly sliced green cabbage

① To prepare steak, combine first 5 ingredients in a small bowl. Score a diamond pattern on both sides of steak. Rub chili powder mixture evenly over steak. Cover and chill 1 hour.
② Prepare grill to medium-high heat.
③ Place steak on a grill rack coated with cooking spray; grill 8 minutes on each side or until desired degree of doneness. Remove from heat; let stand 10 minutes. Cut steak diagonally across grain into thin slices.
④ To prepare salsa, combine avocado and next 7 ingredients in a medium bowl.
⑤ Warm tortillas according to package directions. Spoon steak mixture evenly over each of 8 tortillas. Top each taco with ¼ cup salsa and ¼ cup cabbage. Yield: 4 servings (serving size: 2 tacos).

CALORIES 353; FAT 16g (sat 4.3g, mono 7.6g, poly 1.7g); PROTEIN 27.9g; CARB 27.7g; FIBER 6.8g; CHOL 40mg; IRON 2.5mg; SODIUM 593mg; CALC 78mg

STAFF FAVORITE • QUICK & EASY

Heirloom Tomato and Herb Pappardelle

Use any combination of heirloom tomatoes you like—a variety of colors and tastes is ideal. The tasty sauce can double as a bruschetta topping for an easy appetizer.

- 12 ounces uncooked pappardelle (wide ribbon pasta)
- ¼ cup extra-virgin olive oil, divided
- 2 cups thinly sliced shallots (about 2 large)
- 4 garlic cloves, thinly sliced
- 1 tablespoon chopped fresh oregano
- 2 teaspoons chopped fresh rosemary
- 2 teaspoons chopped fresh thyme
- 1 teaspoon kosher salt
- ½ teaspoon freshly ground black pepper
- 4 pounds heirloom tomatoes, seeded and cut into ½-inch pieces
- ½ cup (2 ounces) shaved pecorino cheese

1 Cook pasta according to package directions, omitting salt and fat. Drain.
2 While pasta cooks, heat 2 tablespoons olive oil in a large nonstick skillet over medium-high heat. Add shallots to pan; sauté 5 minutes, stirring occasionally. Add garlic; sauté 2 minutes. Reduce heat to medium. Add oregano and next 5 ingredients; cook 2 minutes or until thoroughly heated. Arrange 1 cup pasta onto each of 6 plates. Top each serving with about 1⅓ cups tomato mixture; drizzle each with 1 teaspoon remaining oil. Divide cheese evenly among servings. Yield: 6 servings.

CALORIES 397; FAT 13g (sat 3.2g, mono 7.4g, poly 1.3g); PROTEIN 14g; CARB 59.1g; FIBER 5.5g; CHOL 10mg; IRON 3.2mg; SODIUM 448mg; CALC 158mg

Storage Tip

Tomatoes For the brightest taste and juiciest texture, store tomatoes in a single layer, stem sides up, at room temperature and away from direct sunlight for up to 4 days. Do not refrigerate as the cold environment diminishes flavor and turns the flesh mealy.

Mexican Succotash

- 1 poblano chile
- 2 cups shelled fresh lima beans (about 2 pounds unshelled beans)
- 1 tablespoon olive oil
- 1 cup finely chopped Vidalia or other sweet onion
- 1 cup finely chopped red bell pepper
- ½ cup finely chopped green bell pepper
- 3 garlic cloves, minced
- 2 cups fresh corn kernels
- 1 cup grape tomatoes, halved
- ¼ cup chopped fresh cilantro
- 2 tablespoons fresh lemon juice
- ½ teaspoon salt
- ⅛ teaspoon freshly ground black pepper
- Cilantro sprigs (optional)

1 Preheat broiler.
2 Cut poblano chile in half lengthwise; discard seeds and membranes. Place chile halves, skin sides up, on a foil-lined baking sheet; flatten with hand. Broil 10 minutes or until blackened. Place in a zip-top plastic bag; seal. Let stand 5 minutes. Peel, chop, and set aside.
3 Place beans in a medium saucepan; cover with water. Bring to a boil; reduce heat to medium, and cook 25 minutes or until tender. Drain.
4 Heat oil in a large nonstick skillet over medium-high heat. Add onion and bell peppers; sauté 6 minutes. Add garlic; sauté 1 minute. Stir in beans and corn, and sauté 6 minutes or until corn is tender. Add poblano and tomatoes; cook 2 minutes. Remove from heat; stir in chopped cilantro and next 3 ingredients. Garnish with cilantro sprigs, if desired. Yield: 8 servings (serving size: about ¾ cup).

CALORIES 243; FAT 2.9g (sat 0.4g, mono 1.4g, poly 0.5g); PROTEIN 12.1g; CARB 45.1g; FIBER 12.5g; CHOL 0mg; IRON 3.3mg; SODIUM 163mg; CALC 53mg

Storage Tip

Shell Beans Refrigerate unshelled beans in a breathable (not airtight) plastic bag for up to 5 days. Or shell beans, refrigerate in an airtight container, and use within 2 days.

Warm Oysters with Champagne Sabayon

If you've had this trendy dish at a restaurant, you know "sabayon" refers to a simple frothy custard of egg yolks and wine (in this case, Champagne). The saltiness of oysters varies by species; taste one first, then season accordingly.

- ¼ cup dry Champagne or other dry sparkling wine
- ½ teaspoon sugar
- 2 large egg yolks
- 2 teaspoons finely diced shallots
- ½ teaspoon chopped fresh thyme
- ⅛ teaspoon kosher salt
- ⅛ teaspoon freshly ground black pepper
- 12 oysters on the half shell
  Small thyme sprigs (optional)

1 Place first 3 ingredients in top of a double boiler; stir with a whisk. Cook over simmering water until thick and mixture reaches 160° (about 5 minutes), stirring constantly with a whisk. Remove from heat. Stir in shallots and next 3 ingredients. Cool slightly.
2 Preheat broiler.
3 Arrange oysters on a jelly-roll pan. Broil 3 minutes or just until edges begin to curl. Top with sabayon. Garnish with thyme sprigs, if desired. Yield: 6 servings (serving size: 2 oysters and 2 teaspoons sabayon).

CALORIES 102; FAT 3.8g (sat 1g, mono 1g, poly 1.1g); PROTEIN 10.4g; CARB 5.9g; FIBER 0g; CHOL 118mg; IRON 5.3mg; SODIUM 149mg; CALC 17mg .

QUICK & EASY
Spicy Pickled Okra

If you're lucky enough to find purple okra, use it solo or in combination with standard green pods—but know that the longer the pickling time, the less vibrant the color. Serve on a relish tray, with sandwiches in place of pickle spears, or as a bloody Mary garnish. A jar makes a unique hostess gift.

- 1½ pounds okra
- 4 garlic cloves
- 4 fresh dill sprigs
- 2 cups cider vinegar
- 1¾ cups water
- 3 tablespoons sugar
- 1½ tablespoons kosher salt
- 1½ tablespoons mustard seeds
- 1 teaspoon crushed red pepper

1 Divide okra, garlic, and dill evenly among 4 (1-pint) jars.
2 Combine vinegar and remaining ingredients in a saucepan; bring to a boil. Cook 1 minute or until sugar dissolves. Remove from heat; let stand 5 minutes. Carefully pour vinegar mixture into jars, leaving about ¼ inch at top. Seal jars; refrigerate 3 days before serving. Yield: about 4 cups (serving size: ⅓ cup).

CALORIES 22; FAT 0.1g (sat 0g, mono 0g, poly 0.1g); PROTEIN 1g; CARB 4.6g; FIBER 1.6g; CHOL 0mg; IRON 0.4mg; SODIUM 181mg; CALC 42mg

MAKE AHEAD
Concord Grape Jam

Usually found only at farmers' markets, Concord grapes have a full, intense flavor. They are a slip-skin variety, which means the skins can be pinched off easily.

- 3 pounds fresh Concord grapes, stemmed (about 8 cups)
- ¾ cup sugar, divided
- 2 teaspoons grated lemon rind
- 4 teaspoons fresh lemon juice

1 Pinch grapes to separate pulp from skins. Place skins in a bowl; set aside. Place grape pulp and ¼ cup sugar in a medium saucepan; bring to a boil. Reduce heat; simmer 10 minutes or until seeds begin to separate from pulp.
2 Press pulp mixture through a fine sieve into a bowl. Discard seeds. Place skins, remaining ½ cup sugar, rind, juice, and pulp in saucepan; bring to a boil. Reduce heat; simmer until reduced to 2½ cups (about 2 hours and 45 minutes), stirring occasionally. Pour into a bowl; cool. Cover and store in refrigerator up to 2 weeks. Yield: about 2½ cups (serving size: 2 tablespoons).

CALORIES 56; FAT 0.1g (sat 0.1g, mono 0g, poly 0g); PROTEIN 0.3g; CARB 14.4g; FIBER 0.4g; CHOL 0mg; IRON 0.1mg; SODIUM 1mg; CALC 6mg

Dinner Tonight

These Mediterranean and Asian-inspired meals come together in a snap.

Pizza Provençal

························30 minutes

Serve with artichoke–green bean salad. Place 2 cups (2-inch) cut green beans in boiling water; cook 5 minutes or until crisp-tender. Drain and rinse with cold water; drain. Place beans in a small bowl. Drain 1 (6½-ounce) jar marinated artichoke hearts, reserving marinade. Thinly slice artichoke hearts; add to beans. Add reserved marinade, 1 tablespoon fresh lemon juice, ¼ teaspoon black pepper, and ⅛ teaspoon salt to bowl; toss to coat.

- ¼   cup niçoise olives, pitted
- 3   tablespoons fresh basil leaves
- 3   tablespoons drained oil-packed sun-dried tomatoes
- 1   teaspoon grated lemon rind
- 2   tablespoons fresh lemon juice
- 1½ teaspoons minced fresh garlic
- 1   teaspoon water
- 1   (16-ounce) loaf Italian bread, split in half horizontally
- 2   cups thinly sliced roasted skinless, boneless chicken breast
- ¾   cup (3 ounces) crumbled goat cheese
- 2   tablespoons chopped fresh basil

❶ Preheat oven to 450°.
❷ Place first 7 ingredients in a food processor; process until smooth. Place bottom half of bread, cut side up, on a baking sheet (reserve top half for another use). Spread olive mixture over bread. Arrange chicken over bread; sprinkle with cheese. Bake at 450° for 10 minutes or until heated. Sprinkle with basil. Yield: 4 servings (serving size: 1 piece).

CALORIES 330; FAT 10.7g (sat 4.4g, mono 3.8g, poly 1.6g); PROTEIN 23.2g; CARB 34.4g; FIBER 2.3g; CHOL 46mg; IRON 3mg; SODIUM 595mg; CALC 98mg

Coconut and Basil Steamed Mussels

·······························20 minutes

Steamed spinach and scallion rice complete this Asian-themed dinner. Combine 1 cup water, ½ cup jasmine rice, 1 teaspoon butter, ¼ teaspoon kosher salt, and 1 thinly sliced green onion in a small saucepan; bring to a boil. Cover, reduce heat, and simmer 15 minutes; remove from heat. Let stand 5 minutes. Fluff with a fork.

- 2   teaspoons canola oil
- ¼   cup minced shallots
- 2   teaspoons bottled minced garlic
- 1   cup light coconut milk
- ⅔   cup water
- ⅓   cup fat-free, less-sodium chicken broth
- ¼   cup torn fresh basil
- 1   tablespoon fresh lime juice
- 1   teaspoon dark brown sugar
- 1   teaspoon fish sauce
- ½   to 1 teaspoon Sriracha (hot chile sauce, such as Huy Fong)
- 24 mussels (about 1 pound), scrubbed and debearded
- Thinly sliced fresh basil (optional)

❶ Heat a Dutch oven over medium heat. Add oil to pan, swirling to coat. Add shallots and garlic to pan; cook 2 minutes or until tender, stirring frequently. Stir in coconut milk and next 7 ingredients; bring to a boil. Add mussels to pan; cover and cook 5 minutes or until shells open. Discard any unopened shells.
❷ Remove mussels from pan with a slotted spoon, reserving broth mixture. Divide mussels between 2 serving bowls; keep warm. Bring broth mixture to a boil; cook 5 minutes. Pour 1 cup sauce over each bowl. Sprinkle with sliced basil, if desired. Yield: 2 servings.

CALORIES 308; FAT 15.1g (sat 6.8g, mono 5g, poly 3.2g); PROTEIN 25.5g; CARB 19.4g; FIBER 0.5g; CHOL 54mg; IRON 8.8mg; SODIUM 996mg; CALC 75mg

Caramelized Scallops

·····························20 minutes

Serve with wide rice noodles and sugar snap peas. Steam 6 ounces sugar snap peas 2 minutes or until crisp-tender; place in bowl. Add ¼ teaspoon salt, ¼ teaspoon black pepper, and ½ teaspoon toasted sesame oil to peas; toss well. Sprinkle with ¼ teaspoon toasted sesame seeds.

- 3½ teaspoons sugar, divided
- 5   teaspoons water, divided
- 1   tablespoon fish sauce
- 1   teaspoon minced fresh ginger
- 2   teaspoons fresh lime juice
- ½   teaspoon minced fresh garlic
- ⅛   teaspoon crushed red pepper
- Cooking spray
- ⅛   teaspoon freshly ground black pepper
- 6   large sea scallops (about 12 ounces)
- 1   teaspoon chopped fresh mint
- 2   lime wedges

❶ Combine ½ teaspoon sugar, 1 tablespoon water, fish sauce, and next 4 ingredients in a small bowl.
❷ Combine remaining 1 tablespoon sugar and remaining 2 teaspoons water in a small heavy saucepan over medium-high heat; cook until sugar dissolves. Continue cooking 2 minutes or until golden (do not stir). Remove from heat; carefully add fish sauce mixture, stirring constantly. Keep warm.
❸ Heat a medium skillet over medium-high heat. Coat pan with cooking spray. Sprinkle black pepper over scallops; add scallops to pan. Cook 1½ minutes on each side or until desired degree of doneness. Add sauce; toss well. Sprinkle with mint. Serve with lime wedges. Yield: 2 servings (serving size: 3 scallops).

CALORIES 185; FAT 1.3g (sat 0.1g, mono 0.1g, poly 0.5g); PROTEIN 29.2g; CARB 13.2g; FIBER 0.4g; CHOL 56mg; IRON 0.6mg; SODIUM 844mg; CALC 44mg

Pasta with Zucchini and Toasted Almonds

···················*20 minutes*

Try substituting zesty Parmigiano-Reggiano for pecorino Romano. Serve with olive tapenade breadsticks. Combine 1 tablespoon extra-virgin olive oil, 1½ teaspoons minced garlic, 1 teaspoon fresh lemon juice, ¼ teaspoon salt, ⅛ teaspoon freshly ground black pepper, and 15 finely chopped pitted kalamata olives in a small bowl. Spread olive mixture over 1 (11-ounce) can refrigerated breadsticks dough. Twist each breadstick; bake at 375° for 15 minutes or until browned.

    2   cups cherry tomatoes, halved
    2   tablespoons minced shallots
    1   teaspoon minced fresh thyme
    2   teaspoons fresh lemon juice
    ¾   teaspoon kosher salt
    ½   teaspoon freshly ground black
        pepper
    ¼   teaspoon sugar
    5   teaspoons extra-virgin olive oil,
        divided
    1   (9-ounce) package refrigerated
        linguine
    1½ teaspoons bottled minced garlic
    3   cups chopped zucchini
        (about 1 pound)
    ¾   cup fat-free, less-sodium chicken
        broth
    3   tablespoons chopped fresh mint,
        divided
    ⅓   cup (1½ ounces) grated fresh
        pecorino Romano cheese
    3   tablespoons sliced almonds,
        toasted

❶ Combine first 7 ingredients in a medium bowl. Add 2 teaspoons oil, tossing to coat.
❷ Cook pasta according to package directions, omitting salt and fat. Drain well.
❸ Heat a large nonstick skillet over medium-high heat. Add remaining 1 tablespoon oil to pan, swirling to coat.

Add garlic to pan; sauté 30 seconds. Add zucchini; sauté 3 minutes or until crisp-tender. Add broth; bring to a simmer. Stir in pasta and 1½ tablespoons mint; toss well. Remove from heat; stir in tomato mixture. Place 1½ cups pasta mixture in each of 4 bowls; top evenly with remaining 1½ tablespoons mint. Sprinkle each serving with 4 teaspoons cheese and 2 teaspoons almonds. Yield: 4 servings.

CALORIES 344; FAT 12.7g (sat 3.1g, mono 6.6g, poly 2g); PROTEIN 14g; CARB 45.5g; FIBER 5.3g; CHOL 58mg; IRON 3.4mg; SODIUM 601mg; CALC 163mg

Greek Steak Pitas

···················*20 minutes*

Creamy hummus rounds out this meal. Place 1 cup rinsed and drained canned chickpeas, 2 tablespoons lemon juice, 1 tablespoon tahini (roasted sesame seed paste), ¼ teaspoon salt, and ⅛ teaspoon ground red pepper in a food processor; process until well blended. Gradually add 3 tablespoons extra-virgin olive oil; process until smooth. Serve with red pepper slices and baby carrots.

    ½   cup red wine vinegar
    1   teaspoon Greek seasoning
        (such as McCormick)
    ⅛   teaspoon black pepper
    1   (1-pound) flank steak, trimmed
    ½   teaspoon kosher salt, divided
    1   teaspoon butter
    1   teaspoon olive oil
    2   tablespoons lemon juice
    1   teaspoon minced garlic
    1   (6-ounce) package fresh baby
        spinach
    4   (6-inch) pitas, cut in half
    ½   cup thinly sliced red onion
    24 slices English cucumber
    ½   cup (2 ounces) crumbled feta
        cheese

❶ Combine first 3 ingredients in a large zip-top plastic bag; add steak to bag. Marinate 3 minutes, turning once.

Remove steak from bag; discard marinade. Sprinkle steak with ¼ teaspoon salt. Heat a large skillet over medium-high heat. Add butter and oil. Add steak; cook 5 minutes on each side or until desired doneness. Let stand 2 minutes. Cut steak across grain into thin slices.
❷ Return pan to heat. Add juice, garlic, and spinach; sauté 1 minute. Remove from heat; add remaining ¼ teaspoon salt.
❸ Spoon 2 tablespoons spinach mixture into each pita half. Place 1 tablespoon onion, 3 cucumber slices, and 1½ ounces steak in each pita half; sprinkle 1 tablespoon cheese in each pita half. Yield: 4 servings (serving size: 2 filled pita halves).

CALORIES 427; FAT 13.3g (sat 6.5g, mono 4.7g, poly 0.6g); PROTEIN 35.5g; CARB 39.1g; FIBER 2.6g; CHOL 53mg; IRON 6mg; SODIUM 730mg; CALC 215mg

Roasted Rosemary Shrimp with Arugula and White Bean Salad

···················*30 minutes*

Buy peeled and deveined shrimp to save time with prep work. Serve with garlic ciabatta. Heat 4 teaspoons olive oil in a small saucepan over medium-low heat. Add 1 thinly sliced garlic clove; cook until garlic begins to turn golden, stirring frequently. Remove from heat. Discard garlic; stir in ⅛ teaspoon salt. Heat a grill pan over medium-high heat; coat pan with cooking spray. Add 4 (½-inch-thick) slices ciabatta bread to pan, and cook 2 minutes on each side or until lightly browned. Brush one side of each slice with garlic oil.

SHRIMP:

    2   tablespoons olive oil
    1   tablespoon fresh lemon juice
    2   teaspoons minced fresh rosemary
    ½   teaspoon kosher salt
    ¼   teaspoon black pepper
    3   garlic cloves, crushed
    1½ pounds jumbo shrimp, peeled and
        deveined

SALAD:

- 2 tablespoons fresh lemon juice
- 1 tablespoon extra-virgin olive oil
- ½ teaspoon minced fresh garlic
- ¼ teaspoon kosher salt
- ⅛ teaspoon black pepper
- 5 cups arugula leaves
- ½ cup vertically sliced red onion
- 1 (15-ounce) can cannellini beans, rinsed and drained

1 Preheat oven to 400°.

2 To prepare shrimp, combine first 6 ingredients in a medium bowl; stir with a whisk. Add shrimp to bowl; toss well. Cover and refrigerate 10 minutes.

3 Arrange shrimp on a jelly-roll pan. Bake at 400° for 10 minutes or until shrimp are done.

4 To prepare salad, combine 2 tablespoons juice and next 4 ingredients in a large bowl; stir with a whisk. Add arugula, onion, and beans to bowl; toss well. Place salad and shrimp on each of 4 plates. Yield: 4 servings (serving size: 1½ cups salad and about 6 shrimp).

CALORIES 334; FAT 13.6g (sat 2g, mono 7.8g, poly 2.5g); PROTEIN 37.7g; CARB 13.6g; FIBER 3g; CHOL 259mg; IRON 5.4mg; SODIUM 690mg; CALC 156mg

QUICK & EASY
Beef Lettuce Wraps

······················30 minutes

Soba noodle salad complements the meaty wraps. Cook 6 ounces soba noodles according to package directions, omitting salt and fat; drain well. Combine noodles, ⅓ cup chopped green onions, and ⅓ cup matchstick-cut carrots in a large bowl. Combine 1½ tablespoons rice vinegar, 1 tablespoon sesame oil, 1 tablespoon fish sauce, 1 tablespoon low-sodium soy sauce, 2 teaspoons sambal oelek, and 1 teaspoon brown sugar in a small bowl, stirring well with a whisk. Drizzle vinegar mixture over noodle mixture; toss well.

- Cooking spray
- 1 (1-pound) flank steak, trimmed
- ¼ teaspoon kosher salt
- ¼ teaspoon freshly ground black pepper
- 3 tablespoons fresh lime juice
- 2 tablespoons fish sauce
- 4 teaspoons dark brown sugar
- 1 jalapeño pepper, seeded and minced
- 8 Bibb lettuce leaves
- 1 cup thinly sliced red onion
- 1 cup torn fresh mint
- ½ cup matchstick-cut English cucumber
- ½ cup torn fresh cilantro
- 2 tablespoons chopped unsalted, dry-roasted peanuts

1 Heat a grill pan over medium-high heat. Coat pan with cooking spray. Sprinkle steak with salt and pepper. Place steak in pan; cook 5 minutes on each side or until desired degree of doneness. Remove from pan; let stand 10 minutes. Cut steak diagonally across grain into thin slices.

2 Combine juice and next 3 ingredients in a medium bowl, stirring with a whisk. Reserve 4 teaspoons juice mixture in a small serving bowl. Pour remaining juice mixture in a large bowl; add steak, tossing to coat. Place 1½ ounces beef in center of each lettuce leaf; top each with 2 tablespoons onion, 2 tablespoons mint, 1 tablespoon cucumber, and 1 tablespoon cilantro. Sprinkle evenly with peanuts; roll up. Serve with reserved juice mixture. Yield: 4 servings (serving size: 2 wraps and 1 teaspoon sauce).

CALORIES 224; FAT 8.1g (sat 2.7g, mono 3.4g, poly 1g); PROTEIN 27g; CARB 11.2g; FIBER 2g; CHOL 39mg; IRON 2.6mg; SODIUM 755mg; CALC 61mg

QUICK & EASY
Barbecued Pork Chops

······················40 minutes

You can use mirin or vermouth in place of sake in this dish. For kimchi-style slaw, combine ¼ cup rice wine vinegar, 1 to 2 teaspoons Sriracha, 2 teaspoons minced garlic, 1 teaspoon minced fresh ginger, 1 teaspoon canola oil, 1 teaspoon kosher salt, and ½ teaspoon sugar in a large bowl; stir with a whisk. Add 4 cups shredded Napa cabbage and ½ cup thinly sliced green onions; toss to coat.

- 2 tablespoons dark brown sugar
- 2 tablespoons low-sodium soy sauce
- 1 tablespoon dark sesame oil
- 1 tablespoon pineapple juice
- 2 teaspoons minced fresh garlic
- 1½ teaspoons sake (rice wine)
- ¼ teaspoon crushed red pepper
- ¼ teaspoon freshly ground black pepper
- 4 (4-ounce) bone-in pork chops (about ½ inch thick)
- Cooking spray
- ¼ teaspoon kosher salt
- 1 teaspoon sesame seeds, toasted

1 Combine first 8 ingredients in a zip-top plastic bag; add pork to bag. Seal, and marinate at room temperature 25 minutes.

2 Heat a grill pan over medium-high heat. Coat pan with cooking spray. Remove pork from bag; reserve marinade. Sprinkle pork with salt. Cook pork 3 minutes on each side or until done. Pour reserved marinade into a small saucepan; bring to a boil. Reduce heat, and simmer 2 minutes or until thickened. Brush pork with reduced marinade; sprinkle with sesame seeds. Yield: 4 servings (serving size: 1 pork chop).

CALORIES 195; FAT 9.4g (sat 2.5g, mono 3.9g, poly 2.4g); PROTEIN 17.7g; CARB 8.9g; FIBER 0.3g; CHOL 49mg; IRON 1mg; SODIUM 433mg; CALC 31mg

Feta-Stuffed Turkey Burgers

·····················*30 minutes*

Substitute 2 to 3 teaspoons chopped fresh oregano for dried in the burger, if you'd like. Pair with sautéed zucchini. Heat 2 teaspoons olive oil in a skillet over medium-high heat. Add 2 cups sliced zucchini and 2 minced garlic cloves; sauté 5 minutes. Add 2 teaspoons lemon juice, ¼ teaspoon salt, and ⅛ teaspoon black pepper.

¼ cup finely chopped red onion
1 teaspoon dried oregano
1 teaspoon grated lemon rind
½ teaspoon salt
¼ teaspoon freshly ground black pepper
1 pound ground turkey
6 tablespoons (1½ ounces) crumbled feta cheese
Cooking spray
¼ cup grated English cucumber
¼ cup plain fat-free yogurt
1 tablespoon chopped fresh mint
4 (¼-inch-thick) slices tomato
4 green leaf lettuce leaves
4 (2-ounce) Kaiser rolls or hamburger buns

❶ Combine first 6 ingredients. Divide mixture into 4 portions. Indent center of each portion; place 1½ tablespoons feta into each. Fold turkey mixture around cheese; shape each portion into a ¹/₂-inch-thick patty.
❷ Heat grill pan over medium-high heat. Coat pan with cooking spray. Add patties; cook 5 minutes on each side.
❸ Combine cucumber, yogurt, and mint in a small bowl. Arrange 1 turkey patty, 1 tomato slice, 1 lettuce leaf, and 2 tablespoons yogurt mixture on bottom half of each roll. Top with top halves of rolls. Yield: 4 servings.

CALORIES 386; FAT 13.7g (sat 4.5g, mono 4.3g, poly 3g); PROTEIN 30.2g; CARB 34g; FIBER 2.3g; CHOL 109mg; IRON 3.9mg; SODIUM 897mg; CALC 198mg

Make Every Bite Count

The key to eating smart is enjoying foods rich in nutrients and modest in calories. Follow our tips for making healthful choices and recipes that yield flavorful dividends.

Grilled Pork Tenderloin with Green Mango

Green mangoes are not fully ripe, and they lend sour flavor to Southeast Asian dishes. Their tartness contrasts with sweet carrot, refreshing mint and basil, and fiery peppers. Use an equal amount of unpeeled green apples if you can't find green mangoes.

PORK:
¼ cup pineapple juice
2 tablespoons finely chopped peeled fresh ginger
1 tablespoon low-sodium soy sauce
1 tablespoon sake (rice wine) or dry sherry
4 large garlic cloves, minced
1 (1-pound) pork tenderloin, trimmed
¼ teaspoon salt
¼ teaspoon freshly ground black pepper
Cooking spray

SALAD:
½ cup shredded carrot
⅓ cup chopped fresh mint
⅓ cup chopped fresh basil
¼ cup chopped fresh cilantro
½ teaspoon kosher salt
¼ teaspoon crushed red pepper
1 large green (unripe) mango, peeled and shredded
1 jalapeño pepper, finely chopped

REMAINING INGREDIENTS:
8 Boston lettuce leaves
1 cup mung bean sprouts

❶ Prepare grill to medium-high heat.
❷ To prepare pork, combine first 6 ingredients in a large zip-top plastic bag; seal. Marinate in refrigerator 1 hour, turning occasionally. Remove pork from bag; discard marinade. Sprinkle pork evenly with salt and black pepper.
❸ Place pork on grill rack coated with cooking spray. Grill 22 minutes or until a thermometer registers 155°, turning occasionally. Remove from heat; let stand 10 minutes. Cut pork into ¹/₂-inch-thick slices; cut each slice into thin strips, and keep warm.
❹ To prepare salad, combine carrot and next 7 ingredients in a medium bowl; toss well.
❺ Place about 1¹/₂ ounces pork on each of 8 lettuce leaves; top each serving evenly with ¼ cup mango mixture and 2 tablespoon bean sprouts. Yield: 4 servings (serving size: 2 filled lettuce leaves).

CALORIES 219; FAT 5.5g (sat 1.8g, mono 2g, poly 0.6g); PROTEIN 24.6g; CARB 16.8g; FIBER 2.2g; CHOL 65mg; IRON 2.1mg; SODIUM 545mg; CALC 39mg

Asian Snap Pea Salad with Sesame-Orange Dressing

Vitamin C from the orange juice, bell pepper, and peas helps your body absorb the iron in this salad. Serve with stir-fried chicken breast and brown rice or buckwheat noodles to complement the nutrient-rich package.

DRESSING:

- 1 large orange
- 1 tablespoon rice vinegar
- 2 teaspoons low-sodium soy sauce
- 1½ teaspoons dark sesame oil
- 1 teaspoon brown sugar
- 1 teaspoon hot chile sauce (such as Sriracha)

SALAD:

- 2 teaspoons canola oil
- 1½ cups thinly sliced red bell pepper
- ¾ cup thinly sliced carrot
- 12 ounces sugar snap peas, trimmed
- ½ teaspoon kosher salt
- ½ cup diagonally cut green onions
- 1 (6-ounce) package fresh baby spinach
- 1 teaspoon sesame seeds, toasted

❶ To prepare dressing, grate 1 teaspoon rind; squeeze ⅓ cup juice from orange over a bowl. Set rind aside. Combine juice, vinegar, and next 4 ingredients in a small bowl; stir with a whisk.

❷ To prepare salad, heat 2 teaspoons canola oil in a large nonstick skillet over medium-high heat. Add bell pepper and carrot to pan; sauté 1 minute, stirring occasionally. Add reserved orange rind, sugar snap peas, and salt to pan; sauté 2 minutes, stirring occasionally. Transfer pea mixture to a large bowl; cool 5 minutes. Stir in green onions and spinach. Pour dressing over salad; toss gently to coat. Sprinkle with sesame seeds. Serve immediately. Yield: 6 servings (serving size: 1⅓ cups).

CALORIES 98; FAT 3.1g (sat 0.3g, mono 1.5g, poly 1.1g); PROTEIN 3g; CARB 15.7g; FIBER 4.5g; CHOL 0mg; IRON 2.1mg; SODIUM 318mg; CALC 83mg

3 Steps to Nutritional Riches

1. Base meals on items from the grocery store perimeter. "Shopping from the outer edge of the store is the easiest step to increase the nutrient quotient of what you eat," says Andrew Drewnowski, PhD, director of the Center for Public Health Nutrition at Seattle's University of Washington. That's because the perimeter of the supermarket features whole foods—produce; meats, poultry, and fish; and dairy products—that are inherently healthful. Fresh fruits and vegetables, typically in store perimeter areas, are among the best nutritional bargains you can choose. You'll also want to shop the aisles containing 100 percent whole-grain breads, pasta, and whole grains.

2. Be inspired by international cuisine. Take a cue from cultures known for fresh, healthful fare, such as Indian, Latin, Asian, or Mediterranean. "Since meat has traditionally been a luxury, many cultures evolved clever ways to supplement with vegetables, legumes, and grains," says Chef Raghavan Iyer, *Cooking Light* Nutrition Essentials advisory panelist. For example, a classic Vietnamese dish might marinate thinly sliced lean pork (with vitamin B_{12}, iron, and quality protein) in fruit juice, soy sauce, and aromatics, and then combine it with carrots, fresh herbs, green mango, and mung beans (all contributing fiber, vitamins, and antioxidants)—like Grilled Pork Tenderloin with Green Mango on page 152.

3. Focus on the good-for-you nutrients foods provide. Instead of opting for fat- or sugar-free foods, choose items for what they do contain. "The 'don't eat this' message is negative," says Heather Bauer, RD, and *Cooking Light* Nutrition Essentials advisory panelist. "A nutrient-rich approach includes many foods and is more informative than the old nutrition speak." For example, instead of telling clients to limit saturated fat, Bauer offers valuable information by telling them what cuts of meat are the leanest along with some healthful preparation ideas.

> "Shopping from the outer edge of the store is the easiest step to increase the nutrient quotient of what you eat."
>
> —Andrew Drewnowski, PhD,
> director of the Center for Public Health Nutrition,
> University of Washington

Take Two

Which food in each pair offers the best nutritional package?

1 OUNCE WHOLE WHITE WHEAT

66 calories
1.7 grams fiber
Enriched with
B vitamins and iron

1 OUNCE 100 PERCENT WHOLE-GRAIN BREAD

60 calories
3 grams fiber
Also enriched, plus anti-oxidants, magnesium, zinc, and other nutrients from the whole grain

Many "whole white wheat" breads are made with mostly refined flours, so the product is not 100 percent whole grain (unless labeled as such), which means you miss out on the many nutrients whole grains offer.

1 CUP BLACKBERRIES

62 calories
7.4 grams fiber
31 milligrams vitamin C

1 CUP GRAPES

110 calories
0.3 gram fiber
17 milligrams vitamin C

Both are great choices, but the berries have more going for them, like high fiber and nearly half a day's worth of vitamin C for fewer calories. If you regularly eat any fresh fruit, you get extra credit.

1 CUP SPINACH

16 calories
1.6 grams fiber
338 micrograms vitamin A
20 milligrams vitamin C
2 milligrams iron

1 CUP SHREDDED ICEBERG LETTUCE

10 calories
0.9 gram fiber
18 micrograms vitamin A
2 milligrams vitamin C
0.3 milligram iron

Spinach corners the nutrient-rich market for salads. Add vitamin C, from strawberries or bell peppers, to the mix to help your body absorb available iron.

3 OUNCES CANNED ALBACORE TUNA (DRAINED)

85 calories
22 grams protein
0.4 gram omega-3 fats
0 IU vitamin D
0 milligrams calcium

3 OUNCES CANNED WILD SALMON (DRAINED)

130 calories
17 grams protein
1.7 grams omega-3 fats
191 IU vitamin D
203 milligrams calcium

Although it has 45 calories more than tuna, salmon offers one-fifth of a day's calcium needs, plus nearly half your daily requirement for vitamin D, a nutrient not found in many foods. Salmon also offers heart-healthy omega-3s.

Blueberry-Orange Parfaits

This snack comes together in a few minutes if you purchase orange sections from the refrigerated part of the produce section. To make ahead, prepare parfaits and refrigerate, covered, for up to 4 hours; sprinkle with wheat germ just before serving.

- 1½ tablespoons Demerara or turbinado sugar
- ½ teaspoon grated orange rind
- 2 (7-ounce) containers reduced-fat plain Greek-style yogurt
- 2 cups fresh blueberries
- 2 cups orange sections (about 2 large)
- ¼ cup wheat germ

① Combine first 3 ingredients in a small bowl, stirring until blended. Spoon ¼ cup blueberries into each of 4 tall glasses. Spoon about 2½ tablespoons yogurt mixture over blueberries in each glass. Add ¼ cup orange sections to each serving. Repeat layers with remaining blueberries, yogurt mixture, and orange sections. Sprinkle 1 tablespoon wheat germ over each serving; serve immediately. Yield: 4 servings (serving size: 1 parfait).

CALORIES 186; FAT 3g (sat 1.6g, mono 0.1g, poly 0.5g); PROTEIN 11.8g; CARB 31.9g; FIBER 4.2g; CHOL 5mg; IRON 1mg; SODIUM 34mg; CALC 125mg

Bulgur Salad with Edamame and Cherry Tomatoes

The vitamin C from the lemon juice aids iron absorption. Round out the meal with grilled chicken, lemony hummus, and toasted 100 percent whole wheat pita wedges. Substitute fresh shelled fava beans for edamame, if you like. Fava beans also supply protein, fiber, and B vitamins.

- 1 cup uncooked bulgur
- 1 cup boiling water
- 1 cup frozen shelled edamame (green soybeans)
- 1 pound yellow and red cherry tomatoes, halved
- 1 cup finely chopped fresh flat-leaf parsley
- ⅓ cup finely chopped fresh mint
- 2 tablespoons chopped fresh dill
- 1 cup chopped green onions
- ¼ cup fresh lemon juice
- ¼ cup extra-virgin olive oil
- 1 teaspoon kosher salt
- ½ teaspoon freshly ground black pepper

① Combine bulgur and 1 cup boiling water in a large bowl. Cover and let stand 1 hour or until bulgur is tender. ② Cook edamame in boiling water 3 minutes or until crisp-tender. Drain. Add edamame, tomatoes, and remaining ingredients to bulgur; toss well. Let stand at room temperature 1 hour before serving. Yield: 6 servings (serving size: 1¼ cups).

CALORIES 208; FAT 10.5g (sat 1.3g, mono 6.7g, poly 1.2g); PROTEIN 6.3g; CARB 25.4g; FIBER 7.1g; CHOL 0mg; IRON 2.2mg; SODIUM 332mg; CALC 59mg

Grilled Tomato and Brie Sandwiches

These sandwiches make the most of juicy, flavorful summer tomatoes. Serve with grapes or carrot sticks.

- 8 (1-ounce) slices 100% whole-grain bread (about ¼ inch thick)
- 1 teaspoon olive oil
- 1 garlic clove, halved
- 2 teaspoons country-style Dijon mustard
- 4 ounces Brie cheese, thinly sliced
- 1⅓ cups packaged baby arugula and spinach greens (such as Dole)
- 8 (¼-inch-thick) slices beefsteak tomato
- Cooking spray

① Prepare grill to high heat. ② Brush one side of each bread slice with oil; rub cut sides of garlic over oil. Spread ½ teaspoon mustard on each of 4 bread slices, oil side down. Top each bread slice with 1 ounce cheese, ⅓ cup greens, and 2 tomato slices. Top each with remaining 4 bread slices, oil side up. ③ Place sandwiches on grill rack coated with cooking spray; grill 2 minutes on each side or until lightly toasted and cheese melts. Yield: 4 servings (serving size: 1 sandwich).

CALORIES 234; FAT 10.1g (sat 5.1g, mono 3.1g, poly 1g); PROTEIN 11g; CARB 26.9g; FIBER 6.5g; CHOL 28mg; IRON 1.8mg; SODIUM 445mg; CALC 210mg

Reader Recipes

Bigger is better when it comes to these chocolate chip cookies.

Raised in what she describes as a traditional, close-knit Italian family in Chicago, Marie Rizzio was exposed to great food from an early age. Her mother was a prolific home cook, baking fresh bread and preparing meals nearly every day. "When I grew up, I was determined to become as good a cook as my mom," she says.

From that auspicious start, Rizzio has found much success in the kitchen. After retiring to Michigan, she began entering recipe contests as a hobby. From her first win, a local newspaper contest, she went national, eventually taking home grand prizes from an oyster cook-off in Maryland, a Quaker Oats contest, and the National Chicken Cooking Contest.

Her advice for recipe-creation success? "You have to have a good audience for your cooking. My husband loves to eat and will eat anything, so that encourages me to experiment."

It was experimentation that yielded these lower-calorie cookies. Chocolate chip is Rizzio's favorite, and she tried egg whites for soft, puffy texture without extra fat, and a reduced amount of granulated sugar with brown sugar mixed in for deeper flavor. Even the size of these cookies helps: "Eating one giant cookie takes away the urge to eat two or three cookies," Rizzio says.

MAKE AHEAD • FREEZABLE
Giant Chocolate Chunk Cookies

"My grandkids love these cookies because they're nice and big, with lots of chocolate chips. They're easy to freeze—just wrap individually in heavy-duty plastic wrap, and store in a zip-top bag."

—Marie Rizzio,
Interlochen, Michigan

- 5 ounces all-purpose flour (about 1 cup plus 2 tablespoons)
- ½ teaspoon baking soda
- ¼ teaspoon salt
- ⅓ cup granulated sugar
- ⅓ cup packed brown sugar
- ¼ cup butter, softened
- 1 teaspoon vanilla extract
- 2 large egg whites
- ¼ cup semisweet chocolate chips
- Cooking spray

❶ Weigh or lightly spoon flour into dry measuring cups; level with a knife. Combine flour, soda, and salt in a small bowl; stir with a whisk.
❷ Place sugars and butter in a large bowl; beat with a mixer at medium speed until light and fluffy. Add vanilla and egg whites; beat well. Add flour mixture; beat at low speed until well blended. Stir in chocolate chips. Cover and refrigerate 1 hour or until firm.
❸ Preheat oven to 350°.
❹ Divide dough into 6 equal portions; place dough portions 2 inches apart on a baking sheet coated with cooking spray. Bake at 350° for 14 minutes or until golden brown. Cool 2 minutes on pan; cool on a wire rack. Yield: 6 cookies (serving size: 1 cookie).

CALORIES 279; FAT 9.7g (sat 6g, mono 2.7g, poly 0.4g); PROTEIN 4g; CARB 44.8g; FIBER 1g; CHOL 20mg; IRON 1.6mg; SODIUM 281mg; CALC 16mg

QUICK & EASY • FREEZABLE
Kathie's Zucchini Muffins

"I was looking for something healthy the kids could grab for breakfast on the way out the door and came up with these muffins. The kids are grown now, but I still enjoy making these. Sometimes I add raisins, nuts, or dried cranberries for variety."

—Kathleen Lehner,
Montgomery Village, Maryland

- 4.75 ounces whole wheat flour (about 1 cup)
- 3 ounces all-purpose flour (about ⅔ cup)
- ½ cup sugar
- 1 teaspoon ground cinnamon
- 1¼ teaspoons baking powder
- ½ teaspoon baking soda
- ¼ teaspoon salt
- 1⅓ cups shredded zucchini
- ½ cup fat-free milk
- 2 tablespoons canola oil
- 2 tablespoons honey
- 1 large egg
- Cooking spray
- 1 tablespoon sugar
- ¼ teaspoon ground cinnamon

❶ Preheat oven to 400°.
❷ Weigh or lightly spoon flours into dry measuring cups; level with a knife. Combine whole wheat flour and next 6 ingredients in a large bowl; stir with a whisk. Combine zucchini and next 4 ingredients in a small bowl; stir until blended. Make a well in center of flour mixture; add milk mixture, stirring just until moist. Spoon batter into 12 muffin cups coated with cooking spray.
❸ Combine 1 tablespoon sugar and ¼ teaspoon cinnamon; sprinkle over tops of muffins. Bake at 400° for 15 minutes or until golden. Remove from pans immediately; cool on a wire rack. Yield: 12 servings (serving size: 1 muffin).

CALORIES 145; FAT 3.1g (sat 0.4g, mono 1.6g, poly 0.9g); PROTEIN 3.5g; CARB 27.1g; FIBER 1.8g; CHOL 21mg; IRON 1.1mg; SODIUM 154mg; CALC 58mg

QUICK & EASY
Sesame-Orange Shrimp and Chicken Stir-Fry

"Stir-fries are an easy way to get more vegetables into my 4- and 6-year-olds' diets. After years of experimenting to get the best flavor and consistency for a versatile sauce, I was finally satisfied with this combination of ingredients. The taste is slightly sweet with subtle flavors that complement all those fresh vegetables. There's a surprising hint of ground red pepper along with the nutty flavor of the dark sesame oil."

—Rachel Spear,
Casper, Wyoming

SAUCE:
- 1 cup water
- 1/3 cup low-sodium soy sauce
- 1/4 cup cornstarch
- 1/4 cup orange juice
- 1 tablespoon sugar
- 1/2 teaspoon ground ginger
- 1/2 teaspoon dark sesame oil
- 1/4 teaspoon kosher salt
- 1/4 teaspoon ground red pepper
- 1/4 teaspoon freshly ground black pepper
- 1 (14-ounce) can fat-free, less-sodium chicken broth

STIR-FRY:
- 2 tablespoons olive oil, divided
- 12 ounces skinless, boneless chicken breast, cut into 1-inch pieces
- 2 cups coarsely chopped broccoli florets
- 1 cup chopped carrot
- 1 cup mushrooms, halved
- 1 cup snow peas, trimmed
- 1/2 cup chopped onion
- 2 garlic cloves, chopped
- 1 1/2 pounds medium shrimp, cooked and peeled
- 3 cups hot cooked long-grain rice

1 To prepare sauce, combine first 11 ingredients in a large bowl, stirring with a whisk. Set aside.
2 To prepare stir-fry, heat 1 tablespoon olive oil in a large nonstick skillet over medium-high heat. Add chicken to pan, and stir-fry 4 minutes or until done. Remove chicken from pan, and keep warm. Add remaining 1 tablespoon olive oil to pan. Add broccoli and next 5 ingredients to pan; stir-fry 4 minutes or until vegetables are crisp-tender. Return chicken to pan, and stir in shrimp. Add sauce, and bring to a boil. Reduce heat, and simmer for 5 minutes or until sauce thickens. Serve over rice. Yield: 6 servings (serving size: about 1 cup chicken mixture and 1/2 cup rice).

CALORIES 340; FAT 7.3g (sat 1.3g, mono 4.1g, poly 1.3g); PROTEIN 28.6g; CARB 38.6g; FIBER 2.7g; CHOL 142mg; IRON 4.1mg; SODIUM 864mg; CALC 77mg

QUICK & EASY
Feta and Green Onion Couscous Cakes over Tomato-Olive Salad

"This recipe came about when I wanted to use up leftovers I had around the kitchen. It's a great way to highlight the flavor of fresh summer tomatoes."

—Kathleen Kanen,
Birmingham, Alabama

CAKES:
- 1/3 cup uncooked whole wheat couscous
- 1/2 cup boiling water
- 1/4 cup (1 ounce) crumbled feta cheese
- 3 tablespoons egg substitute
- 2 tablespoons finely chopped green onions
- 1/8 teaspoon freshly ground black pepper
- 2 teaspoons olive oil
- Cooking spray

SALAD:
- 2/3 cup chopped seeded tomato
- 2 tablespoons chopped pitted kalamata olives
- 2 tablespoons chopped fresh parsley
- 2 teaspoons red wine vinegar
- 1/2 teaspoon olive oil
- 1/8 teaspoon freshly ground black pepper
- 3 cups gourmet salad greens

1 To prepare cakes, place couscous in a medium bowl; stir in 1/2 cup boiling water. Cover and let stand 5 minutes or until liquid is absorbed. Fluff with a fork. Cool slightly. Add cheese and next 3 ingredients. Heat 2 teaspoons oil in a large nonstick skillet coated with cooking spray over medium-high heat. Spoon about 1/3 cup couscous mixture into 4 mounds in pan. Lightly press with a spatula to flatten to 1/2 inch. Cook 2 minutes or until lightly browned. Coat tops of cakes with cooking spray. Carefully turn cakes over; cook 2 minutes or until heated.
2 To prepare salad, combine tomato and next 5 ingredients. Arrange 1 1/2 cups greens on each of 2 plates. Top each serving with 1/2 cup tomato mixture; arrange 2 cakes over tomato mixture. Yield: 2 servings.

CALORIES 289; FAT 14g (sat 3.6g, mono 8.1g, poly 1.8g); PROTEIN 10.7g; CARB 30.6g; FIBER 4.4g; CHOL 13mg; IRON 2.7mg; SODIUM 478mg; CALC 154mg

Chicken

Learn four simple cooking techniques that will add variety to your weeknight repertoire.

STAFF FAVORITE
Pan-Fried Chicken
(pictured on page 222)

The key to success with this recipe is even heat. If the oil gets too hot, the chicken may brown too quickly before fully cooking. You can lower the heat, or brown the chicken on the stovetop and then cook in a 350° oven until done. If the oil is not hot enough, the chicken will absorb too much of it.

- 1 cup all-purpose flour
- ½ cup whole wheat flour
- 1 teaspoon ground ginger
- ½ teaspoon hot paprika
- ½ teaspoon ground cinnamon
- ½ teaspoon freshly ground nutmeg
- ½ teaspoon fine sea salt
- 2 bone-in chicken breast halves, skinned
- 2 bone-in chicken thighs, skinned
- 2 chicken drumsticks, skinned
- ¼ cup peanut oil

1 Sift together first 6 ingredients; place mixture in a large zip-top plastic bag. Sprinkle salt evenly over chicken. Add chicken, 1 piece at a time, to bag; seal. Shake bag to coat chicken. Remove chicken from bag, shaking off excess flour. Place chicken on a cooling rack; place rack in a jelly-roll pan. Reserve remaining flour mixture. Loosely cover chicken; chill 1½ hours. Let chicken stand at room temperature 30 minutes. Return chicken, one piece at a time, to flour mixture, shaking bag to coat chicken. Discard excess flour mixture.
2 Heat oil in a skillet over medium-high heat. Add chicken to pan. Reduce heat to medium-low; cook 25 minutes or until done, carefully turning every 5 minutes.

3 Line a clean cooling rack with brown paper bags; arrange chicken in a single layer on bags. Let stand 5 minutes. Yield: 4 servings (serving size: 1 chicken breast half or 1 thigh and 1 drumstick).

CALORIES 245; FAT 10.1g (sat 2g, mono 4.1g, poly 3g); PROTEIN 28.2g; CARB 9g; FIBER 0.8g; CHOL 87mg; IRON 1.8mg; SODIUM 240mg; CALC 17mg

---

Step By Step:
How to Pan-Fry Chicken

A. Remove skin from chicken. Be sure to sprinkle the meat directly with salt, then dredge it in the seasoned flour mixture. Refrigerate the chicken to help the breading adhere.
B. Let the chicken stand at room temperature to take the chill off. Dredge it once more in the seasoned flour.

C. Heat oil. Add chicken to pan, and cook until done.
D. Transfer the chicken to a cooling rack covered with brown paper bags (paper towels make the chicken steam and become soggy). Let stand about 5 minutes before serving.

QUICK & EASY
Sautéed Chicken Breasts

Skinless, boneless chicken breast halves are convenient and affordable. For variety, pair this familiar favorite with one of our stellar sauces, such as the Parsley Pesto, page 160.

- 2 tablespoons extra-virgin olive oil
- 4 (6-ounce) skinless, boneless chicken breast halves
- ½ teaspoon kosher salt
- ½ teaspoon freshly ground black pepper

1 Heat a large skillet over medium-high heat; add oil, swirling to coat. Sprinkle chicken evenly on both sides with salt and pepper. Add chicken to pan; cook 4 minutes on each side or until golden brown and done.

CALORIES 202; FAT 9.8g (sat 1.8g, mono 6g, poly 1.4g); PROTEIN 26.7g; CARB 0.2g; FIBER 0.1g; CHOL 73mg; IRON 1mg; SODIUM 359mg; CALC 14mg

---

Step By Step:
How to Sauté Skinless, Boneless Chicken Breasts

"Sauté" is a French term that refers to cooking food quickly in a hot pan in a small amount of fat. Skinless, boneless chicken breast halves are great candidates for this cooking method.

A. Heat pan over medium-high heat. Add oil (or other fat) to the hot pan. Place chicken breast halves in pan, and cook about 4 minutes on each side or until done. (If the pan doesn't sizzle when chicken is added, it's not hot enough.)
B. Because this is one of the simplest and most familiar preparations, busy cooks often turn to skinless, boneless chicken breasts for weeknight dinners. Add interest to your menu by preparing any of a variety of equally simple no-cook or quick-cooking sauces on page 160.

Step By Step:
How to Grill Chicken

A. Prepare the grill for indirect grilling with one hot side and one side without a direct source of heat.

B. If you plan to baste with a glaze as the chicken cooks, remove the skin before cooking; this allows the flesh to absorb the flavor of the glaze and brown nicely at the same time. (Chicken that is not glazed should be grilled with the skin on to shield the meat and keep it moist.)

C. Brown the chicken over direct heat. Then cook it over indirect heat, brushing it with glaze (if using) each time it's turned. Be sure to let the chicken stand 10 minutes before serving.

Apricot-Glazed Grilled Chicken

      3 tablespoons apricot preserves
      2 tablespoons red wine vinegar
   1½ tablespoons extra-virgin olive oil
      1 garlic clove, minced
      2 bone-in chicken breast halves, skinned
      2 bone-in chicken thighs, skinned
      2 chicken drumsticks, skinned
      ½ teaspoon fine sea salt
      ¼ teaspoon freshly ground black pepper
         Cooking spray

1 Combine first 4 ingredients in a small bowl, stirring well.

2 Prepare grill for indirect grilling. If using a gas grill, heat one side to medium-high and leave one side with no heat. If using a charcoal grill, arrange hot coals on one side of charcoal grate, leaving other side empty.

3 Let chicken stand at room temperature 30 minutes. Sprinkle chicken evenly with salt and pepper. Place chicken, meaty sides down, on a grill rack coated with cooking spray over direct heat; grill 5 minutes or until browned.

4 Turn chicken over; baste with apricot mixture. Grill 5 minutes over direct heat or until browned. Turn chicken over, moving it over indirect heat; baste with apricot mixture. Cover and cook 15 minutes. Turn chicken over; baste with apricot mixture. Cook 20 minutes or until done. Yield: 4 servings (serving size: 1 chicken breast half or 1 thigh and 1 drumstick).

CALORIES 247; FAT 10.7g (sat 2.3g, mono 5.7g, poly 1.8g); PROTEIN 26.5g; CARB 10g; FIBER 0.1g; CHOL 82mg; IRON 1.2mg; SODIUM 370mg; CALC 18mg

ASIAN-GLAZED GRILLED CHICKEN VARIATION:

Combine 2 tablespoons hoisin sauce, 1 tablespoon honey, 1 tablespoon dark sesame oil, 1 teaspoon sambal oelek (or other hot chile sauce), and 3 minced garlic cloves, stirring well until blended. Prepare Apricot-Glazed Grilled Chicken, omitting apricot preserves, vinegar, olive oil, and garlic. Baste chicken with hoisin mixture after each turn. Yield: 4 servings (serving size: 1 chicken breast half or 1 thigh and 1 drumstick).

CALORIES 242; FAT 10.5g (sat 2.3g, mono 3.4g, poly 2.7g); PROTEIN 26.6g; CARB 8.7g; FIBER 0.1g; CHOL 82mg; IRON 1.1mg; SODIUM 476mg; CALC 17mg

Grilling chicken is an easy way to transform this humble food. You'll get the best results if you let the chicken stand at room temperature before grilling.

Dress Up Chicken Breasts With...Pan Sauces

WHITE WINE SAUCE: Heat a skillet over medium-high heat. Coat pan with cooking spray. Add $1/3$ cup finely chopped onion to pan; sauté 2 minutes, stirring frequently. Stir in $1/2$ cup fat-free, less-sodium chicken broth, $1/4$ cup dry white wine, and 2 tablespoons white wine vinegar; bring to a boil. Cook until reduced to $1/4$ cup (about 5 minutes). Remove from heat; stir in 2 tablespoons butter and 2 teaspoons finely chopped fresh chives. Yield: 6 tablespoons (serving size: $1^{1}/2$ tablespoons).

CALORIES 59; FAT 5.7g (sat 3.6g, mono 1.5g, poly 0.2g); PROTEIN 0.6g; CARB 1.6g; FIBER 0.4g; CHOL 15mg; IRON 0.2mg; SODIUM 90mg; CALC 8mg

SPICY ORANGE SAUCE: Heat a skillet over medium-high heat; coat with cooking spray. Add 1 tablespoon grated ginger; sauté 1 minute, stirring constantly. Stir in $2/3$ cup fat-free, less-sodium chicken broth, 3 tablespoons orange marmalade, and $1^{1}/2$ tablespoons low-sodium soy sauce; bring to a boil. Cook until mixture is slightly thick. Stir in $1^{1}/2$ teaspoons fresh lemon juice and $3/4$ teaspoon sambal oelek (or other hot chile sauce). Yield: about $3/4$ cup (serving size: about 3 tablespoons).

CALORIES 45; FAT 0.1g (sat 0g, mono 0.1g, poly 0g); PROTEIN 0.8g; CARB 11.2g; FIBER 0.4g; CHOL 0mg; IRON 0.2mg; SODIUM 273mg; CALC 10mg

TANGY MUSTARD SAUCE: Heat 2 teaspoons olive oil in a skillet over medium-high heat. Add 2 minced garlic cloves to pan; sauté 30 seconds, stirring constantly. Stir in $1/4$ cup dry white wine, $1/4$ cup fat-free, less-sodium chicken broth, 2 tablespoons maple syrup, and 2 tablespoons Dijon mustard; bring to a boil. Cook until reduced to $1/4$ cup (about 5 minutes), stirring occasionally. Stir in $3/4$ teaspoon chopped fresh rosemary and $1/2$ teaspoon freshly ground black pepper. Yield: $1/4$ cup (serving size: 1 tablespoon).

CALORIES 54; FAT 2.3g (sat 0.3g, mono 1.7g, poly 0.3g); PROTEIN 0.3g; CARB 8.2g; FIBER 0.2g; CHOL 0mg; IRON 0.3mg; SODIUM 87mg; CALC 13mg

Or Try Our No-Cook Sauces

PARSLEY PESTO: Place 2 cups fresh flat-leaf parsley leaves, 2 tablespoons toasted pine nuts, $1^{1}/2$ tablespoons grated fresh Parmigiano-Reggiano cheese, 1 teaspoon extra-virgin olive oil, and $1/4$ teaspoon salt in a food processor; process until smooth. Yield: $1/2$ cup (serving size: 2 tablespoons).

CALORIES 59; FAT 4.8g (sat 0.7g, mono 1.9g, poly 1.6g); PROTEIN 2.3g; CARB 2.8g; FIBER 1.2g; CHOL 2mg; IRON 2.1mg; SODIUM 211mg; CALC 64mg

CREAMY WHITE SAUCE: Combine $1/4$ cup canola mayonnaise, 2 teaspoons white vinegar, 1 teaspoon fresh lemon juice, $1/2$ teaspoon freshly ground black pepper, $1/4$ teaspoon salt, and 1 minced garlic clove, stirring well. Yield: about $1/3$ cup (serving size: about 4 teaspoons).

CALORIES 47; FAT 4.5g (sat 0g, mono 2.5g, poly 1.5g); PROTEIN 0.1g; CARB 0.5g; FIBER 0.1g; CHOL 0mg; IRON 0mg; SODIUM 238mg; CALC 2mg

CLASSIC VINAIGRETTE: Combine $1^{1}/2$ tablespoons red wine vinegar, 1 tablespoon chopped shallots, $1/4$ teaspoon salt, 1 tablespoon Dijon mustard, and $1/8$ teaspoon pepper. Gradually add 3 tablespoons extra-virgin olive oil, stirring until incorporated. Yield: 6 tablespoons (serving size: $1^{1}/2$ tablespoons).

CALORIES 94; FAT 10.1g (sat 1.4g, mono 7.4g, poly 1.1g); PROTEIN 0.1g; CARB 0.7g; FIBER 0g; CHOL 0mg; IRON 0.1mg; SODIUM 178mg; CALC 2mg

Herb Roast Chicken

- 1 (4$1/2$-pound) whole roasting chicken
- $3/4$ teaspoon fine sea salt, divided
- $3/4$ teaspoon freshly ground black pepper, divided
- 1 lemon, halved
- 2 tablespoons butter, softened
- 2 tablespoons minced shallots
- 2 teaspoons chopped fresh rosemary
- 2 teaspoons chopped fresh thyme
- Cooking spray
- $3/4$ cup water

1 Preheat oven to 450°.

2 Remove giblets and neck from chicken cavity; discard. Trim excess fat from chicken. Loosen skin from breast and drumsticks by inserting fingers, gently pushing between skin and meat. Sprinkle $1/4$ teaspoon salt and $1/2$ teaspoon pepper inside body cavity. Squeeze lemon juice into body cavity; place lemon halves in body cavity. Combine butter and next 3 ingredients stirring with a fork until well blended. Combine remaining $1/2$ teaspoon salt and remaining $1/4$ teaspoon pepper in a small bowl; rub salt mixture evenly under skin over breast and drumstick meat. Rub butter mixture evenly under skin over breast and drumstick meat. Tie ends of legs together with twine. Lift wing tips up and over back, and tuck under chicken.

3 Place chicken, breast side up, on a rack coated with cooking spray; place rack in a roasting pan. Pour $3/4$ cup water into roasting pan. Bake chicken at 450° for 1 hour or until a thermometer inserted in meaty part of thigh registers 160°. Remove chicken from pan; let stand, breast side down, 15 minutes. Remove skin; discard.

4 Place a large zip-top plastic bag inside a 4-cup glass measure. Pour drippings through a sieve into bag; discard solids. Let drippings stand 10 minutes (fat will rise to top). Seal bag; carefully snip off 1 bottom corner of bag. Drain drippings into a medium bowl, stopping before fat layer reaches opening; discard fat. Carve chicken; serve with drippings. Yield:

4 servings (serving size: 1 chicken breast half or 1 thigh and 1 drumstick and 1 tablespoon drippings).

CALORIES 222; FAT 11.4g (sat 5.2g, mono 3.5g, poly 1.5g); PROTEIN 26.6g; CARB 2.3g; FIBER 0.2g; CHOL 97mg; IRON 1.3mg; SODIUM 548mg; CALC 23mg

Step By Step: How to Roast a Whole Chicken

A. Loosen skin from the meat, but don't remove it. The skin shields the meat as it cooks. Season the meat and cavity with salt and pepper. You can also add citrus, herbs, and garlic cloves to the cavity.

B. Truss—or tie—the chicken, so it holds its shape while cooking.

C. Place chicken on a roasting rack; place rack in a roasting pan. Pour a little water into bottom of pan to prevent the drippings, which you'll want to use later, from burning. Bake chicken for about 1 hour or until it's almost done. Remove from oven when it reaches an internal temperature of 160°. Remove chicken from pan; let it stand for 15 to 20 minutes with the breast side down.

TEST KITCHENS SECRETS
Wheat Berry Salad

We'll teach you how to tame the artichokes in a versatile salad.

Test Kitchens Professional Tiffany Vickers knows scooping out the prickly, inedible thistle from a raw artichoke can be tricky and time-consuming. That's why she cooks artichokes first and then removes the formidable thistle. "Roasting artichokes takes away the prickliness and makes removing the fuzzy thistle easier," she says.

Artichokes are available year-round in many grocery stores, and Vickers advises us to choose those heavy for their size, with the stalk attached and tightly packed leaves.

She also offers smart serving options for this salad. For a make-ahead dish, prepare it up to one day ahead and refrigerate; serve as a cold lunch entrée. It also makes a tasty warm side dish for chicken or grilled tuna.

MAKE AHEAD
Wheat Berry Salad

 1 cup uncooked wheat berries (hard winter wheat)
 5 teaspoons fresh lemon juice, divided
 2 teaspoons olive oil, divided
 4 medium artichokes
 ¼ teaspoon salt, divided
 Cooking spray
 1 (1-ounce) prosciutto slice, chopped
 ½ cup chopped onion
 1 garlic clove, minced
 1½ tablespoons jarred roasted kalamata olives, finely chopped
 1 teaspoon chopped fresh parsley
 ½ teaspoon chopped fresh chives
 ¼ teaspoon chopped fresh rosemary

1 Place wheat berries in a medium bowl; cover with water to 2 inches above wheat berries. Cover; let stand 8 hours. Drain. Place wheat berries in a saucepan; cover with water to 2 inches above wheat berries. Bring to a boil, reduce heat, and cook, uncovered, 1 hour or until tender. Drain.
2 Preheat oven to 450°.
3 Combine 2 teaspoons juice and 1 teaspoon oil in a small bowl. Trim about 2 inches from top of each artichoke; cut artichokes in half horizontally. Brush cut sides with juice mixture; sprinkle with ⅛ teaspoon salt. Arrange artichokes, cut sides up, on a baking sheet coated with cooking spray; bake at 450° for 15 minutes. Turn artichokes; bake 15 minutes or until artichokes are browned and tender. Cool slightly. Peel stem; trim an additional ½ inch from top. Discard outer leaves. Remove fuzzy thistle from bottom with a spoon; quarter artichoke hearts.
4 Heat remaining 1 teaspoon oil in a saucepan over medium heat. Add prosciutto; cook 3 minutes or until browned. Add onion; cook 3 minutes, stirring occasionally. Stir in garlic; cook 1 minute. Remove from heat; stir in prepared wheat berries, remaining 1 tablespoon juice, remaining ⅛ teaspoon salt, artichokes, olives, and remaining ingredients. Serve warm or at room temperature. Yield: 4 servings (serving size: 1 cup).

CALORIES 282; FAT 6.9g (sat 1g, mono 3.6g, poly 1g); PROTEIN 12.3g; CARB 51.5g; FIBER 13.3g; CHOL 4mg; IRON 1.9mg; SODIUM 556mg; CALC 67mg

Lemon-Thyme Cornmeal Quick Bread

Our makeover of Lemon-Thyme Cornmeal Quick Bread rescues a California reader's ideal summertime treat.

For Amy Loflin, from San Rafael, California, the sweet lemon and subtle herb flavors of Lemon-Thyme Cornmeal Quick Bread epitomize summer, and she loves the idea of enjoying it often with a cup of tea. But she simply couldn't—not with the excessive amount of butter it contained, which she felt "completely overwhelmed the recipe."

One and one-half sticks of butter, plus three whole eggs, contributed to the weightiness of the original recipe, not to mention its high amount of unhealthy saturated fat.

The Solution:

• **Omit the eggs.** We changed from whole eggs to egg substitute, which cut a little more than 1 gram of fat per serving (and 0.4 gram saturated fat).

• **Substitute oil for butter.** Using 1/3 cup plus 2 tablespoons of canola oil in place of 3/4 cup butter slashed 24 calories, almost 3 grams of total fat, and—most importantly—changed the ratio of healthful mono- and polyunsaturate fats in the recipe so that we eliminated 6.6 grams of saturated fat.

• **Drizzle on flavor.** We wanted to give the bread some buttery flavor, so we drizzled on a prudent 1 tablespoon midway through the cook time. This added back a modest 8 calories, 1 gram of fat, and 0.6 gram saturated fat—and using butter in this way allows a small amount to have a bigger flavor impact.

• **Use less nuts.** Since pine nuts have an assertive flavor, we used half the amount of the original recipe without sacrificing taste. That change cut another 10 calories and almost 1 gram of fat.

serving size: 1 slice		
	before	after
CALORIES PER SERVING	249	207
TOTAL FAT	14.6g	10.5g
SATURATED FAT	7.7g	1.3g

MAKE AHEAD • FREEZABLE

Lemon-Thyme Cornmeal Quick Bread

(pictured on page 222)

For the best texture, be sure to choose regular or finely ground cornmeal. Avoid stone-ground cornmeal as it is too coarse for this delicate bread.

- 1.5 ounces all-purpose flour (about 1/3 cup)
- 1 cup fine yellow cornmeal
- 1 teaspoon baking powder
- 3/4 teaspoon kosher salt
- 3/4 cup egg substitute
- 2/3 cup sugar
- 1/3 cup plus 2 tablespoons canola oil
- 1 tablespoon chopped fresh thyme
- 1 tablespoon grated lemon rind
- 2 tablespoons fresh lemon juice
- 2 tablespoons pine nuts, toasted and divided
  Cooking spray
- 1 tablespoon butter, melted

❶ Preheat oven to 325°.
❷ Weigh or lightly spoon flour into a dry measuring cup; level with a knife. Combine flour and next 3 ingredients in a medium bowl, stirring with a whisk.
❸ Place egg substitute, sugar, and oil in a large bowl; beat with a mixer at medium-high speed 1 minute or until well blended. Add thyme, rind, and juice; beat at low speed until combined. Add flour mixture; beat just until combined. Chop 1 tablespoon nuts; stir into batter.
❹ Pour batter into a 9 x 5–inch loaf pan coated with cooking spray. Sprinkle evenly with remaining 1 tablespoon whole nuts. Bake at 325° for 30 minutes. Remove pan from oven (do not turn oven off). Drizzle butter evenly over batter. Bake an additional 20 minutes or until a wooden pick inserted in center comes out clean. Cool in pan 5 minutes on a wire rack; remove from pan. Cool completely on wire rack. Yield: 12 servings (serving size: 1 slice).

CALORIES 207; FAT 10.5g (sat 1.3g, mono 5.6g, poly 3.1g); PROTEIN 3g; CARB 25.3g; FIBER 0.6g; CHOL 3mg; IRON 0.9mg; SODIUM 188mg; CALC 36mg

"The top crust was something to get excited about. The drizzled butter creates a lovely crispness without being greasy, and the balance of lemon and thyme is perfect."

—Amy Loflin
San Rafael, California

"How I Stretch My Food Budget"

Senior Food Editor Ann Taylor Pittman shares her money-saving tips.

Like so many people, Ann Taylor Pittman has tightened her food budget. "While I'm well aware there are lots of foods that cost next to nothing, as an editor at this magazine, I'm not willing to sacrifice taste and freshness to save a few dollars," Pittman said. "Nor am I willing to feed my family foods high in fat and sodium. So I aim for the best value in terms of quality, freshness, and sound nutrition. I feel my family reaps greater benefits in return." These are the tips upon which she relies.

QUICK & EASY ▪ MAKE AHEAD
New York–Style Pizza Sauce

Our pizza and calzone recipes use all of this stir-together, no-cook sauce.

- 7 tablespoons water
- 2 tablespoons chopped fresh basil
- 1½ tablespoons extra-virgin olive oil
- 2 teaspoons dried oregano
- 1½ teaspoons sugar
- 1 teaspoon minced garlic
- 1 (14.5-ounce) can petite-cut diced tomatoes, undrained
- 1 (6-ounce) can tomato paste

❶ Combine all ingredients in a medium bowl; stir with a whisk. Yield: 2⅔ cups (serving size: about ¼ cup).

CALORIES 40; FAT 1.9g (sat 0.3g, mono 1.4g, poly 0.2g); PROTEIN 1g; CARB 5.6g; FIBER 1.4g; CHOL 0mg; IRON 0.7mg; SODIUM 170mg; CALC 17mg

MAKE AHEAD ▪ FREEZABLE
Homemade Pizza Dough

Making pizza dough is economical, fun, and healthful since you control the ingredients. This recipe yields enough dough to make two pizzas, or one pizza and four large calzones. **Bonus: A homemade pizza crust costs less than store-bought.**

- 1 package active dry yeast (about 2¼ teaspoons)
- 1 cup warm water (100° to 110°)
- 1¼ cups cold water
- 2 tablespoons olive oil
- 1 teaspoon sugar
- 1 teaspoon salt
- 26.1 ounces (about 5½ cups) unbleached bread flour, divided
  Cooking spray

❶ Dissolve yeast in 1 cup warm water in a small bowl; let stand 5 minutes. Combine 1¼ cups cold water and next 3 ingredients in a small bowl; stir with a whisk.
❷ Weigh or lightly spoon 24.9 ounces (about 5¼ cups) flour into dry measuring cups; level with a knife. Combine flour, yeast mixture, and cold water mixture in bowl of a stand mixer fitted with a dough hook. Mix on low 8 minutes or until dough begins to form. Let rest 2 minutes; mix on low 6 minutes or until dough is smooth. Turn dough out onto a floured surface. Knead until smooth and elastic (about 2 minutes); add enough of remaining 1.2 ounces (about ¼ cup) flour, 1 tablespoon at a time, to prevent dough from sticking to hands (dough will feel sticky).
❸ Divide dough in half; place each portion in a large zip-top bag coated with cooking spray. Seal and chill overnight or up to 2 days. Let stand at room temperature for 1 hour. Yield: 2 crusts, 14 servings.
NOTE: You can freeze the dough in heavy-duty, freezer-safe zip-top plastic bags for up to 2 months; thaw dough overnight in the refrigerator.

CALORIES 214; FAT 2.9g (sat 0.4g, mono 1.5g, poly 0.6g); PROTEIN 6.6g; CARB 39.5g; FIBER 1.4g; CHOL 0mg; IRON 2.5mg; SODIUM 170mg; CALC 8mg

MAKE AHEAD
Pita Salad with Tomatoes, Cucumber, and Herbs

- 3 (7-inch) pitas
- 4 cups coarsely chopped romaine lettuce
- 2 cups diced English cucumber
- 2 cups halved cherry tomatoes
- ⅔ cup (3 ounces) crumbled feta cheese
- ½ cup finely chopped red onion
- ½ cup chopped fresh mint
- ¼ cup thinly sliced green onions
- ¼ cup finely chopped fresh flat-leaf parsley
- 6 tablespoons fresh lemon juice
- 1 teaspoon sugar
- 1 teaspoon freshly ground black pepper
- ½ teaspoon kosher salt
- ¼ cup extra-virgin olive oil

❶ Preheat oven to 375°.
❷ Arrange pitas on a baking sheet. Bake at 375° for 14 minutes or until crisp, turning after 7 minutes. Set aside; cool.
❸ Combine lettuce and next 7 ingredients in a bowl. Break pitas into pieces. Add pitas to salad; toss gently to combine.
❹ Combine juice and next 3 ingredients in a bowl; gradually add oil, stirring constantly with a whisk. Drizzle dressing over salad; toss well to coat. Let stand 30 minutes; serve at room temperature. Yield: 8 servings (serving size: 1¼ cups).

CALORIES 183; FAT 10g (sat 2.9g, mono 5.6g, poly 1g); PROTEIN 4.9g; CARB 19.6g; FIBER 2.3g; CHOL 11mg; IRON 1.5mg; SODIUM 386mg; CALC 107mg

Grilled Spice-Rubbed Whole Chicken

Trim your food budget by purchasing a whole chicken rather than cut-up pieces, a precooked chicken, or skinless, boneless cuts. **Bonus: Stretch leftover chicken in pasta salad or Pita Salad with Tomatoes, Cucumber, and Herbs, page 163.**

1½ teaspoons brown sugar
1¼ teaspoons ground cumin
1 teaspoon kosher salt
½ teaspoon freshly ground black pepper
½ teaspoon paprika
½ teaspoon dried thyme
½ teaspoon chili powder
1 (4-pound) whole chicken
Cooking spray

1 Prepare grill for indirect grilling. If using a gas grill, heat one side to medium-high and leave one side with no heat. If using a charcoal grill, arrange hot coals on either side of charcoal grate, leaving an empty space in middle.
2 Combine first 7 ingredients; set aside.
3 Remove and discard giblets and neck from chicken. Trim excess fat. Place chicken, breast side down, on a cutting surface. Cut chicken in half lengthwise along backbone, cutting to, but not through, other side. Turn chicken over. Starting at neck cavity, loosen skin from breast and drumsticks by inserting fingers, gently pushing between skin and meat. Rub spice mixture under skin. Gently press skin to secure.
4 Place chicken, breast side down, on grill rack coated with cooking spray over direct heat; cover and cook 7 minutes. Turn chicken over; cook 7 minutes. Move chicken over indirect heat; cover and cook 45 minutes or until a thermometer inserted in meaty part of thigh registers 165°. Transfer chicken to a cutting board; let rest 10 minutes. Discard skin. Yield: 4 servings (serving size: 1 breast half or 1 thigh and 1 drumstick).

CALORIES 270; FAT 6.5g (sat 1.6g, mono 1.9g, poly 1.6g); PROTEIN 47.3g; CARB 2.6g; FIBER 0.6g; CHOL 150mg; IRON 2.8mg; SODIUM 657mg; CALC 40mg

WINE NOTE: An economical meal can include wine. With this meal, look to Australia. The Little Penguin Chardonnay 2008 ($6) has juicy stone fruit and mango flavors that couple nicely with the chicken's sweet meat, while a touch of toasty oak helps it integrate with smoky grilled flavors and eclectic spices.

Stir-Fried Beef with Broccoli and Bell Peppers

1 pound flank steak, trimmed
2 tablespoons low-sodium soy sauce
1 teaspoon minced garlic
½ teaspoon freshly ground black pepper
3½ tablespoons water, divided
2 tablespoons oyster sauce
¼ teaspoon crushed red pepper
¾ pound broccoli
2 tablespoons canola oil, divided
1 large red bell pepper, halved, seeded, and cut into 1-inch pieces (about 1½ cups)
4 cups hot cooked long-grain rice

1 Cut steak in half lengthwise. Cut each half across the grain into ⅛-inch-thick slices. Combine beef, soy sauce, garlic, and black pepper; toss well. Cover and refrigerate 30 minutes.
2 Combine 1½ tablespoons water, oyster sauce, and crushed red pepper in a small bowl; set aside.
3 Cut broccoli into florets. Peel broccoli stems; cut stems diagonally into ¼-inch-thick slices.
4 Heat 1 tablespoon oil in a large non-stick skillet over medium-high heat. Add beef mixture to skillet; cook 3 minutes or until beef is browned, stirring constantly. Remove from heat. Transfer beef mixture to a bowl.
5 Heat remaining 1 tablespoon oil in pan over medium-high heat. Add broccoli; cook 2 minutes, stirring constantly. Add remaining 2 tablespoons water; cook 1 minute, stirring constantly. Add bell pepper; cook 30 seconds, stirring constantly. Return beef mixture to pan. Stir in oyster sauce mixture; cook until thoroughly heated. Serve over rice. Yield: 6 servings (serving size: about 1 cup stir-fry and ⅔ cup rice).

CALORIES 323; FAT 10.7g (sat 2.7g, mono 5.1g, poly 1.8g); PROTEIN 21.2g; CARB 35.2g; FIBER 2.8g; CHOL 26mg; IRON 3.2mg; SODIUM 273mg; CALC 62mg

Ways to Stretch Your Food Budget

"Eat more meatless meals."

Meat accounts for the most expense at my grocery store visits, so I've started making one or two vegetarian dinners a week to cut costs. Dishes based on pantry staples like rice, whole grains, beans, and legumes are protein-rich, filling, and inexpensive; add seasonal produce for crunch, freshness, and color. A bonus: Research shows that eating more plant-based foods may lower your risk for heart disease, diabetes, and some cancers.

"Make a meal plan."

This strategy has been the most challenging to consistently employ but has made the biggest dent in my budget. The idea may sound simple, but it requires forethought, diligence, and willpower. My meal planning involves me sitting down once a week and planning all the meals for that week, and then shopping only for the items I need to prepare those meals. (Lots of people swear by shopping at bulk wholesale clubs, but I don't have the storage space for that.) Allow for leftovers in your meal plan, and be realistic about how many nights you might eat out or be too busy to cook. Not only does this strategy cut down on the amount of food you buy at the grocery store, but it also decreases the amount of food you waste.

"Do it yourself."

For maximum savings, skip convenience products as you pay a premium for the work that's done for you. For just a few extra minutes, I know I can save by chopping my own produce, for example. On the weekends when I have extra time, or some nights after putting the kids to bed, I do a little work that puts me ahead for the next day, like making a pizza dough that sits in the fridge overnight (page 163).

"Learn to stretch meat, poultry, and fish."

Instead of making protein the center of the plate, use it sparingly for flavor and texture—almost as if it's a condiment. Extend beef by tossing a conservative amount in a vegetable-rich stir-fry, for example, or combine a small quantity of shrimp with pasta. Pizzas, calzones, pasta bakes, and casseroles are easy dishes that use this strategy to great effect.

"Eat in season."

Out-of-season produce is costly and lacks flavor. Skip it; instead choose fruits and vegetables that are in season. When produce is at its peak, there's an abundance of it—and you can find it for a bargain. In the summer, my family and I enjoy tomatoes, cucumbers, fresh herbs, bell peppers, and more. During fall and winter, we look to winter squashes; dark, leafy greens; citrus; and sweet potatoes. And in spring, we love berries, asparagus, artichokes, and fresh peas. We hardly feel deprived when our budget allows for such riches.

Spinach and Ricotta Pizza

Humble ingredients create a deliciously rich and satisfying entrée. **Bonus: Going meatless saves you money.**

  1 portion Homemade Pizza Dough (page 163)
     Cooking spray
  1 tablespoon extra-virgin olive oil
  ¾ cup New York–Style Pizza Sauce (page 163)
  2 tablespoons grated fresh Parmesan cheese
  1½ cups loosely packed baby spinach leaves
  1 teaspoon minced garlic
  1¼ cups (5 ounces) shredded part-skim mozzarella cheese
  ⅓ cup part-skim ricotta cheese
  2 plum tomatoes, cored and thinly sliced

❶ Remove Homemade Pizza Dough from refrigerator; let stand at room temperature 1 hour.
❷ Preheat oven to 500°.
❸ Coat a 12-inch perforated pizza pan with cooking spray.
❹ Place dough on a lightly floured surface; roll into a 12-inch circle. Transfer dough to prepared pan, shaking off excess flour. Brush dough evenly with oil. Spread New York–Style Pizza Sauce evenly over dough, leaving a ¼-inch border. Sprinkle with Parmesan; top evenly with spinach and garlic. Sprinkle mozzarella over spinach. Spoon teaspoonfuls of ricotta over mozzarella. Bake at 500° for 12 minutes or until mozzarella melts and crust browns. Let stand 5 minutes; top with tomato slices. Cut into 6 wedges. Yield: 6 servings (serving size: 1 wedge).

CALORIES 397; FAT 13g (sat 4.9g, mono 5.9g, poly 1.3g); PROTEIN 17.2g; CARB 52.6g; FIBER 3g; CHOL 19mg; IRON 3.7mg; SODIUM 459mg; CALC 259mg

Grilled Pepper, Onion, and Sausage Calzones

Use sweet turkey Italian sausage for sensitive palates. Serve with a spinach salad to use greens left after making the pizza on page 165. **Bonus: These kid-friendly stuffed breads offer a clever way to stretch Italian sausage and sweet summer vegetables over multiple servings.**

- 1 portion Homemade Pizza Dough (page 163)
- 1 Vidalia or other sweet onion, cut into ½-inch-thick slices (about 14 ounces)
- 1 red bell pepper, quartered
- 1 yellow bell pepper, quartered
  Cooking spray
- 1 pound hot Italian turkey sausage links
- 1¾ cups plus 3 tablespoons New York–Style Pizza Sauce (page 163), divided
- 1⅓ cups (about 5 ounces) shredded part-skim mozzarella cheese

❶ Remove Homemade Pizza Dough from refrigerator; let stand at room temperature 1 hour.
❷ Prepare grill to medium-high heat.
❸ Coat onion slices and bell pepper pieces with cooking spray. Place vegetables and sausages on a grill rack coated with cooking spray. Grill vegetables 4 minutes on each side or until browned; grill sausages 8 minutes or until done, turning occasionally to brown on all sides. Remove vegetables and sausages from grill; cool slightly. Cut onion slices in half; cut bell pepper pieces into ½-inch strips. Cut sausages diagonally into thin slices.
❹ Preheat oven to 500°.
❺ Place dough on a lightly floured surface; divide dough into 4 equal portions. Roll each portion into a 9 x 5-inch rectangle. Spread ¼ cup New York–Style Pizza Sauce evenly over each rectangle, leaving a ¼-inch border. Arrange sausage evenly over half of each rectangle; top evenly with onion and bell peppers. Sprinkle each calzone with ⅓ cup cheese. Fold other half of dough over filling; press edges together with a fork to seal.
❻ Place calzones on a baking sheet coated with cooking spray. Coat calzones with cooking spray. Bake at 500° for 15 minutes or until golden brown. Remove from oven; let stand 5 minutes. Cut each calzone in half; serve with remaining New York–Style Pizza Sauce. Yield: 8 servings (serving size: ½ calzone and 5½ teaspoons sauce).

CALORIES 398; FAT 13.6g (sat 4.4g, mono 5.7g, poly 2.2g); PROTEIN 21.5g; CARB 48g; FIBER 4.3g; CHOL 44mg; IRON 3.8mg; SODIUM 759mg; CALC 186mg

Wheat Berry Salad with Goat Cheese

Taking a cue from traditional tabbouleh, this dish uses lots of peak-season vegetables, tart lemon juice, and pungent fresh herbs. Serve with toasted pita wedges. **Bonus: Cucumbers, fresh herbs, and tomatoes are in season now so they're less expensive.**

- 1¼ cups uncooked wheat berries (hard winter wheat)
- 2½ cups chopped English cucumber
- ⅔ cup thinly sliced green onions
- 1½ cups loosely packed chopped arugula
- 6 tablespoons minced fresh flat-leaf parsley
- 1 pint grape tomatoes, halved
- 1 tablespoon grated lemon rind
- 3 tablespoons fresh lemon juice
- 1 teaspoon kosher salt
- ½ teaspoon freshly ground black pepper
- ½ teaspoon sugar
- 2 tablespoons extra-virgin olive oil
- ¾ cup (3 ounces) crumbled goat cheese

❶ Place wheat berries in a medium bowl; cover with water to 2 inches above wheat berries. Cover and let stand 8 hours. Drain.
❷ Place wheat berries in a medium saucepan; cover with water to 2 inches above wheat berries. Bring to a boil, reduce heat, and cook, uncovered, 1 hour or until tender. Drain and rinse with cold water; drain well. Place wheat berries in a large bowl; add cucumber and next 4 ingredients.
❸ Combine rind and next 4 ingredients in a bowl; gradually add oil, stirring constantly with a whisk. Drizzle dressing over salad; toss well to coat. Stir in cheese. Let stand at least 30 minutes; serve at room temperature. Yield: 6 servings (serving size: about 1⅓ cups).

CALORIES 253; FAT 9.7g (sat 3.7g, mono 4.4g, poly 0.9g); PROTEIN 9.2g; CARB 35.7g; FIBER 6.8g; CHOL 11mg; IRON 1.2mg; SODIUM 401mg; CALC 79mg

"Meat accounts for the most expense at my grocery store visits, so I've started making one or two vegetarian dinners a week to cut costs."

—Ann Taylor Pittman
Senior Food Editor

The Price of Convenience

In an ideal world, you might make everything from scratch. In the real world, however, you sometimes need a little head start. Know, though, that with convenience comes a heftier price tag.

Fresh Garlic
14 cents per ounce

Bottled Minced Garlic
35 cents per ounce

USE THIS INGREDIENT IN: *Stir-Fried Beef with Broccoli and Bell Peppers (page 164); Spinach and Ricotta Pizza (page 165)*

Whole Broccoli
$1.69 per pound

Precut Broccoli Florets
$3.36 per pound

USE THIS INGREDIENT IN: *Stir-Fried Beef with Broccoli and Bell Peppers (page 164)*

Homemade Pizza Dough
$1.62 per two 12-inch crusts

Refrigerated Pizza Dough
$5.18 per two 11-ounce crusts

Packaged Pizza Crusts
$4.79 per two 12-inch crusts

USE THIS INGREDIENT IN: *Spinach and Ricotta Pizza (page 165); Grilled Pepper, Onion, and Sausage Calzones (page 166)*

Whole Chicken
$1.28 per pound

Cut-Up Whole Chicken
$1.69 per pound

Skinless, Boneless Chicken Breasts
$5.49 per pound

Rotisserie Chicken
$2.88 per pound

USE THIS INGREDIENT IN: *Grilled Spice-Rubbed Whole Chicken (page 164)*

Protein Power

Learn how this nutrient does more than support strong muscles, and try our healthful recipes highlighting good sources.

PROTEIN IS A HARDWORKING NUTRIENT, responsible for maintaining strong immune systems, regulating enzyme production and water balance, and promoting healthy skin and hair, just to name a few of its tasks. What's more, multiple studies indicate it's the most satiating nutrient, meaning you'll feel fuller longer with a little protein at meals.

The good news is you're probably consuming plenty of protein. The downside is you may be lacking *quality* protein—that is, protein offering a host of beneficial nutrients such as minerals, heart-healthy fats, fiber, and antioxidants. Here, you'll discover how protein factors into more than just muscle mass, and how to put together a nutrient-rich package for your health.

Quinoa and Pistachio Salad with Moroccan Pesto

Quinoa [KEEN-wah] is a quick-cooking whole grain supplying protein, iron, and vitamin E. Pair this side dish with simple grilled chicken or fish. For a vegetarian entrée option, use organic vegetable broth and add one (15½-ounce) can of rinsed, drained chickpeas to ramp up the protein.

 1 red bell pepper
 1 cup uncooked quinoa
 1 cup fat-free, less-sodium chicken broth
 ½ cup water
 ½ cup fresh orange juice
 ⅓ cup coarsely chopped fresh cilantro
 ¼ cup extra-virgin olive oil
 2 tablespoons coarsely chopped fresh flat-leaf parsley
 3 tablespoons fresh lemon juice
 ½ teaspoon ground cumin
 ¼ teaspoon kosher salt
 ¼ teaspoon ground red pepper
 2 large garlic cloves, coarsely chopped
 12 oil-cured olives, pitted and chopped
 ¼ cup chopped pistachios

❶ Preheat broiler.
❷ Cut red bell pepper in half lengthwise; discard seeds and membranes. Place pepper halves, skin sides up, on a foil-lined baking sheet; flatten with hand. Broil 12 minutes or until blackened. Place in a zip-top plastic bag; seal. Let stand 10 minutes. Peel and chop.
❸ Place quinoa, broth, ½ cup water, and juice in a large saucepan; bring to a boil. Cover, reduce heat, and simmer 12 minutes or until liquid is absorbed.
❹ Place cilantro and next 7 ingredients in a food processor; process until smooth. Combine bell pepper, quinoa mixture, cilantro mixture, and olives in a large bowl. Sprinkle with nuts. Yield: 6 servings (serving size: ¾ cup).

CALORIES 263; FAT 15.8g (sat 2.2g, mono 8.3g, poly 2.4g); PROTEIN 5.8g; CARB 28.2g; FIBER 4g; CHOL 0mg; IRON 3.3mg; SODIUM 318mg; CALC 36mg

Grilled Pork Tenderloin with Salsa Verde

Pork tenderloin is a tender, lean cut of meat offering about 75 percent of a day's protein needs in a prudent 4-ounce serving.

 2 (1-pound) pork tenderloins, trimmed and cut into ¾-inch slices
    Cooking spray
 ½ teaspoon salt
 ½ teaspoon freshly ground black pepper, divided
 1½ cups diced green tomato
 ¼ cup chopped fresh flat-leaf parsley
 3 tablespoons thinly sliced fresh chives
 2 tablespoons fresh lemon juice
 2 tablespoons extra-virgin olive oil
 1 tablespoon capers
 1 teaspoon chopped fresh oregano
 1 teaspoon chopped fresh thyme
 1 teaspoon sugar
 1 garlic clove, minced

❶ Prepare grill to medium-high heat.
❷ Arrange pork slices in a single layer between 2 sheets of heavy-duty plastic wrap; pound to ½-inch thickness using a meat mallet or small heavy skillet. Lightly coat pork with cooking spray; sprinkle with salt and ¼ teaspoon pepper. Place pork on a grill rack; grill pork 2 minutes on each side or until done.
❸ Place tomato and remaining ingredients in a food processor; pulse until minced. Stir in remaining ¼ teaspoon pepper. Serve with pork. Yield: 6 servings (serving size: 4 ounces pork and 2 tablespoons salsa).

CALORIES 235; FAT 9.9g (sat 2.5g, mono 5.7g, poly 1.3g); PROTEIN 32.3g; CARB 3.2g; FIBER 0.5g; CHOL 98mg; IRON 2.2mg; SODIUM 320mg; CALC 21mg

All About Protein

Protein Basics

A single protein is made up of a combination of up to 20 types of smaller building blocks called amino acids, which are strung together like links on a chain. When you eat proteins, you disassemble these links, rearrange them, and rebuild them to go about their work in your body.

You can manufacture many amino acids from breaking down and repackaging other amino acids; however, nine amino acids are called "essential" because your body can't make them and they must be obtained from food. Meat, fish, poultry, dairy products, and eggs contain all the essential amino acids; therefore, they are known as "complete" proteins. Vegetables, grains, legumes, and nuts also contain amino acids, but they usually lack one or more, making them "incomplete" proteins.

How Much Is Needed?

Health organizations offer different ways of counting protein. For example, the Institute of Medicine advises about 46 to 56 grams of protein a day for women and men, respectively, while the Food Guide Pyramid recommends about 5 ounces of protein daily for an average adult woman on a 2,000-calorie diet. This means one (6-ounce) skinless, boneless chicken breast and a large hard-boiled egg satisfy these daily protein recommendations. (For most healthy adults, consuming more protein in a day shouldn't be a health concern.)

But science seems to indicate a call for reexamining protein needs. When researchers at Loma Linda University in California examined diets of more than 1,800 women during a 25-year period, they found those with the highest protein intakes were least likely to experience a fractured bone. Also, according to research by Robert Heaney, PhD, of Creighton University in Omaha,

Nebraska, optimal protein intake for bone health is likely higher than current recommendations, particularly for older individuals—a conclusion supported by a study published in *Public Health Nutrition* last summer. Perhaps we'll see a change in the forthcoming Dietary Guidelines for Americans (out in early 2010) or when the Institute of Medicine offers new nutrient intake references. There's no doubt, however, that more research is needed to tease out optimal protein requirements for health.

Choosing Proteins for Optimum Health

Opt for variety, balance, and moderation among nuts, seeds, grains, legumes, fish, meats, and poultry for meal planning. This approach offers a host of vitamins and minerals, plus fiber, antioxidants, and certain types of fats. What's more, emphasizing plant-based proteins at meals will boost fiber intake and likely protect your ticker. A bonus: You'll feel fuller longer, regardless of the type of protein.

The best approach is to include one good source of the nutrient at each meal or snack for optimum health. For example, have an egg at breakfast, some fat-free, plain yogurt as a snack, a chicken salad for lunch, and sautéed shrimp with your pasta at dinner. For other examples, enjoy these recipes to incorporate healthful proteins in your diet.

Superlative Protein Sources

Quality sources of protein exist in just about every food group (except fruits), even if the protein is incomplete. Here's a rundown of some of the other nutrients you gain from these good sources.

Beef, pork, game, and lamb: These sources also offer highly absorbable iron, plus vitamins B_{12}, B_6, and zinc. Choose lean cuts for the least saturated fat.

Poultry: Skinless poultry is a good choice for B vitamins like niacin, B_{12}, and B_6; zinc; potassium; iron; and phosphorus.

Eggs: For little saturated fat, eggs offer iron and vitamin B_{12}, plus trace amounts of many vitamins and minerals.

Fish and shellfish: Fatty fish, like trout or salmon, provide omega-3 fatty acids, which are associated with health benefits. Generally, fish and shellfish offer niacin, iron, selenium, and zinc.

Dairy products: Low-fat or fat-free milks, cheeses, and yogurts all supply essential B vitamins like riboflavin and niacin, vitamins A and D, calcium, phosphorus, and potassium.

Legumes (beans, lentils, and peas): Options from this group are nutritional powerhouses. Besides fiber, legumes generally contain folate, iron, zinc, potassium, and phosphorus, plus scores of antioxidants.

Nuts and seeds: Nuts and seeds provide fiber, heart-healthy fats, phosphorus, potassium, iron, and zinc.

Swap Carbs for Proteins to Protect Your Heart

Results from a 2005 study found swapping some carbohydrates (like potatoes, for example) for a mix of healthful meat- and plant-based proteins improved triglyceride and cholesterol levels while lowering blood pressure. The OmniHeart trial (www.omniheart.org) studied the effects of three similar diets on 164 adults for six weeks; one diet was high in protein (half the protein was plant-based), one high in carbohydrates, and one high in unsaturated fats. Those who raised protein intakes to 25 percent of calories (thereby reducing carbohydrate intakes) exhibited the biggest dip in "bad" or LDL cholesterol and triglyceride levels, helping lower their estimated 10-year heart disease risk rate by 21 percent—the most of any of the three diet groups.

Bison Ribeye Kebabs

The ribeye cut of bison is surprisingly lean, and it yields tender results when grilled. Bison has a deeper, richer flavor than beef, and it stands up well to the piney rosemary.

- ¼ cup extra-virgin olive oil
- 2 tablespoons finely chopped fresh rosemary
- 1 tablespoon coarsely ground black pepper
- 2 large garlic cloves, minced
- 1 pound bison ribeye, trimmed and cut into 1¼-inch cubes
- ½ teaspoon salt
- Cooking spray

❶ Combine first 5 ingredients in a large bowl; toss well to coat. Cover and refrigerate for 45 minutes.
❷ Prepare grill to medium-high heat.
❸ Remove bison from marinade; discard remaining marinade. Thread bison evenly onto each of 4 (12-inch) skewers, and sprinkle with salt. Place skewers on a grill rack coated with cooking spray, and grill 3 minutes on each side or until desired degree of doneness. Serve immediately. Yield: 4 servings (serving size: 2 skewers).

CALORIES 163; FAT 6.2g (sat 2.3g, mono 2.9g, poly 0.4g); PROTEIN 25.1g; CARB 0.2g; FIBER 0.1g; CHOL 67mg; IRON 2.5mg; SODIUM 335mg; CALC 7mg

---

QUICK & EASY
Quick Panzanella with Chicken

A skinless chicken breast half is a protein powerhouse; a serving of this salad offers almost 44 grams of protein (about a day's worth). Plus, poultry offers B vitamins, zinc, iron, and vitamin B12.

- 4 (6-ounce) skinless, boneless chicken breast halves
- ¾ teaspoon salt, divided
- ½ teaspoon freshly ground black pepper, divided
- Cooking spray
- 2 cups (1-inch) cubed tomato
- 2 cups diced ciabatta bread (about 4 ounces)
- 1 cup thinly sliced celery (2 stalks)
- ½ cup fresh basil leaves, torn
- 2 tablespoons extra-virgin olive oil
- 2 tablespoons red wine vinegar
- 1 small red onion, thinly sliced
- ½ English cucumber, halved lengthwise and thinly sliced (about 1 cup)

❶ Heat a grill pan over medium-high heat. Sprinkle chicken evenly with ¼ teaspoon salt and ¼ teaspoon pepper. Coat pan with cooking spray. Add chicken to pan; cook 6 minutes on each side or until done. Remove from heat, and chop.
❷ Place tomato in a large bowl; sprinkle with remaining ½ teaspoon salt and remaining ¼ teaspoon pepper. Let stand 5 minutes. Add chicken, bread, and remaining ingredients to tomato mixture, tossing well to combine. Serve immediately. Yield: 4 servings (serving size: about 2½ cups).

CALORIES 385; FAT 13g (sat 2.4g, mono 7.5g, poly 2g); PROTEIN 43.5g; CARB 23g; FIBER 2.6g; CHOL 108mg; IRON 3mg; SODIUM 757mg; CALC 50mg

---

QUICK & EASY ● MAKE AHEAD
Spiced Pecans

Nuts are considered a quality protein, and they offer plenty of good-for-you fats along with some fiber. According to the USDA's Food Guide Pyramid, a ½-ounce portion counts as one serving of protein. Serve as a snack, or sprinkle over salad greens for a sweet and crunchy topper.

- 1 large egg white
- 1 teaspoon water
- 2 cups pecan halves
- ½ cup sugar
- 1 teaspoon ground cinnamon
- ½ teaspoon ground allspice
- ⅛ teaspoon freshly ground black pepper
- Cooking spray

❶ Preheat oven to 250°.
❷ Combine egg white and 1 teaspoon water in a small bowl, stirring with a whisk until frothy. Stir in pecans. Add sugar and next 3 ingredients, tossing to coat. Spread nut mixture on a jelly-roll pan coated with cooking spray. Bake at 250° for 45 minutes or until dry, stirring once. Cool completely. Yield: 2 cups (serving size: 2 tablespoons or ½ ounce).

CALORIES 119; FAT 9.7g (sat 0.8g, mono 5.5g, poly 2.9g); PROTEIN 1.5g; CARB 8.3g; FIBER 1.4g; CHOL 0mg; IRON 0.4mg; SODIUM 4mg; CALC 12mg

Asparagus Salad with Soft Poached Eggs, Prosciutto, and Lemon-Chive Vinaigrette

Eggs are a great source of protein plus zinc, iron, and lutein. Serve with 100 percent whole-grain toast and a fresh fruit salad for a filling brunch.

1½ tablespoons fresh lemon juice
2¼ teaspoons freshly grated Parmigiano-Reggiano cheese
1 teaspoon minced fresh chives
½ teaspoon minced garlic
¼ teaspoon kosher salt
¼ teaspoon freshly ground black pepper
¼ teaspoon Dijon mustard
3 tablespoons extra-virgin olive oil
1 pound asparagus, trimmed
8 thin slices prosciutto (about 2 ounces)
4 large eggs
Cooking spray
4 teaspoons chopped fresh chives (optional)

❶ Combine first 7 ingredients in a small bowl, stirring with a whisk. Gradually add oil, stirring well with a whisk.
❷ Steam asparagus, covered, 3 minutes. Drain and rinse under cold water; drain. Arrange 2 prosciutto slices in center of each of 4 plates. Arrange asparagus spears evenly over prosciutto.
❸ Add water to a large skillet, filling two-thirds full; bring to a boil. Reduce heat; simmer. Break eggs into each of 4 (6-ounce) custard cups coated with cooking spray. Place custard cups in simmering water in pan. Cover pan; cook 10 minutes. Remove custard cups from water; carefully remove eggs from cups. Arrange 1 egg over each serving, and drizzle with about 1 tablespoon dressing. Sprinkle each serving with 1 teaspoon chives, if desired. Yield: 4 servings.

CALORIES 219; FAT 16.7g (sat 3.6g, mono 10g, poly 2g); PROTEIN 12.3g; CARB 6g; FIBER 2.5g; CHOL 221mg; IRON 1.6mg; SODIUM 417mg; CALC 64mg

---

Feast for the Fourth

There's plenty to celebrate with our casual outdoor menu, including tips on how you can do much of the cooking ahead.

FOURTH OF JULY FÊTE MENU

(Serves 8)

Watermelon and Cucumber Tonic

Grilled Pork Chops with Shallot Butter

Confetti Couscous

Marinated Summer Beans

Berry-Peach Cobbler with Sugared Almonds

Countdown to the Fourth

Prepare some items in advance so the menu comes together easily.

Up to 2 days ahead:
• Make shallot butter.

Up to 1 day ahead:
• Make juice mixture for beverages.
• Prepare couscous side dish.
• Marinate beans.

2 hours before dinner:
• Combine oil and herbs for pork.

30 minutes ahead:
• Assemble cobbler.
• Light grill.

15 minutes ahead:
• Preheat oven for cobbler.

As guests arrive:
• Place cobbler in oven.
• Combine drink ingredients in a pitcher.
• Grill pork.

STAFF FAVORITE • MAKE AHEAD
Watermelon and Cucumber Tonic

(pictured on page 227)

A reinterpretation of the familiar gin and tonic, this cocktail includes fresh watermelon and cucumber juices for a refreshing taste. Hendrick's, a small-batch Scottish gin that's infused with the flavor of cucumber and rose petals, is ideal for this recipe. For even better results, try premium tonic water, such as Fever-Tree or Q Tonic. Serve any remaining juice mixture (which you can make a day ahead) over ice for guests who prefer a nonalcoholic drink.

6 cups cubed seeded watermelon, divided
¼ cup fresh mint leaves, divided
¼ cup fresh lemon juice, divided
1 English cucumber, peeled, sliced, and divided (about 3 cups)
2½ cups tonic water, chilled
1¼ cups gin

❶ Place half each of watermelon, mint, juice, and cucumber in a blender or food processor; process until smooth. Line a fine sieve with 4 layers of cheesecloth, allowing cheesecloth to extend over edges; strain watermelon mixture through prepared sieve over a bowl, reserving juice mixture. Gather edges of cheesecloth together. Holding cheesecloth over sieve, squeeze to release remaining juice mixture. Discard solids. Repeat procedure with remaining watermelon, mint, juice, and cucumber.
❷ Combine 2½ cups juice mixture, tonic water, and gin, stirring well to combine. (Reserve any remaining juice mixture for another use.) Serve over ice. Yield: 8 servings (serving size: about ¾ cup).

CALORIES 135; FAT 0g; PROTEIN 0.5g; CARB 13.9g; FIBER 0.7g; CHOL 0mg; IRON 0.2mg; SODIUM 7mg; CALC 5mg

Grilled Pork Chops with Shallot Butter

If made ahead, allow the butter to come to room temperature before spreading over the pork. You can also combine the oil and herbs a couple of hours in advance.

- 8 (7-ounce) bone-in center-cut pork chops
- 1 teaspoon salt, divided
- ¾ teaspoon freshly ground black pepper
- 2 tablespoons extra-virgin olive oil
- 2 teaspoons finely chopped fresh chives
- 1 teaspoon finely chopped fresh thyme
- 1 teaspoon finely chopped fresh rosemary
- 3 garlic cloves, minced
- 2 tablespoons butter, softened
- 2½ teaspoons minced shallots
- ¼ teaspoon grated lemon rind

❶ Prepare grill to medium-high heat.
❷ Sprinkle both sides of pork evenly with ½ teaspoon salt and pepper. Combine oil and next 4 ingredients, stirring well. Rub oil mixture evenly over both sides of pork. Place pork on grill rack; grill 6 minutes on each side or until a thermometer inserted in thickest part of pork registers 155°. Remove pork from grill; let stand 5 minutes. Sprinkle with remaining ½ teaspoon salt.
❸ Combine butter, shallots, and lemon rind, stirring well. Spread about 1 teaspoon butter mixture over each pork chop; let pork stand an additional 5 minutes. Yield: 8 servings (serving size: 1 pork chop).

CALORIES 208; FAT 12.2g (sat 4.5g, mono 5.9g, poly 0.9g); PROTEIN 22.5g; CARB 0.7g; FIBER 0.1g; CHOL 68mg; IRON 0.7mg; SODIUM 360mg; CALC 28mg

Confetti Couscous

Serve this salad chilled or at room temperature. You can prepare the recipe up to a day ahead, but stir in the basil just before serving.

- 2 baby eggplants, cut into ½-inch-thick slices
- 2 yellow squashes, cut into ½-inch-thick slices
- 2 red bell peppers, seeded and cut into quarters
- ⅓ cup extra-virgin olive oil, divided
- 1 teaspoon salt, divided
- ½ teaspoon freshly ground black pepper, divided
- 2 cups water
- 1½ cups fat-free, less-sodium chicken broth
- 2 cups uncooked Israeli couscous
- 3 tablespoons red wine vinegar
- 1½ tablespoons Dijon mustard
- ½ cup chopped fresh basil

❶ Prepare grill to medium-high heat.
❷ Brush eggplant, squash, and bell peppers evenly with 4 teaspoons oil. Sprinkle evenly with ¼ teaspoon salt and ¼ teaspoon black pepper. Place vegetables on grill rack; grill 3 minutes on each side or until slightly charred. Cool and chop. Place vegetables in a large bowl.
❸ Bring 2 cups water and broth to a boil in a medium saucepan. Stir in couscous. Reduce heat, and simmer 8 minutes or until couscous is tender. Drain and rinse with cold water. Add couscous, remaining ¾ teaspoon salt, and remaining ¼ teaspoon pepper to vegetable mixture; toss. Combine vinegar and mustard in a medium bowl, stirring well. Gradually add remaining ¼ cup oil to vinegar mixture, stirring constantly with a whisk. Drizzle vinegar mixture over couscous mixture; toss to coat. Stir in basil. Yield: 8 servings (serving size: 1 cup).

CALORIES 271; FAT 9.8g (sat 1.4g, mono 6.7g, poly 1.5g); PROTEIN 6.8g; CARB 39.3g; FIBER 4.6g; CHOL 0mg; IRON 1mg; SODIUM 453mg; CALC 29mg

Marinated Summer Beans

The beauty of this side is that the recipe can be prepared up to one day ahead; as they sit, the beans absorb more flavor.

- 3½ teaspoons salt, divided
- 1 pound fresh green beans, trimmed
- 1 pound fresh wax beans, trimmed
- 3 tablespoons chopped fresh flat-leaf parsley
- 2 tablespoons extra-virgin olive oil
- 1 tablespoon grated lemon rind
- 2 tablespoons fresh lemon juice
- 1 teaspoon chile paste with garlic (such as sambal oelek)
- 1 garlic clove, minced

❶ Add 1 tablespoon salt and beans to a large saucepan of boiling water; cook 6 minutes or until crisp-tender. Drain; rinse with cold water. Drain. Combine remaining ½ teaspoon salt, parsley, and remaining ingredients in a large bowl. Add beans to bowl; toss well. Chill at least 1 hour, tossing occasionally. Yield: 8 servings (serving size: 1 cup).

CALORIES 68; FAT 3.7g (sat 0.5g, mono 2.5g, poly 0.6g); PROTEIN 2.2g; CARB 8.9g; FIBER 4g; CHOL 0mg; IRON 1.3mg; SODIUM 199mg; CALC 46mg

Berry-Peach Cobbler with Sugared Almonds
(pictured on page 225)

A delicious combination of blueberries, blackberries, and peaches yields a sweet, juicy dessert that's the epitome of summer.

FILLING:
- 3 (6-ounce) packages fresh blueberries
- 3 (5.6-ounce) packages fresh blackberries
- 3 medium peaches, peeled and sliced
- Cooking spray
- ⅔ cup granulated sugar
- 2½ tablespoons cornstarch
- 3 tablespoons fresh lemon juice
- ⅛ teaspoon salt

TOPPING:

- 4.5 ounces all-purpose flour (about 1 cup)
- ¼ cup granulated sugar
- 2 tablespoons cornstarch
- ½ teaspoon baking powder
- ⅛ teaspoon salt
- 6 tablespoons chilled butter, cut into small pieces
- ½ cup half-and-half
- ⅓ cup sliced almonds
- 3 tablespoons turbinado sugar
- 1 tablespoon egg white

REMAINING INGREDIENT:

- 4 cups vanilla fat-free ice cream

❶ Preheat oven to 350°.

❷ To prepare filling, combine blueberries, blackberries, and peaches in a 13 x 9-inch baking dish lightly coated with cooking spray. Sprinkle ⅔ cup granulated sugar, 2½ tablespoons cornstarch, juice, and ⅛ teaspoon salt over fruit; toss gently to combine.

❸ To prepare topping, weigh or lightly spoon flour into a dry measuring cup; level with a knife. Combine flour and next 4 ingredients, stirring well. Cut butter into flour mixture with a pastry blender or two knives until mixture resembles coarse meal. Add half-and-half; gently knead dough just until moistened. Drop dough by spoonfuls evenly over top of filling. Combine almonds, turbinado sugar, and egg white; sprinkle over top. Bake at 350° for 50 minutes or until topping is browned. Let stand 10 minutes. Serve with ice cream. Yield: 12 servings (serving size: 1 cup cobbler and ⅓ cup ice cream).

CALORIES 321; FAT 8.9g (sat 4.5g, mono 2.7g, poly 0.8g); PROTEIN 5.3g; CARB 58.9g; FIBER 4.2g; CHOL 19mg; IRON 1.1mg; SODIUM 147mg; CALC 101mg

Salads

How to make delicious and healthful versions of international classics.

French Frisée Salad with Bacon and Poached Eggs

If you can't find frisée, substitute a salad blend that includes frisée or radicchio.

- 4 (1-ounce) slices rye bread, cut into ½-inch cubes
- 6 slices applewood-smoked bacon, cut crosswise into ½-inch-thick pieces
- ⅓ cup white wine vinegar
- 1 tablespoon chopped fresh tarragon
- 3 tablespoons olive oil
- ¼ teaspoon kosher salt
- ¼ teaspoon freshly ground black pepper
- 1 head frisée, torn (about 8 ounces)
- 1 tablespoon white vinegar
- 4 large eggs
- Cracked black pepper (optional)

❶ Preheat oven to 400°.

❷ Arrange bread in a single layer on a baking sheet; bake at 400° for 20 minutes or until toasted, turning once. Cool.

❸ Cook bacon in a skillet over medium heat until crisp, stirring occasionally. Remove bacon from pan, reserving 1 tablespoon drippings; set bacon aside. Combine 1 tablespoon drippings, white wine vinegar, and next 4 ingredients in a large bowl, stirring with a whisk. Add croutons, bacon, and frisée, tossing to coat. Place 2 cups salad mixture on each of 4 plates.

❹ Add water to a large skillet, filling two-thirds full; bring to a boil. Reduce heat; simmer. Add white vinegar. Break eggs into pan; cook 3 minutes or until desired degree of doneness. Carefully remove eggs from pan using a slotted spoon; top each serving with 1 poached egg. Sprinkle with cracked pepper, if desired. Yield: 4 servings.

CALORIES 344; FAT 23.5g (sat 5.6g, mono 12.5g, poly 2.6g); PROTEIN 14.5g; CARB 18g; FIBER 2.3g; CHOL 227mg; IRON 2.4mg; SODIUM 765mg; CALC 101mg

Pick the Perfect Greens

When you make a tossed salad, first choose which lettuce or salad greens you'll use. Many choices are available, so it helps to know what flavor and texture to expect and what type of dressing works best with different greens. Most lettuces or salad greens fall into a few broad categories.

Hearty lettuces, such as romaine and iceberg, are good choices for heavier, thick and creamy dressings, such as Caesar or blue cheese.

Peppery greens include arugula and watercress. These lettuces pack a spicy punch, so they can stand up to other strong flavors, like lamb or steak. These lettuces also make a tasty addition to salads with milder lettuces.

Mild lettuces include butter lettuces, such as Boston and Bibb, spinach, leafy green and red, and mâche. These are mild in flavor and tend to be delicate, so pair them with tart vinaigrettes and other assertive flavors.

Bitter greens include radicchio (although it's a vibrant red color), escarole, endive, and frisée. These lettuces have a pleasantly bitter flavor. Pair them with fatty ingredients, such as bacon, nuts, and good-quality oil, or sweet ingredients, such as fruits. The fat and sweetness balance the bitterness of the greens.

Grilled Chicken Salad

Inspired by the popular curried chicken salad, this recipe calls for an Indian tandoori-style yogurt marinade for the chicken. Then it's grilled, chopped, and stirred together with tangy dressing, which includes store-bought mango chutney. If you prefer more spicy heat, add a bit more ground red pepper.

1½ cups 2% reduced-fat Greek-style yogurt (such as Fage)
1 tablespoon canola oil
1 tablespoon grated peeled fresh ginger
3 garlic cloves, minced
¾ teaspoon salt, divided
½ teaspoon ground red pepper
4 bone-in chicken breast halves, skinned
Cooking spray
1 cup seedless green grapes
½ cup chopped red onion
½ cup mango chutney
⅓ cup finely chopped celery
⅓ cup canola mayonnaise (such as Spectrum organic)
3 tablespoons fresh lemon juice

❶ Combine first 4 ingredients, stirring to combine. Stir in ¼ teaspoon salt and pepper. Place yogurt mixture in a heavy-duty zip-top plastic bag. Add chicken to bag; seal. Marinate in refrigerator 2 hours, turning occasionally.
❷ Prepare grill to medium-high heat.
❸ Remove chicken from bag; discard marinade. Place chicken, breast sides down, on grill rack coated with cooking spray; grill 10 minutes or until browned. Turn chicken over; grill 20 minutes or until a thermometer inserted in meaty part of breast registers 160°. Remove chicken from grill; let stand 10 minutes. Remove meat from bones; discard bones. Coarsely chop chicken and place in a medium bowl. Sprinkle chicken with remaining ½ teaspoon salt.
❹ Add grapes and remaining ingredients to chicken mixture; toss mixture gently to combine. Chill 30 minutes. Yield: 5 servings (serving size: about 1 cup).

CALORIES 430; FAT 18.6g (sat 2.7g, mono 6.2g, poly 8.8g); PROTEIN 28.9g; CARB 35.1g; FIBER 1g; CHOL 68mg; IRON 1mg; SODIUM 718mg; CALC 100mg

WINE NOTE: With just a bit of heat from the ground red pepper and sweet-tart mango chutney, this salad matches perfectly with a glass of chilled Hogue Riesling 2007 ($9) from Washington. The tropical fruit and pear flavors nicely echo the chutney, while the wine's refreshing sweetness and fresh acidity add zip and textural contrast to the creamy consistency of the chicken salad.

How to Make Whole-Grain Salads

You're likely aware of the health benefits of eating whole grains, and salads are a clever way to work more into your diet. Try our recipe based on bulgur wheat, Minty Bulgur Wheat and Peach Salad (at right), or improvise with your favorite grains.

Hearty whole grains offer a pleasantly chewy texture when cooked. Varieties include farro and wheat berries. Cook them according to the package directions, and toss with your favorite chopped fresh herbs and a tangy vinaigrette. Fresh chopped raw vegetables, such as radish or carrot, add additional crunch, or you can roast winter squash or root vegetables and toss them in. Shaved or crumbled cheese adds a rich, creamy contrast.

Other whole grains, such as pearled barley, bulgur, and quinoa, are more familiar and make a versatile base for salads, as well. Since these grains absorb excess liquid, add small amounts of a sharp dressing such as a vinaigrette. Thick, creamy dressings may be too heavy for these grains. Add chopped raw vegetables and toasted nuts or seeds for texture.

MAKE AHEAD
Minty Bulgur Wheat and Peach Salad

Jicama adds crunch to this salad. You can add toasted pecans or almonds for even more texture. Make the salad up to one day ahead; serve with grilled chicken or pork.

2 cups boiling water
1 cup uncooked bulgur wheat
3 tablespoons fresh lemon juice
2 tablespoons fresh lime juice
2 tablespoons extra-virgin olive oil
1 tablespoon honey
½ teaspoon salt
¼ teaspoon freshly ground black pepper
2 cups diced, peeled peaches (about 2 medium)
2 cups diced, peeled jicama
1 cup finely chopped fresh mint

❶ Combine boiling water and bulgur in a large bowl; let stand 1 hour or until water is absorbed. Combine lemon juice and next 5 ingredients, stirring well with a whisk. Add peaches, jicama, and mint to bulgur; toss to combine. Drizzle dressing mixture over bulgur mixture; toss to coat. Chill 1 hour. Yield: 8 servings (serving size: about 1 cup).

CALORIES 162; FAT 5.7g (sat 0.8g, mono 3.7g, poly 0.7g); PROTEIN 3.3g; CARB 27.6g; FIBER 6.6g; CHOL 0mg; IRON 2.2mg; SODIUM 156mg; CALC 34mg

---

How to Make a Tastier Salad

Grilling adds a smoky, charred flavor to foods. For example, grilling chicken will yield tastier chicken salad than simply boiling the meat.

Roasting caramelizes natural sugars in meats and vegetables, so roasted ingredients add a more nuanced flavor than raw.

Sautéing ingredients cooks them quickly, browning the exterior and intensifying their natural flavors.

Marinating ingredients before or after cooking introduces additional flavor.

Middle Eastern Eggplant Salad

Reminiscent of baba ghanoush, this salad can be served alongside roasted or grilled meats or as a dip with crackers or flatbread.

- 2 medium red bell peppers
- 1 medium tomato, peeled and seeded
- 3 tablespoons no-salt-added tomato paste
- 2 tablespoons water
- ½ teaspoon salt, divided
- Dash of ground red pepper
- 3 garlic cloves, thinly sliced
- ¼ cup olive oil
- 1 pound eggplant, cut into (1-inch) cubes
- ¼ teaspoon freshly ground black pepper

1 Preheat broiler.

2 Cut bell peppers in half lengthwise; discard seeds and membranes. Place pepper halves, skin sides up, on a foil-lined baking sheet; flatten with hand. Broil 12 minutes or until blackened. Place in a zip-top plastic bag; seal. Let stand 10 minutes. Peel and chop.

3 Place tomato in a blender; process until smooth. Place tomato puree, tomato paste, 2 tablespoons water, ¼ teaspoon salt, ground red pepper, and garlic in a blender; process until smooth.

4 Heat oil in a saucepan over medium heat. Add eggplant; cook 30 minutes or until tender, stirring frequently. Stir in bell pepper and tomato mixture. Cook 5 minutes. Stir in remaining ¼ teaspoon salt and black pepper. Yield: 4 servings (serving size: ½ cup).

CALORIES 182; FAT 14.1g (sat 2g, mono 9.9g, poly 1.7g); PROTEIN 2.7g; CARB 14.6g; FIBER 6g; CHOL 0mg; IRON 1.2mg; SODIUM 315mg; CALC 25mg

Pasta Night Menu
serves 6

Using the blender for the salad dressing helps this meal come together quickly. A simple, bright-tasting pasta entrée doesn't upstage the stellar salad, allowing it to be the star of the meal.

Caesar Salad

Lemon spaghetti
Cook 12 ounces spaghetti according to package directions, omitting salt and fat. Drain; place pasta in a large bowl. Combine 1 teaspoon grated lemon rind, ¼ cup fresh lemon juice, ¼ cup extra-virgin olive oil, ¾ teaspoon salt, and ¼ teaspoon crushed red pepper, stirring with a whisk. Drizzle juice mixture over pasta; toss well to coat. Sprinkle pasta with 2 ounces shaved Parmigiano-Reggiano cheese and ¼ cup chopped fresh flat-leaf parsley.

Garlic breadsticks

Pinot grigio

Vanilla low-fat ice cream with sliced peaches and toasted pine nuts

Caesar Salad

Add grilled shrimp or chicken to make this an entrée salad, or serve it with your favorite pasta toss. Egg yolks enrich and bind this tasty dressing. Be sure to look for pasteurized eggs since they are not cooked in this recipe.

- 5 tablespoons extra-virgin olive oil, divided
- 4 cups (1-inch) cubed French bread (about 4 ounces)
- 1 (2-ounce) can anchovy fillets, drained
- 2 tablespoons grated fresh Parmigiano-Reggiano cheese
- 2 tablespoons red wine vinegar
- 2 large pasteurized egg yolks
- 1 garlic clove
- 6 cups torn romaine hearts
- ¼ teaspoon kosher salt

1 Preheat oven to 350°.

2 Combine 1 tablespoon oil and bread in a large bowl, tossing to coat. Arrange bread in a single layer on a baking sheet; bake at 350° for 15 minutes or until golden. Cool.

3 Pat anchovy fillets dry with a paper towel. Place fillets, cheese, and next 3 ingredients in a blender; process until smooth. With blender on, add remaining ¼ cup oil, 1 tablespoon at a time; process until smooth. Combine croutons and lettuce in a large bowl. Drizzle lettuce and croutons evenly with dressing; toss to coat. Sprinkle salad mixture evenly with salt; toss to combine. Serve immediately. Yield: 6 servings (serving size: 1 cup).

CALORIES 205; FAT 14.4g (sat 2.6g, mono 9.3g, poly 1.9g); PROTEIN 6.5g; CARB 13g; FIBER 1.6g; CHOL 76mg; IRON 1.8mg; SODIUM 496mg; CALC 70mg

How to Add Crunch to Salads

Homemade croutons are a great way to add flavor and texture to salads, and they're healthier than store-bought because you control the amount of fat and sodium. Start with day-old bread, and cut it into uniform cubes. Drizzle the cubes with olive oil (or coat them with cooking spray) and toss, then bake until golden and crisp. You can do this for up to two days ahead, and store them in an airtight container.

You can also add textural contrast to salads by tossing in seeds, such as pumpkin or sunflower, toasted nuts, or chopped crunchy vegetables, such as uncooked zucchini, cucumber, or bell pepper.

Dinner Tonight

Put dinner on the table in a flash with these fast, fresh meals.

Bow Ties with Tomatoes, Feta, and Balsamic Dressing
··20 minutes

Serve with pan-grilled asparagus. Combine 1 teaspoon extra-virgin olive oil, ¼ teaspoon salt, ⅛ teaspoon freshly ground black pepper, and 1 pound trimmed asparagus. Heat a grill pan over medium-high heat. Coat pan with cooking spray. Add asparagus; cook 5 minutes or until tender, turning once.

- 6   ounces uncooked farfalle (bow tie pasta)
- 2   cups grape tomatoes, halved
- 1   cup seedless green grapes, halved
- ⅓   cup thinly sliced fresh basil leaves
- 2   tablespoons white balsamic vinegar
- 2   tablespoons chopped shallots
- 2   teaspoons capers
- 1   teaspoon Dijon mustard
- ½   teaspoon bottled minced garlic
- ½   teaspoon salt
- ¼   teaspoon black pepper
- 4   teaspoons extra-virgin olive oil
- 1   (4-ounce) package crumbled reduced-fat feta cheese

❶ Cook pasta according to package directions, omitting salt and fat. Drain. Combine cooked pasta, tomatoes, grapes, and basil in a large bowl.
❷ While pasta cooks, combine vinegar and next 6 ingredients in a bowl, stirring with a whisk. Gradually add oil to vinegar mixture, stirring constantly. Drizzle vinaigrette over pasta mixture; toss well to coat. Add cheese; toss to combine. Yield: 4 servings (serving size: 2 cups).

CALORIES 320; FAT 9.9g (sat 3.8g, mono 3.6g, poly 0.7g); PROTEIN 14g; CARB 45.6g; FIBER 3.4g; CHOL 10mg; IRON 2mg; SODIUM 822mg; CALC 130mg

Pan-Seared Shrimp Po'boys
··20 minutes

Carrot and cabbage slaw makes for a crunchy side dish. Combine 4 cups shredded green cabbage and 1 cup shredded carrot in a large bowl. Combine 3 tablespoons reduced-fat mayonnaise, 1 tablespoon cider vinegar, and ¼ teaspoon celery seeds in a small bowl. Add mayonnaise mixture to cabbage mixture; stir well.

- ⅓   cup reduced-fat mayonnaise
- 2   tablespoons sweet pickle relish
- 1   tablespoon chopped shallots
- 1   teaspoon capers, chopped
- ¼   teaspoon hot pepper sauce (such as Tabasco)
- 1   pound peeled and deveined large shrimp
- 1½ teaspoons salt-free Cajun seasoning
- 2   teaspoons olive oil
- 4   (2½-ounce) hoagie rolls
- ½   cup shredded romaine lettuce
- 8   thin tomato slices
- 4   thin red onion slices

❶ Combine first 5 ingredients in a small bowl. Heat a large nonstick skillet over medium-high heat. Combine shrimp and Cajun seasoning in a bowl; toss well. Add oil to pan, and swirl to coat. Add shrimp to pan; cook 2 minutes on each side or until done.
❷ Cut each roll in half horizontally. Top bottom half of each roll with 2 tablespoons lettuce, 2 tomato slices, 1 onion slice, and one quarter of shrimp. Spread top half of each roll with about 2 tablespoons mayonnaise mixture; place on top of sandwich. Yield: 4 servings (serving size: 1 sandwich).

CALORIES 401; FAT 12.1g (sat 2.8g, mono 4.6g, poly 3.2g); PROTEIN 30.7g; CARB 44.2g; FIBER 2.7g; CHOL 172mg; IRON 4.4mg; SODIUM 944; CALC 152mg

Snapper with Grilled Mango Salsa
··30 minutes

For a twist in the mango salsa, use lime instead of lemon juice. For orange-scented couscous, bring ¾ cup fresh orange juice, ½ cup water, and 1 tablespoon olive oil to a boil in a saucepan. Stir in 1 cup uncooked couscous, ¼ teaspoon salt, and ⅛ teaspoon black pepper. Remove from heat, cover, and let stand 5 minutes. Fluff with a fork.

- 6   (½-inch-thick) mango wedges (1 mango)
- 3   (¼-inch-thick) slices red onion
- 2   teaspoons olive oil, divided
- Cooking spray
- ¼   cup diced peeled avocado
- 1   tablespoon chopped fresh mint
- 2   teaspoons fresh lemon juice
- ½   teaspoon salt, divided
- ¼   teaspoon freshly ground black pepper, divided
- 4   (6-ounce) yellowtail snapper or other firm white fish fillets
- Mint sprigs (optional)

❶ Prepare grill to medium-high heat.
❷ Brush mango and onion with 1 teaspoon oil. Place mango and onion on a grill rack coated with cooking spray; cover and grill 3 minutes on each side or until tender. Chop onion and mango. Combine onion, mango, avocado, mint, juice, ¼ teaspoon salt, and ⅛ teaspoon pepper in a medium bowl.
❸ Brush fish with remaining 1 teaspoon oil; sprinkle with remaining ¼ teaspoon salt and remaining ⅛ teaspoon pepper. Place fish on grill rack; grill 4 minutes on each side or until fish flakes easily when tested with a fork or until desired degree of doneness. Serve with mango mixture. Garnish with mint sprigs, if desired. Yield: 4 servings (serving size: 1 fillet and ⅓ cup salsa).

CALORIES 246; FAT 6.1g (sat 1g, mono 3g, poly 1.2g); PROTEIN 35.8g; CARB 11.2g; FIBER 1.6g; CHOL 63mg; IRON 0.6mg; SODIUM 402mg; CALC 67mg

Cheddar Burgers with Red Onion Jam
·····················•30 minutes

For heightened flavor, add ¼ teaspoon black pepper to the beef. Serve with baked chips and blue cheese dip. Combine ½ cup (2 ounces) low-fat crumbled blue cheese, ⅓ cup reduced-fat sour cream, 2 tablespoons canola mayonnaise, and 1 teaspoon red wine vinegar in a bowl. Mash with a fork.

JAM:
- 1 teaspoon olive oil
- 4 cups vertically sliced red onion
- 4 teaspoons sugar
- 4 teaspoons red wine vinegar
- ¾ teaspoon chopped fresh thyme

BURGERS:
- ¾ teaspoon chopped fresh oregano
- ½ teaspoon salt
- ¼ teaspoon garlic powder
- 1 pound extra-lean ground round
- Cooking spray
- 4 (½-ounce) slices white Cheddar cheese
- 4 (1½-ounce) hamburger buns, toasted
- 4 teaspoons canola mayonnaise

❶ Prepare grill to medium-high heat.
❷ To prepare jam, heat a large nonstick skillet over medium-high heat. Add oil to pan; swirl to coat. Add onion; sauté 5 minutes. Reduce heat to medium-low; stir in sugar, vinegar, and thyme. Cover and cook 10 minutes or until onion is very tender. Remove from heat.
❸ To prepare burgers, combine oregano and next 3 ingredients. Divide mixture into 4 equal portions, shaping each into a ½-inch-thick patty. Place on a grill rack coated with cooking spray; cook 2 minutes. Turn patties over. Place 1 cheese slice on each patty; cook 2 minutes or until done.
❹ Spread cut sides of each bun with ½ teaspoon mayonnaise. Place 1 patty on bottom half of each bun; top each with ¼ cup onion jam and bun top. Yield: 4 servings (serving size: 1 burger).

CALORIES 395; FAT 13.9g (sat 5.7g, mono 5.2g, poly 1.6g); PROTEIN 33.8g; CARB 36.1g; FIBER 3g; CHOL 75mg; IRON 3.3mg; SODIUM 696mg; CALC 190mg

Sausage, Pepper, and Mushroom Pizza
·····················•30 minutes

Sautéed broccoli rabe brings pleasant bitter notes to the meal. Bring lightly salted water to a boil in a large saucepan. Add 4 cups chopped broccoli rabe; cook 2 minutes. Drain and rinse with cold water; drain well. Heat a large nonstick skillet over medium-high heat. Add 1 tablespoon olive oil to pan; swirl to coat. Add broccoli rabe and ¼ teaspoon crushed red pepper to pan; sauté 2 minutes or until thoroughly heated. Sprinkle with ¼ teaspoon salt.

- 1 (4-ounce) sweet Italian sausage link
- 1 cup thinly sliced onion
- ½ cup thinly sliced red bell pepper
- 1 (8-ounce) package presliced exotic mushroom blend (such as shiitake, cremini, and oyster)
- 2 garlic cloves, minced
- 1 (14-ounce) prepared pizza crust (such as Boboli)
- ½ cup fat-free pasta sauce
- ¾ cup (3 ounces) shredded part-skim mozzarella cheese
- 2 tablespoons thinly sliced fresh basil

❶ Preheat oven to 450°.
❷ Remove casing from sausage. Cook sausage in a large nonstick skillet over medium-high heat until browned, stirring to crumble. Add onion, pepper, and mushrooms to pan; sauté 8 minutes or until tender. Stir in garlic; sauté 1 minute. Place crust on a large baking sheet. Spread pasta sauce evenly over crust, leaving a ¼-inch border. Top evenly with mushroom mixture. Sprinkle evenly with cheese. Bake at 450° for 8 minutes. Remove from oven; sprinkle evenly with basil. Cut pizza into 8 wedges. Yield: 4 servings (serving size: 2 wedges).

CALORIES 400; FAT 10.9g (sat 4.6g, mono 4.7g, poly 0.9g); PROTEIN 23.8g; CARB 52g; FIBER 3g; CHOL 20mg; IRON 3.5mg; SODIUM 943mg; CALC 451mg

Roast Chicken Salad with Peaches, Goat Cheese, and Pecans
·····················•30 minutes

Serve with herbed bread. Unroll the dough from a (13.8-ounce) can refrigerated pizza crust. Fold dough in half; pat into a 9-inch square. Let rest 15 minutes. Brush dough with 1 tablespoon extra-virgin olive oil. Sprinkle evenly with 2 teaspoons chopped fresh thyme, 2 teaspoons chopped fresh rosemary, ¼ teaspoon kosher salt, and ¼ teaspoon freshly ground black pepper. Bake at 350° for 11 minutes or until golden.

- 2½ tablespoons balsamic vinegar
- 1½ tablespoons extra-virgin olive oil
- 1½ tablespoons minced shallots
- 2½ teaspoons fresh lemon juice
- 2½ teaspoons maple syrup
- ¾ teaspoon Dijon mustard
- ¼ teaspoon kosher salt
- ¼ teaspoon freshly ground black pepper
- 2 cups shredded skinless, boneless rotisserie chicken breast
- 2 cups sliced peeled peaches
- ½ cup vertically sliced red onion
- ¼ cup chopped pecans, toasted
- 1 (5-ounce) package gourmet salad greens
- 2 tablespoons crumbled goat cheese

❶ Combine first 8 ingredients; stir with a whisk.
❷ Combine chicken and next 4 ingredients in a large bowl. Add vinegar mixture; toss gently. Sprinkle with cheese. Yield: 4 servings (serving size: about 1¾ cups salad and 1½ teaspoons cheese).

CALORIES 285; FAT 14g (sat 2.4g, mono 7.8g, poly 2.8g); PROTEIN 24.6g; CARB 16g; FIBER 2.9g; CHOL 61mg; IRON 1.9mg; SODIUM 203mg; CALC 54mg

Beef and Sugar Snap Stir-Fry

··*30 minutes*

(pictured on page 226)

Serve this quick stir-fry over steamed rice with green onions to round out your meal. Cook 1 cup white rice according to package directions, omitting salt and fat. Remove from heat; stir in ¾ cup chopped green onions and 1 teaspoon toasted sesame seeds.

  3 tablespoons rice vinegar, divided
  2 tablespoons low-sodium soy sauce, divided
  1 (1-pound) flank steak, trimmed and thinly sliced across grain
  2 teaspoons sugar
  2 teaspoons hoisin sauce
  ¼ teaspoon salt
  ¼ teaspoon crushed red pepper
  2 teaspoons toasted sesame oil, divided
  1 cup chopped onion
  1 teaspoon bottled minced ginger
  ½ teaspoon minced garlic
  1 cup chopped red bell pepper
  ½ cup matchstick-cut carrot
  1 (8-ounce) package fresh sugar snap peas
  ⅓ cup chopped green onions

❶ Combine 1 tablespoon vinegar, 1 tablespoon soy sauce, and beef in a large bowl. Combine remaining 2 tablespoons vinegar, remaining 1 tablespoon soy sauce, sugar, and next 3 ingredients in a small bowl; stir with a whisk.
❷ Heat a large nonstick skillet over medium-high heat. Add 1 teaspoon oil to pan, and swirl to coat. Add beef mixture to pan; stir-fry 2 minutes or until done. Place beef mixture in a bowl. Heat remaining 1 teaspoon oil in pan over medium-high heat. Add onion to pan, and sauté 1 minute. Add ginger and garlic; sauté 15 seconds. Stir in bell pepper, carrot, and peas; sauté 3 minutes. Add vinegar mixture and beef mixture to pan; cook 2 minutes or until thoroughly heated. Remove from heat; stir in green onions. Yield: 4 servings (serving size: 1½ cups).

CALORIES 254; FAT 8.2g (sat 2.7g, mono 2.2g, poly 0.4g); PROTEIN 26.6g; CARB 16.7g; FIBER 3.4g; CHOL 37mg; IRON 2.7mg; SODIUM 526mg; CALC 63mg

Chicken, Mushroom, and Gruyère Quesadillas

··*30 minutes*

Watermelon-jicama salad is a refreshing side dish. Combine 4 cups (½-inch) cubed seedless watermelon, 1½ cups (½-inch) cubed peeled jicama, 1 cup chopped English cucumber, and ½ cup chopped red onion. Add 2 tablespoons fresh lemon juice, 2 teaspoons sugar, and 1 teaspoon olive oil, and toss well.

  1 teaspoon olive oil
  1 cup presliced mushrooms
  ½ cup thinly sliced onion
  ⅛ teaspoon salt
  ⅛ teaspoon freshly ground black pepper
  1 teaspoon bottled minced garlic
  1 tablespoon sherry or red wine vinegar
  2 (10-inch) fat-free flour tortillas
  1 cup shredded cooked chicken breast (about 8 ounces)
  1 cup arugula
  ½ cup (2 ounces) shredded Gruyère cheese
     Cooking spray

❶ Heat a large nonstick skillet over medium-high heat. Add oil to pan, and swirl to coat. Add mushrooms and next 3 ingredients to pan; sauté 5 minutes. Stir in garlic; sauté 30 seconds. Add vinegar, and cook 30 seconds or until liquid almost evaporates.
❷ Arrange half of mushroom mixture over half of each tortilla. Top each tortilla with ½ cup chicken, ½ cup arugula, and ¼ cup cheese; fold tortillas in half.
❸ Wipe pan clean with a paper towel. Heat pan over medium heat. Coat pan with cooking spray. Add tortillas to pan. Place a heavy skillet on top of tortillas; cook 2 minutes on each side or until crisp. Yield: 4 servings (serving size: ½ quesadilla).

CALORIES 270; FAT 8.9g (sat 3.7g, mono 3g, poly 0.8g); PROTEIN 25.2g; CARB 20.3g; FIBER 3g; CHOL 64mg; IRON 1.7mg; SODIUM 391mg; CALC 242mg

Choice Ingredient: Jicama

Learn: Jicama (HEE-kah-ma) is an edible root that resembles a turnip. It has thin brown skin and crisp, juicy, white flesh that's mild in flavor (think of a cross between a water chestnut and a pear). Jicama is native to Mexico, where it's sometimes referred to as yam bean, Mexican turnip, or Mexican potato. The plant is a member of the bean family, and its vine can grow up to 20 feet in length. (The root is the only edible portion of the plant, though; its leaves and seeds contain a mild toxin.) In Central America, jicama is often sold by street vendors, eaten raw, and seasoned with lemon or lime juice and chili powder.

Purchase: Find jicama year-round in the produce section of many supermarkets and Latin American markets. Select firm, dry jicama roots. The skin should not appear shriveled, bruised, or blemished.

Use: Remove skin with a sharp vegetable peeler, then cut the white flesh into cubes or strips according to your recipe. Because jicama does not brown or become soggy after cutting, it makes a nice addition to crudité platters and salads. It's also good added raw to sushi rolls in place of cucumber for crunch, or included in stir-fries as it performs best with quick-cooking methods that allow it to maintain crispness.

Store: Store jicama unpeeled in a plastic bag in the refrigerator for up to two weeks.

Barbecue Chicken with Mustard Glaze
························· *40 minutes*

An assortment of spices mixed with common condiments makes a thick, tangy-sweet glaze with a hint of smokiness. Grilled summer squash makes a light, fresh side. Cut 2 zucchini and 1 yellow squash lengthwise into ¼-inch-thick slices. Brush with 2 teaspoons olive oil; sprinkle with ¼ teaspoon salt and ⅛ teaspoon freshly ground black pepper. Grill 3 minutes on each side or until tender.

- 2 tablespoons dark brown sugar
- 2 teaspoons garlic powder
- 2 teaspoons chili powder
- 1 teaspoon smoked paprika
- ½ teaspoon salt
- ¼ cup ketchup
- 1 tablespoon dark brown sugar
- 1 tablespoon sherry or red wine vinegar
- 1 tablespoon Dijon mustard
- 8 (6-ounce) skinless, bone-in chicken thighs
- Cooking spray

1 Combine first 5 ingredients in a small bowl. Combine ketchup and next 3 ingredients in a small bowl; stir with a whisk.
2 Heat a large grill pan over medium-high heat. Rub spice mixture evenly over chicken thighs. Coat pan with cooking spray. Add chicken to pan; cook 12 minutes. Turn chicken over. Brush with half of ketchup mixture; cook 12 minutes. Turn chicken over. Brush with remaining ketchup mixture; cook 2 minutes or until a thermometer registers 165°. Yield: 4 servings (serving size: 2 chicken thighs).

CALORIES 226; FAT 5.5g (sat 1.4g, mono 1.7g, poly 1.4g); PROTEIN 27.7g; CARB 15.4g; FIBER 0.4g; CHOL 115mg; IRON 1.9mg; SODIUM 651mg; CALC 28mg

When purchasing ingredients for Corn, Clam, and Mussel Chowder, look for mussels with tightly closed shells.

Corn, Clam, and Mussel Chowder
························· *40 minutes*

A tomato and fennel salad completes the meal. Combine 4 cups torn romaine lettuce, 1 cup halved cherry tomatoes, and 1 cup sliced fennel bulb in a large bowl. Combine 1½ tablespoons balsamic vinegar, 2 teaspoons honey, 1 teaspoon Dijon mustard, ¼ teaspoon salt, and ⅛ teaspoon freshly ground black pepper in a small bowl. Gradually add 1 tablespoon extra-virgin olive oil, stirring constantly with a whisk. Pour vinaigrette over lettuce mixture; toss well.

- 2 bacon slices, chopped
- 1 cup chopped onion
- ¾ cup chopped celery
- ¾ teaspoon chopped fresh thyme
- 2 cups diced red potato
- 2 (8-ounce) bottles clam juice
- 2 cups fresh corn kernels
- 20 mussels (about 1 pound), scrubbed and debearded
- ¾ cup half-and-half
- ½ cup 2% reduced-fat milk
- 3 tablespoons all-purpose flour
- 2 (6½-ounce) cans minced clams, liquid reserved
- ¼ teaspoon salt
- Thyme sprigs (optional)

1 Heat a large Dutch oven over medium heat. Add bacon to pan; cook 5 minutes or until browned, stirring occasionally. Add onion, celery, and chopped thyme to pan; cook 8 minutes or until softened, stirring frequently. Add potato and bottled juice; bring to a boil. Reduce heat to medium-low; cook, covered, 9 minutes or until potatoes are tender.
2 Stir in corn and mussels; bring to a boil. Cover and cook 5 minutes or until mussels open; discard any unopened shells. Combine half-and-half, milk, and flour in a small bowl; stir with a whisk. Stir half-and-half mixture and clams into pan; cook 2 minutes or until slightly thickened. Stir in 2 tablespoons reserved clam liquid and salt. Garnish with thyme sprigs, if desired. Yield: 6 servings (serving size: 1½ cups).

CALORIES 233; FAT 7.3g (sat 3.4g, mono 1.7g, poly 1.4g); PROTEIN 14.3g; CARB 29.6g; FIBER 3g; CHOL 37mg; IRON 3.6mg; SODIUM 674mg; CALC 99mg

Pick a Bouquet of Basil

The season's most versatile herb will enliven your cooking. Here's how to use it with abandon.

MAKE AHEAD
Lime Basil Sorbet

A traditional salt and ice electric freezer works best for this sorbet, as opposed to a tabletop freezer, which won't freeze the mixture firmly enough. Use sweet Italian or lemon basil.

1½ cups sugar
2 cups fresh lime juice, divided (about 15 limes)
½ cup light-colored corn syrup
¾ cup packed fresh basil leaves, coarsely chopped
2 cups water
1 tablespoon grated lime rind
Finely grated lime rind (optional)

1 Combine sugar, 1 cup juice, and corn syrup in a medium saucepan over medium-high heat. Cook 2 minutes or until sugar melts, stirring constantly. Stir in basil. Cook 30 seconds. Remove from heat. Pour mixture into a bowl. Add remaining 1 cup juice, 2 cups water, and 1 tablespoon rind. Cover and chill. Strain mixture through a fine sieve; discard solids. Pour mixture into a freezer can of an ice-cream freezer; freeze according to manufacturer's instructions. Spoon mixture into a freezer-safe container; cover and freeze 1 hour or until firm. Garnish with finely grated rind, if desired. Yield: 8 servings (serving size: ½ cup).

CALORIES 220; FAT 0.1g (sat 0g, mono 0g, poly 0.1g); PROTEIN 0.4g; CARB 58.7g; FIBER 0.5g; CHOL 0mg; IRON 0.2mg; SODIUM 14mg; CALC 19mg

STAFF FAVORITE
Phyllo Pizza with Feta, Basil, and Tomatoes

Salty cheese, tomatoes, and basil make this a savory treat. Pair with a tossed green salad for a light summer supper.

½ cup (2 ounces) shredded part-skim mozzarella cheese
½ cup (2 ounces) finely crumbled reduced-fat feta cheese
¼ cup (1 ounce) grated fresh Parmigiano-Reggiano cheese
1 tablespoon chopped fresh oregano
¼ teaspoon salt
⅛ teaspoon freshly ground black pepper
10 (18 x 14-inch) sheets frozen phyllo dough, thawed
Cooking spray
2 cups thinly sliced plum tomato
⅓ cup thinly sliced green onions
¼ cup fresh basil leaves

1 Preheat oven to 375°.
2 Combine first 6 ingredients in a bowl.
3 Cut phyllo sheets in half crosswise. Working with 1 phyllo sheet half at a time (cover remaining dough to keep from drying), place phyllo sheet on a baking sheet coated with cooking spray. Coat phyllo sheet with cooking spray. Repeat with 2 more layers of phyllo. Sprinkle with 2 tablespoons cheese mixture. Repeat layers 5 times, ending with 2 phyllo sheets. Coat top phyllo sheet with cooking spray; sprinkle with 2 tablespoons cheese mixture. Pat tomato slices with a paper towel. Arrange tomato slices on top of cheese, leaving a 1-inch border. Sprinkle with onions and remaining 6 tablespoons cheese mixture. Bake at 375° for 20 minutes or until golden. Sprinkle with basil leaves. Yield: 6 servings (serving size: 2 slices).

CALORIES 195; FAT 6.7g (sat 3.2g, mono 2.1g, poly 0.5g); PROTEIN 9.3g; CARB 24.6g; FIBER 1.9g; CHOL 11mg; IRON 1.7mg; SODIUM 526mg; CALC 158mg

WINE NOTE: A good wine for this dish won't overwhelm the delicate phyllo but will stand up to the salty cheeses and fresh basil. A favorite that fills the bill: Veramonte Sauvignon Blanc Reserva from the Casablanca Valley of Chile. The 2008 is $11.

Best Bets with Basil

There are more than 60 types of basil, all members of the mint family. Here are three you're most likely to see at gourmet groceries, farmers' markets, and nurseries.

Purple Opal
What to know: Its large, dark purple leaves offer mildly spicy hints of clove, licorice, mint, and cinnamon.
Best uses: Its complexity shines in salads, baked goods, and beverages.

Sweet Italian
What to know: This selection (aka Sweet Genovese) is the most common variety of basil, known for its licorice-clove flavor.
Best uses: Its clean, bright flavor makes it an ideal match for fresh tomatoes, or use it in Italian or Thai dishes.

Thai
What to know: Its small, pointed leaves with serrated edges have a peppery anise flavor.
Best uses: A hint of spicy heat makes this basil at home in Asian dishes.

Basil Parmesan Dip with Pita Chips

Basil and Parmesan are a classic flavor combination typically found in pesto. We've added sour cream to create a creamy alternative to snack on.

    4   (6-inch) pitas
        Cooking spray
    ½   teaspoon freshly ground black
        pepper, divided
    ¼   teaspoon salt
    1   cup lightly packed fresh basil leaves
        (about ½ ounce)
    ¾   cup finely grated Parmigiano-
        Reggiano cheese
    ¾   cup reduced-fat sour cream
    2   teaspoons fresh lemon juice
    1   garlic clove, minced
        Basil sprigs (optional)

1 Preheat oven to 375°.
2 Split pitas; cut each half into 8 wedges. Place wedges on a baking sheet. Coat with cooking spray, and sprinkle with ¼ teaspoon pepper and salt. Bake at 375° for 12 minutes or until crisp.
3 Place remaining ¼ teaspoon pepper, basil, and next 4 ingredients in a blender or food processor; process until smooth. Scrape into a serving bowl using a rubber spatula. Garnish with basil sprigs, if desired. Serve with pita chips. Yield: 8 servings (serving size: 2½ tablespoons dip and 8 pita chips).

CALORIES 153; FAT 5.3g (sat 3.1g, mono 0.7g, poly 0.3g); PROTEIN 6.8g; CARB 19.1g; FIBER 0.9g; CHOL 18mg; IRON 1.1mg; SODIUM 362mg; CALC 156mg

Sicilian Pesto

Pesto is a sure sign of summer in Italy's Liguria region, where sweet basil grows in fragrant fields. Farther south, in Sicily, the locals add crushed red pepper and chopped tomatoes to their pesto. It's nice served with crusty bread or tossed with hot pasta and shrimp or poultry.

    ¼   cup pine nuts
    3   garlic cloves
    4   cups loosely packed fresh basil
        leaves (about 2 ounces)
    ¼   cup extra-virgin olive oil
    ½   teaspoon kosher salt
    ¼   teaspoon freshly ground black
        pepper
    ⅛   teaspoon crushed red pepper
    ½   cup (2 ounces) grated fresh
        Parmigiano-Reggiano cheese
    2   cups chopped seeded tomato,
        drained (about 2 large)

1 Heat a small skillet over medium heat. Add nuts to pan; cook 4 minutes or until lightly toasted, stirring constantly. Remove from pan.
2 Place nuts and garlic in a food processor; process until minced. Add basil and next 4 ingredients; process until blended, scraping sides occasionally. Add cheese; process until smooth. Spoon into a bowl; fold in tomato. Yield: 20 servings (serving size: 2 tablespoons).

CALORIES 51; FAT 4.6g (sat 0.8g, mono 2.7g, poly 0.9g); PROTEIN 1.4g; CARB 1.5g; FIBER 0.6g; CHOL 1mg; IRON 0.4mg; SODIUM 82mg; CALC 41mg

Purple Basil Lemonade

In this recipe, basil is crushed with sugar to release the oils. If you don't have a mortar and pestle, process the basil, sugar, and about ¼ cup of the water in a food processor or blender.

    4   cups water
    ½   cup fresh lemon juice
    ½   cup loosely packed fresh purple
        basil leaves (about ¼ ounce)
    6   tablespoons sugar
    4   cups ice
    4   fresh purple basil sprigs

1 Combine 4 cups water and juice in a large bowl. Place ½ cup basil and sugar in a mortar; pound with pestle until a paste forms. Add sugar mixture to juice mixture; stir until sugar dissolves. Strain mixture through a sieve over a bowl; discard solids. Place 1 cup ice in each of 4 glasses. Pour about 1 cup lemonade into each glass; garnish each serving with 1 basil sprig. Yield: 4 servings.

CALORIES 82; FAT 0g; PROTEIN 0.3g; CARB 21.6g; FIBER 0.4g; CHOL 0mg; IRON 0.2mg; SODIUM 5mg; CALC 16mg

Produce tip

Save the Bounty. Fresh basil is best used within a couple of days after harvest. You can dry it, but these methods better preserve its flavor:

- Puree basil with a little olive oil in a food processor (or prepare pesto). Freeze in ice cube trays; store the pesto cubes in a heavy-duty zip-top plastic bag in the freezer for up to 3 months.
- Layer whole leaves in a jar, sprinkling each layer with a little salt, and cover with olive oil. Refrigerate for up to 3 months.

Purple Basil Parmesan Biscuits

(pictured on page 227)

Chopped purple basil flecks these biscuits with color. Standard sweet Italian basil would do as well. For tender biscuits, stop cutting the butter into the dough when the mixture has pea-size nuggets.

    9   ounces all-purpose flour
        (about 2 cups)
    2   tablespoons sugar
    4   teaspoons baking powder
    1   teaspoon salt
    ¼   cup chilled butter, cut into small
        pieces
    ⅔   cup chopped fresh purple basil
    ½   cup (2 ounces) finely grated
        Parmigiano-Reggiano cheese
    ⅔   cup fat-free milk
    1   large egg
        Cooking spray

❶ Preheat oven to 425°.
❷ Weigh or lightly spoon flour into dry measuring cups; level with a knife. Combine flour and next 3 ingredients in a medium bowl, stirring with a whisk. Cut in butter with a pastry blender or 2 knives until mixture resembles coarse meal. Stir in basil and cheese. Combine milk and egg in a small bowl, stirring with a whisk. Add milk mixture to flour mixture; stir just until moist. Turn dough out onto a floured surface; pat to 1-inch-thick circle. Cut with a 2-inch biscuit cutter into 12 biscuits. Place biscuits on a baking sheet coated with cooking spray. Bake at 425° for 15 minutes. Remove from oven, and cool. Yield: 12 biscuits (serving size: 1 biscuit).

CALORIES 145; FAT 5.4g (sat 3.2g, mono 1.3g, poly 0.3g); PROTEIN 4.6g; CARB 19.5g; FIBER 0.7g; CHOL 31mg; IRON 1.3mg; SODIUM 448mg; CALC 156mg

Reader Recipes

A schoolteacher turned cooking instructor scores top marks for an Asian-inspired pasta dish. *Plus*, burgers, salmon salad, cookies, and more.

Amy Sokol made a career as an elementary school teacher in San Antonio, but she became a self-taught "foodie" outside the classroom. She no longer separates work and play. Combining her love of cooking with her teaching experience, she launched a business called Cooking with Care. "I teach people how to make simple, healthy meals, both in my home and at nearby grocery and kitchenware stores," she says.

Sokol's passion for cooking motivated her to create this quick and easy Asian-inspired dish. "My two daughters love yakisoba noodles at our local sushi restaurant. I figured I could make a lighter version at home for less money." When Sokol found soba noodles at the grocery store, she was delighted to learn they are made of buckwheat, "a healthful way for our family to enjoy pasta at dinner," she says. "I've taught this recipe in my classes, and it always goes over well."

Soba Noodles with Chicken and Vegetables

"I love to experiment with the variety of Asian condiments I keep on hand. It's more economical and healthier to use small amounts of a few sauces than using a bottled stir-fry sauce. I serve this with a fruit salad of pineapple, mango, and kiwifruit. If you prefer a vegetable side dish, steamed sugar snap peas or snow peas are a great choice."

—Amy Sokol,
San Antonio, Texas

    ½   cup fat-free, less-sodium chicken
        broth
    3   tablespoons low-sodium soy sauce
    2   tablespoons oyster sauce
    2   tablespoons mirin (sweet rice wine)
    1   teaspoon Sriracha (hot chile sauce,
        such as Huy Fong)
    1   (12-ounce) package soba
        (buckwheat noodles)
    1   tablespoon canola oil
    1   teaspoon minced garlic
    1   teaspoon grated peeled fresh ginger
    1   pound chicken breast tenders,
        cut into bite-sized pieces
    2   large zucchini, cut into julienne
        strips (about 2 cups)
    1   large carrot, cut into julienne strips
    1   tablespoon sesame seeds, toasted

❶ Combine first 5 ingredients in a bowl.
❷ Prepare noodles according to package directions, omitting salt and fat. Drain and rinse with cold water; drain.
❸ Heat oil in a large nonstick skillet over medium-high heat. Add garlic, ginger, and chicken to pan; sauté 3 minutes, stirring constantly. Add broth mixture, zucchini, and carrot; cook 3 minutes, stirring constantly. Add noodles; cook 2 minutes or until thoroughly heated, tossing well. Sprinkle with sesame seeds. Yield: 6 servings (serving size: 1⅓ cups noodle mixture and ½ teaspoon seeds).

CALORIES 353; FAT 5.2g (sat 0.8g, mono 2.2g, poly 1.6g); PROTEIN 25.7g; CARB 47.4g; FIBER 2.4g; CHOL 44mg; IRON 4mg; SODIUM 754mg; CALC 29mg

Casual Mexican Meal Menu
serves 6

Serve this stress-free menu to your family on a busy weeknight, or present it to guests at a relaxed backyard get-together. Enjoy corn tortillas as a breadlike side, or spoon the shrimp mixture into them for hearty tacos.

Grilled Fiesta Shrimp

Glazed grilled pineapple

Combine 2 tablespoons dark brown sugar, ½ teaspoon grated lime rind, 1 tablespoon fresh lime juice, and 1 tablespoon melted butter in a small saucepan; cook over medium heat 2 minutes or until syrupy. Cut 1 trimmed, cored pineapple lengthwise into 12 long spears. Place pineapple on a grill rack coated with cooking spray. Brush half of glaze over pineapple; grill 1 to 2 minutes. Turn pineapple over; brush with remaining glaze, and grill 1 to 2 minutes.

Corn tortillas

Margaritas

Mango sorbet

QUICK & EASY
Grilled Fiesta Shrimp

"Sometimes my husband and I like to add a dash of ground red pepper to the shrimp to turn up the heat."

—Marchelle Falkner, Birmingham, Alabama

2 pounds large shrimp, peeled and deveined
1 tablespoon olive oil
2 teaspoons Creole seasoning, divided
½ cup (2 ounces) preshredded Mexican-blend or Cheddar cheese
½ cup drained canned whole-kernel corn with sweet peppers (such as Green Giant)
3 tablespoons chopped fresh cilantro
1 (15-ounce) can black beans, rinsed and drained
4 cups hot cooked long-grain rice

① Prepare grill to medium-high heat.
② Arrange shrimp in center of a large piece of heavy-duty aluminum foil. Drizzle oil over shrimp; sprinkle with 1 teaspoon Creole seasoning, tossing to coat. Top shrimp with cheese and next 3 ingredients; sprinkle with the remaining 1 teaspoon Creole seasoning. Fold opposite ends of foil together; crimp to seal.
③ Place foil packet on prepared grill; cover and cook 15 minutes or until shrimp are done. Serve over hot cooked rice. Yield: 6 servings (serving size: about ¾ cup of the shrimp mixture and about ⅔ cup rice).

CALORIES 391; FAT 8.3g (sat 2.9g, mono 2.6g, poly 1.3g); PROTEIN 37.6g; CARB 40.3g; FIBER 2.9g; CHOL 238mg; IRON 5.6mg; SODIUM 687mg; CALC 160mg

Pancetta and Swiss Cheese–Stuffed Burgers with Pesto Mayonnaise

"This is my answer to the bacon cheeseburgers we were eating way too often at our house. Stuffing the burger allows you to use a smaller amount of high-fat ingredients but in a way that still makes a big impact. And as far as my husband is concerned, stuffing anything with bacon is never a bad idea."

—Jill Simmons, Suisun City, California

Cooking spray
1 ounce pancetta, chopped into ¼-inch pieces (about 2 slices)
⅓ cup diced onion
2 garlic cloves, minced
½ teaspoon freshly ground black pepper
¼ teaspoon salt
¼ teaspoon dried Italian seasoning
1 pound ground round
½ cup (2 ounces) shredded reduced-fat Swiss cheese (such as Sargento)
3 tablespoons light mayonnaise
1 tablespoon commercial pesto
4 (2-ounce) whole-wheat hamburger buns

① Prepare grill or broiler.
② Heat a large nonstick skillet over medium heat. Coat pan with cooking spray. Add pancetta to pan; cook 4 minutes or until crisp. Remove pancetta from pan, reserving drippings in pan; set pancetta aside. Add onion and garlic to pan; cook 5 minutes or until softened, stirring frequently. Combine onion mixture, pepper, and next 3 ingredients in a bowl. Shape beef mixture into 8 (¼-inch-thick) patties. Top each of 4 patties with pancetta and 2 tablespoons Swiss cheese, leaving a ¼-inch border around edge. Top with remaining 4 patties; pinch edges to seal.
③ Place patties on grill rack or broiler pan coated with cooking spray; cook 5 minutes. Turn and cook 5 minutes or until a meat thermometer inserted in center measures 160°. Combine mayonnaise and pesto. Spread about 1 tablespoon of mayonnaise mixture on bottom half of each bun. Top each serving with 1 patty and top half of bun. Yield: 4 servings (serving size: 1 burger).

CALORIES 444; FAT 18.3g (sat 6.2g, mono 7.3g, poly 3.1g); PROTEIN 39.9g; CARB 30g; FIBER 3.4g; CHOL 82mg; IRON 4.4mg; SODIUM 687mg; CALC 229mg

Grilled Salmon and Spinach Salad

"This meal is perfect for the summer. It's an attractive dish to serve guests, too. The sweet citrus vinaigrette can be made earlier in the day and stored in the refrigerator."

—Arlene Ghent,
New Haven, Connecticut

VINAIGRETTE:
- ¼ cup fresh orange juice
- 2 tablespoons olive oil
- 2 tablespoons balsamic blend seasoned rice vinegar (such as Nakano)
- ½ teaspoon honey mustard
- ½ teaspoon black pepper
- 1 garlic clove, minced

SALAD:
- 2 tablespoons fresh lemon juice
- 4 (6-ounce) salmon fillets (about 1 inch thick)
- 2 teaspoons black pepper
- Cooking spray
- 1 (6-ounce) package fresh spinach
- 4 oranges, each peeled and cut into 6 slices

❶ Preheat grill to medium-high heat.
❷ To prepare vinaigrette, combine first 6 ingredients in a large bowl; stir well with a whisk.
❸ To prepare salad, drizzle lemon juice over fillets; sprinkle with 2 teaspoons pepper. Place fillets, skin sides up, on a grill rack coated with cooking spray; grill 5 minutes on each side or until fish flakes easily when tested with a fork or until desired degree of doneness. Remove skin from fillets; discard.
❹ Add spinach to vinaigrette in bowl; toss well. Place 2 cups spinach mixture on each of 4 serving plates; arrange 1 fillet and 6 orange slices on top of greens. Yield: 4 servings.

CALORIES 474; FAT 25.7g (sat 4.7g, mono 11.6g, poly 7.7g); PROTEIN 36.2g; CARB 27.5g; FIBER 8.4g; CHOL 100mg; IRON 2.5mg; SODIUM 286mg; CALC 129mg

---

MAKE AHEAD • FREEZABLE

Banana-Oatmeal Chocolate Chip Cookies

"Mashed ripe banana adds sweetness and flavor to these chocolate chip cookies. I found I could reduce the usual amount of sugar and butter."

—Cathy Brixen,
Phoenix, Arizona

- ½ cup mashed ripe banana (about 1 medium)
- ½ cup packed brown sugar
- ¼ cup butter, softened
- ¼ cup granulated sugar
- 1 teaspoon vanilla extract
- 1 large egg
- 5.6 ounces all-purpose flour (about 1¼ cups)
- 2 cups old-fashioned oats
- 1 teaspoon baking soda
- ½ teaspoon salt
- ½ cup semisweet chocolate chips
- Cooking spray

❶ Preheat oven to 350°.
❷ Combine first 5 ingredients in a large bowl; beat with a mixer at medium speed until smooth. Add egg; beat well.
❸ Weigh or lightly spoon flour into dry measuring cups; level with a knife. Combine flour and next 3 ingredients in a medium bowl, stirring with a whisk. Add flour mixture to banana mixture in bowl; beat with a mixer at medium speed until well blended. Stir in chocolate chips.
❹ Drop batter by heaping tablespoonfuls 2 inches apart onto baking sheets coated with cooking spray. Bake at 350° for 18 minutes or until golden. Cool on pans 2 minutes. Remove cookies from pans; cool completely on wire racks. Yield: 2 dozen (serving size: 1 cookie).

CALORIES 115; FAT 3.6g (sat 2g, mono 1.1g, poly 0.3g); PROTEIN 2g; CARB 19.1g; FIBER 1.2g; CHOL 14mg; IRON 0.9mg; SODIUM 121mg; CALC 10mg

---

Apricot-Glazed Chicken Thighs

"I adapted this recipe from one of my family's favorite holiday appetizers for roasted chicken wings. They loved the glaze, so I tested it with bone-in chicken thighs. Now it's one of my go-to recipes for cookouts all summer long."

—Mary Bone,
Little Rock, Arkansas

- Cooking spray
- ½ teaspoon minced garlic
- ¾ cup apricot-pineapple preserves
- 1 tablespoon white vinegar
- ½ teaspoon dried rosemary, crushed
- ¼ teaspoon onion powder
- ¼ teaspoon dried oregano
- ¾ teaspoon salt, divided
- ¼ teaspoon pepper, divided
- 12 chicken thighs (about 4 pounds), skinned

❶ Preheat grill.
❷ Heat a small saucepan over medium-high heat. Coat pan with cooking spray. Add garlic to pan; cook 30 seconds. Stir in preserves and next 4 ingredients, and bring mixture to a boil. Reduce heat, and cook 5 minutes, stirring occasionally. Stir in ¼ teaspoon salt and ⅛ teaspoon pepper.
❸ Sprinkle chicken with remaining ½ teaspoon salt and ⅛ teaspoon pepper. Combine chicken and ½ cup preserves mixture in a large bowl; toss well to coat. Arrange chicken on a grill rack coated with cooking spray; grill 5 minutes. Turn chicken thighs over, and brush chicken with remaining ¼ cup preserves mixture. Grill an additional 5 minutes or until done. Yield: 6 servings (serving size: 2 thighs).

CALORIES 266; FAT 5.4g (sat 1.4g, mono 1.7g, poly 1.3g); PROTEIN 27.2g; CARB 26.3g; FIBER 0.1g; CHOL 115mg; IRON 1.5mg; SODIUM 414mg; CALC 17mg

The Summer Pleasures of Fresh Trout

Line-caught or supermarket-bought, trout is a prize worth savoring. Our recipes cast this fine fish in seven sensational dishes.

FOR MANY AVID FLY FISHERMEN, the pursuit of trout is far more important than dining on the catch. In places such as Montana's Rock Creek, east of Missoula, a July day of casting and netting the cutthroat, rainbow, brook, and brown trout that run thick in the stream is supremely satisfying.

"People say if God were to design a trout stream, it would look like Rock Creek," says Joe Sowerby, outfitter for Montana Fly Fishing Connection. Much of the fishing here is catch-and-release, and Sowerby says that's fine; he's in it for the love of the sport. He relishes the art of casting a line and the knowledge required to identify which insects the trout prefer. "It's a very primal challenge—to fool the trout," Sowerby says.

"There is also the solitude. You leave the cell phone behind, stare at a stretch of water, and lose yourself for the day." But for the rest of us, the joy is in the eating. And in the summer, fresh trout is plentiful in markets. What you'll find is typically farm-raised (see "Selection Tips," at right). Fresh trout has an incredibly mild, slightly sweet flavor that our simple, quick-to-prepare recipes highlight. Whether you grill, roast, pan-fry, steam, smoke, or sauté trout, it's a deliciously adaptable choice, and you'll savor the results.

STAFF FAVORITE • QUICK & EASY
Pan-Fried Trout with Fresh Herb Salad

We use flat-leaf parsley, tarragon, basil, and chives for the salad, but you can use any combination of your favorite herbs. Serve with lemon slices, if you like.

- 4 (6-ounce) trout fillets
- ½ teaspoon salt
- ¼ teaspoon freshly ground black pepper
- 1 tablespoon extra-virgin olive oil, divided
- Cooking spray
- 1½ cups mixed fresh herbs
- 1 tablespoon fresh lemon juice
- ⅛ teaspoon salt

① Score skin side of fish. Sprinkle fish with ½ teaspoon salt and pepper. Heat 1 teaspoon oil in a large cast-iron or non-stick skillet coated with cooking spray over medium heat. Add fish, skin sides down, to pan; cook 4 minutes or until skin is crisp. Turn fish over; cook 1 minute or until fish flakes easily when tested with a fork or until desired degree of doneness.

② Combine herbs, remaining 2 teaspoons oil, juice, and ⅛ teaspoon salt in a medium bowl; toss gently to coat. Serve salad over fish. Yield: 4 servings (serving size: 1 fillet and about ⅓ cup salad).

CALORIES 219; FAT 8.8g (sat 2.9g, mono 3.9g, poly 0.9g); PROTEIN 33.5g; CARB 1.9g; FIBER 0.6g; CHOL 74mg; IRON 3.2mg; SODIUM 469mg; CALC 45mg

MAKE AHEAD
Smoked Trout, Watercress, and Orange Salad

Peppery watercress and sweet oranges play beautifully off the rich flavor of smoked trout.

- ½ cup vertically sliced red onion
- 1 teaspoon grated orange rind
- ⅓ cup fresh orange juice (about 2 oranges)
- 1 tablespoon extra-virgin olive oil
- ⅛ teaspoon salt
- 6 cups trimmed watercress (about 3 ounces)
- 1½ cups Smoked Trout (page 187)
- 1 cup orange sections (about 2 oranges)

① Combine first 5 ingredients in a large bowl. Add watercress and remaining ingredients; toss gently to coat. Yield: 4 servings (serving size: about 1½ cups).

CALORIES 169; FAT 5.7g (sat 1.5g, mono 3.1g, poly 0.6g); PROTEIN 15.2g; CARB 15.9g; FIBER 2.1g; CHOL 31mg; IRON 1.4mg; SODIUM 407mg; CALC 73mg

Selection Tips

In the wild, common trout varieties include brown, brook, and rainbow. In the market, however, you'll likely find farm-raised rainbow trout. Occasionally fishmongers offer wild trout, which is probably from saltwater sources rather than lakes or streams. Seagoing rainbow trout, for instance, is sometimes marketed as wild steelhead trout. Regardless, trout varieties tend to share common taste characteristics and are interchangeable in most recipes.

Trout can have white or orange-pink flesh, depending on its diet. The flesh should be firm, uniformly colored, and unblemished, and the skin should be shiny and slippery. Whole trout should have clear, bright eyes that haven't clouded or sunken into the head. Whether whole or filleted, trout should have a fresh, nearly neutral smell, not strong, fishy, or hinting of ammonia.

Hazelnut-Crusted Trout

The nut-and-breadcrumb crust brings welcome texture to the fish. Enjoy with steamed Broccolini.

- ¼ cup panko (Japanese breadcrumbs)
- 2 tablespoons finely chopped hazelnuts, toasted
- ½ teaspoon salt
- ½ teaspoon grated lemon rind
- ½ teaspoon minced fresh thyme
- ¼ teaspoon freshly ground black pepper

Cooking spray
- 4 (6-ounce) trout fillets

Lemon wedges (optional)

1. Preheat oven to 400°.
2. Combine first 6 ingredients in a small bowl.
3. Line a baking sheet with foil; coat foil with cooking spray. Arrange trout in a single layer on baking sheet. Sprinkle hazelnut mixture evenly over trout. Bake at 400° for 10 minutes or until fish flakes easily when tested with a fork or until desired degree of doneness. Serve with lemon wedges, if desired. Yield: 4 servings (serving size: 1 fillet).

CALORIES 215; FAT 7.5g (sat 2.6g, mono 3g, poly 0.8g); PROTEIN 33.8g; CARB 3.2g; FIBER 0.5g; CHOL 74mg; IRON 2.7mg; SODIUM 401mg; CALC 22mg

WINE NOTE: Chardonnay tastes wonderful in the company of nuts (it's because both are rich). For this recipe, choose a chardonnay that's also fresh, clean, dry, and simple (not to mention a steal). The 2006 Fortant de France Chardonnay from the south of France is $12.

Baked Trout with Olive-Tomato Relish

You can find manzanilla olives at specialty grocers or gourmet stores. You can substitute kalamata olives. Serve this dish with sautéed haricots verts and yellow wax beans tossed with toasted hazelnuts.

- 1 cup finely chopped tomato
- ¼ cup coarsely chopped pitted manzanilla (or green) olives (about 6 olives)
- 1 tablespoon capers, drained
- 1 teaspoon extra-virgin olive oil
- ¼ teaspoon minced garlic

Cooking spray
- 4 (6-ounce) trout fillets
- 2 tablespoons minced fresh parsley
- ½ teaspoon salt
- ¼ teaspoon freshly ground black pepper

1. Preheat oven to 400°.
2. Combine first 5 ingredients in a small bowl.
3. Line a baking sheet with foil; coat foil with cooking spray. Place fish, skin sides down, on prepared baking sheet. Sprinkle evenly with parsley, salt, and pepper. Bake at 400° for 8 minutes or until fish flakes easily when tested with a fork or until desired degree of doneness. Serve with olive mixture. Yield: 4 servings (serving size: 1 fillet and 6 tablespoons olive mixture).

CALORIES 215; FAT 8g (sat 2.6g, mono 3.4g, poly 1.1g); PROTEIN 33.3g; CARB 3.2g; FIBER 0.7g; CHOL 74mg; IRON 2.9mg; SODIUM 625mg; CALC 23mg

Grilled Trout with Rosemary and Garlic

This simple presentation is a go-to summer recipe that allows the flavor of the fish to shine. If you like, substitute thyme for rosemary.

- 1 tablespoon chopped fresh rosemary
- 1 tablespoon minced garlic
- 1 teaspoon olive oil
- ½ teaspoon salt
- 4 (8-ounce) dressed whole trout
- 4 (6-inch) fresh rosemary sprigs

Cooking spray

1. Prepare grill to medium-high heat.
2. Combine first 4 ingredients in a small bowl.
3. Cut 3 diagonal slits on each side of fish, and rub rosemary mixture evenly over fish. Place 1 rosemary sprig in cavity of each fish. Place fish on grill rack coated with cooking spray; grill 4 minutes on each side or until fish flakes easily when tested with a fork or until desired degree of doneness. Yield: 4 servings (serving size: 1 trout).

CALORIES 252; FAT 8.2g (sat 3.4g, mono 2.7g, poly 0.8g); PROTEIN 43.9g; CARB 0.8g; FIBER 0.1g; CHOL 99mg; IRON 3.5mg; SODIUM 423mg; CALC 28mg

Mild trout lends itself to bold accompaniments and anchors a zesty summer dinner.

Smoked Trout

Use in salads, on crackers with cream cheese as an hors d'oeuvre, or on bagels for brunch. Let the brine solution cool first before pouring it over the trout. You can choose trout fillets instead of the butterflied trout; fillets will cook faster.

BRINE:
- 3 cups boiling water
- 1 cup packed brown sugar
- ½ cup kosher salt
- ½ teaspoon freshly ground black pepper
- 3 sprigs fresh thyme
- 2 (4-inch) orange rind strips

REMAINING INGREDIENTS:
- 2 (10-ounce) dressed whole rainbow trout
- 2 cups wood chips
- Cooking spray

❶ To prepare brine, combine first 6 ingredients in a large bowl; stir until sugar and salt dissolve. Combine water mixture and fish in a 13 x 9-inch baking dish. Cover and refrigerate overnight.
❷ Soak wood chips in water 1 hour. Drain wood chips well.
❸ Prepare grill for indirect grilling, heating one side to medium-high and leaving one side with no heat. Pierce bottom of a disposable aluminum foil pan several times with a knife. Place pan on heated side of grill; add wood chips to pan.
❹ Remove fish from brine; discard brine. Rinse fish with cold water; pat dry with paper towels.
❺ Coat a grill rack with cooking spray; place on grill. Place fish, skin sides down, on unheated side; cover and grill 15 minutes or until fish flakes easily when tested with a fork or until desired degree of doneness. Flake fish with fork. Discard skin. Yield: 3 cups flaked trout meat (serving size: ½ cup).

CALORIES 113; FAT 2.9g (sat 1.4g, mono 0.8g, poly 0.3g); PROTEIN 18.2g; CARB 3.6g; FIBER 0g; CHOL 41mg; IRON 1.5mg; SODIUM 431mg; CALC 12mg

Smoked Trout and New Potato Salad

- 1 pound small red potatoes, quartered
- ½ cup reduced-fat sour cream
- ¼ cup reduced-fat mayonnaise
- 3 tablespoons red wine vinegar
- ¼ teaspoon salt
- ¼ teaspoon freshly ground black pepper
- 1½ cups Smoked Trout (at left)
- ½ cup chopped green onions
- 2 tablespoons finely chopped fresh parsley
- 2 tablespoons finely chopped fresh chives
- 2 teaspoons finely chopped fresh tarragon

❶ Place potatoes in a medium saucepan; cover with water. Bring to a boil. Reduce heat; simmer 10 minutes or until tender. Drain; cool.
❷ Combine sour cream and next 4 ingredients in a large bowl, stirring well with a whisk. Add potatoes, Smoked Trout, and remaining ingredients; toss gently to coat. Yield: 6 servings (serving size: about ¾ cup).

CALORIES 166; FAT 5.4g (sat 2.3g, mono 1.1g, poly 1g); PROTEIN 11.7g; CARB 19g; FIBER 1.7g; CHOL 31mg; IRON 1.6mg; SODIUM 421mg; CALC 56mg

TEST KITCHENS SECRETS
Rainier Cherry Crumble

Here's how to easily pit cherries for a stellar Rainier Cherry Crumble

Test Kitchen Professional Mary Drennen Ankar keeps it simple when developing recipes. She convinced us that even when starting with fresh cherries, this stone fruit crumble is a snap to prepare. Her tip: "With the flat side of a chef's knife, lightly hit each cherry. Then you can easily pull the stem and pit from the fresh cherry," she says.

Rainier Cherry Crumble

Rainier cherries are the very sweet offspring of sweet-tart Bing cherries. If you can't find Rainier cherries, you can substitute the Bing variety, but you'll likely need to add a little sugar to the filling to balance the tartness.

- Cooking spray
- 2 tablespoons cornstarch
- 2 tablespoons fresh lemon juice
- Dash of salt
- 3 pounds very sweet cherries, such as Rainier, pitted
- 4.5 ounces all-purpose flour (about 1 cup)
- 1 cup packed light brown sugar
- 1 tablespoon finely chopped almonds, toasted
- ¼ teaspoon ground cinnamon
- ⅛ teaspoon salt
- 7 tablespoons chilled butter, cut into small pieces

❶ Preheat oven to 400°.
❷ Place a 9-inch cast-iron skillet in preheated oven; heat 5 minutes. Remove pan from oven, and lightly coat with cooking spray.
❸ Combine cornstarch and next 3 ingredients in a large bowl, tossing well to coat. Pour cherry mixture into prepared preheated pan.
❹ Weigh or lightly spoon flour into a dry measuring cup; level with a knife. Combine flour and next 4 ingredients in a medium bowl; cut in butter with a pastry blender or 2 knives until mixture resembles coarse meal. Sprinkle flour mixture over cherries. Place skillet on a jelly-roll pan. Bake at 400° for 35 minutes or until filling is thick and bubbly and topping is browned. Remove from oven; let stand 20 minutes. Serve warm. Yield: 10 servings (serving size: about ⅔ cup).

CALORIES 298; FAT 8.9g (sat 5.1g, mono 2.3g, poly 0.4g); PROTEIN 3.5g; CARB 54.5g; FIBER 3.4g; CHOL 21mg; IRON 1.4mg; SODIUM 110mg; CALC 45mg

Pennsylvania Dutch Potato Salad

We make healthful tweaks to a reader's Pennsylvania Dutch potato salad just in time for picnics.

Part of Shirley Schmuhl's marriage proposal from her husband, Ray, included a request for this potato salad. "We dated a few times before his mother passed away," says Schmuhl, a flexible benefit plan analyst from Marietta, Georgia. "He gave me some of her cookbooks, one of them containing this recipe. He asked if I'd marry him and would I please learn to make this potato salad. I happily agreed." Soon enough, Ray's family recipes became her favorites, too. "I fell in love with the salad because of its sweet and tart flavors and beautiful presentation. I've been making it for 52 years and would be forever indebted if you could lighten it," she says.

With 1 cup sugar, 6 bacon slices, and ¼ cup bacon grease, this salad tipped the scales for calories, total fat, and saturated fat.

The Solution:

• We halved the amount of sugar in the dressing to ½ cup, shaving 48 calories per serving. To maintain sweetness, a characteristic note in many Pennsylvania Dutch recipes, we added 2 tablespoons cider vinegar to the dressing without adding additional calories.

• We halved the amount of bacon, and to extend the hearty, smoky flavor, we used the applewood-smoked variety. This change eliminated 12 calories and about 60 milligrams of sodium per serving.

• We also halved the amount of bacon drippings in the dressing. A mere 2 tablespoons maintained the dressing's body and cut about 29 calories, 3.2 grams of fat, and 1.2 grams of unhealthful saturated fat per serving.

• A few tweaks balanced flavors in this sweet-tart side. For example, we used the same amount of salt, but used the kosher type for a cleaner taste; this substitution cut 30 milligrams of sodium per serving. With less fat to cut the acidity, we reduced the white vinegar slightly. We doubled the amount of black pepper to add punch.

serving size: 1¼ cups		
	before	after
CALORIES PER SERVING	364	265
TOTAL FAT	12.1g	7.5g
SATURATED FAT	4.3g	2.7g
SODIUM	356mg	260mg

Pennsylvania Dutch Potato Salad

Try this potato salad for something different; the dressing's bacon drippings barely temper the sweet-tart notes from sugar, cider vinegar, and white vinegar. We halved the amount of bacon and bacon grease to cut calories and saturated fat, so a few slices of flavorful applewood-smoked bacon stand in to extend flavor. Serve warm or slightly cool.

2¾   pounds Yukon gold potatoes
2   cups chopped yellow onion
½   cup chopped celery
½   cup shredded carrot
2   large hard-boiled eggs, chopped
3   applewood-smoked bacon slices, diced
½   cup sugar
½   cup water
¼   cup white vinegar
2   tablespoons cider vinegar
½   teaspoon kosher salt
½   teaspoon freshly ground black pepper
¼   teaspoon dry mustard
2   large eggs, lightly beaten
3   tablespoons chopped fresh parsley

❶ Place potatoes in a large saucepan; cover with water. Bring to a boil. Reduce heat; simmer 15 minutes or until tender. Cool 10 minutes; peel and chop. Combine potatoes, onion, and next 3 ingredients in a large bowl.

❷ Cook bacon in a large nonstick skillet over medium heat until crisp, stirring occasionally. Remove bacon from pan with a slotted spoon, reserving 2 tablespoons drippings in pan. Combine sugar and next 7 ingredients; stir with a whisk. Add sugar mixture to pan; cook 8 minutes over medium heat or until slightly thick, stirring constantly with a whisk. Pour sugar mixture over potato mixture, stirring gently to combine. Add reserved bacon and parsley; toss gently to coat. Serve warm or at room temperature. Yield: 8 servings (serving size: 1¼ cups).

CALORIES 265; FAT 7.5g (sat 2.7g, mono 2.4g, poly 0.7g); PROTEIN 8g; CARB 43.1g; FIBER 2.8g; CHOL 113mg; IRON 1.7mg; SODIUM 260mg; CALC 46mg

"The new potato salad has the same substantial quality as the original. The smoky bacon, tart vinegar, and egg flavors we love are still prominent."

—Shirley Schmuhl
Marietta, Georgia

Garden-Fresh Salsas, Chutneys & Relishes

Zesty homemade condiments showcase the season's fruits and vegetables and bring exciting new flavors to your next dinner.

Salsa

Salsa is the Spanish word for sauce. The most traditional type is made from tomatoes, onions, cilantro, and chiles. Yet the term applies to a chunky (or sometimes pureed) mix of vegetables and/or fruits, herbs, and spices—fresh or cooked. Ranging in spiciness from mild to fiery, salsa is a common accompaniment for Latin dishes.

MAKE AHEAD
Fiery Grilled Peach and Habanero Salsa

Refrigerate for up to three days.

- 4 large peeled peaches, halved and pitted (about 1 pound)
- 2 (¼-inch-thick) slices red onion
- Cooking spray
- 2 tablespoons chopped fresh cilantro
- 1 tablespoon fresh lime juice
- 1 teaspoon sugar
- 1 teaspoon grated orange rind
- 1 teaspoon finely chopped seeded habanero pepper
- ½ teaspoon salt

❶ Prepare grill to medium-high heat.
❷ Lightly coat peaches and onion with cooking spray. Place peaches and onion on grill rack coated with cooking spray; grill peaches 2 minutes on each side. Cool and chop peaches. Grill onion 3 minutes on each side. Cool and chop onion. Combine peaches, onion, cilantro, and remaining ingredients in a medium bowl; toss well. Let stand 15 minutes. Yield: 15 servings (serving size: ¼ cup).

CALORIES 20; FAT 0.1g (sat 0g, mono 0g, poly 0g); PROTEIN 0.4g; CARB 5g; FIBER 0.7g; CHOL 0mg; IRON 0.1mg; SODIUM 78mg; CALC 4mg

---

MAKE AHEAD
Roasted Poblano and Tomato Salsa

This salsa pairs well with tortilla chips, steak, chicken, and tacos. Store chilled for up to three days.

- 2 poblano chiles
- 3 cups chopped seeded tomato
- ½ cup finely chopped onion
- 2 tablespoons chopped fresh cilantro
- 1 tablespoon fresh lime juice
- 1 teaspoon extra-virgin olive oil
- ½ teaspoon salt

❶ Preheat broiler.
❷ Place chiles on a foil-lined baking sheet; broil 3 inches from heat 8 minutes or until blackened, turning after 6 minutes. Place in a heavy-duty zip-top plastic bag; seal. Let stand 15 minutes. Peel and discard skins; chop chiles. Combine chiles, tomato, and remaining ingredients in a medium bowl; toss well. Yield: 12 servings (serving size: ¼ cup).

CALORIES 18; FAT 0.5g (sat 0.1g, mono 0.3g, poly 0.1g); PROTEIN 0.6g; CARB 3.2g; FIBER 0.8g; CHOL 0mg; IRON 0.2mg; SODIUM 100mg; CALC 7mg

---

STAFF FAVORITE ▪ QUICK & EASY
MAKE AHEAD
Citrus-Avocado Salsa

Lemon and lime rind add floral flavor notes, keeping the salsa mildly tangy. Serve with seared scallops, grilled duck or chicken breasts, or grilled or sautéed shrimp. Keep refrigerated for up to two days. If not using immediately, add a squeeze of lime juice to help prevent the avocado from turning brown.

- 3 cups coarsely chopped orange sections (about 6 oranges)
- ½ cup diced peeled avocado (about 1 small)
- ¼ cup finely chopped red onion
- 1 teaspoon grated lemon rind
- 1 teaspoon grated lime rind
- ¼ teaspoon salt
- 1 serrano chile, seeded and minced

❶ Combine all ingredients in a medium bowl; toss well. Yield: 16 servings (serving size: ¼ cup).

CALORIES 24; FAT 0.8g (sat 0.1g, mono 0.5g, poly 0.1g); PROTEIN 0.4g; CARB 4.5g; FIBER 1g; CHOL 0mg; IRON 0.1mg; SODIUM 37mg; CALC 15mg

Ginger-Nectarine Salsa

Ginger adds a piquant note to sweet nectarines. Serve with grilled pork, chicken, or salmon. This salsa keeps for up to three days in the fridge.

2⅔ cups chopped nectarine
½ cup finely chopped green onions
¼ cup golden raisins
1 tablespoon cider vinegar
1 teaspoon minced peeled fresh ginger
¼ teaspoon salt
¼ teaspoon minced garlic
¼ teaspoon freshly ground black pepper

❶ Combine all ingredients in a bowl; toss well. Cover and chill at least 1 hour. Yield: 20 servings (serving size: 2 tablespoons).

CALORIES 17; FAT 0.1g (sat 0g, mono 0g, poly 0g); PROTEIN 0.4g; CARB 4.1g; FIBER 0.5g; CHOL 0mg; IRON 0.1mg; SODIUM 30mg; CALC 4mg

Tomato Chow-Chow

Chow-chow is a traditional Southern relish of summer vegetables cooked in a vinegar mixture. Serve with beans, field peas, ham, grilled chicken, or hamburgers.

1½ cups white vinegar
1 cup sugar
12 black peppercorns
6 whole allspice
1 (3-inch) cinnamon stick
4 cups chopped seeded tomato (about 1½ pounds)
2 cups chopped green cabbage
1 cup chopped green bell pepper
1 cup chopped onion
½ cup chopped celery
¾ teaspoon salt
1 serrano chile, minced

❶ Combine first 5 ingredients in a large saucepan; bring to a boil. Cook 1 minute. Add tomato and remaining ingredients; bring to a boil. Cook 20 minutes, stirring occasionally. Cool to room temperature; discard cinnamon. Place tomato mixture in a medium bowl; cover and chill. Yield: 14 servings (serving size: ¼ cup).

CALORIES 78; FAT 0.2g (sat 0g, mono 0g, poly 0.1g); PROTEIN 0.8g; CARB 18.6g; FIBER 1.3g; CHOL 0mg; IRON 0.3mg; SODIUM 133mg; CALC 15mg

Relish

Relish features chopped, cooked, or pickled vegetables or fruits. Vinegar is often a prominent ingredient in relish, which can also contain sugar and spices. Relish is considered more tart than chutney or salsa, and it's often paired with American fare like burgers, hot dogs, field peas and beans, and grilled chicken.

Pan-Roasted Corn and Tomato Relish

Serve this smoky relish with steak, chicken, or grilled striped bass. Refrigerate for up to three days.

1 tablespoon olive oil
¼ cup chopped shallots
2 garlic cloves, minced
2 cups fresh corn kernels (about 2 ears)
2 cups cherry tomatoes, quartered (about 1 pint)
¼ cup chopped fresh basil
1 tablespoon cider vinegar
½ teaspoon salt

❶ Heat oil in a large cast-iron skillet over high heat. Add shallots and garlic; sauté 1 minute. Add corn; sauté 5 minutes or until corn is lightly browned. Add tomatoes; sauté 2 minutes. Remove from heat. Place corn mixture in a medium bowl; cool to room temperature. Stir in basil, vinegar, and salt. Yield: 10 servings (serving size: ¼ cup).

CALORIES 47; FAT 1.8g (sat 0.3g, mono 1.2g, poly 0.3g); PROTEIN 1.4g; CARB 7.5g; FIBER 1.2g; CHOL 0mg; IRON 0.3mg; SODIUM 123mg; CALC 8mg

Curried Pineapple and Stone Fruit Chutney

Spoon this chutney, which keeps for up to one week in the refrigerator, over ham steaks or pork tenderloin.

1 tablespoon canola oil
2 tablespoons minced peeled fresh ginger
4 garlic cloves, minced
1 cup chopped onion
1 cup chopped red bell pepper
2 tablespoons minced seeded jalapeño pepper
2 teaspoons curry powder
2 cups diced fresh pineapple
¾ cup chopped peeled peach (about 1)
¾ cup chopped peeled nectarine (about 1)
¾ cup cider vinegar
½ cup dried cranberries
½ cup packed brown sugar
⅓ cup granulated sugar
½ teaspoon salt

❶ Heat oil in a large nonstick skillet over medium-high heat. Add ginger and garlic; sauté 30 seconds. Add onion and peppers; sauté 4 minutes or until tender. Stir in curry powder; cook 1 minute. Add pineapple and remaining ingredients; bring to a boil. Reduce heat, and simmer 30 minutes or until mixture thickens. Serve at room temperature or chilled. Yield: 28 servings (serving size: 2 tablespoons).

CALORIES 51; FAT 0.6g (sat 0.1g, mono 0.3g, poly 0.2g); PROTEIN 0.3g; CARB 11.5g; FIBER 0.6g; CHOL 0mg; IRON 0.3mg; SODIUM 44mg; CALC 9mg

Chutney

Indian in origin, the term **chutney** comes from the Hindi word *chatni*. The condiment became popular in the West during the 19th century, while India was under British rule. A fruit- or vegetable-based sauce, chutney can be fresh or cooked, mild or spicy. It's often thicker than relish because it's typically cooked longer and contains more sugar.

Prime Pairings

Salsas, chutneys, and relishes make dinner planning a snap. Just cook simply seasoned meat, poultry, or fish, then serve it with one of our bold-flavored, bright-colored condiments.

◄ Grilled Chicken Breast

BEST WITH: Ginger-Nectarine Salsa; Pan-Roasted Corn and Tomato Relish; Citrus-Avocado Salsa; Fiery Grilled Peach and Habanero Salsa; Roasted Poblano and Tomato Salsa; Tomato Chow-Chow

Prepare grill to medium-high heat. Sprinkle 4 (6-ounce) skinless, boneless chicken breast halves with ½ teaspoon salt and ¼ teaspoon freshly ground black pepper. Place chicken on grill rack coated with cooking spray. Grill chicken 6 minutes on each side or until done.

CALORIES 183; FAT 4g (sat 1.1g, mono 1.4g, poly 0.9g); PROTEIN 34g; CARB 0.1g; FIBER 0g; CHOL 94mg; IRON 1.2mg; SODIUM 373mg; CALC 17mg

◄ Grilled Striped Bass

BEST WITH: Fiery Grilled Peach and Habanero Salsa; Ginger-Nectarine Salsa

Prepare grill to medium-high heat. Sprinkle 4 (6-ounce) striped bass fillets with ½ teaspoon salt and ¼ teaspoon freshly ground black pepper. Place fish on a grill rack coated with cooking spray; grill 4 minutes on each side or until fish flakes easily or until desired degree of doneness.

CALORIES 159; FAT 3.8g (sat 0.8g, mono 1.1g, poly 1.3g); PROTEIN 29g; CARB 0.1g; FIBER 0g; CHOL 131mg; IRON 1.4mg; SODIUM 403mg; CALC 25mg

◄ Roasted Pork Tenderloin

BEST WITH: Ginger-Nectarine Salsa; Fiery Grilled Peach and Habanero Salsa; Curried Pineapple and Stone Fruit Chutney

Sprinkle ½ teaspoon salt and ¼ teaspoon freshly ground black pepper over 1 (1-pound) pork tenderloin. Heat a large skillet over medium-high heat. Add 1 tablespoon olive oil to pan; swirl to coat. Add pork to pan; cook 3 minutes, browning on all sides. Bake pork at 400° for 22 minutes or until a thermometer registers 155° (slightly pink). Let stand 10 minutes before cutting across grain into thin slices.

CALORIES 170; FAT 7.5g (sat 1.9g, mono 4.1g, poly 0.7g); PROTEIN 24g; CARB 0.1g; FIBER 0g; CHOL 67mg; IRON 1.3mg; SODIUM 338mg; CALC 6mg

◄ Grilled Flank Steak

BEST WITH: Pan-Roasted Corn and Tomato Relish; Roasted Poblano and Tomato Salsa

Prepare grill to medium-high heat. Sprinkle 1 (1-pound) flank steak with ½ teaspoon salt and ½ teaspoon freshly ground black pepper. Grill steak 8 minutes on each side or until desired degree of doneness. Let steak stand 10 minutes before cutting diagonally across grain into thin slices.

CALORIES 152; FAT 5.5g (sat 2.3g, mono 2.2g, poly 0.2g); PROTEIN 23.8g; CARB 0.2g; FIBER 0.1g; CHOL 37mg; IRON 1.5mg; SODIUM 341mg; CALC 18mg

Share a Taste of Greece

Enjoy a meze party featuring Greek-inspired salads, skewers, finger foods, and spreads.

AT ANY TIME OF DAY, hungry Greeks may stop at a taverna to enjoy a *meze* (meh-ZAY), loosely translated as "appetizer."

Similar to Spanish tapas, mezes continue the tradition in Mediterranean countries of small-plate pleasures that incorporate the particular ingredients of each national cuisine. In Greece, characteristic elements include lemon, garlic, mint, parsley, oregano, olives, olive oil, and vegetables such as tomatoes, cucumbers, artichokes, and beets.

The flavors and the format lend themselves to entertaining, especially in the lighter days of summer. Here, an assortment of meze recipes creates a convivial spread—with small-plate dishes, the fun lies in the variety.

MAKE AHEAD
Eggplant with Capers and Red Peppers

1 medium eggplant (about 1¼ pounds)
1 medium red bell pepper
¼ cup finely chopped red onion
3 tablespoons capers
2 tablespoons chopped fresh flat-leaf parsley
2 tablespoons fresh lemon juice
1 tablespoon extra-virgin olive oil
¼ teaspoon salt
¼ teaspoon crushed red pepper
¼ teaspoon freshly ground black pepper
2 garlic cloves, minced

1 Preheat broiler.
2 Pierce eggplant several times with a fork; place on a foil-lined baking sheet. Broil 30 minutes or until blackened, turning frequently. Cool eggplant slightly; peel and chop.
3 Cut bell pepper in half lengthwise, and discard seeds and membranes. Place pepper halves, skin sides up, on a foil-lined baking sheet; flatten with hand. Broil 15 minutes or until blackened. Place in a zip-top plastic bag; seal. Let stand 15 minutes. Peel and chop.
4 Combine eggplant, bell pepper, onion, and remaining ingredients in a medium bowl; toss well. Yield: 8 servings (serving size: about ⅓ cup).

CALORIES 43; FAT 2g (sat 0.3g, mono 1.3g, poly 0.4g); PROTEIN 1.2g; CARB 6.6g; FIBER 3.1g; CHOL 0mg; IRON 0.4mg; SODIUM 172mg; CALC 14mg

QUICK & EASY
Tzatziki

Use thick, Greek-style yogurt in this dish, pronounced "dzah-DZEE-kee."

2 cups plain 2% low-fat Greek-style yogurt
¾ cup shredded seeded peeled cucumber
3 tablespoons chopped fresh mint
2 tablespoons chopped fresh dill
1 tablespoon extra-virgin olive oil
1 tablespoon fresh lemon juice
¼ teaspoon salt
3 garlic cloves, minced

1 Combine all ingredients in a medium bowl, stirring well. Yield: 8 servings (serving size: about ¼ cup).

CALORIES 60; FAT 3g (sat 1.2g, mono 1.3g, poly 0.3g); PROTEIN 5.5g; CARB 3.4g; FIBER 0.2g; CHOL 3mg; IRON 0.1mg; SODIUM 95mg; CALC 62mg

MEZE MENU
(Serves 8)

Eggplant with Capers and Red Peppers

Tzatziki

Bulgur, Mint, and Parsley Salad

Bread Salad with Mint and Tomatoes

Beet and Arugula Salad with Kefalotyri

Artichoke and Eggplant Skewers

Spiced Chicken Skewers with Lemon Vinaigrette

Lamb-Stuffed Grape Leaves

Mussels with Tomato and Dill

WINE NOTE: This menu brings together bright, summery Mediterranean flavors. Wines that develop along with a cuisine often make the perfect match, and this is especially true of Greek wines. Moschofilero is a pink-skinned local grape capable of making white or rosé wines, like the organically grown Domaine Spiropoulos Meliasto Moschofilero Rosé 2007 ($13). This dry, crisp rosé is ideal with delicate fish and chicken dishes. As a red option, try the widely available Boutari Naoussa 2005 ($17), with dark cherry fruit and underlying mushroom, earthy, and meaty flavors that will marry nicely with flavorful meats, as in the menu's Lamb-Stuffed Grape Leaves.

No-Cook, Ready-to-Eat Greek Treats

Round out your meze offerings with a few ready-to-eat foods that complement the Greek theme.

Olives: Have a bowl of kalamata olives—one of the most common and familiar (to Americans) Greek olives—on hand for easy party snacking. If available, include other Greek varieties, such as *agrinion* and *amphissa*, though other Mediterranean olives, like France's *niçoise* and Spain's *manzanillas* will also make nice additions.

Pitas: They're a must-have for a Greek-inspired spread. Cut into wedges and use for dips such as Tzatziki (page 192) or to pair with cheese.

Cheese: Offer a wedge of *kefalotyri*, a hard Greek cheese sometimes likened to Parmigiano-Reggiano. *Kasseri* can be mild or sharp. Salty, tangy feta cheese is the most widely available Greek cheese.

Nuts: Set out bowls of nuts such as almonds and walnuts, which are particularly popular in Greek cuisine.

Beverages: Include ouzo among your bar offerings. An anise-flavored liqueur, it's a traditional beverage for many meze dishes. Greek beer, such as Mythos, also makes a fine accompaniment, as does a crisp, Greek rosé wine or a deeply flavored red (see Wine Note, page 192).

MAKE AHEAD

Bulgur, Mint, and Parsley Salad

Light, herby, and vibrantly flavored, this salad makes a fine addition to a meze spread.

- 1 cup uncooked bulgur
- 1 cup boiling water
- 3 tablespoons fresh lemon juice
- 2 tablespoons extra-virgin olive oil
- 3 garlic cloves, minced
- 3 cups chopped tomato (about 2 large)
- 1¼ cups chopped seeded peeled cucumber (about 1 medium)
- 1 cup chopped fresh parsley
- ½ cup chopped green onions (about 3)
- ¼ cup chopped fresh mint
- ¾ teaspoon salt
- ½ teaspoon freshly ground black pepper

❶ Combine bulgur and 1 cup boiling water in a medium bowl. Cover and let stand 30 minutes or until tender. Stir in juice, oil, and garlic. Cool to room temperature.

❷ Combine bulgur mixture, tomato, and remaining ingredients in a large bowl; toss gently to coat. Yield: 8 servings (serving size: about 1 cup).

CALORIES 113; FAT 4g (sat 0.6g, mono 2.6g, poly 0.7g); PROTEIN 3.3g; CARB 18.4g; FIBER 4.7g; CHOL 0mg; IRON 1.3mg; SODIUM 234mg; CALC 36mg

Bread Salad with Mint and Tomatoes

This fresh, simple salad is coated in a pleasantly tart lemon juice dressing. Serve immediately to prevent the bread from becoming too soggy.

- 6 tablespoons fresh lemon juice (about 2 lemons)
- 1½ tablespoons extra-virgin olive oil
- ½ teaspoon salt
- ½ teaspoon freshly ground black pepper
- 2 garlic cloves, minced
- 3 cups chopped tomato (about 3 medium)
- 1¼ cups chopped seeded peeled cucumber
- ½ cup sliced green onions (about 3)
- ⅓ cup chopped fresh flat-leaf parsley
- ¼ cup chopped fresh mint
- 1 tablespoon chopped fresh cilantro
- 2 (6-inch) pitas, toasted and torn into bite-sized pieces

❶ Combine first 5 ingredients in a large bowl, stirring well with a whisk. Add tomato and remaining ingredients; toss gently to coat. Serve immediately. Yield: 8 servings (serving size: about ¾ cup).

CALORIES 87; FAT 2.9g (sat 0.4g, mono 1.9g, poly 0.5g); PROTEIN 2.8g; CARB 13.9g; FIBER 1.5g; CHOL 0mg; IRON 1.3mg; SODIUM 197mg; CALC 29mg

Beet and Arugula Salad with Kefalotyri

Kefalotyri is a hard, salty Greek cheese (Parmigiano-Reggiano can sub in a pinch). For more visual appeal, use golden and red beets.

- 3 beets (about 1 pound)
- 2 tablespoons red wine vinegar
- 1 teaspoon extra-virgin olive oil
- ½ teaspoon salt
- ½ teaspoon freshly ground black pepper
- 6 cups arugula
- ¼ cup (1 ounce) shaved fresh kefalotyri cheese

❶ Preheat oven to 425°.

❷ Leave root and 1-inch stem on beets; scrub with a brush. Place beets in a baking dish; bake at 425° for 1 hour and 10 minutes or until tender. Cool; peel and cut into ¼-inch-thick slices.

❸ Combine vinegar and next 3 ingredients, stirring with a whisk. Arrange beet slices in a single layer on a platter. Drizzle beets with half of vinegar mixture.

❹ Combine remaining vinegar mixture and arugula in a large bowl; toss gently to coat. Top beets with arugula mixture. Sprinkle with cheese. Yield: 8 servings (serving size: about ½ cup beet mixture and 1½ teaspoons cheese).

CALORIES 50; FAT 1.8g (sat 0.7g, mono 0.7g, poly 0.2g); PROTEIN 2.7g; CARB 6.2g; FIBER 1.9g; CHOL 3mg; IRON 0.7mg; SODIUM 250mg; CALC 73mg

Artichoke and Eggplant Skewers

We use frozen artichoke hearts for convenience. Use fresh baby artichoke hearts, if you like, but blanch them first in boiling water with lemon juice for eight minutes or just until barely tender; quarter and arrange on skewers. Serve with Tzatziki (page 192).

- 3 tablespoons fresh lemon juice
- 1 teaspoon chopped fresh oregano
- 4 teaspoons extra-virgin olive oil
- 2 garlic cloves, minced
- 6 frozen artichoke hearts, thawed and quartered
- 24 (1-inch) cubes eggplant (about ¾ pound)
- 24 cherry tomatoes
  Cooking spray
- ¼ teaspoon salt
- ¼ teaspoon freshly ground black pepper
  Lemon wedges (optional)

❶ Prepare grill to medium-high heat.
❷ Combine first 4 ingredients in a small bowl; stir well with a whisk.
❸ Thread artichoke hearts, eggplant, and tomatoes alternately onto each of 8 (10-inch) skewers. Place skewers on grill rack coated with cooking spray, and grill 6 minutes or until tender, turning frequently. Place skewers on a platter; brush with juice mixture. Sprinkle with salt and pepper. Serve with lemon wedges, if desired. Yield: 8 servings (serving size: 1 skewer).

CALORIES 45; FAT 2.5g (sat 0.3g, mono 1.7g, poly 0.3g); PROTEIN 1.1g; CARB 5.7g; FIBER 2.4g; CHOL 0mg; IRON 0.3mg; SODIUM 80mg; CALC 14mg

Spiced Chicken Skewers with Lemon Vinaigrette

Toasting the spices before grinding brings out their oils and makes them more potent.

- 1½ pounds skinless, boneless chicken breast, cut into bite-sized pieces
- 1 tablespoon cumin seeds
- 1 tablespoon coriander seeds
- ½ teaspoon salt, divided
- ½ teaspoon paprika
- ½ teaspoon freshly ground black pepper, divided
- ¼ teaspoon crushed red pepper
- 1 tablespoon thinly sliced green onions
- 2 tablespoons fresh lemon juice
- 1 tablespoon extra-virgin olive oil
- 1 garlic clove, minced
  Cooking spray
- 8 lemon wedges (optional)

❶ Prepare grill to medium-high heat.
❷ Thread chicken pieces evenly onto 16 (6-inch) skewers.
❸ Place cumin and coriander in a small nonstick pan over medium heat; cook 1 minute or until toasted, stirring frequently. Place spice mixture in a spice or coffee grinder; pulse 3 times or until coarsely ground. Combine ground spices, ¼ teaspoon salt, paprika, ¼ teaspoon black pepper, and crushed red pepper in a small bowl, stirring with a whisk. Spread spice mixture onto a large plate; lightly roll each skewer in spice mixture.
❹ Combine remaining ¼ teaspoon salt, remaining ¼ teaspoon black pepper, onions, and next 3 ingredients in a small bowl; stir well with a whisk.
❺ Place skewers on grill rack coated with cooking spray. Grill 8 minutes or until done, turning occasionally. Arrange skewers on a platter; drizzle with juice mixture. Serve with lemon wedges, if desired. Yield: 8 servings (serving size: 2 skewers).

CALORIES 114; FAT 4.1g (sat 0.8g, mono 2.1g, poly 0.7g); PROTEIN 17.5g; CARB 1.4g; FIBER 0.5g; CHOL 47mg; IRON 1.3mg; SODIUM 190mg; CALC 23mg

Lamb-Stuffed Grape Leaves

Serve at room temperature.

  Cooking spray
- 1½ cups finely chopped yellow onion (about 1 medium)
- ½ cup chopped green onions (about 3)
- ½ cup uncooked long-grain rice
- 2 tablespoons pine nuts
- ½ cup water
- 2 tablespoons chopped fresh parsley
- 2 tablespoons chopped fresh mint
- 2 tablespoons chopped fresh dill
- 2 tablespoons golden raisins
- ¼ teaspoon salt
- ¼ teaspoon freshly ground black pepper
- 3 ounces lean ground lamb
- 30 bottled large grape leaves

❶ Heat a large nonstick skillet over medium heat. Coat pan with cooking spray. Add yellow onion to pan; cook 4 minutes, stirring occasionally. Add green onions, rice, and nuts; cook 2 minutes, stirring frequently. Stir in ½ cup water and next 6 ingredients; bring to a boil. Cover, reduce heat, and simmer 8 minutes or until liquid is absorbed. Remove from heat; cool. Stir in lamb.
❷ Rinse grape leaves with cold water; drain well. Pat dry with paper towels. Remove stems; discard.
❸ Spoon 1 tablespoon rice mixture onto center of each grape leaf. Bring 2 opposite points of leaf to center; fold over filling. Beginning at 1 short side, roll up leaf tightly, jelly-roll fashion. Place stuffed grape leaves, seam sides down, in a vegetable steamer. Steam 1 hour and 30 minutes. Yield: 8 servings (serving size: about 3 rolls).

CALORIES 111; FAT 3.3g (sat 0.8g, mono 1g, poly 1g); PROTEIN 4g; CARB 16.8g; FIBER 1.2g; CHOL 7mg; IRON 1.1mg; SODIUM 513mg; CALC 65mg

Mussels with Tomato and Dill

Add this tasty hot dish to your spread.

Cooking spray
¾ cup finely chopped yellow onion
2 cups coarsely chopped seeded peeled tomato
1 cup dry white wine
¼ cup chopped fresh dill
1 teaspoon red wine vinegar
¼ teaspoon dried oregano
⅛ teaspoon crushed red pepper
2 pounds medium mussels, scrubbed and debearded
½ teaspoon freshly ground black pepper
Crumbled feta cheese (optional)
Fresh dill sprigs (optional)

❶ Heat a large nonstick skillet over medium heat. Coat pan with cooking spray. Add onion to pan; cook 7 minutes, stirring occasionally. Add tomato and next 5 ingredients; bring to a boil. Reduce heat, and simmer 10 minutes or until liquid almost evaporates. Add mussels; cover and cook 4 minutes or until shells open. Remove from heat; discard any unopened shells. Sprinkle with black pepper. Divide mussel mixture evenly among 8 shallow bowls. Sprinkle with feta and garnish with dill sprigs, if desired. Serve immediately. Yield: 8 servings (serving size: about 7 mussels).

CALORIES 116; FAT 2.7g (sat 0.5g, mono 0.6g, poly 0.7g); PROTEIN 14.1g; CARB 8.3g; FIBER 0.8g; CHOL 32mg; IRON 4.9mg; SODIUM 331mg; CALC 39mg

---

IN SEASON

The Fascination of Figs

Their sweet, succulent flesh and sumptuous texture amaze and delight like few other fruits. And this collection of recipes captures their charm anew.

Perhaps fresh figs are so desired because they have such a short window of availability. It's imperative to enjoy them during the brief window of mid- to late summer when they're available. What's more, the fruit is incredibly delicate, with a shelf life of two days or less.

Fortunately, luscious figs are not only beautiful, but they're also versatile. Since most varieties have a pleasant sweetness, they're often used interchangeably in recipes. The best all-around fig may be the Black Mission. However, the slightly larger, elongated shape of the Brown Turkey fig makes this variety well-suited for stuffing with salty cheeses. The super-sweet Kadota variety has fewer seeds, which makes it a favorite for jams or preserves. And even though they're nearly perfect eaten out of hand, fresh figs make delightful additions to salads, pan sauces, pizza toppers, or desserts.

Selection and Storage

- Choose figs that are plump and heavy for their size and yield slightly with gentle pressure. The skin will be smooth, and the fruit fragrant.
- Purchase fresh, ripe figs because the fruit doesn't always ripen well once harvested.
- Handle figs carefully to avoid damaging the delicate skin.
- Store figs in a single layer on paper towels; they will keep refrigerated this way, covered with plastic wrap, for about two days.

Ginger-Garlic Chicken with Fresh Fig Pan Sauce
(pictured on page 229)

Serve over jasmine rice to soak up the savory sauce. Grill baby bok choy and carrots for a quick side dish.

4 (6-ounce) skinless, boneless chicken breast halves
1 teaspoon grated peeled fresh ginger
¾ teaspoon kosher salt, divided
1 large garlic clove, grated
1 tablespoon canola oil
2 tablespoons thinly sliced green onion bottoms
1 pound ripe Kadota or Brown Turkey figs, cut into ¼-inch-thick wedges
2 tablespoons rice vinegar
1 teaspoon dark sesame oil
2 tablespoons thinly sliced green onion tops
½ teaspoon sesame seeds, toasted

❶ Place each chicken breast half between 2 sheets of heavy-duty plastic wrap; pound each chicken breast half to ¼-inch thickness using a meat mallet or small heavy skillet.
❷ Combine ginger, ½ teaspoon salt, and garlic in a small bowl; mash with a spoon to form a paste. Rub paste evenly over chicken; cover and chill 20 minutes. Heat a large nonstick skillet over medium-high heat. Add oil to pan; swirl to coat. Add chicken to pan; cook 2 minutes on each side or until done. Remove chicken from pan; keep warm. Add green onion bottoms to pan; sauté 1 minute, stirring frequently. Add figs; sauté 2 minutes, stirring frequently. Stir in remaining ¼ teaspoon salt, vinegar, and sesame oil. Remove from heat; spoon sauce over chicken. Sprinkle with green onion tops and sesame seeds. Yield: 4 servings (serving size: 1 chicken breast half and about ⅓ cup sauce).

CALORIES 318; FAT 7.3g (sat 1.1g, mono 3.2g, poly 2.2g); PROTEIN 40.4g; CARB 22.7g; FIBER 3.5g; CHOL 99mg; IRON 1.8mg; SODIUM 466mg; CALC 65mg

Cantaloupe and Grilled Fig Salad

Contrasting tastes (sweet, salty, tangy) and textures (soft, juicy, crunchy) create an intriguing and beautiful first course.

1½ tablespoons low-sodium soy sauce, divided
9 Black Mission figs, trimmed and halved lengthwise
3 tablespoons fresh lime juice
3 tablespoons honey
1 tablespoon canola oil
¼ teaspoon minced garlic
⅛ teaspoon kosher salt
3 cups baby arugula (about 3 ounces)
3 cups baby spinach (about 3 ounces)
½ cup thinly sliced celery
½ cup thinly vertically sliced red onion
¼ teaspoon freshly ground black pepper
12 thin wedges peeled seeded cantaloupe
3 tablespoons chopped walnuts, toasted

❶ Prepare grill to medium-high heat.
❷ Brush 1½ teaspoons soy sauce over cut sides of figs. Place figs, cut sides down, on a grill rack; grill 1 minute on each side or until lightly browned. Remove from grill.
❸ Combine remaining 1 tablespoon soy sauce, juice, and next 4 ingredients; stir with a whisk.
❹ Combine arugula and next 4 ingredients. Arrange 2 cantaloupe wedges on each of 6 plates. Top each serving with about 1 cup arugula mixture, 3 fig halves, and 1½ teaspoons nuts; drizzle with about 1½ tablespoons dressing. Yield: 6 servings.

CALORIES 187; FAT 5.4g (sat 0.5g, mono 1.8g, poly 2.7g); PROTEIN 3.3g; CARB 35.9g; FIBER 4.2g; CHOL 0mg; IRON 1.4mg; SODIUM 215mg; CALC 85mg

Although fresh figs are used interchangeably in most recipes, each has a subtle but distinctive profile.

STAFF FAVORITE
Fresh Fig Tart

Warmed honey makes an easy, glistening glaze for this dessert. Allow about 30 minutes chilling time once the crust is pressed into the tart pan.

CRUST:
Cooking spray
6.75 ounces all-purpose flour (about 1½ cups)
2 tablespoons sugar
½ teaspoon ground cinnamon
⅛ teaspoon salt
6 tablespoons chilled butter, cut into small pieces
1 teaspoon vanilla extract
1 large egg

FILLING:
2 pounds firm ripe Black Mission figs, trimmed
¼ cup sugar
2 tablespoons all-purpose flour
2 tablespoons honey
¾ cup 2% reduced-fat Greek-style yogurt

❶ Preheat oven to 400°.
❷ To prepare crust, coat a 9-inch round removable-bottom tart pan with cooking spray; set aside. Weigh or lightly spoon 6.75 ounces flour into dry measuring cups; level with a knife. Place 6.75 ounces flour and next 3 ingredients in a food processor; pulse to combine. With processor on, gradually add butter through food chute, processing until mixture resembles wet sand. Combine vanilla and egg in a small bowl; stir with a whisk. With processor on, gradually add egg mixture, processing until dough forms. Turn dough out into prepared pan; gently press into bottom and up sides of pan. Chill 30 minutes.
❸ To prepare filling, thinly slice figs to measure 1½ cups; cut remaining figs into ½-inch pieces (about 5 cups). Combine fig pieces, ¼ cup sugar, and 2 tablespoons flour, tossing to coat figs. Spoon fig mixture into prepared crust. Bake at 400° for 20 minutes; reduce oven temperature to 350° (do not remove tart from oven). Bake an additional 25 minutes or until bubbly. Remove from oven; arrange fig slices over top of tart.
❹ Place honey in a microwave-safe bowl. Microwave at HIGH 1 minute; brush over fig slices. Cool tart slightly on a wire rack. Serve warm with yogurt. Yield: 12 servings (serving size: 1 tart wedge and 1 tablespoon yogurt).

CALORIES 224; FAT 6.6g (sat 4g, mono 1.7g, poly 0.3g); PROTEIN 4.3g; CARB 36.7g; FIBER 2.5g; CHOL 34mg; IRON 1.1mg; SODIUM 77mg; CALC 53mg

How to Cook Fish

Learn six techniques that allow you to create a healthful, delicious dinner in mere minutes.

Stuffed Whole Roasted Yellowtail Snapper

Fennel is often paired with fish, but you can easily substitute chopped, seeded, and peeled tomato, if you prefer. Use this versatile preparation with almost any small whole fish and your favorite fresh herbs.

- 2 (1½-pound) whole cleaned yellowtail snappers (heads and tails intact)
- 2 tablespoons extra-virgin olive oil, divided
- ¼ cup fresh lemon juice, divided
- ½ teaspoon salt
- ¼ teaspoon freshly ground black pepper
  Cooking spray
- 6 tablespoons chopped onion
- 2 tablespoons chopped fennel bulb
- 4 fresh rosemary sprigs
- 4 fresh oregano sprigs

① Preheat oven to 400°.
② Score skin of each fish with 3 diagonal cuts. Rub inside flesh of each fish with 2½ teaspoons olive oil; drizzle each fish with 4½ teaspoons lemon juice. Sprinkle flesh evenly with salt and black pepper. Place both fish on a rimmed baking sheet coated with cooking spray. Place 3 tablespoons onion, 1 tablespoon fennel, 2 rosemary sprigs, and 2 oregano sprigs inside each fish. Rub skin of each fish with ½ teaspoon remaining oil; drizzle each with 1½ teaspoons remaining juice.
③ Roast at 400° for 30 minutes or until fish flakes easily when tested with a fork or until desired degree of doneness. Yield: 4 servings (serving size: about 5 ounces fish and ¼ cup vegetable mixture).

CALORIES 251; FAT 9.2g (sat 1.5g, mono 5.4g, poly 1.6g); PROTEIN 37.5g; CARB 2.7g; FIBER 0.4g; CHOL 67mg; IRON 0.4mg; SODIUM 378mg; CALC 63mg

Selection and Storage

Success with fish starts at the market. Use these tips to inform your choices.

When selecting fillets:
• Choose the freshest fish you can find with translucent, tight flesh that is firm to the touch and smells only faintly of the water from which it came.
• Avoid fish with visible holes or gaps in the flesh.
• Fillets should be chilled but not stored directly on ice. It's advisable to place a barrier, such as a metal pan or plastic bag, between the fish and the ice since flesh that comes in direct contact with ice or water deteriorates more quickly and may become mushy.

When selecting whole fish:
• Look for a fish with clear eyes, shiny scales, pink gills, and moist skin.
• Make sure it has a firm, rigid body—pressing the flesh should not leave an indentation.
• It's OK to store whole fish directly on ice, since they stay fresh longer than fillets or other cuts, but they should be placed on the ice in the position that they swim through the water. For example, round fish, like striped bass, should be placed upright, not on their sides.

Roast a Whole Fish

This is one of the simplest ways to prepare an impressive entrée. First, score the skin. This helps the fish keep its shape nicely as it cooks and contributes to the finished dish.

Next, rub the fish inside and out with a bit of oil, and season with salt and pepper. At this point, it's ready to cook, but you can boost the flavor even more by stuffing herb sprigs, citrus slices, or other zesty ingredients into the cavity. Then place the fish on a large rimmed baking sheet and roast according to the recipe's directions.

Sauté Fish Fillets

This is a super-simple and quick way to prepare fish. To begin, heat your pan over medium-high heat. Coat the pan with cooking spray or add a touch of oil. Season the fish, and when the oil is hot, but not smoking, carefully lay the fish in the pan. It's usually best to place fish flesh side down first. We've also found it best to score the skin diagonally two or three times so it doesn't curl the fillet as it cooks.

Cook the fish a couple of minutes, just until the flesh is golden and the fillets are a little more than half-cooked. (You should see the texture of the fillets become more opaque as they cook.) It's a smart idea to use a timer because fillets can be ready to turn in as little as 90 seconds. When they're set, turn them over to finish cooking, skin side down. This allows you to nicely brown the presentation side of the fish while keeping the flesh tender and succulent.

Sautéed Sole with Browned Butter and Capers

Flounder, a close cousin to sole, is a good substitute in this classic yet simple preparation. You can also use trout or your favorite flaky white fish.

4   (6-ounce) sole fillets
¼   teaspoon salt
¼   teaspoon freshly ground black pepper, divided
Cooking spray
3   tablespoons butter
2   tablespoons minced shallots
1   tablespoon drained capers
2   teaspoons fresh lemon juice

❶ Sprinkle fish evenly with salt and ⅛ teaspoon pepper. Heat a large nonstick skillet over medium-high heat. Coat pan with cooking spray. Add 2 fillets to pan; sauté 1½ minutes or until browned. Carefully turn fillets; sauté 1½ minutes or until fish flakes easily when tested with a fork or until desired degree of doneness. Place fillets on a plate; keep warm. Repeat procedure with cooking spray and remaining fillets.

❷ Melt butter in pan; cook 2 minutes or just until lightly browned. Add shallots to butter; sauté 45 seconds, stirring frequently. Remove from heat; stir in remaining ⅛ teaspoon pepper, capers, and juice. Serve with fish. Yield: 4 servings (serving size: 1 fillet and about 1 tablespoon sauce).

CALORIES 279; FAT 11.2g (sat 6g, mono 2.7g, poly 1.4g); PROTEIN 41.4g; CARB 1.3g; FIBER 0.2g; CHOL 138mg; IRON 0.7mg; SODIUM 451mg; CALC 37mg

Fry Fish

To healthfully mimic crispy, deep-fried fish, dredge fillets in a coarse-textured mixture, such as cornmeal, crushed cornflakes, or ground nuts, and then fry in a small amount of oil over medium-high heat.

Tilapia Tostadas with Roasted Corn Relish

These crisp tostadas have all the appeal of fish tacos, but the flat shape allows you to pile toppings high. Although we broil corn tortillas for the base, substitute flour tortillas, or use prepared shells, if you prefer.

½   cup reduced-fat sour cream
¼   cup green salsa
Cooking spray
1   cup yellow corn kernels
¼   cup finely chopped red bell pepper
¼   cup finely chopped red onion
1½ teaspoons minced seeded jalapeño pepper
¾   teaspoon salt, divided
1   cup diced peeled avocado
2   teaspoons fresh lime juice
1½ pounds tilapia fillets, cut into 2-inch pieces
¼   teaspoon freshly ground black pepper
⅓   cup yellow cornmeal
1   tablespoon canola oil, divided
8   (6-inch) corn tortillas
1   cup packaged angel hair slaw
Lime wedges (optional)

❶ Combine sour cream and salsa.
❷ Heat a large nonstick skillet over medium-high heat. Coat pan with cooking spray. Add corn, bell pepper, onion, jalapeño, and ¼ teaspoon salt to pan; sauté 5 minutes, stirring occasionally. Remove mixture from pan; wipe pan clean with paper towels. Combine avocado and juice; toss gently. Stir avocado mixture into corn mixture.

③ Preheat broiler.

④ Sprinkle fish evenly with remaining ½ teaspoon salt and black pepper. Place cornmeal in a shallow dish; dredge fish in cornmeal. Heat 1½ teaspoons oil in pan over medium-high heat. Add half of fish to pan; cook 3 minutes. Carefully turn fish over; cook 2 minutes or until fish flakes easily when tested with a fork or until desired degree of doneness. Repeat procedure with remaining 1½ teaspoons oil and fish.

⑤ Coat both sides of tortillas with cooking spray. Arrange tortillas in a single layer on baking sheets; broil 2 minutes on each side or until crisp. Place 2 tortillas on each of 4 plates. Arrange 2 tablespoons slaw on each tortilla. Divide fish evenly among tortillas; top each serving with about 3 tablespoons corn relish and about 1½ tablespoons sour cream mixture. Serve with lime wedges, if desired. Yield: 4 servings.

CALORIES 470; FAT 17.1g (sat 4.3g, mono 7.6g, poly 3.3g); PROTEIN 40.4g; CARB 43.7g; FIBER 6.7g; CHOL 96mg; IRON 2.2mg; SODIUM 610mg; CALC 83mg

QUICK & EASY
Grilled Tuna Steaks with Pineapple Salsa

Wild salmon or swordfish would also work well in this recipe.

- 1 cup fresh orange juice
- 2 tablespoons low-sodium soy sauce
- ½ pineapple, peeled, cored, and cut into ½-inch-thick rings
- 1 medium red onion, peeled and cut into ½-inch-thick slices
- Cooking spray
- 4 (6-ounce) tuna steaks
- 1 tablespoon canola oil
- ½ teaspoon salt, divided
- ¼ teaspoon freshly ground black pepper, divided
- 2 tablespoons chopped fresh basil
- 1 tablespoon chopped fresh mint
- 1 tablespoon fresh lime juice
- 1 serrano pepper, seeded and minced
- 4 fresh mint sprigs (optional)

① Prepare grill to medium-high heat.

② Boil orange juice in a small saucepan 15 minutes or until reduced to ¼ cup. Transfer to a small bowl; stir in soy sauce.

③ Place pineapple and onion on a grill rack coated with cooking spray. Grill 5 minutes on each side or until onion is tender. Remove from grill; let stand 5 minutes. Coarsely chop, and transfer to a bowl.

④ Brush both sides of fish evenly with oil; sprinkle evenly with ¼ teaspoon salt and ⅛ teaspoon pepper. Place fish on a grill rack coated with cooking spray; brush with half of juice mixture. Grill 3 minutes; turn fish over. Brush fish with remaining juice mixture; grill 3 minutes or until desired degree of doneness.

⑤ Add remaining ¼ teaspoon salt, remaining ⅛ teaspoon pepper, basil, and next 3 ingredients to pineapple mixture; toss. Serve with fish; garnish with mint sprigs, if desired. Yield: 4 servings (serving size: 1 tuna steak and ½ cup salsa).

CALORIES 243; FAT 5g (sat 0.6g, mono 2.3g, poly 1.5g); PROTEIN 31.4g; CARB 17.8g; FIBER 1.7g; CHOL 57mg; IRON 1.7mg; SODIUM 612mg; CALC 49mg

---

How to
Grill Fish

Grilling adds sublime flavor to fish. Two keys to great results every time: Pick the proper fish, and don't turn it too soon. Meaty fish, like salmon, halibut, and tuna, are the best candidates because they're sturdy enough to hold up on the grill.

Before you start, clean the grate. (Debris left from the last cookout contributes to sticking.) Preheat the grill and grate, and coat the grate well with cooking spray or brush it with oil before adding food. Fish (and most foods) will stick at first, even if you oil the grate, but fillets should also release naturally when they're ready to be turned. If you try to turn and they seem to be sticking, allow a little more time before turning.

Fish needs only salt, pepper, and a little oil to yield delicious results when grilled. But if you want to enhance the flavor, brush it with a glaze as it cooks, or serve with a sauce. (See "Garden-Fresh Salsas, Chutneys & Relishes" on page 189 for some new tastes.)

Assertive marinades can enhance flavor, but if you use them, be sure to keep an eye on the clock. Why? The texture of fish is easily altered by acidic mixtures. Meaty and oily fish, like swordfish, tuna, and salmon, can marinate longer, but more delicate varieties require a shorter exposure. Be sure to follow the recipe exactly for best results.

Swordfish Skewers with Cilantro-Mint Pesto

Although imported swordfish is endangered, the population for North American species is healthy. Check with your fish seller to make sure the fish you purchase was caught in the United States or Canada.

PESTO:
- 1 cup fresh cilantro leaves
- ½ cup fresh mint leaves
- 3 tablespoons fresh orange juice
- 2 tablespoons chopped green onions
- 1 tablespoon fresh lime juice
- 2 teaspoons extra-virgin olive oil
- ¼ teaspoon salt
- 1 garlic clove, minced

SKEWERS:
- 2 teaspoons grated lime rind
- 1 teaspoon grated orange rind
- 2 tablespoons fresh orange juice
- 1 tablespoon fresh lime juice
- 2 teaspoons sugar
- 2 garlic cloves, minced
- 1½ pounds swordfish fillets, cut into 1¼-inch cubes
- 24 cherry tomatoes
- ¼ teaspoon salt
- ¼ teaspoon freshly ground black pepper
- Cooking spray

❶ To prepare pesto, place first 8 ingredients in a food processor; process until smooth. Let stand 30 minutes.
❷ Prepare grill to medium-high heat.
❸ To prepare skewers, combine lime rind and next 5 ingredients in a large zip-top plastic bag. Add fish to bag; seal. Marinate in refrigerator for 30 minutes, turning bag once. Remove fish from bag; discard marinade. Thread fish and tomatoes alternately onto each of 8 (8-inch) skewers; sprinkle evenly with ¼ teaspoon salt and pepper.
❹ Place skewers on a grill rack coated with cooking spray; grill 6 minutes or until desired degree of doneness, turning every 2 minutes. Serve with pesto. Yield: 4 servings (serving size: 2 skewers and about 2 tablespoons pesto).

CALORIES 206; FAT 7.5g (sat 1.7g, mono 3.6g, poly 1.5g); PROTEIN 25g; CARB 9.5g; FIBER 1.8g; CHOL 47mg; IRON 1.8mg; SODIUM 416mg; CALC 31mg

Poached Salmon with Dill-Mustard Sauce

Prepare the sauce up to two days ahead. You can also poach the salmon a couple of hours ahead and serve it chilled, if you prefer. Take care to cook the salmon over even heat, and maintain a constant, steady temperature.

SAUCE:
- 2 tablespoons reduced-fat sour cream
- 1 tablespoon organic canola mayonnaise (such as Spectrum)
- 1½ teaspoons chopped fresh dill
- 1½ teaspoons fresh lemon juice
- 1½ teaspoons country-style Dijon mustard

SALMON:
- 3½ cups dry white wine
- 2 cups water
- ¼ cup fresh lemon juice
- 2 cups thinly sliced onion
- 2 dill sprigs
- 4 (6-ounce) salmon fillets, skin on (about 1 inch thick)
- Dill sprigs (optional)
- Lemon wedges (optional)

❶ To prepare sauce, combine first 5 ingredients in a small bowl, stirring well. Cover and chill 2 hours.
❷ To prepare salmon, heat wine and next 4 ingredients in a large skillet to 150°. Cover and simmer 10 minutes. Add fish to wine mixture; cook at 150° for 12 minutes or until desired degree of doneness. Transfer to a serving platter with a slotted spoon. Serve with sauce. Garnish with dill sprigs and lemon wedges, if desired. Yield: 4 servings (serving size: 1 fillet and about 1½ tablespoons sauce).

CALORIES 286; FAT 18.7g (sat 3.1g, mono 6.4g, poly 3.8g); PROTEIN 26.3g; CARB 3.1g; FIBER 0.4g; CHOL 82mg; IRON 1.2mg; SODIUM 96mg; CALC 68mg

Poaching is a simple preparation that plays up the natural flavor of fish. You need to submerge fillets in a seasoned liquid, and cook gently. We bring the poaching liquid to 150°, add the fish, return the liquid to 150°, and cook at that temperature to the desired degree of doneness. Incidentally, this technique requires no added fat, so it's inherently healthy.

Salt
Here are some simple ways to cut back without losing flavor.

CONGRATULATIONS! If you're cooking at home, you've taken a significant step toward lowering your sodium intake, thereby reducing your risk of heart disease and stroke. Of the 3,600 milligrams of sodium consumed each day by the average American, 77 percent is from processed and restaurant foods. Home cooking accounts for five percent of the daily allotted 2,300 milligrams of sodium for healthy adults.

"Cooking puts you in control of the amount of salt and sodium in food," says *Cooking Light* Nutrition Essentials Advisory Panel Expert Heather Bauer, RD, CDN.

On the following pages, Bauer and Amy Myrdal Miller, MS, RD, of the Culinary Institute of America Greystone (CIA), a premier culinary school, provide tips on how to manage salt and sodium while building flavor with other ingredients and techniques.

The result: Your body—and your taste buds—can get by with less and never know the difference.

QUICK & EASY
Herb and Goat Cheese Omelet

A tender omelet gains a salty boost from goat cheese without adding too much sodium. Serve with seedy whole-grain toast and fresh fruit for a hearty brunch.

- 4 large eggs
- 1 tablespoon water
- ¼ teaspoon freshly ground black pepper, divided
- ⅛ teaspoon salt
- 1 teaspoon chopped fresh parsley
- ½ teaspoon chopped fresh tarragon
- ¼ cup (1 ounce) crumbled goat cheese
- 2 teaspoons olive oil, divided
- ½ cup thinly sliced zucchini
- ½ cup (3 x ¼-inch) julienne-cut red bell pepper
- Dash of salt
- 1 teaspoon chopped fresh chives

❶ Combine eggs and 1 tablespoon water in a bowl, stirring with a whisk. Stir in ⅛ teaspoon pepper and ⅛ teaspoon salt. Combine parsley, tarragon, and goat cheese in a small bowl.

❷ Heat 1 teaspoon olive oil in an 8-inch nonstick skillet over medium heat. Add remaining ⅛ teaspoon pepper, zucchini, bell pepper, and dash of salt to pan; cook 4 minutes or until tender. Remove zucchini mixture from pan; cover and keep warm.

❸ Place ½ teaspoon oil in skillet. Pour half of the egg mixture into pan, and let egg mixture set slightly (do not stir). Carefully loosen set edges of omelet with a spatula, tipping the pan to pour uncooked egg to the sides. Continue this procedure for about 5 seconds or until almost no runny egg remains. Sprinkle half of cheese mixture evenly over omelet; cook omelet 1 minute or until set. Slide omelet onto plate, folding into thirds. Repeat procedure with remaining ½ teaspoon oil, egg mixture, and goat cheese mixture. Sprinkle chives over omelets. Serve with zucchini mixture. Yield: 2 servings (serving size: 1 omelet and ½ cup vegetables).

CALORIES 233; FAT 17.6g (sat 5.8g, mono 7.8g, poly 2g); PROTEIN 16g; CARB 3.6g; FIBER 1g; CHOL 430mg; IRON 2.5mg; SODIUM 416mg; CALC 84mg

QUICK & EASY
Halibut Meunière

Using a bit of salt to season the fish and a little more to boost the pan sauce heightens flavors without going overboard in sodium. A little lemon juice and fresh parsley round out flavors. For another flavor boost, serve with fresh lemon wedges.

- 4 (6-ounce) halibut fillets (about ¾ inch thick)
- ¼ teaspoon black pepper
- ¼ teaspoon salt, divided
- 1 teaspoon all-purpose flour
- 1½ tablespoons butter, divided
- 2 tablespoons fresh lemon juice
- 1 tablespoon finely chopped fresh parsley

❶ Pat fish dry, and sprinkle both sides with pepper and ⅛ teaspoon salt. Sprinkle with flour. Melt 1½ teaspoons butter in a large nonstick skillet over medium heat. Add fish to pan, and cook 5 minutes or until lightly browned. Carefully turn fish over; cook 4 minutes or until fish flakes easily when tested with a fork or until desired degree of doneness. Remove fish from pan; set aside, and keep warm.

❷ Add remaining 1 tablespoon butter to pan, and cook 1 minute or until lightly browned, swirling pan to melt butter evenly and prevent burning. Remove pan from heat; stir in juice. Drizzle juice mixture over fish. Sprinkle fish with remaining ⅛ teaspoon salt. Sprinkle with parsley. Serve immediately. Yield: 4 servings (serving size: 1 fillet and about 1½ teaspoons sauce).

CALORIES 221; FAT 8g (sat 3.2g, mono 2.3g, poly 1.4g); PROTEIN 34.2g; CARB 1.3g; FIBER 0.1g; CHOL 64mg; IRON 1.5mg; SODIUM 266mg; CALC 80mg

Salt Savvy in the Kitchen

Salt provides a precise package of sodium and chloride. These minerals are essential to electrolyte balance in our bodies, and our senses can't do without them. For one thing, nothing else quite satisfies the craving for a salty taste. For another, salt likely excites the sense of smell by enhancing aromas wafting from hot dishes. The smart techniques here make the most of those appealing benefits while minimizing sodium amounts.

1 Use Acids and Fresh Herbs as Flavor Accents.

Stock the pantry with flavor enhancers to boost taste without added sodium. Acids like wine, citrus juices, or vinegars brighten flavors while fresh herbs enliven finished dishes. Miller recommends trying a savory recipe with half the recommended salt, and filling in with other flavors. "For homemade marinara sauce, add a splash of red wine as the sauce simmers, and then sprinkle in some chopped fresh basil at the end," she says. "The alcohol in the wine heightens the flavors of other ingredients, and the fresh basil adds freshness and great aroma. These other ingredients contribute so much flavor that diners won't notice smaller amounts of salt."

2 Excite Taste Buds with Spice Blends and Specialty Salts.

At the CIA, chefs are revising seasoning strategies, Miller says. They have been inspired by global culinary techniques to infuse dishes with flavor without excess salt and sodium.

Miller notes two helpful strategies. One is using toasted spice blends, which offer flavor nuances. The blend is ground, and chefs add a sprinkle during cooking. If the mixture isn't too fiery or assertive, a final flourish of the blend with a dash of salt is added to round flavors. Another option is to add a dash of flavored or specialty salts, like smoked sea salt or *fleur de sel* (a finishing salt from France), which, when added at the end of cooking, puts the salt flavor and texture up front, says Miller.

3 Be Picky About Pantry Staples.

"Most people know many canned foods can have a lot of sodium, but they're always surprised at where else it hides," says Bauer. "It's in breakfast cereals, in salad dressings, in jarred marinara sauce, and in breads, too." Compare brands, and make the better choice. "If one energy bar has 20 milligrams of sodium and another has 250 milligrams, choose the one with less sodium." Same goes for pantry staples like chicken broth, canned tomatoes or beans, pasta sauces, breads, and condiments. Choosing lower-sodium versions of these foods lets you stretch your sodium budget further, so you can add salt to foods that really need it.

4 Let Small Amounts of Salty and High-Sodium Ingredients Shine.

Bauer admits many salt-free foods can be lacking in taste. That's why she advises clients in her nutrition consulting practice to indulge in some higher-sodium ingredients, but to keep amounts small. For example, just a little grated or finely shredded full-flavored cheese makes a powerfully tasty pizza or pasta topper without adding excessive sodium.

Your Daily Dose

Everyone needs a little sodium because it helps maintain healthy fluid and electrolyte balance in the body. But too much elevates your blood pressure, increasing the risk of heart disease and stroke.

Nearly one in three Americans suffer from high blood pressure, and another 28 percent of us are teetering on the edge of developing it.

Most of us, seven out of 10 Americans, according to a new report from the Centers for Disease Control and Prevention, should aim for 1,500 milligrams of sodium (about 2/3 teaspoon) a day. That includes anyone with high blood pressure, those over 40 years of age, and all African Americans. The rest of us can safely tolerate up to 2,300 milligrams of sodium (1 teaspoon) per day.

Chicken and Roquefort Sandwiches

One serving of this entrée contains about one-fourth of your daily sodium allotment. We extend salty Roquefort cheese by mixing it with cream cheese as a spread. A 2-ounce portion size for bread also helps control sodium counts.

- ½ cup (about 3 ounces) tub whipped cream cheese
- ¼ cup (1 ounce) crumbled blue cheese
- 2 tablespoons finely chopped celery
- 1½ teaspoons chopped fresh chives
- 2 teaspoons olive oil
- 2 (6-ounce) skinless, boneless chicken breasts
- ¼ teaspoon coarsely ground black pepper
- ⅛ teaspoon salt
- 1 (8-ounce) baguette
- 2 small heirloom tomatoes, thinly sliced (about 8 ounces)
- ½ cup baby arugula leaves

❶ Combine first 4 ingredients in a bowl.
❷ Heat oil in a nonstick skillet over medium-high heat. Sprinkle chicken with pepper. Add chicken to pan; cook 5 minutes on each side or until chicken is done. Remove from heat; let stand 5 minutes. Cut lengthwise into ⅓-inch-thick strips. Sprinkle evenly with ⅛ teaspoon salt.
❸ Cut baguette in half lengthwise. Spread cheese mixture over cut sides of baguette. Arrange chicken, tomato slices, and arugula evenly over bottom half of baguette; cover with top half. Cut crosswise into 4 equal pieces. Yield: 4 servings (serving size: 1 sandwich).

CALORIES 392; FAT 15.8g (sat 7g, mono 5.2g, poly 1.2g); PROTEIN 27.9g; CARB 35.1g; FIBER 2.2g; CHOL 84mg; IRON 3.1mg; SODIUM 640mg; CALC 100mg

Egyptian-Spiced Chicken

This spice blend, known as *dukka* (DOO-kah) in Egypt, combines sesame and cumin seeds plus nuts, and often other spices. The blend gains a roasted note when the spices and nuts are toasted. Then a little salt on the chicken brings out the robust flavors of the blend.

¼   cup sliced almonds
¼   cup sesame seeds
2   teaspoons cumin seeds
2   tablespoons fresh thyme leaves
1   teaspoon black peppercorns
2   large egg whites, lightly beaten
4   (6-ounce) skinless, boneless
     chicken breast halves
¼   teaspoon salt
2   teaspoons olive oil
     Cooking spray

❶ Preheat oven to 350°.
❷ Place first 3 ingredients in a small, dry skillet over medium heat. Cook 2 minutes

or until lightly browned, shaking pan frequently. Remove from heat, and cool slightly. Place nut mixture, thyme, and peppercorns in a spice or coffee grinder; pulse mixture 15 times to coarsely chop.
❸ Place nut mixture in a shallow pan; place egg whites in another shallow pan. Dip chicken in egg white, and sprinkle with salt; dredge in almond mixture. Heat oil in a large nonstick skillet coated with cooking spray over medium-high heat. Add chicken to pan; sauté 2 minutes on each side or until golden. Place chicken on a baking sheet coated with cooking spray, and bake at 350° for 12 minutes or until done. Yield: 4 servings (serving size: 1 breast half).

CALORIES 317; FAT 14g (sat 2.2g, mono 6g, poly 4.5g); PROTEIN 44.9g; CARB 3.8g; FIBER 1g; CHOL 108mg; IRON 3mg; SODIUM 274mg; CALC 58mg

QUICK & EASY
Seared Scallops with Coarse Sea Salt

Watching portion sizes helps keep sodium in check when considering fish and shellfish. With a 6-ounce portion of cooked scallops, we can allot for a dusting of coarse sea salt to highlight their delicate flavor and add a crunchy textural counterpoint to the dish.

12   large sea scallops (about 2 pounds)
⅛   teaspoon freshly ground black pepper
1   tablespoon olive oil
⅛   teaspoon coarse sea salt or finishing
     salt
     Watercress sprigs (optional)

❶ Pat scallops dry with paper towels; sprinkle evenly with pepper. Heat oil in a large cast-iron skillet over medium-high heat. Add scallops to pan; sauté 3 minutes on each side or until done. Remove scallops from pan; sprinkle with salt. Garnish with watercress sprigs, if desired. Yield: 4 servings (serving size: 3 scallops).

CALORIES 231; FAT 5.1g (sat 0.7g, mono 2.6g, poly 1g); PROTEIN 38.4g; CARB 5.6g; FIBER 0.1g; CHOL 75mg; IRON 0.7mg; SODIUM 430mg; CALC 72mg

QUICK & EASY
Garlicky Spaghetti with Beans and Greens

Canned beans are a great pantry staple with lots of protein and fiber. To help reduce sodium in regular canned beans, we rinse and drain them.

8   ounces uncooked spaghetti
¾   teaspoon kosher salt, divided
3   tablespoons extra-virgin olive oil
2   tablespoons minced fresh garlic
½   teaspoon crushed red pepper
2   cups grape tomatoes, halved
1   (16-ounce) can cannellini beans or
     other white beans, rinsed and
     drained
5   ounces arugula leaves
2   tablespoons fresh lemon juice
½   cup (2 ounces) grated Parmesan
     cheese

❶ Cook pasta according to package directions, omitting salt and fat. Drain pasta in a colander over a bowl, reserving ½ cup pasta water. Place pasta in a small bowl. Add ¼ teaspoon salt, tossing gently. Set aside, and keep warm.
❷ Return pan to medium heat. Add oil, garlic, and pepper; cook 2 minutes or until garlic is lightly browned, stirring occasionally. Stir in remaining ½ teaspoon salt, tomatoes, and beans; cook 2 minutes. Add pasta; cook 4 minutes, stirring frequently. Add reserved pasta water and arugula, tossing gently to combine. Remove from heat. Stir in lemon juice and cheese. Serve immediately. Yield: 6 servings (serving size: about 1⅓ cups).

CALORIES 290; FAT 10.5g (sat 2.7g, mono 5.8g, poly 1.3g); PROTEIN 11.3g; CARB 38.1g; FIBER 3.7g; CHOL 8mg; IRON 2.4mg; SODIUM 469mg; CALC 173mg

One Simple Salt Blend, Five Tasty Uses

- Mix with softened butter. Rub under chicken skin before roasting.

- Season cooked shrimp.

- Rim a cocktail glass.

- Sprinkle on roasted or mashed potatoes.

- Mix with extra-virgin olive oil for a dip.

Simple Steak Supper Menu

serves 4

Flavored salt offers a quick way to jazz up the taste of seared or grilled meats, fish, or poultry.

Beef Tenderloin Steaks with **Lemon-Rosemary Salt**

Heat a large nonstick skillet over medium-high heat. Add 1 tablespoon butter to pan, swirling to coat. Add 4 (4-ounce) beef tenderloin steaks to pan; cook 2 minutes on each side or until desired degree of doneness. Remove steaks from pan; let stand 5 minutes. Rub each steak with ¼ teaspoon Lemon-Rosemary Salt.

Mashed potatoes sprinkled with cracked black pepper

Steamed haricots verts or green beans

Zinfandel

Pound cake with fresh berries

QUICK AND EASY • MAKE AHEAD
Lemon-Rosemary Salt

One teaspoon of this herb-enhanced salt has 600 milligrams less sodium than a teaspoon of kosher salt. So if you're seasoning a dish serving four with 1 teaspoon of this blend, for example, you shave 150 milligrams of sodium per serving. Vary the rinds and herbs used; try grated orange rind and fresh thyme or grated lime rind and cilantro for other combinations.

- 8 teaspoons grated lemon rind (about 2 large lemons)
- 4 teaspoons kosher salt
- 1 teaspoon finely chopped fresh rosemary

❶ Combine all ingredients in a mini chopper; pulse 5 times or until well blended. Yield: 2 tablespoons (serving size: 1 teaspoon).

CALORIES 2; FAT 0g; PROTEIN 0g; CARB 0.5g; FIBER 0.3g; CHOL 0mg; IRON 0.1mg; SODIUM 1,255mg; CALC 5mg

Chile Pepper Striped Bass

A little salt sprinkled onto the fillets balances and enhances fiery flavors from the marinade. Panko (Japanese breadcrumbs) has about one-fourth the sodium of dry breadcrumbs but offers the same satisfying crunch to sautéed fish.

- ¼ cup finely chopped seeded Anaheim chile
- 1 teaspoon minced garlic
- ¼ teaspoon ground red pepper
- 5 teaspoons canola oil, divided
- 4 (6-ounce) farmed-raised striped bass fillets (about ½ inch thick)
- 2 large egg whites, lightly beaten
- ⅓ cup panko (Japanese breadcrumbs)
- ½ teaspoon grated lemon rind
- ¼ teaspoon salt
- 4 lemon wedges

❶ Combine first 3 ingredients and 2 teaspoons oil in a large zip-top plastic bag. Add fish to bag; seal and refrigerate 30 minutes.

❷ Remove fish from bag, discarding marinade. Brush chile off fish. Place egg whites in a shallow dish. Combine panko and rind in another shallow dish. Dip fish in egg white; dredge in panko mixture. Repeat procedure with remaining 3 fillets, egg white, and panko mixture. Sprinkle fillets evenly with salt.

❸ Heat remaining 1 tablespoon oil in a large nonstick skillet over medium-high heat. Add fish to pan; sauté 3 minutes or until golden brown. Turn fish over; cook 4 minutes or until fish flakes easily when tested with a fork or until desired degree of doneness. Serve with lemon wedges. Yield: 4 servings (serving size: 1 fillet and 1 lemon wedge).

CALORIES 230; FAT 9.8g (sat 1.3g, mono 4.5g, poly 3g); PROTEIN 29.8g; CARB 3.8g; FIBER 0.3g; CHOL 131mg; IRON 1.4mg; SODIUM 274mg; CALC 26mg

QUICK & EASY
Soy-Glazed Tofu

Added sodium and sugar tame seasoned rice vinegar's tartness, making a nice counterpoint to sesame oil, sweet orange juice, and aromatic orange rind. To serve, drizzle the tofu with the flavorful pan sauce. Add the sauce to plain rice noodles tossed with snow peas, carrots, and bell pepper for a smart entrée.

- 1 (12-ounce) package firm tofu, drained and cut crosswise into 6 slices
- 3 tablespoons seasoned rice vinegar
- 2 tablespoons fresh orange juice
- 2 tablespoons low-sodium soy sauce
- 1 tablespoon brown sugar
- ¼ teaspoon grated orange rind
- 1 teaspoon dark sesame oil
- 2 tablespoons thinly diagonally sliced green onions
- ½ teaspoon sesame seeds, toasted

1 Cut each slice of tofu in half diagonally. Place tofu slices on several layers of paper towels, and cover tofu with additional paper towels; let stand 15 minutes, pressing down occasionally.

2 Combine vinegar and next 4 ingredients in a small saucepan; bring to a boil. Reduce heat and simmer, uncovered, 6 minutes or until thick and syrupy. Heat oil in a large nonstick skillet over medium-high heat. Arrange tofu slices in pan in a single layer; sauté 5 minutes on each side or until golden brown. Remove from heat; pour vinegar mixture over tofu to coat. Sprinkle with green onions and sesame seeds. Serve immediately. Yield: 4 servings (serving size: 3 triangles).

CALORIES 132; FAT 6.5g (sat 1.2g, mono 1.5g, poly 3.6g); PROTEIN 8.9g; CARB 9.2g; FIBER 0.1g; CHOL 0mg; IRON 1.8mg; SODIUM 419mg; CALC 68mg

WINE NOTE: Tofu works with just about every wine, but given the flavors of soy sauce, orange, and sesame, a refreshing white is in order. In particular, sesame and orange both work magnificently with unoaked chardonnay. Try St. Supery Oak Free Chardonnay from Napa Valley, California. The 2008 is $25.

Test Kitchen Secrets

Two simple steps yield juicy, beefy burgers.

Former Test Kitchen professional Mike Wilson has two tips for making leaner beef into tasty, juicy burgers. "It's important to season the ground beef and then let the mixture rest so the salt penetrates the meat. Next, very gingerly pat portions of ground beef into patties so the burgers seem to barely hold together; the cooked burgers will be tender and less dense than if you pack the meat too tightly," Wilson says. Both of his tips work like a charm. Prep the fixings—the horseradish spread and caramelized onion and bacon relish—while the burgers rest in the fridge after seasoning.

STAFF FAVORITE
Cast-Iron Burgers

PATTIES:
- 1 pound ground sirloin
- ½ teaspoon kosher salt

HORSERADISH SPREAD:
- 1 tablespoon canola mayonnaise
- 1 tablespoon Dijon mustard
- 1 tablespoon prepared horseradish
- 2 teaspoons ketchup

RELISH:
- 2 applewood-smoked bacon slices, chopped
- 3 cups vertically sliced yellow onion
- 1 tablespoon finely chopped fresh chives
- 1 teaspoon Worcestershire sauce
- ¼ teaspoon freshly ground black pepper

REMAINING INGREDIENTS:
- Cooking spray
- 4 (1½-ounce) hamburger buns or Kaiser rolls
- 4 (¼-inch-thick) slices tomato
- 1 cup shredded lettuce

1 To prepare patties, divide beef into 4 portions, lightly shaping each into a ½-inch-thick patty. Sprinkle evenly with salt. Cover and refrigerate 30 minutes.

2 To prepare horseradish spread, combine mayonnaise and next 3 ingredients in a small bowl. Set aside.

3 To prepare relish, cook bacon in a large nonstick skillet over medium-low heat until crisp. Remove bacon from pan with a slotted spoon. Add onion to drippings in pan; cook 15 minutes or until golden brown. Combine bacon, onion, chives, Worcestershire sauce, and pepper in a small bowl.

4 Heat a large cast-iron skillet over medium-high heat. Coat pan with cooking spray. Add patties; cook 2 minutes on each side or until desired degree of doneness. Spread 1½ teaspoons horseradish spread on cut sides of each bun half. Top bottom half of each bun with 1 patty, ¼ cup relish, 1 tomato slice, ¼ cup lettuce, and top half of bun. Yield: 4 burgers (serving size: 1 burger).

CALORIES 351; FAT 12g (sat 3.5g, mono 3.4g, poly 3.2g); PROTEIN 29.2g; CARB 32.7g; FIBER 3g; CHOL 66mg; IRON 3.7mg; SODIUM 788mg; CALC 91mg

Fresh Ways with Fresh Herbs

Whether you pick them from your windowsill or buy them at the farmers' market, no other ingredient does more to make food taste like summer. Here are new recipes for salads, sides, entrées, and condiments that vividly capture their bright, distinctive tastes.

QUICK & EASY • MAKE AHEAD
Cilantro-Walnut Pesto

Place plastic wrap directly on surface of leftover pesto to prevent browning.

- 3 garlic cloves
- 3 cups packed fresh cilantro leaves and tender stems (about 3 ounces)
- ¼ cup chopped walnuts, toasted
- 2 tablespoons white wine vinegar
- ½ teaspoon salt
- ¼ cup organic vegetable broth (such as Swanson)
- 3 tablespoons extra-virgin olive oil

❶ Place garlic in a food processor; pulse 10 times or until minced. Add cilantro and next 3 ingredients to processor; process 15 seconds. Combine broth and oil in a small bowl. With processor on, slowly pour broth mixture through food chute; process until well blended. Yield: 16 servings (serving size: 1 tablespoon).

CALORIES 37; FAT 3.9g (sat 0.5g, mono 2.1g, poly 1.2g); PROTEIN 0.4g; CARB 0.7g; FIBER 0.3g; CHOL 0mg; IRON 0.2mg; SODIUM 85mg; CALC 6mg

QUICK & EASY
Cherry Tomato and Herb Salad

Four kinds of chopped leaves give this simple salad complex flavor.

- 2 tablespoons fresh lemon juice
- 1 tablespoon extra-virgin olive oil
- ½ teaspoon Dijon mustard
- ½ teaspoon honey
- ¼ teaspoon salt
- ¼ teaspoon freshly ground black pepper
- 8 cups torn Boston lettuce (about 2 large heads)
- 2 cups multicolored cherry tomatoes, halved
- 1 tablespoon chopped fresh basil
- 1 tablespoon chopped fresh chives
- 1 tablespoon chopped fresh flat-leaf parsley
- 1 tablespoon chopped fresh thyme

❶ Combine first 6 ingredients in a small bowl, stirring with a whisk. Combine lettuce and remaining ingredients in a large bowl; toss gently to combine. Drizzle juice mixture over salad; toss gently to coat. Yield: 6 servings (serving size: about 1²/₃ cups).

CALORIES 41; FAT 2.6g (sat 0.4g, mono 1.7g, poly 0.4g); PROTEIN 1.3g; CARB 4.4g; FIBER 1.3g; CHOL 0mg; IRON 0.9mg; SODIUM 114mg; CALC 31mg

MAKE AHEAD
Thyme Corn Bread

Familiar bread recipes taste brand new with the addition of even a small spoonful of herbs. Stir them in right before baking.

- 4.5 ounces all-purpose flour (about 1 cup)
- ¾ cup yellow cornmeal
- 1 tablespoon sugar
- 1 teaspoon baking soda
- ¾ teaspoon salt
- ¾ cup reduced-fat buttermilk
- 2 tablespoons canola oil
- 1 large egg
- ½ cup fresh corn kernels (about 1 ear)
- 1½ tablespoons fresh thyme leaves
   Cooking spray

❶ Preheat oven to 350°.
❷ Weigh or lightly spoon flour into a dry measuring cup; level with a knife. Combine flour and next 4 ingredients in a bowl. Make a well in center of mixture. Combine buttermilk, oil, and egg in a bowl; stir in corn and thyme. Add buttermilk mixture to flour mixture; stir just until moist.
❸ Spoon batter into an 8-inch square baking pan lightly coated with cooking spray. Bake at 350° for 25 minutes or until corn bread is lightly browned and begins to pull away from sides of pan. Cool in pan 5 minutes on a wire rack. Yield: 9 servings (serving size: 1 piece).

CALORIES 161; FAT 4.4g (sat 0.7g, mono 2.3g, poly 1.1g); PROTEIN 4.2g; CARB 25.5g; FIBER 0.9g; CHOL 25mg; IRON 1.1mg; SODIUM 364mg; CALC 39mg

Herb Highlights

Since each herb has its own distinctive flavor profile, certain food pairings work particularly well. If you want to branch out with a substitute, follow our suggestions below.

Herb	Taste	Use	Substitutes
basil	Slightly peppery	Mediterranean dishes; tomato-based sauces, soups, stews, and salads; beef; chicken; seafood	Oregano
chives	Mild onion flavor	Meats; seafood; soups; stews; sauces; egg dishes	Green onion tops
cilantro	Slightly citrusy	Asian and Latin dishes; salsas; soups; stews	Parsley
dill	Tangy and sweet	Seafood; chicken; vegetables; soups	Tarragon
oregano	Pungent; sweet yet peppery	Mediterranean dishes; seafood; tomato-based dishes	Marjoram
parsley	Lightly peppery; grassy	An all-purpose herb suitable as a finishing garnish for many dishes	Chervil, cilantro
rosemary	Piney	Beef; chicken; lamb; pork; breads; shrimp	Thyme
sage	Pleasantly bitter; musty	Pork; chicken; stews; poultry stuffing	Marjoram, rosemary
tarragon	Licorice notes	Seafood; chicken; eggs; sauces	Chervil, parsley
thyme	Floral; slightly lemony	Beef; chicken; mushrooms; pork; breads	Marjoram, oregano, rosemary

Toasted Pita Salad

This Mediterranean-style salad highlights the pungent, peppery tang of oregano.

- 2 (6-inch) pitas, split in half horizontally
- 3 cups chopped tomato (about 4 medium)
- 1½ cups chopped English cucumber
- ¼ cup finely chopped red onion
- ¼ cup chopped fresh oregano
- 2 tablespoons chopped fresh flat-leaf parsley
- 2 tablespoons fresh lime juice
- 1 teaspoon ground cumin
- 4 teaspoons extra-virgin olive oil
- ½ teaspoon salt
- ½ teaspoon freshly ground black pepper
- ½ teaspoon honey

❶ Preheat oven to 350°.
❷ Place pitas on a baking sheet; bake at 350° for 10 minutes or until crisp. Cool completely; break into small pieces.
❸ Combine tomato and next 4 ingredients in a large bowl. Combine lime juice and remaining ingredients in a small bowl, stirring with a whisk. Pour juice mixture over tomato mixture; toss gently. Add pita pieces to bowl; toss gently. Let stand 10 minutes before serving. Yield: 6 servings (serving size: about 1 cup).

CALORIES 111; FAT 3.5g (sat 0.5g, mono 2.3g, poly 0.5g); PROTEIN 3.8g; CARB 17.5g; FIBER 2.1g; CHOL 0mg; IRON 1.4mg; SODIUM 256mg; CALC 42mg

---

Grow Your Own

Packaged fresh herbs can be costly, particularly if there's waste—for example, you buy a bunch of herbs for a recipe and only use a few tablespoons; the rest languishes before you can use it. One solution: Grow herbs at home. If you don't want to devote space in your garden—or don't have a garden—grow them indoors. We recommend these tips from experience:
• Start small, with an indoor pot or two, until you find whether your home is well-suited for hosting potted herbs.
• Position your pots in windows with southern exposure for the most sunlight.
• Be careful not to overwater herbs. Add water only when the soil is dry. Yellowing leaves can be an indicator of overwatering.
• We've found it easier to buy healthy seedlings from a nursery rather than starting from scratch and planting seeds.
• Herbs that tend to flourish indoors include mint, rosemary, chives, and oregano.

Having your own herb supply at home also means less waste since you can snip and use precisely what you need for a recipe.

Rosemary Grilled Steak with Tomato Jam

Fresh rosemary brings pleasant pine notes to grilled beef. If you don't have time to make the jam, use bottled tomato chutney instead. Extra rosemary sprigs make a lovely garnish.

- 1 teaspoon canola oil
- 1 tablespoon finely chopped shallots
- 1 teaspoon minced garlic, divided
- ¾ cup finely chopped tomato
- 2 tablespoons water
- 1 tablespoon white balsamic vinegar
- ⅛ teaspoon salt
- ¼ teaspoon freshly ground black pepper, divided
- 1 teaspoon minced fresh rosemary
- ¼ teaspoon salt
- 2 (4-ounce) beef tenderloin steaks, trimmed (1 inch thick)
- Cooking spray

❶ Prepare grill to medium-high heat.
❷ Heat a small nonstick skillet over medium heat. Add oil to pan, swirling to coat. Add shallots to pan; cook 3 minutes, stirring occasionally. Stir in ½ teaspoon garlic; cook 1 minute, stirring frequently. Add tomato and next 3 ingredients; bring to a boil. Reduce heat, and simmer 12 minutes or until liquid almost evaporates. Stir in ⅛ teaspoon pepper, and keep warm.
❸ Combine remaining ½ teaspoon minced garlic, remaining ⅛ teaspoon pepper, rosemary, and ¼ teaspoon salt in a small bowl.
❹ Place steaks on grill rack coated with cooking spray; grill 3 minutes. Turn steaks over. Sprinkle evenly with rosemary mixture, and grill 3 minutes or until desired degree of doneness. Serve with tomato jam. Yield: 2 servings (serving size: 1 steak and 2 tablespoons tomato jam).

CALORIES 168; FAT 6.5g (sat 1.7g, mono 2.9g, poly 0.8g); PROTEIN 22.9g; CARB 5.7g; FIBER 0.9g; CHOL 60mg; IRON 3.1mg; SODIUM 504mg; CALC 19mg

Continued on page 241

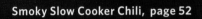
Smoky Slow Cooker Chili, page 52

Smothered Steak Burgers, page 19, and Shoestring Fries with Garlicky Dijon Mayo, page 20

Deep Dark Chocolate Biscotti, page 58

Roasted Vegetable Couscous with Chickpeas and Onion–Pine Nut Topping, page 44

Spaghetti with Tomato Sauce, page 72

Broccoli and Chicken
Noodle Soup, page 80

Almond-Stuffed Chicken,
page 54

Herbed Passover Rolls, page 106

Baked Shrimp with Feta, page 103

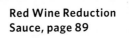
Red Wine Reduction
Sauce, page 89

Cilantro-Lime Chicken with Avocado Salsa,
page 81

Chicken and Feta Tabbouleh,
page 83

Chicken and Strawberry Salad,
page 115

Limoncello-Mint Sorbet with
Fresh Blackberries, page 134

Broiled Salmon with Peppercorn-Lime
Rub, page 116

Butterscotch Bars, page 104

Steak and Fennel Sandwiches,
page 112

Prosciutto-Melon Bites with
Lime Drizzle, page 132

Pan-Fried Chicken, page 158, and Potato Salad with Herbs and Grilled Summer Squash, page 137

Lemon-Thyme Cornmeal Quick Bread, page 162

Tomato Flatbread with Goat Cheese, page 146

Lemon Verbena Gimlet
Cocktails, page 138

Lobster Rolls, page 141

Berry-Peach Cobbler with Sugared
Almonds, page 172

Beef and Sugar Snap
Stir-Fry, page 178

Watermelon and Cucumber
Tonic, page 171

Purple Basil Parmesan
Biscuits, page 182

Jerk-Spiced Shrimp, page 244

Gazpacho with Shrimp and
Avocado Relish, page 243

Ginger-Garlic Chicken with
Fresh Fig Pan Sauce, page 195

Tartines with Cheese, Peppers, and Chard, page 255

Pain Perdu, page 276

Spice-Rubbed Braised
Beef, page 252

Beer-Braised Beef with Onion, Carrot,
and Turnips, page 294

Amaretto Apple Streusel
Cupcakes, page 321

Singapore-Style
Noodles, page 292

Roasted Brussels Sprouts
and Apples, page 330

Maple-Brined Turkey
Breast with Mushroom
Pan Gravy, page 327

Vanilla-Bourbon Pumpkin Tart,
page 334

Salmon with Satsuma-Soy
Glaze, page 327

Pecan Pie with Spiked Cream,
page 340

Fontina-Stuffed Potato
Skins, page 331

Chicken and Wild Rice Salad
with Almonds, page 369

Beer-Battered Fish and Chips,
page 381

Potato-Apple Latkes, page 371

Grilled Snapper with Orange-Tarragon Butter

Compound butter—butter mixed with other ingredients such as herbs and acids like wine or citrus juices—adds bright yet rich flavor to meat, poultry, fish, or vegetables. Use thyme, chives, or rosemary instead of tarragon, if you prefer. Keep the leftover butter mixture in the refrigerator for several days, and use it on steamed vegetables, shrimp, poultry, or meats.

- ½ teaspoon canola oil
- 4 (6-ounce) yellowtail snapper fillets
- ½ teaspoon salt
- ⅛ teaspoon paprika
- ⅛ teaspoon freshly ground black pepper
  Cooking spray
- 2 tablespoons Orange-Tarragon Butter

❶ Prepare grill to medium-high heat.
❷ Brush oil evenly over fish. Sprinkle fish with salt, paprika, and pepper. Place fish on grill rack coated with cooking spray; grill 3 minutes on each side or until fish flakes easily when tested with a fork or until desired degree of doneness. Cut butter into 4 equal portions; place 1 portion on top of each fillet. Yield: 4 servings (serving size: 1 fillet and 1½ teaspoons butter mixture).

CALORIES 227; FAT 8.6g (sat 4.1g, mono 2.2g, poly 1.2g); PROTEIN 35g; CARB 0.3g; FIBER 0.1g; CHOL 78mg; IRON 0.3mg; SODIUM 444mg; CALC 58mg

ORANGE-TARRAGON BUTTER:

- ¼ cup butter, softened
- 1 tablespoon finely chopped fresh tarragon
- ¼ teaspoon grated orange rind
- 2 teaspoons fresh orange juice

❶ Combine all ingredients in a small bowl. Place butter mixture on a long sheet of plastic wrap, and roll into a 3-inch log, covering completely. Freeze for 10 minutes or until firm. Yield:

8 servings (serving size: 1½ teaspoons butter mixture).

CALORIES 51; FAT 5.7g (sat 3.6g, mono 1.5g, poly 0.2g); PROTEIN 0.1g; CARB 0.2g; FIBER 0g; CHOL 15mg; IRON 0mg; SODIUM 40mg; CALC 3mg

Iceberg Wedge with Buttermilk-Herb Dressing

Bottled salad dressings are typically made with dried herbs, but we use fresh thyme, parsley, and chives to make a simple dressing special.

- ¾ cup reduced-fat buttermilk
- ½ cup reduced-fat mayonnaise
- ¼ cup chopped fresh chives
- 2 tablespoons chopped fresh flat-leaf parsley
- 1 tablespoon chopped fresh thyme
- 2 tablespoons white wine vinegar
- ¼ teaspoon salt
- ¼ teaspoon black pepper
- 1 garlic clove, minced
- 1 (1¼-pound) head iceberg lettuce, trimmed and cut into 6 wedges
- 24 grape tomatoes, halved
- ⅓ cup thinly sliced red onion
- 1-inch pieces fresh chives (optional)

❶ Place first 9 ingredients in a blender; process 45 seconds or until herbs are finely chopped.
❷ Place 1 lettuce wedge on each of 6 plates. Drizzle each wedge with 3 tablespoons dressing; top each serving with 8 tomato halves. Divide onion evenly among servings. Garnish with chive pieces, if desired. Yield: 6 servings.

CALORIES 58; FAT 0.9g (sat 0.4g, mono 0.2g, poly 0.2g); PROTEIN 2.8g; CARB 11.5g; FIBER 2g; CHOL 2mg; IRON 0.8mg; SODIUM 276mg; CALC 74mg

Storage tips

Wrap herbs in damp paper towels; store in partly sealed plastic bags so moisture can escape. Set cut ends of leafy herbs like parsley or cilantro into a glass with 1 inch water; cover loosely with plastic.

Dinner Tonight

From summertime soup to great grilled tastes, we have meals to suit your schedule.

Prosciutto, Lettuce, and Tomato Sandwiches
· *20 minutes*

For a zesty and pretty garnish, attach 1 small sweet gherkin pickle to the top of each sandwich with a toothpick. A toss-together fruit salad makes a speedy side. Combine 1 teaspoon fresh lime rind, 1 tablespoon fresh lime juice, 1 tablespoon honey, and a dash of salt; drizzle over 4 cups mixed precut fruit.

- 8 (1-ounce) slices 100% whole-grain bread
- ¼ cup canola mayonnaise
- 2 tablespoons chopped fresh basil
- 1 teaspoon Dijon mustard
- 1 small garlic clove, minced
- 1 cup baby romaine lettuce leaves
- 8 (¼-inch-thick) slices tomato
- 3 ounces very thin slices prosciutto

❶ Preheat broiler.
❷ Arrange bread slices in a single layer on a baking sheet. Broil bread slices 2 minutes on each side or until toasted.
❸ Combine mayonnaise and next 3 ingredients; spread mayonnaise mixture evenly over 4 bread slices. Layer ¼ cup lettuce and 2 tomato slices over each serving; top evenly with prosciutto and remaining bread. Yield: 4 servings (serving size: 1 sandwich).

CALORIES 243; FAT 9.4g (sat 1.4g, mono 4.6g, poly 2.4g); PROTEIN 11.8g; CARB 28.4g; FIBER 4.3g; CHOL 19mg; IRON 2.5mg; SODIUM 808mg; CALC 62mg

Cavatappi with Bacon and Summer Vegetables

· *20 minutes*

Serve with a mixed greens salad. Combine 1 tablespoon balsamic vinegar, 1 tablespoon orange juice, 2 teaspoons honey, ½ teaspoon Dijon mustard, ¼ teaspoon salt, and ⅛ teaspoon pepper. Whisk in 1 tablespoon extra-virgin olive oil. Toss with 6 cups mixed salad greens.

- 8 ounces uncooked cavatappi
- 4 slices center-cut bacon, chopped
- 2 teaspoons olive oil
- 1 cup prechopped onion
- 1 teaspoon bottled minced garlic
- 1 zucchini, quartered lengthwise and cut into ¼-inch-thick slices
- 1 cup fresh corn kernels (about 2 ears)
- 1 pint grape tomatoes
- ½ cup (2 ounces) shaved Parmigiano-Reggiano cheese, divided
- ¼ cup small fresh basil leaves
- ½ teaspoon salt
- ¼ teaspoon black pepper

❶ Cook pasta according to package directions, omitting salt and fat; drain.
❷ While pasta cooks, cook bacon in a large nonstick skillet over medium-high heat 5 minutes or until crisp. Remove bacon from pan with a slotted spoon, reserving drippings in pan; add oil to drippings. Add onion and garlic to pan; cook 2 minutes, stirring occasionally. Add zucchini; cook 3 minutes, stirring occasionally. Stir in corn and tomatoes; cook 5 minutes or until tomatoes burst, stirring occasionally. Add pasta to tomato mixture; toss. Cook 1 minute or until thoroughly heated, stirring frequently. Remove from heat. Add bacon, ¼ cup cheese, basil, salt, and pepper; toss. Sprinkle with remaining cheese. Yield: 4 servings (serving size: about 2 cups pasta mixture and 1 tablespoon cheese).

CALORIES 248; FAT 8.4g (sat 3.3g, mono 2.9g, poly 0.8g); PROTEIN 12.8g; CARB 32.6g; FIBER 4g; CHOL 15mg; IRON 1.7mg; SODIUM 626mg; CALC 203mg

Spicy Sweet-and-Sour Pork

· *20 minutes*

A bed of coconut rice is an ideal accompaniment. Combine 1 cup uncooked basmati rice, 1¼ cups water, ½ cup light coconut milk, and ¼ teaspoon salt in a small saucepan; bring to a boil. Cover, reduce heat, and simmer 16 minutes or until liquid is absorbed.

- ¼ cup slivered almonds
- 1 pound pork tenderloin, cut into ¾-inch cubes
- 2 tablespoons cornstarch, divided
- 3 tablespoons low-sodium soy sauce, divided
- 1 (8-ounce) can pineapple chunks in juice, undrained
- ¼ cup cider vinegar
- ¼ cup sugar
- 2 tablespoons ketchup
- 2 teaspoons Sriracha (hot chile sauce, such as Huy Fong)
- 1 tablespoon canola oil
- 1 cup prechopped onion
- 1 teaspoon bottled minced ginger
- ½ teaspoon bottled minced garlic
- 1 cup chopped green bell pepper
- ¼ cup slivered green onions

❶ Preheat oven to 400°.
❷ Place almonds on a baking sheet; bake at 400° for 4 minutes or until toasted. Set aside.
❸ While almonds cook, combine pork, 1 tablespoon cornstarch, and 1 tablespoon soy sauce; toss well to coat. Drain pineapple in a sieve over a bowl, reserving juice. Combine juice, remaining 1 tablespoon cornstarch, remaining 2 tablespoons soy sauce, vinegar, and next 3 ingredients, stirring with a whisk.
❹ Heat a large nonstick skillet over medium-high heat. Add canola oil to pan; swirl to coat. Add pork to pan; sauté 3 minutes, stirring frequently. Add 1 cup onion, ginger, and garlic; sauté 1 minute. Stir in pineapple and bell pepper; sauté 3 minutes, stirring frequently. Stir in vinegar mixture; bring to a boil. Cook 1 minute, stirring constantly. Sprinkle with almonds and green onions. Yield: 4 servings (serving size: about 1½ cups).

CALORIES 347; FAT 11g (sat 1.9g, mono 6g, poly 2.3g); PROTEIN 27g; CARB 35.9g; FIBER 3g; CHOL 74mg; IRON 2.5mg; SODIUM 582mg; CALC 54mg

Salmon with Hoisin Glaze

· *20 minutes*

Enjoy garlicky-spicy snow peas on the side. Heat 1 teaspoon canola oil in a large nonstick skillet over medium-high heat. Add 1 pound snow peas and ¼ teaspoon salt; sauté 2 minutes. Stir in 2 teaspoons bottled minced garlic and ¼ teaspoon crushed red pepper; sauté 1 minute. Stir in ¼ teaspoon sugar; sauté 1 minute. Remove from heat; drizzle with ½ teaspoon dark sesame oil.

- 2 tablespoons hoisin sauce
- 2 teaspoons low-sodium soy sauce
- ½ teaspoon dark sesame oil
- 4 (6-ounce) skinless wild salmon fillets
  Cooking spray
- 1 teaspoon sesame seeds
  Lemon rind strips (optional)

❶ Preheat oven to 400°.
❷ Combine first 3 ingredients in a shallow dish. Add fish to dish, turning to coat. Marinate at room temperature 8 minutes, turning occasionally.
❸ Remove fish from marinade; discard marinade. Place fish on a baking sheet coated with cooking spray. Sprinkle fish evenly with sesame seeds. Bake at 400° for 8 minutes or until fish flakes easily when tested with a fork. Garnish with rind, if desired. Yield: 4 servings (serving size: 1 fillet).

CALORIES 255; FAT 11.7g (sat 2.7g, mono 4.8g, poly 2.8g); PROTEIN 31.5g; CARB 3.9g; FIBER 0.3g; CHOL 81mg; IRON 0.7mg; SODIUM 285mg; CALC 26mg

Gazpacho with Shrimp and Avocado Relish

30 minutes

(pictured on page 229)

Serve with grilled garlic bread. Heat a grill pan over medium-high heat. Brush 4 (1-ounce) slices French bread with 1 tablespoon olive oil. Add bread to pan; cook 1½ minutes on each side. Rub toast with cut sides of a halved garlic clove.

SOUP:

- 1 pound peeled and deveined large shrimp
- ¾ cup chopped red bell pepper
- ¼ cup chopped fresh cilantro
- 3 tablespoons chopped red onion
- 2 tablespoons fresh lemon juice
- ¾ teaspoon salt
- ½ teaspoon hot pepper sauce
- 1 pound plum tomatoes, seeded and chopped
- 1 medium cucumber, peeled and chopped
- 1 garlic clove
- 1 (11.5-ounce) can low-sodium vegetable juice

RELISH:

- ¼ cup finely chopped red bell pepper
- 2 tablespoons chopped fresh cilantro
- 1 tablespoon finely chopped red onion
- 1 teaspoon fresh lemon juice
- 1 ripe peeled avocado, diced

❶ To prepare soup, cook shrimp in boiling water 2 minutes or until done. Drain and rinse under cold water; coarsely chop shrimp.

❷ Place ¾ cup bell pepper and next 9 ingredients in a blender; process until smooth. Stir in shrimp.

❸ To prepare relish, combine ¼ cup bell pepper and remaining ingredients. Top soup with relish. Yield: 4 servings (serving size: 1 cup soup and about ⅓ cup relish).

CALORIES 250; FAT 9g (sat 1.4g, mono 4.6g, poly 1.7g); PROTEIN 26g; CARB 17.5g; FIBER 6.2g; CHOL 172mg; IRON 3.9mg; SODIUM 675mg; CALC 105mg

Mushroom and Sweet Onion Cheesesteaks

30 minutes

Serve with a cucumber salad. Combine 1 thinly sliced English cucumber, ¼ cup sliced red onion, 1 tablespoon sugar, 1 tablespoon cider vinegar, and ¼ teaspoon salt.

- 2 teaspoons olive oil, divided
- 12 ounces top round steak, cut into thin strips
- 1½ cups thinly vertically sliced Vidalia or other sweet onion
- 1 teaspoon bottled minced garlic
- 1 (8-ounce) package presliced mushrooms
- ¼ cup Madeira wine
- ½ cup green bell pepper strips
- ½ cup red bell pepper strips
- 1 teaspoon Worcestershire sauce
- ¼ teaspoon salt
- ¼ teaspoon black pepper
- 1 cup (4 ounces) shredded reduced-fat Cheddar cheese
- 4 (2-ounce) ciabatta rolls

❶ Heat a large nonstick skillet over medium-high heat. Add 1 teaspoon oil to pan; swirl to coat. Add steak to pan; cook 2 minutes or until browned, turning occasionally. Remove steak from pan. Add remaining 1 teaspoon oil to pan; swirl to coat. Add onion and garlic to pan; sauté 1 minute, stirring occasionally. Add mushrooms; sauté 6 minutes. Stir in wine; cook until liquid evaporates (about 1 minute). Add bell peppers; sauté 4 minutes. Return steak to pan. Stir in Worcestershire, salt, and black pepper; cook 1 minute or until thoroughly heated. Remove from heat. Sprinkle mixture with cheese; stir until cheese melts. Divide mixture evenly among rolls. Yield: 4 servings (serving size: 1 sandwich).

CALORIES 419; FAT 15.7g (sat 6.3g, mono 6.7g, poly 0.9g); PROTEIN 35.3g; CARB 35.6g; FIBER 3.4g; CHOL 65mg; IRON 3.7mg; SODIUM 660mg; CALC 343mg

Asian Beef Rolls

30 minutes

Serve with spicy ginger noodles. Combine 3 cups hot cooked linguine, 1 tablespoon canola oil, 1½ teaspoons grated peeled fresh ginger, 1 teaspoon dark sesame oil, ½ teaspoon salt, and ½ teaspoon crushed red pepper.

- 1 pound flank steak, trimmed
- ¼ cup low-sodium soy sauce
- 2½ tablespoons rice wine vinegar, divided
- 2 tablespoons mirin (sweet rice wine)
- 1 teaspoon dark sesame oil
- 48 (1½-inch-long) pieces green onion tops (about 16 onions)
- 48 (1½-inch-long) red bell pepper strips (about 1 large pepper)
- Cooking spray

❶ Cut steak diagonally across grain into 16 thin slices. Combine steak, soy sauce, 1 tablespoon vinegar, mirin, and sesame oil in a shallow dish. Marinate steak 10 minutes, turning occasionally.

❷ Remove steak from marinade, reserving marinade. Place 1 steak slice on a cutting board or work surface; arrange 3 green onion pieces and 3 bell pepper strips on end of steak slice. Roll up; set aside, seam side down. Repeat procedure with remaining steak strips, onion pieces, and bell pepper pieces.

❸ Heat a grill pan over medium-high heat. Coat pan with cooking spray. Place beef rolls in pan, seam sides down; cook 7 minutes, turning once.

❹ While beef rolls cook, bring reserved marinade to a boil over medium-high heat; cook 3 minutes. Remove from heat; stir in remaining 1½ tablespoons vinegar. Drizzle sauce over rolls. Yield: 4 servings (serving size: 4 rolls).

CALORIES 204; FAT 6.8g (sat 2.5g, mono 2.7g, poly 0.8g); PROTEIN 25.4g; CARB 7.7g; FIBER 1.5g; CHOL 37mg; IRON 2.3mg; SODIUM 589mg; CALC 38mg

Skillet Chicken Souvlaki

························*30 minutes*

To make the salad, combine 5 cups torn romaine lettuce, ⅓ cup sliced red onion, and 3 sliced pepperoncini peppers. Combine 2 tablespoons red wine vinegar, 2 tablespoons olive oil, and ¼ teaspoon salt; toss with salad. Top with ¼ cup crumbled feta cheese and 3 tablespoons halved kalamata olives.

- 1 tablespoon olive oil, divided
- 1 pound skinless, boneless chicken breast, thinly sliced
- ½ teaspoon salt
- ¼ teaspoon freshly ground black pepper
- 1½ cups vertically sliced onion (about 1 medium)
- 1 cup thinly sliced green bell pepper (about 1)
- 2 teaspoons bottled minced garlic
- ½ teaspoon dried oregano
- ½ cup grated English cucumber
- ¼ cup 2% Greek-style yogurt (such as Fage)
- ¼ cup reduced-fat sour cream
- 1 tablespoon chopped fresh flat-leaf parsley
- ½ teaspoon grated lemon rind
- 1 teaspoon fresh lemon juice
- ⅛ teaspoon salt
- 4 (6-inch) whole-wheat soft pitas, cut in half
- 2 plum tomatoes, thinly sliced

❶ Heat 2 teaspoons oil in a large nonstick skillet over medium-high heat. Sprinkle chicken with ½ teaspoon salt and black pepper. Add chicken to pan; sauté 5 minutes or until done. Remove from pan.
❷ Add remaining 1 teaspoon oil to pan. Add onion and bell pepper; sauté 3 minutes. Add chicken, garlic, and oregano; cook 30 seconds.
❸ Combine cucumber and next 6 ingredients. Serve chicken mixture with yogurt sauce, warmed pita, and tomato slices. Yield: 4 servings (serving size: 1 cup chicken mixture, ¼ cup sauce, 1 pita, and about ¼ cup tomatoes).

CALORIES 361; FAT 7.4g (sat 2.3g, mono 3.3g, poly 0.8g); PROTEIN 35.1g; CARB 39g; FIBER 4.7g; CHOL 72mg; IRON 3.1mg; SODIUM 589mg; CALC 105mg

Lemon-Oregano Lamb Chops

························*40 minutes*

Nestle an oregano sprig under each serving for a lively garnish. A side of orzo pilaf rounds out the menu. Combine 2 cups cooked orzo, ¼ cup crumbled feta cheese, ¼ cup finely chopped red onion, ¼ cup finely chopped carrot, 3 tablespoons chopped fresh flat-leaf parsley, 1 tablespoon red wine vinegar, 1 tablespoon extra-virgin olive oil, ¼ teaspoon salt, and ⅛ teaspoon black pepper; toss well to coat.

- 2 tablespoons fresh lemon juice
- 1 teaspoon extra-virgin olive oil
- ½ teaspoon dried oregano
- 1 garlic clove, minced
- 8 (4-ounce) lamb loin chops, trimmed
- ½ teaspoon salt
- ¼ teaspoon freshly ground black pepper
- Cooking spray

❶ Combine first 4 ingredients in a large zip-top plastic bag. Add lamb to bag, turning to coat. Seal and marinate at room temperature 15 minutes, turning occasionally.
❷ Heat a grill pan over medium-high heat. Remove lamb from marinade; discard marinade. Sprinkle lamb evenly with salt and pepper. Coat pan with cooking spray. Add lamb to pan, and cook for 3 minutes on each side or until desired degree of doneness. Yield: 4 servings (serving size: 2 chops).

CALORIES 220; FAT 10.4g (sat 3.5g, mono 4.9g, poly 0.7g); PROTEIN 28.7g; CARB 1.1g; FIBER 0.2g; CHOL 90mg; IRON 2.1mg; SODIUM 375mg; CALC 23mg

Jerk-Spiced Shrimp

························*40 minutes*

(pictured on page 228)

Serve a refreshing fruit salsa on the side to tame the fiery spice of the shrimp. Combine 2 cups chopped fresh pineapple, ½ cup chopped cucumber, ½ cup vertically sliced red onion, 2 tablespoons chopped fresh cilantro, and 2 teaspoons cider vinegar.

- 1 tablespoon sugar
- 1 tablespoon paprika
- ½ teaspoon salt
- ½ teaspoon garlic powder
- ½ teaspoon ground red pepper
- ¼ teaspoon ground thyme
- ⅛ teaspoon ground allspice
- 2 tablespoons olive oil
- 1½ pounds peeled and deveined large shrimp
- Cooking spray

❶ Prepare grill to medium-high heat.
❷ Combine first 7 ingredients. Combine oil and shrimp in a large bowl; toss well to coat. Sprinkle spice mixture over shrimp; toss to coat. Thread shrimp evenly onto 8 (8-inch) skewers. Place skewers on a grill rack coated with cooking spray; grill 6 minutes or until done, turning once. Yield: 4 servings (serving size: 2 skewers).

CALORIES 260; FAT 9.9g (sat 1.5g, mono 5.4g, poly 1.9g); PROTEIN 34.9g; CARB 6g; FIBER 0.7g; CHOL 259mg; IRON 4.5mg; SODIUM 549mg; CALC 94mg

Tuscan Pork Kebabs

······················*40 minutes*

Sautéed chard makes a simple side. Heat a large skillet over medium-high heat. Add 1 tablespoon olive oil to pan, and swirl to coat. Add 8 cups chopped stemmed Swiss chard, 1 tablespoon minced garlic, and ⅛ teaspoon salt; sauté for 5 minutes or until chard wilts.

 4 teaspoons olive oil
 1 tablespoon grated lemon rind
 ½ teaspoon salt
 ½ teaspoon freshly ground black pepper
 2 garlic cloves, crushed
 1 pound pork tenderloin, trimmed and cut into 1-inch cubes
 16 (1-inch) pieces red bell pepper
 16 (1-inch) pieces yellow bell pepper
   Cooking spray

1 Prepare grill to medium-high heat.
2 Combine first 5 ingredients in a large bowl, stirring well. Add pork; marinate at room temperature 15 minutes, tossing occasionally.
3 Thread pork and bell peppers alternately onto each of 8 (8-inch) skewers. Place skewers on a grill rack coated with cooking spray; grill 10 minutes or until pork is done, turning occasionally. Yield: 4 servings (serving size: 2 kebabs).

CALORIES 198; FAT 8.8g (sat 2.1g, mono 4.9g, poly 0.9g); PROTEIN 24.7g; CARB 4.5g; FIBER 1.5g; CHOL 67mg; IRON 1.6mg; SODIUM 346mg; CALC 15mg

Reader Recipes

From pancakes and panzanella to burritos and biscotti, readers share their secrets for healthier family favorites.

Angela Ricciardi, a tutor coordinator at Plymouth State University in New Hampshire, loves to experiment in her home kitchen. She especially enjoys the tradition of cooking Saturday morning breakfast. But when her husband, John, discovered his cholesterol levels were high, she decided to alter some of their breakfast options.

Ricciardi started with the pancake and waffle recipes she'd been making for years. "I took a look at our favorite recipes and thought about ways to make them more heart-healthy," she says. She substituted fat-free vanilla yogurt for vegetable oil to lower the amount of fat and calories in the pancakes, and the extra calcium from the yogurt improved the nutritional value. Fresh blueberries added color, and a hint of vanilla boosted the flavor. "These pancakes are heartier and not as sweet as traditional pancakes. In place of maple syrup, sometimes we'll dust them with a little powdered sugar," says Ricciardi. With a few simple changes, the Ricciardis' Saturday breakfasts are more healthful, but just as delicious.

Blueberry Pancakes

"For variety, we substitute sliced bananas or chocolate chips for the blueberries for a special treat. Since these pancakes reheat well in the toaster oven, we often make a big batch and enjoy all week."

—Angela Ricciardi,
Plymouth, New Hampshire

 2.25 ounces all-purpose flour (about ½ cup)
 2.38 ounces whole wheat flour (about ½ cup)
 1 tablespoon sugar
 1 teaspoon baking powder
 ½ teaspoon baking soda
 ⅛ teaspoon salt
 ⅛ teaspoon ground nutmeg
 ¾ cup vanilla fat-free yogurt
 2 tablespoons butter, melted
 2 teaspoons fresh lemon juice
 ½ teaspoon vanilla extract
 2 large eggs, lightly beaten
 1 cup fresh blueberries

1 Weigh or lightly spoon flours into dry measuring cups; level with a knife. Combine flours and next 5 ingredients in a large bowl, stirring well with a whisk. Combine yogurt and next 4 ingredients in a small bowl; add to flour mixture, stirring until smooth.
2 Pour about ¼ cup batter per pancake onto a hot nonstick griddle or nonstick skillet. Top each pancake with 2 tablespoons blueberries. Cook 2 minutes or until tops are covered with bubbles and edges look cooked. Carefully turn pancakes over; cook 2 minutes or until bottoms are lightly browned. Yield: 4 servings (serving size: 2 pancakes).

CALORIES 272; FAT 8.8g (sat 4.5g, mono 2.5g, poly 0.8g); PROTEIN 9.5g; CARB 40.1g; FIBER 3.2g; CHOL 122mg; IRON 2mg; SODIUM 403mg; CALC 192mg

"The small amount of rich white chocolate makes this biscotti feel like an indulgence."

—Shelly Huckey,
Mount Pleasant, South Carolina

Summer Biscotti

"The lemon zest adds a bright citrus flavor that is perfect with a cold drink on a warm summer day. You can substitute milk for the fat-free half-and-half if you don't keep it on hand. Store the cookies in a single layer in an airtight container."

—Shelly Huckey,
Mount Pleasant, South Carolina

- 6 tablespoons sugar
- 2 tablespoons butter, softened
- 1½ teaspoons grated lemon rind
- ¼ teaspoon vanilla extract
- 1 large egg
- 1 large egg white
- 4.5 ounces all-purpose flour (about 1 cup)
- ¾ teaspoon baking powder
- ⅛ teaspoon salt
- ½ cup white chocolate chips, divided
- ⅓ cup chopped pecans
- Cooking spray
- 1 tablespoon fat-free half-and-half

1 Place first 4 ingredients in a large bowl; beat with a mixer at high speed 2 minutes until well blended. Add egg and egg white, one at a time, beating well after each addition.

2 Weigh or lightly spoon flour into a dry measuring cup; level with a knife. Combine flour, baking powder, and salt in a small bowl, stirring well with a whisk. Add flour mixture to sugar mixture, stirring until blended. Stir in ¼ cup chips and pecans (dough will be sticky). Cover and chill 30 minutes.

3 Preheat oven to 325°.

4 Turn dough out onto a heavily floured surface. With floured hands, shape dough into a 9 x 4–inch log, and pat to ½-inch thickness. Place log on a baking sheet coated with cooking spray. Bake at 325° for 30 minutes. Remove log from pan; cool 10 minutes on a wire rack. Cut log crosswise into 18 (½-inch-thick) slices. Place, cut sides down, on baking sheet. Bake at 325° for 15 minutes or until lightly browned. Cool completely on wire rack.

5 Place remaining ¼ cup chips in a glass measuring cup; microwave at HIGH 30 seconds or just until melted. Add half-and-half; stir until smooth. Drizzle over biscotti. Yield: 18 biscotti (serving size: 1 biscotto).

CALORIES 95; FAT 4.1g (sat 1.8g, mono 1.3g, poly 0.6g); PROTEIN 1.6g; CARB 13.3g; FIBER 0.5g; CHOL 15mg; IRON 0.5mg; SODIUM 50mg; CALC 20mg

Sesame Shrimp Scampi

"This dish has a great balance of sweet and tangy flavors. Don't be tempted to skip the brining step. It gives the shrimp a wonderful fresh taste and texture."

—Donna Kelly, Provo, Utah

- 8 cups ice water
- 3 tablespoons kosher salt
- 2 pounds large shrimp, peeled and deveined (about 50 shrimp)
- 12 ounces uncooked fettuccine
- ¼ cup water
- 2 tablespoons cornstarch
- ½ cup shiitake sesame vinaigrette (such as Annie's Naturals)
- 1 tablespoon peanut oil
- 1½ teaspoons butter
- 3 garlic cloves, minced
- ¼ cup chopped fresh basil
- 1 tablespoon sesame seeds, toasted

1 Combine 8 cups ice water and salt in a large bowl; stir until salt dissolves. Add shrimp; cover and refrigerate 30 minutes. Drain shrimp; discard brine. Rinse and pat dry.

2 Cook pasta according to package directions, omitting salt and fat. Drain and keep warm.

3 Combine ¼ cup water and cornstarch in a small bowl. Add vinaigrette, stirring with a whisk until well blended.

4 Heat oil in a large skillet over high heat. Add shrimp to pan; stir-fry 2 minutes. Add butter and garlic to pan; stir-fry 1 minute. Reduce heat to low. Add cornstarch mixture to pan; bring to a boil. Cook 1 minute, stirring constantly. Remove from heat; stir in basil. Serve shrimp mixture over pasta; sprinkle with sesame seeds. Yield: 6 servings (serving size: 1 cup pasta, about ¾ cup shrimp mixture, and ½ teaspoon sesame seeds).

CALORIES 472; FAT 13.1g (sat 2.5g, mono 3.3g, poly 6g); PROTEIN 38.6g; CARB 48.7g; FIBER 2.3g; CHOL 232mg; IRON 5.5mg; SODIUM 579mg; CALC 98mg

Mediterranean Plate Menu

serves 3

This entire meal comes together in less than an hour. The classic bread salad allows you to make the most of ripe summer tomatoes, cucumbers, and fresh basil. The menu easily doubles if you're cooking for more.

Panzanella Salad

Simple seared scallops

Heat a large cast-iron skillet over high heat. Arrange 18 ounces sea scallops over paper towels; pat scallops dry with paper towels. Sprinkle scallops evenly with ½ teaspoon kosher salt and ¼ teaspoon freshly ground black pepper. Add scallops to pan; cook 1½ minutes on each side or until desired degree of doneness. Drizzle evenly with 2 teaspoons extra-virgin olive oil and ½ teaspoon fresh lemon juice.

Fettuccine tossed with olive oil

Sauvignon blanc

Lemon sorbet

QUICK & EASY
Panzanella Salad

"This salad takes advantage of juicy summer tomatoes. The cucumber and olives add extra flavor and texture. I like to mash the minced garlic and salt together with a knife so they distribute evenly throughout the salad."

—Nicolette Manescalchi,
Minneapolis, Minnesota

- 3 ounces sourdough bread, cut into 1-inch cubes (2 [1½-ounce] slices)
- ¼ cup white wine vinegar
- 2 teaspoons extra-virgin olive oil
- ¼ teaspoon freshly ground black pepper
- ⅛ teaspoon kosher salt
- 1 garlic clove, minced
- ⅓ cup thinly sliced red onion
- 2 tablespoons coarsely chopped pitted kalamata olives (about 8)
- 2 tablespoons thinly sliced fresh basil
- 1 tomato, cut into 1-inch pieces
- ½ English cucumber, halved and thinly sliced (about 1 cup)

❶ Preheat oven to 350°.
❷ Place bread cubes in a jelly-roll pan; bake at 350° for 10 minutes or until crisp, stirring once. Cool completely.
❸ Combine vinegar and next 4 ingredients in a large bowl. Add bread cubes, onion, and remaining ingredients, tossing gently to coat. Serve immediately. Yield: 3 servings (serving size: 2 cups).

CALORIES 172; FAT 6.4g (sat 0.9g, mono 4.3g, poly 0.9g); PROTEIN 4.8g; CARB 24.8g; FIBER 2.5g; CHOL 0mg; IRON 1.5mg; SODIUM 433mg; CALC 42mg

QUICK & EASY
Quick Breakfast Burritos

"Use as much ground red pepper as you want depending on how hot and spicy you like your food. Add a spinach salad with tomatoes and avocados, and this dish is transformed into a wonderful lunch."

—Heather Demeritte,
Scottsdale, Arizona

PICO DE GALLO:
- 1½ cups chopped tomato (about 1 large)
- ½ cup chopped green onions
- ½ cup chopped fresh cilantro
- 2 teaspoons fresh lemon juice
- ⅛ teaspoon salt
- ⅛ teaspoon black pepper
- Dash of crushed red pepper

BURRITOS:
- ¼ teaspoon chopped fresh oregano
- ⅛ teaspoon salt
- ⅛ teaspoon black pepper
- 4 large eggs, lightly beaten
- Dash of ground red pepper
- Cooking spray
- ¼ cup chopped onion
- 1 (2-ounce) can diced green chiles
- 4 (6-inch) corn tortillas
- ½ cup (2 ounces) shredded colby-Jack cheese

❶ To prepare pico de gallo, combine first 7 ingredients in a small bowl.
❷ To prepare burritos, combine oregano and next 4 ingredients in a small bowl, stirring well with a whisk.
❸ Heat a large nonstick skillet over medium heat. Coat pan with cooking spray. Add egg mixture, ¼ cup onion, and green chiles to pan. Cook 3 minutes or until eggs are set, stirring frequently. Remove pan from heat; stir egg mixture well.
❹ Heat tortillas according to package directions. Divide egg mixture evenly among tortillas. Top each serving with 2 tablespoons cheese and about ⅓ cup pico de gallo. Yield: 4 servings (serving size: 1 burrito).

CALORIES 197; FAT 10.8g (sat 4.5g, mono 3.5g, poly 1.2g); PROTEIN 12.7g; CARB 14.3g; FIBER 2.4g; CHOL 258mg; IRON 1.7mg; SODIUM 372mg; CALC 170mg

> "I created this recipe because I needed an easy, satisfying breakfast."

—Heather Demeritte,
Scottsdale, Arizona

Lemon-Ginger Fried Chicken

We give a nutritional makeover to a reader's Lemon-Ginger Fried Chicken.

The great taste of Lemon-Ginger Fried Chicken made it a favorite of Robby Champion from Staunton, Virginia, for years. In 1987, when Champion and her husband, Jim, discovered the recipe, it didn't have nutrition information. "We absolutely love this dish, but it's easy to tell it isn't as healthful as we would like it to be," she says. They tried to lighten the recipe several times without success. "We are trying to lead more healthful lives and want to enjoy this meal without feeling guilty," she explains.

With one whole chicken serving two people, portions were oversized, yielding high calorie, fat, saturated fat, and sodium counts.

The Solution:

• For starters, the gargantuan portion sizes had to be brought down to size. A serving now includes either one breast half or one thigh plus one drumstick; this brought the calories per serving down by about 300.

• Removing the skin from the meat and double-dredging the chicken maintained a crisp crust while shaving 317 calories, 17.4 grams of fat, and 4.7 grams of artery-clogging saturated fat per serving.

• To bring sodium under control, we swapped fat-free, less-sodium chicken broth for the regular version, and used 1 teaspoon kosher salt to season the four-serving yield. This trimmed 494 milligrams of sodium per serving.

serving size: 1 breast half, or 1 thigh plus 1 drumstick		
	before	after
CALORIES PER SERVING	891	375
TOTAL FAT	45g	15.5g
SATURATED FAT	9.3g	3.3g
SODIUM	1,179mg	578mg

Lemon-Ginger Fried Chicken

Giving the chicken a double coat of the flour mixture creates a golden crust (without the skin) when pan-fried. We use lemon rind instead of the lemon extract called for in the original.

- 1 teaspoon grated lemon rind
- 1 cup fresh lemon juice (about 4 lemons)
- 2 teaspoons minced peeled fresh ginger
- 1½ teaspoons minced garlic
- 2 bone-in chicken breast halves, skinned
- 2 bone-in chicken thighs, skinned
- 2 chicken drumsticks, skinned
- 4.5 ounces all-purpose flour (about 1 cup)
- 2 teaspoons ground ginger
- 1 teaspoon paprika
- ½ teaspoon ground red pepper
- 1 teaspoon kosher salt
- ½ teaspoon freshly ground black pepper
- ¼ cup peanut oil
- ¼ cup fat-free, less-sodium chicken broth
- 2 tablespoons brown sugar
- 1 lemon, thinly sliced

① Place first 7 ingredients in a large zip-top plastic bag; seal and shake to coat. Marinate in refrigerator 1 hour, turning bag occasionally.

② Sift together flour and next 3 ingredients. Place flour mixture in a large zip-top plastic bag. Remove chicken from marinade bag, reserving marinade. Sprinkle salt and black pepper evenly over chicken. Add chicken, one piece at a time, to flour mixture; seal bag and shake to coat chicken. Remove chicken from bag, shaking off excess flour mixture. Reserve remaining flour mixture. Place chicken on a wire rack; place rack in a jelly-roll pan. Cover and refrigerate 1½ hours. Let stand at room temperature 30 minutes.

③ Preheat oven to 350°.

④ Return chicken, one piece at a time, to flour mixture; seal bag and shake to coat chicken. Remove chicken from bag, shaking off excess flour mixture. Discard remaining flour mixture.

⑤ Heat oil in a large ovenproof skillet over medium-high heat. Add chicken to pan; cook 3 minutes or until golden, turning once. Arrange chicken in single layer in a shallow roasting pan. Discard remaining oil in pan. Combine broth and reserved marinade in a small bowl; pour broth mixture into pan. Sprinkle chicken evenly with sugar, and top with lemon slices. Bake at 350° for 45 minutes or until golden and a thermometer registers 165°. Yield: 4 servings (serving size: 1 breast half or 1 thigh plus 1 drumstick).

CALORIES 375; FAT 15.5g (sat 3.3g, mono 6.6g, poly 4.7g); PROTEIN 30.8g; CARB 30.5g; FIBER 2.4g; CHOL 85mg; IRON 2.6mg; SODIUM 578mg; CALC 48mg

> "Flouring skinless chicken twice gives it a wonderful crust. I'm thrilled the new version maintains the flavor and texture of the original."
>
> —Robby Champion, Staunton, Virginia

The *Cooking Light* Join-the-Party Planning Kit

Pick a party below, then use our handy guide for no-stress success.

LATE SUMMER IS A GREAT TIME to enjoy company, but you don't want to be stuck at the stove while your guests have all the fun. The trick: make-ahead menus. Drinks and dishes you can prepare in advance free you to mingle. We offer food for three kinds of gatherings. Choose one, or mix and match. Our make-ahead strategies ensure your party won't start without you.

PARTY 1
COCKTAIL PARTY MENU

(Serves 12)

The right mix of old friends and new acquaintances yields a good cocktail party, and here's what makes a good one perfect: really delicious finger food. Our eclectic make-ahead menu ranges from the Italian marriage of polenta and mushrooms to an Asian blend of teriyaki and wasabi flavors. And we offer the Watermelon Bellini. Consider it your new end-of-summer house cocktail to kick off the festivities.

Mushroom Polenta Canapés

Beef Teriyaki Crisps with Wasabi Mayonnaise

Corn Cups with Salsa Shrimp Salad

Watermelon Bellinis

Game Plan

Up to 2 days ahead:
• Marinate flank steak.
• Cook and chill polenta.

Up to 1 day ahead:
• Cut and freeze watermelon.
• Bake corn cups.
• Make salsa shrimp salad.
• Prepare wasabi mixture.
• Cook mushroom mixture.
• Cook steak.

1 hour ahead:
• Broil polenta.
• Slice steak and let stand at room temperature.

30 minutes ahead:
• Top polenta with reheated mushrooms and cheese.
• Assemble beef teriyaki crisps.
• Fill corn cups with shrimp salad.

As guests arrive:
• Top cups and crisps with fresh herbs.
• Prepare Bellinis.

MAKE AHEAD
Beef Teriyaki Crisps with Wasabi Mayonnaise

Prepare the mayonnaise mixture and cook the steak up to a day in advance. There's no need to reheat it; just slice the steak about an hour ahead, and leave at room temperature.

STEAK:
- ¼ cup fresh orange juice
- ¼ cup low-sodium soy sauce
- 2 tablespoons mirin (sweet rice wine)
- 2 tablespoons honey
- 2 teaspoons grated peeled fresh ginger
- ½ pound flank steak, trimmed
- Cooking spray

REMAINING INGREDIENTS:
- ½ cup reduced-fat mayonnaise
- 2 teaspoons wasabi paste
- 2 teaspoons rice vinegar
- 24 baked rice crackers
- Fresh chive pieces (optional)

❶ To prepare steak, combine first 6 ingredients in a large zip-top plastic bag; seal. Marinate in refrigerator 24 hours, turning occasionally.

❷ Remove steak from bag, and discard marinade. Heat a grill pan over medium-high heat. Coat pan with cooking spray. Add steak to pan; cook 6 minutes on each side or until desired degree of doneness. Remove steak; let stand 10 minutes. Cut steak diagonally across grain into thin slices; cut slices into 2-inch pieces.

❸ Combine mayonnaise, wasabi paste, and vinegar, stirring well. Spoon ¾ teaspoon mayonnaise mixture onto each cracker. Divide steak evenly among crackers; top each with ¼ teaspoon mayonnaise mixture. Garnish with chives, if desired. Yield: 12 servings (serving size: 2 topped crisps).

CALORIES 71; FAT 2.6g (sat 0.5g, mono 0.4g, poly 0.7g); PROTEIN 4.2g; CARB 7.1g; FIBER 0g; CHOL 7mg; IRON 0.3mg; SODIUM 166mg; CALC 3mg

Mushroom Polenta Canapés

Nutty Gruyère cheese complements earthy mushrooms. Prepare and chill the polenta up to two days in advance; broil close to serving. Make the mushroom mixture up to a day ahead. You can serve this as an appetizer with Spice-Rubbed Braised Beef (page 252), or as a simple side dish—just omit the mushrooms and cheese, cut the polenta into 20 rectangles, and serve two per plate.

POLENTA:

4½ cups water
1½ cups quick-cooking polenta
1 teaspoon salt
Cooking spray
1 tablespoon butter, melted
½ cup (2 ounces) shredded Gruyère cheese

TOPPING:

1 cup boiling water
½ ounce dried porcini mushrooms
1 tablespoon butter
⅓ cup thinly sliced shallots
⅛ teaspoon crushed red pepper
1 cup sliced shiitake mushroom caps (about 3½ ounces)
1 cup sliced cremini mushrooms (about 3½ ounces)
1 teaspoon dry vermouth or dry white wine
½ teaspoon minced fresh thyme
¼ teaspoon salt
¼ teaspoon freshly ground black pepper
¼ cup (1 ounce) shaved Gruyère cheese

1 To prepare polenta, bring 4½ cups water to a boil in a medium saucepan. Gradually add polenta and 1 teaspoon salt, stirring constantly with a whisk. Reduce heat to low; cook 3 minutes or until thick, stirring frequently. Spoon polenta into a 13 x 9–inch baking pan coated with cooking spray, spreading evenly. Press plastic wrap onto surface of polenta; chill 1 hour or until firm.

2 Preheat broiler.

3 Invert polenta onto a baking sheet coated with cooking spray. Cut polenta into 36 rectangles (leave polenta on baking sheet). Broil 5 minutes. Turn polenta over. Brush polenta with 1 tablespoon butter. Broil 5 minutes. Sprinkle ½ cup shredded cheese evenly over rectangles; broil 5 minutes or until cheese melts.

4 To prepare topping, combine 1 cup boiling water and porcini mushrooms in a bowl; cover and let stand 15 minutes. Drain; chop mushrooms.

5 Melt 1 tablespoon butter in a large nonstick skillet over medium heat. Add shallots to pan; cook 4 minutes or until tender, stirring frequently. Stir in red pepper; cook 30 seconds. Add porcini, shiitake, and cremini mushrooms; cook over medium-high heat 10 minutes or until liquid evaporates, stirring occasionally. Stir in vermouth, thyme, ¼ teaspoon salt, and black pepper; cook 2 minutes, stirring frequently.

6 Spoon 1 teaspoon mushroom mixture on top of each polenta rectangle; top rectangles evenly with shaved cheese. Yield: 12 servings (serving size: 3 canapés).

CALORIES 124; FAT 4.2g (sat 2.6g, mono 1.2g, poly 0.2g); PROTEIN 4.3g; CARB 12.3g; FIBER 2.4g; CHOL 13mg; IRON 0.4mg; SODIUM 284mg; CALC 75mg

Corn Cups with Salsa Shrimp Salad

For the best flavor, use fresh salsa verde from the refrigerated section of the supermarket. Use chipotle chile powder in the masa dough if you want more spicy heat or ancho chile powder for bittersweet fruity notes. Bake the cups the day before the party, and store at room temperature in an airtight container. Fill cups shortly before serving so they keep their crunch. Garnish with additional chopped green onions, if you like. Serve along with other finger foods or as a festive appetizer at a dinner party featuring Spice-Rubbed Braised Beef (page 252).

CUPS:

⅔ cup masa harina (about 2½ ounces)
¼ teaspoon salt
¼ teaspoon ancho or chipotle chile powder
6 tablespoons warm water
4 teaspoons butter, melted
Cooking spray

SALAD:

½ cup chopped cooked shrimp (about 4 ounces)
¼ cup fresh or frozen corn kernels, thawed
¼ cup fresh salsa verde, drained
2 tablespoons finely chopped celery
1 tablespoon chopped green onions
2 tablespoons reduced-fat mayonnaise

1 To prepare cups, weigh or lightly spoon masa harina into dry measuring cups; level with a knife. Combine masa, salt, and chile powder in a medium bowl, stirring with a whisk. Stir in 6 tablespoons warm water and butter; stir thoroughly to combine. Turn dough out onto a clean surface; knead lightly 1 minute. Cover dough; let rest 30 minutes.

2 Preheat oven to 400°.

3 Place dough on a sheet of plastic wrap; cover with another sheet of plastic wrap. Roll dough, still covered, to ⅛-inch thickness. Remove top sheet of plastic wrap. Cut 24 rounds from dough using a 2½-inch round cutter. Coat 24 miniature muffin cups with cooking spray. Place 1 dough round in each muffin cup, gently pressing into bottom and up sides of cup. Bake at 400° for 14 minutes or until crisp and dry. Cool in pans on a wire rack. Remove corn cups from pans.

4 To prepare salad, combine shrimp and remaining ingredients; cover with plastic wrap, and chill 20 minutes. Spoon 2 teaspoons salsa shrimp salad into each corn cup. Yield: 12 servings (serving size: 2 filled cups).

CALORIES 54; FAT 2g (sat 0.9g, mono 0.4g, poly 0.5g); PROTEIN 2.7g; CARB 6.8g; FIBER 0.7g; CHOL 22mg; IRON 0.5mg; SODIUM 120mg; CALC 18mg

Watermelon Bellinis

This drink is a twist on the classic Bellini, a post–World War II cocktail of white peach puree and Champagne, first mixed at Harry's Bar in Venice. Freezing the watermelon before pureeing lends the drink a slightly slushy consistency. If you prefer a smoother texture, simply chill the watermelon. You can easily double this recipe to serve a larger crowd. Serve in Champagne flutes.

> 3 cups cubed seeded watermelon, frozen
> 2 tablespoons sugar
> 2 tablespoons fresh lemon juice
> 3 cups chilled prosecco or other sparkling wine, divided
> Julienne-cut lemon rind (optional)

❶ Place watermelon, sugar, juice, and 1 cup wine in a blender; process until smooth. Pour about ⅓ cup watermelon mixture into each of 8 glasses. Pour ¼ cup remaining wine into each glass. Garnish with lemon rind, if desired. Serve immediately. Yield: 8 servings.

CALORIES 94; FAT 0.1g (sat 0g, mono 0g, poly 0g); PROTEIN 0.4g; CARB 9.3g; FIBER 0.2g; CHOL 0mg; IRON 0.1mg; SODIUM 1mg; CALC 4mg

---

PARTY 2
MIX & MATCH DINNER PARTY MENU

(Serves 10)

Our menu's core recipes (braised beef and coleslaw salad) are great on their own, or served with a hearty bread. They're also versatile enough to pair with our appetizers, sides, and desserts. Start with the basic recipes, then upgrade your meal with one or more of our three options.

Spice-Rubbed Braised Beef

Chopped Coleslaw Salad

Crusty sourdough bread

Crios de Susana Balbo Malbec

Appetizer Upgrade:
*Add **Corn Cups with Salsa Shrimp Salad***
(page 250)
or
Mushroom Polenta Canapés
(page 250)

Side Dish Upgrade:
Add polenta (page 250)

Dessert Upgrade:
*Add **Cocoa Nib Meringues***
(page 254)
or
Lemon-Rosemary Olive Oil Cake
(page 253)

Start with the core recipes (braised beef and coleslaw salad), then add other menu items (see menu at left) as needed.

Game Plan

Up to 2 weeks ahead:
• Bake and freeze unglazed olive oil cake, if using.

Up to 3 days ahead:
• Prepare beef braising liquid.

Up to 2 days ahead:
• Cook and chill polenta, if using.

Up to 1 day ahead:
• Bake meringues, if using.
• Cook mushroom mixture for polenta canapés.

1 day ahead:
• Thaw cake in refrigerator.

The night before:
• Rub beef with spice mixture.

2 hours ahead:
• Prepare coleslaw salad.
• Reheat braising liquid; add beef and braise.

30 minutes ahead:
• Glaze cake.
• Broil polenta (for canapés).
• Top polenta canapés with mushrooms and cheese.

Just before serving:
• Broil polenta (for side dish).

Continued

Spice-Rubbed Braised Beef
(pictured on page 231)

You can make the sauce up to three days ahead—just reheat it before adding the roast.

ROAST:

- 1 tablespoon paprika
- 1 tablespoon dark brown sugar
- 2 teaspoons garlic powder
- 1 teaspoon salt
- 1 teaspoon dry mustard
- ½ teaspoon ground red pepper
- 1 (3-pound) boneless chuck roast, trimmed

SAUCE:

- Cooking spray
- 1 cup chopped onion
- ¼ teaspoon crushed red pepper
- 3 garlic cloves, minced
- 1 (28-ounce) can whole tomatoes, undrained
- ½ cup water
- 6 tablespoons dark brown sugar
- ¼ cup red wine vinegar
- 1 tablespoon tomato paste
- ½ teaspoon salt
- ½ teaspoon freshly ground black pepper

❶ To prepare roast, combine first 6 ingredients; rub over roast. Place roast in a large zip-top plastic bag. Seal and refrigerate 1 hour or overnight.
❷ To prepare sauce, heat a large Dutch oven over medium heat. Coat pan with cooking spray. Add onion, crushed red pepper, and minced garlic; cook 3 minutes, stirring frequently. Place tomatoes in blender, and process until smooth. Add pureed tomatoes, ½ cup water, and next 3 ingredients to pan, and bring to a boil. Reduce heat, and simmer 30 minutes, stirring occasionally. Stir in ½ teaspoon salt and ½ teaspoon black pepper.
❸ Preheat oven to 325°.
❹ Remove roast from bag. Add roast to sauce in pan. Cover and bake at 325° for 2½ hours or until tender. Serve with sauce. Yield: 10 servings (serving size: 3 ounces beef and about ⅓ cup sauce).

CALORIES 262; FAT 10.8g (sat 3.6g, mono 4.8g, poly 0.5g); PROTEIN 25.1g; CARB 15.7g; FIBER 1.4g; CHOL 76mg; IRON 4.3mg; SODIUM 508mg; CALC 48mg

Chopped Coleslaw Salad

The mustard seeds will begin to pop in the pan as they toast. Make the salad two hours ahead so the flavors meld. The warm dressing won't wilt the hardy cabbage, but it will make the leaves crisp-tender as they marinate.

- 2 tablespoons mustard seeds
- ⅓ cup sugar
- ⅓ cup white wine vinegar
- 1 tablespoon prepared mustard
- ¾ teaspoon salt
- 2 cups green cabbage, cut into 1-inch pieces
- 2 cups red cabbage, cut into 1-inch pieces
- 1 cup julienne-cut red bell pepper
- ½ cup vertically sliced red onion
- ¼ cup (1-inch) slices green onions

❶ Place mustard seeds in a small saucepan over medium heat; cook, partially covered, 2 minutes or until lightly toasted. Remove mustard seeds from pan. Add sugar and vinegar to pan; bring to a boil over high heat. Remove pan from heat; stir in mustard and salt. Combine mustard seeds, vinegar mixture, green cabbage, and remaining ingredients; toss well. Cover and chill 2 hours, stirring occasionally. Yield: 10 servings (serving size: ⅔ cup).

CALORIES 51; FAT 0.6g (sat 0.1g, mono 0.5g, poly 0g); PROTEIN 1.2g; CARB 11.5g; FIBER 1.9g; CHOL 0mg; IRON 0.4mg; SODIUM 202mg; CALC 28mg

PARTY 3
DESSERT & COFFEE MENU

(Serves 12)

Sometimes you want to skip the formalities and get straight to the fun stuff, and a dessert party lets you do just that. This sweet spread offers a little something for everyone: lightly glazed, herb-scented cake; bittersweet cocoa meringues; and a galette featuring ripe, late-summer plums. Make the desserts beforehand, then simply put on fresh coffee and pour prosecco once the guests arrive. It's a recipe for pure pleasure.

Lemon-Rosemary Olive Oil Cake

Plum Galette with Armagnac Cream

Cocoa Nib Meringues

Coffee

Prosecco or cava

Game Plan:

Up to 2 weeks ahead:
- Bake and freeze unglazed olive oil cake.

Up to 1 day ahead:
- Prepare galette dough, and chill.
- Cook plum filling.
- Bake meringues.

1 day ahead:
- Thaw cake in refrigerator.

3 hours ahead:
- Shape and bake galette.
- Bring cake to room temperature.

30 minutes ahead:
- Glaze cake.

15 minutes ahead:
- Mix Armagnac cream.

As guests arrive:
- Make coffee.

Lemon-Rosemary Olive Oil Cake

Rosemary lends evergreen essence, while olive oil enhances the flavor and maintains the moist texture of this Mediterranean-inspired cake. Casual yet elegant, it's a fine finish for a dinner party, though it also makes a well-chosen addition to a dessert buffet. You can prepare it up to two weeks ahead and freeze, unglazed; top thawed cake with glaze before serving to your guests.

Cooking spray
2 tablespoons all-purpose flour
13.5 ounces all-purpose flour (about 3 cups)
1½ tablespoons finely chopped fresh rosemary
2 teaspoons baking powder
½ teaspoon baking soda
½ teaspoon salt
1½ cups granulated sugar
½ cup olive oil
½ cup fat-free milk
2 teaspoons grated lemon rind
¼ cup fresh lemon juice
½ teaspoon vanilla extract
¼ teaspoon lemon extract
3 large eggs
1 cup powdered sugar
1 tablespoon fresh lemon juice
Fresh rosemary sprig (optional)

❶ Preheat oven to 350°.
❷ Coat a 10-inch tube pan with cooking spray; dust with 2 tablespoons flour. Weigh or lightly spoon 13.5 ounces flour (about 3 cups) into dry measuring cups; level with a knife. Combine flour and next 4 ingredients in a large bowl.
❸ Place granulated sugar and next 7 ingredients in a medium bowl; beat with a mixer at low speed 2 minutes or until smooth. Add to flour mixture; beat until blended.
❹ Pour batter into prepared pan. Bake at 350° for 45 minutes or until a wooden pick inserted in center comes out clean. Cool in pan for 15 minutes on a wire rack, and remove from pan. Cool completely on wire rack. Combine powdered sugar and lemon juice, stirring until smooth. Drizzle sugar mixture over cake. Garnish with rosemary sprig, if desired. Yield: 16 servings (serving size: 1 slice).

CALORIES 265; FAT 7.9g (sat 1.3g, mono 5.3g, poly 0.9g); PROTEIN 3.9g; CARB 45.1g; FIBER 0.7g; CHOL 40mg; IRON 1.3mg; SODIUM 211mg; CALC 20mg

Plum Galette with Armagnac Cream

Armagnac is a brandy that hails from southwest France and is often paired with plums, both fresh and dried.

GALETTE:
6 ounces all-purpose flour (about 1⅓ cups)
3 tablespoons whole wheat pastry flour
2 teaspoons granulated sugar
¼ teaspoon salt
8 tablespoons chilled butter, cut into small pieces
¼ cup ice water
3 pounds ripe plums, quartered
9 tablespoons brown sugar, divided
¼ cup Armagnac or cognac
1 vanilla bean, halved
1 (1-ounce) slice whole wheat bread
2 tablespoons butter, melted

CREAM:
1 cup light sour cream
⅓ cup powdered sugar
2 tablespoons whole milk
2 tablespoons Armagnac or cognac
1 teaspoon vanilla extract

❶ To prepare galette, weigh or lightly spoon flours into dry measuring cups; level with a knife. Combine flours, granulated sugar, and salt in a medium bowl, and cut in butter with a pastry blender or 2 knives until mixture resembles coarse meal. Add ice water; stir just until moist. Pat dough into a 7-inch circle on plastic wrap; cover. Chill 15 minutes.
❷ Combine plums, ½ cup brown sugar, ¼ cup Armagnac, and vanilla bean in a large skillet over medium heat, and cook for 10 minutes or until plums are tender, stirring occasionally. Cool to room temperature.
❸ Preheat oven to 300°.
❹ Tear bread into 1-inch pieces. Place on baking sheet; bake at 300° for 30 minutes or until dry and golden. Place bread in a food processor; process until coarse crumbs measure ¼ cup.
❺ Increase oven to 425°.
❻ Unwrap and place dough on a baking sheet. Roll dough into a 15-inch circle; sprinkle dough with breadcrumbs, leaving a 2-inch border. Arrange plum mixture over crumbs. Fold edges of dough over plum mixture (dough will only partially cover plum mixture). Brush dough edges and top of fruit with melted butter; sprinkle with remaining 1 tablespoon brown sugar. Bake at 425° for 15 minutes. Reduce oven temperature to 375° (do not remove galette from oven); bake an additional 20 minutes or until bubbly and edges are golden. Cool 5 minutes on pan; loosen galette from pan. Cool an additional 30 minutes on pan.
❼ To prepare cream, combine sour cream and remaining ingredients in a small bowl, stirring with a whisk. Serve over galette slices. Yield: 12 servings (serving size: 1 galette slice and 1½ teaspoons cream).

CALORIES 277; FAT 11.4g (sat 7.4g, mono 2.5g, poly 0.4g); PROTEIN 4g; CARB 35.9g; FIBER 3g; CHOL 25mg; IRON 1.2mg; SODIUM 149mg; CALC 34mg

Cocoa Nib Meringues

Cocoa nibs are roasted cocoa beans, broken into small pieces; they add a bittersweet crunch. Look for them on the baking aisle at specialty stores or large supermarkets. Superfine sugar dissolves easily into the meringue for a supple texture. If you can't find superfine sugar, process granulated sugar in a blender for a minute or two. Store meringues in an airtight container for up to one day. Serve as a crowd-pleasing follow-up to the Spice-Rubbed Braised Beef (page 252).

- ½ teaspoon cream of tartar
- 3 large egg whites
- ½ cup superfine sugar
- 2 tablespoons unsweetened cocoa
- 2 teaspoons cocoa nibs
- 1 teaspoon instant espresso granules or 2 teaspoons instant coffee granules
- Dash of salt
- 1 teaspoon unsweetened cocoa (optional)

❶ Preheat oven to 225°.
❷ Line a baking sheet with parchment paper.
❸ Place cream of tartar and egg whites in a large bowl; beat with a mixer at high speed until foamy. Gradually add superfine sugar, 1 tablespoon at a time, beating until stiff peaks form. Add 2 tablespoons unsweetened cocoa, cocoa nibs, espresso granules, and salt; beat just until blended.
❹ Drop batter by tablespoonfuls onto prepared baking sheet. Bake at 225° for 1 hour. Turn oven off (do not remove pan from oven); cool meringues in closed oven at least 8 hours or until crisp. Carefully remove meringues from paper. Sprinkle with 1 teaspoon unsweetened cocoa, if desired. Yield: 36 meringues (serving size: 1 meringue).

CALORIES 14; FAT 0.1g (sat 0.1g, mono 0g, poly 0g); PROTEIN 0.4g; CARB 3.1g; FIBER 0.1g; CHOL 0mg; IRON 0.1mg; SODIUM 9mg; CALC 1mg

The Carb-Lover's Guide to Using Your Noodles
(and Potatoes and Breads and Whole Grains)

CARBS COMFORT AND SATISFY. And when we eat them as whole foods they deliver good nutrition, too. Minimally processed starches and grains provide vitamins, minerals, quality protein, and disease-fighting phytochemicals. They also supply the glucose that fuels our bodies and brains. (All this goes for the humble potato, too.)

Of course, not all carbs need be enjoyed whole: At times, only sublimely slippery semolina pasta or a gloriously crunchy white-flour baguette will do. Whatever you want, follow our ideas and recipes to get more good carbs into your diet. Comfort and satisfaction guaranteed.

Noodles

Noodles are more nutritious than you might think. For plain pasta, check the label for 100% semolina, a high-protein wheat. One cooked cup has about as much fiber as a slice of whole wheat bread and more protein than an egg.

Penne with Sage and Mushrooms

- 1 whole garlic head
- 2 tablespoons plus 1 teaspoon olive oil, divided
- 2½ cups boiling water, divided
- ½ ounce dried wild mushroom blend (about ¾ cup)
- 8 ounces uncooked 100 percent whole-grain penne pasta
- ¼ cup fresh sage leaves
- 2½ cups sliced cremini mushrooms (about 6 ounces)
- ½ teaspoon salt
- ½ teaspoon freshly ground black pepper
- 1 cup fat-free, less-sodium chicken broth
- 2 ounces fresh Parmigiano-Reggiano cheese, divided

❶ Preheat oven to 400°.
❷ Cut top off garlic head. Place in a small baking dish, and drizzle with 1 teaspoon oil; cover with foil, and bake at 400° for 45 minutes. Remove dish from oven. Add ½ cup boiling water to dish; cover and let stand 30 minutes. Separate cloves; squeeze to extract garlic pulp into water. Discard skins. Mash garlic pulp mixture with a fork, and set aside.
❸ Combine remaining 2 cups boiling water and dried mushrooms in a bowl; cover and let stand 30 minutes. Rinse mushrooms; drain well, and roughly chop. Set aside.
❹ Cook pasta according to package directions, omitting salt and fat.
❺ Heat remaining 2 tablespoons oil in a large nonstick skillet over medium-high heat. Add sage to pan; sauté 1 minute or until crisp and browned. Remove from pan using a slotted spoon; set aside. Add cremini mushrooms, salt, and pepper to pan; sauté 4 minutes. Add garlic mixture, chopped mushrooms, and broth to pan; cook 5 minutes or until liquid is reduced by about half. Grate 1½ ounces cheese. Add pasta and grated cheese to pan; stir to combine. Cover and let stand 5 minutes. Thinly shave remaining

^{1}/$_2$ ounce cheese; top each serving evenly with cheese shavings and sage leaves. Yield: 4 servings (serving size: 1^3/$_4$ cups).

CALORIES 350; FAT 13g (sat 2.9g, mono 6.6g, poly 2.5g); PROTEIN 14.6g; CARB 51.1g; FIBER 7.8g; CHOL 9mg; IRON 3mg; SODIUM 550mg; CALC 183mg

Tomato and Walnut Pesto Rotini

- 3 cups loosely packed fresh basil leaves
- ^{1}/$_3$ cup chopped walnuts, toasted
- ^{1}/$_4$ cup (1 ounce) grated fresh Parmigiano-Reggiano cheese
- ^{1}/$_4$ cup (1 ounce) grated fresh pecorino Romano cheese
- 2 tablespoons fresh lemon juice
- 2 teaspoons minced garlic
- ^{3}/$_4$ teaspoon salt, divided
- ^{1}/$_4$ teaspoon freshly ground black pepper, divided
- 2 tablespoons extra-virgin olive oil
- 5 ounces uncooked rotini (corkscrew-shaped pasta)
- 5 ounces uncooked multigrain rotini (corkscrew-shaped pasta)
- 1 cup cherry tomatoes, quartered

❶ Place first 6 ingredients, ^{1}/$_4$ teaspoon salt, and ^{1}/$_8$ teaspoon pepper in a food processor; process until smooth, scraping sides of bowl occasionally. Gradually add oil through food chute with food processor on; process until smooth.
❷ Cook pastas according to package directions, omitting salt and fat. Drain in a colander over a bowl, reserving ^{3}/$_4$ cup cooking liquid. Combine pastas, pesto mixture, tomatoes, reserved cooking liquid, remaining ^{1}/$_2$ teaspoon salt, and remaining ^{1}/$_8$ teaspoon pepper in a large bowl; toss well. Yield: 5 servings (serving size: 1 cup).

CALORIES 341; FAT 13.6g (sat 2.8g, mono 5.8g, poly 4g); PROTEIN 13.8g; CARB 44.3g; FIBER 4.7g; CHOL 9mg; IRON 2.9mg; SODIUM 482mg; CALC 163mg

---

Good to Great Noodle Choices

Whole-grain pastas have more fiber and good-for-you antioxidants than semolina. If the texture is too hearty, mix 50-50 with semolina noodles. The key to loving whole wheat pasta is pairing its dense, chewy texture with a gutsy sauce—zesty, caper-flecked tomato, for instance, or sage and brown butter.

Bread

Bread varies widely in nutritional value. There are lots of options beyond breads made only of enriched white flour (sometimes colored brown with sugars). Whole grains like oats or rye, which are full of flavor, contain the most nutritious parts of the grain—the bran, germ, and endosperm. That makes them rich in B vitamins, minerals, and antioxidants.

Tartines with Cheese, Peppers, and Chard

(pictured on page 230)

A tartine is an open-faced sandwich. This recipe demands a hearty bread (one topped with seeds and intact grains adds a nutritional bonus); it's the best match for the herbed cheese topping.

- 1 large red bell pepper
- 1 tablespoon olive oil
- 3 cups chopped Swiss chard leaves (about 1 bunch)
- ^{1}/$_4$ teaspoon salt
- ^{1}/$_8$ teaspoon crushed red pepper
- ^{1}/$_4$ teaspoon black pepper, divided
- 2 garlic cloves, thinly sliced
- 4 (1.5-ounce) slices rustic 100 percent whole-grain bread
- 2 teaspoons chopped fresh chives
- ^{1}/$_2$ teaspoon chopped fresh thyme
- 2 ounces soft goat cheese

---

❶ Preheat broiler.
❷ Cut bell pepper in half lengthwise; discard seeds and membranes. Place pepper halves, skin sides up, on a foil-lined baking sheet; flatten with hand. Broil 10 minutes or until blackened. Place in a zip-top plastic bag; seal. Let stand 5 minutes. Peel and cut into strips.
❸ Heat oil in a large nonstick skillet over medium-high heat. Add chard, salt, crushed red pepper, ^{1}/$_8$ teaspoon black pepper, and garlic to pan; sauté 1^1/$_2$ minutes or until chard wilts, stirring frequently.
❹ Arrange bread in a single layer on a baking sheet; broil 3 minutes on each side. Combine chives, thyme, cheese, and remaining ^{1}/$_8$ teaspoon pepper in a small bowl; spread 2 teaspoons cheese mixture over one side of each bread slice. Arrange roasted pepper slices evenly over cheese; top with chard mixture. Yield: 2 servings (serving size: 2 tartines).

CALORIES 323; FAT 14.4g (sat 5.1g, mono 6.3g, poly 1g); PROTEIN 12.3g; CARB 43.4g; FIBER 15.2g; CHOL 13mg; IRON 4.2mg; SODIUM 718mg; CALC 330mg

---

Good to Great Bread Choices

If you're not a fan of whole-grain bread, consider a bread that contains at least some whole grains—millet, pumpernickel, or multigrain combinations, for example. These have more nutrients than refined white breads. On packaged bread, check the ingredient label for whole grains. In bakeries, just ask.

Pita Bread Salad

It takes just two pita rounds to make this salad, a variation on Italian panzanella. Toasting the pitas with the Middle Eastern spice mix known as za'atar enhances the nutty whole-grain flavor.

- 2 (6-inch) whole wheat pitas, each cut into 10 wedges
  Cooking spray
- 1½ teaspoons za'atar
- ½ teaspoon salt, divided
- ¾ teaspoon chopped garlic
- 2 tablespoons fresh lemon juice
- ½ teaspoon ground sumac
- 3 tablespoons extra-virgin olive oil
- 2 cups chopped cucumber
- 2 cups chopped tomato
- ½ cup loosely packed fresh flat-leaf parsley, chopped
- ¼ cup thinly diagonally sliced green onions
- ¼ cup loosely packed fresh mint, chopped
- ¼ teaspoon black pepper

❶ Preheat oven to 350°.
❷ Arrange pita wedges in a single layer on a baking sheet; lightly coat with cooking spray. Sprinkle pita evenly with za'atar and ¼ teaspoon salt. Bake at 350° for 15 minutes or until crisp and golden. Cool and break into 1-inch pieces.
❸ Combine remaining ¼ teaspoon salt and garlic on a dry surface. Mash with the side of a knife to form a paste. Combine garlic mixture, juice, and sumac in a large bowl; stir with a whisk. Slowly whisk in olive oil. Add cucumber and remaining ingredients to bowl; toss well to coat. Let stand 10 minutes. Add pita pieces; toss well to coat. Serve immediately. Yield: 4 servings (serving size: 1¾ cups).

CALORIES 215; FAT 11.4g (sat 1.6g, mono 7.6g, poly 1.5g); PROTEIN 5.2g; CARB 26.2g; FIBER 5.4g; CHOL 0mg; IRON 3.1mg; SODIUM 480mg; CALC 60mg

Potatoes

Potatoes are the most misunderstood of high-carb foods, probably because Americans like to skin them, deep-fry them, butter them, cream them, and generally load them with fat. But the potato is a natural health food with fiber, vitamin C, potassium, and iron.

MAKE AHEAD
All-American Potato Salad

- 1 tablespoon kosher salt, divided
- 5 medium Yukon gold potatoes (about 2 pounds 6 ounces)
- 1¼ cups diced red bell pepper (1 large)
- ½ cup canola mayonnaise
- ¼ cup diced celery
- 2 tablespoons chopped green onions
- ½ teaspoon freshly ground black pepper
- 3 large hard-boiled eggs, diced

❶ Combine 2 teaspoons salt and potatoes in a large saucepan; cover with cold water. Bring to a boil; cook 25 minutes or until potatoes are tender. Drain; rinse with cold water. Drain and let cool; cut into 1-inch pieces. Combine potatoes, remaining 1 teaspoon salt, bell pepper, and remaining ingredients in a large bowl; toss gently to coat. Yield: 6 servings (serving size: 1½ cups).

CALORIES 259; FAT 17.2g (sat 2.1g, mono 9g, poly 4.4g); PROTEIN 6.8g; CARB 23.4g; FIBER 3.1g; CHOL 112mg; IRON 1.5mg; SODIUM 559mg; CALC 36mg

---

Good to Great Potato Choices

Besides plenty of good-for-you nutrients, potatoes also supply resistant starch, a carbohydrate that helps regulate blood sugar and keeps the digestive system healthy. (Legumes and lentils are other sources of this super starch.) Roasted potatoes add some resistant starch to your diet, but a cool potato salad gives you even more.

Spiced Potatoes and Green Beans

- 1 New Mexican chile
- 2 tablespoons canola oil
- ½ teaspoon brown mustard seeds
- 1 cup finely chopped onion
- 2 teaspoons minced garlic
- 1 teaspoon ground cumin
- 1 teaspoon ground coriander
- 1 teaspoon minced peeled fresh ginger
- ¼ teaspoon ground turmeric
- 1 pound Yukon gold or red potatoes, cut into ½-inch pieces
- ½ cup water
- ¾ teaspoon salt
- 8 ounces green beans, trimmed and cut into 1-inch pieces
- ¼ cup chopped fresh cilantro

❶ Place chile in a spice or coffee grinder; process until finely ground (about 1 teaspoon).
❷ Heat oil in a large nonstick skillet over medium-high heat. Add mustard seeds to pan; sauté 30 seconds or until seeds begin to pop. Add onion; sauté 2 minutes or until lightly browned. Stir in ground chile, garlic, and next 4 ingredients; cook 30 seconds, stirring constantly. Stir in potatoes; cook 2 minutes. Add ½ cup water and salt, and bring to a boil. Reduce heat to medium-low and simmer, covered, 8 minutes or until potatoes are tender. Add beans, and cover and cook 5 minutes or until beans are crisp-tender. Stir in cilantro. Yield: 5 servings (serving size: 1½ cups).

CALORIES 154; FAT 5.8g (sat 0.4g, mono 3.3g, poly 1.7g); PROTEIN 3.3g; CARB 22.7g; FIBER 3.6g; CHOL 0mg; IRON 1.3mg; SODIUM 379mg; CALC 38mg

Grains

Grains like bulgur, farro, and barley are easy to prepare and packed with slowly digested complex carbohydrates, fiber, and antioxidants. (Brown and wild rices count, too.) Regular consumption boosts digestive health and may cut heart disease and type 2 diabetes risks.

Barley Risotto with Eggplant and Tomatoes

- 6 cups (½-inch) diced eggplant
- 1 pint cherry tomatoes
- 3 tablespoons olive oil, divided
- ½ teaspoon black pepper, divided
- 5 cups fat-free, less-sodium chicken broth
- 2 cups water
- 1½ cups finely chopped onion
- 1 cup uncooked pearl barley
- 2 teaspoons minced garlic
- ½ cup dry white wine
- ¼ teaspoon salt
- ½ cup (2 ounces) crumbled soft goat cheese
- ¼ cup thinly sliced fresh basil
- ¼ cup pine nuts, toasted

① Preheat oven to 400°.
② Combine eggplant, tomatoes, 2 tablespoons oil, and ¼ teaspoon pepper in a bowl; toss to coat. Arrange mixture in a single layer on a jelly-roll pan. Bake at 400° for 20 minutes or until tomatoes begin to collapse and eggplant is tender.
③ Combine broth and 2 cups water in a medium saucepan; bring to a simmer (do not boil). Keep warm over low heat.
④ Heat remaining 1 tablespoon oil in a large nonstick skillet over medium-high heat. Add onion to pan; sauté 4 minutes or until onion begins to brown. Stir in barley and garlic; cook 1 minute. Add wine; cook 1 minute or until liquid almost evaporates, stirring constantly. Add 1 cup broth mixture to pan; bring to a boil, stirring frequently. Cook 5 minutes or until liquid is nearly absorbed, stirring constantly. Add remaining broth mixture, 1 cup at a time, stirring constantly until each portion of broth mixture is absorbed before adding the next (about 40 minutes total). Gently stir in eggplant mixture, remaining ¼ teaspoon pepper, and salt. Top with cheese, basil, and nuts. Yield: 4 servings (serving size: 1¼ cups risotto, 2 tablespoons cheese, 1 tablespoon basil, and 1 tablespoon nuts).

CALORIES 453; FAT 20.3g (sat 4.2g, mono 9.9g, poly 4.6g); PROTEIN 14.5g; CARB 57.5g; FIBER 15.5g; CHOL 7mg; IRON 3.4mg; SODIUM 697mg; CALC 93mg

Kibbeh Meatballs with Spiced Yogurt Sauce

- 1½ cups plain nonfat Greek-style yogurt
- 1 cup shredded seeded cucumber
- ½ teaspoon ground cumin
- ½ teaspoon minced garlic
- ⅛ teaspoon salt
- ⅛ teaspoon black pepper
- ¾ cup uncooked bulgur
- 2 cups cold water
- 1 pound lean ground lamb (20% fat)
- ¼ cup minced shallots
- ¼ cup minced fresh parsley
- ¾ teaspoon salt
- ½ teaspoon ground cumin
- ½ teaspoon ground allspice
- ½ teaspoon ground cinnamon
- ¼ teaspoon ground red pepper
- 1 tablespoon olive oil

① Combine first 6 ingredients; chill.
② Combine bulgur and 2 cups water in a medium bowl. Let stand 30 minutes; drain bulgur through a fine sieve, pressing out excess liquid. Place bulgur, lamb, and next 7 ingredients in a food processor; process just until smooth. Cover and chill 30 minutes. Form lamb mixture into 20 (2½-inch) football-shaped meatballs.
③ Heat oil in nonstick skillet over medium-high heat. Add meatballs to pan; cook 12 minutes, browning on all sides. Serve with sauce. Yield: 10 servings (serving size: 2 meatballs and 3 tablespoons sauce).

CALORIES 161; FAT 7.7g (sat 2.7g, mono 3.6g, poly 0.6g); PROTEIN 12.2g; CARB 10.8g; FIBER 2.3g; CHOL 30mg; IRON 1.1mg; SODIUM 248mg; CALC 43mg

Dinner Tonight

Seven stopwatch-tested menus from the *Cooking Light* Kitchen

---

Shopping List

Oven-Fried Chicken Parmesan
panko (Japanese breadcrumbs)
tomato-basil pasta sauce
all-purpose flour
dried oregano
olive oil
cooking spray
large eggs
2 ounces Parmigiano-Reggiano cheese
3 ounces shredded part-skim mozzarella cheese
4 (6-ounce) skinless, boneless chicken breast halves

Romaine Salad
romaine lettuce
1 lemon
honey
Dijon mustard
olive oil

Basic Polenta
2 cups fat-free, less-sodium chicken broth
instant dry polenta
2% milk

Game Plan

- Preheat oven.
- While oven heats:
  - Make dressing for salad.
  - Bread chicken.
- While chicken bakes:
  - Make polenta.
- Toss salad just before serving.

Oven-Fried Chicken Parmesan with Romaine Salad and Basic Polenta
···*30 minutes*

Simple Sub: Use an equal amount of fresh breadcrumbs in place of panko.
Flavor Hit: Parmigiano-Reggiano cheese offers richness and complexity.

- ¼ cup all-purpose flour
- ½ teaspoon dried oregano
- ¼ teaspoon salt
- 2 large egg whites, lightly beaten
- ¾ cup panko (Japanese breadcrumbs)
- 4 (6-ounce) skinless, boneless chicken breast halves
- 2 tablespoons olive oil, divided
- Cooking spray
- ½ cup jarred tomato-basil pasta sauce
- ½ cup (2 ounces) grated Parmigiano-Reggiano cheese
- ¾ cup (3 ounces) shredded part-skim mozzarella cheese

1 Preheat oven to 450°.
2 Combine first 3 ingredients in a shallow dish; place egg whites in a bowl. Place panko in a shallow dish. Dredge 1 breast half in flour mixture. Dip in egg whites; dredge in panko. Repeat procedure with remaining chicken, flour mixture, egg whites, and panko.
3 Heat 1 tablespoon oil in a large oven-proof skillet over medium-high heat. Add chicken to pan; cook 2 minutes. Add remaining 1 tablespoon oil. Turn chicken over; cook 2 minutes. Coat chicken with cooking spray; place pan in oven. Bake at 450° for 5 minutes. Turn chicken over; top each breast half with 2 tablespoons sauce, 2 tablespoons Parmigiano-Reggiano, and 3 tablespoons mozzarella. Bake 6 minutes or until chicken is done. Yield: 4 servings (serving size: 1 breast half).

CALORIES 401; FAT 16.9g (sat 6.4g, mono 7.6g, poly 1.3g); PROTEIN 44.4g; CARB 15.9g; FIBER 0.6g; CHOL 95mg; IRON 1.8mg; SODIUM 719mg; CALC 352mg

---

ROMAINE SALAD:
Whisk together 2 tablespoons fresh lemon juice, 1 tablespoon olive oil, 2 teaspoons honey, 1 teaspoon Dijon mustard, ¼ teaspoon salt, and ⅛ teaspoon black pepper. Drizzle over 6 cups torn romaine lettuce; toss well.

BASIC POLENTA:
Bring 2 cups fat-free, less-sodium chicken broth and 1 cup 2% milk to a boil in a medium saucepan. Gradually whisk in ¾ cup instant dry polenta. Cook 5 minutes or until thick, stirring constantly.

Shopping List

Pork Noodle Salad
1 red bell pepper
carrots
green onions
basil
bottled ground fresh ginger
bottled minced garlic
6 ounces rice vermicelli
rice vinegar
mirin
fish sauce
hoisin sauce
sugar
cooking spray
dry-roasted peanuts
4 (4-ounce) boneless center-cut pork loin chops

Soy-Buttered Sugar Snap Peas
1 pound sugar snap peas
1 lemon
low-sodium soy sauce
butter

Game Plan

- While broiler preheats and water comes to a boil:
  - Slice bell pepper, onions, and basil.
  - Prepare hoisin mixture.
- While noodles and pork cook:
  - Chop peanuts.
  - Prepare sugar snap peas.

Pork Noodle Salad with Soy-Buttered Sugar Snap Peas

·····················*30 minutes*

- 6 ounces uncooked rice vermicelli
- ¼ cup rice vinegar
- 1 tablespoon sugar
- 3 tablespoons mirin
- 2 tablespoons water
- 1 tablespoon fish sauce
- 1 cup julienne-cut carrots
- ¾ cup thinly sliced red bell pepper (about 1 small pepper)
- ½ cup thinly sliced green onions
- ⅓ cup thinly sliced fresh basil
- ¼ cup chopped dry-roasted peanuts
- 2 tablespoons hoisin sauce
- 1 teaspoon rice vinegar
- 1 teaspoon bottled ground fresh ginger
- ½ teaspoon bottled minced garlic
- 4 (4-ounce) boneless center-cut pork loin chops
- ¼ teaspoon salt
- ⅛ teaspoon black pepper
- Cooking spray

1 Preheat broiler.

2 Cook noodles according to package directions. Drain and rinse under cold water; drain. Place noodles in a large bowl. Add ¼ cup vinegar and next 4 ingredients; toss well. Top with carrots and next 4 ingredients.

3 Combine hoisin and next 3 ingredients. Sprinkle pork evenly with salt and black pepper; place on a broiler pan coated with cooking spray. Brush half of hoisin mixture over pork; broil 3 minutes. Turn pork over. Brush remaining hoisin mixture over pork; broil 3 minutes or until done. Serve pork thinly sliced over salad. Yield: 4 servings (serving size: about 1¾ cups salad and 1 pork chop).

CALORIES 457; FAT 11.7g (sat 3.1g, mono 4.6g, poly 1.7g); PROTEIN 29.9g; CARB 50.8g; FIBER 3.1g; CHOL 65mg; IRON 2.4mg; SODIUM 703mg; CALC 65mg

---

SOY-BUTTERED SUGAR SNAP PEAS:

Steam 1 pound sugar snap peas 3 minutes or until crisp-tender; drain and place in a bowl. Combine 5 teaspoons melted butter, 1 tablespoon low-sodium soy sauce, 1 teaspoon lemon juice, and ⅛ teaspoon black pepper. Drizzle butter mixture over peas; toss to coat.

Shopping List

Moroccan Pita Sandwiches
1 onion
green leaf lettuce
3 medium tomatoes
garlic
1 lemon
pita bread
tomato paste
tahini
cooking spray
ground coriander
fennel seeds
ground cumin
ground cinnamon
ground ginger
12 ounces ground round
large egg
1 cup fat-free Greek-style yogurt

Carrot-Currant Slaw
1 lemon
carrots
green onions
dried currants
olive oil
ground cumin
ground red pepper

Game Plan

- Preheat oven.
- While oven heats:
  - Grate carrots.
  - Make patties.
- While patties brown in the skillet:
  - Grate lemon rind.
  - Juice lemon.
- While patties finish cooking in oven:
  - Make sauce.
  - Toss together salad.

Moroccan Pita Sandwiches with Carrot-Currant Slaw

·····················*40 minutes*

PATTIES:

- ⅓ cup finely chopped onion
- 2 tablespoons tomato paste
- ½ teaspoon salt
- ½ teaspoon ground coriander
- ½ teaspoon fennel seeds, crushed
- ¼ teaspoon ground cumin
- ¼ teaspoon ground cinnamon
- ⅛ teaspoon ground ginger
- 12 ounces ground round
- 1 large egg
- Cooking spray

SAUCE:

- 1 cup fat-free Greek-style yogurt
- 2 teaspoons tahini (sesame seed paste)
- ½ teaspoon grated lemon rind
- 1 teaspoon fresh lemon juice
- ⅛ teaspoon salt
- 1 garlic clove, minced

REMAINING INGREDIENTS:

- 4 (6-inch) pitas, halved
- 8 green leaf lettuce leaves
- 16 (¼-inch) slices tomato

1 Preheat oven to 400°.

2 To prepare patties, combine first 10 ingredients. Divide into 8 equal portions; shape each into a ¼-inch-thick patty. Heat a large nonstick skillet over medium-high heat. Coat pan with cooking spray. Add 4 patties to pan; cook 5 minutes or until browned, turning occasionally. Arrange patties on a baking sheet. Repeat procedure with remaining patties. Bake at 400° for 5 minutes or until done.

3 To prepare sauce, combine yogurt and next 5 ingredients. Spoon 2 tablespoons sauce into each pita half; top with 1 lettuce leaf, 2 tomato slices, and 1 patty. Yield: 4 servings (serving size: 2 pita halves).

CALORIES 370; FAT 9.1g (sat 3.3g, mono 3.9g, poly 0.9g); PROTEIN 31.2g; CARB 39.6g; FIBER 2.1g; CHOL 31mg; IRON 4.9mg; SODIUM 633mg; CALC 99mg

CARROT-CURRANT SLAW:

Combine 2 tablespoons lemon juice, 1½ teaspoons olive oil, ½ teaspoon ground cumin, ¼ teaspoon salt, ⅛ teaspoon ground red pepper, and ⅛ teaspoon black pepper in a large bowl. Stir in 4 cups shredded carrots, ½ cup chopped green onions, and ½ cup currants.

Shopping List

Fresh Tomato, Sausage, and Pecorino Pasta

1¼ pounds tomatoes
1 medium onion
garlic
fresh basil
olive oil
8 ounces penne pasta
8 ounces sweet Italian sausage
pecorino Romano cheese

Lemony Green Beans

1 pound green beans
1 lemon
extra-virgin olive oil

Game Plan

- While water comes to a boil:
  - Slice onion.
  - Chop tomatoes.
  - Trim green beans.
- While pasta cooks:
  - Cook sauce.
  - Grate cheese.
  - Steam green beans.
  - Tear basil.
- Toss pasta and green bean mixtures.

Fresh Tomato, Sausage, and Pecorino Pasta with Lemony Green Beans

·······································*40 minutes*

Ripe, late-summer tomatoes are juicy and delicious in this entrée, with no seeding or peeling necessary.

Simple Sub: Any short pasta—tubes such as mostaccioli or ziti, or shapes such as campanelle or rotini—will work in this dish.

Flavor Hit: Pecorino Romano is a pungent sheep's milk cheese that contributes big flavor; you can also use milder Parmigiano-Reggiano or Asiago.

8	ounces uncooked penne
8	ounces sweet Italian sausage
2	teaspoons olive oil
1	cup vertically sliced onion
2	teaspoons minced garlic
1¼	pounds tomatoes, chopped
6	tablespoons grated fresh pecorino Romano cheese, divided
¼	teaspoon salt
⅛	teaspoon black pepper
¼	cup torn fresh basil leaves

❶ Cook pasta according to package directions, omitting salt and fat; drain.

❷ Heat a large nonstick skillet over medium-high heat. Remove casings from sausage. Add oil to pan, swirling to coat. Add sausage and onion to pan; cook 4 minutes, stirring to crumble sausage. Add garlic; cook 2 minutes. Stir in tomatoes; cook 2 minutes. Remove from heat; stir in pasta, 2 tablespoons cheese, salt, and pepper. Sprinkle with remaining ¼ cup cheese and basil. Yield: 4 servings (serving size: about 2 cups pasta mixture, 1 tablespoon cheese, and 1 tablespoon basil).

CALORIES 389; FAT 10.7g (sat 4g, mono 4.5g, poly 0.7g); PROTEIN 21.6g; CARB 53.5g; FIBER 4.5g; CHOL 27mg; IRON 3.3mg; SODIUM 595mg; CALC 159mg

---

LEMONY GREEN BEANS:

Steam 1 pound trimmed green beans 5 minutes or until crisp-tender. Drain and rinse with cold water; drain and place in a bowl. Add 1 teaspoon grated lemon rind, 1 tablespoon fresh lemon juice, 1½ teaspoons extra-virgin olive oil, ½ teaspoon salt and ¼ teaspoon black pepper, and toss well.

WINE NOTE: Italian sausage craves a clean-tasting wine with the substance to complement the rest of the dish without overwhelming it. The smoky 2006 San Lorenzo Verdicchio Vigna Delle Oche ($23) is a great choice.

Shopping List

Cold Sesame Noodles with Chicken and Cucumbers

2 medium cucumbers
green onions
bottled ground fresh ginger
8 ounces dried udon noodles
rice vinegar
dark sesame oil
low-sodium soy sauce
sambal oelek or chile paste with garlic
honey
dry-roasted peanuts
rotisserie chicken

Baby Spinach Salad

8 cups baby spinach
1 small red onion
radishes
rice vinegar
canola oil
sugar
crushed red pepper

Game Plan

- While water comes to a boil:
  - Chop chicken.
  - Seed and slice cucumbers.
- While noodles cook:
  - Prepare dressing for noodles and salad.
- Toss noodle mixture and salad just before serving.

Cold Sesame Noodles with Chicken and Cucumbers with Baby Spinach Salad

·····················*30 minutes*

We use dried udon noodles; if using fresh noodles, you'll need about 11 ounces.
Simple Sub: Try an equal amount of soba in place of udon.
Shopping Tip: Look for nutty, fragrant dark sesame oil in the Asian foods section of your supermarket.
Vegetarian Swap: Replace the chicken with packaged baked or smoked tofu, cut into cubes.

8 ounces uncooked dried udon noodles
¼ cup rice vinegar
2 tablespoons dark sesame oil
2 tablespoons low-sodium soy sauce
1 tablespoon honey
2 teaspoons sambal oelek or chile paste with garlic
½ teaspoon bottled ground fresh ginger
2 cups shredded skinless, boneless rotisserie chicken breast
2 medium cucumbers, halved lengthwise and sliced
6 tablespoons chopped green onions
3 tablespoons chopped dry-roasted peanuts

❶ Cook noodles according to package directions, omitting salt and fat. Drain and rinse under cold water; drain.
❷ Combine rice vinegar and next 5 ingredients in a large bowl, and stir with a whisk. Add noodles, chicken, and cucumbers to bowl; toss gently to coat. Top with green onions and peanuts. Yield: 6 servings (serving size: about 1 cup noodle mixture, 1 tablespoon onions, and 1½ teaspoon peanuts).

CALORIES 302; FAT 9.2g (sat 1.4g, mono 3.3g, poly 2.8g); PROTEIN 21.5g; CARB 32.6g; FIBER 3.1g; CHOL 40mg; IRON 2.3mg; SODIUM 301mg; CALC 34mg

BABY SPINACH SALAD:
Combine 8 cups baby spinach, ½ cup thinly sliced red onion, and ½ cup quartered radishes. Whisk together 1½ tablespoons rice vinegar, 2 teaspoons canola oil, 1 teaspoon sugar, ¼ teaspoon salt, and ¼ teaspoon crushed red pepper. Drizzle dressing over salad; toss to coat.

WINE NOTE: Floral, zippy white wines from Argentina, like the 2007 Alamos Torrontes ($10), pair incredibly well with Asian-inspired dishes.

Shopping List

Barbecue Sirloin and Blue Cheese Salad
2 large shallots
1 large cucumber
1 red bell pepper
Bibb lettuce
chili powder
ground cumin
garlic powder
cooking spray
extra-virgin olive oil
white wine vinegar
Dijon mustard
1 pound lean sirloin steak
2 ounces blue cheese

Garlic–Olive Oil Bread
Italian-style hoagie rolls
extra-virgin olive oil
garlic powder

Game Plan

- While oven preheats:
  - Rub steak with spice mixture.
  - Heat grill pan.
- While steak cooks:
  - Prepare vinaigrette.
  - Prepare lettuce.
  - Slice cucumber, bell pepper, and onion.
- While steak rests:
  - Toss salad.
  - Bake bread.

Barbecue Sirloin and Blue Cheese Salad with Garlic–Olive Oil Bread

·····················*30 minutes*

Prep Pointer: Allow the steak to rest after cooking so the juices reabsorb, keeping the meat moist.

2 teaspoons chili powder
¾ teaspoon ground cumin
½ teaspoon garlic powder
½ teaspoon salt, divided
¼ teaspoon black pepper, divided
1 pound lean sirloin steak, trimmed
Cooking spray
2 tablespoons white wine vinegar
2 teaspoons Dijon mustard
1 tablespoon extra-virgin olive oil
6 cups torn Bibb lettuce
¾ cup thinly sliced peeled cucumber
1 cup red bell pepper strips
½ cup thinly sliced shallots
½ cup (2 ounces) crumbled blue cheese

❶ Combine chili powder, cumin, garlic powder, ¼ teaspoon salt, and ⅛ teaspoon black pepper; rub evenly over both sides of steak.
❷ Heat a grill pan over medium-high heat. Coat pan with cooking spray. Add steak to pan; cook 5 minutes. Turn steak over; cook 4 minutes or until desired degree of doneness. Place steak on a cutting board; let stand 5 minutes. Cut across grain into thin slices.
❸ Combine vinegar, mustard, remaining ¼ teaspoon salt, and remaining ⅛ teaspoon black pepper in a bowl, stirring with a whisk. Gradually add oil, stirring with a whisk. Combine lettuce and next 3 ingredients in a bowl. Drizzle vinaigrette over salad; toss gently to coat. Top salad with steak and cheese. Yield: 4 servings (serving size: about 1½ cups salad, 3 ounces steak, and 2 tablespoons cheese).

CALORIES 269; FAT 12.4g (sat 4.9g, mono 5.4g, poly 0.8g); PROTEIN 29.5g; CARB 9.4g; FIBER 2.6g; CHOL 57mg; IRON 2.8mg; SODIUM 671mg; CALC 141mg

GARLIC–OLIVE OIL BREAD:

Preheat oven to 425°. Slice 2 Italian-style hoagie rolls in half horizontally. Combine 1½ tablespoons extra-virgin olive oil and 1 teaspoon garlic powder; brush evenly over cut sides of rolls. Bake at 425° for 7 minutes or until toasted.

Shopping List

Cincinnati Turkey Chili

prechopped onion
1 green bell pepper
bottled minced garlic
spaghetti
tomato paste
fat-free, less-sodium chicken broth
1 (15-ounce) can kidney beans
1 (14.5-ounce) can diced tomatoes
semisweet chocolate
chili powder
ground cumin
dried oregano
ground cinnamon
ground allspice
cooking spray
8 ounces lean ground turkey
3 ounces sharp Cheddar cheese

Jack-Corn Muffins

1 ear corn
1 (8.5-ounce) package corn muffin mix
cooking spray
1% milk
large eggs
2 ounces Monterey Jack cheese with jalapeño peppers

Game Plan

- While oven heats and water comes to a boil:
  - Chop bell pepper and chocolate.
  - Shred cheeses.
  - Rinse and drain beans.
- While pasta cooks:
  - Cook chili.
  - Mix muffin batter.
- While chili simmers:
  - Cook muffins.

Cincinnati Turkey Chili with Jack-Corn Muffins

·············40 minutes

Flavor Hit: A touch of chocolate adds body and richness.

Make-Ahead Tip: Freeze individual portions of leftover chili for up to two months; thaw overnight and reheat over medium-low heat.

     4 ounces uncooked spaghetti
        Cooking spray
     8 ounces lean ground turkey
   1½ cups prechopped onion, divided
     1 cup chopped green bell pepper
     1 tablespoon bottled minced garlic
     1 tablespoon chili powder
     2 tablespoons tomato paste
     1 teaspoon ground cumin
     1 teaspoon dried oregano
     ¼ teaspoon ground cinnamon
     ⅛ teaspoon ground allspice
     ½ cup fat-free, less-sodium chicken broth
     1 (15-ounce) can kidney beans, rinsed and drained
     1 (14.5-ounce) can diced tomatoes, undrained
   2½ tablespoons chopped semisweet chocolate
     ¼ teaspoon salt
     ¾ cup (3 ounces) shredded sharp Cheddar cheese

❶ Cook pasta according to package dir-ections, omitting salt and fat. Drain; set aside.

❷ Heat a Dutch oven over medium-high heat. Coat pan with cooking spray. Add turkey; cook 3 minutes, stirring to crumble. Add 1 cup onion, bell pepper, and garlic; sauté 3 minutes. Stir in chili powder and next 5 ingredients; cook 1 minute. Add broth, beans, and tomatoes; bring to a boil. Cover, reduce heat, and simmer 20 minutes, stirring occasionally. Remove from heat; stir in chocolate and salt. Serve chili over spaghetti; top with remaining ½ cup onion and cheese. Yield:

4 servings (serving size: about ½ cup spaghetti, 1½ cups chili, 2 tablespoons onion, and 3 tablespoons cheese).

CALORIES 408; FAT 13.8g (sat 6.6g, mono 4.3g, poly 1.7g); PROTEIN 24.5g; CARB 47.4g; FIBER 7.9g; CHOL 67mg; IRON 3.7mg; SODIUM 765mg; CALC 237mg

JACK-CORN MUFFINS:

Preheat oven to 400°. Combine 1 (8.5-ounce) package corn muffin mix, ½ cup shredded Monterey Jack cheese with jalapeño peppers, ½ cup corn kernels, ½ cup 1% low-fat milk, and 1 large egg. Divide batter evenly among 8 muffin cups coated with cooking spray. Bake at 400° for 16 minutes or until browned.

Ice Cream with Dark Chocolate Sauce

This simple dessert makes an indulgent finale to any meal. Chill leftover sauce, and reheat it in the microwave.

     6 ounces finely chopped bittersweet chocolate
     6 tablespoons water
   2½ tablespoons sugar
        Dash of salt
     6 cups vanilla fat-free ice cream

❶ Place chocolate in a large bowl; set aside.

❷ Combine water, sugar, and salt in a small saucepan over medium-high heat; bring to a boil, stirring until sugar dissolves. Pour hot sugar mixture over chocolate; stir gently until smooth. Spoon ¾ cup ice cream into each of 8 bowls; top each serving with 2 tablespoons sauce. Yield: 8 servings.

CALORIES 256; FAT 9.1g (sat 4.6g, mono 3.1g, poly 0.3g); PROTEIN 6g; CARB 43g; FIBER 3g; CHOL 0mg; IRON 0.6mg; SODIUM 116mg; CALC 150mg

Simple Additions

Chicken Breasts with Tomatoes and Olives

Kalamata and picholine olives add salty savor. Serve over couscous, with dressed greens on the side.

4 (6-ounce) skinless, boneless chicken breast halves

+

1 cup multicolored cherry or grape tomatoes, halved

+

3 tablespoons oil and vinegar dressing, divided

20 olives, halved

+

½ cup (2 ounces) crumbled feta cheese

Directions: Prepare grill to medium-high heat. Sprinkle chicken evenly with ¼ teaspoon salt and ¼ teaspoon freshly ground black pepper. Place chicken on grill rack coated with cooking spray, and grill 6 minutes on each side or until chicken is done. Keep warm. Combine tomatoes, 1½ tablespoons dressing, and olives in a medium skillet over medium heat, and cook 2 minutes or until tomatoes soften slightly and mixture is thoroughly heated, stirring occasionally. Brush chicken with remaining 1½ tablespoons dressing. Cut each chicken breast half into ¾-inch slices. Top each chicken breast half with ¼ cup tomato mixture. Sprinkle each serving with 2 tablespoons cheese and torn basil leaves, if desired. Yield: 4 servings.

CALORIES 348; FAT 17.3g (sat 4.4g, mono 5g, poly 1.2g); PROTEIN 41.9g; CARB 3.9g; FIBER 0.6g; CHOL 111mg; IRON 1.6mg; SODIUM 810mg; CALC 100mg

Grilled Salmon with Smoky Tomato Salsa

If you prefer a milder relish, remove the seeds from the jalapeño before grilling.

4 (6-ounce) skinless salmon fillets

+

4 large plum tomatoes, halved

+

1 small red onion, cut into ½-inch slices

+

1 jalapeño pepper, halved

+

1 lime, divided

Directions: Prepare grill to medium-high heat. Sprinkle fillets with ¼ teaspoon salt and ¼ teaspoon black pepper. Place on grill rack coated with cooking spray, and grill 4 minutes on each side or until desired degree of doneness. Place tomatoes, onion, and jalapeño on grill rack coated with cooking spray; grill tomatoes, cut sides down, 6 minutes. Turn; grill 1 minute. Grill onion and jalapeño 6 minutes on each side or until lightly browned. Remove from grill, and cool slightly. Coarsely chop tomatoes and onion; finely chop jalapeño. Combine tomatoes, onion, jalapeño, ¼ teaspoon salt, ¼ teaspoon black pepper, and juice from ½ lime. Serve salsa over fish. Garnish with lime wedges. Yield: 4 servings (serving size: 1 fillet and about ½ cup salsa).

CALORIES 336; FAT 18.6g (sat 3.7g, mono 6.6g, poly 6.8g); PROTEIN 34.7g; CARB 6.2g; FIBER 1.7g; CHOL 100mg; IRON 0.9mg; SODIUM 399mg; CALC 32mg

Grilled Pork Tenderloin Roulade

Searing gives the pork a pleasant char, acting almost like an extra ingredient. The filling is adaptable; substitute fresh rosemary for thyme, if you prefer.

 +  +

1 (1-pound) pork tenderloin, trimmed

¼ cup chopped shallots

¼ cup crumbled goat cheese

 +

3 tablespoons chopped walnuts, toasted

2 teaspoons chopped fresh thyme

Directions: Prepare grill to medium heat. Slice tenderloin lengthwise, cutting to, but not through, other side. Open halves, laying tenderloin flat. Place tenderloin between 2 sheets of plastic wrap; pound to ½-inch thickness using a meat mallet or heavy skillet. Sprinkle shallots, cheese, walnuts, and thyme on tenderloin. Roll up, starting with long side; secure pork at 1-inch intervals with twine. Sprinkle with ¼ teaspoon salt and ¼ teaspoon black pepper. Place pork on grill rack coated with cooking spray. Grill 27 minutes or until a thermometer registers 155°, turning after 13 minutes. Remove from grill; lightly cover with foil. Let stand 10 minutes; cut crosswise into 8 slices. Yield: 4 servings (serving size: 2 slices).

CALORIES 206; FAT 9.6g (sat 3.1g, mono 2.7g, poly 3.1g); PROTEIN 26.5g; CARB 2.8g; FIBER 0.5g; CHOL 79mg; IRON 1.9mg; SODIUM 242mg; CALC 38mg

Great Big Flavors from the Last Grilling Days of Summer

Send the last lazy days of the season out in style by grilling peak-quality vegetables and fruits, even fish and shellfish.

MAKE AHEAD
Grilled Corn and Potato Chowder

1 pound small red potatoes, quartered
1 tablespoon salt, divided
3 tablespoons softened butter, divided
4 ears shucked corn
Cooking spray
¾ cup finely chopped onion
⅛ teaspoon ground red pepper
3 cups 2% reduced-fat milk
½ cup half-and-half
2 fresh thyme sprigs
3 tablespoons finely chopped fresh chives
1½ teaspoons chopped fresh thyme
½ teaspoon freshly ground black pepper

1. Preheat grill to medium-high heat.
2. Place a grill basket on grill.
3. Place potatoes and 2 teaspoons salt in a saucepan; cover with water. Bring to a boil; cook 2 minutes. Remove from heat. Let potatoes stand in hot water 5 minutes. Drain; cut into ¼-inch cubes.
4. Melt 1 tablespoon butter; brush evenly over corn. Place corn on grill rack coated with cooking spray. Place potatoes in grill basket coated with cooking spray. Grill corn and potatoes 15 minutes or until slightly charred, turning occasionally. Cool corn slightly; cut kernels from cobs. Place 1 cup corn kernels in a food processor; process until smooth.
5. Melt remaining 2 tablespoons butter in a medium saucepan over medium-high heat. Add onion; sauté 3 minutes, stirring occasionally. Add remaining 1 teaspoon salt and red pepper; cook 30 seconds, stirring frequently. Stir in potatoes, remaining corn kernels, pureed corn, milk, half-and-half, and thyme sprigs; bring to a simmer. Reduce heat; simmer 20 minutes, stirring occasionally. Discard thyme sprigs. Stir in chives and remaining ingredients. Yield: 6 servings (serving size: 1 cup).

CALORIES 268; FAT 12.3g (sat 6.6g, mono 2.2g, poly 0.4g); PROTEIN 9.9g; CARB 33.8g; FIBER 3.1g; CHOL 32mg; IRON 1mg; SODIUM 599mg; CALC 214mg

WINE NOTE: This creamy chowder calls for a smooth, full-bodied white, like a French chardonnay. Lulu B. Chardonnay Vin de Pays d'Oc 2008 ($10) mixes apple fruitiness with buttery and smoky nuances—a perfect match for grilled corn—while the acidity balances the creaminess.

Stilton Burgers

2 teaspoons olive oil
4 cups sliced onion (about 12 ounces)
½ teaspoon salt, divided
1 pound ground sirloin
2 tablespoons grated onion
2 tablespoons Worcestershire sauce
⅛ teaspoon ground black pepper
2 garlic cloves, minced
Cooking spray
¼ cup crumbled Stilton cheese
4 (2-ounce) French hamburger rolls, split
4 green leaf lettuce leaves
4 (¼-inch-thick) slices tomato

1. Preheat grill to medium-high heat.
2. Heat a large skillet over medium heat. Add oil to pan. Add sliced onion and ¼ teaspoon salt; cook 18 minutes or until golden, stirring occasionally.
3. Combine remaining ¼ teaspoon salt, beef, and next 4 ingredients; toss gently. Divide mixture into 4 equal portions, shaping each into a ½-inch-thick patty.
4. Place patties on a grill rack lightly coated with cooking spray; grill 4 minutes on each side or until desired degree of doneness. Top each patty with 1 tablespoon cheese during last 2 minutes of cooking.
5. Place cut sides of rolls on grill rack; grill 1 minute. Place bottom halves of rolls on 4 plates; top each serving with 1 lettuce leaf, 1 tomato slice, 1 patty, ¼ cup onion mixture, and 1 roll top. Yield: 4 servings (serving size: 1 burger).

CALORIES 393; FAT 15g (sat 6.3g, mono 6g, poly 0.6g); PROTEIN 28.3g; CARB 35.3g; FIBER 2.1g; CHOL 75mg; IRON 5.1mg; SODIUM 849mg; CALC 142mg

Smoky Mussels and Clams with White Wine Broth

Be sure to soak the wood chips in water before adding them to the grill so they'll smolder with flavorful smoke as the shellfish steam. We like the subtle, almost sweet flavor of applewood, though you can try hickory for a more assertive taste. If using a gas grill, place wood chips inside a small disposable aluminum pan; cover with foil, and perforate the foil. Place the container on the cooking grate with the Dutch oven in step 3.

- 1 cup wood chips
- 2 tablespoons extra-virgin olive oil
- 1/3 cup chopped shallots
- 6 garlic cloves, sliced
- 2 cups chopped, seeded, peeled tomato
- 1/2 cup dry white wine
- 3 fresh thyme sprigs
- 1 (8-ounce) bottle clam juice
- 1 1/2 pounds littleneck clams
- 2 pounds mussels, scrubbed and debearded
- 8 (1/2-ounce) slices French bread baguette
- Cooking spray
- 3 tablespoons butter
- 3 tablespoons finely chopped fresh flat-leaf parsley
- 1 tablespoon chopped fresh thyme

① Soak wood chips in water 30 minutes; drain well.

② Preheat grill to medium-high heat.

③ Place wood chips on hot coals. Place a large Dutch oven on grill rack. Close grill lid; heat 2 minutes. Add oil to pan, swirling to coat. Add shallots and garlic to pan; sauté 2 minutes, stirring frequently. Add tomato; close grill lid, and cook 3 minutes. Remove grill lid. Add wine; bring to a boil. Cook 5 minutes or until reduced to 2 tablespoons, stirring occasionally. Add thyme, juice, and clams; close grill lid, and cook 5 minutes. Remove grill lid. Stir in mussels; close grill lid, and cook 5 minutes. Coat bread slices with cooking spray; grill 1 minute on each side or until toasted.

④ Remove clams and mussels from pan using a slotted spoon, reserving cooking liquid in pan; discard any unopened shells. Cover clams and mussels; keep warm. Discard thyme sprigs. Bring reserved cooking liquid to a boil. Cook 15 minutes or until reduced to 3/4 cup; remove from heat. Add butter, parsley, and chopped thyme, stirring until smooth. Return mussels and clams to pan; toss to coat. Serve with grilled bread. Yield: 4 servings (serving size: about 2 cups clams and mussels, about 1/4 cup broth, and 2 bread slices).

CALORIES 402; FAT 19.5g (sat 7.1g, mono 8g, poly 2.3g); PROTEIN 26.6g; CARB 30.6g; FIBER 2g; CHOL 76mg; IRON 14.4mg; SODIUM 773mg; CALC 105mg

Pork, Pineapple, and Anaheim Chile Salad with Avocado

PORK:
- 3/4 teaspoon ground coriander
- 3/4 teaspoon ground cumin
- 1/2 teaspoon kosher salt
- 1/2 teaspoon freshly ground black pepper
- 1 (1-pound) pork tenderloin, trimmed
- 1 tablespoon olive oil
- Cooking spray

VINAIGRETTE:
- 1 1/2 tablespoons chopped fresh cilantro
- 1 1/2 tablespoons fresh lime juice
- 1 tablespoon olive oil
- 1 tablespoon water
- 1/2 teaspoon kosher salt
- 1/2 teaspoon sugar
- 1/2 teaspoon ground black pepper
- 1 garlic clove, minced

SALAD:
- 1/2 fresh pineapple, peeled, cored, and cut into (1/2-inch-thick) rings
- 1 red bell pepper, seeded and halved
- 2 Anaheim chiles
- 12 Boston lettuce leaves
- 3/4 cup cubed avocado

① Preheat grill to medium-high heat.

② To prepare pork, combine first 4 ingredients. Brush pork with 1 tablespoon oil; rub spice mixture over pork.

③ Place pork on grill rack coated with cooking spray, and grill for 20 minutes or until thermometer registers 155° (slightly pink), turning pork occasionally. Transfer to a cutting board, and let rest for 10 minutes. Cut pork crosswise into thin slices.

④ To prepare vinaigrette, combine cilantro and next 7 ingredients in a bowl, stirring well with a whisk.

⑤ To prepare salad, place pineapple, bell pepper, skin sides down, and chiles on a grill rack lightly coated with cooking spray; grill 5 minutes. Turn pineapple and chiles; grill 5 minutes. Place bell pepper and chiles in a zip-top plastic bag; seal. Let stand 10 minutes. Remove pepper and chiles from bag. Seed chiles. Peel pepper and chiles, and finely chop. Chop pineapple. Place pepper, chiles, and pineapple in a bowl. Drizzle with vinaigrette; toss. Arrange 2 lettuce leaves on each of 6 plates. Divide pork evenly among salads. Spoon 1/2 cup pineapple mixture over each serving, and sprinkle each serving with 2 tablespoons avocado. Serve immediately. Yield: 6 servings.

CALORIES 235; FAT 11.8g (sat 2.2g, mono 7.2g, poly 1.3g); PROTEIN 17.1g; CARB 17.3g; FIBER 4.7g; CHOL 42mg; IRON 2.1mg; SODIUM 363mg; CALC 41mg

WINE NOTE: Ponzi Pinot Gris 2008 ($17) from Oregon has flavors of pear, guava, and pineapple that complement this salad. American pinot gris is usually richer than Italian pinot grigio, making it well matched for this savory-sweet salad.

Halibut with Grilled Tomato and Olive Relish

Mild halibut pairs nicely with this tangy relish. Any other meaty, firm fish, such as wild salmon or striped bass, will also work.

2½ tablespoons extra-virgin olive oil, divided
1 (12-ounce) beefsteak tomato, halved crosswise and seeded
¾ teaspoon salt, divided
½ teaspoon freshly ground black pepper, divided
  Cooking spray
2 tablespoons thinly sliced fresh basil
1 tablespoon chopped fresh oregano
1½ tablespoons finely chopped shallots
½ teaspoon grated lemon rind
1½ teaspoons fresh lemon juice
2 ounces pitted green olives, coarsely chopped
1 garlic clove, minced
4 (6-ounce) halibut fillets

① Preheat grill to medium-high heat.
② Brush 1½ teaspoons oil over cut sides of tomato; sprinkle evenly with ⅛ teaspoon salt and ⅛ teaspoon pepper. Place tomato, cut sides down, on grill rack coated with cooking spray. Cover and grill 8 minutes. Cool slightly; peel and chop tomato. Combine chopped tomato, ⅛ teaspoon salt, ⅛ teaspoon pepper, 1 tablespoon oil, basil, and next 6 ingredients; toss gently.
③ Brush fillets evenly with remaining 1 tablespoon oil; sprinkle evenly with remaining ½ teaspoon salt and remaining ¼ teaspoon pepper. Place fillets, flesh sides down, on grill rack coated with cooking spray. Grill 5 minutes; turn and grill 3 minutes or until fish flakes when tested with a fork or until desired degree of doneness. Serve with relish. Yield: 4 servings (serving size: 1 fillet and about ⅓ cup relish).

CALORIES 318; FAT 16.3g (sat 2.2g, mono 10.3g, poly 2.6g); PROTEIN 35.3g; CARB 6.7g; FIBER 1.2g; CHOL 52mg; IRON 2mg; SODIUM 770mg; CALC 97mg

Charred Vegetable Salad

Although you can successfully prepare this colorful end-of-summer salad on a gas grill, charcoal will imbue the vegetables with extra flavor. You can easily substitute white wine vinegar for the champagne vinegar without compromising the flavor of the dish.

2 red bell peppers, halved and seeded
1½ pounds eggplant, cut into (½-inch-thick) slices (about 2 medium)
1 sweet onion, cut into 8 wedges
1 pint cherry tomatoes
½ teaspoon freshly ground black pepper, divided
3 tablespoons extra-virgin olive oil, divided
¾ teaspoon salt, divided
  Cooking spray
1 tablespoon champagne vinegar
½ teaspoon sugar
2 garlic cloves, minced
1 ounce oil-cured olives (about 12), pitted and halved
¼ cup fresh small basil leaves
1 tablespoon finely chopped fresh chives

① Preheat grill to medium-high heat.
② Combine first 4 ingredients, ¼ teaspoon black pepper, 1 tablespoon oil, and ¼ teaspoon salt. Place bell peppers, skin sides down, and onion on grill rack coated with cooking spray; grill 10 minutes. Turn onion; add eggplant to grill. Remove bell peppers. Place bell peppers in a zip-top bag; seal. Let stand 10 minutes. Grill eggplant and onion 5 minutes; remove onion. Turn eggplant; grill 5 minutes. Remove eggplant. Add tomatoes to a grill basket; grill 5 minutes. Remove bell peppers from bag. Peel and discard skins; slice lengthwise.
③ Combine ¼ teaspoon salt, vinegar, and sugar. Slowly add remaining 2 tablespoons oil, stirring with a whisk. Combine vegetables, vinegar mixture, garlic, and olives. Sprinkle with remaining

¼ teaspoon salt, remaining ¼ teaspoon pepper, basil, and chives. Yield: 8 servings (serving size: about ¾ cup).

CALORIES 99; FAT 5.9g (sat 0.8g, mono 4g, poly 0.8g); PROTEIN 2g; CARB 11.7g; FIBER 4.7g; CHOL 0mg; IRON 0.9mg; SODIUM 258mg; CALC 23mg

Caramelized Fresh Figs with Sweet Cream

Honey-coated figs caramelize on the grill to star in this simple dessert.

2 teaspoons honey
8 large fresh figs, cut in half lengthwise
  Cooking spray
¼ cup crème fraîche
½ teaspoon sugar

① Preheat grill to high heat.
② Brush honey on cut sides of figs. Lightly spray cut sides of figs with cooking spray.
③ Place figs, cut sides down, on grill rack, and grill 3 minutes or until grill marks appear. Remove from grill. Combine crème fraîche and sugar; spoon over figs. Yield: 4 servings (serving size: 4 fig halves and 1 tablespoon sauce).

CALORIES 159; FAT 5.6g (sat 3.3g, mono 1.7g, poly 0.4g); PROTEIN 1.4g; CARB 28g; FIBER 3.7g; CHOL 14mg; IRON 0.5mg; SODIUM 6mg; CALC 45mg

SuperFast

Here are a handful of 20-minute dishes hot from the Test Kitchens.

Quick-cooking seafood for busy weeknights, featuring pan sautéing for browned, flaky fish; lemon juice for bright taste; toasted sesame seeds to add instant Asian flair; and capers for briny, salty notes.

Blackened Cumin-Cayenne Tilapia

Use your broiler to make already quick-cooking fish fillets an even speedier dinner option. Serve with sautéed spinach and roasted new potato wedges.

- 1 tablespoon olive oil
- 4 (6-ounce) tilapia fillets
- 2 teaspoons ground cumin
- ½ teaspoon salt
- ½ teaspoon garlic powder
- ½ teaspoon ground red pepper
- ¼ teaspoon freshly ground black pepper
- Cooking spray

1 Preheat broiler.
2 Rub oil evenly over fish. Combine cumin and next 4 ingredients; sprinkle over fish. Arrange fish on a broiler pan coated with cooking spray; broil 5 minutes or until fish flakes easily when tested with a fork or desired degree of doneness. Yield: 4 servings (serving size: 1 fillet).

CALORIES 159; FAT 5.8g (sat 1.2g, mono 3.1g, poly 0.9g); PROTEIN 25.9g; CARB 0.9g; FIBER 0.5g; CHOL 64mg; IRON 1.1mg; SODIUM 364mg; CALC 22mg

Double-Sesame Grilled Tuna

You can serve the tuna with quick-cooking rice and steamed baby bok choy to round out your meal.

- ¼ cup low-sodium soy sauce
- 2 tablespoons finely chopped green onions
- 2 teaspoons toasted sesame seeds
- 2 teaspoons dark sesame oil
- 1 teaspoon chili oil
- 4 (6-ounce) tuna steaks (about ¾-inch thick)
- Cooking spray

1 Combine first 5 ingredients in a large zip-top plastic bag. Add tuna; seal and let stand 10 minutes, turning steaks occasionally.
2 Heat a grill pan over medium-high heat. Coat pan with cooking spray. Remove tuna from bag; discard marinade. Add tuna to pan; cook 5 minutes or until desired degree of doneness, turning once. Yield: 4 servings (serving size: 1 tuna steak).

CALORIES 208; FAT 8.4g (sat 1.9g, mono 2.6g, poly 2.7g); PROTEIN 30.3g; CARB 1g; FIBER 0.2g; CHOL 48mg; IRON 1.6mg; SODIUM 317mg; CALC 20mg

Creole Shrimp and Sausage Stew

Serve with crusty bread and hot sauce.

- 2 teaspoons olive oil
- 1 cup chopped green bell pepper
- 1 cup thinly sliced turkey smoked sausage (about 6 ounces)
- 1 teaspoon bottled minced garlic
- ¾ cup fat-free, less-sodium chicken broth
- 1 (10-ounce) can diced tomatoes and green chiles, undrained (such as Rotel)
- 8 ounces peeled and deveined medium shrimp
- 1 (15-ounce) can organic kidney beans, rinsed and drained
- 2 tablespoons chopped fresh parsley

1 Heat a large saucepan over medium-high heat. Add oil to pan, swirling to coat. Add bell pepper, sausage, and garlic to pan; sauté 3 minutes or until bell pepper is tender, stirring occasionally. Add broth and tomatoes; bring to a boil. Stir in shrimp and beans; cover, reduce heat, and simmer 6 minutes or until shrimp are done. Sprinkle with parsley. Yield: 4 servings (serving size: about 1 cup).

CALORIES 191; FAT 6g (sat 1.7g, mono 2.7g, poly 1g); PROTEIN 21.3g; CARB 13.2g; FIBER 3.5g; CHOL 97mg; IRON 2.9mg; SODIUM 694mg; CALC 127mg

Crispy Skin Salmon with Fiery Asian Slaw

Be sure to purchase skin-on salmon fillets for the best flavor and texture.

- 4 (6-ounce) salmon fillets
- ¾ teaspoon salt, divided
- ¼ teaspoon black pepper
- Cooking spray
- ¼ cup fresh orange juice
- 1 tablespoon rice vinegar
- 1 tablespoon balsamic vinegar
- 1 tablespoon olive oil
- 2 teaspoons Sriracha (hot chile sauce)
- 1 teaspoon bottled ground fresh ginger
- ½ teaspoon honey
- ½ cup chopped fresh cilantro
- 1 (16-ounce) package cabbage-and-carrot coleslaw
- 1 tablespoon toasted sesame seeds

1 Heat a large nonstick skillet over medium-high heat. Sprinkle salmon fillets evenly with ¼ teaspoon salt and pepper. Coat pan with cooking spray. Place salmon in pan, skin sides down; cook 4 minutes. Turn salmon over; cook 3 minutes. Add juice to pan; cook 30 seconds or until liquid almost evaporates and fish flakes easily when tested with a fork.
2 While fish cooks, combine rice vinegar and next 5 ingredients in a large bowl, stirring with a whisk. Add remaining ½ teaspoon salt, cilantro, and coleslaw; toss well to coat. Sprinkle with sesame seeds. Serve salmon with slaw. Yield: 4 servings (serving size: about 1 cup slaw and 1 fillet).

CALORIES 302; FAT 14.8g (sat 2.8g, mono 6.8g, poly 2.8g); PROTEIN 29.2g; CARB 12g; FIBER 3.2g; CHOL 65mg; IRON 5.5mg; SODIUM 577mg; CALC 66mg

Halibut Sandwiches with Spicy Tartar Sauce

- 2 tablespoons all-purpose flour
- ½ teaspoon salt
- ½ teaspoon ground coriander
- ⅛ teaspoon black pepper
- 4 (6-ounce) skinless halibut fillets
- 1 tablespoon olive oil
- ¼ cup canola mayonnaise
- 2 tablespoons dill pickle relish
- ⅛ teaspoon ground red pepper
- 4 (2-ounce) Kaiser or sandwich rolls, toasted
- 8 (¼-inch-thick) slices tomato
- 4 (¼-inch-thick) slices red onion

❶ Combine first 4 ingredients in a shallow dish. Dredge fish in flour mixture, shaking off excess.
❷ Heat a large nonstick skillet over medium-high heat. Add oil to pan, swirling to coat. Add fish to pan; cook 3 minutes on each side or until fish flakes easily when tested with a fork.
❸ While fish cooks, combine mayonnaise, relish, and red pepper. Spread about 1 teaspoon mayonnaise mixture over cut side of each roll half. Layer 2 tomato slices, 1 onion slice, and 1 fillet on bottom of each roll; top with top halves of rolls. Yield: 4 servings (serving size: 1 sandwich).

CALORIES 455; FAT 14.2g (sat 1.4g, mono 6.9g, poly 4.1g); PROTEIN 40.5g; CARB 38.1g; FIBER 2.1g; CHOL 52mg; IRON 3.6mg; SODIUM 852mg; CALC 138mg

Greek Mahimahi

- 4 (6-ounce) mahimahi or other firm white fish fillets (about 1 inch thick), skinned
- 1 teaspoon black pepper, divided
- ½ teaspoon salt, divided
- Cooking spray
- 2 cups tomato wedges
- ¼ cup thinly vertically sliced red onion
- 3 tablespoons halved pitted kalamata olives

- 2 tablespoons chopped fresh parsley
- 1 tablespoon red wine vinegar
- 2 teaspoons extra-virgin olive oil
- 1 teaspoon chopped fresh oregano

❶ Heat a nonstick skillet over medium-high heat. Sprinkle fish with ½ teaspoon pepper and ¼ teaspoon salt. Coat pan with cooking spray. Place fish in pan; cook 4 minutes on each side or until fish flakes easily when tested with a fork or until desired degree of doneness. Remove fish from pan; let stand 3 minutes.
❷ While fish cooks, combine remaining ½ teaspoon pepper, remaining ¼ teaspoon salt, tomato, and remaining ingredients, tossing well. Serve salad with fish. Yield: 4 servings (serving size: 1 fillet and ¾ cup salad).

CALORIES 213; FAT 6.6g (sat 1g, mono 4.1g, poly 0.9g); PROTEIN 31.5g; CARB 5.9g; FIBER 1.6g; CHOL 120mg; IRON 2.4mg; SODIUM 692mg; CALC 46mg

Pan-Sautéed Trout with Capers

Serve over orzo to catch all the sauce.

- 4 (6-ounce) trout fillets, halved
- ½ teaspoon salt
- ¼ teaspoon black pepper
- Cooking spray
- ⅓ cup dry white wine
- 2 teaspoons grated lemon rind
- 2 tablespoons fresh lemon juice
- 1 tablespoon capers
- ⅛ teaspoon dried herbes de Provence
- 1 tablespoon chilled butter, cut into small pieces
- 2 tablespoons chopped fresh flat-leaf parsley

❶ Heat a large nonstick skillet over medium-high heat. Sprinkle fish evenly with salt and pepper. Coat pan with cooking spray. Add fish to pan; cook 2 minutes on each side or until fish flakes easily when tested with a fork. Remove fish from pan, and keep warm. Add wine and next 4 ingredients to pan; cook 30

seconds, stirring constantly. Remove pan from heat. Add butter to pan, stirring constantly with a whisk until butter melts and sauce is smooth. Serve sauce over fish; sprinkle with parsley. Yield: 4 servings (serving size: 2 fillet halves and about 1½ tablespoons sauce).

CALORIES 280; FAT 14g (sat 3.8g, mono 6.2g, poly 2.6g); PROTEIN 35.1g; CARB 1.5g; FIBER 0.4g; CHOL 104mg; IRON 2.8mg; SODIUM 465mg; CALC 83mg

EASY COOKING
Start with a Tub of... Supermarket Pesto

Its garlicky, herb-kissed flavor is like nothing else. Grab a refrigerated container (it's near the fresh pasta in most markets) to jump-start these recipes.

Tomato-Provolone Sandwiches with Pesto Mayo

- 3 tablespoons organic canola mayonnaise (such as Spectrum)
- 5 teaspoons refrigerated pesto
- 8 (1½-ounce) slices sourdough bread
- 4 (½-ounce) slices provolone cheese
- 1 cup arugula leaves
- 8 (¼-inch-thick) slices tomato
- ¼ teaspoon freshly ground black pepper
- ⅛ teaspoon salt

❶ Preheat broiler.
❷ Combine mayonnaise and pesto in a bowl, stirring well.
❸ Arrange bread in a single layer on a baking sheet. Broil bread 2 minutes or until toasted. Turn bread over; place 1 cheese slice on each of 4 bread slices. Broil 1 minute or until cheese is bubbly.

Spread about 2 teaspoons pesto mixture over each cheese-topped bread slice. Arrange ¼ cup arugula and 2 tomato slices over pesto mixture; sprinkle tomato slices evenly with pepper and salt. Spread about 1½ teaspoons of remaining pesto mixture evenly over one side of each remaining bread slice; place 1 slice, pesto-side down, on top of each sandwich. Yield: 4 servings (serving size: 1 sandwich).

CALORIES 329; FAT 16.7g (sat 3.4g, mono 5.8g, poly 6.3g); PROTEIN 11g; CARB 35.7g; FIBER 2.9g; CHOL 16mg; IRON 3.3mg; SODIUM 630mg; CALC 194mg

QUICK & EASY
Pesto Caesar Salad

    3 ounces French bread baguette,
       cut into ½-inch cubes
    1½ teaspoons extra-virgin olive oil
       Cooking spray
    2 ounces Parmigiano-Reggiano
       cheese
    ¼ cup organic canola mayonnaise
       (such as Spectrum)
    3 tablespoons refrigerated pesto
    4 teaspoons water
    2 teaspoons fresh lemon juice
    1 teaspoon anchovy paste
    ½ teaspoon Worcestershire sauce
    ½ teaspoon Dijon mustard
    ⅛ teaspoon hot pepper sauce
       (such as Tabasco)
    1 garlic clove, minced
    12 cups torn romaine lettuce

❶ Preheat oven to 400°.
❷ Place bread in a large bowl; drizzle with oil. Toss to coat. Arrange bread in a single layer on a baking sheet coated with cooking spray. Bake at 400° for 10 minutes or until golden, turning once.
❸ Grate 2 tablespoons cheese; shave remaining cheese to equal about 6 tablespoons. Set shaved cheese aside.
❹ Combine grated cheese, mayonnaise, and next 8 ingredients in a medium bowl, stirring well with a whisk. Combine croutons and lettuce in a large bowl. Drizzle mayonnaise mixture over lettuce mixture; toss to coat.

❺ Place 1⅓ cups salad on each of 6 plates; top each serving with 1 tablespoon shaved cheese. Yield: 6 servings.

CALORIES 202; FAT 14.3g (sat 2.3g, mono 6.2g, poly 5.4g); PROTEIN 6.2g; CARB 13.6g; FIBER 2.9g; CHOL 15mg; IRON 1.9mg; SODIUM 331mg; CALC 131mg

QUICK & EASY • KID FRIENDLY
Chicken, Red Grape, and Pesto Pizza

Romano cheese, similar to Parmigiano-Reggiano, is a tangy contrast to the grapes.

    1 (11-ounce) can refrigerated thin-
       crust pizza dough
       Cooking spray
    ⅓ cup refrigerated pesto
    1½ cups seedless red grapes, halved
    8 ounces shredded skinless, boneless
       rotisserie chicken breast
    3 garlic cloves, thinly sliced
    4 ounces fresh mozzarella cheese,
       thinly sliced
    3 tablespoons grated Romano cheese
    ¼ teaspoon black pepper
    ¼ cup sliced green onions

❶ Preheat oven to 425°.
❷ On a lightly floured surface, pat dough into a 12-inch circle; gently place dough on a pizza pan coated with cooking spray. Spread pesto evenly over dough, leaving a ½-inch border around edges. Arrange grapes evenly over dough; top evenly with chicken. Top with garlic and mozzarella; sprinkle with Romano and pepper. Bake at 425° for 20 minutes or until crust is golden brown. Sprinkle with onions. Cut into 12 wedges. Yield: 6 servings (serving size: 2 wedges).

CALORIES 364; FAT 14.4g (sat 4.8g, mono 6.3g, poly 1.4g); PROTEIN 22.6g; CARB 34.6g; FIBER 1.7g; CHOL 55mg; IRON 2.5mg; SODIUM 562mg; CALC 191mg

WINE NOTE: The eclectic flavors of this pizza make it an ideal match for a fun white blend like Seven Daughters Winemaker's Blend White, NV ($12). Great acidity balances the pesto, with its rich olive oil, nuts, and cheese.

QUICK & EASY
Sautéed Halibut with Lemon-Pesto Butter

Make extra lemon-herb butter. It's delicious tossed with steamed green beans or hot cooked rice or pasta. Garnish with fresh basil.

    3 tablespoons butter, softened
    1 tablespoon refrigerated pesto
    1½ teaspoons finely chopped fresh basil
    1 teaspoon finely chopped shallots
    ½ teaspoon grated lemon rind
    4 (6-ounce) skinless halibut fillets
    ¼ teaspoon salt
    ⅛ teaspoon freshly ground black
       pepper
       Cooking spray

❶ Combine first 5 ingredients in a small bowl, stirring until well blended.
❷ Heat a large nonstick skillet over medium-high heat. Sprinkle fillets evenly on both sides with salt and pepper. Coat pan with cooking spray. Add fillets to pan; sauté 5 minutes on each side or until fish flakes easily with a fork or until desired degree of doneness. Serve fish with butter mixture. Yield: 4 servings (serving size: 1 fillet and about 1 tablespoon butter mixture).

CALORIES 274; FAT 14g (sat 6.2g, mono 4.7g, poly 1.7g); PROTEIN 34.6g; CARB 0.6g; FIBER 0.2g; CHOL 76mg; IRON 1.5mg; SODIUM 330mg; CALC 90mg

Pesto Pointers

In a side-by-side tasting, we tried several prepared pestos, some shelf-stable and others refrigerated. Although the color and flavor varied widely, we preferred the more vivid fresh basil taste and brighter green color of the refrigerated sauces packaged in plastic tubs, regardless of the brand.

Mac 'n' Cheese Basics

At last! We reveal the secret to smooth—not grainy—cheese sauce, plus other surefire tips for an all-American staple.

THE SECRET TO SUBLIME MAC 'N' CHEESE is a smooth, creamy cheese sauce. Here, you'll see how to nail it every time. This comes from hard-won experience, as we've produced a grainy, broken sauce during more than one recipe test. Once you've mastered the sauce, get creative. Start with our outrageously good stovetop variation. Then try spooning saucy pasta into a casserole and broiling it until golden; toss in veggies and bacon for a delicious difference. It's even better when you top it with buttery breadcrumbs before baking.

The Basics

Temperature is crucial to a successful sauce.
If the cheese gets too hot, the sauce can curdle or develop a grainy texture.

Pick the perfect cheese for best texture.
Hard, aged cheeses don't melt easily or smoothly, especially in lower-fat recipes.

Punch up the flavor and add color.
Stir in tomatoes, green onions, roasted bell peppers, sautéed squash, grilled eggplant, or your favorite vegetables.

Add flavor and texture with tasty toppings.
Top with buttery fresh breadcrumbs, extra cheese, or a mixture.

Salt pasta cooking water.
This barely bumps up the sodium but makes a big difference in the overall flavor.

Nutrition Notes

■ Each recipe provides about ¼ of your daily calcium needs.
■ Boost heart-healthy protein by adding tofu, cooked chicken, turkey sausage, or sautéed shrimp.

QUICK & EASY
Creamy Rigatoni with Gruyère and Brie

This is yummy just off the stove, but top with crumbs and bake if you like. You can substitute your favorite Swiss cheese for the Gruyère, and most soft-ripened cheeses can work in place of the Brie—just be sure to remove the rind.

3½ teaspoons salt, divided
12 ounces rigatoni pasta
3 tablespoons all-purpose flour
2 cups 2% reduced-fat milk, divided
1 tablespoon butter
1¼ cups (5 ounces) finely shredded Gruyère cheese
3 ounces soft-ripened Brie cheese, rind removed
½ teaspoon freshly ground black pepper
Fresh flat-leaf parsley leaves (optional)

❶ Bring 6 quarts water to a boil in a large saucepan. Add 1 tablespoon salt and pasta; cook 6 minutes or until al dente. Drain.
❷ Place flour in a medium saucepan over medium heat; add ½ cup milk, stirring with a whisk until smooth. Gradually add remaining 1½ cups milk to pan, stirring with a whisk; bring to a boil, stirring constantly with a whisk. Cook 2 minutes or until slightly thick, stirring constantly; stir in butter. Remove from heat; let stand 4 minutes or until sauce cools to 155°. Add cheeses; stir until smooth. Stir in remaining ½ teaspoon salt, pepper, and pasta. Garnish with parsley, if desired. Yield: 6 servings (serving size: 1 cup).

CALORIES 424; FAT 15.6g (sat 9.2g, mono 4.4g, poly 0.7g); PROTEIN 21g; CARB 49.9g; FIBER 1.9g; CHOL 51mg; IRON 2.2mg; SODIUM 544mg; CALC 383mg

Cavatappi with Tomatoes

1 teaspoon chopped fresh thyme
½ teaspoon freshly ground black pepper
2 pints grape tomatoes, halved
Cooking spray
2¼ teaspoons salt, divided
1 pound cavatappi pasta
2 slices applewood-smoked bacon, finely chopped
1 cup finely chopped onion
6 tablespoons all-purpose flour
2 teaspoons minced fresh garlic (about 2 cloves)
4 cups fat-free milk, divided
1½ cups (6 ounces) finely shredded fontina cheese
¾ cup (3 ounces) crumbled blue cheese
¼ cup chopped fresh chives
1½ cups panko (Japanese breadcrumbs)
1 tablespoon butter, melted

❶ Preheat oven to 250°.
❷ Combine first 3 ingredients on a jelly-roll pan lightly coated with cooking spray. Bake at 250° for 3 hours. Preheat broiler.
❸ Bring 6 quarts water to a boil. Add 2 teaspoons salt and pasta; cook 8 minutes or until al dente. Drain.
❹ Cook bacon in a saucepan; remove. Cook onion in drippings 4 minutes. Add flour and garlic; cook 1 minute. Stir in

1 cup milk. Gradually add remaining 3 cups milk; bring to a boil. Cook 1 minute, stirring constantly. Remove from heat; let stand 4 minutes. Stir in cheeses. Add remaining ¼ teaspoon salt, bacon, tomatoes, and chives. Add pasta. Divide among 8 (10-ounce) ramekins lightly coated with cooking spray. Combine panko and butter; sprinkle over pasta. Broil 5 minutes. Yield: 8 servings (serving size: 1 ramekin).

CALORIES 500; FAT 15.5g (sat 8.4g, mono 4.6g, poly 1.3g); PROTEIN 24.7g; CARB 65.2g; FIBER 3.5g; CHOL 45mg; IRON 3mg; SODIUM 755mg; CALC 328mg

STAFF FAVORITE • QUICK & EASY
KID FRIENDLY
Bacon Mac

3¼ teaspoons salt, divided
 12 ounces strozzapreti or penne pasta
  4 teaspoons all-purpose flour
1½ cups fat-free milk, divided
  2 cups finely shredded sharp Cheddar cheese, divided
 ¼ cup sliced green onions
  1 teaspoon hot sauce
 ¼ teaspoon pepper
  2 slices center-cut bacon, cooked and crumbled
     Cooking spray

❶ Preheat broiler.
❷ Bring 6 quarts water and 1 tablespoon salt to a boil. Add pasta; cook 8 minutes or until al dente; drain.
❸ Combine flour and ½ cup milk in a saucepan over medium heat. Gradually add remaining 1 cup milk; bring to a boil. Cook 1 minute, stirring constantly. Remove from heat; let stand 4 minutes or until it cools to 155°. Stir in 1½ cups cheese. Add ¼ teaspoon salt, onions, and next 3 ingredients; stir. Add pasta; toss. Spoon into a 2-quart broiler-safe dish coated with cooking spray; top with remaining ½ cup cheese. Broil 7 minutes. Yield: 6 servings (serving size: about 1 cup).

CALORIES 399; FAT 13.8g (sat 8.5g, mono 4g, poly 0.8g); PROTEIN 20g; CARB 48.7g; FIBER 2g; CHOL 44mg; IRON 2.1mg; SODIUM 544mg; CALC 358mg

4 Steps to Silky Smooth Cheese Sauce

1 Start with a slurry. Heavy sauces are often based on a roux made of butter and flour. But our recipes use butter judiciously in order to keep saturated fat in check. That's why our cheese sauces start by combining flour with a small amount of milk, a mixture known as a slurry. Be sure to stir it with a whisk until smooth—lumps are your enemy.

2 Thicken the sauce. Combine the slurry and remaining milk in a saucepan, and bring to a boil over medium heat. Cook until the sauce thickens and coats the back of a spoon, stirring constantly with a whisk. Moderate heat and constant stirring will help you avoid scorching the milk.

3 Stir in the cheese. Moist, semisoft cheeses, such as mozzarella or Monterey Jack, usually melt easily, but be careful when working with low-moisture semifirm, firm, or aged cheeses like Cheddar or Gruyère. Finely shred these (so they'll melt quickly), and make sure the mixture to which you add them is not above 155° so the cheese melts without separating.

4 Season and serve. Once your sauce is stable, focus on the flavor. Stir in salt, pepper, and additional ingredients, such as hot sauce, meats, vegetables, or herbs; taste for balance. Remember to work quickly, and add hot pasta into the sauce so you can bake or serve before it has time to seize.

Feed 4 For Less Than $10

These inspired recipes help you watch your pennies—and be delectably creative.

$2.36 per serving; $9.45 total

QUICK & EASY • KID FRIENDLY
Quick Meat Loaf

Preparing a free-form loaf and cooking it on a broiler pan cuts cook time, compared to standard recipes. Smashed red-skinned potatoes and simple steamed broccoli spears round out the meal.

⅓	cup chopped green onions
3	tablespoons dry breadcrumbs
2	teaspoons minced garlic
½	teaspoon salt
½	teaspoon dry mustard
¼	teaspoon freshly ground black pepper
¼	teaspoon crushed red pepper
1	pound ground sirloin
1	large egg, lightly beaten
6	tablespoons ketchup, divided
	Cooking spray

❶ Preheat oven to 400°.
❷ Combine first 9 ingredients in a large bowl; add ¼ cup ketchup. Mix beef mixture with hands just until combined. Shape beef mixture into a 9 x 4-inch loaf on a broiler pan coated with cooking spray. Bake at 400° for 20 minutes. Brush top of meat loaf with remaining 2 tablespoons ketchup. Bake 7 additional minutes or until done. Slice loaf into 8 equal pieces. Yield: 4 servings (serving size: 2 slices).

CALORIES 267; FAT 13.1g (sat 5.1g, mono 5.5g, poly 0.7g); PROTEIN 25.6g; CARB 10.8g; FIBER 0.7g; CHOL 127mg; IRON 3.4mg; SODIUM 679mg; CALC 44mg

SMASHED POTATOES:
Place 1½ pounds cubed red potatoes in a saucepan; cover with water. Bring to a boil. Reduce heat; simmer 20 minutes. Drain; return potatoes to pan. Add 2 tablespoons butter, ½ cup 1% low-fat milk, ½ teaspoon salt, and ¼ teaspoon black pepper. Mash with potato masher to desired consistency.

BROCCOLI:
Cut 1 (1½-pound) broccoli head into spears. Steam broccoli 6 minutes or until crisp-tender. Sprinkle with ¼ teaspoon salt.

WINE NOTE: A value-priced cabernet or merlot, like Crane Lake Cabernet Sauvignon 2005 ($4), tends to be straightforward, lighter-bodied, and lower in tannins, ideal with the lean ground beef in this traditional baked meat loaf.

$2.43 per serving; $9.73 total

KID FRIENDLY
Pan-Fried Pork Chops and Homemade Applesauce

Granny Smith or Braeburn apples work well in the sauce. Or try a combination; use more Granny Smith for a tart flavor or more Braeburn for sweetness. Serve with green beans.

APPLESAUCE:

1	tablespoon butter
3	apples, peeled, cored, and coarsely chopped (about 4 cups chopped)
½	cup water
3	tablespoons sugar
2	tablespoons fresh lemon juice
⅛	teaspoon salt

PORK:

½	cup all-purpose flour
4	(5-ounce) bone-in center-cut pork chops
¾	teaspoon salt
½	teaspoon freshly ground black pepper
2	tablespoons canola oil

❶ To prepare applesauce, melt butter in a medium saucepan over medium heat. Add apples to pan; cook 4 minutes, stirring frequently. Add ½ cup water and next 3 ingredients to pan; cook 25 minutes, stirring occasionally. Cover and cook 25 minutes or until apples are tender. Mash gently with the back of a spoon.
❷ To prepare pork, heat a large nonstick skillet over medium-high heat. Place flour in a shallow dish. Sprinkle pork evenly with ¾ teaspoon salt and pepper; dredge pork in flour. Add oil to pan, swirling to coat. Add pork to pan; cook 5 minutes or until golden. Turn pork over; cook 3 minutes or until desired degree of doneness. Serve with applesauce. Yield: 4 servings (serving size: 1 pork chop and ¼ cup applesauce).

CALORIES 402; FAT 17.6g (sat 4.8g, mono 8.5g, poly 3.6g); PROTEIN 32.6g; CARB 28.4g; FIBER 1.6g; CHOL 95mg; IRON 0.5mg; SODIUM 631mg; CALC 8mg

GREEN BEANS:
Steam 1 pound trimmed green beans 5 minutes or until crisp-tender. Toss with ¼ teaspoon salt and ¼ teaspoon freshly ground black pepper.

What Is Budget Cooking?

All the prices for our Budget Cooking sections are derived from midsized-city supermarkets. For specialty or highly perishable ingredients, like some Asian sauces or fresh herbs, we account for the entire cost of the ingredient. For staples and other ingredients, we include the cost for only the amount used. Salt, pepper, and cooking spray are freebies.

$2.08 per serving; $8.33 total

Butternut Squash Soup

SOUP:

1 tablespoon butter
3½ cups cubed peeled butternut squash (about 1½ pounds)
¾ cup chopped carrot
½ cup chopped sweet onion
2½ cups fat-free, less-sodium chicken broth
¼ cup half-and-half
⅛ teaspoon salt

TOASTS:

4 (1-ounce) slices French bread
3 ounces thinly sliced Swiss cheese

❶ To prepare soup, melt butter in a large saucepan over medium-high heat. Add squash, carrot, and onion; sauté 12 minutes. Add broth, and bring to a boil. Cover, reduce heat, and simmer 30 minutes. Remove from heat; stir in half-and-half and salt.

❷ Preheat broiler.

❸ Place squash mixture in a blender. Remove center piece of blender lid (to allow steam to escape), and secure blender lid on blender. Place a clean towel over opening in blender lid (to avoid splatters). Blend until smooth.

❹ To prepare toasts, arrange bread on a baking sheet. Broil 1 minute or until lightly toasted. Turn bread over, and top evenly with Swiss cheese. Broil 1 minute or until bubbly. Serve toasts with soup. Yield: 4 servings (serving size: about 1 cup soup and 1 toast).

CALORIES 297; FAT 10.7g (sat 6.7g, mono 2.3g, poly 0.4g); PROTEIN 11.8g; CARB 42.4g; FIBER 4.9g; CHOL 33mg; IRON 2.3mg; SODIUM 645mg; CALC 315mg

SPINACH SALAD:

Combine 2 tablespoons fresh lemon juice, 1 tablespoon extra-virgin olive oil, 1 teaspoon sugar, ¼ teaspoon salt, and ¼ teaspoon black pepper in a large bowl; stir with a whisk. Add 6 cups fresh spinach and ½ cup vertically sliced red onion, and toss to coat.

$2.43 per serving; $9.72 total

Chicken and Dumplings

This generous serving of soup is chock-full of vegetables and hearty enough to pass as a complete meal.

BROTH:

12 cups cold water
1 tablespoon whole black peppercorns
4 chicken leg quarters, skinned
3 celery stalks, sliced
2 medium carrots, peeled and sliced
2 bay leaves
1 large onion, peeled and cut into 8 wedges

DUMPLINGS:

4.5 ounces all-purpose flour (about 1 cup), divided
1 teaspoon baking powder
¼ teaspoon salt
¼ cup chilled butter, cut into small pieces
3 tablespoons buttermilk

REMAINING INGREDIENTS:

Cooking spray
1½ cups chopped onion
1 cup thinly sliced celery
¾ cup (¼-inch-thick) slices carrot
¾ teaspoon salt
1 tablespoon all-purpose flour
2 tablespoons finely chopped fresh chives

❶ To prepare broth, combine first 7 ingredients in a large stockpot; bring to a boil. Reduce heat to medium-low, and simmer 2 hours, skimming as necessary. Remove chicken from broth; cool. Remove meat from bones. Shred meat; set aside. Discard bones. Strain broth through a sieve over a bowl; discard solids. Place broth in a large saucepan; bring to a boil. Cook until reduced to 6 cups (about 8 minutes).

❷ To prepare dumplings, weigh or lightly spoon 4.5 ounces (about 1 cup) flour into a dry measuring cup; level with a knife. Combine 3.4 ounces (¾ cup) flour, baking powder, and ¼ teaspoon salt; stir with a whisk. Cut in butter with a pastry blender or two knives until mixture resembles coarse meal. Add buttermilk; stir to combine. Turn dough out onto a lightly floured surface; knead 5 times, adding remaining 1.1 ounces (¼ cup) flour as needed. Divide mixture into 24 equal portions.

❸ Heat a large Dutch oven over medium-high heat. Coat pan with cooking spray. Add chopped onion, celery, and carrot to pan; sauté 4 minutes, stirring occasionally. Add broth and ¾ teaspoon salt; bring to a boil. Reduce heat, and simmer 20 minutes or until vegetables are tender. Drop dumplings into pan; cover and cook 10 minutes or until dumplings are done, stirring occasionally. Remove ¼ cup liquid from pan; stir in 1 tablespoon flour. Return chicken to pan. Add flour mixture to pan; bring to a boil. Cook 1 minute or until slightly thick, stirring occasionally. Remove from heat; stir in chives. Yield: 4 servings (serving size: about 2 cups).

CALORIES 457; FAT 19.7g (sat 9.6g, mono 5.7g, poly 2.4g); PROTEIN 31.8g; CARB 37.1g; FIBER 3.5g; CHOL 129mg; IRON 3.5mg; SODIUM 906mg; CALC 142mg

Breakfast, Lunch, and Dinner in... New Orleans

NEW ORLEANS, no matter how battered by circumstance, keeps on cooking. For almost three centuries, it has suffered fires, floods, and battles under the flags of three nations. Hurricane Katrina dealt perhaps the biggest blow, yet since 2005 the city has become a hotbed of experimentation in schooling, housing redevelopment, and, of course, cuisine. New Orleans is now home to more restaurants than before the storm, testament to the role of food here, a fact all the more amazing given that the population hasn't fully rebounded and tourism remains down by about 16 percent.

Something old, something new, and always uniquely local: that's New Orleans—its food and its cooks. Take celebrated Chef Donald Link, author of *Real Cajun* and proprietor of Cochon and Herbsaint, two popular restaurants. Link is a German Cajun from western Louisiana who sells Italian-style cured meats (and a remarkable duck pastrami) at his celebrated new charcuterie and sandwich shop, Cochon Butcher. "New Orleans," Link says with wry understatement, "is a city that has had a lot of culinary influences."

Long may it be that way. Those of us who might have worried about New Orleans can rest assured that the city's food culture (steeped, admittedly, in equal parts butter and tradition) remains unbowed.

For this first in a series of Breakfast, Lunch, and Dinner visits to great food destinations, we chose three iconic specialties from the Big Easy: each emblematic, each delicious, and each, now, lightened up for a brighter, healthier tomorrow.

Something old, something new, and always uniquely local: that's New Orleans—its food and its cooks.

Breakfast

KID FRIENDLY

Pain Perdu

(pictured on page 230)

Find the city's take on French toast at Café Adelaide (cafeadelaide.com). Our lightened version uses reduced-fat milk and only 4 teaspoons of butter.

- ¾ cup 2% reduced-fat milk
- 2 tablespoons granulated sugar, divided
- ½ teaspoon ground cinnamon
- 1½ teaspoons vanilla extract
- ¼ teaspoon grated whole nutmeg
- ⅛ teaspoon salt
- 3 large eggs, lightly beaten
- 8 (1-ounce) slices diagonally cut day-old French bread (about 1 inch thick)
- 2 cups sliced strawberries
- 2 teaspoons grated orange rind
- 4 teaspoons butter, divided
- 2 tablespoons powdered sugar

1 Combine milk, 1 tablespoon sugar, cinnamon, and next 4 ingredients in a large bowl; stir with a whisk. Place bread slices in a 13 x 9-inch baking dish; pour egg mixture over bread; turn to coat. Let stand at room temperature 20 minutes, turning occasionally, until egg is absorbed.

2 Combine strawberries, remaining 1 tablespoon sugar, and rind in a small bowl. Let stand 20 minutes.

3 Melt 2 teaspoons butter in a large nonstick skillet over medium heat. Add 4 bread slices to pan; cook 3½ minutes on each side or until golden. Repeat procedure with remaining butter and bread.

4 Place 2 bread slices on each of 4 plates. Sprinkle each serving with 1½ teaspoons powdered sugar; top each with ½ cup strawberry mixture. Yield: 4 servings.

CALORIES 349; FAT 10.2g (sat 4.5g, mono 3.4g, poly 1.1g); PROTEIN 11.7g; CARB 52g; FIBER 3.4g; CHOL 172mg; IRON 2.8mg; SODIUM 540mg; CALC 136mg

The Origin of the Muffuletta

In 1906 the first muffuletta was created at the Central Grocery on Decatur Street. This hubcap-sized bit of business (one is big enough for two or even a small family) offers testimony to the Sicilians whose grocery shops once dominated the French Quarter. Now, as then, Central Grocery serves a delicious muffuletta composed of Italian cured meats and provolone layered on round bread, then topped with a tangy olive spread. Seating is scant; for a more relaxed experience, try an upscale (and smaller) version made with house-cured meats and high-quality cheese at Link's Cochon Butcher (cochonbutcher.com).

Lunch

MAKE AHEAD
Muffulettas

We captured the essence of this sandwich by swapping some of the high-sodium, high-fat meats for chicken breast, which allows for a satisfying portion. These sandwiches can be prepared the day before and brown-bagged for lunch. The olive salad—which some consider the best part—will moisten the bread overnight.

1½ cups bottled giardiniera, drained and chopped (about 6 ounces)
2 tablespoons red wine vinegar
2 tablespoons extra-virgin olive oil
10 pimiento-stuffed manzanilla (or green) olives, chopped
1 garlic clove, minced
4 (2-ounce) Kaiser rolls, cut in half horizontally
4 (½-ounce) slices reduced-fat provolone cheese
4 ounces skinless, boneless rotisserie chicken breast, sliced (about 1 breast)
4 thin slices Genoa salami (about 1½ ounces)
4 thin slices ham (about 2 ounces)

1 Combine first 5 ingredients in a bowl; mix well.
2 Layer bottom half of each roll with 1 provolone cheese slice, 1 ounce chicken, 1 salami slice, and 1 ham slice; top each portion with about ⅓ cup olive mixture and top halves of rolls. Wrap each sandwich tightly in plastic wrap; chill at least 1 hour or overnight. Remove plastic wrap, and cut each sandwich in half. Yield: 4 servings (serving size: 2 sandwich halves).

CALORIES 352; FAT 16.9g (sat 4.5g, mono 9.1g, poly 2g); PROTEIN 22.2g; CARB 27.1g; FIBER 1.2g; CHOL 47mg; IRON 2.7mg; SODIUM 947mg; CALC 166mg

Dinner
Shrimp Étouffée

Our take on this classic still achieves strong flavor but with salt-free Cajun seasoning and less butter in the roux. Home cooks might not easily find crawfish in their grocery, but shrimp make a great substitute. Étouffée is a popular dish in many of the city's enduring restaurants, including Galatoire's (galatoires.com).

4 tablespoons butter, softened
1 cup chopped onion
1 cup chopped green bell pepper
¾ cup chopped celery
3 garlic cloves, minced
1.1 ounces all-purpose flour (about ¼ cup)
2 teaspoons salt-free Cajun seasoning
¼ teaspoon dried thyme
2 (8-ounce) bottles clam juice
¾ cup chopped tomato
1 teaspoon Worcestershire sauce
½ cup chopped green onions
½ teaspoon salt
1 pound large shrimp, peeled and deveined
2⅔ cups hot cooked long-grain rice
Hot sauce (optional)

1 Melt 1 tablespoon butter in a Dutch oven over medium heat. Add onion and next 3 ingredients to pan; cook 8 minutes or until very tender and onion begins to brown, stirring frequently. Place onion mixture in a bowl. Melt remaining 3 tablespoons butter in pan. Stir in flour; cook 6 minutes or until flour turns a deep rust color, stirring constantly. Stir in Cajun seasoning, thyme, and clam juice; cook 1 minute. Stir in onion mixture, tomato, and Worcestershire sauce; simmer 15 minutes or until thick. Add green onions, salt, and shrimp; cook 6 minutes or until shrimp are done, stirring occasionally. Serve over hot cooked rice. Serve with hot sauce, if desired. Yield: 4 servings (serving size: 1¼ cups étouffée and ⅔ cup rice).

CALORIES 453; FAT 14g (sat 7.7g, mono 3.4g, poly 1.4g); PROTEIN 28.7g; CARB 51.6g; FIBER 3.2g; CHOL 206mg; IRON 6mg; SODIUM 842mg; CALC 126mg

Étouffée is a seasoned stew, often roux-based, that is traditionally made from crawfish harvested from Louisiana wetlands.

Snacking the Healthy Way

Improve mood and energy, and build a healthful bridge between meals.

The moment a favorite snack hits your taste buds, your brain sends out soothing *ahh* chemicals. For many of us, guilt soon follows. Yet it's easy to snack smart—and with pleasure. The right snacks supply important nutrients, keep you satisfied between meals, boost energy, and lift your mood.

Good Creamy Choice

QUICK & EASY
Warm Cranberry-Walnut Brie

Dip into the luscious melted cheese with trans fat–free 100 percent whole-grain or wheat crackers.

- 1 (8-ounce) round Brie cheese
- 2 tablespoons dried cranberries
- 1 teaspoon chopped fresh thyme
- 1 teaspoon chopped walnuts, toasted
- 40 low-sodium 100 percent whole wheat crackers (such as Triscuit)

❶ Preheat oven to 350°.
❷ Using a serrated knife, remove topmost rind from cheese; discard rind. Place cheese, cut side up, in a small ovenproof baking dish; sprinkle with cranberries and thyme. Top evenly with nuts. Bake at 350° for 15 minutes or until cheese is soft and warm. Serve immediately with crackers. Yield: 8 servings (serving size: about 1 ounce cheese mixture and 5 crackers).

CALORIES 188; FAT 11.6g (sat 5.6g, mono 2.4g, poly 0.7g); PROTEIN 7.9g; CARB 15g; FIBER 2.1g; CHOL 28mg; IRON 1.1mg; SODIUM 291mg; CALC 54mg

Good Salty Choice

QUICK & EASY • MAKE AHEAD
Rosemary Roasted Almonds

- 1 tablespoon finely chopped fresh rosemary
- 1 tablespoon extra-virgin olive oil
- 1 teaspoon chile powder
- ¾ teaspoon kosher salt
- Dash of ground red pepper
- 1 (10-ounce) bag whole almonds (about 2 cups)

❶ Preheat oven to 325°.
❷ Combine all ingredients in a medium bowl; toss to coat. Arrange nut mixture in a single layer on a baking sheet lined with foil. Bake at 325° for 20 minutes or until lightly toasted. Cool to room temperature. Yield: 2 cups (serving size: about 2 tablespoons).

CALORIES 111; FAT 9.9g (sat 0.8g, mono 6.3g, poly 2.3g); PROTEIN 3.8g; CARB 3.6g; FIBER 2.1g; CHOL 0mg; IRON 0.8mg; SODIUM 94mg; CALC 45mg

Good Sweet Choice

QUICK & EASY • KID FRIENDLY
Chocolate Hazelnut Bark

- ¾ cup hazelnuts (about 4 ounces)
- ⅓ cup dried cherries, coarsely chopped
- 2 tablespoons finely chopped crystallized ginger
- 6 ounces bittersweet chocolate, chopped

❶ Preheat oven to 350°.
❷ Place hazelnuts on a baking sheet. Bake at 350° for 20 minutes, stirring once halfway through cooking. Turn nuts out onto a towel. Roll up towel; rub off skins. Coarsely chop nuts. Combine nuts, cherries, and ginger in a medium bowl.
❸ Place chocolate in a microwave-safe measuring cup. Microwave at HIGH 1 minute or until chocolate melts, stirring every 15 seconds. Add to nut mixture, stirring just until combined. Spread mixture evenly on a jelly-roll pan lined with foil; freeze 1 hour. Break into pieces; serve immediately. Yield: about 12 ounces (serving size: 1 ounce).

CALORIES 139; FAT 8.8g (sat 2.5g, mono 3.9g, poly 0.7g); PROTEIN 2.1g; CARB 15.4g; FIBER 1.4g; CHOL 0mg; IRON 0.8mg; SODIUM 5mg; CALC 19mg

---

What Science Says About Snacking

It's good for you. The 5,000-subject-strong National Health and Nutrition Examination Survey found that people who ate snacks in addition to three meals a day had higher levels of nutrients in their diets.

Don't deny yourself. When Belgian researchers told 68 women to either enjoy or refuse their favorite snack, the refusers ate more of the forbidden snack once they were given the green light a day later. Sensible snacking helps you avoid bingeing.

Size it right. Research has shown snackers will eat more if a larger portion is offered to them, so don't plop down on the sofa with a bag of chips and tell yourself you'll stop at just a few. Measure out a serving, then enjoy.

Include protein. Eating a snack with protein rather than just carbs can help curb hunger, keeping daily calories in check. Good options include an ounce of nuts or a small fat-free yogurt.

Don't drink your snack. When Purdue researchers gave 20 people an apple, applesauce, or apple juice, those who drank their snack were the quickest to report being hungry.

Watch out for low-fat claims. Low-fat does not necessarily mean low-calorie. The label can give you a sense of false security, setting off overeating. Treat low-fat foods like any others, and enjoy in moderation.

Our Favorite Dietitian-Approved Snacks

True North Pecan Almond Peanut Clusters: A serving has 170 calories, 11 grams of "good" fat, and just 75 milligrams of sodium.

Vitatops: Most of these soft muffin tops have about 100 calories, 4 grams of protein, and 5 grams of fiber, and all flavors are trans fat free.

Fruit: No surprise, huh? Try a Pink Lady apple or Anjou pear—both are in season in the fall. Grapes and bananas are other good options.

Build Your Own Portable 100-Calorie Snacks

Snack packs are big business. Last year, 190 new 100-calorie-pack products hit the market. They're great because they help satisfy cravings for tempting foods with smart portions. But few are nutritional powerhouses. If you want something that satisfies, saves money, and offers a nutritional boost, make your own pre-portioned snacks.

3½ cups 94% fat-free microwave popcorn: One of your three servings of whole grains.

1⅓ ounces pitted olives: This fruit satisfies a salty craving and supplies a decent amount of heart-healthy fats.

¼ cup hummus with 4 carrot sticks: Five grams of filling fiber mean you won't go hungry for a while.

Mood-Boosting Snacks

Half a 100% whole-grain bagel with 1 tablespoon peanut butter: 240 calories. Carbohydrates trigger the release of feel-good chemicals. Pick quality carbs, like whole grains with fiber, for a longer-lasting high.

½ cup shelled edamame: 100 calories. Folate-rich foods like edamame may even out moods: In a few small studies, people with higher levels of folate in their systems reported less mood variability.

8 ounces low-fat plain yogurt: 140 calories. Several studies link vitamin B12 deficiency to depression. While it's not an antidepressant, B12-rich low-fat yogurt might help lift a bad mood, and its live bacteria are your friends.

Chocolate Chip Cannoli

Our version of the Sicilian sweet has all the classic's crunch and creaminess—crispy, lightly sweetened shells filled with homemade ricotta and chopped chocolate—without the calories and saturated fat.

No self-respecting cannoli can really be "light," and it takes some work to make cannoli lighter. For starters, the crisp shell is made with plenty of fat (i.e., lard) and flour and then deep-fried in (you guessed it) more fat. The shell is filled with a creamy ricotta mixture, sugar, and sometimes ground spices or candied citrus. Chopped chocolate or nuts—or both—are stirred into the filling or sprinkled on top.

Our lighter version takes the "no" out of the cannoli with easy phyllo-based shells (follow our method to make your own cannoli molds), a simple lower-fat homemade ricotta, and a hint of semisweet chocolate. The best part: You can make the filling and shells ahead, and assemble while the espresso brews. Family and friends will be impressed, and they won't even guess these treats are lighter than the classic version.

serving size: 1 cannoli	before	after
CALORIES PER SERVING	726	340
TOTAL FAT	64.3g	12g
SATURATED FAT	25.2g	7.4g
BEFORE	Deep-fried pastry, Full-fat ricotta mixture	
AFTER	Baked phyllo shells, Lower-fat ricotta mixture	

Chocolate Chip Cannoli

We prefer the fresh taste of this recipe's homemade ricotta, which can be made up to four days ahead. If you don't have time to make ricotta from scratch, substitute 4 cups part-skim ricotta, and proceed to step 3.

RICOTTA:
- 1 gallon 1% low-fat milk
- 4 cups low-fat buttermilk
- ¼ teaspoon kosher salt
- ⅔ cup granulated sugar
- ½ teaspoon vanilla extract
- 6 ounces fromage blanc

SHELLS:
- Cooking spray
- ⅓ cup granulated sugar
- ½ teaspoon ground cinnamon
- 6 (18 x 14-inch) sheets frozen phyllo dough, thawed
- 3 tablespoons butter, melted

REMAINING INGREDIENTS:
- 2 ounces semisweet chocolate, divided
- 2 tablespoons sifted powdered sugar

❶ To prepare ricotta, line a large colander or sieve with 3 layers of dampened cheesecloth, allowing cheesecloth to extend over outside edges of colander, and place colander in a large bowl.
❷ Combine milk and buttermilk in a large, heavy stockpot. Cook over medium heat until a candy thermometer reaches 170°, gently stirring constantly. As soon as milk mixture reaches 170°, stop stirring (whey and curds will separate at this point). Continue to cook, without stirring, until thermometer reaches 190°. (Be sure not to stir, or curds that have formed will break apart). Immediately remove pan from heat. (Bottom of pan may be slightly scorched.) Pour milk mixture into cheesecloth-lined colander. Drain over bowl 5 minutes, and discard liquid (whey). Gather edges of cheesecloth together, and tie securely. Hang cheesecloth bundle from kitchen faucet, and drain 12 minutes or just until whey stops dripping. Scrape ricotta into a medium bowl. Sprinkle with salt, and toss gently with a fork to combine. Cool to room temperature.

Grated chocolate pumps up flavor in every bite

Butter and sugar help crisp up phyllo shells when baked

Finely chopped chocolate has richer flavor than minichips

❸ Add ⅔ cup of granulated sugar, vanilla extract, and fromage blanc to ricotta; beat with a mixer at medium speed until combined. Cover mixture, and refrigerate.

❹ To prepare shells, preheat oven to 375°.

❺ Cut out 12 (12 x 4–inch) pieces of heavy-duty aluminum foil. Using your index fingers as a guide, loosely roll up each foil piece jelly-roll fashion to form a cylinder with a 1-inch opening. Lightly coat outside of each cylinder with cooking spray. Combine ⅓ cup granulated sugar and ½ teaspoon ground cinnamon in a small bowl.

❻ Place 1 phyllo sheet on a large cutting board or work surface (cover remaining dough to prevent drying); lightly brush with butter. Sprinkle evenly with 2 teaspoons sugar mixture. Repeat layers once. Cut phyllo stack lengthwise into 4 equal strips. Place a foil cylinder at bottom of 1 phyllo strip; roll up jelly-roll fashion around cylinder. Lightly coat with cooking spray. Place on a parchment paper–lined baking sheet. Repeat procedure with remaining phyllo, butter, sugar mixture, and foil cylinders. Bake at 375° for 12 minutes or until lightly browned; cool completely on a wire rack. Carefully remove foil cylinders from phyllo shells by twisting ends of foil in opposite directions and gently pulling foil from shells.

❼ Finely chop 1½ ounces chocolate. Combine ricotta mixture and chopped chocolate in a bowl. Transfer mixture to a large zip-top plastic bag; snip off ½-inch of 1 corner of bag. Pipe ricotta mixture evenly into each of 12 prepared shells (about ⅓ cup). Grate remaining ½ ounce chocolate. Dust cannoli evenly with powdered sugar and grated chocolate; serve immediately. Yield: 12 servings (serving size: 1 cannoli).

CALORIES 340; FAT 12g (sat 7.4g, mono 2.7g, poly 0.4g); PROTEIN 13.7g; CARB 45.5g; FIBER 0.5g; CHOL 26mg; IRON 1mg; SODIUM 401mg; CALC 506mg

3 Essential Steps for Homemade Cannoli

1 Immerse the tip of a thermometer 2 inches into ricotta liquid to ensure an accurate reading. (Be patient—it may take up to 20 minutes to reach 170 degrees.)

2 Hang the cheesecloth bag over the sink to allow the whey to drain. The ricotta is ready when whey drips infrequently, yielding a barely moist cheese perfect for blending.

3 Make phyllo molds by rolling heavy-duty foil into cylinders. Lightly coat cylinders with cooking spray before rolling and wrapping dough around molds.

Dinner-Worthy Tofu Dishes

Hardworking soybean curd adapts to any flavor profile, works in a variety of cooking methods, and supplies protein and heart-healthy fats. We show you how to season and prepare it with worldly new twists for exciting, tasty entrées. Try just one, and you'll never make another bland tofu recipe again.

Tofu Banh Mi

Allow 8 hours to marinate the tofu—it soaks up savory flavor from soy sauce and heat from fresh ginger for this riff on a popular Vietnamese sandwich. Serve with Sriracha (hot chile sauce) if you prefer more fire.

- 1 (14-ounce) package water-packed firm tofu, drained
- 2 tablespoons low-sodium soy sauce
- 2 teaspoons finely grated peeled fresh ginger
- ⅓ cup rice vinegar
- ¼ cup sugar
- 1 teaspoon kosher salt
- 1¼ cups (3-inch) matchstick-cut carrot
- 1 cup sliced shiitake mushroom caps
- ¼ teaspoon freshly ground black pepper
- 1 julienne-cut green onions
- 1 cucumber, peeled, halved lengthwise, and thinly sliced (about 2 cups)
- 2 tablespoons canola oil
- 1 (12-ounce) loaf French bread
- ½ cup fresh cilantro sprigs
- 2 jalapeño peppers, thinly sliced

❶ Cut tofu crosswise into 8 (½-inch-thick) slices. Arrange tofu on several layers of paper towels. Top with several more layers of paper towels; top with a cast-iron skillet or other heavy pan. Let stand 30 minutes. Remove tofu from paper towels.

❷ Combine soy sauce and ginger in a 13 x 9-inch baking dish. Arrange tofu slices in a single layer in soy mixture. Cover and refrigerate 8 hours or overnight, turning once.

❸ Combine vinegar, sugar, and salt in a medium bowl, stirring until sugar and salt dissolve. Add carrot and next 4 ingredients; toss well. Let stand 30 minutes, stirring occasionally. Drain carrot mixture through a sieve; drain thoroughly.

❹ Heat oil in a large nonstick skillet over medium-high heat. Remove tofu from marinade, and discard marinade. Pat tofu slices dry with paper towels. Add tofu slices to pan; sauté 4 minutes on each side or until crisp and golden.

❺ Preheat broiler.

❻ Cut bread in half lengthwise. Open halves, laying bread cut sides up on a baking sheet. Broil 2 minutes or until lightly browned. Place tofu slices on bottom half of bread; top with carrot mixture, cilantro, and jalapeño slices. Top with top half of bread. Cut loaf crosswise into 6 equal pieces. Yield: 6 servings (serving size: 1 sandwich).

CALORIES 369; FAT 14.1g (sat 1.8g, mono 5.2g, poly 6.1g); PROTEIN 11.9g; CARB 49.6g; FIBER 5g; CHOL 0mg; IRON 2.6mg; SODIUM 367mg; CALC 147mg

WINE NOTE: The herbaceous quality of Monkey Bay Sauvignon Blanc 2007 ($11) echoes the jalapeño peppers and green onions in our Tofu Banh Mi, while the wine's lemony acidity helps it stand up to the rice vinegar–pickled vegetables.

Test Kitchen Tip

Store leftover unprepared tofu in an airtight container. Cover tofu with water and refrigerate, covered, for up to 5 days. Change water daily.

Pan-Crisped Tofu with Greens and Peanut Dressing

This sweet-salty dressing deliciously turns crisp tofu and salad greens into a light lunch or dinner. Allow 30 minutes in your prep time for pressing the tofu.

- ⅓ cup white miso (soybean paste)
- ⅓ cup mirin (sweet rice wine)
- ⅓ cup rice vinegar
- 1 tablespoon finely grated peeled fresh ginger
- ½ cup chopped dry-roasted peanuts, divided
- 5 tablespoons canola oil, divided
- 2 (14-ounce) packages water-packed firm tofu, drained
- 8 cups gourmet salad greens
- Minced fresh chives (optional)

❶ Combine first 4 ingredients, ¼ cup peanuts, and 3 tablespoons oil in a small bowl; stir with a whisk.

❷ Cut each tofu block crosswise into 8 (½-inch-thick) slices. Arrange tofu on several layers of paper towels. Top with several more layers of paper towels; top with a cast-iron skillet or other heavy pan. Let stand 30 minutes. Remove tofu from paper towels.

❸ Heat 1 tablespoon oil in a large non-stick skillet over medium-high heat. Add 8 tofu slices to pan; sauté 4 minutes on each side or until crisp and golden. Remove from pan, and drain tofu on paper towels. Repeat procedure with remaining 1 tablespoon oil and remaining 8 tofu slices. Place 1 cup greens on each of 8 plates. Top each serving with 2 tofu slices, 3 tablespoons miso mixture, and 1½ teaspoons chopped peanuts. Garnish each serving with chives, if desired. Yield: 8 servings.

CALORIES 266; FAT 18g (sat 1.8g, mono 8.3g, poly 6.8g); PROTEIN 13.9g; CARB 13g; FIBER 4.1g; CHOL 0mg; IRON 3mg; SODIUM 375mg; CALC 227mg

Korean-Inspired Sautéed Tofu

- 2 tablespoons rice vinegar
- 2 tablespoons mirin (sweet rice wine)
- 1 tablespoon low-sodium soy sauce
- 1 teaspoon dark sesame oil
- 1/8 teaspoon kosher salt
- 1/4 teaspoon ground red pepper, divided
- 1 (14-ounce) package water-packed soft tofu, drained
- 2 tablespoons canola oil, divided
- 1 ounce fresh ginger, peeled and julienne-cut
- 3 tablespoons diagonally sliced green onions
- 1 teaspoon minced fresh garlic
- 1/4 teaspoon kosher salt
- 1 teaspoon sesame seeds

1 Combine first 5 ingredients and 1/8 teaspoon ground red pepper in a medium bowl; stir with a whisk.

2 Cut tofu crosswise into 8 (1/2-inch-thick) slices. Arrange tofu on several layers of paper towels. Top with several more layers of paper towels; top with a cast-iron skillet or other heavy pan. Let stand 30 minutes. Remove tofu from paper towels. Cut tofu into (1-inch) cubes. Sprinkle tofu with remaining 1/8 teaspoon red pepper.

3 Heat 1 tablespoon canola oil in a large nonstick skillet over medium-high heat. Add tofu to pan; sauté 8 minutes or until crisp, carefully turning to brown on all sides. Remove tofu from pan; keep warm. Heat remaining 1 tablespoon canola oil in pan. Add ginger and green onions to pan; sauté 30 seconds. Add garlic to pan; sauté 30 seconds or just until golden. Add ginger mixture to vinegar mixture; stir well. Pour vinegar mixture over tofu; sprinkle evenly with 1/4 teaspoon salt and sesame seeds. Yield: 6 servings (serving size: about 1/2 cup).

CALORIES 128; FAT 9.1g (sat 0.9g, mono 3.9g, poly 3.7g); PROTEIN 6.3g; CARB 4.9g; FIBER 0.5g; CHOL 0mg; IRON 1.1mg; SODIUM 208mg; CALC 135mg

How to Press Tofu

Just as cheese is made from cow's milk curds, tofu is soybean curd made from cultured soymilk. (Silken tofu, or Japanese-style tofu, is made by a slightly different process, resulting in smooth, custardy tofu.) A quick press of the block between paper towels removes extra water, resulting in a firmer curd. Pressed tofu works especially well in two applications: for marinating, perhaps because extra water doesn't dilute marinade flavors, and for cooking methods like grilling, pan-frying, or baking, where it maintains its shape and yields appealingly chewy or crisp textures. Follow our tips for pressing success.

1 Cut drained tofu as the recipe directs.

2 Lay tofu flat on a few absorbent heavy-duty paper towels.

3 Top with another layer of paper towels; place a heavy pan on top.

4 Let sit, pressing occasionally on the pan so the tofu releases excess moisture.

Fiery Tofu and Coconut Curry Soup

Inspired by similar soups from Thailand and Malaysia, this version balances fiery flavor with sweet and sour back notes. The crisp-tender vegetables offer a pleasant texture contrast to the custardlike tofu.

    2   tablespoons canola oil
    2   teaspoons minced garlic
    ¼   cup red curry paste
    1   tablespoon dark brown sugar
    2   (13.5-ounce) cans light coconut milk
   2½   cups organic vegetable broth
    ¼   cup fresh lime juice
    ¼   cup thinly sliced peeled fresh ginger
    2   tablespoons low-sodium soy sauce
    2   cups thinly sliced carrot (about 4)
   1½   cups (1-inch) pieces green beans
        (8 ounces)
    1   (14-ounce) package water-packed
        soft tofu, drained and cut into
        (1-inch) cubes
    ¾   cup fresh cilantro leaves

1 Heat oil in a large saucepan over medium-high heat. Add garlic to pan; sauté 30 seconds or until lightly browned. Add curry paste; sauté 1 minute, stirring constantly. Add brown sugar; cook 1 minute. Stir in coconut milk and next 4 ingredients. Reduce heat to low; cover and simmer 1 hour. Add carrot; cook 6 minutes. Add beans, and cook 4 minutes or until vegetables are crisp-tender. Add tofu to pan, and cook 2 minutes. Garnish with cilantro leaves. Yield: 6 servings (serving size: 1⅓ cups soup and 2 tablespoons cilantro).

CALORIES 224; FAT 14.4g (sat 7.4g, mono 3.3g, poly 2.8g); PROTEIN 7.6g; CARB 21g; FIBER 3g; CHOL 0mg; IRON 2mg; SODIUM 690mg; CALC 114mg

KITCHEN HOW-TO
Get the Most Flavor from Garlic

The secret is matching the preparation to the desired effect. Mincing yields a bolder flavor than crushing, while roasting gives garlic a sweet-nutty dimension. Yet for all its robustness, garlic must be treated gently in a sauté. The most common error cooks make is hurriedly burning it in a too-hot pan, which renders an unpleasantly bitter, almost sour taste. When sautéing garlic, avoid burning by adding it to the pan after other ingredients have softened. When properly done, garlic will become a light golden color and cast an enticing fragrance.

Purchase: Grip garlic to find a firm head, and make sure the bulb shows no signs of green sprouting.

Store: Keep garlic in a cool, dry, dark place. A whole head can last up to two months, but watch for drying (cloves will feel shrunken) and bitter green sprouts.

Peel garlic by placing side of knife on a clove; lightly tap with fist to loosen skin. Then you can:

• **Crush It…** for mild flavor. Lay a peeled clove on a cutting board, place the side of a chef's knife on top, and firmly press with a fist. Use crushed cloves in recipes to release aromatic oils without overpowering other ingredients.

• **Make a Paste…** for robust taste. After mincing, continue finely cutting, then use the side of a chef's knife to mash the garlic into a paste. Garlic paste can be spread on toasted bread or mixed into soups or dips.

• **Mince It…** for bold results. Make thin, lengthwise cuts through a peeled clove, then cut strips crosswise. Minced garlic suffuses dishes with vivid flavor, whether raw in a vinaigrette or briefly sautéed for a sauce.

• **Roast It…** for a mellow sweetness. Remove outer layer of the papery skin from a whole garlic head. Wrap in foil, and bake at 350° for 1 hour; cool. Pull cloves apart, squeeze garlic out, then use paste as a spread or stir into sauces or vinaigrettes.

Our All-Time Favorite Herbed Cheese Pizza

Chewy, tender crust, rich Greek cheese, and subtly spiced tomato sauce make this a pie you'll love, too.

STAFF FAVORITE
Herbed Cheese Pizza

DOUGH:

- 9.5 ounces bread flour, divided (about 2 cups)
- 2 cups warm water (100° to 110°), divided
- 1 teaspoon sugar
- 2 packages dry yeast (about 4½ teaspoons)
- 14.6 ounces all-purpose flour, divided (about 3¼ cups)
- 1 teaspoon salt
- 2 teaspoons olive oil
- Cooking spray

TOPPING:

- 2 teaspoons dried oregano
- 2 teaspoons ground cumin
- 1 teaspoon hot paprika
- ¾ teaspoon coarsely ground black pepper, divided
- 1 teaspoon olive oil
- 1 cup finely chopped onion
- ½ teaspoon salt
- 5 garlic cloves, minced
- 1 bay leaf
- 1 (28-ounce) can diced tomatoes
- 10 ounces sliced kasseri cheese
- 3 tablespoons minced fresh parsley

1 To prepare dough, weigh or lightly spoon bread flour into dry measuring cups; level with a knife. Combine 4.75 ounces (about 1 cup) bread flour, 1 cup warm water, sugar, and yeast in a bowl; let stand 15 minutes.

2 Weigh or lightly spoon all-purpose flour into dry measuring cups; level with a knife. Combine 13.5 ounces (about

3 cups) all-purpose flour, remaining 4.75 ounces (about 1 cup) bread flour, and 1 teaspoon salt in a large bowl; make a well in center. Add yeast mixture, remaining 1 cup warm water, and 2 teaspoons oil to flour mixture; stir well. Turn dough out onto a floured surface. Knead until smooth and elastic (about 10 minutes); add enough of remaining flour, 1 tablespoon at a time, to prevent dough from sticking to hands.

3 Place dough in a large bowl coated with cooking spray, turning to coat top. Cover and let rise in a warm place (85°), free from drafts, for 45 minutes or until doubled in size. (Press two fingers into dough. If indentation remains, dough has risen enough.) Punch dough down; divide dough into 8 equal portions. Cover and let rest 20 minutes.

4 To prepare topping, combine oregano, cumin, paprika, and ½ teaspoon black pepper. Heat a large skillet over medium-high heat. Add 1 teaspoon olive oil to pan. Add onion; sauté 3 minutes. Add ½ teaspoon salt, remaining ¼ teaspoon black pepper, garlic, bay leaf, and tomatoes; bring to a boil. Reduce heat, and simmer 15 minutes or until thick. Remove from heat; discard bay leaf.

5 Preheat oven to 450°.

6 Working with 1 dough portion at a time (cover remaining dough to keep from drying), roll each portion into a 6-inch circle on a lightly floured surface; place circle on a baking sheet coated with cooking spray. Repeat procedure with remaining dough portions. Top each crust with ¼ cup tomato mixture, 1¼ ounces cheese, and ½ teaspoon oregano mixture. Bake at 450° for 12 minutes or until crusts are lightly browned. Sprinkle evenly with parsley. Yield: 8 servings (serving size: 1 pizza).

CALORIES 493; FAT 13.7g (sat 7.9g, mono 1.4g, poly 0.4g); PROTEIN 19.4g; CARB 73.9g; FIBER 5.1g; CHOL 38mg; IRON 5.2mg; SODIUM 917mg; CALC 296mg

Reader Recipes

Readers always have a good story about the inspiration behind their recipes. Many are better-for-you spins on family favorites or dishes from friends. Darlene Babcock started making this green salad when her friend Helen shared it with her years ago. "It goes together quickly for weeknight suppers and is so versatile. I just add whatever fresh vegetables I have on hand, so it's never the same salad twice."

QUICK & EASY
Darlene's Healthy Salad

"What makes this different from other salads is the tartness of the vinegar: I toss the greens with vinegar first, then add the olive oil and other seasonings. I like the extra crunch from the sunflower seeds; it's such a nice contrast to the creamy texture of the avocado."

—Darlene Babcock,
Walnut Creek, California

- 12 cups chopped romaine lettuce (about 1 large head)
- 2 cups thinly sliced cucumber (about 1 large)
- 1 cup vertically sliced red onion
- ½ cup thinly sliced radishes (about 3)
- ⅔ cup vertically sliced peeled ripe avocado (about 1)
- ¼ teaspoon black pepper, divided
- ¼ cup red wine vinegar
- 3 tablespoons extra-virgin olive oil
- ¼ teaspoon salt
- 2 tablespoons sunflower seed kernels

1 Place lettuce in a large bowl; layer cucumber, onion, radishes, and avocado on top of lettuce. Sprinkle ⅛ teaspoon pepper over avocado; refrigerate 15 minutes or up to 1 hour.

Continued

2 Pour vinegar over salad, tossing gently to coat. Gradually add oil, salt, and remaining ⅛ teaspoon pepper to salad; toss well. Sprinkle with sunflower seed kernels. Yield: 7 servings (serving size: 2 cups).

CALORIES 137; FAT 11.9g (sat 1.7g, mono 7.3g, poly 2.3g); PROTEIN 2.5g; CARB 7.6g; FIBER 4.1g; CHOL 0mg; IRON 1.5mg; SODIUM 106mg; CALC 44mg

QUICK & EASY • FREEZABLE
KID FRIENDLY
Blueberry Power Smoothie

"One morning I added tofu to my smoothie, and my little sister (who always wants what big sis is having) never even detected the 'secret' ingredient. This recipe makes two large servings, so sometimes I freeze one serving and have it for dessert later with a dollop of whipped cream."

—Anne Emig,
Grand Rapids, Michigan

  1 cup fresh or frozen blueberries
⅔ cup fat-free milk
½ cup reduced-fat firm silken tofu (about 4 ounces)
  2 tablespoons raspberry spread (such as Polaner All Fruit)
  1 (6-ounce) carton raspberry low-fat yogurt

1 Place all ingredients in a blender; process until smooth. Yield: 2 servings (serving size: 1¼ cups).

CALORIES 202; FAT 1.3g (sat 0.6g, mono 0.1g, poly 0.3g); PROTEIN 9.4g; CARB 38.2g; FIBER 2.3g; CHOL 6mg; IRON 1.6mg; SODIUM 134mg; CALC 231mg

Special Occasion Recipe

MAKE AHEAD
Windowpane Potato Chips

  2 medium baking potatoes
Cooking spray
Assorted fresh herb sprigs (such as dill, chives, and sage)
½ teaspoon salt

1 Preheat oven to 400°.
2 Set mandoline on thinnest slicing setting. Cut each potato lengthwise into 28 slices using mandoline. Arrange potato slices in a single layer on several layers of paper towels. Cover with additional paper towels; press lightly. Let stand 5 minutes.
3 Arrange 14 potato slices in a single layer on each of 2 baking sheets coated with cooking spray. Place a small herb sprig on each potato slice; cover with another potato slice. Press gently to adhere. Coat potato stacks with cooking spray. Sprinkle evenly with salt. Working with one sheet at a time, cover potato stacks with parchment paper. Place an empty baking sheet on top of parchment paper; set a cast-iron or heavy ovenproof skillet on second baking sheet. Bake at 400° for 25 minutes.
4 Remove skillet. Remove baking sheets from oven; remove top baking sheet and parchment paper. Remove browned potato chips from pan; place on a wire rack. Turn any unbrowned potato chips over on sheet. Replace parchment paper and top baking sheet; return pan to oven. Replace skillet on top of baking sheet. Bake 5 minutes or until browned. Cool chips on wire racks. Repeat procedure with remaining potatoes. Store chips in an airtight container up to 2 days. Yield: 7 servings (serving size: 4 chips).

CALORIES 53; FAT 0.3g (sat 0g, mono 0.1g, poly 0.1g); PROTEIN 1.7g; CARB 11.3g; FIBER 1.4g; CHOL 0mg; IRON 1.3mg; SODIUM 180mg; CALC 34mg

How to Make Picture-Perfect Chips

1 With mandoline adjusted to the thinnest setting, cut the potato lengthwise into paper-thin slices. You'll discard the first few smaller slices. (Tip: Buy an extra potato for practice.)

2 Arrange half of potato slices on a baking sheet. Top each slice with an herb sprig that fits into the center. Top each piece with another potato slice of the same size.

3 To ensure the potato slices seal around the herbs and cook into a flat disk, weigh down the baking sheet with another baking sheet and a cast-iron or other heavy skillet.

10 Little Secrets of Portion Control

Overeating is all in your mind. Meet the researcher who is uncovering all the ways that "hidden persuaders" work.

AMONG ALL THE WAYS TO CHANGE YOUR DIET for the better, portion control sounds like the one thought up by a pocket-protector-wearing nutrition nerd patrolling the school cafeteria. To be portion-preoccupied means to be tyrannized by food scales and little tape measures: Is this chicken breast bigger than a pack of cards? Portion policing runs against the ideal of a relaxed, balanced, real-world diet in which healthy food choices bring satisfaction without too much worry about quantity.

But the man whose research introduced the world to the 100-calorie snack pack—now a multimillion-dollar slice of the food market—begs to differ. To Cornell University food psychologist Brian Wansink, PhD, portion awareness is the key to making sure that more of the 200 food choices we make each day are closer to what our thinking brain—as opposed to our instinctive brain—would like.

The cards are stacked against most Americans. Our bodies think we're still hunter-gatherers threatened by imminent famine at the end of every season—even as we drive the minivan to Costco. Our supermarkets offer tens of thousands of products, often sold in packages that could feed a small nomadic tribe.

"When it comes to portion control, you can count on your brain not being very interested and your body not being very well calibrated," Wansink says. Result: We often overeat in 100 or 200-calorie increments, which over time adds up to a weight gain that seems like a mystery to the eater. And here's the rub, according to Wansink: Most of us know what we're supposed to eat, and how much of it. We just ignore what we know. We eat, he says, "mindlessly."

"People think education and awareness are the answer to a better diet, but they're not," Wansink says. Consider even the simplest dietary "rules": More than a fifth of Americans probably know we're supposed to eat two to four servings of fruit each day, but only about 20 percent actually do it. We fail in part, Wansink says, because we're bombarded by subtle and not-so-subtle cues that trigger instinctive as opposed to conscious eating behavior. Much as behavioral science is used to explain why Americans make illogical decisions about money, Wansink specializes in what could be called behavioral home economics. See "10 Tips for Portion Control" on page 288 for some simple solutions.

Nutty Warm Brussels Sprouts Salad

Pulse a (1 1/2-ounce) slice of bread in the food processor to make 1/3 cup fresh breadcrumbs.

- 1 1/2 teaspoons extra-virgin olive oil, divided
- 1 garlic clove, minced
- 1/3 cup fresh breadcrumbs
- 3/4 pound Brussels sprouts, trimmed and halved (about 8 cups)
- 1/4 teaspoon salt
- 1/8 teaspoon freshly ground black pepper
- 1 1/2 tablespoons finely chopped walnuts, toasted
- 1/2 ounce shaved Asiago cheese

① Heat 1 teaspoon oil in a large nonstick skillet over medium heat. Add garlic, and cook 1 minute or just until golden, stirring constantly. Add breadcrumbs; cook 1 minute or until lightly browned, stirring constantly. Transfer garlic mixture to a small bowl.

② Separate leaves from Brussels sprouts; quarter cores. Heat remaining 1/2 teaspoon oil in pan over medium heat. Add leaves and cores to pan; cook 8 minutes or just until leaves wilt and cores are crisp-tender, stirring frequently. Remove from heat; toss with breadcrumb mixture, salt, and pepper. Top with walnuts and cheese. Yield: 6 servings (serving size: 3/4 cup).

CALORIES 71; FAT 3.1g (sat 0.6g, mono 1.1g, poly 1.1g); PROTEIN 3.5g; CARB 8.9g; FIBER 2.3g; CHOL 1mg; IRON 1mg; SODIUM 160mg; CALC 47mg

10 Tips for Portion Control

1 Before Eating, Divide the Plate

Here's a simple rule to portion a plate properly: Divide it in half. Automatically fill one side with fruits or vegetables, leaving the rest for equal parts protein and starch. This way, you begin to see what a properly balanced meal looks like. Spaghetti and meatballs? Steak and potatoes? They're only half a meal, incomplete without fruits and vegetables.

2 Pre-Portion Tempting Treats

The bigger the package, the more food you'll pour out of it. When two groups were given half- or 1-pound bags of M&Ms to eat while watching TV, those given the 1-pound bag ate nearly twice as much.

3 Head Off the Mindless Munch

Five minutes after eating at an Italian restaurant, 31 percent of people couldn't remember how much bread they ate. If you're worried you might do the same, have the bread removed from the table.

4 Downsize Your Dishes

If you're one of the 54 percent of Americans who eat until their plates are clean, make sure those plates are modestly sized. On a standard 8- to 10-inch dinner plate, a portion of spaghetti looks like a meal. On a 12- to 14-inch dinner plate, it looks meager, so you're likely to dish out a bigger portion to fill the plate. When researchers gave study participants 34- or 17-ounce bowls and told them to help themselves to ice cream, those with the bigger bowls dished out 31 percent more.

5 Limit Your Choices

The more options you have, the more you want to try. In one study, researchers gave two groups jellybeans to snack on while they watched a movie. One group got six colors, neatly divided into compartments; jellybeans for the other group were jumbled together. Those given a mix ate nearly two times more.

6 Use Your Power for Good

Most homes have a "nutritional gate-keeper" who controls 72 percent of the food eaten by everyone else. The person who chooses food, buys it, and prepares it wields power. If that's you, take advantage of it.

7 Avoid a See-Food Diet

Office workers who kept candy in clear dishes on their desks dipped in for a sample 71 percent more often than those who kept their candy out of sight.

8 Turn Off the Television

The Vast Wasteland leads to vast waists. It's not just the couch-sitting. TV distracts you from how much you're eating, and the more you watch, the more you're likely to eat. In a study comparing how much popcorn viewers ate during either a half-hour show or an hour-long show, those who watched more television ate 28 percent more popcorn.

9 Think Before You Drink

Pour cranberry juice into two glasses of equal volume: one short and wide, the other tall and thin. Most people pour 19 percent more cranberry juice in the short glass because the eye is a poor judge of volume in relation to height and width.

10 Serve Good-for-You Foods Family-Style

Not all portion-control strategies are about eating less. You can have as much as you want of some foods. Place the foods you want your family to eat more of—salads and vegetable sides—within easy reach on the dining table.

The Big Fat Business of 100-Calorie Portion Control

The 100-calorie snack pack, an invention of Cornell's Brian Wansink, rocked the food market when Kraft sold $75 million worth of Oreo Thin Crisps and Wheat Thin Minis in the first year. Now there are hundreds of similar products.

• "We did research in the mid-1990s that showed mini-sized food packages could lead 70 percent of people to eat less," Wansink says. He took the concept to major food companies, but no takers. Then in 2004 Kraft rolled out its snacks, and the market exploded.

• Is the trend fading? Brandweek reported this year that 100-calorie sales were down, possibly because of perceived high cost in the recession. Critics question whether snackers actually eat less or just keep opening packs until they're full.

• Wansink is confident. "There are people whom it doesn't help and there's the issue of packaging waste, but I'm so overwhelmed by the people 100-calorie packs have helped that I'm willing to overlook it."

How to Build a Better Bowl of Noodles

Introducing the *Cooking Light* guide to transforming plain noodles into exciting, festive feasts.

THE NOODLE BOWL is the world's most perfect one-dish meal. Noodles are cheap, nourishing, easy to prepare, and versatile, blending with a multitude of foods and flavors. These recipes showcase some of the tastiest versions we've had the pleasure of slurping. Use them as a starting point, then experiment. Success boils down to three basic elements: the noodles, the sauce, and the extras.

Japan

Thick, springy udon is one of the country's most popular comfort foods.

The Noodle
Search out fresh noodles if you can, but dried work in a pinch. And the noodles are available in a range of sizes—we love the jumbo's texture.

The Sauce
Dashi, seaweed broth infused with bonito flakes (shaved, dried fish), tastes fresh and of the sea. To rev up the flavor, infuse the broth with fresh ginger, mushrooms, and a sweet-tart combo of salty soy sauce, vinegar, and sugar.

The Extras
Our finishing touches include poached shrimp, dried mushrooms (rehydrated in the broth, of course), and thin slivers of green onions. Any combination will do. In Japan you'll also often find tempura or tofu in the bowl.

Udon Soup with Shrimp

Fat, chewy udon noodles are a mainstay in this basic, soul-warming soup. Although homemade dashi (Japanese seaweed broth) is part of the easy beauty of this dish, you can substitute instant dashi in a pinch. If you take that shortcut, infuse the broth with fresh ginger.

- 2 large sheets kombu (kelp)
- 2 quarts cold water
- 1 cup bonito flakes (about ¼ ounce)
- 1 (1-inch) piece fresh ginger, peeled and thinly sliced
- 1 ounce dried mushroom blend
- 1 (14-ounce) package fresh jumbo udon noodles
- 2 green onions, trimmed
- 1 tablespoon sugar
- 2½ tablespoons low-sodium soy sauce
- 2 tablespoons rice vinegar
- 1 pound medium shrimp, peeled and deveined

1 Wipe kombu clean with a cloth; cut sheeting lengthwise into 3-inch pieces. Place kombu in a large saucepan over medium-high heat; cover with 2 quarts cold water. Heat mixture to 180° or until tiny bubbles form around edge (do not boil). Reduce heat to medium-low, and simmer 20 minutes. Remove from heat; discard kombu. Stir in bonito and ginger; let stand 10 minutes or until bonito sinks. Strain through a cheesecloth-lined colander over a bowl; discard solids.

2 Wipe pan clean. Return broth to pan; bring to a boil. Remove from heat. Stir in mushrooms; let stand 20 minutes. Strain mixture through a cheesecloth-lined colander over a bowl, reserving mushrooms and broth. Wipe pan clean. Return broth to pan; bring to a simmer. Coarsely chop mushrooms.

3 Cook noodles according to package directions; drain. Cut onions into 1-inch pieces; cut each piece in half lengthwise. Cut onion pieces lengthwise into thin strips. Combine sugar, soy sauce, and vinegar in a small bowl, stirring well. Add shrimp to broth; cook 1 minute. Stir in mushrooms; cook 30 seconds. Remove from heat; stir in vinegar mixture. Place about 1 cup noodles in each of 4 bowls; top with 2 cups broth mixture. Divide onion strips evenly among bowls. Yield: 4 servings.

CALORIES 429; FAT 3g (sat 0.5g, mono 0.4g, poly 1.2g); PROTEIN 28.9g; CARB 65.5g; FIBER 2.2g; CHOL 147mg; IRON 4.3mg; SODIUM 994mg; CALC 74mg

Chinese-style barbecue, char siu, is robust with sweet, salty, and spicy flavors working in concert. The light, fresh noodles provide a smooth counterpoint.

China

Many provinces boast regional interpretations of *char siu*, a ubiquitous—and utterly delicious—roast pork.

The Noodle

Long, translucent rice noodles, common in southern China, anchor this Cantonese-style dish. Medium-width rice sticks work well, soaking up the tart, salty sauce and providing a soft, slick contrast to the sliced pork.

The Sauce

A simple dressing that echoes the flavors in the pork—soy, sesame oil, chile paste, garlic, acid, and a little sugar—moistens and flavors the noodles.

The Extras

Chinese barbecued pork hits all the right notes: sweet, sour, spicy, and salty, all at once. And the meat is meltingly tender. Torn fresh cilantro and mint leaves add a dash of color and fresh flavor.

Char Siu over Sesame Noodles

½ cup low-sodium soy sauce, divided
¼ cup honey
3 tablespoons rice vinegar
3 tablespoons dark sesame oil, divided
2 tablespoons hoisin sauce
2 tablespoons chile paste with garlic (such as sambal oelek), divided
5 garlic cloves, divided
1 (1¼-pound) boneless pork shoulder (Boston butt), trimmed
12 ounces (¼-inch-thick) uncooked rice sticks (rice-flour noodles)
¼ cup fresh lime juice
1½ tablespoons sugar
3 tablespoons torn fresh cilantro leaves
3 tablespoons torn fresh mint leaves

1 Combine ¼ cup soy sauce, honey, vinegar, 1 tablespoon oil, hoisin, 1 tablespoon chile paste, and 3 garlic cloves, stirring well with a whisk; place mixture in a heavy-duty zip-top plastic bag. Place pork in bag; seal. Marinate in refrigerator 8 hours or overnight, turning occasionally.

2 Preheat oven to 450°.

3 Remove pork from bag; reserve marinade. Place a roasting rack in a small roasting pan; fill pan with water to a depth of ½ inch. Place pork on rack. Roast pork at 450° for 15 minutes. Baste pork with some of reserved marinade. Turn pork over; baste. Reduce oven temperature to 400°. Cook pork an additional 40 minutes, basting every 10 minutes.

Discard remaining marinade. Let pork stand 10 minutes; thinly slice.

4 Prepare noodles according to package directions; drain. Combine remaining ¼ cup soy sauce, remaining 2 tablespoons oil, remaining 1 tablespoon chile paste, remaining 2 garlic cloves, juice, and sugar in a large bowl, stirring well. Add noodles to bowl; toss to coat. Divide noodles evenly among each of 6 bowls. Combine cilantro and mint; sprinkle about 1 tablespoon herb mixture over each serving. Divide pork evenly among bowls. Yield: 6 servings.

CALORIES 428; FAT 13.3g (sat 3.4g, mono 5.4g, poly 3g); PROTEIN 15.8g; CARB 60.1g; FIBER 0.6g; CHOL 42mg; IRON 2.4mg; SODIUM 623mg; CALC 33mg

Italy

Pastas offer a canvas for transforming simple ingredients into edible masterpieces and supremely satisfying meals.

The Noodle

Bucatini (fat, hollow noodles like spaghetti) adds heft to this dish and carries the sauce well. Long fusilli would be another fun noodle option to stand up to the chunky mushroom mixture. Or press fettuccine or *pappardelle* into service if you can't find the other pastas.

The Sauce

Think of the porcini soaking liquid as a flavorful broth to use as the foundation for a rich, meaty-tasting sauce. A little sherry adds complexity. Finish with a touch of heavy cream and some of the starchy pasta water.

The Extras

If you have access to wild mushrooms, toss them in. Otherwise, look for an exotic blend and combine with crumbled Parmigiano-Reggiano and sage. A final splash of truffle oil takes this over the top.

Bucatini with Mushrooms

Substitute long fusilli or fettuccine if you can't find bucatini. Dried porcini mushrooms and truffle oil supply rich earthiness. Use leftover truffle oil to drizzle over pizzas, polenta, or salad greens.

- ½ cup dried porcini mushrooms (about ½ ounce)
- ⅔ cup boiling water
- 8 ounces uncooked bucatini
- 3½ teaspoons salt, divided
- 1 tablespoon butter
- ¼ cup finely chopped shallots
- 2 (4-ounce) packages exotic mushroom blend, coarsely chopped
- 2 garlic cloves, minced
- 2 tablespoons dry sherry
- 2 ounces Parmigiano-Reggiano cheese, divided
- ¼ cup heavy whipping cream
- 1 teaspoon finely chopped fresh sage
- ½ teaspoon cracked black pepper
- 1 teaspoon truffle oil
- Fresh sage sprigs (optional)

❶ Rinse porcini thoroughly. Combine porcini and ⅔ cup boiling water in a bowl; cover and let stand 30 minutes. Drain in a sieve over a bowl, reserving ¼ cup soaking liquid. Chop porcini.
❷ Cook pasta with 1 tablespoon salt in boiling water 10 minutes or until al dente; drain in a colander over a bowl, reserving ¼ cup cooking liquid.
❸ Melt butter in a large skillet over medium-high heat. Add shallots, mushroom blend, and garlic; sauté 5 minutes, stirring frequently. Stir in porcini, sherry, and ¼ teaspoon salt; cook 1 minute or until liquid evaporates.
❹ Finely grate 1 ounce cheese; crumble remaining cheese. Reduce heat to medium. Stir in pasta, ¼ cup reserved cooking liquid, ¼ cup reserved porcini soaking liquid, remaining ¼ teaspoon salt, ¼ cup grated cheese, cream, chopped sage, and pepper; toss well to combine. Drizzle with oil; toss. Place about 1¼ cups pasta mixture on each of 4 plates; top each serving with about 1 tablespoon crumbled cheese. Garnish with sage sprigs, if desired. Yield: 4 servings.

CALORIES 393; FAT 14.2g (sat 7.9g, mono 4.3g, poly 0.9g); PROTEIN 15.8g; CARB 49.3g; FIBER 3.4g; CHOL 38mg; IRON 3.1mg; SODIUM 733mg; CALC 201mg

WINE NOTE: Like most Chiantis, Cecchi Natio Chianti 2007 ($16) is a medium-bodied, versatile red. What makes this one special is that the ripe cherry fruit is underscored by a sensuous, rustic structure that plays especially well with the ingredients in this dish. Even better, the clear, refreshing acidity of this wine, made with organic grapes, cuts right through the rich truffle oil and butter.

Malaysia

Malaysian food is a melting pot of flavors and traditions. Inspired by traditional street food, this fiery dish reflects the country's tapestry of colorful cuisine.

The Noodle
Here Chinese lo mein egg noodles star in this spicy stir-fry. Their dramatic length and chunky texture make them perfect for the thick sauce. You can substitute dried linguine for lo mein.

The Sauce
Blazing chile paste and sweet bean sauce, a salty-sugary brew of fermented soybeans, mix to render incomparable flavor. The latter is usually available at Asian markets; try hoisin sauce or *kecap manis* if you can't find it. Look for the sweet bean sauce and noodles (which are sometimes frozen) at Asian markets.

The Extras
Sautéed baby bok choy adds a slight crunch, and its little green leaves perk up the color of this bowl. Drain extra-firm tofu, cut it into chunks, and toss with the noodles to boost protein and cut the heat.

Spicy Malaysian-Style Stir-Fried Noodles

This popular Southeast Asian street fare is known as *mee goreng* (fried noodles).

- 1 (14-ounce) package water-packed extra-firm tofu, drained
- 1 (1-pound) package fresh Chinese lo mein egg noodles
- 2 tablespoons dark sesame oil
- 4 garlic cloves, minced
- ¼ teaspoon salt
- 4 heads baby bok choy, trimmed and cut crosswise into 2-inch-thick strips
- 1 tablespoon sugar
- 3 tablespoons chile paste with garlic (such as sambal oelek)
- 2 tablespoons fresh lime juice
- 2 tablespoons sweet bean sauce
- 2 tablespoons low-sodium soy sauce

❶ Line a plate with a triple layer of paper towels; top with tofu. Place a triple layer of paper towels on top of tofu; top with another plate. Let stand 20 minutes. Cut tofu into ½-inch cubes.
❷ Cook noodles in a large pan of boiling water 3 minutes or until done; drain in a colander over a bowl, reserving 1 cup cooking liquid. Wipe pan with paper towels. Heat oil in pan over medium heat. Add garlic to pan; cook 30 seconds, stirring constantly. Add salt and bok choy; cook 30 seconds, stirring frequently. Stir in ½ cup reserved cooking liquid; bring to a boil. Reduce heat, and cook 4 minutes.
❸ Combine sugar and remaining ingredients, stirring until combined. Add noodles, remaining ½ cup cooking liquid, and sugar mixture to pan; toss to combine. Cook 30 seconds or until thoroughly heated, tossing to coat. Add tofu; toss to combine. Serve immediately. Yield: 6 servings (serving size: 1⅔ cups).

CALORIES 359; FAT 9.5g (sat 1.4g, mono 2.6g, poly 4.2g); PROTEIN 15.1g; CARB 53g; FIBER 2.1g; CHOL 17mg; IRON 3.4mg; SODIUM 617mg; CALC 65mg

Thailand

Bright-flavored bowls of stir-fried noodles are the national fast food.

The Noodle

Rice noodles are a staple of Thai food and available in a variety of widths. Although seasoned variations exist, we like the plain, wide, flat noodles in stir-fries such as this. If shopping in an Asian grocery, look for pad thai noodles designated as "XL." At supermarkets, they'll be marked "wide."

The Sauce

The piquant base comes from the prototypical Thai flavor trinity: soy sauce, fish sauce, and garlicky chile paste. Lime juice cut with brown sugar adds zing.

The Extras

Toss the noodles with flavorful lime-marinated chicken breast. Then top with thinly sliced lemongrass, raw shallots, and torn basil leaves for a lively flavor.

QUICK & EASY
Thai Rice Noodles with Chicken

- ¼ cup fresh lime juice, divided
- 2 (6-ounce) skinless, boneless chicken breast halves, cut into ¾-inch cubes
- 8 ounces ½-inch-thick rice noodles
- 1 tablespoon brown sugar
- 1 tablespoon water
- 1 tablespoon fish sauce
- 1 tablespoon low-sodium soy sauce
- 1½ teaspoons fresh chile paste with garlic (such as sambal oelek)
- ¼ teaspoon salt, divided
- 4 teaspoons canola oil, divided
- 3 tablespoons thinly diagonally sliced green onions
- 1 teaspoon grated peeled fresh ginger
- 1 teaspoon minced garlic
- ½ cup torn fresh basil leaves
- ¼ cup very thinly sliced lemongrass (tough outer stalks removed)
- ¼ cup very thinly vertically sliced shallots

❶ Combine 2 tablespoons juice and chicken in a bowl. Let stand 15 minutes.
❷ Soak noodles in hot water 15 minutes or until somewhat soft but still slightly chewy. Drain well.
❸ Combine remaining 2 tablespoons juice, sugar, and next 4 ingredients. Stir in ⅛ teaspoon salt.
❹ Heat a large wok or skillet over medium-high heat. Add 1 teaspoon oil to pan, swirling to coat. Remove chicken from juice; discard juice. Add chicken to pan; stir-fry 4 minutes or until done. Transfer to a large bowl; sprinkle with remaining ⅛ teaspoon salt. Add remaining 1 tablespoon oil to pan. Add green onions, ginger, and garlic; stir-fry 45 seconds or just until golden and fragrant. Add noodles; cook 30 seconds, tossing well. Stir in sugar mixture. Add chicken; cook 30 seconds. Place 1¼ cups noodle mixture on each of 4 plates. Top each with 2 tablespoons basil, 1 tablespoon lemongrass, and 1 tablespoon shallots. Yield: 4 servings.

CALORIES 343; FAT 5.5g (sat 0.6g, mono 2.9g, poly 1.6g); PROTEIN 17.5g; CARB 54.4g; FIBER 0.7g; CHOL 34mg; IRON 2.1mg; SODIUM 615mg; CALC 36mg

Singapore

A worldly array of Southeast Asian ingredients jostles together to create a uniquely cosmopolitan taste.

The Noodle

Super-thin rice vermicelli soaks up the vivid and tasty curry-tinged sauce. It also provides a textural contrast to the chunky ingredients in this dish.

The Sauce

A raucous assortment of flavors defines the sauce—soy sauce, vinegar, hoisin, and chiles. And fresh, homemade curry powder informs each bite.

The Extras

A savory mixture of roasted green onion pieces, chunks of bacon, and briny-sweet shrimp adds an extra dimension of satisfaction.

Singapore-Style Noodles

(pictured on page 233)

Although our curry powder blend packs a particular punch, you can substitute 1 teaspoon spicy-hot Madras curry powder and omit the cumin, coriander, mustard, clove, and ground red pepper. We tested this recipe with Wai Wai brand noodles because we like the texture. They're thinner than most supermarket brands, which will work just fine, though you may need to soak them a minute longer.

- 5 ounces uncooked rice vermicelli
- ¼ teaspoon cumin seeds
- ⅛ teaspoon coriander seeds
- ⅛ teaspoon mustard seeds
- 1 whole clove
- ⅛ teaspoon ground red pepper
- 1 cup (1-inch) pieces green onions
- 5 teaspoons canola oil, divided
- 5 bacon slices, cut into 1-inch pieces
- Cooking spray
- 1 pound large tail-on shrimp, peeled and deveined
- ¼ teaspoon black pepper
- ¼ teaspoon salt, divided
- 2 tablespoons low-sodium soy sauce
- 1 tablespoon rice wine vinegar
- 1 tablespoon hoisin sauce
- 2 teaspoons chili garlic sauce (such as Lee Kum Kee)
- 1½ teaspoons grated peeled fresh ginger, divided
- 1 cup (1½-inch) julienne-cut red bell pepper

❶ Soak noodles in warm water 2 minutes. Drain well. Combine cumin and next 3 ingredients in a spice or coffee grinder; pulse until finely ground. Stir in red pepper.
❷ Preheat broiler.
❸ Combine green onions, 2 teaspoons oil, and bacon. Place onion mixture on a rimmed baking sheet coated with cooking spray. Broil 5 minutes. Add shrimp to mixture; toss. Arrange shrimp in a single layer. Broil 5 minutes or until shrimp and

bacon are done. Transfer mixture to a bowl using a slotted spoon. Stir in black pepper and 1/8 teaspoon salt.

❹ Combine cumin mixture, remaining 1/8 teaspoon salt, soy sauce, vinegar, hoisin, chili garlic sauce, and 1/2 teaspoon ginger. Heat remaining 1 tablespoon oil in a large nonstick skillet over medium-high heat. Add bell pepper to pan; sauté 2 minutes. Add remaining 1 teaspoon ginger; sauté 45 seconds. Add to shrimp mixture.

❺ Return skillet to medium-high heat. Add soy sauce mixture and noodles; cook 1 minute or until thoroughly heated, tossing to coat. Place about 3/4 cup noodles on each of 4 plates. Top each serving with about 1 cup shrimp mixture. Serve immediately. Yield: 4 servings.

CALORIES 468; FAT 21.5g (sat 5.2g, mono 9.4g, poly 4g); PROTEIN 30.2g; CARB 34.1g; FIBER 1.5g; CHOL 192mg; IRON 4.3mg; SODIUM 843mg; CALC 84mg

Spain

The Catalonian palate spotlights smoky seasonings, briny seafood, and fresh-from-the-field produce.

The Noodle

Thin, coiled wheat noodles, called *fideos*, are interchangeable with dried angel hair pasta—use either in this recipe. The distinct toasty flavor of this classic dish comes when you break the noodles into pieces, brown them, then cook in broth.

The Sauce

Sausage, garlic, tomatoes, and smoked paprika provide the basis for the sauce. Then add tangy wine, broth, and briny liquid from the mussels, and reduce it to intensify the flavors. To finish and enrich the sauce, stir in a touch of cream.

The Extras

A close cousin to paella, this dish uses pasta instead of rice. And similarly, *fideo* bowls often include fish and shellfish. We chose mussels, but you can toss in other seafood, if you prefer.

Fideos with Chorizo and Mussels

Available at tienda.com, *pimentón de la Vera* is traditional Spanish smoked paprika with a more delicate, nuanced flavor than American smoked paprika, which works if you have it. Be sure to use dried Spanish chorizo instead of the fresh Mexican-style sausage.

  4 cups fat-free, less-sodium chicken broth, divided
1/8 teaspoon dried thyme
  3 tablespoons olive oil
  8 ounces uncooked angel hair pasta or fideos, broken into 1 1/2-inch pieces
     Cooking spray
1 1/2 cups chopped onion
  1 cup chopped green bell pepper
1/2 cup finely diced Spanish chorizo sausage (about 2.75 ounces)
  1 large garlic clove, thinly sliced
  2 cups chopped tomato
1/2 teaspoon sugar
1/2 teaspoon pimentón de la Vera (Spanish smoked paprika)
1/8 teaspoon salt
1/2 cup dry white wine
  2 pounds medium mussels, scrubbed and debearded
1/4 cup heavy cream
  2 tablespoons chopped fresh parsley

❶ Bring broth and thyme to a simmer in a small saucepan; cover and keep warm.
❷ Heat oil in a large skillet over medium-high heat. Add noodles to pan; cook 3 minutes or until golden and fragrant, stirring constantly. Transfer to a bowl.
❸ Heat a large Dutch oven over medium-high heat. Coat pan with cooking spray. Add onion and next 3 ingredients to pan; sauté 6 minutes or until vegetables are tender, stirring occasionally. Add tomato and next 3 ingredients; cook 1 minute. Add wine and 1 cup broth to pan; bring to a boil. Add mussels to pan. Cook, covered, 3 minutes or until shells open.

Discard any unopened shells. Transfer mussels with a slotted spoon to a bowl; keep warm. Return tomato mixture to a boil; reduce heat, and simmer 3 minutes or until liquid is reduced by about half. Remove from heat; stir in cream.
❹ Add pasta and 1 1/2 cups broth to skillet; bring to a boil. Cover and cook 3 minutes. Add remaining 1 1/2 cups broth to pasta mixture; cover and cook 3 minutes. Uncover; cook 2 minutes or until liquid is absorbed and pasta is tender. Place about 3/4 cup pasta in each of 6 shallow bowls. Top each serving with about 1/2 cup tomato mixture; divide mussels evenly among servings. Sprinkle with parsley. Yield: 6 servings.

CALORIES 442; FAT 18.2g (sat 5.3g, mono 8.5g, poly 2.8g); PROTEIN 28.6g; CARB 41.6g; FIBER 3.6g; CHOL 147mg; IRON 7.9mg; SODIUM 753mg; CALC 85mg

WINE NOTE: Let the Spanish influences in this dish inspire you. Albariño, the unique white wine of northern Spain, pairs perfectly. Martin Codax Albariño 2008 ($15) has crisp citrus and pear notes. Floral aromas and mineral nuances resonate with mussels but stand up to spicy chorizo.

Feed 4 for Less Than $10

Here are four affordable, delicious meals prepared on a budget.

$1.60 per serving; $9.28 total
Sausage and Caramelized Onion Bread Pudding

If your supermarket offers turkey Italian sausage in the butcher case, purchase one or two links to equal 4 ounces. If starting with a package of several sausages, freeze leftover links up to two months for later use.

1⅓ cups 1% low-fat milk
¼ teaspoon dry mustard
⅛ teaspoon salt
2 large eggs
1 large egg white
8 (1-ounce) slices day-old French bread, cut into 1-inch cubes
Cooking spray
2 cups chopped yellow onion
¼ cup apple juice
4 ounces turkey Italian sausage
¾ cup (3 ounces) shredded sharp Cheddar cheese

❶ Combine first 5 ingredients in a large bowl; stir well with a whisk. Add bread; toss gently to coat. Let bread mixture stand 20 minutes.
❷ Preheat oven to 350°.
❸ Heat a large nonstick skillet over medium heat. Coat pan with cooking spray. Add onion to pan; cook 10 minutes, stirring occasionally. Add juice; cook 5 minutes, stirring occasionally. Remove casings from sausage. Crumble sausage into pan; cook 5 minutes or until browned, stirring frequently. Remove from heat; let stand 5 minutes.
❹ Add sausage mixture and cheese to bread mixture; stir well to combine. Spoon into an 8-inch square baking dish coated with cooking spray. Bake at 350° for 40 minutes or until set and lightly browned. Let stand 10 minutes before serving. Yield: 4 servings (serving size: 1 piece).

CALORIES 419; FAT 14.6g (sat 7g, mono 4.9g, poly 1.3g); PROTEIN 25.6g; CARB 46.4g; FIBER 2.7g; CHOL 156mg; IRON 3.5mg; SODIUM 892mg; CALC 311mg

SAUTÉED ZUCCHINI:
Heat a large nonstick skillet over medium-high heat. Add 1 tablespoon canola oil to pan; swirl to coat. Add 1 pound thinly sliced zucchini to pan; sauté 4 minutes or until zucchini is lightly browned, stirring occasionally. Sprinkle with ¼ teaspoon salt and ¼ teaspoon black pepper.

$2.50 per serving; $7.25 total
Adobo Chicken

1 tablespoon canola oil
8 bone-in chicken thighs, skinned
2 cups chopped onion
5 garlic cloves, minced
6 tablespoons low-sodium soy sauce
3 tablespoons water
3 tablespoons white vinegar
2 tablespoons honey
½ teaspoon black pepper
1 bay leaf
3 cups hot cooked long-grain rice

❶ Heat oil in a large nonstick skillet over medium-high heat. Add chicken to pan; sauté 4 minutes on each side or until browned. Remove chicken from pan. Add onion to pan; sauté 3 minutes. Add garlic; sauté 1 minute, stirring frequently.
❷ Return chicken to pan. Add soy sauce and next 5 ingredients; bring to a boil. Reduce heat to medium; cover and cook 12 minutes. Uncover and cook 20 minutes or until chicken is done and sauce thickens. Discard bay leaf. Serve over rice. Yield: 4 servings (serving size: 2 thighs and about 6 tablespoons sauce).

CALORIES 483; FAT 14.7g (sat 3.4g, mono 6.3g, poly 3.6g); PROTEIN 33.1g; CARB 53g; FIBER 2.2g; CHOL 99mg; IRON 3.8mg; SODIUM 888mg; CALC 55mg

$2.32 per serving; $9.99 total
KID FRIENDLY
Beer-Braised Beef with Onion, Carrot, and Turnips
(pictured on page 232)

Ask your butcher to cut a 1-pound roast for you, or buy a larger one and freeze the rest. Use a dark beer that's not too strong; stout will overpower the other ingredients.

3 tablespoons all-purpose flour
1½ tablespoons canola oil
1 (1-pound) boneless chuck roast, trimmed
1 teaspoon salt, divided
½ teaspoon black pepper
1 cup fat-free, less-sodium beef broth
4 garlic cloves, crushed
1 (12-ounce) bottle dark beer
1 bay leaf
3 carrots, peeled and cut diagonally into ½-inch-thick slices
9 ounces small turnips, peeled and cut into wedges
1 medium onion, peeled and cut into wedges
¼ cup chopped fresh flat-leaf parsley

❶ Preheat oven to 300°.
❷ Place flour in a shallow dish. Heat oil in a Dutch oven over medium-high heat. Sprinkle beef evenly on all sides with ½ teaspoon salt and pepper; dredge in flour. Add beef to pan; cook 10 minutes, turning to brown on all sides. Add broth and next 3 ingredients, scraping pan to remove browned bits; bring to a boil. Cover and bake at 300° for 1½ hours. Add carrots; cover and cook 25 minutes. Add remaining ½ teaspoon salt, turnips, and onion; cover and cook an additional 1 hour and 5 minutes or until vegetables are tender and beef is fork-tender.
❸ Remove beef and vegetables from pan; discard bay leaf. Cover beef mixture; keep warm. Let cooking liquid stand 10 minutes. Place a zip-top plastic bag inside a 2-cup glass measure. Pour cooking liquid into bag; let stand 10 minutes (fat will

rise to top). Seal bag; carefully snip off 1 bottom corner of bag. Drain cooking liquid into a medium bowl, stopping before fat layer reaches opening; discard fat. Serve cooking liquid with beef and vegetables. Sprinkle each serving with 1 tablespoon parsley. Yield: 4 servings (serving size: 3 ounces beef, 1 cup vegetables, and about ½ cup cooking liquid).

CALORIES 383; FAT 19.7g (sat 6g, mono 9.1g, poly 2.2g); PROTEIN 24.4g; CARB 21g; FIBER 3.6g; CHOL 70mg; IRON 2.9mg; SODIUM 815mg; CALC 68mg

BEER NOTE: Grab a 6-pack of Warsteiner Premium Dunkel ($8/6-pack) and you'll have five bottles left after making Beer-Braised Beef with Onion, Carrot, and Turnips. The word "dunkel" means "dark" in German, and the toasted malt that gives this beer its duskiness also makes it a good match for the chuck roast. A touch of hop bitterness balances nicely with the sweet root vegetables.

$1.81 per serving; $6.39 total
Pork-Potato Hash with Eggs

Pork sold as "country-style ribs" is not always from the rib section; it can be cut from a pork shoulder roast, too. Either way, it's economical and generally cut into individual "ribs," making it easy for you to ask your butcher for just the number you need.

- 12 ounces pork country-style ribs (about 2 ribs)
- 1¼ teaspoons salt, divided
- ½ teaspoon freshly ground black pepper
  Cooking spray
- 2½ cups water
- 6 garlic cloves, crushed
- 1 tablespoon olive oil
- 4 cups (½-inch) cubed red potatoes (about 1½ pounds)
- 1 cup chopped onion
- 4 large eggs
- ¼ teaspoon ground red pepper
- 3 tablespoons thinly diagonally sliced green onions

1 Heat a 12-inch cast-iron skillet over medium-high heat. Sprinkle pork evenly with ½ teaspoon salt and black pepper. Coat pan with cooking spray. Add pork to pan; cook 2 minutes on each side or until browned. Add 2½ cups water and garlic to pan; bring to a boil. Cover, reduce heat to low, and simmer 1 hour or until pork is fork-tender. Remove pork from pan, reserving cooking liquid and garlic. Place cooking liquid in a bowl. Cool pork slightly. Remove meat from bones; shred with two forks.
2 Wipe pan clean with paper towels. Heat oil in pan over medium-high heat. Add potatoes and onion to pan, and sauté 8 minutes or until browned, stirring frequently. Add cooking liquid and garlic to potato mixture, and bring to a boil. Reduce heat to medium, and cook, uncovered, 20 minutes or until potatoes are tender and liquid evaporates. Stir in shredded pork and ½ teaspoon salt. Working with one egg at a time, carefully crack eggs over potato mixture, about 1 inch apart in pan. Sprinkle eggs evenly with remaining ¼ teaspoon salt and red pepper. Cover, reduce heat, and cook 3 minutes or until desired degree of doneness. Sprinkle with green onions. Yield: 4 servings (serving size: 1 egg and about 1½ cups hash).

CALORIES 334; FAT 13.8g (sat 4g, mono 6.6g, poly 1.6g); PROTEIN 20.2g; CARB 33.2g; FIBER 3.9g; CHOL 244mg; IRON 3mg; SODIUM 845mg; CALC 75mg

GREEN SALAD:
Shave 1 carrot into ribbons using a vegetable peeler. Combine carrot and 6 cups torn romaine lettuce. Whisk together 2 tablespoons olive oil, 1½ tablespoons fresh lemon juice, 1 teaspoon honey, ¼ teaspoon salt, and ¼ teaspoon freshly ground black pepper. Toss dressing with salad.

Start with a Can of... Refrigerated French Bread Dough

Unfurl and roll it thin to transform this ordinary ingredient into crisp pizza crust, breadsticks, flatbread, and more.

QUICK & EASY ▪ MAKE AHEAD
KID FRIENDLY
Grissini

- 1 (11-ounce) can refrigerated French bread dough
- 2 tablespoons olive oil, divided
- ¼ cup (1 ounce) finely grated Parmigiano-Reggiano cheese
- 2 tablespoons lightly toasted sesame seeds
- 1 tablespoon poppy seeds
- ½ teaspoon freshly ground black pepper
- ¼ teaspoon kosher salt
  Cooking spray

1 Preheat oven to 425°.
2 Find lengthwise seam in dough. Beginning at seam, gently unroll dough into a rectangle on a lightly floured surface. Roll into a 15 x 13–inch rectangle on a lightly floured surface. Brush evenly with 1 tablespoon oil. Combine cheese and next 4 ingredients, stirring well; sprinkle half of mixture evenly over dough, pressing gently to adhere. Turn dough over. Brush with remaining 1 tablespoon oil; sprinkle with remaining cheese mixture. Cut lengthwise into 48 thin strips (about ¼-inch-thick) using a pizza cutter. Place strips on baking sheets coated with cooking spray. Bake in batches at 425° for 4 minutes or until golden and crisp. Yield: 12 servings (serving size: 4 breadsticks).

CALORIES 107; FAT 4.7g (sat 1.1g, mono 2.4g, poly 0.9g); PROTEIN 3.7g; CARB 12.8g; FIBER 0.3g; CHOL 2mg; IRON 0.9mg; SODIUM 249mg; CALC 52mg

QUICK & EASY
Sausage and Egg Flatbread

With its lemony arugula garnish, this light entrée would be good for brunch or Sunday supper.

- 1 (11-ounce) can refrigerated French bread dough
- 2 teaspoons cornmeal
- 2/3 cup chopped onion
- 1 (4-ounce) turkey Italian sausage, casing removed, crumbled
- 1/2 cup (2 ounces) shredded fontina cheese
- 6 large eggs
- 1/4 teaspoon kosher salt
- 1/8 teaspoon freshly ground black pepper
- 2 cups arugula
- 2 teaspoons fresh lemon juice
- 1 teaspoon extra-virgin olive oil

1 Preheat oven to 400°.
2 Find lengthwise seam in dough. Beginning at seam, gently unroll dough into a rectangle on a lightly floured surface. Cut dough crosswise into 2 equal portions. Roll each portion into a 15 x 6-inch rectangle on a lightly floured surface. Place each rectangle on a baking sheet sprinkled with 1 teaspoon cornmeal.
3 Heat a nonstick skillet over medium heat. Add onion and turkey Italian sausage to pan; cook 4 minutes or until lightly browned, stirring to crumble. Divide sausage mixture evenly between rectangles, spreading evenly down length of dough, leaving a 1/4-inch border on each; top each rectangle evenly with 1/4 cup cheese. Bake at 400° for 10 minutes or until lightly browned. Remove from oven. Break 3 eggs onto each flatbread, spacing evenly lengthwise; sprinkle evenly with salt and freshly ground black pepper. Bake an additional 5 minutes or until eggs are set. Turn oven off; leave flatbreads in oven with oven door closed for 4 minutes or until desired degree of doneness. Remove from oven.

4 Combine arugula, juice, and oil; toss. Arrange arugula mixture evenly over flatbreads. Cut each flatbread crosswise into 3 squares; serve immediately. Yield: 6 servings (serving size: 1 square).

CALORIES 288; FAT 12.3g (sat 4.7g, mono 4.8g, poly 1.4g); PROTEIN 17.1g; CARB 27.7g; FIBER 0.6g; CHOL 234mg; IRON 2.7mg; SODIUM 676mg; CALC 94mg

MAKE AHEAD • KID FRIENDLY
Savory Sausage Breakfast Rolls

These rolls hit the spot on a chilly fall morning. We like reduced-fat pork sausage, but turkey sausage also works.

- 1 (11-ounce) can refrigerated French bread dough
- 2 tablespoons butter, melted
- 2 teaspoons chopped fresh sage
- 1/4 teaspoon salt
- 8 ounces reduced-fat pork sausage, cooked and crumbled (such as Jimmy Dean)
- 3/4 cup (3 ounces) shredded Gruyère cheese
- Cooking spray

1 Preheat oven to 350°.
2 Find lengthwise seam in dough. Beginning at seam, gently unroll dough into a rectangle on a lightly floured surface. Roll dough into a 13 x 8-inch rectangle; brush with butter, leaving a 1/2-inch border. Combine sage, salt, and sausage. Sprinkle sausage mixture evenly over dough, leaving a 1/2-inch border; top with cheese. Starting with a long side, roll dough up, jelly-roll fashion; press seam to seal (do not seal ends of roll). Cut 1 (1/2-inch-thick) crosswise slice from each end; discard. Slice roll crosswise into 12 (1/2-inch-thick) pieces; arrange in a 13 x 9-inch baking dish coated with cooking spray. Bake at 350° for 28 minutes or until golden. Yield: 6 servings (serving size: 2 rolls).

CALORIES 312; FAT 16.8g (sat 7.9g, mono 6.4g, poly 1.2g); PROTEIN 15.5g; CARB 24.8g; FIBER 0g; CHOL 52mg; IRON 1.8mg; SODIUM 738mg; CALC 146mg

> ## Best Buy
> We sampled several products and preferred the flavor and texture of the refrigerated French bread dough. Make sure to start with chilled dough and tug gently to separate the layers as you go.

QUICK & EASY • KID FRIENDLY
Bacon, Onion, and Mushroom Pizza

- 1 (11-ounce) can refrigerated French bread dough
- 2 teaspoons yellow cornmeal
- 2 teaspoons olive oil
- 2 cups vertically sliced onions (about 2 small)
- 1 (8-ounce) package presliced cremini mushrooms
- 1 1/2 cups (6 ounces) shredded white Cheddar cheese
- 6 bacon slices, cooked and coarsely crumbled
- 1/2 cup finely chopped fresh flat-leaf parsley

1 Preheat oven to 425°.
2 Find lengthwise seam in dough. Beginning at seam, gently unroll dough into a rectangle on a lightly floured surface. Stretch dough into a 12-inch circle on a lightly floured surface; transfer to a round pizza pan or large baking sheet sprinkled with 2 teaspoons cornmeal.
3 Heat a large nonstick skillet over medium-high heat. Add oil to pan, swirling to coat. Add onion; sauté 8 minutes, stirring occasionally. Place onion in a bowl. Add mushrooms to pan; sauté 8 minutes or until liquid almost evaporates. Add mushrooms to onion mixture; toss. Spread onion mixture evenly over prepared dough, leaving a 1/4-inch border. Sprinkle evenly with cheese and bacon. Bake at 425° for 15 minutes or until crust is lightly browned. Sprinkle with parsley. Cut into 12 wedges. Yield: 6 servings (serving size: 2 wedges).

CALORIES 316; FAT 14.9g (sat 6.6g, mono 5.5g, poly 1g); PROTEIN 15.6g; CARB 31.1g; FIBER 0.9g; CHOL 37mg; IRON 1.9mg; SODIUM 682mg; CALC 224mg

Mediterranean Main Dishes

Venture beyond the expected hummus and tabbouleh with these authentic recipes featuring ingredients you can find at the supermarket down the street.

Turkish Carrots and Lentils (*Zeytinyağli Havuç*)

Slightly sweet and spicy, ground Aleppo pepper brightens the sauce, while carrots and yogurt lighten earthy lentils. Serve with a simple romaine salad.

- 3 tablespoons extra-virgin olive oil
- 1½ cups thinly sliced onion
- 1 garlic clove, minced
- 1 tablespoon tomato paste
- ½ teaspoon ground Aleppo pepper
- 1 pound carrots, halved lengthwise and thinly sliced (about 3 cups)
- ¾ teaspoon sea salt, divided
- 3 cups water
- 1 cup uncooked dried green lentils
- ¼ teaspoon freshly ground black pepper
- ¼ cup Greek-style yogurt (such as Fage)
  Fresh dill sprigs (optional)

❶ Heat oil in a large saucepan over medium heat. Add onion; cook 9 minutes or until lightly browned, stirring occasionally. Add garlic; cook 1 minute. Stir in tomato paste and Aleppo pepper; cook 30 seconds. Stir in carrots and ¼ teaspoon salt; cook 1 minute. Remove from heat.
❷ Combine 3 cups water and lentils in a large saucepan, and bring to a boil. Cover, reduce heat, and simmer 30 minutes. Uncover, increase heat to medium-high, and stir in onion mixture; cook 2 minutes or until liquid almost evaporates. Stir in remaining ½ teaspoon salt and black pepper. Cover with a kitchen towel, and cool to room temperature.

Serve with yogurt. Garnish with dill, if desired. Yield: 4 servings (serving size: about 1 cup lentil mixture and 1 tablespoon yogurt).

CALORIES 357; FAT 12.2g (sat 2.8g, mono 7.7g, poly 1.2g); PROTEIN 17.4g; CARB 48.6g; FIBER 10.6g; CHOL 3mg; IRON 5mg; SODIUM 549mg; CALC 64mg

Koshari

SAUCE:
- 1 tablespoon extra-virgin olive oil
- 1 cup finely chopped onion
- 1½ tablespoons minced garlic
- ½ teaspoon sea salt
- ½ teaspoon freshly ground black pepper
- ½ teaspoon crushed red pepper
- 2 (14.5-ounce) cans diced tomatoes, undrained

KOSHARI:
- 3 tablespoons extra-virgin olive oil
- 3 cups thinly sliced onion
- ½ cup uncooked vermicelli, broken into 1-inch pieces
- 5 cups water
- 1¼ cups dried lentils or yellow split peas
- 2½ cups hot cooked long-grain rice
- 1 teaspoon sea salt

❶ To prepare sauce, heat 1 tablespoon oil in a large saucepan over medium heat. Add chopped onion to pan, and cook 15 minutes or until golden, stirring occasionally. Add garlic; cook 2 minutes. Stir in ½ teaspoon salt and next 3 ingredients; cook 10 minutes or until slightly thick. Transfer tomato mixture to a food processor; process 1 minute or until smooth. Keep warm. Wipe skillet dry with paper towels.
❷ To prepare koshari, heat 3 tablespoons oil in pan over medium heat. Add sliced onion; cook 15 minutes or until deep golden brown, stirring frequently. Remove onion with a slotted spoon to several layers of paper towels; set aside. Return pan to medium heat. Add vermicelli; sauté 2 minutes or until golden brown, stirring frequently. Set aside.

❸ Combine 5 cups water and lentils in a medium saucepan; bring to a boil. Cover, reduce heat, and simmer 30 minutes or until lentils are tender. Remove from heat; add vermicelli, stirring well to combine. Wrap a clean kitchen towel around lid, and cover lentil mixture; let stand 10 minutes or until vermicelli is tender. Add rice and 1 teaspoon salt to lentil mixture; fluff with a fork. Serve immediately with sauce and onions. Yield: 8 servings (serving size: ¾ cup lentil mixture, ⅓ cup sauce, and 2 tablespoons onion mixture).

CALORIES 292; FAT 7.7g (sat 1g, mono 5g, poly 0.8g); PROTEIN 10.2g; CARB 47.5g; FIBER 7.6g; CHOL 0mg; IRON 3mg; SODIUM 569mg; CALC 53mg

Bulgur-Pepper Patties (*Batirik*)

- 2¼ cups finely chopped peeled tomato
- ¾ cup uncooked fine bulgur
- ½ cup coarsely grated onion
- ¼ cup coarsely grated green bell pepper
- 1 teaspoon canned tomato puree
- ¾ cup shelled dry-roasted pistachios, finely ground
- 1 tablespoon finely chopped fresh flat-leaf parsley
- 2 teaspoons finely chopped fresh oregano
- 1 teaspoon ground Aleppo pepper
- ¾ teaspoon fine sea salt
  Chopped fresh parsley (optional)

❶ Combine first 5 ingredients in a large bowl; let stand 15 minutes. Add pistachios and next 4 ingredients; mix well. Press bulgur mixture into a ¼-cup dry measuring cup; unmold onto a platter. Repeat with remaining bulgur mixture to form 12 patties total. Chill 15 minutes; shape each bulgur portion into a 2½-inch patty. Top with chopped parsley, if desired. Yield: 6 servings (serving size: 2 patties).

CALORIES 172; FAT 7.8g (sat 1g, mono 3.9g, poly 2.4g); PROTEIN 6.5g; CARB 22.1g; FIBER 6.1g; CHOL 0mg; IRON 1.4mg; SODIUM 364mg; CALC 38mg

Foolproof Flatbreads

Homemade breads are at the heart of Moroccan cuisine and culture: Used as serving utensils to scoop up food at meals, they're also a symbol of hospitality since bread is shared with guests. Carry on the Mediterranean tradition by welcoming diners to your table with Moroccan Flatbreads (at right), substantial enough for an entrée or as a partner for soup or salad. Add cheese or herbs to vary the filling. Follow these steps for working with the dough and shaping the breads.

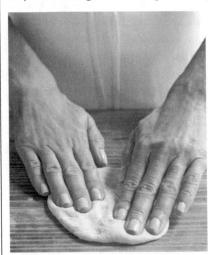

1 Lightly spray your hands with cooking spray, if needed, to avoid tearing the dough. Carefully flatten each dough portion to a 6½-inch round; the dough will be delicate and very thin at this point.

2 Fold the dough to make a square package: Fold 2 opposite sides over filling; then fold one short side over dough and one short side under dough. Lightly press the square to seal.

3 Because the dough is tender and thin, it crisps and browns nicely when heated. Carefully turn flatbreads over when golden and slightly crisp on bottom.

Moroccan Flatbreads (*R'ghayef*)

Check the "use by" date on yeast to ensure it is still good. If the yeast–warm liquid mixture does not swell or bubble after 5 minutes, start over with new yeast. Pair these veggie-stuffed flatbreads with a bell pepper and feta cheese salad with olives for an inspired North African meal. Make up to one day ahead; reheat breads in a warm oven. A leftover flatbread with soup makes a good light lunch.

- ½ teaspoon dry yeast
- ¾ cup plus 1 tablespoon warm water (100° to 110°)
- 9 ounces all-purpose flour (about 2 cups)
- ¾ teaspoon sea salt
- Cooking spray
- 2 cups chopped onion
- ½ cup finely chopped fresh flat-leaf parsley
- 2 tablespoons extra-virgin olive oil
- 2 teaspoons paprika
- 1 teaspoon ground cumin
- ½ teaspoon sea salt
- ¼ teaspoon crushed red pepper
- 1 teaspoon canola oil, divided

❶ Dissolve yeast in warm water in a large bowl; let stand 5 minutes. Weigh or lightly spoon flour into dry measuring cups; level with a knife. Add flour and ¾ teaspoon salt to yeast mixture; stir with a wooden spoon until smooth. Turn dough out onto a lightly floured surface; knead 3 minutes. Shape dough into a ball; invert bowl over dough, and let stand 15 minutes. Uncover; knead dough 3 minutes. Divide dough into 8 equal portions, shaping each into a ball; lightly coat with cooking spray. Cover with plastic wrap; let stand 30 minutes.

❷ Combine onion and next 6 ingredients in a bowl.

❸ Working with one dough portion at a time (cover remaining dough to prevent drying), carefully flatten each portion into a 6½-inch circle (dough will be delicate). Spoon 2 tablespoons onion mixture in center of dough. Fold sides of dough over filling (see "Foolproof Flatbreads," page 298). Fold one short side under dough. Fold other short side over dough. Gently press square of dough to seal. Repeat procedure with remaining dough portions and onion mixture.

❹ Heat ½ teaspoon oil in a large non-stick skillet over medium heat. Add 4 flatbreads to pan; cook 2 minutes on each side or until crisp and golden. Transfer flatbreads to a parchment paper-lined platter. Repeat procedure with remaining ½ teaspoon oil and 4 flatbreads. Serve immediately. Yield: 4 servings (serving size: 2 flatbreads).

CALORIES 331; FAT 8.9g (sat 1.2g, mono 5.7g, poly 1.3g); PROTEIN 7.8g; CARB 54.5g; FIBER 3.6g; CHOL 0mg; IRON 3.9mg; SODIUM 730mg; CALC 40mg

Heart of a Farm, Soul of a Kitchen

The dedicated artisans, gardeners, and chefs of Tennessee's Blackberry Farm bring the "eat fresh and local" ideal to delicious life.

IF IN THIS CRAZY, MODERN WORLD YOU ARE comforted by the idea of truly fresh, truly local food, be sure to visit Blackberry Farm, a 4,200-acre piece of Tennessee foothills Eden. In season, the inn's foragers scour the property for wild creasy greens, ramps, elderberries, and morels. A master gardener grows hundreds of varieties of heirloom beans, squash, beets, lettuce, and has even inoculated a grove of hazelnut trees with spore that may become some of the world's few cultivated black truffles. A shepherd tends a herd of sheep and crafts their milk into both the yogurt you'll have at breakfast and the sumptuous cheeses with which you'll finish your dinner. Butchers like Michael Sullivan cure a vast array of house salumi, and "jam lady" Maggie Davidson turns the wild blackberries that give this special place its name into a sweet preserve you will never forget.

As one of the 126 guests at this luxurious country inn, you may find the energy to hike one of the eight trails that disappear into forest. It builds an appetite and an appreciation for what has been carved out of this lovely Smoky Mountains landscape. Or you may relax, crisscrossing the tended lawns and gardens surrounding the central inn; winding paths lead from spa to tennis courts, and from fly-fishing stream to swimming pool. This is not farm life, in other words, but it has at its heart a farm, and the most interesting road is the one that takes you to dinner.

Set off early for a culinary tour, and you will get a firsthand look at this inn's ambitious farm-to-table program, which is the foundation of its signature "Foothills Cuisine." A team of in-house artisans grows, collects, and handcrafts all the ingredients needed to create their vision of super-local, haute-Smoky refinement.

Roasted Root Vegetables with Sorghum and Cider

1 cup pearl onions, peeled
16 baby carrots, peeled and cut in half lengthwise (about 1 pound)
12 baby turnips, peeled and cut in half lengthwise (about 1 pound)
2 teaspoons canola oil
2 tablespoons sorghum
2 tablespoons cider vinegar
1 tablespoon chopped fresh chives
½ teaspoon kosher salt
¼ teaspoon freshly ground black pepper

❶ Preheat oven to 450°.

❷ Place onions, carrots, and turnips on a jelly-roll pan. Drizzle with oil, and toss gently to coat. Bake at 450° for 15 minutes.

❸ Combine sorghum and vinegar. Drizzle half of sorghum mixture over carrot mixture, and toss gently to coat. Bake an additional 15 minutes or until vegetables are tender. Drizzle with remaining sorghum mixture. Sprinkle evenly with chives, salt, and pepper. Yield: 8 servings (serving size: ½ cup).

CALORIES 77; FAT 1.3g (sat 0.1g, mono 0.7g, poly 0.4g); PROTEIN 1.2g; CARB 15.9g; FIBER 2.7g; CHOL 0mg; IRON 1mg; SODIUM 205mg; CALC 50mg

Bourbon and Orange–Glazed Ham

Blackberry Farm uses Benton's country ham, from artisanal producers based in Tennessee. We call for a lower-sodium ham in this dish, but if your diet allows it, try Benton's (bentonshams.com) or another artisanal ham.

1 (8½-pound) 33%-less-sodium smoked, fully cooked ham
8 cups apple cider
2 cups fresh orange juice (about 8 medium oranges)
¾ cup bourbon
½ cup sorghum
4 black peppercorns
1 bay leaf
¼ teaspoon salt
   Cooking spray
1 cup water

① Place ham in a large stockpot; add cider and enough water to cover ham. Bring to a simmer; simmer 30 minutes. Discard cider mixture; cool ham 20 minutes. Cover and chill 8 hours. Trim rind and most of fat, leaving a ¼-inch layer of fat. Score outside of ham in a diamond pattern.
② Combine juice and next 4 ingredients in a saucepan; bring to a boil. Reduce heat; simmer until reduced to 1½ cups (about 35 minutes). Remove from heat; stir in salt.
③ Preheat oven to 350°.
④ Place ham on a rack coated with cooking spray. Pour 1 cup water into a shallow roasting pan; place rack in pan. Brush ham with juice mixture. Bake at 350° for 30 minutes. Reduce oven temperature to 300° (do not remove ham from oven); bake ham an additional 1½ hours or until a thermometer registers 140°, brushing with juice mixture every 30 minutes. Let stand 15 minutes before slicing. Yield: 34 servings (serving size: 3 ounces ham).

CALORIES 156; FAT 6.1g (sat 2g, mono 2.9g, poly 0.7g); PROTEIN 14.3g; CARB 7.9g; FIBER 0g; CHOL 51mg; IRON 1mg; SODIUM 873mg; CALC 11mg

Honey Buttermilk Rolls

1 teaspoon sugar
1 package dry yeast
½ cup warm water (100° to 110°)
17.8 ounces bread flour (about 3¾ cups), divided
¾ cup buttermilk
3 tablespoons honey
2 tablespoons butter, melted
1 teaspoon salt
   Cooking spray

① Dissolve sugar and yeast in warm water in a large bowl; let stand 5 minutes or until foamy. Weigh or lightly spoon flour into dry measuring cups; level with a knife. Add 9.5 ounces (2 cups) flour, buttermilk, and next 3 ingredients to yeast mixture; beat with a mixer at medium speed until smooth. Stir in 5.9 ounces (about 1¼ cups) flour to form a soft dough. Turn out onto a floured surface. Knead until smooth and elastic (about 8 minutes); add enough of remaining flour, 1 tablespoon at a time, to prevent dough from sticking to hands (dough will feel sticky).
② Place dough in a bowl coated with cooking spray; turn to coat top. Cover and let rise in a warm place (85°), free from drafts, 45 minutes or until doubled in size. (Gently press two fingers into dough. If indentation remains, dough has risen enough.) Punch dough down; cover and let rest 5 minutes. Divide into 24 pieces. Shape into balls. Place balls 2 inches apart on parchment-lined baking sheets. Cover; let rise 20 minutes or until doubled in size.
③ Preheat oven to 350°.
④ Uncover dough; make a (¼-inch-deep) cut in each ball using a knife. Bake at 350° for 18 minutes or until golden, rotating baking sheets after 9 minutes. Remove rolls from baking sheets; cool on wire racks. Yield: 2 dozen (serving size: 1 roll).

CALORIES 99; FAT 1.6g (sat 0.8g, mono 0.3g, poly 0.2g); PROTEIN 2.9g; CARB 18.1g; FIBER 0.6g; CHOL 4mg; IRON 0.3mg; SODIUM 113mg; CALC 4mg

Shaved Fall Vegetable Salad with Cider Vinaigrette

Sparkling cider and cider vinegar amplify the apple flavor in this fresh seasonal salad.

1 (1-pound) butternut squash, trimmed and cut into (1-inch-thick) slices
1 (12-ounce) celery root, trimmed and cut into (1-inch-thick) slices
1 large Granny Smith apple (about 7 ounces), cored and cut into (1-inch-thick) slices
1 large carrot, peeled
½ teaspoon kosher salt, divided
2 tablespoons cider vinegar
2 tablespoons sparkling apple cider
½ teaspoon honey
6 tablespoons grapeseed or canola oil
4 cups trimmed arugula leaves
½ teaspoon freshly ground black pepper

① Hold each squash slice by an end; shave into ribbons with a vegetable peeler to measure 4½ cups. Repeat procedure with celery root, shaving to measure 1½ cups. Repeat procedure with apple, shaving to measure 1 cup. Repeat procedure with carrot, shaving to measure ½ cup. Combine vegetable ribbons in a large bowl; add ¼ teaspoon salt, tossing to combine.
② Combine remaining ¼ teaspoon salt, vinegar, cider, and honey, stirring with a whisk. Gradually add oil, stirring constantly with a whisk. Add vinegar mixture to squash mixture, tossing gently to coat. Let stand 30 minutes. Add arugula just before serving, tossing to combine. Sprinkle with pepper. Yield: 8 servings (serving size: 1 cup).

CALORIES 155; FAT 10.4g (sat 1.5g, mono 7.4g, poly 1.2g); PROTEIN 1.6g; CARB 15.9g; FIBER 2.8g; CHOL 0mg; IRON 0.9mg; SODIUM 171mg; CALC 62mg

Wild Rice with Apples

If Pink Lady apples aren't available, use any crisp, sweet apple, such as Honeycrisp or Macoun, or try an heirloom variety.

- 2 tablespoons butter, divided
- 2 cups chopped Pink Lady apple
- 1 cup chopped leek
- 2 garlic cloves, minced
- 3 cups fat-free, less-sodium chicken broth
- 2 cups water
- 1 cup apple cider
- 1 teaspoon chopped fresh thyme
- 2 cups uncooked wild rice
- $\frac{1}{3}$ cup chopped pecans, toasted
- $\frac{3}{4}$ teaspoon kosher salt
- $\frac{1}{2}$ teaspoon freshly ground black pepper

❶ Melt 1 tablespoon butter in a large saucepan over medium-high heat. Add apple; sauté 7 minutes or until tender and lightly browned. Remove from pan.
❷ Reduce heat to medium. Melt remaining 1 tablespoon butter in pan. Add leek; cook 5 minutes or until tender, stirring occasionally. Add garlic; cook 30 seconds, stirring occasionally. Stir in broth and next 3 ingredients; bring to a boil. Stir in rice; reduce heat, and simmer 55 minutes or until liquid is absorbed. Drain and discard excess liquid. Return rice mixture to pan over medium heat. Stir in apple, pecans, salt, and pepper; cook 2 minutes or until thoroughly heated. Yield: 8 servings (serving size: about $\frac{3}{4}$ cup).

CALORIES 243; FAT 6.9g (sat 2.2g, mono 2.8g, poly 1.5g); PROTEIN 7.2g; CARB 40.5g; FIBER 3.6g; CHOL 8mg; IRON 1.2mg; SODIUM 370mg; CALC 23mg

Sumac-Dusted Bison with Chanterelle Sauce and Beets

Lean, tender, and mild, bison steaks—sometimes labeled buffalo—pair well with the earthy sauce. Find bison steaks at some gourmet grocers and specialty markets, or online at localharvest.org or blackwing.com.

BEETS:
- 24 baby beets (about 3 pounds)
- $\frac{1}{4}$ cup water
- $\frac{1}{2}$ teaspoon extra-virgin olive oil
- $\frac{1}{8}$ teaspoon salt
- $\frac{1}{8}$ teaspoon freshly ground black pepper

BISON:
- 8 (4-ounce) bison tenderloin steaks (about $\frac{3}{4}$ inch thick)
- $\frac{1}{2}$ teaspoon salt
- $\frac{1}{2}$ teaspoon freshly ground black pepper
- 2 tablespoons canola oil, divided
- 1 tablespoon ground sumac

SAUCE:
- 2 teaspoons canola oil
- 2 cups sliced fresh chanterelle mushrooms
- 1 tablespoon minced shallots
- $\frac{1}{4}$ teaspoon salt
- $\frac{1}{8}$ teaspoon freshly ground black pepper
- 1 small garlic clove, minced
- 1 tablespoon tomato paste
- 2 cups fat-free, less-sodium beef broth
- 1 tablespoon minced fresh parsley
- 1 tablespoon bourbon
- 1 teaspoon minced fresh thyme
- 1 teaspoon all-purpose flour
- 2 teaspoons water
- 1 tablespoon chilled butter, cut into small pieces

❶ Preheat oven to 350°.
❷ To prepare beets, leave root and 1-inch stem on beets; scrub with a brush. Place in a 13 x 9-inch baking dish; add $\frac{1}{4}$ cup water. Cover and bake at 350° for 45 minutes or until tender. Drain; cool slightly. Trim off roots; rub off skins. Cut each beet in half lengthwise; place in a bowl. Drizzle with olive oil; sprinkle evenly with $\frac{1}{8}$ teaspoon salt and $\frac{1}{8}$ teaspoon pepper, tossing gently to coat.
❸ To prepare bison, sprinkle both sides of bison with $\frac{1}{2}$ teaspoon salt and $\frac{1}{2}$ teaspoon pepper. Heat 1 tablespoon canola oil in a large nonstick skillet over medium-high heat. Add half of bison to pan; cook 2 minutes on each side or until browned. Repeat procedure with remaining bison and 1 tablespoon canola oil. Place bison on a broiler pan; sprinkle with sumac. Bake at 350° for 8 minutes or until desired degree of doneness.
❹ To prepare sauce, heat 2 teaspoons canola oil in a large nonstick skillet over medium-high heat. Add mushrooms and next 4 ingredients; sauté 4 minutes or until tender. Add tomato paste; cook 1 minute, stirring frequently. Add broth and next 3 ingredients; bring to a boil. Reduce heat; simmer 5 minutes. Combine flour and 2 teaspoons water; add flour mixture to mushroom mixture. Bring to a boil over medium heat; cook 1 minute, stirring constantly. Remove from heat. Gradually add butter to mushroom mixture, stirring until butter melts. Serve sauce with bison and beets. Yield: 8 servings (serving size: 6 beet halves, 1 bison steak, and about 2 tablespoons sauce).

CALORIES 274; FAT 8.7g (sat 2.1g, mono 4.1g, poly 1.7g); PROTEIN 28.5g; CARB 19.1g; FIBER 1.7g; CHOL 74mg; IRON 4.7mg; SODIUM 564mg; CALC 41mg

Butternut Squash Soup with Spiced Seeds

You'll find pumpkinseed kernels—also called *pepitas*—at gourmet grocers and Mexican markets.

1 tablespoon powdered sugar
1 tablespoon brown sugar
1 tablespoon egg white, lightly beaten
¼ teaspoon water
⅛ teaspoon salt
⅛ teaspoon ground cinnamon
Dash of ground red pepper
¾ cup unsalted pumpkinseed kernels
Cooking spray
1 (3½-pound) butternut squash
1 tablespoon canola oil
¾ teaspoon kosher salt, divided
4 cups fat-free, less-sodium chicken broth
2 cups water

❶ Preheat oven to 300°.
❷ Combine first 7 ingredients in a small bowl. Add seeds to sugar mixture, stirring to coat. Spread seed mixture evenly on a baking sheet lined with parchment paper and coated with cooking spray. Bake at 300° for 15 minutes. Stir mixture; bake an additional 15 minutes. Place parchment on a wire rack; cool pumpkinseed mixture. Break into small pieces; set aside.
❸ Preheat oven to 350°.
❹ Cut squash in half lengthwise; discard seeds and membrane. Brush oil over cut sides of squash; sprinkle cut sides with ¼ teaspoon salt. Place squash, cut sides down, on a jelly-roll pan. Bake at 350° for 1 hour and 20 minutes or until squash is tender. Cool slightly. Scoop out squash pulp from skins; discard skins.
❺ Place squash pulp and broth in a blender. Remove center piece of blender lid (to allow steam to escape); secure blender lid on blender. Place a clean towel over opening in blender lid (to avoid splatters). Blend until smooth. Pour pureed mixture into a medium saucepan; stir in 2 cups water and remaining ½ teaspoon salt. Cook over medium-high heat 5 minutes or until thoroughly heated. Top each serving with seeds. Yield: 8 servings (serving size: 1 cup soup and 2 tablespoons spiced seeds).

CALORIES 130; FAT 3.1g (sat 0.4g, mono 1.4g, poly 1.1g); PROTEIN 3.5g; CARB 25.2g; FIBER 3.6g; CHOL 0mg; IRON 1.4mg; SODIUM 449mg; CALC 84mg

Steamed Butternut Squash Pudding

Blackberry chefs top this pudding with sabayon featuring vanilla-infused whiskey. At the Farm, the chefs flavor a 1.5-liter bottle of Jack Daniel's whiskey for three weeks. Our adaptation cuts the infusion time back to four days; you can let the mixture stand for even less time, though the vanilla flavor will be milder.

1 (1-pound) butternut squash
Cooking spray
1 cup turbinado sugar
¼ cup butter, softened
3 large eggs
3 tablespoons fresh lemon juice
9 ounces all-purpose flour (about 2 cups)
2¼ teaspoons baking powder
1 teaspoon grated peeled fresh ginger
¾ teaspoon salt
½ teaspoon ground cinnamon
¼ teaspoon ground allspice
Vanilla Jack Sabayon (at right)

❶ Preheat oven to 400°.
❷ Cut squash in half lengthwise; discard seeds and membrane. Place squash, cut sides down, on a baking sheet coated with cooking spray; bake at 400° for 55 minutes or until tender. Cool slightly. Scoop out squash pulp from skins; discard skins. Mash pulp.
❸ Preheat oven to 325°.
❹ Place sugar and butter in a large bowl; beat with a mixer at medium speed until blended. Add eggs, 1 at a time; beat after each addition. Add squash and juice; beat until combined.
❺ Weigh or lightly spoon flour into dry measuring cups; level with a knife. Combine flour and next 5 ingredients in a medium bowl; stir with a whisk. Add flour mixture to squash mixture; beat until just combined. Spoon about ⅓ cup batter into each of 12 (6-ounce) ramekins coated with cooking spray. Place 6 ramekins in each of 2 (13 x 9-inch) baking dishes. Add hot water to pans to a depth of 1 inch. Cover pans loosely with heavy-duty foil coated with cooking spray.
❻ Bake at 325° for 22 minutes or until a wooden pick inserted in center comes out clean. Cool completely on a wire rack. Serve with Vanilla Jack Sabayon. Yield: 12 servings (serving size: 1 steamed pudding and 4 teaspoons Vanilla Jack Sabayon).

CALORIES 208; FAT 5.5g (sat 2.9g, mono 1.8g, poly 0.5g); PROTEIN 5g; CARB 34g; FIBER 1.2g; CHOL 85mg; IRON 1.7mg; SODIUM 318mg; CALC 80mg

Vanilla Jack Sabayon

¼ cup whiskey or bourbon
1 (2-inch) piece vanilla bean
¼ cup turbinado sugar
¼ cup water
⅛ teaspoon salt
2 large eggs

❶ Place whiskey and vanilla bean in a microwave-safe bowl. Microwave at HIGH 30 seconds. Cover bowl with plastic wrap; let stand up to 4 days. Strain mixture through a sieve into a bowl; discard bean.
❷ Combine infused whiskey, sugar, and remaining ingredients in the top of a double boiler. Cook over simmering water until thick and mixture reaches 160° (about 6 minutes), stirring constantly with a whisk. Remove from heat; place top of double boiler in a large ice-filled bowl, stirring whiskey mixture to cool (about 5 minutes). Serve with Steamed Butternut Squash Pudding. Yield: 12 servings (serving size: 4 teaspoons).

CALORIES 34; FAT 0.8g (sat 0.3g, mono 0.3g, poly 0.1g); PROTEIN 1.1g; CARB 3.1g; FIBER 0g; CHOL 35mg; IRON 0.2mg; SODIUM 36mg; CALC 4mg

Easy Ideas for a Healthy Breakfast

Here are some quick-fix and make-ahead options for this essential meal.

Some days a sit-down breakfast feels like something that belongs in a museum exhibit. Between getting to work, kids to school, or both, who has time to make a morning meal? You do. We've assembled recipes and ready-made options that will help you have a quick, healthy breakfast on the table (or in your tote bag) so you can rise and really shine.

Liquid Start

QUICK & EASY ▪ KID FRIENDLY

Pineapple Lassi

A frothy South Indian yogurt-based beverage, lassi often contains seasonal fruit and spices. This recipe yields a drink that's a bit thinner than the average smoothie.

- 2   cups vanilla low-fat yogurt
- 1   cup canned crushed pineapple in juice, undrained
- ¼   cup light coconut milk
- ⅛   to ¼ teaspoon bottled ground fresh ginger (such as Spice World)
- 6   ice cubes

❶ Place all ingredients in a blender; process until well blended. Serve immediately. Yield: 3 servings (serving size: about 1½ cups).

CALORIES 177; FAT 3.1g (sat 2.3g, mono 0.6g, poly 0.1g); PROTEIN 8.7g; CARB 30.1g; FIBER 0.7g; CHOL 8mg; IRON 0.5mg; SODIUM 114mg; CALC 293mg

Crunchy Start

QUICK & EASY ▪ MAKE AHEAD
KID FRIENDLY

Molasses-Almond Granola

Subdivide the batch into individual servings so it's ready when you are.

- 2   cups regular oats
- ½   cup sliced almonds
- 2   tablespoons wheat germ
- ½   teaspoon sea salt
- ¼   teaspoon ground cinnamon
- ⅓   cup dried currants
  Cooking spray
- ¼   cup dried cranberries
- 2   tablespoons sugar
- 5   tablespoons blackstrap molasses
- 3   tablespoons canola oil
- 1¼ teaspoons vanilla extract

❶ Preheat oven to 325°.
❷ Place first 3 ingredients in a food processor; pulse 10 times or until coarsely chopped. Combine oat mixture, salt, and cinnamon in a medium bowl; toss well. Spread oat mixture on a baking sheet; bake at 325° for 20 minutes or until lightly browned, stirring occasionally. Remove mixture from baking sheet; stir in currants.
❸ Cover a baking sheet with parchment paper; coat paper with cooking spray. Combine cranberries and remaining ingredients in a small saucepan over medium heat. Cook 4 minutes or until sugar dissolves, stirring frequently. Pour cranberry mixture over oat mixture, tossing to coat. Spread granola evenly on prepared baking sheet. Bake at 325° for 15 minutes or until mixture is lightly browned. Remove granola from oven, and cool completely. Break into small pieces. Store granola in an airtight container in refrigerator for up to 2 weeks. Yield: 3 cups (serving size: ⅓ cup).

CALORIES 214; FAT 8.8g (sat 0.8g, mono 4.8g, poly 2.4g); PROTEIN 4.5g; CARB 31.4g; FIBER 2.9g; CHOL 0mg; IRON 1.7mg; SODIUM 133mg; CALC 53mg

Box Cereals Our Dietitian Recommends

Best kids' cereal: Kix (1¼ cups: 110 calories, 3 grams fiber, 2 grams protein) Kix has some whole grains (whole-grain corn is the second ingredient on the ingredients list, after cornmeal). Plus, it doesn't add extrasugary calories with fruit or yogurt clusters, mini cookies, or candy bits. For a slightly sweetened cereal, this is one you can feel good about feeding your kids.

Best granola option: Mona's Original Granola (⅓ cup: 140 calories, 3 grams fiber, 4 grams protein) Seeds and nuts make granola a good source of good fats; low-fat granola removes them. Instead, pick up a box of this. You'll find A-list ingredients—sunflower seeds, wheat germ, almonds, dried fruit, and whole-grain oats—and not a speck of trans fats.

Best flake cereal: Raisin Bran (1 cup: 190 calories, 7 grams fiber, 5 grams protein) This classic choice sits smartly in the middle of the spectrum between plain flakes and overly accessorized blends. It ups the flavor factor with raisins, even as it keeps it real nutritionally. The first ingredient is whole wheat, so you get all the nutritional benefits of whole grain, plus a fiber bonus from the raisins and wheat bran.

The Best-for-You, Best-Tasting Yogurts

Nonfat and low-fat yogurts are great sources of protein and calcium. But they can also be sugar-delivery systems. Yogurt is concentrated milk, and milk contains about 12 grams of natural sugar (lactose) per serving. More than 25 grams of sugar per serving in a yogurt may mean added sugars, often in the form of jelly-like fruit on the bottom. You're better off customizing your cup with fresh or dried fruit, or choosing flavored varieties that aren't aimed at your sweet tooth.

Best plain: Chobani Non-Fat Plain
(6 ounces: 100 calories, 18 grams protein, 200 mg calcium)

Besides being loaded with 18 grams of satiating protein, this boasts the creamy thickness of Greek-style yogurt, with the watery whey strained out. This nonfat version keeps both calorie and saturated fat counts well within reasonable ranges.

Best flavored: Stonyfield Farm Organic Lowfat Blueberry
(6 ounces: 120 calories, 6 grams protein, 250 mg calcium, and 80 IU vitamin D)

Organic milk is the first ingredient; blueberries are the second. What's not to love? (Other flavors are similarly simple.) This has a modest amount of sugar, plus bone-strengthening vitamin D.

Best yogurt drink: Lifeway Organic Low-Fat Kefir
(1 cup: 160 calories, 11 grams protein, 300 mg calcium, and 100 IU vitamin D)

Technically, kefir (of Turkish origin, meaning "good feeling") is a cultured milk drink, not a yogurt. But it has similar flavor and a nutritional edge over other yogurt drinks: more protein and vitamin D, with less sugar.

Bake Ahead and Freeze
MAKE AHEAD • FREEZABLE
KID FREINDLY

Ham and Cheese Corn Muffins

7½ ounces all-purpose flour
(about 1⅔ cups)

1 cup yellow cornmeal

1 tablespoon sugar

1¼ teaspoons baking soda

½ teaspoon salt

⅛ teaspoon ground red pepper

1¼ cups low-fat buttermilk

½ cup egg substitute

3 tablespoons canola oil

¾ cup (3 ounces) reduced-fat shredded sharp Cheddar cheese

½ cup finely chopped green onions (about 1 bunch)

½ cup frozen whole-kernel corn, thawed

⅓ cup (2 ounces) diced extralean ham

Cooking spray

❶ Preheat oven to 350°.

❷ Weigh or lightly spoon flour into dry measuring cups; level with a knife. Combine flour and next 5 ingredients in a medium bowl; stir with a whisk. Make a well in center of mixture. Combine buttermilk, egg substitute, and oil; add to flour mixture, stirring just until moist. Fold in cheese and next 3 ingredients.

❸ Spoon batter into 12 muffin cups coated with cooking spray. Bake at 350° for 23 minutes or until a wooden pick inserted in center comes out clean. Remove muffins from pan; place on a wire rack. Yield: 12 muffins (serving size: 1 muffin).

CALORIES 204; FAT 6.2g (sat 1.7g, mono 2.8g, poly 1.4g); PROTEIN 8.1g; CARB 28.7g; FIBER 1.1g; CHOL 10mg; IRON 1.5mg; SODIUM 378mg; CALC 92mg

Creamy Soup Basics

Rich, silky soups don't have to be loaded with saturated fat. Follow our tips for no-guilt soups that sing.

THERE'S A COMMON NOTION AMONG CHEFS: Fat equals flavor. True, yet when making soup, throwing in cream and butter is not the only route to success. In fact, these recipes are based on aromatic ingredients, like onions and garlic, sautéed in heart-healthy olive oil, and we use dairy products (which are higher in saturated fat) in judicious ways to enrich the underlying flavor rather than carry it. From there it's simple to build on the foundation and create a bounty of hearty, comforting, and tasty soups.

Tuscan-Style Potato Soup

  2 heads garlic
2½ tablespoons olive oil, divided
  2 cups finely chopped onion, divided
  ½ teaspoon freshly ground black
     pepper
  ¼ teaspoon salt, divided
2¼ pounds cubed peeled Yukon gold
     potato (about 6 cups)
  4 cups fat-free, less-sodium
     chicken broth
  1 cup half-and-half
  4 ounces pecorino Romano cheese,
     divided
  6 ounces hot Italian sausage,
     casings removed
  1 ounce pancetta, finely chopped
  1 cup chopped kale
  ¼ cup fresh sage leaves
  2 tablespoons pine nuts, toasted

1 Preheat oven to 400°.
2 Cut off pointed end of each garlic head to partially reveal cloves (do not peel or separate cloves); place each head in center of a small sheet of heavy-duty aluminum foil. Drizzle ½ teaspoon oil over each head; wrap each in foil. Bake at 400° for 45 minutes; cool 10 minutes. Squeeze to extract pulp; discard skins.

3 Heat 2 teaspoons oil in a Dutch oven over medium-high heat. Add 1½ cups onion; cook 4 minutes, stirring frequently. Stir in pepper, ⅛ teaspoon salt, and potato; sauté 2 minutes. Add broth; bring to a boil. Reduce heat, and simmer 20 minutes or until potatoes are very tender, stirring occasionally. Place a food mill over a large bowl; pour potato mixture and garlic pulp into food mill. Press mixture through food mill; return mixture to pan. Stir in half-and-half. Finely grate 2 ounces cheese to yield ½ cup; stir into soup. Cook over medium heat 5 minutes or until thoroughly heated.
4 Heat 1½ teaspoons oil in a large skillet over medium heat. Add remaining ½ cup onion; cook 6 minutes, stirring frequently. Stir in remaining ⅛ teaspoon salt, sausage, and pancetta; cook 8 minutes or until browned, stirring to crumble sausage.
5 Cook kale in boiling water 4 minutes; strain through a sieve over a bowl, reserving ¼ cup cooking liquid. Grate 1 ounce cheese. Place kale, reserved cooking liquid, grated cheese, sage, and nuts in a food processor; process until finely ground. With processor on, gradually add remaining 1 tablespoon oil through food chute, processing until combined. Ladle 1 cup soup into each of 6 bowls; top each serving with 3 tablespoons sausage mixture. Drizzle each serving with about 4 teaspoons kale mixture; shave remaining 1 ounce cheese evenly over soup. Yield: 6 servings.

CALORIES 456; FAT 23.2g (sat 9.2g, mono 9.3g, poly 2.4g); PROTEIN 18.3g; CARB 43.8g; FIBER 4.2g; CHOL 46mg; IRON 2.8mg; SODIUM 871mg; CALC 311mg

The Basics

Add a punch of fresh flavor and color by garnishing with herbs. Scatter small, whole leaves or use torn larger leaves like basil, cilantro, or sage for a homey, rustic effect, or simply sprinkle with a mélange of chopped fresh herbs. You can also finish with a flavorful drizzle of pesto.

Turn an appetizer soup into an entrée. Simply increase the portion size, or shave on a little extra cheese. Or serve with cheesy toasts.

Crisp toppings provide a tasty contrast to smooth soups. Try homemade croutons, toasted nuts or seeds, or crumbled bacon or pancetta.

Nutrition Notes

■ Thicken soups with pureed vegetables instead of roux to minimize saturated fat.
■ Use heart-smart oil, like walnut, pumpkinseed, or olive, to garnish and add flavor to soups.

MAKE AHEAD
Black Bean Soup

1 cup dried black beans
2½ tablespoons extra-virgin olive
   oil, divided
¾ cup chopped onion
7 garlic cloves, minced and
   divided
2½ cups fat-free, less-sodium
   chicken broth
2 cups water
¼ cup no-salt-added tomato paste
1 teaspoon dried oregano
¾ teaspoon salt
¾ teaspoon ground cumin
¼ teaspoon ground red pepper
1 (4-ounce) can chopped green
   chiles
1 cup fresh cilantro leaves
½ jalapeño pepper, seeded
¼ cup crema Mexicana
3 hard-cooked large eggs, peeled
   and finely chopped
Fresh cilantro leaves (optional)

❶ Sort and wash beans, and place in a
large Dutch oven. Cover with water; cover
and let stand 8 hours. Drain beans.
❷ Heat 1½ teaspoons oil in a Dutch oven
over medium heat. Add onion; cook
4 minutes, stirring often. Add 5 garlic
cloves; cook 1 minute. Increase heat to
medium-high. Add beans, broth, and
next 7 ingredients; bring to a boil. Cover,
reduce heat, and simmer 1 hour or until
beans are tender. Let stand 10 minutes.
❸ Place half of bean mixture in a blender. Remove center piece of blender lid;
secure blender lid on blender. Place a
clean towel over opening in blender lid.
Process until smooth. Pour into a large
bowl. Repeat procedure with remaining
mixture. Return soup to pan; cook 5 minutes, stirring often.
❹ Finely chop 1 cup cilantro and jalapeño. Combine remaining 2 tablespoons
oil, remaining 2 garlic cloves, cilantro,
jalapeño, and crema. Ladle 1¼ cups
soup into each of 4 bowls; top each with
2 tablespoons crema mixture. Sprinkle

soup with eggs. Garnish with cilantro
leaves, if desired. Yield: 4 servings.

CALORIES 369; FAT 18.4g (sat 5.8g, mono 7.8g, poly 1.8g);
PROTEIN 17.5g; CARB 34.7g; FIBER 11.8g; CHOL 173mg;
IRON 4.8mg; SODIUM 829mg; CALC 114mg

MAKE AHEAD
Creamy Celeriac Soup

2 tablespoons butter
4 ounces French bread baguette, cut
   into (1-inch) cubes
1 tablespoon olive oil
3 cups sliced leek
2 tablespoons all-purpose flour
5 cups (1-inch) cubed peeled celeriac
   (celery root)
4 cups fat-free, less-sodium
   chicken broth
½ cup half-and-half
½ teaspoon black pepper
¼ teaspoon salt
Fresh parsley sprigs (optional)

❶ Preheat oven to 350°.
❷ Melt butter; toss with bread on a baking sheet. Bake at 350° for 20 minutes or
until golden.
❸ Heat oil in a Dutch oven over medium
heat. Add leek; cook 10 minutes, stirring
often. Stir in flour; cook 2 minutes, stirring well. Add celeriac and broth; bring
to a simmer. Cook 30 minutes. Let stand
10 minutes.
❹ Place half of mixture in blender.
Remove center piece of blender lid, and
secure blender lid on blender. Place a
clean towel over opening in lid. Process
until smooth. Strain pureed mixture
through a sieve over a bowl; discard
solids. Repeat procedure with remaining celeriac mixture.
❺ Return soup to pan over medium
heat; stir in half-and-half, pepper, and
salt. Cook 5 minutes. Serve with croutons. Garnish with parsley, if desired.
Yield: 4 servings (serving size: 1½ cups
soup and ½ cup croutons).

CALORIES 356; FAT 14.1g (sat 6.6g, mono 4.3g, poly 1.3g);
PROTEIN 11.1g; CARB 48.8g; FIBER 6.5g; CHOL 26mg;
IRON 4.5mg; SODIUM 906mg; CALC 185mg

3 Steps to Healthy, Creamy Soups

1 Frame the foundation. Our recipes begin by sautéing aromatic ingredients in
olive oil. This step coaxes the most flavor
from pungent onions and garlic, and provides the building blocks for the soups.

2 Simmer until soft. Next, add your star
veggies—starches like potatoes or dried
beans are popular, but most any vegetables work. Finally, add broth or other
liquid, season, and simmer until tender.

3 Puree. The hallmark of a creamy soup
is the smooth texture, so once the veggies are cooked, puree them. Blenders,
food processors, food mills, or immersion blenders can all do the trick, but the
ingredients determine the tool.

Breakfast, Lunch, and Dinner in... Chicago

First known for its modern architecture—the steel-boned skyscraper was invented here—Chicago now is a bustling, innovative food town.

CARL SANDBURG'S DESCRIPTION OF CHICAGO as the "city of big shoulders" also works for its favorite foods: big pizzas, big sandwiches, big kielbasa and beef dogs, big almost anything you could eat. Pizzas are deep-dish, like bread bowls. Italian sandwiches are heavy with beef. But this is not the whole story, nor the latest chapter. Chicago has a progressive culinary soul, according to Laurent Gras, chef at the acclaimed Lincoln Park restaurant L20. "It does not have a culinary wall," Gras says, by which he means that it absorbs the foods of its diverse citizens and also looks beyond the seemingly limitless horizon of Lake Michigan to the rest of the world. Thus did Rick Bayless, of Frontera Grill, become one of the most serious students of Mexican cuisine. Thus did Charlie Trotter become an early pioneer of all-vegetable tasting menus at his eponymous restaurant. Thus did Grant Achatz of the stunning restaurant Alinea become the country's top practitioner of molecular gastronomy. Here, *Cooking Light* takes on three classic Chicago favorites.

Breakfast

STAFF FAVORITE • KID FRIENDLY
Cinnamon Rolls

On Sunday morning, lines snake down Belmont Avenue for the sweet, spicy, heavenly cinnamon rolls at Ann Sather's (annsather.com), where its namesake owner began baking a Chicago classic breakfast favorite in 1945. Our version lightens them by using fat-free milk, not whole, and less butter in the dough.

ROLLS:

- 1   cup warm fat-free milk (100° to 110°)
- 6   tablespoons melted butter, divided
- ⅓   cup granulated sugar, divided
- 1   package quick-rise yeast
- 16.9   ounces all-purpose flour (about 3¾ cups), divided
- 1   large egg, lightly beaten
- ¼   teaspoon salt
-     Cooking spray
- ⅔   cup packed brown sugar
- 1½   tablespoons ground cinnamon

ICING:

- 3   tablespoons butter, softened
- 2   tablespoons heavy cream
- ½   teaspoon vanilla extract
- 1   cup powdered sugar

❶ To prepare rolls, combine milk, 3 tablespoons melted butter, 1 tablespoon granulated sugar, and yeast in a large bowl; let stand 5 minutes. Weigh or lightly spoon flour into dry measuring cups; level with a knife. Add egg and remaining granulated sugar to bowl. Stir in 4.5 ounces (1 cup) flour; let stand 10 minutes.

❷ Add 11.25 ounces (about 2½ cups) flour and salt to milk mixture; stir until a soft dough forms (dough will be sticky). Turn out onto a lightly floured surface. Knead until smooth and elastic (about 6 minutes); add enough of remaining flour, 1 tablespoon at a time, to prevent dough from sticking to hands. Place dough in a large bowl coated with cooking spray; turn to coat top. Cover and let rise in a warm place (85°), free from drafts, 35 minutes or until doubled in size. (Gently press two fingers into dough. If indentation remains, dough has risen enough.) Punch dough down; cover and let rise 35 minutes or until doubled in size. Punch dough down; cover and let rest 5 minutes.

❸ Combine brown sugar and cinnamon. Turn dough out onto a lightly floured surface; roll dough into an 18 x 11–inch rectangle. Brush remaining 3 tablespoons melted butter over dough; sprinkle evenly with brown sugar mixture. Beginning at one long side, roll up dough tightly, jelly-roll fashion; pinch seam to seal (do not seal ends of roll). Cut dough into 18 (1-inch) slices. Arrange 9 slices in each of 2 (8-inch) square baking dishes coated with cooking spray. Cover and let rise 35 minutes or until doubled in size.

❹ Preheat oven to 350°.

❺ Uncover rolls. Bake at 350° for 22 minutes or until lightly browned. Cool 10 minutes in dishes on a wire rack. Turn rolls out onto wire rack; cool 5 minutes. Turn rolls over.

❻ To prepare icing, combine 3 tablespoons softened butter and cream; stir with a whisk. Stir in vanilla. Gradually add powdered sugar; stir until blended. Spread icing over rolls; serve warm. Yield: 18 servings (serving size: 1 roll).

CALORIES 234; FAT 6.8g (sat 4.1g, mono 1.8g, poly 0.4g); PROTEIN 3.8g; CARB 39.6g; FIBER 1.1g; CHOL 28mg; IRON 1.7mg; SODIUM 87mg; CALC 40mg

Lunch

Italian Beef Sandwiches

Legend has it that Depression-era cooks stretched tougher cuts by roasting and simmering them in spices, slicing the meat paper thin, and stacking it into a split Italian roll. Choose toppings—such as giardiniera (a spicy Italian pepper mix) or sweet sautéed peppers—at Al's Beef (alsbeef.com), which traces its history to 1938. Specify dry or a side of "gravy" (a dipping jus of thin, aromatic broth). Our version lowers the sodium by trimming the salt in the jus. If you can't find Italian rolls, substitute a sturdy bread that will soak up the juices in this moist, delightfully messy sandwich.

    1 teaspoon dried Italian seasoning
    1 teaspoon crushed red pepper
    1 (2½ pound) rump roast, trimmed
    1 (14-ounce) can fat-free, less-sodium
       beef broth
    1 garlic clove, minced
    2 teaspoons olive oil
    1 cup coarsely chopped green bell
       pepper (about 1 medium)
    8 (2-ounce) Italian rolls
       Giardiniera (pickled vegetables),
       chopped (optional)

❶ Combine first 5 ingredients in a large zip-top bag, and marinate in the refrigerator overnight.

❷ Place beef and marinade in an electric slow cooker; cook on LOW 8 hours or until beef is tender. Place beef on a cutting board (reserve cooking liquid); let stand 10 minutes. Thinly slice beef; place in a shallow dish. Pour cooking liquid over beef.

❸ Heat oil in a large nonstick skillet over medium-high heat. Add bell pepper to pan; sauté 5 minutes or until tender. Slice rolls lengthwise, cutting to, but not through, other side. Hollow out top and bottom halves of rolls, leaving a ¾-inch-thick shell; reserve the torn bread for another use. Arrange about 3 ounces beef and 2 tablespoons bell peppers on each roll. Drizzle 1 tablespoon cooking liquid

over beef and peppers; top with giardiniera, if desired. Serve with remaining 2½ cups cooking liquid for dipping. Yield: 8 servings (serving size: 1 sandwich and about ⅓ cup cooking liquid).

CALORIES 386; FAT 11.3g (sat 3.4g, mono 4.8g, poly 1.2g); PROTEIN 39.4g; CARB 29.2g; FIBER 1.8g; CHOL 102mg; IRON 5.4mg; SODIUM 479mg; CALC 52mg

Dinner

Chicago Deep-Dish Pizza

Deep-dish pizza is the archetypal Chicago food. Pizzeria Uno (unos.com) is credited with creating the distinctive pie in 1943. The thick crust is an impressive piece of dough architecture, able to handle thick layers of cheese, meat, vegetables, and tomato sauce. The *Cooking Light* version reduces the amount of oil typically found in a deep-dish crust, adding cornmeal for the crunch that is lost when fat is reduced. We sprinkle a little bit of mozzarella on the top, although many traditional Chicago deep-dish pies keep the cheese on the bottom in a thick, oozing layer.

     2 teaspoons sugar
     1 package dry yeast
        (about 2¼ teaspoons)
     1 cup warm water (100° to 110°)
     1 tablespoon extra-virgin olive oil
  12.4 ounces all-purpose flour
        (about 2¾ cups), divided
     ¼ cup yellow cornmeal
     ½ teaspoon salt
        Cooking spray
     2 cups (8 ounces) shredded part-skim
        mozzarella cheese, divided
     2 precooked mild Italian chicken
        sausages (about 6 ounces),
        casings removed, chopped
     1 (28-ounce) can whole tomatoes,
        drained
    1½ teaspoons chopped fresh oregano
    1½ teaspoons chopped fresh basil
     2 cups thinly sliced mushrooms
        (about 6 ounces)
     ¾ cup chopped green bell pepper
     ¾ cup chopped red bell pepper

❶ Dissolve sugar and yeast in warm water in a large bowl; let stand 5 minutes. Stir in oil.

❷ Weigh or lightly spoon flour into dry measuring cups; level with a knife. Combine 11.25 ounces (about 2½ cups) flour, cornmeal, and salt in a bowl. Stir flour mixture into yeast mixture until dough forms a ball. Turn dough out onto a lightly floured surface. Knead until smooth and elastic (about 5 minutes); add enough of remaining flour, 1 tablespoon at a time, to prevent dough from sticking to hands (dough will feel sticky).

❸ Place dough in a large bowl coated with cooking spray, turning to coat top. Cover and let rise in a warm place (85°), free from drafts, 45 minutes or until doubled in size. (Gently press two fingers into dough. If indentation remains, dough has risen enough.) Punch dough down; cover and let rest 5 minutes. Roll dough into an 15 x 11–inch rectangle on a lightly floured surface. Place dough in a 13 x 9–inch baking dish coated with cooking spray; press dough up sides of dish. Spread 1½ cups cheese evenly over dough. Arrange chopped sausage evenly over cheese.

❹ Preheat oven to 400°.

❺ Chop tomatoes; place in a sieve. Stir in oregano and basil; drain tomato mixture 10 minutes.

❻ Heat a large nonstick skillet over medium heat. Coat pan with cooking spray. Add mushrooms to pan; cook 5 minutes, stirring occasionally. Stir in bell peppers; cook 8 minutes or until tender, stirring occasionally. Arrange vegetables over sausage; spoon tomato mixture evenly over vegetables and sausage. Sprinkle evenly with remaining ½ cup cheese. Bake at 400° for 25 minutes or until crust browns and cheese bubbles. Cool 5 minutes before cutting. Yield: 8 servings (serving size: 1 piece).

CALORIES 330; FAT 9.2g (sat 4.6g, mono 3.2g, poly 1g); PROTEIN 17.8g; CARB 44g; FIBER 3.2g; CHOL 31mg; IRON 3.9mg; SODIUM 365mg; CALC 244mg

Dinner Tonight

Here are seven stopwatch-tested menus from the *Cooking Light* Test Kitchens.

Shopping List

Seafood Cakes with Mustard Crema
red onion
celery
fresh parsley
stone-ground mustard
canola oil
panko
8 ounces medium shrimp
8 ounces lump crabmeat
1 ounce Parmigiano-Reggiano cheese
light sour cream
eggs

Watercress Salad
1 lemon
2 bunches watercress
olive oil
white wine vinegar
sugar

Game Plan

- Prepare sauce.
- While onion and celery cook:
  - Combine seafood mixture, and form into patties.
  - Trim watercress.
- While seafood patties cook:
  - Prepare vinaigrette.
  - Toss salad.

Seafood Cakes with Mustard Crema and Watercress Salad

···*30 minutes*

Make-Ahead Tip: Form the patties, and hold in the fridge up to 1 day.
Flavor Hit: Stone-ground mustard lends sharp, slightly spicy flavor to the sauce.
Time-Saver: Use prechopped onion and celery from your supermarket.
Buy the Best: We've discovered that some cheeses labeled "Parmigiano-Reggiano" have a waxy texture and lack the characteristic granular feel and yummy salt crystals of premium Parm-Regg. To avoid this, shop at a store that lets you sample.

⅓ cup light sour cream
6 tablespoons chopped fresh parsley, divided
1 tablespoon stone-ground mustard
½ teaspoon black pepper, divided
7 teaspoons canola oil, divided
¼ cup finely chopped red onion
¼ cup finely chopped celery
8 ounces peeled and deveined medium shrimp, chopped
8 ounces lump crabmeat, drained and shell pieces removed
¼ cup (1 ounce) grated fresh Parmigiano-Reggiano cheese
¼ teaspoon salt
2 large egg whites, lightly beaten
1 large egg, lightly beaten
1 cup panko (Japanese breadcrumbs)

❶ Combine sour cream, 2 tablespoons parsley, mustard, and ⅛ teaspoon pepper, stirring with a whisk until blended. Set aside.
❷ Heat a large nonstick skillet over medium heat. Add 1 teaspoon canola oil to pan, swirling to coat. Add onion and celery; cook 5 minutes or until tender, stirring occasionally. Remove from heat; cool slightly.
❸ Combine shrimp and crab in a large bowl. Stir in onion mixture, remaining pepper, remaining ¼ cup parsley, cheese, and next 3 ingredients; stir gently. Add panko; stir gently. Divide mixture into 8 equal portions; flatten to ½-inch-thick patties.
❹ Heat skillet over medium-high heat. Add remaining 2 tablespoons oil to pan, swirling to coat. Add patties to pan; cook 3 minutes or until lightly browned. Carefully turn over; cook 3 minutes or until done. Serve with sauce. Yield: 4 servings (serving size: 2 cakes and about 4 teaspoons sauce).

CALORIES 337; FAT 15.2g (sat 3.5g, mono 6.1g, poly 3.4g); PROTEIN 32.1g; CARB 16.1g; FIBER 1.4g; CHOL 207mg; IRON 2.6mg; SODIUM 679mg; CALC 196mg

WATERCRESS SALAD:
Combine 1 teaspoon grated lemon rind, 1 tablespoon lemon juice, 1 tablespoon olive oil, 1 teaspoon white wine vinegar, ¼ teaspoon salt, ¼ teaspoon sugar, and ¼ teaspoon pepper. Toss with 5 cups trimmed watercress.

Shopping List

Shrimp and Pine Nut Spaghetti
fresh basil
all-purpose flour
ground nutmeg
8 ounces spaghetti
pine nuts
Dijon mustard
12 ounces medium shrimp
1% milk
2 ounces Parmigiano-Reggiano cheese

Wilted Tomatoes
2 pints grape tomatoes
olive oil
balsamic vinegar

Game Plan

- While water comes to a boil:
  - Grate cheese.
- While pasta cooks:
  - Toast nuts.
  - Prepare sauce.
  - Chop and tear basil.
  - Cook tomatoes.

Continued

Shrimp and Pine Nut Spaghetti with Wilted Tomatoes

·······························*30 minutes*

Because the noodles will quickly absorb the creamy sauce, it's best to serve this calcium-rich entrée right away. It's also good with rotisserie chicken.

Flavor Hit: Toasting nuts intensifies their flavor.

Time-Saver: Purchase prepeeled and deveined shrimp from the seafood counter.

Simple Sub: Use Asiago cheese to create a sauce with slightly sharper notes.

> 8 ounces uncooked spaghetti
> 12 ounces peeled and deveined medium shrimp
> 2 tablespoons pine nuts
> 1 cup 1% low-fat milk, divided
> 1 tablespoon all-purpose flour
> ½ teaspoon Dijon mustard
> ¼ teaspoon ground nutmeg
> ¼ teaspoon salt
> ¼ teaspoon freshly ground black pepper
> ½ cup (2 ounces) grated fresh Parmigiano-Reggiano cheese
> ⅓ cup finely chopped fresh basil
> ¼ cup torn fresh basil leaves

❶ Bring 4 quarts water to a boil in a large saucepan. Add pasta; cook 7 minutes. Add shrimp to pan; cook 3 minutes or until shrimp are done and pasta is al dente. Drain; keep warm.

❷ While pasta cooks, heat a small nonstick skillet over medium heat. Add nuts to pan; cook 2 minutes or until lightly browned.

❸ Combine ½ cup milk and flour in a large saucepan, stirring with a whisk until well blended. Place pan over medium heat; gradually stir in remaining ½ cup milk. Stir in mustard and nutmeg. Bring to a boil; reduce heat to medium-low, and cook 5 minutes or until mixture begins to thicken, stirring constantly. Stir in salt and pepper; cook 1 minute. Add drained pasta mixture, cheese, and chopped basil, tossing gently to combine. Sprinkle with nuts and torn basil. Serve immediately. Yield: 4 servings (serving size: about 1 cup).

CALORIES 421; FAT 9.7g (sat 3.4g, mono 2.4g, poly 2.5g); PROTEIN 32.7g; CARB 49.1g; FIBER 2.3g; CHOL 141mg; IRON 4.6mg; SODIUM 550mg; CALC 310mg

WILTED TOMATOES:

Heat 1 teaspoon olive oil in a large nonstick skillet over medium-high heat. Add 2 pints grape tomatoes, and sauté 3 minutes or until skins begin to burst. Stir in 1 teaspoon balsamic vinegar, ⅛ teaspoon salt, and ⅛ teaspoon black pepper.

Shopping List

Eggplant and Goat Cheese Sandwiches
1 small eggplant
1 large red bell pepper
baby arugula
ciabatta bread
olive oil
refrigerated pesto
2 ounces soft goat cheese

Tomato-Parmesan Soup
2 cups boxed tomato soup
dried basil
half-and-half
Parmigiano-Reggiano cheese

Game Plan

• While broiler heats:
  • Slice eggplant.
  • Halve and seed bell pepper.
  • Slice bread.
• While vegetables broil:
  • Prepare arugula.
  • Heat soup.

Eggplant and Goat Cheese Sandwiches with Tomato-Parmesan Soup

·······························*40 minutes*

You can peel the eggplant, but the sandwiches are prettier with the deep-purple skin intact.

Buy the Best: Look for firm, deeply colored eggplant with no dents or soft spots.

Make-Ahead Tip: Hearty ciabatta holds up well, making this a good brown-bag lunch option.

Flavor Hit: Purchased pesto offers basil, Parmesan, garlic, and olive oil tastes in one handy ingredient.

> 8 (½-inch-thick) eggplant slices
> 2 teaspoons olive oil, divided
> 1 large red bell pepper
> 4 (1-ounce) slices ciabatta bread
> 2 tablespoons refrigerated pesto
> 1 cup baby arugula
> ⅛ teaspoon freshly ground black pepper
> ¼ cup (2 ounces) soft goat cheese

❶ Preheat broiler.

❷ Arrange eggplant slices in a single layer on a foil-lined baking sheet. Brush both sides of eggplant with 1 teaspoon oil. Cut bell pepper in half lengthwise; discard seeds and membrane. Arrange bell pepper halves, skin sides up, on baking sheet with eggplant; flatten with hand. Broil 4 minutes; turn eggplant over (do not turn bell pepper over). Broil an additional 4 minutes; remove eggplant from pan. Broil bell pepper an additional 7 minutes or until blackened. Place bell pepper in a zip-top plastic bag; seal. Let stand 15 minutes; peel and discard skin.

❸ Broil bread slices 2 minutes or until lightly browned, turning once. Spread 1 tablespoon pesto on each of 2 bread slices. Layer each bread slice, pesto side up, with 2 eggplant slices, 1 bell pepper half, and 2 eggplant slices. Toss arugula with remaining 1 teaspoon oil and black pepper; divide arugula mixture evenly between sandwiches. Spread 2 tablespoons goat cheese over each of 2 remaining bread slices; place, cheese side down, on sandwiches. Yield: 2 servings (serving size: 1 sandwich).

CALORIES 395; FAT 20.4g (sat 6.4g, mono 11.6g, poly 1.4g); PROTEIN 14g; CARB 43.1g; FIBER 6.7g; CHOL 18mg; IRON 3.5mg; SODIUM 635mg; CALC 108mg

TOMATO-PARMESAN SOUP:

Combine 2 cups commercial boxed tomato soup, ¼ cup half-and-half, ½ teaspoon dried basil, and ⅛ teaspoon freshly ground black pepper. Cook in a small saucepan over medium heat 8 minutes or until thoroughly heated. Stir in 2 tablespoons grated fresh Parmigiano-Reggiano cheese.

Shopping List

Two-Bean Soup with Kale
1 onion
carrots
celery
garlic
1 bunch kale
fresh rosemary
olive oil
red wine vinegar
1 quart vegetable broth
2 (15-ounce) cans no-salt-added cannellini beans
1 (15-ounce) can no-salt-added black beans

Cheese-Tomato Toasts
ciabatta bread
2 plum tomatoes
Parmigiano-Reggiano cheese

Game Plan

• While vegetables sauté:
  • Preheat broiler.
  • Chop kale.
  • Puree beans.
  • Chop rosemary.
• While soup simmers:
  • Shred cheese.
  • Slice tomato.
  • Broil toasts.

Two-Bean Soup with Kale with Cheese-Tomato Toasts
·····································•*30 minutes*

This hearty vegetarian soup warms up chilly nights. Use any type of canned beans you happen to have on hand, and add rotisserie chicken or Italian sausage for a heftier dish, if you prefer.
Simple Sub: Swiss chard, mustard greens, or escarole can stand in for kale.
Flavor Hit: A small amount of red wine vinegar brightens the taste of the soup.
Prep Pointer: Stir in fresh herbs at the end of cooking to keep their flavor vibrant.

3   tablespoons olive oil
1   cup chopped onion
½   cup chopped carrot
½   cup chopped celery
½   teaspoon salt, divided
2   garlic cloves, minced
4   cups organic vegetable broth (such as Emeril's), divided
7   cups stemmed, chopped kale (about 1 bunch)
2   (15-ounce) cans no-salt-added cannellini beans, rinsed, drained, and divided
1   (15-ounce) can no-salt-added black beans, rinsed and drained
½   teaspoon freshly ground black pepper
1   tablespoon red wine vinegar
1   teaspoon chopped fresh rosemary

❶ Heat a large Dutch oven over medium-high heat. Add oil to pan, swirling to coat. Add onion, carrot, and celery, and sauté 6 minutes or until tender. Stir in ¼ teaspoon salt and garlic; cook 1 minute. Stir in 3 cups broth and kale. Bring to a boil; cover, reduce heat, and simmer 3 minutes or until kale is crisp-tender. **❷** Place half of cannellini beans and remaining 1 cup broth in a blender or food processor; process until smooth. Add pureed bean mixture, remaining cannellini beans, black beans, and

pepper to soup. Bring to a boil; reduce heat, and simmer 5 minutes. Stir in remaining ¼ teaspoon salt, vinegar, and rosemary. Yield: 6 servings (serving size: about 1¼ cups).

CALORIES 250; FAT 10.4g (sat 1.4g, mono 5.5g, poly 2.2g); PROTEIN 11.8g; CARB 30.5g; FIBER 9.2g; CHOL 0mg; IRON 3.8mg; SODIUM 593mg; CALC 189mg

CHEESE-TOMATO TOASTS:

Broil 4 (1-ounce) slices ciabatta bread 1 minute. Turn bread over; top each slice with 2 thin plum tomato slices and 1 tablespoon shredded Parmigiano-Reggiano cheese. Broil 2 minutes or until cheese melts.

The Scoop on Kale

When choosing hearty greens like kale, select those with crisp-feeling leaves that have no signs of yellowing edges, yellow spots, or wilted leaves.

Wrap unwashed greens in damp paper towels, and refrigerate in a plastic bag up to 5 days.

Those curly leaves can trap a lot of dirt. Be sure to rinse them several times until no dirt or grit remains.

You'll need to remove and discard the tough, fibrous stems before chopping the leaves.

Shopping List

Noodles with Roast Pork and Almond Sauce

fresh ginger
green onions
fresh mint
canola oil
8 ounces fettuccine
almond butter
low-sodium soy sauce
rice vinegar
chili garlic sauce
½ pound pork tenderloin

Honey Oranges

4 large oranges
honey
ground allspice

Game Plan

- While oven preheats:
  - Bring water to a boil.
  - Season pork.
  - Mince ginger.
- While pork cooks:
  - Cook pasta.
  - Slice green onions.
  - Chop mint.
  - Section oranges.
- While pork rests:
  - Prepare sauce.
  - Prepare side dish.

QUICK & EASY

Noodles with Roast Pork and Almond Sauce with Honey Oranges

·······················*40 minutes*

Simple Sub: Replace almond butter with peanut butter.
Time-Saver: Use bottled ground fresh ginger, found in the produce section.
Vegetarian Swap: Omit pork and add roasted tofu and/or edamame.

- ½ teaspoon canola oil
- ½ pound pork tenderloin, trimmed
- ½ teaspoon salt, divided
- ¼ teaspoon black pepper
- 8 ounces uncooked fettuccine
- ¼ cup almond butter
- 2½ tablespoons low-sodium soy sauce
- 2 tablespoons rice vinegar
- 1 tablespoon minced peeled fresh ginger
- 1½ teaspoons chili garlic sauce
- 1 cup thinly sliced green onions
- ⅓ cup finely chopped fresh mint

1 Preheat oven to 425°.
2 Drizzle oil in an ovenproof skillet. Sprinkle pork with ⅛ teaspoon salt and pepper; place pork in pan. Bake at 425° for 10 minutes. Turn pork over, and bake an additional 10 minutes or until a thermometer registers 155°. Place pork on a cutting board; let stand 10 minutes. Shred pork into small pieces.
3 Cook pasta according to package directions, omitting salt and fat. Drain pasta in a colander over a bowl, reserving 2 tablespoons pasta water; keep pasta warm.
4 Combine almond butter, 2 tablespoons pasta water, remaining salt, soy sauce, and next 3 ingredients. Divide pasta evenly among 4 bowls; top evenly with sauce, pork, onions, and mint. Yield: 4 servings (serving size: about 1½ cups).

CALORIES 398; FAT 12.7g (sat 1.9g, mono 7.2g, poly 2.3g); PROTEIN 22.7g; CARB 49.3g; FIBER 3.7g; CHOL 34mg; IRON 3.7mg; SODIUM 763mg; CALC 83mg

HONEY ORANGES:

Peel and section 4 large oranges over a bowl, reserving excess juice. Combine juice, 1 tablespoon honey, and a dash of ground allspice; stir with a whisk. Add orange sections to honey mixture; toss to coat.

WINE NOTE: With a hint of candied nut to complement the almond flavor in this recipe, Hardys Stamp of Australia Chardonnay 2008 ($7) makes a great value pairing. Clean citrus and baking spice notes highlight the dish's pepper and ginger flavors. For the best value, grab the 3-liter box ($19).

Shopping List

Pecan-Crusted Trout
¼ cup pecan halves
panko
olive oil
4 (6-ounce) rainbow trout fillets

Creamy Grits
fat-free, less-sodium chicken broth
quick-cooking grits
2% milk
butter

Sautéed Broccoli Rabe
10 ounces broccoli rabe
garlic
1 lemon
olive oil

Game Plan

- While water for broccoli rabe and broth mixture for grits come to a boil:
  - Grind pecans.
  - Trim broccoli rabe.
  - Bread fillets.
- While fillets cook:
  - Cook grits.
  - Cook broccoli rabe.

Pecan-Crusted Trout with Creamy Grits and Sautéed Broccoli Rabe

......................................*30 minutes*

A pan-fried coating of ground nuts and panko yields crunchy texture. Although we loved the taste of pecans with trout, the breading would also be delicious with cod, halibut, or catfish.

Simple Sub: Use walnuts, hazelnuts, or almonds in place of pecans.

Buy the Best: Choose fish fillets with firm flesh and a sweet (not fishy) smell.

Prep Tip: Blanching the broccoli rabe removes some of its bitterness.

- ¼ cup pecan halves
- ¼ cup panko (Japanese breadcrumbs)
- 1 tablespoon olive oil, divided
- 4 (6-ounce) rainbow trout fillets, halved
- ¼ teaspoon salt
- ¼ teaspoon freshly ground black pepper

❶ Place pecans in a mini chopper or food processor; pulse until pecans are finely ground. Combine pecans and panko in a shallow dish.

❷ Heat 1½ teaspoons oil in a large non-stick skillet over medium-high heat. Sprinkle fish evenly with salt and pepper. Dredge tops of fish in nut mixture, pressing gently to adhere. Place half of fish, breading side down, in pan; cook 4 minutes or until browned. Turn fish over; cook 4 minutes or until fish flakes easily with a fork or until desired degree of doneness. Remove fish from pan; cover and keep warm. Repeat procedure with remaining 1½ teaspoons oil and re-maining fish. Yield: 4 servings (serving size: 2 fillet halves).

CALORIES 267; FAT 15.3g (sat 2.9g, mono 7.2g, poly 4.1g); PROTEIN 27.8g; CARB 3.5g; FIBER 0.8g; CHOL 75mg; IRON 0.6mg; SODIUM 203mg; CALC 91mg

CREAMY GRITS:

Bring 1 cup fat-free, less-sodium chicken broth; 1 cup 2% reduced-fat milk; and ½ teaspoon salt to a boil in a saucepan. Gradually add ½ cup quick-cooking grits, stirring constantly. Cover, reduce heat, and simmer 5 minutes or until thick, stirring occasionally. Stir in 1 tablespoon butter.

SAUTÉED BROCCOLI RABE:

Cook 10 ounces trimmed broccoli rabe in boiling water 2 minutes. Drain and plunge into ice water; drain and pat dry. Cook 2 thinly sliced garlic cloves in 2 tea-spoons olive oil in a nonstick skillet for 1 minute over medium-high heat. Add broccoli rabe and ¼ teaspoon salt; cook 1 minute. Drizzle with 1 tablespoon fresh lemon juice.

Shopping List

Spice-Rubbed Pork Chops
garlic salt
ground coriander
ground cumin
brown sugar
olive oil
2 (4-ounce) boneless pork loin chops

Sweet Potato Wedges
1 large sweet potato
olive oil
garlic salt
paprika

Lemon Green Beans
8 ounces green beans
1 lemon
olive oil

Game Plan

- While oven preheats for potatoes:
  - Coat pork with spice mixture.
  - Trim green beans.
  - Grate lemon rind.
- While potatoes cook:
  - Cook pork.
  - Steam green beans.

Spice-Rubbed Pork Chops with Sweet Potato Wedges and Lemon Green Beans

......................................*40 minutes*

A hint of brown sugar rounds out the flavors of the smoky, robust spice rub. Although this recipe serves two people, you can easily double or even triple the ingredients to serve more.

Time-Saver: Look for microwave-ready bags of fresh green beans or haricots verts in the produce section.

Flavor Hit: Lemon rind adds floral notes to simple steamed green beans.

Simple Sub: Replace coriander with paprika or smoked paprika in the spice rub.

- 2 (4-ounce) boneless pork loin chops (about ¾-inch thick)
- ⅛ teaspoon garlic salt
- ¼ teaspoon ground coriander
- ¼ teaspoon ground cumin
- ¼ teaspoon brown sugar
- 1½ teaspoons olive oil

❶ Heat a nonstick skillet over medium-high heat. Sprinkle pork with garlic salt. Combine coriander, cumin, and sugar in a shallow bowl. Sprinkle spice mixture over 1 side of pork. Add oil to pan, swirling to coat. Add pork to pan, spice side down. Cook 2 minutes or until browned. Turn over, and cook 4 minutes or until done. Yield: 2 servings (serving size: 1 pork chop).

CALORIES 193; FAT 9.8g (sat 2.8g, mono 5.3g, poly 0.8g); PROTEIN 23.9g; CARB 0.7g; FIBER 0.1g; CHOL 65mg; IRON 0.8mg; SODIUM 109mg; CALC 27mg

SWEET POTATO WEDGES:

Cut 1 large peeled sweet potato length-wise into 10 wedges. Combine potato wedges, 1 tablespoon olive oil, ¼ tea-spoon garlic salt, and ¼ teaspoon paprika; toss to coat. Arrange wedges in a single layer on a baking sheet. Bake at 500° for 16 to 20 minutes or until done, turning after 9 minutes.

Continued

LEMON GREEN BEANS:
Steam 8 ounces green beans 5 minutes or until crisp-tender. Toss with 1 teaspoon olive oil, 1 teaspoon grated lemon rind, and ¼ teaspoon salt.

WINE NOTE: Riesling is always a good choice with pork, and the smoky and spicy cumin flavors of this dish benefit from this wine's touch of fruity sweetness. Snoqualmie Winemaker's Select Riesling 2008 ($8) is a super value from Washington state. Its generous apricot fruit handles the robust spice rub, while the honeyed finish and rich texture ensure this wine won't wimp out when pitted with a bit of brown sugar.

QUICK & EASY
Couscous Pilaf

This versatile side dish pairs well with most any entrée.

- 2 teaspoons olive oil
- ½ cup chopped onion
- ½ cup finely chopped red bell pepper
- 1 cup fat-free, less-sodium chicken broth
- 1 cup uncooked couscous
- ¼ teaspoon salt
- ⅛ teaspoon black pepper
- 2 tablespoons pine nuts, toasted

❶ Heat oil in a nonstick skillet over medium-high heat. Add onion and bell pepper; sauté 7 minutes.
❷ While vegetables cook, bring broth to a boil in a medium saucepan; gradually stir in couscous. Remove from heat; cover and let stand 5 minutes. Fluff with a fork. Stir in onion mixture, salt, and black pepper. Sprinkle with nuts. Yield: 4 servings (serving size: about ¾ cup).

CALORIES 225; FAT 5.5g (sat 0.6g, mono 2.5g, poly 1.8g); PROTEIN 6.8g; CARB 37.1g; FIBER 3.1g; CHOL 0mg; IRON 0.9mg; SODIUM 266mg; CALC 17mg

SuperFast

20-minute dishes hot from the *Cooking Light* Test Kitchens!

Skinless, boneless chicken breasts are perfect for quick everyday meals. Easy ways to add big flavor: chicken broth adds rich flavor to sauces and soups, orzo is a quick-cooking versatile pasta, olive oil is great for sautéing, and black pepper's pungent notes jazz up mild poultry.

QUICK & EASY
Grilled Chicken with Mustard-Tarragon Sauce

A tangy sauce enlivens simple grilled chicken breasts; a hint of sugar balances the flavors.

- 4 (6-ounce) skinless, boneless chicken breast halves
- ½ teaspoon salt, divided
- ¼ teaspoon black pepper, divided
  Cooking spray
- 3 tablespoons minced shallots
- 3 tablespoons Dijon mustard
- 2 tablespoons red wine vinegar
- 2 tablespoons water
- 1 tablespoon extra-virgin olive oil
- 1 teaspoon chopped fresh tarragon
- ½ teaspoon sugar
- 4 cups gourmet salad greens

❶ Heat a grill pan over medium-high heat. Sprinkle chicken evenly with ¼ teaspoon salt and ⅛ teaspoon pepper. Coat pan with cooking spray. Place chicken in pan; cook 6 minutes on each side or until done.
❷ Combine remaining ¼ teaspoon salt, remaining ⅛ teaspoon pepper, shallots, and next 6 ingredients in a bowl, stirring well with a whisk. Serve chicken over greens with sauce. Yield: 4 servings (serving size: 1 breast half, 1 cup greens, and about 2 tablespoons sauce).

CALORIES 231; FAT 7.6g (sat 1.6g, mono 4.1g, poly 1.2g); PROTEIN 35.4g; CARB 3.5g; FIBER 1.3g; CHOL 94mg; IRON 2mg; SODIUM 538mg; CALC 51mg

QUICK & EASY • KID FRIENDLY
Chicken-Orzo Soup

- 1 (32-ounce) container fat-free, less-sodium chicken broth, divided
- ½ cup uncooked orzo
- 2 teaspoons olive oil
- ⅔ cup coarsely chopped carrot
- ½ cup coarsely chopped celery
- ½ cup chopped onion
- ¾ pound skinless, boneless chicken breasts, cut into ½-inch cubes
- 1¼ cups water
- 3 fresh parsley sprigs
- 1 fresh thyme sprig
- 4 cups fresh baby spinach
- 1 tablespoon fresh lemon juice
- ¼ teaspoon salt
- ⅛ teaspoon black pepper

❶ Bring 1¾ cups broth to a boil in a medium saucepan. Add orzo; cook 10 minutes or until done. Drain.
❷ While orzo cooks, heat a large saucepan over medium heat. Add oil to pan, swirling to coat. Add carrot and next 3 ingredients; cook 3 minutes, stirring constantly. Stir in remaining 2¼ cups broth, 1¼ cups water, parsley, and thyme; bring to a boil. Reduce heat; cover and simmer 10 minutes or until vegetables are tender. Discard herb sprigs. Add orzo, spinach, and next 3 ingredients; simmer 1 minute. Yield: 4 servings (serving size: about 1½ cups).

CALORIES 224; FAT 4.7g (sat 0.9g, mono 2.3g, poly 0.7g); PROTEIN 22g; CARB 22.6g; FIBER 3g; CHOL 47mg; IRON 1.5mg; SODIUM 750mg; CALC 43mg

QUICK & EASY
Chicken with Lemon-Caper Sauce

Serve over white and wild rice blend.

- 4 (6-ounce) skinless, boneless chicken breast halves
- ¼ teaspoon salt
- ¼ teaspoon black pepper
- 3 tablespoons all-purpose flour
- 2 tablespoons butter

½ cup fat-free, less-sodium chicken broth

¼ cup fresh lemon juice

2 tablespoons capers, drained

3 tablespoons minced fresh flat-leaf parsley

1 Place chicken between 2 sheets of plastic wrap; pound to an even thickness using a meat mallet or small heavy skillet. Sprinkle chicken evenly with salt and pepper. Place flour in a shallow dish; dredge chicken in flour.

2 Melt butter in a large nonstick skillet over medium-high heat. Add chicken to pan; cook 3 minutes. Turn chicken over. Add broth, juice, and capers; reduce heat to medium, and simmer 3 minutes, basting chicken occasionally with sauce. Sprinkle with parsley; cook 1 minute. Remove chicken from pan; keep warm.

3 Bring sauce to a boil; cook 2 minutes or until thick. Serve over chicken. Yield: 4 servings (serving size: 1 breast half and 1 tablespoon sauce).

CALORIES 267; FAT 7.9g (sat 4.2g, mono 2g, poly 0.7g); PROTEIN 40.5g; CARB 6.4g; FIBER 0.6g; CHOL 114mg; IRON 1.9mg; SODIUM 476mg; CALC 30mg

QUICK & EASY • KID FRIENDLY
Chicken Tacos with Mango-Avocado Salsa

Omit the jalapeño seeds for a mild salsa.

1 teaspoon garlic powder

1 teaspoon paprika

½ teaspoon onion powder

¼ teaspoon ground red pepper

¾ teaspoon salt, divided

4 (6-ounce) skinless, boneless chicken breast halves

1½ teaspoons olive oil

½ cup diced peeled mango

½ cup diced peeled avocado

½ cup chopped tomato

⅓ cup prechopped onion

2 tablespoons chopped fresh cilantro

2 tablespoons fresh lime juice

1 tablespoon minced jalapeño pepper

8 (6-inch) corn tortillas

1 Heat a nonstick skillet over medium-high heat. Combine first 4 ingredients; stir in ½ teaspoon salt. Rub over chicken. Add oil to pan, swirling to coat. Add chicken; cook 4 minutes on each side or until done. Remove chicken from pan; let stand 5 minutes. Cut into ¼-inch-thick slices.

2 While chicken cooks, combine mango and next 6 ingredients; stir in remaining ¼ teaspoon salt.

3 Heat tortillas according to package directions; top with chicken and salsa. Yield: 4 servings (serving size: 2 tortillas, 1 chicken breast half, and ½ cup salsa).

CALORIES 379; FAT 8.2g (sat 1.5g, mono 3.9g, poly 1.7g); PROTEIN 43.4g; CARB 33.1g; FIBER 4.9g; CHOL 99mg; IRON 2.4mg; SODIUM 643mg; CALC 124mg

QUICK & EASY • KID FRIENDLY
Chicken Cacciatore

Serve over a bed of spaghetti or other pasta.

1 pound skinless, boneless chicken breast, cut into bite-sized pieces

1 teaspoon dried oregano

½ teaspoon dried basil

¼ teaspoon crushed red pepper
Cooking spray

2 cups sliced cremini mushrooms

¾ cup prechopped bell pepper

1½ cups tomato-basil pasta sauce

¼ cup dry red wine

¼ teaspoon salt

¼ teaspoon black pepper

½ cup (about 2 ounces) shaved Parmigiano-Reggiano cheese

2 tablespoons thinly sliced fresh basil

1 Heat a large nonstick skillet over medium-high heat. Sprinkle chicken evenly with oregano, dried basil, and red pepper. Coat pan with cooking spray. Add chicken to pan, and sauté 2 minutes or until lightly browned, stirring frequently. Add mushrooms and bell pepper to pan; sauté 5 minutes. Stir in pasta sauce and wine; bring to a simmer. Cover, reduce heat, and simmer

10 minutes. Stir in salt and black pepper. Sprinkle with cheese and fresh basil. Yield: 4 servings (serving size: about 1 cup chicken mixture, 2 tablespoons cheese, and 1½ teaspoons basil).

CALORIES 239; FAT 6g (sat 2.7g, mono 1.4g, poly 0.5g); PROTEIN 34.2g; CARB 11.1g; FIBER 2.6g; CHOL 75mg; IRON 2.1mg; SODIUM 746mg; CALC 266mg

QUICK & EASY
Steamed Chicken and Vegetables with Soy Dipping Sauce

4 (6-ounce) skinless, boneless chicken breast halves

¼ teaspoon salt

¼ teaspoon black pepper

3 cups (2-inch) slices asparagus

1 cup halved sugar snap peas

¼ cup coarsely chopped fresh cilantro

¼ cup low-sodium soy sauce

2 tablespoons rice vinegar

2 tablespoons mirin (sweet rice wine)

½ teaspoon dark sesame oil

1 Sprinkle chicken with salt and pepper; arrange chicken in a large vegetable steamer. Add water to a large saucepan to a depth of 1 inch; bring to a boil. Place steamer in pan; cover and steam chicken 10 minutes. Add asparagus and peas to steamer; cover and cook 2 minutes or until vegetables are crisp-tender.

2 Combine cilantro and remaining ingredients, stirring with a whisk. Serve sauce with chicken and vegetables. Yield: 4 servings (serving size: 1 breast half, about ¾ cup vegetables, and 2 tablespoons sauce).

CALORIES 250; FAT 4.7g (sat 1.2g, mono 1.6g, poly 1.1g); PROTEIN 37.9g; CARB 9.8g; FIBER 2.7g; CHOL 94mg; IRON 3.7mg; SODIUM 766mg; CALC 58mg

Simple Additions

Green Curry Chicken

A full tablespoon of curry paste makes this a boldly spicy dish. Use 2 teaspoons if you prefer milder flavor.

1 cup uncooked
basmati rice

1 pound (1-inch) cubed
chicken breast tenders

2 to 3 teaspoons
green curry paste

1 (14-ounce) can
light coconut milk,
divided

2 cups tricolor
prechopped bell
pepper mix

Directions: Cook rice according to package directions, omitting salt and fat. Stir in ¼ teaspoon salt. Heat a large nonstick skillet over medium-high heat. Coat pan with cooking spray. Sprinkle chicken with ¼ teaspoon salt. Add chicken to pan; sauté 4 minutes or until chicken is lightly browned. Stir in curry paste; cook 1 minute, stirring frequently. Stir in 1 cup coconut milk; bring to a boil. Reduce heat, and simmer 4 minutes or until chicken is done, stirring occasionally. Stir in bell pepper mix, ¼ teaspoon salt, and remaining coconut milk; cook 3 minutes or until vegetables are tender. Serve chicken mixture over rice. Sprinkle with fresh cilantro leaves, if desired. Yield: 4 servings (serving size: about ¾ cup rice and ¾ cup chicken mixture).

CALORIES 282; FAT 6.8g (sat 5.4g, mono 0.4g, poly 0.4g); PROTEIN 29.7g; CARB 25.9g; FIBER 1.5g; CHOL 66mg; IRON 1.7mg; SODIUM 606mg; CALC 20mg

Mushroom Frittata

This vegetarian entrée is ideal for a light breakfast or brunch, but you can also serve it for dinner paired with a simple side salad.

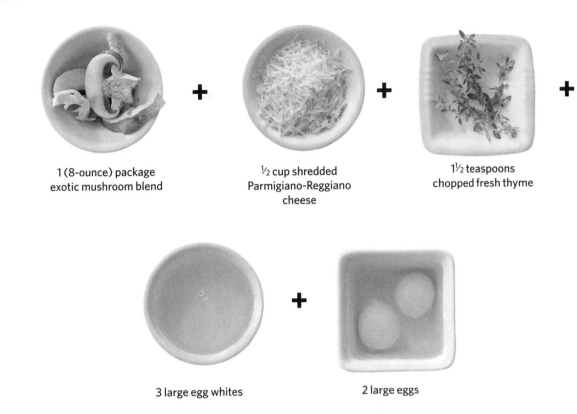

1 (8-ounce) package exotic mushroom blend

+

½ cup shredded Parmigiano-Reggiano cheese

+

1½ teaspoons chopped fresh thyme

+

3 large egg whites

+

2 large eggs

Directions: Preheat broiler. Heat an 8-inch ovenproof skillet over medium-high heat. Coat pan with cooking spray. Add mushrooms to pan; sauté 12 minutes or until lightly browned. Place mushrooms in a medium bowl; cool slightly. Wipe pan clean with paper towels. Combine mushrooms, cheese, thyme, ¼ teaspoon freshly ground black pepper, ⅛ teaspoon salt, egg whites, and eggs in a medium bowl, stirring well with a whisk. Heat pan over medium heat. Coat pan with cooking spray. Add mushroom mixture; cook, covered, 3 minutes or until almost set. Broil 3 minutes or until egg is set. Cut into 4 wedges. Yield: 4 servings (serving size: 1 wedge).

CALORIES 122; FAT 6.4g (sat 3.2g, mono 2.2g, poly 0.4g); PROTEIN 13.3g; CARB 3g; FIBER 0.8g; CHOL 116mg; IRON 0.9mg; SODIUM 401mg; CALC 195mg

Mango Pork with Wild Rice Pilaf

Sweet-tangy chutney works its way into both the meat and the rice in this zesty dish.

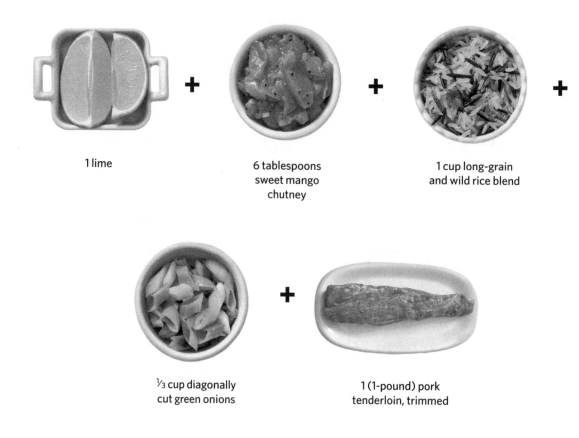

1 lime

+

6 tablespoons
sweet mango
chutney

+

1 cup long-grain
and wild rice blend

+

⅓ cup diagonally
cut green onions

+

1 (1-pound) pork
tenderloin, trimmed

Directions: Preheat oven to 400°. Grate 1 teaspoon lime rind; squeeze 1½ tablespoons lime juice over a small bowl. Combine 1 tablespoon juice, ½ teaspoon rind, and chutney in a medium bowl. Cook rice according to package directions, omitting salt and fat. Stir in onions, 2 tablespoons chutney mixture, 1½ teaspoons juice, ½ teaspoon rind, ¼ teaspoon salt, and ⅛ teaspoon pepper. Sprinkle pork with ¼ teaspoon salt and ⅛ teaspoon pepper. Heat a large ovenproof skillet over medium-high heat. Coat pan with cooking spray. Add pork to pan; cook 4 minutes, browning on all sides. Place pan in oven; bake at 400° for 10 minutes or until thermometer registers 155°. Spoon ¼ cup chutney mixture over pork. Cover loosely with foil; let stand 5 minutes or until temperature reaches 160° (slightly pink). Cut pork into thin slices; serve with rice. Yield: 4 servings (serving size: 3 ounces pork and about ¾ cup rice).

CALORIES 285; FAT 4.1g (sat 1.5g, mono 1.8g, poly 0.4g); PROTEIN 25.3g; CARB 34g; FIBER 1.1g; CHOL 74mg; IRON 2mg; SODIUM 793mg; CALC 23mg

Our Favorite Tarte Tatin

Caramel-bathed apples nestle in a tender crust, while crème fraîche lends a little French tang to this fall classic.

KID FRIENDLY
Tarte Tatin

6.75 ounces all-purpose flour (about 1½ cups)
¼ teaspoon salt
6 tablespoons butter, softened
6 tablespoons water, divided
1 large egg
1 cup sugar
2 pounds Golden Delicious apples, peeled, cored, and quartered (about 6 small)
¼ teaspoon ground cinnamon
10 teaspoons crème fraîche

❶ Weigh or lightly spoon flour into dry measuring cups; level with a knife. Place flour and salt in a medium bowl; cut in butter with a pastry blender or 2 knives until mixture resembles coarse meal. Combine 2 tablespoons water and egg, stirring with a whisk. Add egg mixture to flour mixture, stirring just until moist. Turn dough out onto a large piece of heavy-duty plastic wrap; knead lightly 5 times (dough will be sticky). Pat dough into a disk. Cover with additional plastic wrap; chill 30 minutes.
❷ Combine remaining ¼ cup water and sugar in a 9-inch cast-iron skillet over medium-high heat. Cook 10 minutes or until golden, stirring only until sugar dissolves. Remove from heat; gently stir in small circles to evenly distribute cooked sugar. Let stand 5 minutes.
❸ Arrange apple quarters tightly in a circular pattern over sugar in pan, beginning at outside edge. Cut 2 apple quarters in half, and arrange, points up, in center of pan. Place pan over medium heat; cook 20 minutes (do not stir), pressing apples slightly to extract juices. Remove from heat; let stand 10 minutes. Sprinkle cinnamon over apples.
❹ Preheat oven to 400°.
❺ Remove plastic wrap covering dough. Turn dough onto a lightly floured surface; roll dough into an 11-inch circle. Place over apple mixture, fitting dough between apples and skillet. Bake at 400° for 20 minutes or until lightly browned. Cool 10 minutes. Invert tart onto a plate. Serve with crème fraîche. Yield: 10 servings (serving size: 1 slice tart and 1 teaspoon crème fraîche).

CALORIES 275; FAT 9.3g (sat 5.6g, mono 2g, poly 0.4g); PROTEIN 3.1g; CARB 46.3g; FIBER 1.7g; CHOL 44mg; IRON 1.1mg; SODIUM 115mg; CALC 13mg

Pork and Pinto Bean Nachos

Underneath all the fat in American-style nachos lies some healthy eating. We put a classic fast food into a good nutritional niche.

A plate of nachos satisfies a comfort-food craving. A lot less comforting: That nacho serving exceeds daily needs for sodium, saturated fat, and calories for breakfast, lunch, and dinner.

We saw the good-for-you potential in the traditional toppings of meat, veggies, and avocados, but we didn't want to skimp on the crunchy-salty-cheesy deliciousness in our lighter version. Serve with a cool margarita… and don't feel bad about taking a nice siesta afterward.

serving size: 1 ounce chips, ½ cup beans, ⅓ cup pork, and ½ cup topping		
	before	after
CALORIES PER SERVING	1,258	517
TOTAL FAT	74.6g	26.9g
SATURATED FAT	29g	6.8g
SODIUM	2,199mg	991mg

KID FRIENDLY
Pork and Pinto Bean Nachos

MEAT:
1 (1-pound) pork tenderloin, trimmed
2 tablespoons olive oil, divided
½ teaspoon salt, divided
¼ teaspoon black pepper
Cooking spray
2 tablespoons fresh lime juice
1 teaspoon minced garlic

BEANS:
1 can chipotle chiles in adobo sauce
2 tablespoons water
2 teaspoons fresh lime juice
1 teaspoon chili powder
¼ teaspoon salt
2 (15-ounce) cans pinto beans, rinsed and drained
4 applewood-smoked bacon slices, cooked and crumbled

SALSA:
1½ cups chopped plum tomato
1 cup diced avocado
½ cup chopped jicama
⅓ cup chopped onion
2 tablespoons fresh lime juice
1 tablespoon olive oil
¼ teaspoon salt

REMAINING INGREDIENTS:
6 ounces sturdy tortilla chips (8 cups)
1¼ cups (5 ounces) shredded reduced-fat Colby and Monterey Jack cheese blend
¼ cup chopped fresh cilantro
1 jalapeño pepper, thinly sliced

❶ Preheat oven to 500°.
❷ To prepare pork, rub with 1 tablespoon oil, ¼ teaspoon salt, and black pepper. Place pork in a shallow roasting pan coated with cooking spray. Bake at 500° for 23 minutes or until a thermometer registers 160°. Remove from pan; cool 10 minutes. Shred pork with two forks to measure 2 cups; place in a small bowl. Stir in remaining 1 tablespoon oil, remaining ¼ teaspoon salt, 2 tablespoons juice, and garlic.

Continued

③ To prepare beans, remove 2 chipotle chiles and 1 teaspoon adobo sauce from can; reserve remaining chiles and sauce for another use. Drop chiles through food chute with food processor on; pulse 3 times or until coarsely chopped. Add adobo sauce, water, and next 4 ingredients; process 5 seconds or until smooth. Stir in bacon.

④ Preheat broiler.

⑤ To prepare salsa, combine tomato and next 6 ingredients; toss well to coat.

⑥ Arrange tortilla chips in a single layer on a large rimmed baking sheet. Top evenly with bean mixture; top with meat mixture, and sprinkle with cheese. Broil 4 minutes or until cheese melts. Top evenly with salsa, cilantro, and jalapeño. Serve immediately. Yield: 6 servings (serving size: 1 ounce chips, ½ cup beans, ⅓ cup pork, and ½ cup salsa).

CALORIES 517; FAT 26.9g (sat 6.8g, mono 12.4g, poly 3.3g); PROTEIN 31.4g; CARB 38.4g; FIBER 8.9g; CHOL 66mg; IRON 3.3mg; SODIUM 991mg; CALC 248mg

Special Occasion Recipe

STAFF FAVORITE
Lobster Américaine

Though this recipe requires some involved steps, they're more than worth the effort. .

LOBSTERS:
2   (2-pound) whole Maine lobsters
SAUCE:
1   tablespoon canola oil
½   cup sliced shallots
2   tablespoons sliced garlic
1½ tablespoons black peppercorns
2   tablespoons tomato paste
½   cup brandy
½   cup vermouth
2   cups Shrimp Stock (at right)
¼   cup whipping cream
1   fresh basil sprig

2   fresh tarragon sprigs
½   teaspoon fine sea salt, divided
⅛   teaspoon freshly ground white pepper
BEURRE MONTÉ:
2   tablespoons water
½   cup unsalted butter, cut into large pieces

① To prepare lobsters, plunge a heavy chef's knife through each head just above eyes, making sure knife goes all the way through the head. Pull knife in a downward motion between eyes. Twist off claws where they join bodies; set claws aside. Twist off tails from bodies. Reserve bodies. Place tails on a cutting board; press to flatten. Cut in half lengthwise. Remove vein that runs down center of each tail. Cover and refrigerate tails.

② Bring a large saucepan of water to a boil. Add claws to boiling water; cook 5 minutes. Remove claws from pan, and cool. Separate knuckles from claws. Remove meat from knuckles and claws.

③ To prepare sauce, heat oil in a large, shallow saucepan over medium-high heat. Add lobster bodies to pan; cook 5 minutes, stirring occasionally. Add shallots and garlic; sauté 1 minute. Add peppercorns and tomato paste; reduce heat to medium, and cook 1 minute, stirring constantly. Stir in brandy and vermouth; cook until liquid is reduced by half (about 5 minutes). Add 2 cups Shrimp Stock; bring to a boil. Reduce heat to low, and simmer 10 minutes. Add cream, basil, and tarragon; simmer 5 minutes. Strain mixture through a fine sieve over a bowl. Discard solids. Stir in ¼ teaspoon salt and white pepper. Keep warm.

④ Preheat oven to 350°.

⑤ To prepare beurre monté, bring 2 tablespoons water to a simmer in a small saucepan. Add butter, 1 tablespoon at a time, stirring constantly with a whisk until butter melts.

⑥ Sprinkle remaining ¼ teaspoon salt over tails. Brush 3 tablespoons beurre monté over tails. Arrange tails in a

baking dish. Bake at 350° for 10 minutes or until done. Add claw and knuckle meat to remaining beurre monté; cook over low heat until thoroughly heated.

⑦ Remove tail meat from shells; place one piece of tail meat in each of 4 shallow bowls. Divide knuckle and claw meat evenly among servings, and discard remaining beurre monté. Spoon ½ cup sauce over each serving. Yield: 4 servings.

CALORIES 395; FAT 22.2g (sat 11.1g, mono 7.4g, poly 2.2g); PROTEIN 18g; CARB 12.3g; FIBER 2g; CHOL 130mg; IRON 1.9mg; SODIUM 852mg; CALC 76mg

Shrimp Stock

1½ teaspoons canola oil
1   pound whole small shrimp, unpeeled
¼   cup diced onion
2   tablespoons diced carrot
2   tablespoons diced celery
1   cup tomato paste
5   cups cold water

① Heat oil in a large Dutch oven over medium-high heat. Add shrimp to pan; sauté 2 minutes or until shells turn bright orange. Add onion, carrot, and celery; sauté 3 minutes or until tender. Add tomato paste, stirring well with a wooden spoon. Cook 8 minutes or until tomato paste turns orange, stirring constantly. Add 5 cups water; bring to a boil. Remove from heat.

② Place half of shrimp mixture in a blender. Remove center piece of blender lid (to allow steam to escape); secure blender lid on blender. Place a clean towel over opening in blender lid (to avoid splatters). Blend until smooth. Pour into a large bowl. Repeat procedure with remaining shrimp mixture. Return to pan. Bring to a simmer over medium heat; remove from heat. Let stand 10 minutes. Strain shrimp mixture through a fine sieve over a bowl. Discard solids. Yield: 4 cups (serving size: ½ cup).

CALORIES 41; FAT 1.1g (sat 0.1g, mono 0.6g, poly 0.4g); PROTEIN 2.6g; CARB 6.4g; FIBER 1.5g; CHOL 9mg; IRON 1.1mg; SODIUM 267mg; CALC 15mg

FROM YOUR KITCHEN TO OURS
Reader Recipes

At the heart of Lorraine Fina Stevenski's Italian heritage are family gatherings complete with many traditional recipes. She's created hundreds of dishes over the years, but her favorites always take her back to her roots. "Amaretto is a classic Italian almond-flavored liqueur, so I just couldn't resist adding a hint to my homemade cupcakes."

MAKE AHEAD • FREEZABLE

Amaretto Apple Streusel Cupcakes

(pictured on page 233)

"I've been baking lightened cupcakes for years, so I know that fat is critical for texture and flavor. The small amounts of butter and cream cheese used in this batter make them taste like you aren't sacrificing a thing. These are wonderful served warm."

—Lorraine Fina Stevenski
Clearwater, Florida

CUPCAKES:
Cooking spray
6.75 ounces all-purpose flour (about 1½ cups)
½ teaspoon baking powder
¼ teaspoon salt
¼ teaspoon baking soda
¾ cup granulated sugar
¼ cup (2 ounces) ⅓-less-fat cream cheese, softened
¼ cup butter, softened
2 tablespoons amaretto (almond-flavored liqueur)
1 teaspoon vanilla extract
1 large egg
½ cup reduced-fat sour cream
¼ cup 2% reduced-fat milk
¾ cup finely chopped Gala apple
1 tablespoon all-purpose flour

STREUSEL:
2 tablespoons all-purpose flour
2 tablespoons brown sugar
¼ teaspoon ground cinnamon
2 tablespoons butter, chilled
2 tablespoons sliced almonds
GLAZE:
1 cup powdered sugar
4 teaspoons 2% reduced-fat milk

1 Preheat oven to 350°.
2 Place muffin cup liners in 12 muffin cups; coat with cooking spray.
3 Weigh or lightly spoon 6.75 ounces (about 1½ cups) flour into dry measuring cups; level with a knife. Combine 6.75 ounces flour and next 3 ingredients in a small bowl, stirring with a whisk. Combine granulated sugar, cream cheese, and ¼ cup butter in a large bowl; beat with a mixer at high speed until well blended. Add amaretto, vanilla, and egg to sugar mixture; beat with a mixer at medium speed until well blended. Combine sour cream and ¼ cup milk in a small bowl; stir with a whisk until well blended. Combine apple and 1 tablespoon flour in a small bowl; toss well.
4 Add flour mixture and sour cream mixture alternately to sugar mixture, beginning and ending with flour mixture. Beat just until blended. Fold in apple mixture. Divide batter evenly among prepared muffin cups.
5 To prepare streusel, combine 2 tablespoons flour, brown sugar, and cinnamon in a bowl. Cut in 2 tablespoons butter with a pastry blender or 2 knives until mixture resembles coarse meal; stir in almonds. Sprinkle streusel evenly over cupcakes. Bake at 350° for 27 minutes or until a wooden pick inserted in center comes out clean. Cool in pan 15 minutes on a wire rack, and remove cupcakes from pan.
6 To prepare glaze, combine powdered sugar and 4 teaspoons milk in a bowl, stirring with a whisk. Drizzle over cupcakes. Yield: 12 servings (serving size: 1 cupcake).

CALORIES 256; FAT 9g (sat 5.3g, mono 2.3g, poly 0.5g); PROTEIN 3.5g; CARB 39.9g; FIBER 0.8g; CHOL 40mg; IRON 1mg; SODIUM 172mg; CALC 43mg

MAKE AHEAD • FREEZABLE
KID FRIENDLY

Eileen's Best Banana Bread

"When I finally created a version I was happy with, this bread became a breakfast favorite. My son in college requests a loaf be sent to him regularly."

—Eileen Solberg,
Billings, Montana

3.4 ounces all-purpose flour (about ¾ cup)
3.6 ounces whole-wheat flour (about ¾ cup)
¼ cup flaxseed meal
1 teaspoon baking powder
½ teaspoon salt
½ teaspoon baking soda
1 cup mashed ripe banana
½ cup chopped walnuts
¾ cup sugar
½ cup plain low-fat yogurt
¼ cup canola oil
Cooking spray

1 Preheat oven to 325°.
2 Weigh or lightly spoon flours into dry measuring cups; level with a knife. Combine flours and next 4 ingredients in a large bowl, stirring with a whisk. Combine banana and next 4 ingredients in a small bowl. Add banana mixture to flour mixture, stirring just until moist.
3 Spoon batter into a 9 x 5-inch loaf pan coated with cooking spray. Bake at 325° for 1 hour and 15 minutes or until a wooden pick inserted into center comes out clean. Cool 10 minutes in pan on a wire rack, and remove from pan. Cool on wire rack. Yield: 12 servings (serving size: 1 slice).

CALORIES 212; FAT 9.2g (sat 0.8g, mono 3.7g, poly 4.2g); PROTEIN 4.3g; CARB 30.4g; FIBER 2.6g; CHOL 1mg; IRON 1.1mg; SODIUM 189mg; CALC 60mg

Black Bean-Salsa Chili

"My new and improved chili's spiciness depends on the salsa—use medium or hot salsa if you want to turn up the heat, and if you want it fiery, increase the crushed red pepper."

—Barbara Estabrook,
Rhinelander, Wisconsin

 2 (15-ounce) cans black beans, rinsed, drained, and divided
 ⅔ cup water
 1 tablespoon dark brown sugar
 Cooking spray
 ½ pound ground turkey
 1 cup chopped sweet onion
 ½ cup chopped green bell pepper
 ½ cup chopped red bell pepper
 3 sweet hickory-smoked bacon slices, chopped
 1½ tablespoons chili powder
 1 tablespoon ground cumin
 1 teaspoon dried oregano
 ⅛ teaspoon crushed red pepper
 1½ cups mild salsa
 3 tablespoons tomato paste
 1 (14-ounce) can fat-free, less-sodium beef broth
 ½ cup reduced-fat sour cream
 ¼ cup chopped fresh cilantro
 1 teaspoon fresh lime juice

1 Place 1½ cups beans, ⅔ cup water, and sugar in a food processor; process until smooth. Combine bean puree and remaining beans in a bowl.
2 Heat a large saucepan over medium-high heat. Coat pan with cooking spray. Add turkey; cook 3 minutes or until browned, stirring to crumble. Remove turkey from pan.
3 Add onion and next 3 ingredients to pan; cook 5 minutes or until bacon and onion are lightly browned. Return turkey to pan. Add chili powder and next 3 ingredients to pan; stir well to coat. Stir in bean mixture, salsa, tomato paste, and broth; bring to a boil. Reduce heat; simmer 30 minutes, stirring occasionally.

4 Combine sour cream, cilantro, and juice in a small bowl. Serve chili with sour cream mixture. Yield: 6 servings (serving size: 1 cup chili and about 4 teaspoons sour cream mixture).

CALORIES 199; FAT 6.2g (sat 2.6g, mono 1.9g, poly 1.2g); PROTEIN 14.8g; CARB 22g; FIBER 5.9g; CHOL 34mg; IRON 2.6mg; SODIUM 740mg; CALC 88mg

Spicy Turkey Meat Loaf with Ketchup Topping

To update my mother's meat loaf, I added vegetables for moisture and nutrition. To create flavor without adding fat, I use herbs and spices, including Sriracha for a spicy kick. But I wouldn't dare change the ketchup topping. Mom's used that for more than 50 years!"

—Dan Kailukaitis, Bethesda, Maryland

 1 tablespoon butter
 2 cups chopped onion
 1 (8-ounce) package presliced mushrooms
 3 garlic cloves, chopped
 ¾ cup panko (Japanese breadcrumbs)
 ¼ cup fat-free, less-sodium chicken broth
 3 tablespoons chopped fresh flat-leaf parsley
 1 tablespoon low-sodium soy sauce
 1 tablespoon Sriracha (hot chile sauce, such as Huy Fong)
 1 tablespoon Worcestershire sauce
 ½ teaspoon freshly ground black pepper
 1½ pounds ground turkey breast
 1 large egg, lightly beaten
 Cooking spray
 ½ cup ketchup
 1 tablespoon brown sugar
 ⅛ teaspoon dry mustard
 ⅛ teaspoon ground nutmeg

1 Preheat oven to 350°.
2 Melt butter in a large nonstick skillet over medium heat. Add onion, mushrooms, and garlic to pan; cook 8 minutes, stirring occasionally. Remove from heat; cool 5 minutes.
3 Combine mushroom mixture, panko, and next 8 ingredients in a large bowl; stir well to combine. Shape turkey mixture into a 9 x 5–inch rectangle on a broiler pan coated with cooking spray.
4 Combine ketchup and remaining ingredients in a bowl, stirring with a whisk. Spread ketchup mixture evenly over top of meat loaf; bake at 350° for 40 minutes or until a thermometer registers 160°. Let stand 10 minutes before serving. Yield: 8 servings (serving size: 2 slices).

CALORIES 184; FAT 3.7g (sat 1.6g, mono 1g, poly 0.5g); PROTEIN 23.2g; CARB 15g; FIBER 1.2g; CHOL 69mg; IRON 1.3mg; SODIUM 405mg; CALC 30mg

Holiday Cookbook

A dollop of tradition. A sprinkling of the new. Served up with joy!

Starters & Drinks

Raise a toast, nibble a savory appetizer, then sit down to a comforting soup or seasonal salad. These recipes set the tone for easy holiday entertaining.

MAKE AHEAD
Citrus, Fennel, and Rosemary Olives

A mix of fruity and meaty olives works well in this treatment. They are ideal for cocktail platters, antipasto, snacking, or as a gift when placed in a decorative jar.

- 22 ounces (about 4 cups) assorted olives (such as niçoise, arbequina, kalamata, and picholine)
- 2 cups extra-virgin olive oil
- 1 cup finely chopped fennel bulb
- 1 tablespoon chopped fresh flat-leaf parsley
- 1½ teaspoons chopped fresh rosemary
- 1 teaspoon grated lemon rind
- ¾ teaspoon crushed red pepper
- 3 garlic cloves, minced

❶ Combine all ingredients in a large bowl; stir well to combine. Cover and refrigerate 48 hours. Serve at room temperature. Yield: 5 cups (serving size: 2 tablespoons).
NOTE: Refrigerate up to 1 month.

CALORIES 45; FAT 4.3g (sat 0.6g, mono 3.3g, poly 0.5g); PROTEIN 0.3g; CARB 1.4g; FIBER 0.2g; CHOL 0mg; IRON 0.1mg; SODIUM 200mg; CALC 6mg

Candied Walnut, Pear, and Leafy Green Salad

The sweet, crunchy nuts are great on their own—make a double batch, and give some as a gift.

- ⅓ cup sugar
- ⅔ cup chopped walnuts, toasted
  Cooking spray
- ½ teaspoon kosher salt, divided
- 2 tablespoons white balsamic vinegar
- 1½ teaspoons Dijon mustard
- 3 tablespoons extra-virgin olive oil
- 1 tablespoon capers, chopped
- 4 cups torn green leaf lettuce
- 4 cups chopped romaine lettuce
- 4 cups chopped radicchio
- 1 ripe red Anjou pear, thinly sliced
- ¼ teaspoon freshly ground black pepper

❶ Place sugar in a small, heavy saucepan over medium-high heat; cook until sugar dissolves, stirring gently as needed to dissolve sugar evenly (about 1 minute). Continue cooking 1 minute or until golden (do not stir). Remove from heat; carefully stir in nuts to coat evenly. Spread nuts on a baking sheet coated with cooking spray; separate nuts quickly. Sprinkle with ¼ teaspoon salt. Set aside until cool; break into small pieces.
❷ Combine vinegar and mustard, stirring with a whisk. Gradually add oil, stirring constantly with a whisk. Stir in capers.
❸ Combine lettuces and radicchio; top with pear and candied walnuts. Drizzle dressing evenly over salad; sprinkle with remaining ¼ teaspoon salt and pepper.

Toss gently to combine. Yield: 8 servings (serving size: about 1 cup).

CALORIES 171; FAT 11.6g (sat 1.3g, mono 4.6g, poly 5.2g); PROTEIN 2.7g; CARB 16.3g; FIBER 2.6g; CHOL 0mg; IRON 1mg; SODIUM 177mg; CALC 37mg

WINE NOTE: A crisp white works well with almost any green salad, and Candied Walnut, Pear, and Leafy Green Salad is no exception. 2007 Pinon Vouvray Cuvée Tradition ($16) has a gorgeous nose of honey and lemon peel that resonates perfectly with the candied nuts and pears.

MAKE AHEAD
Winter Sangria

For the best flavor, let the sangria chill overnight. If you can't find satsumas, use tangerines instead.

- 1 cup fresh satsuma orange juice (about 4 satsumas)
- 1 cup satsuma orange sections (about 2 satsumas)
- ⅓ cup Triple Sec (orange-flavored liqueur)
- ¼ cup sugar
- 2 whole cloves
- 1 cinnamon stick
- 1 lemon, cut into 8 wedges
- 1 lime, cut into 8 wedges
- 1 (750-milliliter) bottle fruity red wine

❶ Combine all ingredients in a pitcher, stirring until sugar dissolves. Cover and refrigerate 4 hours or overnight. Yield: 10 servings (serving size: about ⅔ cup).

CALORIES 137; FAT 0.1g (sat 0g, mono 0g, poly 0.1g); PROTEIN 0.3g; CARB 17g; FIBER 0.8g; CHOL 0mg; IRON 0.4mg; SODIUM 4mg; CALC 20mg

Creamy Garlic-Herb Dip

You can prepare this all-purpose dip up to a day ahead. Serve with cauliflower and broccoli florets, carrot and celery sticks, and bell pepper strips.

- ½ cup (4 ounces) ⅓-less-fat cream cheese
- ¼ cup buttermilk
- 2 tablespoons minced fresh chives
- 1 tablespoon minced fresh parsley
- 1 teaspoon grated lemon rind
- ¼ teaspoon salt
- ⅛ teaspoon freshly ground black pepper
- 1 small garlic clove, minced

❶ Combine all ingredients in a bowl, and beat with a mixer at high speed 2 minutes or until smooth. Yield: ¾ cup (serving size: 2 tablespoons).

CALORIES 55; FAT 4.4g (sat 2.9g, mono 1.3g, poly 0.1g); PROTEIN 2.5g; CARB 1.5g; FIBER 0.1g; CHOL 15mg; IRON 0.1mg; SODIUM 195mg; CALC 17mg

Creamy Carrot and Sweet Potato Soup

Make the soup several days in advance, and reheat over medium-low heat.

- 3 tablespoons butter, divided
- 1 cup chopped onion
- ¼ teaspoon ground cinnamon
- ¼ teaspoon ground nutmeg
- 4¾ cups cubed peeled sweet potatoes (about 1½ pounds)
- 3½ cups water
- 3 cups fat-free, less-sodium chicken broth
- 3 cups chopped carrot (about 1 pound)
- ¼ cup half-and-half
- ½ teaspoon salt
- ¼ teaspoon freshly ground black pepper
- ⅓ cup reduced-fat sour cream
- 2 tablespoons chopped fresh flat-leaf parsley

❶ Melt 1 tablespoon butter in a large Dutch oven over medium heat. Add onion to pan; cook 4 minutes or until tender, stirring occasionally. Stir in cinnamon and nutmeg; cook 1 minute, stirring constantly. Move onion mixture to side of pan; add remaining 2 tablespoons butter to open space in pan. Increase heat to medium-high; cook 1 minute or until butter begins to brown. Add sweet potatoes and next 3 ingredients; bring to a boil. Cover, reduce heat, and simmer 35 minutes or until vegetables are tender.
❷ Place half of soup mixture in a blender. Remove center piece of blender lid (to allow steam to escape); secure blender lid on blender. Place a clean towel over opening in blender lid (to avoid splatters). Blend until smooth. Pour into a large bowl. Repeat procedure with remaining soup mixture. Stir in half-and-half, salt, and pepper. Ladle about 1 cup soup into each of 8 bowls; top each serving with about 2 teaspoons sour cream and ¾ teaspoon parsley. Yield: 8 servings.

CALORIES 173; FAT 6.7g (sat 4.1g, mono 1.5g, poly 0.3g); PROTEIN 3.6g; CARB 25.7g; FIBER 5g; CHOL 18mg; IRON 1mg; SODIUM 415mg; CALC 77mg

Pomegranate-Rosemary Royale

This simple twist on the traditional kir royale blends tart-sweet pomegranate juice with subtle herbal notes from a rosemary-infused syrup. Float rosemary leaves on the drinks for a pretty garnish.

- ¼ cup water
- 1 tablespoon sugar
- 2 teaspoons fresh rosemary leaves
- ½ cup pomegranate juice
- 2 cups Champagne or sparkling wine

❶ Combine ¼ cup water and sugar in a small saucepan; bring to a simmer, stirring until sugar dissolves. Remove from heat. Add rosemary; let stand 30 minutes. Strain through a sieve into a bowl; discard solids.
❷ Pour 2 tablespoons pomegranate juice and 1 tablespoon rosemary syrup into 4 Champagne glasses. Top each serving with ½ cup Champagne. Serve immediately. Yield: 4 servings.

CALORIES 115; FAT 0g; PROTEIN 0.1g; CARB 9.5g; FIBER 0g; CHOL 0mg; IRON 0.1mg; SODIUM 4mg; CALC 5mg

Wild Rice and Celery Root Soup

The knobby bulb called celeriac or celery root has a celery-like flavor, but one that is more robust and creamy at the same time.

- 2 tablespoons butter
- 1 cup thinly sliced leek
- ½ cup finely chopped carrot
- 2 tablespoons dry white wine
- 3 cups (½-inch) cubed peeled celeriac (celery root; about ¾ pound)
- 3 cups fat-free, less-sodium chicken broth
- 1 cup water
- ½ teaspoon kosher salt
- ½ teaspoon freshly ground black pepper
- 1¾ cups cooked wild rice
- 2 tablespoons minced fresh chives

❶ Melt butter in a large saucepan over medium heat. Add leek and carrot; cover and cook 5 minutes. Uncover and cook 5 minutes or until tender. Stir in wine, scraping pan to loosen browned bits. Add celeriac and next 4 ingredients; bring to a boil. Cover and cook 10 minutes or until celeriac is tender.
❷ Place 1 cup soup mixture in a blender. Remove center piece of blender lid (to allow steam to escape); secure blender lid on blender. Place a clean towel over opening in blender lid (to avoid splatters). Blend until smooth. Add pureed soup mixture back to saucepan. Add wild rice; cook 15 minutes. Sprinkle with chives. Yield: 8 servings (serving size: about ⅔ cup soup and ¾ teaspoon chives).

CALORIES 90; FAT 3.1g (sat 1.9g, mono 0.8g, poly 0.3g); PROTEIN 2.7g; CARB 13.6g; FIBER 1.8g; CHOL 8mg; IRON 0.8mg; SODIUM 353mg; CALC 29mg

QUICK & EASY

Brussels Sprouts Salad with Warm Bacon Vinaigrette

- ¾ pound Brussels sprouts
- 6 slices applewood-smoked bacon
- ⅓ cup white wine vinegar
- 1½ tablespoons maple syrup
- 2 teaspoons Dijon mustard
- ½ teaspoon salt
- ¼ teaspoon freshly ground black pepper
- 6 cups chopped romaine lettuce
- ¼ cup coarsely chopped pecans, toasted

1 With food processor on, drop Brussels sprouts through food chute of food processor fitted with the slicer attachment. Transfer Brussels sprouts to a bowl.
2 Heat a large nonstick skillet over medium-high heat. Add bacon to pan; cook 5 minutes or until crisp, turning occasionally. Remove bacon from pan, reserving 2 tablespoons drippings in pan; set bacon aside. Reduce heat to medium-low; add vinegar and next 4 ingredients, stirring well to combine. Add Brussels sprouts; cook 1 minute, stirring to coat. Cover and cook 2 minutes. Combine Brussels sprouts mixture and lettuce in a large bowl; toss until well combined. Sprinkle evenly with bacon and pecans. Serve immediately. Yield: 8 servings (serving size: 1 cup).

CALORIES 116; FAT 8.1g (sat 2.2g, mono 3.9g, poly 1.5g); PROTEIN 4.1g; CARB 8.4g; FIBER 2.9g; CHOL 8mg; IRON 1.2mg; SODIUM 286mg; CALC 38mg

Main Dishes

Turkey, of course—two ways. Or have some fun with glazed salmon, spicy lamb, or spinach pie.

MAKE AHEAD • KID FRIENDLY

Honey-Coriander Glazed Ham

- 1½ tablespoons coriander seeds
- 1½ teaspoons cumin seeds
- 2 tablespoons brown sugar
- 1 teaspoon paprika
- 1 (5-pound) 33%-less-sodium smoked, fully cooked, bone-in ham
- 3 tablespoons honey
- 2 tablespoons cider vinegar
- Cooking spray

1 Heat a small skillet over medium heat. Add coriander seeds and cumin seeds to pan; cook 2 minutes or until seeds are golden brown and fragrant, stirring frequently. Place coriander mixture in a spice or coffee grinder; pulse until coarsely ground. Add sugar and paprika; pulse to blend.
2 Trim fat and rind from ham. Score a diamond pattern across top of ham; rub spice mixture evenly over ham.
3 Preheat oven to 350°.
4 Combine honey and vinegar. Place ham, bone end up, in a roasting pan coated with cooking spray. Bake at 350° for 30 minutes. Baste with honey mixture. Bake ham an additional 1 hour or until a thermometer registers 140°. Place ham on serving platter; cover with foil. Let stand 15 minutes before slicing. Yield: 20 servings (serving size: 3 ounces).

CALORIES 137; FAT 6.2g (sat 2g, mono 2.9g, poly 0.7g); PROTEIN 14.3g; CARB 6.1g; FIBER 0.2g; CHOL 51mg; IRON 1mg; SODIUM 872mg; CALC 6mg

Spinach Pie with Goat Cheese, Raisins, and Pine Nuts

- ⅓ cup olive oil, divided
- 2 cups minced onion (about 1 large)
- 5 (9-ounce) packages fresh spinach
- ½ cup golden raisins
- 2 cups (8 ounces) crumbled goat cheese
- ⅓ cup pine nuts, toasted
- ½ teaspoon kosher salt
- ¼ teaspoon ground black pepper
- 12 sheets frozen phyllo dough, thawed
- Cooking spray

1 Heat 3 tablespoons oil in a large Dutch oven over medium heat. Add onion to pan; cook 5 minutes or until browned, stirring occasionally. Add spinach, 1 bag at a time; cook 3 minutes or until spinach wilts, stirring frequently. Simmer spinach mixture 40 minutes or until liquid evaporates. Stir in raisins. Remove from heat; cool completely. Stir in cheese and next 3 ingredients.
2 Preheat oven to 400°.
3 Press 1 phyllo sheet into bottom and up sides of a 13 x 9–inch baking dish coated with cooking spray (cover remaining dough to keep from drying); lightly coat phyllo with cooking spray. Repeat procedure with 7 phyllo sheets. Spread spinach mixture in an even layer onto phyllo. Place 1 phyllo sheet on a large cutting board or work surface (cover remaining dough to keep from drying); lightly brush with 1½ teaspoons oil. Repeat procedure with remaining 3 phyllo sheets and remaining 1½ tablespoons oil. Place phyllo layer over spinach mixture; tuck in sides to enclose spinach fully. Bake at 400° for 30 minutes. Remove from oven; let stand 15 minutes. Yield: 8 servings (serving size: 1 piece).

CALORIES 363; FAT 21.8g (sat 6.6g, mono 9.9g, poly 3.6g); PROTEIN 14.9g; CARB 31.9g; FIBER 6.4g; CHOL 13mg; IRON 5.3mg; SODIUM 480mg; CALC 300mg

Herbed Beef Tenderloin with Two-Onion Jus

    1   (3-pound) beef tenderloin roast, trimmed
    ¾   teaspoon salt
    ¼   teaspoon freshly ground black pepper
    1   tablespoon chopped fresh oregano, divided
    1   teaspoon chopped fresh thyme
    1½ cups chopped sweet onion
    ½   cup chopped shallots
    2   cups fat-free, less-sodium beef broth, divided
    ⅓   cup dry red wine
    ⅓   cup brandy

❶ Let tenderloin stand at room temperature 1 hour.
❷ Preheat oven to 450°.
❸ Rub tenderloin with salt, pepper, 2 teaspoons oregano, and thyme. Set on a rack in a roasting pan; arrange onion and shallots in bottom of pan. Pour 1 cup broth into pan. Bake at 450° for 30 minutes or until thermometer registers 125° or until desired degree of doneness. Let stand 10 minutes before slicing.
❹ Place liquid from roasting pan in a large skillet over medium-high heat, scraping roasting pan to loosen browned bits. Bring to a boil; cook 5 minutes or until liquid evaporates and onion begins to brown. Stir in remaining 1 teaspoon oregano, wine, and brandy. Bring to a boil; cook 2 minutes. Stir in remaining 1 cup broth. Bring to a boil; cook 3 minutes. Serve broth mixture with beef. Yield: 12 servings (serving size: about 3 ounces beef and about 2 tablespoons jus).

CALORIES 208; FAT 9.4g (sat 3.7g, mono 3.9g, poly 0.4g); PROTEIN 24.2g; CARB 3.2g; FIBER 0.4g; CHOL 71mg; IRON 1.7mg; SODIUM 272mg; CALC 26mg

QUICK & EASY
Pork Medallions with Pomegranate-Cherry Sauce

    1   (1-pound) pork tenderloin, trimmed
    ½   teaspoon salt
    ¼   teaspoon freshly ground black pepper
    1   tablespoon olive oil
    ½   cup pomegranate juice
    ⅓   cup dried sweet cherries
    ¼   cup dry red wine
    ¼   cup balsamic vinegar
    1   teaspoon cornstarch
    1   teaspoon water
    1   tablespoon butter

❶ Cut pork crosswise into 12 (1-inch-thick) pieces. Sprinkle both sides of pork with salt and pepper. Heat oil in a large nonstick skillet over medium-high heat. Add pork to pan; cook 4 minutes on each side or until done. Remove pork from pan; keep warm.
❷ Add juice and next 3 ingredients to pan; bring to a boil. Reduce heat to medium; cook 2 minutes. Combine cornstarch and 1 teaspoon water in a small bowl. Add cornstarch mixture to pan; bring to a boil. Cook 1 minute, stirring constantly. Remove pan from heat. Add butter, stirring until butter melts. Return pork to pan, turning to coat. Yield: 4 servings (serving size: 3 medallions and 2 tablespoons sauce).

CALORIES 269; FAT 10.1g (sat 3.6g, mono 4.9g, poly 0.9g); PROTEIN 24.3g; CARB 17.6g; FIBER 1.4g; CHOL 81mg; IRON 1.8mg; SODIUM 384mg; CALC 27mg

WINE NOTE: Stoneleigh Marlborough Pinot Noir 2007 ($16) from New Zealand echoes the fruitiness of this dish, while its light body and soft tannins won't overpower the mild pork.

STAFF FAVORITE
Leg of Lamb with Spicy Harissa

Spice up a holiday dinner with this sultry combo of rich lamb coated with pomegranate molasses and served with a fiery sauce.

HARISSA:
    1   teaspoon crushed red pepper
    1   teaspoon coriander seeds
    ½   teaspoon cumin seeds
    ½   teaspoon caraway seeds
    2   tablespoons olive oil
    1   tablespoon minced garlic
    1½ cups canned whole tomatoes, undrained and finely chopped
    1   tablespoon chopped fresh mint
    ½   teaspoon kosher salt

LAMB:
    ¼   cup pomegranate molasses
    2   tablespoons finely grated ginger
    1   tablespoon minced garlic
    1   tablespoon minced shallots
    1   (2½-pound) rolled boneless leg of lamb, trimmed
    1   teaspoon kosher salt
    ¾   teaspoon freshly ground black pepper

❶ To prepare harissa, place first 4 ingredients in a spice or coffee grinder; process until finely ground. Heat oil in a small saucepan over medium heat. Add 1 tablespoon garlic and spice mixture; cook 1 minute or until garlic is golden and spices are fragrant, stirring frequently. Add tomatoes, mint, and ½ teaspoon salt; reduce heat to low, and simmer 1 hour or until mixture thickens to a paste, stirring occasionally. Remove from heat; chill until ready to use.
❷ Preheat oven to 375°.
❸ To prepare lamb, combine molasses and next 3 ingredients. Unroll lamb; sprinkle 1 teaspoon salt and black pepper over both sides. Spread half of molasses mixture on top of lamb. Reroll lamb; secure at 1-inch intervals with twine. Place on a broiler pan; rub remaining

molasses mixture over outside of lamb. Bake at 375° for 50 minutes or until a thermometer registers 125°. Place roast on a platter; let stand 15 minutes. Serve with harissa. Yield: 8 servings (serving size: about 3 ounces lamb and 2 tablespoons harissa).

CALORIES 244; FAT 9.4g (sat 2.9g, mono 4.9g, poly 0.7g); PROTEIN 20.4g; CARB 17.4g; FIBER 0.9g; CHOL 64mg; IRON 3.3mg; SODIUM 412mg; CALC 61mg

Salmon with Satsuma-Soy Glaze

(pictured on page 236)

Sweet citrus like oranges, tangerines, or clementines can stand in for the brilliant gold satsumas. But keep in mind that satsuma rind is milder than orange rind.

- 1 tablespoon grated satsuma orange rind
- 1 cup fresh satsuma orange juice (about 4 satsumas)
- 6 tablespoons low-sodium soy sauce
- ¼ cup rice vinegar
- 1 tablespoon canola oil
- 1 tablespoon honey
- ½ teaspoon freshly ground black pepper
- ¼ teaspoon crushed red pepper
- 3 (¼-inch) slices peeled fresh ginger
- 6 (6-ounce) skinless salmon fillets (about ½ inch thick)
- 1 tablespoon water
- ½ teaspoon cornstarch
- 2 satsuma oranges, peeled and separated into sections
  Cooking spray
- 2 tablespoons green onion strips

❶ Combine first 9 ingredients in a large zip-top plastic bag. Add salmon to bag; seal. Marinate in refrigerator 1 hour, turning occasionally. Remove salmon from bag, reserving marinade. Strain marinade through a sieve into a bowl; discard solids. Place marinade in a small saucepan over high heat. Bring to a boil; cook until reduced to 1 cup (about 6 minutes). Combine 1 tablespoon water and

cornstarch in a small bowl, stirring with a whisk. Add cornstarch mixture to pan; bring to a boil. Cook 1 minute, stirring constantly. Add orange sections; cook 30 seconds. Set aside; keep warm.
❷ Preheat broiler.
❸ Place salmon on a broiler pan coated with cooking spray; broil 8 minutes or until desired degree of doneness. Serve with sauce. Sprinkle with green onion strips. Yield: 6 servings (serving size: 1 fillet, about ¼ cup sauce, and 1 teaspoon green onion strips).

CALORIES 320; FAT 13.3g (sat 1.9g, mono 5g, poly 5.1g); PROTEIN 35.3g; CARB 12.8g; FIBER 0.9g; CHOL 94mg; IRON 1.7mg; SODIUM 467mg; CALC 45mg

Maple-Brined Turkey Breast with Mushroom Pan Gravy

(pictured on page 234)

Because you're starting with a boneless cut, the brining time is much shorter than if using a whole bird.

- 3 quarts water
- 1½ cups maple syrup
- 1 cup packed brown sugar
- ¾ cup low-sodium soy sauce
- ¼ cup kosher salt
- 1 teaspoon whole black peppercorns
- 6 garlic cloves, crushed
- 3 bay leaves
- 2 (2-pound) boneless turkey breast halves
- 1 teaspoon freshly ground black pepper, divided
  Cooking spray
- 1 tablespoon olive oil
- ¼ cup chopped shallots
- 2 cups finely chopped cremini mushrooms
- 4 cups fat-free, less-sodium chicken broth
- 1 tablespoon all-purpose flour
- 2 tablespoons water
- ¼ cup chilled butter
- 1 tablespoon chopped fresh flat-leaf parsley

❶ Combine first 8 ingredients in a large Dutch oven. Bring to a boil, stirring to dissolve sugar and salt. Cool completely. Add turkey to brine; cover and chill 4 hours.
❷ Preheat oven to 400°.
❸ Remove turkey from brine; discard brine. Rinse turkey; pat dry. Loosen skin from breast by inserting fingers, gently pushing between skin and meat. Rub ½ teaspoon ground pepper under loosened skin. Place on a roasting pan coated with cooking spray.
❹ Bake turkey at 400° for 45 minutes or until a thermometer registers 160°. Remove from oven; cover loosely with foil. Let stand 15 minutes. Remove skin, and discard.
❺ Heat oil in a large nonstick skillet over medium-high heat. Add shallots; sauté 1 minute. Add mushrooms; sauté 6 minutes or until lightly browned. Add broth; bring to a boil, and cook until reduced to 2 cups (about 20 minutes). Combine flour and 2 tablespoons water in a small bowl; stir with a whisk. Stir flour mixture into mushroom mixture; simmer 3 minutes or until slightly thickened, stirring frequently with a whisk. Remove from heat; stir in butter, 1 tablespoon at a time. Stir in parsley and remaining ½ teaspoon ground pepper. Serve gravy with sliced turkey breast. Yield: 8 servings (serving size: about 6 ounces turkey and ¼ cup gravy).

CALORIES 349; FAT 8.8g (sat 4.3g, mono 2.9g, poly 0.8g); PROTEIN 55.4g; CARB 9.3g; FIBER 0.3g; CHOL 164mg; IRON 3.2mg; SODIUM 724mg; CALC 34mg

Classic Roast Turkey and Giblet Gravy

Prepare the Homemade Turkey Broth ahead—a day or two in advance is ideal. In a pinch, use purchased fat-free, less-sodium chicken broth.

- 1 (12-pound) fresh or frozen turkey, thawed
- 3 tablespoons butter, softened
- 2 tablespoons finely chopped fresh sage
- 1 tablespoon chopped fresh thyme
- 1¾ teaspoons kosher salt, divided
- 1 teaspoon dried marjoram
- ¾ teaspoon freshly ground black pepper, divided
- 2½ cups coarsely chopped onion (about 1 medium)
- 1 cup coarsely chopped celery (about 2 stalks)
- 1 medium bunch fresh sage leaves (about ¼ ounce)
- Cooking spray
- 4 cups Homemade Turkey Broth (at right), divided
- 3 tablespoons cornstarch
- 3 tablespoons water

1 Preheat oven to 425°.
2 Remove giblets and neck from turkey; reserve for Homemade Turkey Broth. Pat turkey dry. Trim excess fat. Starting at neck cavity, loosen skin from breast and drumsticks by inserting fingers, gently pushing between skin and meat. Lift wing tips up and over back; tuck under turkey.
3 Combine butter, chopped sage, thyme, 1¼ teaspoons salt, marjoram, and ½ teaspoon pepper; rub mixture under loosened skin and over breast and drumsticks. Place onion, celery, and sage leaves in turkey cavity; tie legs together with kitchen string. Let stand at room temperature 30 minutes. Place turkey, breast side up, on rack of a roasting pan coated with cooking spray. Pour 2 cups Homemade Turkey Broth in bottom of pan; place rack in pan. Bake turkey at 425° for 30 minutes. Reduce heat to 325° (do not remove turkey from oven). Bake at 325° for an additional 1 hour and 45 minutes or until a thermometer inserted into meaty part of thigh registers 165°. Remove turkey from pan; cover loosely with foil. Let turkey stand 20 minutes; discard skin.
4 Place a large zip-top plastic bag inside a 4-cup glass measure. Pour drippings through a fine sieve into bag; let stand 10 minutes (fat will rise to top). Seal bag; carefully snip off 1 bottom corner of bag. Drain drippings into a medium bowl, stopping before fat layer reaches opening; discard fat. Add enough of remaining 2 cups Homemade Turkey Broth to drippings to equal 3 cups. Combine cornstarch and 3 tablespoons water in a small bowl, stirring with a whisk. Bring broth mixture to a boil; stir in cornstarch mixture. Bring to a boil; reduce heat, and simmer 5 minutes or until thickened, stirring frequently. Stir in remaining ½ teaspoon salt and remaining ¼ teaspoon pepper. Serve gravy with turkey. Yield: 12 servings (serving size: about 6 ounces turkey and about ¼ cup gravy).

CALORIES 292; FAT 7.5g (sat 3.3g, mono 1.8g, poly 1.5g); PROTEIN 50.6g; CARB 2.1g; FIBER 0.1g; CHOL 175mg; IRON 3.4mg; SODIUM 410mg; CALC 39mg

Homemade Turkey Broth

Remove the turkey liver from the giblets so your broth won't become bitter. To cool the broth quickly, set the bowl in an ice-water bath and stir it occasionally.
Stock Tip: Freeze any extra broth, and use it in soups, stews, and sauces.

- 1 teaspoon canola oil
- 3 pounds turkey wings, cut into 2-inch pieces
- Giblets and neck from 1 (12-pound) turkey
- 1 cup chopped onion
- ¼ cup chopped celery
- 8 cups water

1 Heat oil in a large Dutch oven over medium-high heat. Add turkey wings, giblets, and neck; sauté 15 minutes or until well browned. Cover and reduce heat to low; cook 5 minutes. Stir in onion and celery; cover and cook 10 minutes, stirring occasionally. Add 8 cups water; bring to a boil. Cover, reduce heat, and simmer 30 minutes. Strain broth through a fine sieve into a large bowl; discard solids. Cool to room temperature. Cover and chill 8 hours or overnight. Skim solidified fat from surface of broth; discard. Yield: 7 servings (serving size: about 1 cup).

CALORIES 8; FAT 0.6g (sat 0.1g, mono 0.2g, poly 0.1g); PROTEIN 0.8g; CARB 0.1g; FIBER 0g; CHOL 3mg; IRON 0.1mg; SODIUM 2mg; CALC 1mg

Sides

Sides can be sublime when earthy sage tops sweet carrots and warm bacon vinaigrette flavors fresh beans.

Sautéed Carrots with Sage

You can easily double, triple, or quadruple this small-yield recipe to feed more.

- 1 teaspoon butter
- 1 teaspoon olive oil
- 1½ cups diagonally sliced carrot
- 2 tablespoons water
- ⅛ teaspoon salt
- ⅛ teaspoon freshly ground black pepper
- 2 teaspoons fresh small sage leaves

1 Melt butter in a large nonstick skillet over medium heat. Add oil to pan, swirling to coat. Add carrot and 2 tablespoons water. Partially cover pan and cook 10 minutes or until carrots are almost tender. Add salt and pepper to pan; increase to medium-high heat. Cook 4 minutes or until carrots are tender and lightly browned, stirring frequently. Sprinkle with sage. Yield: 2 servings (serving size: ½ cup).

CALORIES 75; FAT 4.4g (sat 1.5g, mono 2.2g, poly 0.4g);
PROTEIN 0.9g; CARB 9g; FIBER 2.6g; CHOL 5mg;
IRON 0.3mg; SODIUM 224mg; CALC 35mg

QUICK & EASY

Haricots Verts with Warm Bacon Vinaigrette

Haricots verts are tiny, fresh French green beans. If you can't find them, substitute regular fresh beans, which you'll need to cook a few minutes longer. You can also use white wine vinegar instead of Champagne vinegar, if necessary.

    2   pounds haricots verts, trimmed
    3   slices bacon, chopped
    ¾   cup thinly sliced shallots (about
        2 medium)
   1½   tablespoons toasted walnut oil
    2   teaspoons Champagne vinegar
    1   teaspoon kosher salt
    3   tablespoons chopped walnuts,
        toasted
    1   tablespoon chopped fresh flat-leaf
        parsley

1 Cook beans in boiling water 7 minutes or until crisp-tender. Drain and plunge beans into ice water; drain.
2 Cook bacon in a large nonstick skillet over medium heat until crisp; remove with a slotted spoon. Add shallots to drippings in pan; cook 5 minutes or until tender. Combine shallots and bacon in a large bowl. Add beans to pan; cook 3 minutes or until thoroughly heated. Add beans, oil, vinegar, and salt to bacon mixture; toss to combine. Sprinkle with walnuts and parsley. Yield: 8 servings (serving size: about 1 cup).

CALORIES 108; FAT 6.2g (sat 1.1g, mono 0.8g, poly 3g);
PROTEIN 4.2g; CARB 11.3g; FIBER 4.2g; CHOL 4mg;
IRON 1.5mg; SODIUM 327mg; CALC 51mg

Maple-Pecan Sweet Potatoes

You can make this dish up to two days ahead. Simply bake the potatoes and assemble. Then refrigerate and bake just before serving.

   2¾   pounds sweet potatoes
    ¼   cup half-and-half
    3   tablespoons butter, melted
    3   tablespoons maple syrup
    1   teaspoon kosher salt
    ½   teaspoon freshly ground black
        pepper
    ¼   teaspoon vanilla extract
    ¼   teaspoon ground cinnamon
    ⅛   teaspoon ground allspice
    1   large egg, lightly beaten
        Cooking spray
    ½   cup mini-marshmallows
    2   tablespoons chopped pecans

1 Preheat oven to 400°.
2 Pierce potatoes several times with a fork; place on a foil-lined baking sheet. Bake at 400° for 1 hour or until tender. Cool potatoes slightly; peel and mash in a large bowl.
3 Reduce oven temperature to 350°.
4 Stir half-and-half and next 8 ingredients into sweet potatoes. Spoon mixture into a 2-quart baking dish coated with cooking spray. Bake at 350° for 15 minutes. Sprinkle top with marshmallows and pecans; bake 12 minutes or until marshmallows are slightly melted. Serve immediately. Yield: 8 servings (serving size: ½ cup).

CALORIES 185; FAT 7.3g (sat 3.6g, mono 2.1g, poly 0.7g);
PROTEIN 3.2g; CARB 28g; FIBER 3.4g; CHOL 41mg;
IRON 1mg; SODIUM 315mg; CALC 57mg

Buttery Lemon Broccolini

If you want to get a jump on this recipe, cook the Broccolini four minutes, plunge it into ice water, and refrigerate. Separately prepare the compound butter, and chill it. Then finish cooking the Broccolini in the skillet, and toss it with the butter just before serving.

    4   quarts water
   2½   teaspoons salt, divided
    4   (6-ounce) packages Broccolini
    2   tablespoons butter, softened
    1   teaspoon grated lemon rind
    1   tablespoon fresh lemon juice
    ¼   teaspoon black pepper

1 Bring 4 quarts water to a boil in a large saucepan; add 2 teaspoons salt. Cook Broccolini in batches 5 minutes; remove with a slotted spoon. Drain.
2 Combine butter, rind, and juice, stirring with a fork until well blended. Return Broccolini to pan over medium-high heat, and stir in butter mixture, remaining ½ teaspoon salt, and pepper, tossing gently to coat. Yield: 8 servings (serving size: 3 ounces Broccolini).

CALORIES 61; FAT 2.8g (sat 1.8g, mono 0.7g, poly 0.1g);
PROTEIN 3.1g; CARB 6.3g; FIBER 1.1g; CHOL 8mg;
IRON 0.7mg; SODIUM 250mg; CALC 62mg

Buttermilk-Parmesan Mashed Potatoes

Be sure to purchase a crumbly wedge of Parmigiano-Reggiano for this super-quick potato side dish.

- 2 pounds russet potatoes
- 2/3 cup fat-free milk
- 3 tablespoons butter
- 1/2 cup buttermilk
- 1/3 cup (1 1/2 ounces) grated fresh Parmigiano-Reggiano cheese
- 1/2 teaspoon salt
- 1/4 teaspoon freshly ground black pepper

❶ Prick each potato several times with a fork. Place potatoes in microwave, and cook at HIGH 16 minutes or until tender, turning after 8 minutes. Let stand 2 minutes. Cut each potato in half lengthwise; scoop out flesh with a large spoon, and transfer to a bowl.
❷ Combine milk and butter in a microwave-safe bowl, and microwave at HIGH 2 minutes or until butter melts. Add milk mixture to potatoes; mash with a potato masher to desired consistency. Stir in buttermilk and remaining ingredients. Yield: 6 servings (serving size: 3/4 cup).

CALORIES 240; FAT 7.9g (sat 4.9g, mono 1.9g, poly 0.3g); PROTEIN 7.5g; CARB 35.2g; FIBER 3.5g; CHOL 22mg; IRON 1.7mg; SODIUM 366mg; CALC 117mg

Italian-Style Escarole

Peppery mustard greens and slightly bitter escarole combine with raisins and pungent garlic for a tasty green veggie side.

- 2 tablespoons extra-virgin olive oil
- 2 teaspoons minced fresh garlic
- 1/2 cup golden raisins
- 1 head escarole, chopped (about 1/2 pound)
- 8 ounces mustard greens, chopped
- 1/2 teaspoon salt
- 1/8 teaspoon freshly ground black pepper
- Dash of ground nutmeg (optional)

❶ Heat a large Dutch oven over medium-high heat. Add oil to pan, swirling to coat. Add garlic; sauté 45 seconds, stirring constantly. Stir in raisins; cook 1 minute. Add escarole and mustard greens; sauté 5 minutes or until greens are slightly wilted, tossing occasionally. Remove from heat, and stir in salt, pepper, and nutmeg, if desired. Yield: 8 servings (serving size: 1/2 cup).

CALORIES 99; FAT 4.7g (sat 0.7g, mono 3.3g, poly 0.5g); PROTEIN 2g; CARB 14.4g; FIBER 3g; CHOL 0mg; IRON 1.2mg; SODIUM 216mg; CALC 68mg

Roasted Brussels Sprouts and Apples
(pictured on page 234)

We tested with Fuji apples and love the sweet-tart contrast with the bitter Brussels sprouts. Leave the red skin on for a pretty contrast, or peel the apple, if you prefer.

- 1/2 cup diced apple
- 8 ounces Brussels sprouts, trimmed and quartered
- 2 tablespoons apple cider
- 2 teaspoons olive oil
- 1 teaspoon minced fresh thyme
- 1/4 teaspoon salt
- 1/8 teaspoon freshly ground black pepper

❶ Preheat oven to 375°.
❷ Combine apple and Brussels sprouts in an 11 x 7–inch baking dish. Add apple cider and remaining ingredients; toss well. Bake at 375° for 25 minutes or until sprouts are tender. Yield: 2 servings (serving size: 3/4 cup).

CALORIES 109; FAT 4.9g (sat 0.7g, mono 3.3g, poly 0.7g); PROTEIN 3.6g; CARB 15.8g; FIBER 4.7g; CHOL 0mg; IRON 1.6mg; SODIUM 321mg; CALC 47mg

Bulgur with Dried Cranberries

Serve this lemony bulgur—an American interpretation of Middle Eastern tabbouleh—instead of the more familiar and expected stuffing.

- 1 cup coarse-ground bulgur
- 2 cups (1/4-inch) cubed peeled English cucumber
- 1 cup dried cranberries
- 1/3 cup thinly sliced green onions
- 1 cup finely chopped fresh flat-leaf parsley
- 1 teaspoon grated lemon rind
- 1/3 cup fresh lemon juice
- 1/3 cup extra-virgin olive oil
- 3/4 teaspoon kosher salt
- 3/4 teaspoon freshly ground black pepper

❶ Place bulgur in a large bowl; cover with 2 cups boiling water. Cover; let stand 30 minutes or until liquid is absorbed. Fluff with a fork. Add cucumber and remaining ingredients; toss gently to combine. Yield: 8 servings (serving size: 1 cup).

CALORIES 197; FAT 9.6g (sat 1.3g, mono 6.7g, poly 1.2g); PROTEIN 2.7g; CARB 28.2g; FIBER 4.7g; CHOL 0mg; IRON 1.2mg; SODIUM 186mg; CALC 27mg

Classic Herbed Bread Dressing

You can substitute fat-free, less-sodium chicken broth, but reduce the added salt.

8   cups (¾-inch-cubed) French bread
     baguette (about 12 ounces)
3   tablespoons butter, divided
8   ounces sliced cremini mushrooms
1½   cups chopped onion
1½   cups thinly sliced celery
1½   tablespoons chopped fresh sage
1   tablespoon chopped fresh thyme
½   teaspoon dried marjoram
1   teaspoon kosher salt
½   teaspoon ground black pepper
2   cups Homemade Turkey Broth
     (page 328)
1   large egg, lightly beaten
     Cooking spray

❶ Preheat oven to 325°.
❷ Place bread on a baking sheet; bake at 325° for 25 minutes, stirring once. Place bread in a large bowl; increase oven temperature to 375°.
❸ Melt 2 tablespoons butter in a large skillet over medium heat. Add mushrooms, onion, and celery; cover. Cook 5 minutes. Uncover; cook 17 minutes or until tender. Stir in sage, thyme, and marjoram. Add mushroom mixture, salt, and pepper to bread.
❹ Bring broth to a boil in a small saucepan; boil 15 minutes or until reduced to 1½ cups. Cool to room temperature. Combine broth and egg in a bowl, stirring with a whisk. Add to bread mixture, tossing to coat. Spoon bread mixture into a 3-quart baking dish coated with cooking spray. Cover and bake at 375° for 15 minutes.
❺ Melt remaining 1 tablespoon butter. Uncover dressing; brush with butter. Bake, uncovered, 25 minutes or until top is lightly browned. Yield: 12 servings (serving size: about ¾ cup).

CALORIES 129; FAT 3.9g (sat 2.1g, mono 1g, poly 0.4g); PROTEIN 4.7g; CARB 19.2g; FIBER 1.3g; CHOL 25mg; IRON 1.3mg; SODIUM 381mg; CALC 30mg

Fontina-Stuffed Potato Skins
(pictured on page 237)

Bake potatoes up to two days ahead, and fill with stuffing. Cover and refrigerate. Before serving, let them stand at room temperature for 30 minutes, sprinkle with Parmigiano-Reggiano, and bake.

3¼   pounds russet potatoes
1   cup whole milk
⅓   cup light sour cream
¼   cup reduced-fat buttermilk
1   cup (4 ounces) shredded fontina
     cheese
¼   cup finely chopped chives
2   tablespoons butter
½   teaspoon salt
½   teaspoon black pepper
6   tablespoons grated fresh
     Parmigiano-Reggiano cheese

❶ Preheat oven to 400°.
❷ Pierce potatoes with a fork; bake at 400° for 1 hour or until tender. Cut potatoes in half lengthwise. Scoop out flesh, leaving about a ¼-inch-thick shell. Combine flesh, milk, sour cream, and buttermilk; mash with a potato masher to desired consistency. Stir in fontina and next 4 ingredients. Divide mixture evenly among shells. Place potatoes in a single layer on a baking sheet; sprinkle potatoes evenly with Parmigiano-Reggiano. Bake at 400° for 12 minutes or until heated.
❸ Preheat broiler.
❹ Broil potatoes 2 minutes or until browned and bubbly. Yield: 16 servings (serving size: 1 potato half).

CALORIES 142; FAT 5.4g (sat 3.2g, mono 1.1g, poly 0.2g); PROTEIN 5.8g; CARB 18.4g; FIBER 1.3g; CHOL 17mg; IRON 0.8mg; SODIUM 205mg; CALC 113mg

Desserts

There is so much fruity, chocolaty, tangy, crumbly sweetness to choose from.

Mocha Chocolate Sauce with Pound Cake

An easy, versatile chocolate sauce dresses up store-bought pound cake for a simple dessert offering. For a festive fondue dessert, substitute an orange-flavored liqueur like Triple Sec for the coffee-flavored one (or omit the liqueur altogether), and dunk fresh orange sections, dried apricots, marshmallows, or pretzel rods into the sauce. Or make this as a topping for reduced-fat ice cream.

⅓   cup whole milk
3   ounces premium-quality semisweet
     chocolate, chopped
½   cup powdered sugar
1½   tablespoons light-colored corn syrup
1   tablespoon coffee-flavored liqueur
¼   teaspoon vanilla extract
1   (10.75-ounce) loaf low-fat pound
     cake (such as Sara Lee), cut into
     12 slices
2   cups raspberries

❶ Heat milk in top of a double boiler over medium heat. Add chocolate to pan; cook 2 minutes or until smooth, stirring constantly. Stir in sugar and next 3 ingredients; cook 2 minutes or until smooth, stirring constantly with a whisk. Serve with pound cake and raspberries. Yield: 6 servings (serving size: 2 cake slices, ⅓ cup raspberries, and about 2 tablespoons sauce).

CALORIES 306; FAT 8.2g (sat 3.5g, mono 2g, poly 0.2g); PROTEIN 4.1g; CARB 56.3g; FIBER 4.4g; CHOL 1mg; IRON 3.6mg; SODIUM 217mg; CALC 41mg

Salted Chocolate Ganache Cake

Choose a premium chocolate bar for this simple one-layer cake. Make up to one day ahead, and store in an airtight container.

Cooking spray
2 teaspoons cake flour
5.3 ounces sifted cake flour (about 1¼ cups)
1½ teaspoons baking powder
½ cup packed dark brown sugar
¼ cup butter, softened
1 large egg
¾ cup evaporated fat-free milk
1 teaspoon vanilla extract
2 large egg whites
3 tablespoons dark brown sugar
2½ ounces dark chocolate, divided
1 tablespoon butter
¼ teaspoon sea salt or fleur de sel

❶ Preheat oven to 350°.
❷ Coat 1 (9-inch) round cake pan with cooking spray; dust with 2 teaspoons flour.
❸ Weigh or lightly spoon 5.3 ounces flour into dry measuring cups; level with a knife. Combine flour and baking powder in a bowl; stir with a whisk. Place ½ cup sugar and ¼ cup butter in a large bowl; beat with a mixer at medium speed until well blended (about 5 minutes). Add egg; mix well. Add flour mixture to sugar mixture alternately with milk, beginning and ending with flour mixture. Stir in vanilla.
❹ Beat egg whites with a mixer at high speed until foamy using clean, dry beaters. Gradually add 3 tablespoons sugar, beating until stiff peaks form. Gently fold half of egg white mixture into flour mixture; fold in remaining egg white mixture. Grate ½ ounce chocolate, and fold into batter. Pour batter into prepared pan. Bake at 350° for 23 minutes or until a wooden pick inserted in center comes out clean. Cool in pan 10 minutes. Remove from pan; cool completely on a wire rack.

❺ Chop remaining 2 ounces chocolate. Combine chopped chocolate and 1 tablespoon butter in a microwave-safe bowl. Microwave at MEDIUM 1 minute or until chocolate melts, stirring every 15 seconds. Spread chocolate mixture over top of cake; sprinkle evenly with sea salt. Cut into 8 wedges. Yield: 8 servings (serving size: 1 wedge).

CALORIES 263; FAT 10.9g (sat 6.4g, mono 2.1g, poly 0.4g); PROTEIN 5.3g; CARB 37.6g; FIBER 0.7g; CHOL 47mg; IRON 2.2mg; SODIUM 248mg; CALC 156mg

Cranberry Upside-Down Cake

A tawny butterscotch syrup candies the tart cranberries in the topping.

TOPPING:
Cooking spray
⅓ cup packed brown sugar
2 tablespoons butter
6 ounces fresh or frozen, thawed, cranberries
CAKE:
6.75 ounces all-purpose flour (about 1½ cups)
2 teaspoons baking powder
¼ teaspoon salt
1 cup granulated sugar
½ cup butter, softened
2 large egg yolks
1 teaspoon vanilla extract
½ cup 1% low-fat milk
2 large egg whites

❶ Preheat oven to 350°.
❷ To prepare topping, lightly coat a 9-inch round cake pan with cooking spray. Heat brown sugar and 2 tablespoons butter in a small saucepan over medium heat. Cook 2 minutes or until butter melts and sugar dissolves, stirring occasionally. Pour sugar mixture into prepared cake pan, tilting pan to coat bottom evenly. Arrange cranberries evenly over sugar mixture.
❸ To prepare cake, weigh or lightly spoon flour into dry measuring cups; level with a knife. Combine flour, baking powder, and salt; stir with a whisk. Place granulated sugar and ½ cup butter in a bowl; beat with a mixer at medium speed until well blended and fluffy (about 3 minutes). Add egg yolks, 1 at a time, beating well after each addition. Beat in vanilla. Fold flour mixture into sugar mixture alternately with milk, beginning and ending with flour mixture.
❹ Beat egg whites with a mixer at high speed until stiff peaks form using clean, dry beaters. Gently fold egg whites into batter. Spoon batter over cranberries, spreading evenly. Bake at 350° for 55 minutes or until a wooden pick inserted in center of cake comes out clean. Cool in pan 15 minutes on a wire rack. Loosen cake from sides of pan using a narrow metal spatula. Place a serving plate upside down on top of cake, and invert cake pan onto plate. Let stand 5 minutes, and remove pan. Serve warm. Yield: 12 servings (serving size: 1 wedge).

CALORIES 252; FAT 10.6g (sat 6.3g, mono 2.8g, poly 0.5g); PROTEIN 3.2g; CARB 37.1g; FIBER 1.1g; CHOL 61mg; IRON 1.1mg; SODIUM 217mg; CALC 74mg

---

Carpe the Cranberries:

We love the zingy burst of cranberries, and their crimson hue enlivens a holiday spread. Since they have a short season, available throughout the holidays, freeze a few bags to stock up. Place the fresh fruit on a jelly-roll pan, and freeze. Transfer frozen berries to zip-top plastic bags.

Caramel Apple Pie

TOPPING:

- 1.1 ounces all-purpose flour (about ¼ cup)
- ¼ cup packed light brown sugar
- 2 tablespoons chilled butter, cut into small pieces

CRUST:

- 5.6 ounces all-purpose flour (about 1¼ cups)
- ¼ teaspoon salt
- 3 tablespoons chilled butter, cut into small pieces
- 2 tablespoons chilled vegetable shortening, cut into small pieces
- 3 tablespoons ice water
  Cooking spray

FILLING:

- ¼ cup granulated sugar
- 2 tablespoons cornstarch
- 4 cups thinly sliced peeled Granny Smith apple (about 1¼ pounds)
- 3 cups thinly sliced peeled Fuji apple (about 1 pound)

CARAMEL SAUCE:

- ½ cup fat-free caramel sundae syrup
- ⅛ teaspoon kosher salt

❶ To prepare topping, weigh or lightly spoon 1.1 ounces (about ¼ cup) flour in a dry measuring cup; level with a knife. Place flour, brown sugar, and 2 tablespoons butter in a food processor; pulse 10 times or until crumbly. Transfer topping to a bowl; cover and chill.

❷ To prepare crust, weigh or lightly spoon 5.6 ounces (about 1¼ cups) flour in dry measuring cups; level with a knife. Place flour and ¼ teaspoon salt in a food processor; pulse 2 times or until combined. Add 3 tablespoons butter and shortening; pulse 4 times or until mixture resembles coarse meal. With processor on, add 3 tablespoons water through food chute, processing just until combined (do not form a ball). Press mixture gently into a 4-inch circle on plastic wrap; cover and chill 15 minutes. Slightly overlap 2 sheets of plastic wrap on a slightly damp surface. Unwrap dough, and place on plastic wrap. Cover with 2 additional sheets of overlapping plastic wrap. Roll dough into an 11-inch circle. Freeze dough 5 minutes or until plastic wrap can be easily removed.

❸ Preheat oven to 375°.

❹ Discard top 2 sheets of plastic wrap; let dough stand 1 minute or until pliable. Fit dough, plastic-wrap side up, into a 9-inch pie plate coated with cooking spray. Discard plastic wrap. Press dough into bottom and sides of pan. Fold edges under; flute.

❺ To prepare filling, combine granulated sugar and cornstarch in a bowl; stir with a whisk. Add apples; toss to combine. Arrange apple mixture in crust, mounding slightly in center. Bake at 375° for 25 minutes. Remove from oven; sprinkle evenly with topping. Bake at 375° for 25 additional minutes or until golden. Cool on a wire rack 20 minutes.

❻ To prepare sauce, combine caramel syrup and kosher salt. Slice pie into 12 wedges, and serve with sauce. Yield: 12 servings (serving size: 1 pie wedge and 2 teaspoons sauce).

CALORIES 280; FAT 8.4g (sat 4.5g, mono 2.2g, poly 1g); PROTEIN 2.2g; CARB 49.6g; FIBER 1.7g; CHOL 15mg; IRON 1.1mg; SODIUM 169mg; CALC 14mg

Satsuma Orange Cheesecake

We love showcasing seasonally abundant satsumas, a relative of the mandarin orange. The tang of cream cheese and sour cream in the filling rounds out the citrusy sweetness. Make up to three days ahead.

CRUST:

- Cooking spray
- 4.5 ounces all-purpose flour (about 1 cup)
- ¼ teaspoon baking powder
- ⅛ teaspoon salt
- 3 tablespoons sugar
- 3 tablespoons butter, softened
- 1 large egg yolk

FILLING:

- 1½ cups (12 ounces) fat-free cream cheese, softened
- 1 cup (8 ounces) ⅓-less-fat cream cheese, softened
- ¾ cup sugar
- ¾ cup fat-free sour cream
- 2 tablespoons grated satsuma orange rind
- ¼ cup fresh satsuma orange juice
- 4 large eggs

❶ Preheat oven to 325°.

❷ To prepare crust, lightly coat a 9-inch springform pan with cooking spray. Line bottom of pan with parchment paper.

❸ Weigh or lightly spoon flour into a dry measuring cup; level with a knife. Sift together flour, baking powder, and salt. Place 3 tablespoons sugar and butter in a food processor; process until light and fluffy. Add egg yolk; process until smooth. Add flour mixture to food processor; process just until combined. Firmly press mixture into bottom of prepared pan. Bake at 325° for 25 minutes or until lightly browned. Cool 10 minutes on a wire rack.

❹ Place cream cheeses in food processor; process 30 seconds or until smooth. Add ¾ cup sugar; process 30 seconds. Add sour cream, rind, and juice; process 30 seconds. Add eggs, 1 at a time, processing well after each addition. Scrape down sides of bowl; process 10 seconds. Pour cheese mixture into prepared crust; place pan in a large baking pan. Add hot water to pan to a depth of 1 inch. Bake at 325° for 50 minutes or until cheesecake center barely moves when pan is touched. Turn oven off; let stand 30 minutes. Remove cheesecake from oven; run a knife around outside edge. Cool to room temperature. Cover and chill at least 8 hours. Cut into 12 wedges. Yield: 12 servings (serving size: 1 wedge).

CALORIES 244; FAT 9.4g (sat 5.4g, mono 2.8g, poly 0.5g); PROTEIN 10.6g; CARB 29.4g; FIBER 0.4g; CHOL 113mg; IRON 0.9mg; SODIUM 331mg; CALC 117mg

Gingerbread Cookies

Get a head start by baking cookies up to four days ahead and storing in an airtight container. Frost one day before serving; after frosting is set, pack cookies in airtight containers between layers of wax paper. This dough also makes fine slice-and-bake cookies: Form the dough into two (8-inch) round logs, and chill; slice the chilled logs into ⅛-inch rounds, and bake at 350° for 8 minutes or just until set and golden.

COOKIES:

- 10.1 ounces all-purpose flour (about 2¼ cups)
- 1 teaspoon ground ginger
- 1 teaspoon ground cinnamon
- ½ teaspoon baking powder
- ¼ teaspoon baking soda
- ¼ teaspoon salt
- ¼ teaspoon ground nutmeg
- ½ cup packed brown sugar
- ½ cup butter, softened
- 3 tablespoons molasses
- 1 large egg
- Cooking spray

ICING:

- 1 cup sifted powdered sugar
- 1 tablespoon water

1 To prepare cookies, weigh or lightly spoon flour into measuring cups; level with a knife. Combine flour and next 6 ingredients in a bowl; stir with a whisk. Combine brown sugar, butter, and molasses in a large bowl; beat with a mixer at medium speed 2 minutes. Add egg; beat well. Add flour mixture to sugar mixture; beat at low speed until well blended. Divide dough in half (dough will be sticky). Gently press dough into a 4-inch circle on heavy-duty plastic wrap. Cover with additional plastic wrap; chill 1½ hours.
2 Preheat oven to 350°.
3 Roll each portion of dough to a ⅛-inch thickness on a floured work surface; cut with a 3-inch gingerbread man or woman cookie cutter to form 48 cookies. Place cookies 1 inch apart on a baking sheet coated with cooking spray. Bake at 350° for 8 minutes or until lightly browned. Remove cookies from baking sheet; cool completely on a wire rack.
4 To prepare icing, combine sifted powdered sugar and 1 tablespoon water. Spoon mixture into a zip-top plastic bag. Snip a small hole off corner of bag. Pipe icing onto cookies as desired. Yield: 4 dozen (serving size: 2 cookies).

CALORIES 102; FAT 2.1g (sat 1.3g, mono 0.6g, poly 0.1g); PROTEIN 1.4g; CARB 19.4g; FIBER 0.4g; CHOL 14mg; IRON 0.8mg; SODIUM 67mg; CALC 18mg

Vanilla-Bourbon Pumpkin Tart

(pictured on page 235)

Graham crackers and pecans encrust the spirited, spiced filling. Dollop each serving with sweetened whipped cream.

CRUST:

- ¾ cup graham cracker crumbs (about 5 cookie sheets)
- 1 tablespoon finely chopped pecans
- 1 teaspoon granulated sugar
- 1 tablespoon butter, melted
- Cooking spray

FILLING:

- 1 cup (8 ounces) ⅓-less-fat cream cheese, softened
- ½ cup granulated sugar
- ¼ cup packed light brown sugar
- 1 (15-ounce) can unsweetened pumpkin
- 2 large eggs
- 2 tablespoons bourbon
- 2 teaspoons vanilla extract
- ½ teaspoon salt
- ½ teaspoon ground cinnamon
- ¼ teaspoon ground nutmeg
- ⅛ teaspoon ground allspice

REMAINING INGREDIENTS:

- ⅓ cup cold heavy cream
- 2 teaspoons powdered sugar

1 Preheat oven to 350°.
2 To prepare crust, combine first 3 ingredients in a bowl. Drizzle butter over crumb mixture; stir with a fork. Firmly press into bottom and 1 inch up sides of a 9-inch springform pan coated with cooking spray. Bake at 350° for 8 minutes or until lightly browned; cool on a wire rack.
3 To prepare filling, beat cream cheese, ½ cup granulated sugar, and brown sugar in a large bowl with a mixer at medium speed until smooth. Add pumpkin and eggs; beat until combined, scraping sides of bowl as needed. Add bourbon and next 5 ingredients; beat 1 minute or until combined. Pour cheese mixture into prepared pan. Place pan in a large roasting pan; add hot water to pan to a depth of 1 inch. Bake at 350° for 35 minutes or until center barely moves when side of pan is tapped. Cool completely on wire rack. Cover and refrigerate at least 4 hours or overnight. Place cream and powdered sugar in a small bowl; beat with a mixer at high speed until stiff peaks form. Serve sweetened whipped cream with tart. Yield: 8 servings (serving size: 1 wedge and about 1 tablespoon whipped cream).

CALORIES 284; FAT 14.1g (sat 7.8g, mono 4.4g, poly 0.9g); PROTEIN 6.4g; CARB 32.2g; FIBER 2.7g; CHOL 90mg; IRON 1.1mg; SODIUM 356mg; CALC 54mg

Cardamom-Coconut Crème Caramel

A prime make-ahead option, these delicately flavored custards make a light finish to a hearty Thanksgiving feast.

- Cooking spray
- 1 cup sugar, divided
- 3 tablespoons water
- 2 cups whole milk
- 2 cups flaked sweetened coconut
- 3 green cardamom pods
- 1 cup half-and-half
- ¼ teaspoon salt
- 4 large eggs, lightly beaten

① Lightly coat 8 (6-ounce) custard cups or ramekins with cooking spray. Combine ½ cup sugar and 3 tablespoons water in a small saucepan over medium-high heat; cook 2 minutes or until sugar dissolves, stirring gently as needed to dissolve sugar evenly. Cook an additional 4 minutes or until golden (do not stir). Immediately pour into prepared ramekins, tipping quickly to coat bottoms of cups.
② Preheat oven to 300°.
③ Heat milk, coconut, and cardamom over medium-high heat in a medium, heavy saucepan to 180° or until tiny bubbles form around edge (do not boil). Remove from heat; cover and let stand 15 minutes. Strain milk mixture through a cheesecloth-lined sieve into a medium bowl. Gather edges of cheesecloth together; squeeze over bowl to release moisture. Discard solids.
④ Combine remaining ½ cup sugar, half-and-half, salt, and eggs in a large bowl; gradually add milk mixture, stirring constantly with a whisk. Divide mixture evenly among prepared custard cups. Place in a roasting pan; add hot water to pan to a depth of 1 inch. Bake at 300° for 25 minutes or until center barely moves when ramekin is touched. Cool completely in water. Place plastic wrap on surface of custards; chill at least 6 hours. Loosen edges of custards. Invert custard cups onto plates. Drizzle any remaining caramelized syrup over custards. Yield: 8 servings (serving size: 1 custard).

CALORIES 213; FAT 8.2g (sat 4.3g, mono 1.5g, poly 0.5g); PROTEIN 6g; CARB 29.7g; FIBER 0.1g; CHOL 123mg; IRON 0.5mg; SODIUM 133mg; CALC 114mg

MAKE AHEAD • FREEZABLE
KID FRIENDLY
Pumpkin Ice Cream Torte

Thaw the torte 10 minutes for easier slicing.

- ¾ cup graham cracker crumbs
- 2 tablespoons brown sugar
- 2 tablespoons finely chopped pecans
- 2 tablespoons butter, melted
- Cooking spray
- 1 cup canned unsweetened pumpkin
- 1 teaspoon ground cinnamon
- ½ teaspoon ground allspice
- ⅛ teaspoon ground ginger
- ⅛ teaspoon ground cloves
- 9 cups vanilla low-fat ice cream (about 1½ cartons), divided
- ¼ cup finely chopped pecans, toasted and divided
- ¼ cup jarred caramel topping

① Preheat oven to 350°.
② Combine first 4 ingredients (mixture will be crumbly). Firmly press crumb mixture into bottom of a 9-inch springform pan coated with cooking spray. Bake at 350° for 10 minutes; cool on a wire rack.
③ Combine pumpkin and next 4 ingredients in a bowl. Soften 6 cups ice cream; add to pumpkin mixture, stirring to blend. Spoon half of mixture into prepared pan. Cover with plastic wrap; freeze 1 hour or until firm. Cover and freeze remaining pumpkin ice cream.
④ Soften remaining 3 cups vanilla ice cream; stir in 3 tablespoons pecans. Spread over pumpkin ice cream layer; freeze 1 hour or until firm. Soften remaining 3 cups pumpkin ice cream; spread over vanilla ice cream mixture. Cover; freeze 8 hours or until firm. Cut torte into 12 wedges. Place 1 wedge on each of 12 plates. Place topping in microwave-safe bowl; microwave at HIGH 45 seconds. Top each serving with 1 tablespoon topping; sprinkle with ¼ teaspoon pecans. Yield: 12 servings.

CALORIES 260; FAT 8.2g (sat 3.1g, mono 2.2g, poly 1.1g); PROTEIN 5.6g; CARB 40.9g; FIBER 2.8g; CHOL 13mg; IRON 0.7mg; SODIUM 186mg; CALC 168mg

Tasty Extras

It's the little additions to a meal we love the most—a tangy, aromatic chutney; a warm, toasted scone; a chile-pickled green bean.

MAKE AHEAD
Cranberry, Apple, and Walnut Sauce

Make this sauce up to two weeks ahead. You can use frozen cranberries in place of fresh, if you'd like.

- 1 cup sugar
- ¾ cup fresh orange juice (about 3 oranges)
- ½ cup white wine
- 1 cinnamon stick
- 2 cups diced peeled Granny Smith apple
- 1½ teaspoons minced peeled fresh ginger
- ⅛ teaspoon ground red pepper
- 1 (12-ounce) package fresh cranberries
- 1 tablespoon grated orange rind
- ½ cup coarsely chopped walnuts, toasted

① Combine first 4 ingredients in a large saucepan; bring to a boil. Cook 3 minutes or until sugar dissolves, stirring frequently. Stir in apple and next 3 ingredients; bring to a boil. Reduce heat, and simmer 35 minutes or until sauce thickens. Remove from heat; stir in rind. Cool; stir in walnuts. Yield: 4 cups (serving size: ¼ cup).

CALORIES 96; FAT 2.5g (sat 0.2g, mono 0.3g, poly 1.8g); PROTEIN 0.8g; CARB 19.2g; FIBER 1.4g; CHOL 0mg; IRON 0.2mg; SODIUM 1mg; CALC 9mg

Toasted Almond and Cherry Scones

This bread comes together in less than 30 minutes and is best served warm from the oven. Substitute an equal amount of chopped pistachios or walnuts for the almonds, if you prefer.

- 4.5 ounces all-purpose flour (about 1 cup)
- 3.3 ounces whole wheat pastry flour (about ¾ cup)
- ½ cup old-fashioned rolled oats
- ¼ cup packed brown sugar
- 2 teaspoons baking powder
- ½ teaspoon baking soda
- ½ teaspoon salt
- ½ teaspoon ground cinnamon
- ¼ teaspoon ground allspice
- 5 tablespoons chilled butter, cut into small pieces
- 1 cup fat-free sour cream
- 1 teaspoon vanilla extract
- ⅓ cup chopped dried cherries
- ⅓ cup chopped almonds, toasted
  Cooking spray
- ½ cup powdered sugar
- 4 teaspoons 2% reduced-fat milk

❶ Preheat oven to 400°.
❷ Weigh or lightly spoon flours into dry measuring cups; level with a knife. Place oats in a food processor; process until finely ground. Add flours, brown sugar, and next 5 ingredients to processor; pulse 3 times. Add butter; pulse 5 times or until mixture resembles coarse meal. Add sour cream and vanilla; pulse 3 times or just until combined (do not overmix). Add cherries and nuts; pulse 2 times.
❸ Turn dough out onto a lightly floured surface; knead lightly 3 times. Roll dough to a ½-inch thickness; cut with a 2½-inch biscuit cutter to form 10 rounds. Place rounds 1 inch apart on a baking sheet lightly coated with cooking spray. Bake at 400° for 14 minutes or until golden brown. Remove from baking sheet; cool on a wire rack.
❹ Combine powdered sugar and 4 teaspoons milk, stirring with a whisk. Drizzle powdered sugar glaze over scones. Yield: 10 servings (serving size: 1 scone).

CALORIES 258; FAT 8.7g (sat 3.9g, mono 3.1g, poly 0.9g); PROTEIN 5.7g; CARB 39.3g; FIBER 3.1g; CHOL 19mg; IRON 1.6mg; SODIUM 363mg; CALC 140mg

Fresh Cranberry-Orange Relish

Allow at least one day in the refrigerator to marry the bright, fresh flavors. Make up to three days ahead.

- 1 large orange
- ¼ cup plus 2 tablespoons sugar
- 2 (10-ounce) packages fresh cranberries

❶ Grate orange rind, and place in a food processor. Peel and section orange over bowl of food processor. Add orange sections, sugar, and cranberries to processor; process until coarsely chopped. Cover and refrigerate at least 1 day. Yield: 4 cups (serving size: ¼ cup).

CALORIES 40; FAT 0.1g (sat 0g, mono 0g, poly 0g); PROTEIN 0.3g; CARB 10.4g; FIBER 1.9g; CHOL 0mg; IRON 0.1mg; SODIUM 1mg; CALC 7mg

Spicy Pickled Green Beans

If you're making the recipe for a gift, the beans look gorgeous in tall glass jars.

- 2 cups water
- 2 cups white vinegar
- 3 tablespoons kosher salt
- 1½ tablespoons sugar
- 3 tablespoons thinly sliced garlic (about 8 cloves)
- 8 fresh dill sprigs
- 4 small dried hot red chiles
- 1½ pounds green beans, trimmed

❶ Combine first 4 ingredients in a large saucepan; bring to a boil. Remove from heat; add garlic, dill, and peppers to pan. Let stand 1 minute. Pour vinegar mixture over beans in a large glass bowl; cover and refrigerate 1 week, stirring occasionally. Yield: 26 servings (serving size: 1 ounce [about 4 beans]).

CALORIES 10; FAT 0.1g (sat 0g, mono 0g, poly 0g); PROTEIN 0.6g; CARB 2.4g; FIBER 0.9g; CHOL 0mg; IRON 0.3mg; SODIUM 120mg; CALC 12mg

Spiced Apricot Chutney

Serve with ham, sandwiches, or scones.

- 2 tablespoons canola oil
- 1 cup finely chopped onion
- 1½ teaspoons mustard seeds
- ¼ teaspoon crushed red pepper
- 1½ cups apple juice
- ½ cup dried currants
- ⅓ cup raspberry vinegar
- 2 tablespoons sweetened dried cranberries, finely chopped
- 3 tablespoons honey
- ½ teaspoon ground coriander
- ½ teaspoon ground allspice
- 1 (16-ounce) package dried apricots, finely chopped

❶ Heat oil in a saucepan over medium heat. Add onion to pan, and cook 4 minutes or until tender (do not brown), stirring frequently. Add mustard seeds and pepper; cook 1 minute. Stir in juice and remaining ingredients; bring to a boil. Cover, reduce heat, and simmer 15 minutes. Uncover; cook an additional 5 minutes or until liquid almost evaporates. Yield: 3½ cups (serving size: 1 tablespoon).

CALORIES 39; FAT 0.6g (sat 0g, mono 0.3g, poly 0.2g); PROTEIN 0.4g; CARB 8g; FIBER 0.6g; CHOL 0mg; IRON 0.4mg; SODIUM 1mg; CALC 7mg

Walnut Bread

This recipe yields two loaves, which means you can make one for yourself and give one away with preserves as a tasty gift. Serve any leftovers toasted with a spot of butter and jam.

- 1¼ cups old-fashioned rolled oats
- 1 cup boiling water
- 1 package dry yeast (about 2¼ teaspoons)
- ¼ cup warm water (100° to 110°)
- 1½ cups low-fat buttermilk
- 6 tablespoons honey
- 3 tablespoons canola oil
- 20.3 ounces all-purpose flour (about 4½ cups), divided
- 9 ounces whole wheat pastry flour (about 2 cups)
- 2½ teaspoons salt
- 1 cup finely chopped walnuts
- Cooking spray

❶ Place oats in a food processor; pulse 8 times or until coarsely chopped. Combine chopped oats and 1 cup boiling water in a medium bowl; let stand 10 minutes, stirring occasionally.

❷ Dissolve yeast in ¼ cup warm water in bowl of a stand mixer; let stand 5 minutes. Add buttermilk to oat mixture, stirring to combine. Stir in honey and oil. Add oat mixture to yeast mixture; mix with dough hook attachment until combined. Weigh or lightly spoon 13.5 ounces all-purpose flour (about 3 cups) and whole wheat pastry flour in dry measuring cups; level with a knife. Combine flours and salt. Add flour mixture to buttermilk mixture. Mix dough at medium speed 10 minutes or until smooth and elastic, adding remaining all-purpose flour, ¼ cup at a time, to prevent dough from sticking to sides of bowl. Add walnuts, and mix at medium speed just until combined.

❸ Place dough in a large bowl coated with cooking spray, turning to coat top.

Cover and let rise in a warm place (85°), free from drafts, 1 hour or until doubled in size. (Gently press two fingers into dough. If indentation remains, dough has risen enough.)

❹ Preheat oven to 400°.

❺ Punch dough down; divide in half. Divide each half into 3 equal portions. Working with 1 portion at a time (cover remaining dough to keep from drying), shape each portion into a 14-inch rope. Place 3 ropes lengthwise on a baking sheet coated with cooking spray (do not stretch). Pinch ends together at one end to seal. Braid ropes, and pinch loose ends together to seal. Repeat procedure with remaining dough to form another braid. Cover and let rise 30 minutes or until doubled in size.

❻ Spritz top and sides of loaves lightly with water from a spray bottle. Bake on center rack of oven at 400° for 28 minutes or until deep golden brown. Remove from pan; cool on a wire rack. Yield: 2 loaves, 16 servings per loaf.

CALORIES 150; FAT 4.3g (sat 0.5g, mono 1.2g, poly 2.2g); PROTEIN 4.1g; CARB 24.1g; FIBER 2.1g; CHOL 1mg; IRON 1.5mg; SODIUM 195mg; CALC 27mg

---

NUTRITION MADE EASY
The Truth About the Great American Veggie Burger

It's not a beef-burger substitute: Nothing is. But the best homemade and ready-made veggie burgers deliver a bun-and-patty experience that can be entirely satisfying.

As fancy restaurants concoct hamburgers with short-rib meat, hanger steak, and foie gras, it's time for the veggie burger to quit chasing the beefy bandwagon and settle for life on the light side. Done right, veggie burgers are full of unexpected, delicious, unmeaty flavors and positively packed with nutrition, courtesy of lean vegetable protein and fiber. Here's a short primer.

QUICK & EASY
Our Homemade Quick Black Bean Burger

Serve on a bun with ketchup, spinach leaves, a tomato slice, a slice of Monterey Jack cheese, avocado slices, and onion.

- 1 (2-ounce) hamburger bun, torn into pieces
- 3 tablespoons olive oil, divided
- 2 teaspoons chopped garlic
- 1 (15.25-ounce) can black beans, rinsed and drained
- 1 teaspoon grated lime rind
- ¾ teaspoon chili powder
- ½ teaspoon chopped fresh oregano
- ¼ teaspoon salt
- 1 large egg, lightly beaten
- 1 large egg white, lightly beaten

❶ Place bun in a food processor; process 4 times or until crumbs measure about 1 cup. Transfer to a bowl.

❷ Place 1 tablespoon oil, garlic, and beans in processor; pulse 8 times or until beans make a thick paste. Scrape bean mixture into bowl with breadcrumbs. Stir in rind and remaining ingredients. With moistened hands, divide bean mixture into 4 equal portions (about ⅓ cup mixture per portion), shaping each into a 3-inch patty.

❸ Heat remaining 2 tablespoons oil in a large nonstick skillet over medium-high heat. Add patties to pan; reduce heat to medium, and cook 4 minutes or until bottom edges are browned. Carefully turn patties over; cook 3 minutes or until bottom edges are done. Yield: 4 patties (serving size: 1 patty).

CALORIES 182; FAT 12.3g (sat 1.3g, mono 6.7g, poly 3.6g); PROTEIN 6.6g; CARB 15.6g; FIBER 4.6g; CHOL 53mg; IRON 2mg; SODIUM 448mg; CALC 103mg

Middle Eastern Chickpea Miniburgers

Serve each burger on a whole-grain slider bun with lettuce, crisp radish slices, roasted red bell pepper, and canola-based mayonnaise.

- 1 (8-ounce) red potato
- 3 tablespoons olive oil, divided
- 1 teaspoon minced garlic
- 1 (15.5-ounce) can chickpeas (garbanzo beans), rinsed, drained, and divided
- 1 tablespoon chopped fresh parsley
- ½ teaspoon salt
- ½ teaspoon grated lemon rind
- ½ teaspoon smoked paprika
- ¼ teaspoon freshly ground black pepper
- 2 large egg whites, lightly beaten

❶ Place potato in a saucepan; cover with water. Bring to a boil; cook 20 minutes or until very tender. Drain. Cool slightly. Coarsely chop, and place in a medium bowl. Add 1 tablespoon oil and garlic to bowl; mash potato mixture with a potato masher until slightly chunky. Remove 3 tablespoons chickpeas; place in a small bowl. Add remaining chickpeas to potato mixture; mash until well blended. Stir in remaining 3 tablespoons whole chickpeas, parsley, and remaining ingredients. With moistened hands, divide mixture into 6 equal portions (about ⅓ cup mixture per portion), shaping each into a 3-inch patty.
❷ Heat 1 tablespoon oil in a large nonstick skillet over medium-high heat. Add 3 patties to pan; reduce heat to medium, and cook 4 minutes or until bottoms are golden. Carefully turn patties over; cook 3 minutes or until bottoms are golden and patties are set. Repeat procedure with remaining 1 tablespoon oil and 3 patties. Yield: 3 servings (serving size: 2 patties).

CALORIES 308; FAT 16.2g (sat 1.9g, mono 10.9g, poly 3g); PROTEIN 9g; CARB 32.9g; FIBER 6.5g; CHOL 0mg; IRON 2.6mg; SODIUM 716mg; CALC 54mg

Special Occasion Recipe

Oysters with Pink Peppercorn Mignonette

Oysters are at their delicious best in winter; they spawn in the summer and by winter become sweetest and fattest. Use a small plate and, for an elegant restaurant touch, spread a layer of rock salt on the bottom. The salt evokes the sea and stabilizes the shells.

- ½ cup Champagne vinegar
- 2 tablespoons finely chopped shallots
- 2 teaspoons pink peppercorns, coarsely crushed
- 1½ teaspoons finely chopped fresh tarragon
- 32 oysters on the half shell

❶ Combine first 4 ingredients; chill. Spoon sauce over oysters. Yield: 8 servings (4 oysters and about 4 teaspoons sauce).

CALORIES 47; FAT 1.4g (sat 0.4g, mono 0.2g, poly 0.5g); PROTEIN 4.1g; CARB 4.4g; FIBER 0.2g; CHOL 30mg; IRON 4mg; SODIUM 120mg; CALC 29mg

WINE NOTE: The 2007 Willi Haag Spatlese Brauneberger Juffer Riesling ($15) is spicy and aromatic, perfect with salty oysters.

> Briny oysters on the half shell are a glorious beginning to any celebratory meal.

Learn to Shuck Oysters Like a Pro

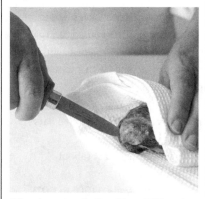

1 Scrub oyster shells with a stiff brush. Hold one oyster, flat shell on top, inside a folded kitchen towel (to protect your hands) on a sturdy surface. Work the tip of an oyster knife into the hinge.

2 Twist the knife sharply until you hear or feel the hinge snap. Carefully slide the knife around the inside surface of the top shell to separate the oyster from the shell; discard top shell.

3 Cautiously cut the muscle under the oyster to release it from the bottom shell (leave oyster on bottom shell for serving). Try not to spill any of the tasty oyster liquor.

RECIPE MAKEOVER
Spaghetti with Pork Bolognese

An Italian classic goes from ristorante to your kitchen table much healthier and just as tasty as the original.

A *ragù alla Bolognese*—or a meat sauce prepared in the Bologna culinary style—is traditionally a tomato, vegetable, and meat mixture simmered carefully to marry flavors and produce a rich sauce. While the technique is flawless, we wanted to update the heavy ingredients (such as plenty of butter, oil, and fatty meats) to bring this classic dish to the right side of healthy.

Our recipe starts with aromatics sautéed in olive oil. To limit the meat's saturated fat and sodium, we use a little pancetta and ground pork with lean pork tenderloin. We use low-fat milk, wine, low-sodium broth, and a Parmigiano-Reggiano rind to harmonize flavors. Instead of high-sodium diced tomatoes, our recipe uses tomato paste and fresh chopped tomatoes. Parmigiano-Reggiano and fresh parsley pep up each serving. Unlike the sweet ground beef and tomato versions at some restaurants, our rendition has pleasing texture and vibrant flavor thanks to the fresh ingredients.

serving size: 1 cup noodles and ¾ cup sauce	before	after
CALORIES PER SERVING	786	512
TOTAL FAT	37.1g	18g
SATURATED FAT	14.7g	6.8g
BEFORE	Butter and olive oil, Ground beef and pork plus pancetta, 3 cups beef broth	
AFTER	Olive oil, Lean and fatty ground pork plus pancetta, 1½ cups low-sodium vegetable broth	

KID FRIENDLY
Spaghetti with Pork Bolognese

A rich sauce with plenty of meat feels like the old-world Italian dish but fits in the new-world nutrition sense. A little liquid remaining in your sauce helps coat the pasta.

- 1½ tablespoons extra-virgin olive oil
- 2 cups finely chopped onion
- ½ cup finely chopped carrot (about 1 medium)
- ½ cup finely chopped celery (about 1 stalk)
- 1½ teaspoons chopped garlic
- 1 teaspoon kosher salt, divided
- 1 bay leaf
- 1 pound ground pork tenderloin
- ¾ pound ground pork
- 2 ounces pancetta, finely diced
- ¼ cup tomato paste
- 2 cups chopped plum tomato (about ½ pound)
- 1½ cups organic vegetable broth (such as Swanson)
- 1 cup dry white wine
- 1 cup 1% low-fat milk
- ⅛ teaspoon grated whole nutmeg
- 1 (2-ounce) piece Parmigiano-Reggiano rind
- 1 (3-inch) cinnamon stick
- ½ teaspoon freshly ground black pepper
- 8 cups hot cooked spaghetti (about 16 ounces uncooked)
- ½ cup (2 ounces) grated fresh Parmigiano-Reggiano
- ½ cup chopped fresh parsley

1 Heat oil in a large Dutch oven over medium heat. Add onion, carrot, celery, garlic, ¼ teaspoon salt, and bay leaf to pan; cook 8 minutes or until vegetables are tender, stirring occasionally. Increase heat to medium-high. Add ground pork tenderloin, ground pork, pancetta, and ¼ teaspoon salt; sauté 8 minutes or until pork loses its pink color. Stir in tomato paste; cook 1 minute. Add tomato and next 5 ingredients; bring to a boil. Reduce heat, and simmer 45 minutes. Add cinnamon; simmer 30 minutes or until most of liquid evaporates. Discard bay leaf, rind, and cinnamon stick; stir in remaining ½ teaspoon salt and pepper. Arrange 1 cup noodles on each of 8 plates; top each with about ¾ cup sauce. Sprinkle each serving with 1 tablespoon grated cheese and 1 tablespoon parsley. Yield: 8 servings.

CALORIES 512; FAT 18g (sat 6.8g, mono 6.8g, poly 1.6g); PROTEIN 34.5g; CARB 51.4g; FIBER 4.5g; CHOL 79mg; IRON 4mg; SODIUM 770mg; CALC 205mg

Build Flavor the Italian Way

These staples add depth.

Adding the **cheese rind** to simmering liquid imbues the sauce with plenty of richness and some flavor-boosting sodium. The garnish of grated cheese is simultaneously savory and slightly sweet.

From tree bark, **cinnamon** is another spice in the Italian arsenal for enlivening sweet and savory cooking. Simmered in the ragù, the cinnamon stick adds subtle flavor.

Our Favorite Pecan Pie with Spiked Cream

Packed with pecans and graced with a bourbon-laced topping, this dish gives ample reason to be thankful this season.

MAKE AHEAD

Pecan Pie with Spiked Cream

(pictured on page 237)

CRUST:

- 4.5 ounces all-purpose flour (about 1 cup), divided
- 3 tablespoons ice water
- 1 teaspoon fresh lemon juice
- 2 tablespoons powdered sugar
- ¼ teaspoon salt
- 3 tablespoons vegetable shortening

FILLING:

- 1 cup brown rice syrup or dark corn syrup
- ¼ cup maple syrup
- 2 tablespoons all-purpose flour
- ¼ teaspoon salt
- 2 large eggs
- 1 large egg white
- ¾ cup pecan halves
- 1 teaspoon vanilla extract

TOPPING:

- ⅔ cup frozen fat-free whipped topping, thawed
- 1 tablespoon bourbon

❶ Preheat oven to 350°.

❷ To prepare crust, weigh or lightly spoon 4.5 ounces (about 1 cup) flour into a dry measuring cup; level with a knife. Combine 1.1 ounces (about ¼ cup) flour, 3 tablespoons ice water, and juice, stirring with a whisk until well blended to form a slurry. Combine remaining 3.4 ounces (about ¾ cup) flour, powdered sugar, and ¼ teaspoon salt in a large bowl; cut in shortening with a pastry blender or 2 knives until mixture resembles coarse meal. Add slurry; toss with a fork until moist. Gently press flour mixture into a 4-inch circle on 2 sheets of overlapping plastic wrap; cover with 2 additional sheets of over-lapping wrap. Roll dough, still covered, into a 12-inch circle. Freeze dough 10 minutes or until wrap can be easily removed.

❸ Remove dough from freezer. Remove top 2 sheets of plastic wrap; let dough stand 1 minute or until pliable. Fit dough, plastic wrap side up, into a 9-inch pie plate, allowing dough to extend over edge. Remove remaining plastic wrap. Press dough into bottom and up sides of pie plate. Fold edges under; flute. Bake at 350° for 8 minutes. Cool on a wire rack.

❹ To prepare filling, place rice syrup and next 5 ingredients in a large bowl; beat with a mixer at medium speed until well blended. Stir in pecans and vanilla. Pour filling into prepared crust. Bake at 350° for 50 minutes or until edges puff and center is set (shield edges of piecrust with foil if crust gets too brown). Cool on rack.

❺ To prepare topping, combine whipped topping and bourbon until blended. Serve with pie. Yield: 10 servings (serving size: 1 wedge and about 1 tablespoon topping).

CALORIES 328; FAT 10.8g (sat 2.2g, mono 4.8g, poly 3g); PROTEIN 4.3g; CARB 53.1g; FIBER 1.3g; CHOL 42mg; IRON 1.2mg; SODIUM 210mg; CALC 29mg

Take Stock

Invest a little time in preparing homemade vegetable stocks (recipes page 341). You'll get a huge payoff from the fresh, pure flavors and less sodium than in many supermarket stocks.

Chickpea and Winter Vegetable Stew

Harissa is a fiery spice paste used in Moroccan cooking. Look for it at Middle Eastern markets.

- 2 teaspoons extra-virgin olive oil
- 1 cup chopped onion
- 1 cup (½-inch) slices leek
- ½ teaspoon ground coriander
- ½ teaspoon caraway seeds, crushed
- ⅛ teaspoon ground cumin
- ⅛ teaspoon ground red pepper
- 1 garlic clove, minced
- 3⅔ cups Simple Vegetable Stock (page 341), divided
- 2 cups (1-inch) cubed peeled butternut squash
- 1 cup (½-inch) slices carrot
- ¾ cup (1-inch) cubed peeled Yukon gold potato
- 1 tablespoon harissa
- 1½ teaspoons tomato paste
- ¾ teaspoon salt
- 1 pound turnips, peeled and each cut into 8 wedges (about 2 medium)
- 1 (15½-ounce) can chickpeas (garbanzo beans), drained
- ¼ cup chopped fresh flat-leaf parsley
- 1½ teaspoons honey
- 1⅓ cups uncooked couscous
- 8 lemon wedges

❶ Heat oil in a large saucepan over medium-high heat. Add onion and leek; sauté 5 minutes. Add coriander and next 4 ingredients; cook 1 minute, stirring constantly. Add 3 cups Simple Vegetable Stock and next 8 ingredients; bring to a boil. Cover, reduce heat, and simmer 30 minutes. Stir in parsley and honey.

2 Remove ²/₃ cup hot cooking liquid from squash mixture. Place cooking liquid and remaining ²/₃ cup stock in a medium bowl. Stir in couscous. Cover and let stand 5 minutes. Fluff with a fork. Serve with lemon wedges. Yield: 8 servings (serving size: ³/₄ cup squash mixture, ¹/₂ cup couscous, and 1 lemon wedge).

CALORIES 264; FAT 2.3g (sat 0.3g, mono 1g, poly 0.6g); PROTEIN 8.3g; CARB 54.5g; FIBER 7.5g; CHOL 0mg; IRON 2.4mg; SODIUM 425mg; CALC 92mg

MAKE AHEAD • FREEZABLE
Simple Vegetable Stock

- 1 whole garlic head
- 10 cups water
- 2 cups (1-inch) slices onion
- 2 cups (1-inch) slices leek
- 1 cup (1-inch) slices carrot
- 1 cup (1-inch) slices celery
- 1 small turnip, peeled and cut into 8 wedges (about ¹/₄ pound)
- ¹/₄ pound cremini mushrooms, halved
- 6 black peppercorns
- 4 fresh parsley sprigs
- 4 fresh thyme sprigs
- 1 bay leaf

1 Cut off pointed end of garlic just to expose cloves.
2 Combine garlic and remaining ingredients in a Dutch oven; bring to a boil. Reduce heat, and simmer 50 minutes. Strain through a fine sieve over a bowl; discard solids. Store in an airtight container in refrigerator up to 1 week. Yield: 7 cups (serving size: 1 cup).

CALORIES 6; FAT 0g; PROTEIN 0.2g; CARB 1.3g; FIBER 0.3g; CHOL 0mg; IRON 0.1mg; SODIUM 4mg; CALC 5mg

MAKE AHEAD • FREEZABLE
Roasted Vegetable Stock

- 1 whole garlic head
- 2 cups (1-inch) slices onion
- 1¹/₂ cups (1-inch) slices carrot
- 1 cup (1-inch) slices celery
- ¹/₂ teaspoon black pepper
- 2 medium turnips, peeled and each cut into 3 wedges
- 2 tablespoons extra-virgin olive oil
- 2 cups (1-inch) slices leek
- 8 ounces whole cremini mushrooms
- ¹/₂ cup dry white wine
- 10 cups water
- 4 fresh parsley sprigs
- 4 fresh thyme sprigs
- 1 bay leaf

1 Preheat oven to 450°.
2 Cut off pointed end of garlic just to expose cloves. Place garlic and next 5 ingredients on a large jelly-roll pan. Drizzle with oil; toss well. Bake at 450° for 10 minutes. Add leek and mushrooms. Bake an additional 35 minutes or until browned and tender, stirring occasionally. Spoon vegetables into a Dutch oven. Pour wine into jelly-roll pan, scraping to loosen browned bits. Add wine mixture, 10 cups water, and remaining ingredients to vegetable mixture; bring to a boil. Reduce heat, and simmer 1 hour, stirring occasionally. Strain through a fine sieve over a bowl; discard solids. Store in an airtight container in refrigerator up to 1 week. Yield: 7 cups (serving size: 1 cup).

CALORIES 50; FAT 4.7g (sat 0.7g, mono 3.3g, poly 0.7g); PROTEIN 0.4g; CARB 2.2g; FIBER 0.4g; CHOL 0mg; IRON 0.2mg; SODIUM 8mg; CALC 9mg

MAKE AHEAD • FREEZABLE
Mushroom Stock

- 2 cups boiling water
- ¹/₂ cup dried porcini mushrooms (about ¹/₂ ounce)
- 1 whole garlic head
- 1 tablespoon extra-virgin olive oil
- 2 cups (1-inch) slices onion
- 2 cups (1-inch) slices leek
- 1 pound cremini mushrooms, quartered
- 4 fresh parsley sprigs
- 4 fresh thyme sprigs
- 10 black peppercorns
- 1 bay leaf
- ¹/₄ cup dry white wine
- 6¹/₂ cups water

1 Combine 2 cups boiling water and porcini mushrooms in a bowl. Cover and let stand 30 minutes or until tender. Strain through a fine sieve over a bowl; reserve 1¹/₂ cups liquid and mushrooms.
2 Cut off pointed end of garlic just to expose cloves; set aside.
3 Heat a Dutch oven over medium-high heat. Add oil to pan, swirling to coat. Add onion and leek; sauté 5 minutes or until tender, stirring occasionally. Add porcini mushrooms, garlic, cremini mushrooms, and next 4 ingredients; sauté 10 minutes or until cremini mushrooms are tender, stirring occasionally. Add wine; cook until liquid evaporates (about 2 minutes). Add reserved 1¹/₂ cups mushroom liquid and 6¹/₂ cups water; bring to a boil. Reduce heat, and simmer 50 minutes. Strain through a fine sieve over a bowl; discard solids. Store in an airtight container in refrigerator up to 1 week. Yield: 6 servings (serving size: 1 cup).

CALORIES 28; FAT 2.4g (sat 0.3g, mono 1.7g, poly 0.3g); PROTEIN 0.5g; CARB 1.6g; FIBER 0.3g; CHOL 0mg; IRON 0.2mg; SODIUM 3mg; CALC 5mg

---

Flavor Boosters

Most of our stocks call for fresh thyme and parsley sprigs, black peppercorns, and bay leaves to balance their flavor. To tailor your broth to suit your tastes:
- To make stock with more pronounced garlic flavor, peel and crush the cloves before simmering.
- Substitute your favorite fresh herbs in place of thyme or parsley.
- For an Asian-style broth, simmer broth with ginger coins, and add 2 tablespoons low-sodium soy sauce after straining.
- For a fiery broth, add one or two halved chiles to the broth as it simmers.

Farro Risotto with Mushrooms

Farro, an ancient Italian wheat grain, adds a pleasant chewiness to this earthy dish. If you can't find it, substitute pearl barley or Arborio rice.

1 cup dried wild mushroom blend (about 1 ounce)
5½ cups Mushroom Stock (page 341)
2 tablespoons extra-virgin olive oil
1½ cups uncooked farro
½ cup finely chopped onion
2 garlic cloves, minced
6 cups sliced cremini mushrooms (about 1 pound)
¾ teaspoon salt, divided
½ cup dry white wine
1 teaspoon chopped fresh thyme
¼ cup (1 ounce) grated fresh Parmigiano-Reggiano cheese
¼ cup chopped fresh flat-leaf parsley
½ teaspoon freshly ground black pepper

❶ Place dried mushrooms in a medium bowl; cover with boiling water. Let stand 30 minutes or until tender; drain. Coarsely chop mushrooms.
❷ Bring Mushroom Stock to a simmer in a small saucepan (do not boil). Keep stock warm over low heat.
❸ Heat a Dutch oven over medium heat. Add oil to pan, swirling to coat. Add farro and onion; cook 5 minutes, stirring occasionally. Add garlic; cook 1 minute, stirring constantly. Add rehydrated mushrooms, cremini mushrooms, and ½ teaspoon salt; sauté 5 minutes or until cremini mushrooms are tender, stirring occasionally. Add wine and thyme, and cook until liquid almost evaporates.
❹ Add ½ cup stock to farro mixture; cook over medium heat 4 minutes or until liquid is nearly absorbed, stirring occasionally. Add 4½ cups stock, ½ cup at a time, stirring occasionally until each portion of stock is absorbed before adding the next (about 40 minutes total).

❺ Add remaining ¼ teaspoon salt, ½ cup stock, cheese, parsley, and pepper; stir until cheese melts. Yield: 6 servings (serving size: 1 cup).

CALORIES 271; FAT 7.1g (sat 1.7g, mono 3.9g, poly 1g); PROTEIN 12.2g; CARB 43.4g; FIBER 8.5g; CHOL 4mg; IRON 1.8mg; SODIUM 378mg; CALC 71mg

WINE NOTE: Serve a sparkling wine with Farro Risotto with Mushrooms— the bubbles match the texture of the grain. Prosecco has become a popular aperitif, but this Soligo Prosecco ($12) is fuller bodied than most, so it stands up well to food. With its vibrant stone fruit flavors, it contrasts pleasantly with the earthy character of the mushrooms that dominate this dish.

Roasted Butternut Soup with Goat Cheese Toasts

Most any winter squash will work in this recipe. We like butternut for the nutty, slightly sweet flavor it lends to the soup. Serve this paired with a hearty salad studded with nuts and seeds for a more filling entrée.

1 (2½-pound) butternut squash
Cooking spray
1 tablespoon extra-virgin olive oil
1½ cups chopped onion
3 garlic cloves, minced
6 cups Roasted Vegetable Stock (page 341)
2 cups coarsely chopped peeled Yukon gold potatoes
2 teaspoons chopped fresh sage
¾ teaspoon salt
¼ teaspoon freshly ground black pepper
1 bay leaf
6 (1-ounce) slices French bread baguette
½ cup (2 ounces) goat cheese, crumbled
1 tablespoon finely chopped fresh chives
2 tablespoons chopped fresh parsley
2 teaspoons honey

❶ Preheat oven to 400°.
❷ Cut squash in half lengthwise; discard seeds. Place squash, cut sides down, on a foil-lined baking sheet coated with cooking spray. Bake at 400° for 30 minutes or until tender. Cool squash. Discard peel; mash pulp.
❸ Heat a Dutch oven over medium-high heat. Add oil to pan, swirling to coat. Add onion; sauté 4 minutes, stirring occasionally. Add garlic; sauté 30 seconds, stirring constantly. Add squash, Roasted Vegetable Stock, and next 5 ingredients; bring to a boil. Reduce heat, and simmer 45 minutes or until potato is tender, stirring occasionally. Let stand 10 minutes. Discard bay leaf.
❹ Preheat broiler.
❺ Place bread slices in a single layer on a baking sheet. Broil 2 minutes or until toasted. Sprinkle about 4 teaspoons cheese on each slice; sprinkle evenly with chives.
❻ Place one-third of vegetable mixture in a blender. Remove center piece of blender lid (to allow steam to escape); secure blender lid on blender. Place a clean towel over opening in blender lid (to avoid splatters). Blend until smooth. Pour into a large bowl. Repeat procedure twice with remaining squash mixture. Return pureed mixture to pan; cook over medium heat 3 minutes or until thoroughly heated. Stir in parsley and honey. Serve with toasts. Yield: 6 servings (serving size: about 1 cup soup and 1 toast).

CALORIES 292; FAT 10.1g (sat 3g, mono 5.7g, poly 1.2g); PROTEIN 7.3g; CARB 47.8g; FIBER 5g; CHOL 7mg; IRON 2.6mg; SODIUM 546mg; CALC 126mg

Great Gratins

Here are the secrets to mastering healthy versions of these piping hot, golden brown, creamy casseroles.

ALTHOUGH THE TERM "GRATIN" IS FRENCH, these rich dishes are mainstays in American cooking. Little wonder. Tender veggies bathed with sauce and topped with a crisp coating are a universal crowd-pleaser. And the varieties and interpretations are countless since the only defining characteristic is the browned top. (The word also refers to shallow dishes in which the food bakes.) This all adds up to good news for you. Just pick your vegetable (or a couple), add a flavorful liquid or sauce, sprinkle the top, and bake. The golden deliciousness is easy to achieve, even while you keep saturated fat in check.

The Basics

Limit the amount of time you bake a light gratin.
Because these sauces rely on lower-fat dairy products like milk, they can curdle if exposed to heat too long. It's best to partially cook the vegetables, assemble the gratin, and bake just until tender; then broil it briefly to brown and crisp the topping.

Although they're often veggie-based, you can cook pasta or other starches au gratin for a change of pace.
Simply follow our four-step guide (on page 344), but use a starch instead of veggies, or combine them. Then let your imagination be your guide.

Transform a gratin into a main dish.
Add protein to create an entrée. Incorporate chopped cooked chicken, ground beef, cooked beans, or tofu before baking.

Nutrition Notes

• Traditional gratins often use copious amounts of heavy cream. Limit saturated fat by substituting milk, broth, or a combination.
• A little full-fat cheese impacts the overall flavor without adding a ton of fat.

Sweet Potato and Butternut Gratin

You can substitute smoked bacon for the pancetta, if you prefer. Assemble up to 2 days ahead, but leave off the Gruyère, cover, and refrigerate. Then top it and bake.

 2 tablespoons butter
 1 ounce pancetta, chopped
 ¼ cup chopped shallots
 2 garlic cloves, minced
 1.38 ounces all-purpose flour, divided (about 5 tablespoons)
 1 teaspoon chopped fresh thyme
 2 cups 2% reduced-fat milk
 ¾ cup (3 ounces) grated fresh Parmigiano-Reggiano cheese
 ½ teaspoon salt
 ½ teaspoon freshly ground black pepper
 ⅛ teaspoon ground red pepper
 1 pound baking potato, peeled and cut into ⅛-inch-thick slices
 8 ounces sweet potato, peeled and cut into ⅛-inch-thick slices
 8 ounces butternut squash, peeled and cut into ⅛-inch-thick slices
 Cooking spray
 ⅓ cup (1½ ounces) shredded Gruyère cheese

❶ Melt butter in a small saucepan over medium-high heat. Add pancetta; cook 1 minute. Add shallots and garlic, and cook 2 minutes, stirring constantly. Weigh or lightly spoon 1.1 ounces (about ¼ cup) flour into a dry measuring cup; level with a knife. Add to pan; cook 2 minutes, stirring constantly with a whisk. Stir in thyme. Gradually add milk, stirring constantly with a whisk; cook over medium heat until slightly thick (about 3 minutes), stirring constantly. Stir in Parmigiano-Reggiano; cook 3 minutes or until cheese melts. Stir in salt and peppers. Remove from heat.
❷ Preheat oven to 375°.
❸ Cook baking potato in boiling water 4 minutes or until almost tender; remove with a slotted spoon. Cook sweet potato in boiling water 4 minutes or until almost tender; remove with a slotted spoon. Cook butternut squash in boiling water 4 minutes or until almost tender; drain. Sprinkle vegetables evenly with remaining 1 tablespoon flour. Arrange potatoes and squash in alternating layers in a broiler-safe 11 x 7-inch baking dish coated with cooking spray; spoon sauce over potato mixture. Top with Gruyère. Bake at 375° for 40 minutes.
❹ Preheat broiler. Broil 3 minutes or until golden. Let stand 10 minutes. Yield: 8 servings (serving size: about ½ cup).

CALORIES 220; FAT 8.7g (sat 5.2g, mono 2.2g, poly 0.3g); PROTEIN 9.7g; CARB 26.2g; FIBER 2.6g; CHOL 25mg; IRON 1.3mg; SODIUM 418mg; CALC 259mg

4 Steps to Gorgeous, Tasty Gratins

1 Slice or dice ingredients into uniform shapes and sizes. You can choose the size and shape of your veggies so long as they're all the same. That way they will cook evenly. Thin or thick slices work just as well as small- to medium-sized cubes. Of course, thicker, larger pieces will take a little more time to cook.

2 Partially cook. Once you cut the vegetables, partially cook them in milk, broth, or water until they're almost tender. This cuts down on the amount of time the dish has to bake once assembled. If you want to get a jump start on the recipe, you can prepare and assemble the gratin, but leave the topping off.

3 Arrange in baking dish, and top with breadcrumbs, cheese, or a combination. Breadcrumbs will brown easily and become crisp if they're tossed with a bit of butter. Cheese browns well, too. You can also add finely chopped nuts to the topping.

4 Cook until browned and bubbly. The word "gratin" actually refers to the browned bits on top of any food prepared in this style, so this is the heart of the dish. Broiling for the last few minutes ensures a nice browned top.

Turnip-Parsnip Gratin

A mandoline will slice the veggies into uniform thickness and make quick work of it.

- 3¾ cups (⅛-inch-thick) slices peeled turnip
- 3¾ cups (⅛-inch-thick) slices peeled parsnip
- 6 cups water
- Cooking spray
- 1 cup whole milk
- ⅓ cup fat-free, less-sodium chicken broth
- 2 tablespoons all-purpose flour
- 1 teaspoon kosher salt
- ½ teaspoon freshly ground black pepper
- 1 cup (4 ounces) shredded Gruyère cheese
- 2 tablespoons butter
- ¼ cup panko (Japanese breadcrumbs)

1 Preheat oven to 400°.

2 Combine first 3 ingredients in a large saucepan; bring to a boil. Reduce heat, and simmer 7 minutes or until almost tender. Drain; let stand 5 minutes. Arrange about ½ cup vegetable mixture into each of 8 (5½-inch) round gratin dishes coated with cooking spray.

3 Combine milk and next 4 ingredients in a saucepan over medium-high heat; bring to a simmer. Cook 4 minutes, stirring constantly with a whisk until thick. Remove from heat; add cheese, stirring with a whisk until smooth. Spoon about 3 tablespoons sauce over each serving.

4 Melt butter in a medium skillet over medium-high heat. Add panko; toast 2 minutes, stirring constantly. Sprinkle breadcrumb mixture evenly over cheese mixture. Place dishes on a baking sheet. Bake at 400° for 15 minutes or until bubbly and golden brown on top. Let stand 5 minutes before serving. Yield: 8 servings (serving size: 1 gratin).

CALORIES 196; FAT 8.8g (sat 5.1g, mono 2.5g, poly 0.5g); PROTEIN 7.6g; CARB 22.8g; FIBER 5.3g; CHOL 26mg; IRON 0.9mg; SODIUM 424mg; CALC 236mg

Potato Gratin

Inspired by the French classic potatoes *dauphinoise,* this dish is rich, gooey, and comforting. Yukon gold potatoes lend a buttery flavor, but russets will work, too.

- 1 garlic clove, peeled and halved
- 1 tablespoon unsalted butter, softened
- 2½ cups whole milk
- 2 tablespoons minced shallots
- ¼ teaspoon kosher salt
- ¼ teaspoon freshly ground black pepper
- Dash of grated whole nutmeg
- 2 pounds Yukon gold potatoes, peeled and cut into ⅛-inch-thick slices
- ½ cup (2 ounces) shredded Gruyère cheese
- ¼ cup (1 ounce) grated fresh Parmigiano-Reggiano cheese

❶ Preheat oven to 375°.
❷ Rub a broiler-safe 11 x 7–inch baking dish with garlic; discard garlic. Coat dish with butter. Combine milk and next 5 ingredients in a skillet; bring to a simmer. Cook 8 minutes or until potatoes are almost tender. Spoon potato mixture into prepared baking dish. Sprinkle with cheeses. Bake at 375° for 35 minutes.
❸ Preheat broiler. Broil 3 minutes or until golden. Let stand 10 minutes. Yield: 8 servings (serving size: about ½ cup).

CALORIES 198; FAT 7.2g (sat 4.3g, mono 2g, poly 0.4g); PROTEIN 8.7g; CARB 24.1g; FIBER 1.4g; CHOL 22mg; IRON 1.1mg; SODIUM 311mg; CALC 204mg

Breakfast, Lunch, and Dinner in... Los Angeles

Fresh ingredients, international flavors, and top-notch chefs, like Suzanne Goin of Lucques, are the stars of L.A.'s food scene.

LOS ANGELES' REPUTATION for fad diets and la-la land power lunches is deserved, but it obscures the deeper fact of its exceptional food. Yes, certain Angelenos entertain magical ideas about the power of, say, acai berries, to give them an edge in the hyper-body-conscious showbiz world. But on the bright, sunny West Coast, health is naturally a priority, and good food a focus.

"People in Los Angeles really do have an orientation to eating more healthfully," says Pat Saperstein, founder of the blog Eating L.A. "They think about it every day, and so there are likely to be more places where you can find healthier choices than in other cities."

L.A. cuisine is also heavily influenced by its wildly diverse population, with accents ranging from Latino to Armenian to Japanese. Strip-mall spots serve ethereal house-made Korean tofu. Haute fusion restaurants offer small-plate paragons of perfection. World cuisines are blended and tweaked for the city's legions of adventurous eaters.

Breakfast

QUICK & EASY • KID FRIENDLY
Banana-Agave Smoothie

Whether or not you're glowing from an early-morning Pilates class, the classic L.A. morning meal on the go is a smoothie, eminently portable and fruit-packed. The classic spot to pick one up is Beverly Hills Juice (beverlyhillsjuice.com), just beyond the Beverly Hills city limits. Since 1975, this unassuming white-tiled storefront has served wheatgrass shots and thick, banana-blended smoothies to a toned, health-conscious crowd. For a refreshing "shake," as they're called, try banana-sunflower seed with coconut-apple-mint juice. Robeks (robeks.com), based in nearby Manhattan Beach, offers a kaleidoscopic array of tropical fruit smoothies; standouts are the Mahalo Mango, with papaya juice, mango, and pineapple sherbet, and the signature Hummingbird, with guava juice, mangoes, strawberries, and bananas. Thick and fruity, this shake is a simple, quick breakfast ideal for fast-paced yet health-minded Los Angeles residents, or anyone looking to eat and get out the door in a hurry.

- 1 cup plain fat-free yogurt
- ⅓ cup fresh or frozen blueberries, thawed
- 2 teaspoons light-colored agave nectar
- 1 chilled sliced ripe banana

❶ Place all ingredients in a blender; process until smooth. Yield: 1 serving (serving size: 1¼ cups).

CALORIES 273; FAT 0.3g (sat 0g, mono 0.1g, poly 0.2g); PROTEIN 11.3g; CARB 65.3g; FIBER 4.3g; CHOL 5mg; IRON 0mg; SODIUM 135mg; CALC 300mg

Lunch

Carne Asada Taco with Avocado Pico de Gallo

On a warm L.A. day, lunch is best when it's light, spicy, and quick. Angelenos are passionate about the offerings of taco trucks, and you can find them throughout the city, each with its own take on the classic. Equally exceptional versions are offered at tiny sit-down diners. The menu at Señor Fish (senorfishla.com), in Eagle Rock, contains 11 different choices; don't miss the kicky carne asada tacos and the grilled scallop tacos. Along with a funky crowd, it has a terrific porch. If you don't have a gas stove to cook the tortillas, char them slightly in a grill pan over high heat.

- ¼ cup fresh lime juice (about 2 medium)
- 1 (1-pound) skirt steak, trimmed
- 1 teaspoon ground cumin
- ½ teaspoon kosher salt
- ½ teaspoon ground red pepper
- Cooking spray
- 1 cup diced seeded plum tomato
- ¼ cup diced onion
- 3 tablespoons finely chopped fresh cilantro
- 1 tablespoon diced seeded jalapeño pepper
- 1 tablespoon fresh lime juice
- 1 garlic clove, minced
- ¾ cup diced avocado (about 1 medium)
- ¼ teaspoon kosher salt
- 8 corn tortillas
- Lime wedges (optional)

❶ Combine ¼ cup juice and steak in a shallow dish. Sprinkle cumin, ½ teaspoon salt, and red pepper over both sides of steak. Cover and marinate in refrigerator 3 hours.

❷ Heat grill pan over high heat. Coat pan with cooking spray. Add steak to pan; cook 3 minutes on each side or until desired degree of doneness. Let stand at least 10 minutes. Cut steak into ½-inch pieces.

❸ Combine tomato and next 5 ingredients in a bowl. Gently stir in avocado and ¼ teaspoon salt.

❹ Heat tortillas over gas flame 15 seconds on each side or until charred on edges. Divide steak evenly among tortillas. Top with pico de gallo. Serve with lime wedges, if desired. Yield: 4 servings (serving size: 2 steak-filled tortillas and ¼ cup pico de gallo).

CALORIES 372; FAT 15.8g (sat 4.1g, mono 8.4g, poly 1.6g); PROTEIN 27.6g; CARB 32.6g; FIBER 5g; CHOL 50mg; IRON 4mg; SODIUM 505mg; CALC 115mg

Dinner

Spaghetti with Caramelized Onion and Radicchio

Although they helped invent fusion cuisine, influential L.A. chefs have moved beyond it. Their "Cal-Med" style blends Mediterranean ingredients with farm-fresh Southern California produce. Taste some of the best at Chef Mark Peel's Campanile (campanilerestaurant.com) or at Chef Suzanne Goin's beloved and low-key Lucques (lucques.com).

- 1 tablespoon olive oil
- 6 cups thinly sliced yellow onion (about 1¾ pounds)
- ½ teaspoon crushed red pepper
- 6 garlic cloves, minced
- ½ cup dry white wine
- 1 pound uncooked spaghetti
- 3½ cups thinly sliced radicchio (about 1 head)
- 2 tablespoons chopped fresh flat-leaf parsley
- 2 teaspoons chopped fresh oregano
- 1 teaspoon salt
- ½ teaspoon freshly ground black pepper
- ¾ cup (3 ounces) crumbled Parmigiano-Reggiano cheese

❶ Heat oil in a large Dutch oven over medium-high heat. Add onion; sauté 15 minutes or until almost tender, stirring frequently. Reduce heat to medium-low; cook until deep golden (about 20 minutes), stirring occasionally. Add red pepper and garlic. Cook 3 minutes, stirring occasionally. Add wine; cook 4 minutes or until liquid evaporates.

❷ Cook pasta according to package directions, omitting salt and fat. Drain pasta in a colander over a bowl, reserving ½ cup cooking liquid. Add reserved cooking liquid, pasta, radicchio, parsley, and oregano to onion mixture. Sprinkle with salt and black pepper; toss to combine. Top with cheese. Yield: 8 servings (serving size: about 1¼ cups pasta mixture and 1½ tablespoons cheese).

CALORIES 300; FAT 5.8g (sat 2.3g, mono 2.3g, poly 0.7g); PROTEIN 12.1g; CARB 49.7g; FIBER 4.1g; CHOL 9mg; IRON 2.5mg; SODIUM 468mg; CALC 160mg

L.A. cuisine is also heavily influenced by its wildly diverse population, with accents ranging from Latino to Armenian to Japanese.

Feed 4 for Less Than $10

Fall flavors and ingredients lend themselves to tasty but economical eating.

$2.12 per serving; $8.47 total
Stewed Pork and Squash

- 1 tablespoon canola oil
- ¾ cup chopped onion
- 1 medium garlic clove, minced
- 1 pound boneless pork shoulder, cut into ½-inch pieces
- 1½ tablespoons chili powder
- 1 teaspoon ground cumin
- ½ teaspoon salt
- ¼ teaspoon ground red pepper
- 1½ cups fat-free, less-sodium chicken broth
- 1 (15-ounce) can stewed tomatoes, undrained
- 4 cups cubed peeled butternut squash (about 1½ pounds)

① Heat oil in a large saucepan over medium-high heat. Add onion and garlic; sauté 2 minutes, stirring frequently. Add pork; cook 5 minutes, browning on all sides. Stir in chili powder and next 3 ingredients; cook 30 seconds, stirring constantly. Stir in broth and tomatoes; bring to a simmer. Cover, reduce heat, and simmer 1½ hours or until pork is almost tender, stirring occasionally. Stir in squash; simmer 30 minutes or until pork and squash are tender. Yield: 4 servings (serving size: 1½ cups).

CALORIES 393; FAT 16g (sat 4.6g, mono 7.5g, poly 2.2g); PROTEIN 28g; CARB 37.9g; FIBER 6.6g; CHOL 89mg; IRON 4.9mg; SODIUM 768mg; CALC 186mg

CORN MUFFINS:

Combine 2.25 ounces (about ½ cup) all-purpose flour, ⅓ cup yellow cornmeal, 1 tablespoon sugar, 1 teaspoon baking powder, and ¼ teaspoon salt in a medium bowl; stir with a whisk. Combine ⅓ cup low-fat buttermilk, 2 tablespoons melted butter, and 1 large egg white; add to flour mixture, stirring just until moist. Spoon batter into 4 muffin cups coated with cooking spray. Bake at 425° for 12 minutes or until muffins spring back when lightly touched.

$2.41 per serving; $9.65 total
Beef-Barley Soup

A generous portion of this hearty soup is satisfying as a one-dish meal. If chuck roast is on sale, purchase a large one and freeze the rest for later. If not, ask your butcher to cut off only the amount you need.

- Cooking spray
- ¾ pound boneless chuck roast, trimmed and cut into ½-inch pieces
- 1½ cups thinly sliced carrot
- 1½ cups thinly sliced celery
- ⅔ cup chopped onion
- 1 (8-ounce) package presliced mushrooms
- 4 cups fat-free, less-sodium beef broth
- 1 bay leaf
- ⅔ cup uncooked pearl barley
- ½ teaspoon salt
- ½ teaspoon black pepper

① Heat a Dutch oven over medium-high heat. Coat pan with cooking spray. Add beef to pan; cook 4 minutes or until browned, stirring frequently. Remove beef from pan. Add carrot and next 3 ingredients to pan; cook 6 minutes or until liquid almost evaporates. Add beef, broth, and bay leaf. Bring to a simmer over medium-high heat. Cover, reduce heat, and simmer 1½ hours or until beef is tender, stirring occasionally. Stir in barley; cover and simmer 30 minutes or until tender. Stir in salt and pepper. Discard bay leaf. Yield: 4 servings (serving size: 2 cups).

CALORIES 341; FAT 11.4g (sat 4.3g, mono 4.6g, poly 0.8g); PROTEIN 24.1g; CARB 36.2g; FIBER 8.2g; CHOL 53mg; IRON 2.8mg; SODIUM 837mg; CALC 61mg

$2.32 per serving; $9.26 total
Dan Dan Noodles

- 1 pound frozen fresh wide Chinese egg noodles, thawed
- 2 tablespoons canola oil
- ⅓ cup dry-roasted peanuts
- 3 tablespoons low-sodium soy sauce
- 1 tablespoon sambal oelek (ground fresh chile paste)
- 1 teaspoon sugar
- 2 garlic cloves
- 1 (½-inch) piece fresh ginger, peeled
- 8 ounces lean ground pork
- ⅛ teaspoon salt
- 3 tablespoons fresh lime juice
- ¾ cup thinly diagonally sliced green onions
- 1¼ cups chopped seeded peeled cucumber
- ¼ cup chopped fresh cilantro

① Cook noodles in 6 quarts boiling water 3 minutes. Drain in a colander over a bowl, reserving ¾ cup cooking liquid. Place noodles in a large bowl.
② Heat oil in a large nonstick skillet over medium-high heat. Add peanuts to pan; sauté 2 minutes or until fragrant. Remove from heat; cool slightly. Combine peanut mixture, soy sauce, and next 4 ingredients in a mini chopper; process until finely ground.
③ Cook pork and salt in skillet over medium-high heat 8 minutes or until done, stirring to crumble. Add peanut mixture and ¾ cup cooking liquid to pork; bring to a boil. Cook 1 minute, stirring frequently. Add pork mixture, juice, and onions to noodles; toss well. Place about 1¾ cup noodle mixture in each of 4 bowls; top each serving with 5 tablespoons cucumber and 1 tablespoon cilantro. Yield: 4 servings.

CALORIES 541; FAT 17.2g (sat 3.5g, mono 8.2g, poly 4.2g); PROTEIN 31g; CARB 66.1g; FIBER 3.9g; CHOL 43mg; IRON 1.6mg; SODIUM 914mg; CALC 54mg

$2.10 per serving; $8.40 total
Bistro Braised Chicken

- 1 tablespoon butter, divided
- 8 (4-ounce) bone-in chicken thighs, skinned
- 1 cup thinly sliced carrot
- ¾ cup chopped onion
- ½ cup thinly sliced celery
- 8 pitted dried plums, chopped
- ½ teaspoon dried thyme
- ¼ teaspoon dried sage
- 2 teaspoons Dijon mustard
- 1 (14-ounce) can fat-free, less-sodium chicken broth
- ¾ cup water
- ½ teaspoon salt
- ½ teaspoon black pepper
- 4 cups hot cooked egg noodles

1 Melt 1 teaspoon butter in a large skillet over medium heat. Add chicken to pan; cook 6 minutes, browning on both sides. Remove chicken from pan; keep warm.

2 Add remaining 2 teaspoons butter to pan, swirling until butter melts. Add carrot and next 3 ingredients; cook 4 minutes or until vegetables begin to soften, stirring frequently. Stir in thyme and sage; cook 30 seconds. Stir in mustard. Add broth and ¾ cup water, scraping pan to loosen browned bits; bring to a simmer.

3 Return chicken to pan. Cover, reduce heat, and simmer 35 minutes. Uncover, increase heat to medium-high, and simmer until sauce is reduced by half (about 10 minutes). Stir in salt and pepper. Serve over noodles. Yield: 4 servings (serving size: 1 cup egg noodles, 2 chicken thighs, and about ½ cup vegetable mixture.)

CALORIES 483; FAT 11.5g (sat 4.3g, mono 3.9g, poly 1.8g); PROTEIN 36.9g; CARB 57.3g; FIBER 5g; CHOL 189mg; IRON 3.7mg; SODIUM 765mg; CALC 76mg

WINE NOTE: This simple dinner deserves a tasty, affordable wine. Astica Chardonnay 2008 ($6), from Argentina, is made without the use of oak, making it a nice, fruity match for the dried plums in this stew.

Dinner Tonight

Here are seven stopwatch-tested menus from the *Cooking Light* Test Kitchens.

Shopping List

Red Onion, Potato, and Goat Cheese Pizza
7 ounces fingerling potatoes
1 medium red onion
garlic
fresh thyme
olive oil
cornmeal
1 (13.5-ounce) can refrigerated pizza crust dough
1 cup shredded part-skim mozzarella cheese
3 ounces goat cheese

Romaine-Radicchio Salad
garlic
romaine lettuce
radicchio
balsamic vinegar
extra-virgin olive oil
dried oregano

Game Plan

- While water for potatoes comes to a boil:
  - Slice onion.
  - Crumble cheese.
  - Mince garlic (for pizza and salad).
- While potatoes cook:
  - Sauté onion.
  - Roll out pizza dough.
- While pizza bakes:
  - Prepare vinaigrette.
  - Toss salad.

Picking Good Potatoes

When buying potatoes of any type, look for firm texture, smooth skin with no green coloration, and no sprouts. Fingerlings are any type bred to be small, long, and, well, vaguely finger-shaped.

Red Onion, Potato, and Goat Cheese Pizza with Romaine-Radicchio Salad
······················*40 minutes*

The sweetness of red onions is tempered by tangy goat cheese in this carb-lover's pizza. Use any color fingerling potatoes you like—blue or purple varieties are particularly dramatic.

Prep Pointer: If the dough is difficult to roll out, let it rest for about 5 minutes, and then try again.

Simple Sub: In place of goat cheese, try feta or queso fresco.

Flavor Hit: Fresh thyme is sprinkled on after the pizza is baked to keep the color and taste vibrant.

- 7 ounces fingerling potatoes (about 5 potatoes)
- 1 teaspoon olive oil
- 1 medium red onion, cut into ½-inch-thick slices
- 1 (13.8-ounce) can refrigerated pizza crust dough
- 2 tablespoons cornmeal
- 1 cup (4 ounces) shredded part-skim mozzarella cheese
- ¾ cup (3 ounces) crumbled goat cheese
- 1 garlic clove, minced
- 1½ teaspoons fresh thyme leaves

1 Preheat oven to 450°.

2 Place potatoes in a saucepan; cover with water. Bring to a boil. Cook 10 minutes or until just tender; drain. Cool slightly; cut potatoes crosswise into ¼-inch slices.

3 Heat oil in a large nonstick skillet over medium-high heat. Add onion to pan, and sauté 8 minutes or until tender.

4 Roll dough out on a lightly floured surface to a 14 x 10-inch rectangle. Sprinkle cornmeal over a large baking sheet; place dough on baking sheet. Sprinkle mozzarella evenly over dough. Arrange potatoes and onion over mozzarella; top evenly with goat cheese and garlic. Bake in lower third of oven at 450° for 15 minutes or until browned. Sprinkle with thyme; cut into 12 pieces. Yield: 6 servings (serving size: 2 pieces).

CALORIES 314; FAT 10.3g (sat 4.9g, mono 3.7g, poly 0.6g); PROTEIN 14.4g; CARB 39.8g; FIBER 1.8g; CHOL 22mg; IRON 2.4mg; SODIUM 599mg; CALC 173mg

ROMAINE-RADICCHIO SALAD:

Combine 2 tablespoons balsamic vinegar, 2 tablespoons extra-virgin olive oil, 1 teaspoon minced garlic, $\frac{1}{4}$ teaspoon salt, and $\frac{1}{8}$ teaspoon dried oregano in a large bowl, stirring with a whisk. Add 5 cups thinly sliced romaine lettuce and 2 cups thinly sliced radicchio; toss to coat. Sprinkle with freshly ground black pepper.

Shopping List

Black Pepper and Molasses Pulled Chicken Sandwiches
ketchup
cider vinegar
prepared mustard
molasses
chili powder
ground cumin
ground ginger
dill pickle chips
2-ounce sandwich rolls
12 ounces skinless, boneless chicken thighs

Mango Slaw
4 cups packaged cabbage-and-carrot coleslaw
1 mango
1 small red onion
canola mayonnaise
cider vinegar
sugar

Game Plan

• While chicken mixture cooks:
  • Split rolls.
  • Prepare slaw; chill until ready to serve.

QUICK & EASY • KID FRIENDLY

Black Pepper and Molasses Pulled Chicken Sandwiches with Mango Slaw

·······································*30 minutes*

This sauce delivers great barbecue taste. Chili powder and cumin add smokiness, while ketchup and molasses provide sweetness. 'Cue lovers in North Carolina put the slaw on the sandwich. Try it for a change.

Simple Sub: Try pork tenderloin in place of chicken thighs.

Flavor Hit: Molasses adds body and sweet, subtly bitter notes to the sauce.

Make-Ahead Tip: Double the chicken mixture, and freeze half for up to one month.

3	tablespoons ketchup
1	tablespoon cider vinegar
1	tablespoon prepared mustard
1	tablespoon molasses
$\frac{3}{4}$	teaspoon chili powder
$\frac{1}{2}$	teaspoon ground cumin
$\frac{1}{4}$	teaspoon freshly ground black pepper
$\frac{1}{8}$	teaspoon ground ginger
12	ounces skinless, boneless chicken thighs, cut into 2-inch pieces
4	(2-ounce) sandwich rolls, cut in half horizontally
12	dill pickle chips

1 Combine first 9 ingredients in a medium saucepan; bring to a boil. Reduce heat to medium-low; cover and cook, stirring occasionally, 23 minutes or until chicken is done and tender. Remove from heat; shred with 2 forks to measure 2 cups meat. Place $\frac{1}{2}$ cup chicken on bottom half of each roll. Top each with 3 pickles and top half of roll. Yield: 4 servings (serving size: 1 sandwich).

CALORIES 294; FAT 6.5g (sat 1.5g, mono 2.6g, poly 1.4g); PROTEIN 22g; CARB 35.6g; FIBER 1.8g; CHOL 71mg; IRON 3.1mg; SODIUM 698mg; CALC 105mg

MANGO SLAW:

Combine 4 cups packaged cabbage-and-carrot coleslaw, 1 cup chopped mango, and $\frac{1}{4}$ cup vertically sliced red onion in a large bowl. Add $\frac{1}{4}$ cup canola mayonnaise, 1 tablespoon cider vinegar, 1 tablespoon sugar, and $\frac{1}{4}$ teaspoon salt; toss well to coat.

BEER NOTE: Apricots are a popular fruit among brewers of beer, and for very good reason. Their distinctive fruity flavor is especially refreshing with grilled, spicy, and barbecue-style dishes. Magic Hat #9 from Vermont ($8/6-pack) has more subtle apricot notes, finishing crisp and dry.

Shopping List

Greek Pasta with Meatballs
garlic
fresh parsley
2 cups orzo pasta
2 cups marinara sauce
plain dry breadcrumbs
dried oregano
ground cinnamon
olive oil
1 pound lean ground lamb
large eggs
3 ounces feta cheese

Fennel-Onion Salad
1 large fennel bulb
1 small red onion
1 lemon
extra-virgin olive oil
Dijon mustard

Game Plan

• While water for orzo comes to a boil:
  • Combine lamb with seasonings.
  • Form meatballs.
• While orzo cooks:
  • Brown meatballs.
• While meatballs bake in oven:
  • Prepare salad.

Continued

Greek Pasta with Meatballs with Fennel-Onion Salad
·······································*30 minutes*

This riff on spaghetti and meatballs uses rice-shaped pasta, ground lamb, and feta cheese.

Flavor Hit: Sharp and tangy feta cheese is a fitting complement to spiced lamb.

Simple Sub: Substitute ground beef or turkey for lamb; add more breadcrumbs as needed.

Make-Ahead Tip: Brown meatballs, freeze on a tray, and store in a zip-top bag one month.

- ⅓ cup plain dry breadcrumbs
- ½ teaspoon dried oregano
- ¼ teaspoon salt
- ¼ teaspoon ground cinnamon
- ¼ teaspoon freshly ground black pepper
- 1 pound lean ground lamb
- 1 garlic clove, minced
- 2 tablespoons chopped fresh parsley, divided
- 2 large egg whites
- 1½ teaspoons olive oil
- 2 cups jarred marinara sauce
- ¾ cup (3 ounces) crumbled feta cheese
- 2 cups hot cooked orzo

❶ Preheat oven to 375°.

❷ Combine first 7 ingredients in a medium bowl; stir in 1½ tablespoons parsley. Add egg whites, stirring mixture until just combined. Shape mixture into 12 (1-inch) meatballs; cover and chill meatballs 5 minutes.

❸ Heat oil in a large ovenproof skillet over medium-high heat. Add meatballs to pan; cook 8 minutes, turning to brown on all sides. Drain well; wipe pan clean with paper towels. Return meatballs to pan. Spoon marinara sauce over meatballs; sprinkle with cheese. Bake at 375° for 11 minutes or until meatballs are done. Sprinkle with remaining 1½ teaspoons parsley. Serve over orzo. Yield:

4 servings (serving size: ½ cup orzo, 3 meatballs, and ½ cup sauce).

CALORIES 486; FAT 14.1g (sat 5.7g, mono 4.5g, poly 0.8g); PROTEIN 37.4g; CARB 50.7g; FIBER 3.9g; CHOL 94mg; IRON 5.8mg; SODIUM 919mg; CALC 164mg

FENNEL-ONION SALAD:
Combine 2 cups vertically sliced fennel bulb and ½ cup vertically sliced red onion in a medium bowl. Combine 1½ tablespoons extra-virgin olive oil, 1 tablespoon fresh lemon juice, ¼ teaspoon kosher salt, ¼ teaspoon freshly ground black pepper, and ¼ teaspoon Dijon mustard. Drizzle over salad; toss to combine.

Shopping List

Asian Turkey Cabbage Cups
fresh ginger
green onions
fresh cilantro
fresh mint
2 limes
1 jalapeño pepper
1 head napa cabbage
brown sugar
olive oil
dark sesame oil
fish sauce
unsalted dry-roasted peanuts
1¼ pounds ground turkey

Rice Noodle Salad
1 English cucumber
1 small red bell pepper
1 lime
fresh mint
6 ounces rice noodles
rice vinegar
crushed red pepper
sugar

Game Plan

- While water for noodles comes to a boil:
  - Cook turkey.
  - Chop herbs and jalapeño.
- While noodles cook:
  - Combine turkey with seasonings.
  - Prepare cucumber and bell pepper.
  - Prepare dressing for salad.

Asian Turkey Cabbage Cups with Rice Noodle Salad
·······································*30 minutes*

Cool, crisp napa (Chinese) cabbage leaves cradle a hot and spicy herbed filling in this quick dish.

Time-Saver: Use bottled fresh ginger from the produce section.

Buy the Best: We prefer Three Crabs brand fish sauce, available at Asian markets.

Vegetarian Swap: Omit fish sauce; substitute crumbled extra-firm tofu for the turkey.

- 1 teaspoon grated peeled fresh ginger
- 1¼ pounds ground turkey
- ½ cup thinly sliced green onions
- 1 tablespoon brown sugar
- 2 tablespoons chopped fresh cilantro
- 2 tablespoons chopped fresh mint
- 2 tablespoons fresh lime juice
- 1½ tablespoons fish sauce
- 2 teaspoons olive oil
- 1 teaspoon dark sesame oil
- 1 jalapeño pepper, finely chopped
- 12 large napa (Chinese) cabbage leaves (about 8 ounces)
- ¼ cup chopped unsalted, dry-roasted peanuts

❶ Heat a large nonstick skillet over medium heat. Add ginger and turkey to pan; cook 7 minutes or until turkey is done, stirring frequently. Drain turkey mixture; place in a large bowl. Add green onions and next 8 ingredients; toss well. Spoon ⅓ cup turkey mixture into each cabbage leaf. Top with peanuts. Yield: 4 servings (serving size: 3 filled cabbage cups).

CALORIES 267; FAT 13.6g (sat 3.7g, mono 6.4g, poly 2.7g); PROTEIN 30.3g; CARB 7.6g; FIBER 1.4g; CHOL 89mg; IRON 1.8mg; SODIUM 637mg; CALC 111mg

RICE NOODLE SALAD:
Cook 6 ounces rice noodles according to package directions. Drain and rinse with cold water; drain. Combine noodles, ⅔ cup chopped English cucumber, and ⅔ cup red bell pepper strips. Whisk

together 1 tablespoon fresh lime juice, 1 teaspoon rice vinegar, ¼ teaspoon crushed red pepper, and ¼ teaspoon sugar; toss with noodle mixture and 2 tablespoons chopped fresh mint.

WINE NOTE: A dish laced with ginger, mint, and lime wants a highly aromatic wine partner. Chenin blanc is a natural. Dry Creek Vineyard's 2008 version from Clarksburg, California ($12), is loaded with peach and mango flavors that create an exotic buzz with the ginger, plus a hint of sweetness that handles the spice.

Shopping List

Seafood Arrabbiata
1 small onion
garlic
fresh parsley
fresh basil
8 ounces linguine
extra-virgin olive oil
crushed red pepper
tomato paste
1 (14.5-ounce) can petite-cut diced
    tomatoes
1 bottle clam juice
6 ounces bay scallops
6 ounces peeled and deveined medium
    shrimp
12 littleneck clams
12 mussels

Garlic Broccoli Rabe
1 bunch broccoli rabe
garlic
1 lemon
olive oil

Game Plan

- While water for pasta comes to a boil:
  - Chop onion.
  - Mince garlic.
  - Drain tomatoes.
- Blanch broccoli rabe; remove with a slotted spoon, then add pasta.
- While pasta cooks:
  - Prepare sauce for pasta.
  - Prepare side dish.

Seafood Arrabbiata with Garlic Broccoli Rabe

·······························*40 minutes*

Italian for "angry," arrabbiata is a spicy tomato sauce. For true fury, use ½ teaspoon crushed red pepper.
Time-Saver: Use 2 to 3 teaspoons bottled minced garlic in place of the 3 cloves.
Simple Sub: This recipe is equally good with fettuccine or spaghetti.
Flavor Hit: The sauce's characteristic spicy flavor comes from crushed red pepper.

8   ounces uncooked linguine
2   tablespoons extra-virgin olive oil, divided
6   ounces bay scallops
6   ounces peeled and deveined medium shrimp
½   cup chopped onion
¼   to ½ teaspoon crushed red pepper
3   garlic cloves, minced
2   tablespoons tomato paste
1   (14.5-ounce) can petite-cut diced tomatoes, drained
½   cup clam juice
12 littleneck clams
12 mussels, scrubbed and debearded
2   tablespoons chopped fresh parsley
1   tablespoon thinly sliced fresh basil

❶ Cook pasta according to package directions, omitting salt and fat; drain.
❷ While pasta cooks, heat 1 tablespoon oil in a large nonstick skillet over medium-high heat. Add scallops and shrimp to pan; cook 3 minutes. Remove scallop mixture from pan; keep warm. Heat remaining 1 tablespoon oil in pan over medium-high heat. Add onion, red pepper, and garlic; cook 2 minutes. Add tomato paste and tomatoes; bring to a boil, and cook 2 minutes. Add clam juice; cook 1 minute. Add clams; cover, reduce heat to medium, and cook 4 minutes. Add mussels; cover and cook 3 minutes or until clams and mussels open. Discard any unopened

---

shells. Stir in scallop mixture and parsley; cook 1 minute or until thoroughly heated. Serve over pasta. Sprinkle with basil. Yield: 4 servings (serving size: about 2 cups).

CALORIES 444; FAT 10g (sat 1.6g, mono 5.3g, poly 1.5g); PROTEIN 34g; CARB 54g; FIBER 3.9g; CHOL 102mg; IRON 9.3mg; SODIUM 447mg; CALC 95mg

GARLIC BROCCOLI RABE:
Cook 1 bunch broccoli rabe in boiling water 1 minute; drain well. Heat 1 tablespoon olive oil in a large nonstick skillet over medium-high heat. Add 3 sliced garlic cloves; sauté 1 minute. Add broccoli rabe and ¼ teaspoon salt; cook 1 minute. Sprinkle with 1½ teaspoons grated lemon rind.

Shopping List

Halibut with Spicy Mint-Cilantro Chutney
1 serrano pepper
fresh cilantro
fresh mint
green onions
1 lemon
fresh ginger
garlic
sugar
cumin seeds
garam masala
canola oil
butter
2% Greek-style yogurt
⅓-less-fat cream cheese
4 (6-ounce) skinless halibut fillets

Basmati-Green Pea Rice
green onions
1 cup basmati rice
frozen green peas

Game Plan

- While water for rice comes to a boil:
  - Make chutney.
- While rice cooks:
  - Coat fish in spice mixture.
  - Rinse peas to thaw.
  - Cook fish.
  - Chop onions for rice.

Continued

Halibut with Spicy Mint-Cilantro Chutney with Basmati–Green Pea Rice

·························*30 minutes*

Traditional Indian cuisine provides the theme for this speedy menu. A fiery sauce accompanies fish that's coated in a fragrant spice blend. If you're wary of spicy-hot food, remove and discard all the seeds and membranes from the serrano.

Buy the Best: Greek yogurt is thick and creamy, yielding a chutney with pleasing body.

Flavor Hit: Garam masala is an Indian spice blend that boasts pungent, sweet, and smoky flavors.

1	serrano pepper, halved
½	cup fresh cilantro leaves
½	cup chopped green onions
¼	cup 2% Greek-style yogurt (such as Fage)
4	teaspoons ⅓-less-fat cream cheese
1½	teaspoons fresh lemon juice
½	teaspoon minced peeled fresh ginger
⅛	teaspoon salt
⅛	teaspoon sugar
⅛	teaspoon cumin seeds
1	garlic clove, crushed
2	tablespoons chopped fresh mint
½	teaspoon garam masala
¼	teaspoon salt
4	(6-ounce) skinless halibut fillets
1	tablespoon canola oil
1	tablespoon butter

❶ Remove seeds from half of serrano pepper; leave seeds in other half of pepper. Place both pepper halves in a mini food processor; pulse 5 times or until minced. Add cilantro and next 9 ingredients; process until smooth. Stir in mint. ❷ Heat a large nonstick skillet over medium-high heat. Combine garam masala and ¼ teaspoon salt; sprinkle evenly over fish. Add oil and butter to pan, swirling until butter melts. Add

fish to pan; cook 3 minutes on each side or until desired degree of doneness. Serve chutney with fish. Yield: 4 servings (serving size: 1 fillet and ¼ cup chutney).

CALORIES 286; FAT 11.6g (sat 3.4g, mono 4.4g, poly 2.5g); PROTEIN 37.9g; CARB 5.6g; FIBER 1.1g; CHOL 66mg; IRON 2.1mg; SODIUM 362mg; CALC 123mg

BASMATI–GREEN PEA RICE:
Bring 1¾ cups water and ½ teaspoon salt to a boil in a medium saucepan. Stir in 1 cup uncooked basmati rice; cover, reduce heat to low, and cook 20 minutes or until liquid is absorbed and rice is tender. Stir in ¼ cup thawed frozen green peas and 2 tablespoons chopped green onions.

Shopping List

Chicken-Butternut Tagine
1 large onion
small butternut squash
garlic
olive oil
ground cumin
paprika
ground turmeric
ground cinnamon
ground ginger
2 cups fat-free, less-sodium chicken broth
picholine olives
8 dried plums
1 pound skinless, boneless chicken breasts

Pistachio Couscous
1 lemon
¾ cup fat-free, less-sodium chicken broth
¾ cup couscous
pistachios

Game Plan
- While onion cooks:
  - Trim and cut chicken.
  - Cube squash.
  - Halve olives.
  - Chop plums.
- While tagine simmers:
  - Prepare couscous.

Chicken-Butternut Tagine with Pistachio Couscous

·························*40 minutes*

Sweet, smoky, and salty flavors blend beautifully in this quick adaptation of a classic Moroccan dish.

Vegetarian Swap: Omit the chicken, double the squash, and use vegetable broth.

Flavor Hit: A hint of cinnamon adds subtle sweetness that rounds out the flavor from the headier spices.

Prep Pointer: Pit olives by pressing them with the flat side of a chef's knife.

1	tablespoon olive oil
2	cups chopped onion
2	teaspoons ground cumin
1	teaspoon paprika
1	teaspoon ground turmeric
¼	teaspoon salt
¼	teaspoon ground cinnamon
¼	teaspoon ground ginger
2	garlic cloves, minced
1	pound skinless, boneless chicken breast, cut into bite-sized pieces
2	cups fat-free, less-sodium chicken broth
8	ounces peeled cubed butternut squash
⅓	cup halved pitted picholine olives (about 3 ounces)
8	pitted dried plums, chopped
	Fresh flat-leaf parsley leaves (optional)

❶ Heat oil in a Dutch oven over medium heat. Add onion; cook 8 minutes or until golden, stirring occasionally. Stir in cumin and next 7 ingredients; cook 1 minute, stirring constantly. Stir in broth and next 3 ingredients; bring to a boil. Cover, reduce heat to medium-low, and simmer 10 minutes or until squash is tender. Garnish with parsley, if desired. Yield: 4 servings (serving size: 1¼ cups).

CALORIES 309; FAT 8.8g (sat 0.9g, mono 5.3g, poly 1.6g); PROTEIN 29.8g; CARB 29.7g; FIBER 5.2g; CHOL 66mg; IRON 2.9mg; SODIUM 782mg; CALC 90mg

The Best Butternuts

Choose a squash that feels heavy for its size, one that's firm to the touch with no dark or soft spots.

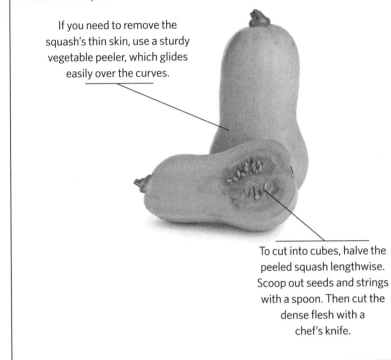

If you need to remove the squash's thin skin, use a sturdy vegetable peeler, which glides easily over the curves.

To cut into cubes, halve the peeled squash lengthwise. Scoop out seeds and strings with a spoon. Then cut the dense flesh with a chef's knife.

PISTACHIO COUSCOUS:

Bring ³⁄₄ cup fat-free, less-sodium chicken broth to a boil in a small saucepan. Stir in ³⁄₄ cup uncooked couscous; cover and remove from heat. Let stand 5 minutes; fluff with a fork. Stir in 1 teaspoon grated lemon rind and ¹⁄₄ cup chopped pistachios.

WINE NOTE: Warm Moroccan spices are a perfect match for the grapes that go into spicy red Rhône blends: syrah, grenache, mourvèdre. But with the sweet plums and squash, you want a fruitier version—one from California, preferably heavy on juicy grenache. Go for Beckmen Vineyards 2007 Cuvée le Bec ($20), full of cherries and black pepper.

QUICK & EASY • MAKE AHEAD
Pita Chips with Goat Cheese Dip

Refrigerate leftover dip up to three days; chips keep about one day.

2 (6-inch) pitas
Olive oil–flavored cooking spray
¹⁄₄ cup (2 ounces) garlic-and-herb goat cheese spread, softened
1 tablespoon 1% low-fat milk

1 Preheat oven to 425°.
2 Cut each pita into 8 wedges. Arrange pita wedges in a single layer on a baking sheet. Coat pita wedges with cooking spray. Bake pita wedges at 425° for 7 minutes or until crisp.
3 Combine cheese spread and milk, stirring until well blended. Serve dip with pita chips. Yield: 4 servings (serving size: 4 pita chips and about 1 tablespoon dip).

CALORIES 122; FAT 3.4g (sat 2.1g, mono 0.7g, poly 0.2g); PROTEIN 5.5g; CARB 17g; FIBER 0.7g; CHOL 7mg; IRON 1.1mg; SODIUM 215mg; CALC 50mg

---

Reader Recipes

Trisha Kruse created this quick sheet cake after harvesting 20 pumpkins from her garden last fall. Here, she's adapted her recipe using canned pumpkin for the sake of convenience.

MAKE AHEAD • KID FRIENDLY
Frosted Pumpkin Cake

"When I bake this cake, the smells and tastes remind me of everything I like about autumn: chilly evenings, harvest time, Halloween, and Thanksgiving."
—Trisha Kruse, Eagle, Idaho

CAKE:
10.1 ounces all-purpose flour (about 2¼ cups)
2½ teaspoons baking powder
2 teaspoons ground cinnamon
¹⁄₄ teaspoon salt
1 cup packed brown sugar
¹⁄₄ cup butter, softened
1 teaspoon vanilla extract
2 large eggs
1 (15-ounce) can pumpkin puree
Cooking spray
FROSTING:
2 tablespoons butter, softened
¹⁄₂ teaspoon vanilla extract
1 (8-ounce) package ¹⁄₃-less-fat cream cheese
2 cups sifted powdered sugar

1 Preheat oven to 350°.
2 To prepare cake, weigh or lightly spoon flour into dry measuring cups; level with a knife. Combine flour and next 3 ingredients in a small bowl, stirring with a whisk.
3 Combine brown sugar, ¹⁄₄ cup butter, and 1 teaspoon vanilla in a large bowl; beat with a mixer at medium speed until well combined. Add eggs, 1 at a time, to sugar mixture; beat well after each

Continued

addition. Add pumpkin; mix well. Fold in flour mixture. Spread batter into a 13 x 9–inch baking pan coated with cooking spray. Bake at 350° for 25 minutes or until a wooden pick inserted into center comes out clean. Cool completely in pan on a wire rack.

❹ To prepare frosting, combine 2 tablespoons butter, $\frac{1}{2}$ teaspoon vanilla, and cream cheese in a medium bowl; beat with a mixer at medium speed until combined. Gradually add powdered sugar, beating until well combined. Spread frosting evenly over top of cake. Yield: 24 servings (serving size: 1 piece).

CALORIES 178; FAT 5.5 (sat 3.3g, mono 1.3g, poly 0.3g); PROTEIN 3g; CARB 30g; FIBER 0.9g; CHOL 32mg; IRON 1.2mg; SODIUM 135mg; CALC 62mg

Sweet Potato Chicken Curry

"If I have fresh tomatoes on hand, I add a traditional Nepalese salsa seasoned with garlic, ground coriander, and cumin."

—Danielle Stephenson, Lakeville, Minnesota

- 2 teaspoons curry powder
- 1 teaspoon ground coriander
- 1 teaspoon ground turmeric
- $\frac{1}{2}$ teaspoon salt
- $\frac{1}{2}$ teaspoon black pepper
- $\frac{1}{4}$ teaspoon ground red pepper
- 1 bay leaf
- $1\frac{1}{2}$ teaspoons olive oil
- $1\frac{1}{2}$ pounds skinless, boneless chicken breast, cut into 1-inch pieces
- $1\frac{1}{2}$ cups vertically sliced onion
- $1\frac{1}{2}$ teaspoons minced peeled fresh ginger
- 2 garlic cloves, minced
- 1 (14-ounce) can fat-free, less-sodium chicken broth
- 1 (14.5-ounce) can diced tomatoes, undrained
- 2 cups ($\frac{1}{2}$-inch) cubed peeled sweet potato
- $\frac{3}{4}$ cup canned chickpeas, rinsed and drained
- $\frac{1}{2}$ cup frozen green peas
- 1 tablespoon fresh lemon juice

❶ Combine first 7 ingredients in a small bowl.

❷ Heat oil in a large Dutch oven over medium-high heat. Add chicken to pan; sauté 5 minutes or until browned, stirring occasionally. Remove chicken from pan. Reduce heat to medium. Add onion to pan; cook 10 minutes or until tender, stirring frequently. Increase heat to medium-high; return chicken to pan. Cook 1 minute, stirring occasionally. Stir in ginger and garlic; cook 1 minute, stirring constantly. Add curry powder mixture; cook 2 minutes, stirring constantly. Add broth and tomatoes; bring to a boil. Cover, reduce heat, and simmer 1 hour. Stir in potato and chickpeas. Cook, uncovered, 30 minutes. Add peas; cook 5 minutes or until thoroughly heated. Remove from heat; stir in juice. Discard bay leaf. Yield: 7 servings (serving size: about 1 cup).

CALORIES 196; FAT 3.9g (sat 0.9g, mono 1.6g, poly 0.8g); PROTEIN 23g; CARB 16.9g; FIBER 3.5g; CHOL 54mg; IRON 1.9mg; SODIUM 467mg; CALC 46mg

Roasted Tomato Tortilla Soup

"It's easy for [daughter-in-law] Melissa and me to keep each other motivated since she, my son, and four grandchildren live next door. Ripe tomatoes work best in this soup. Pat the vegetables dry with paper towels before broiling them. Lightly coat the tortilla strips with cooking spray so they crisp and brown evenly."

—Eleanor Childers, Escondido, California

- 5 medium tomatoes, cut in half (about $1\frac{1}{2}$ pounds)
- 2 (6-inch) Anaheim chiles
- 7 ($\frac{1}{4}$-inch-thick) slices onion
- 2 large garlic cloves, halved
- Cooking spray
- 8 (6-inch) white corn tortillas, cut into $\frac{1}{2}$-inch strips
- 1 tablespoon chopped fresh cilantro
- 2 teaspoons ground cumin
- $\frac{1}{2}$ teaspoon sugar
- $\frac{1}{2}$ teaspoon salt
- $\frac{1}{4}$ teaspoon freshly ground black pepper
- 3 (14-ounce) cans fat-free, less-sodium chicken broth
- $\frac{1}{2}$ cup diced ripe avocado
- $\frac{1}{2}$ cup (2 ounces) shredded queso fresco
- 8 fresh cilantro sprigs

❶ Preheat broiler.

❷ Arrange tomatoes, cut sides down, on a foil-lined baking sheet. Cut chiles in half lengthwise; discard seeds and membranes. Place chiles, skin sides up, on baking sheet; flatten with hand. Broil 15 minutes or until blackened. Remove from oven; let stand 15 minutes. Peel tomatoes and chiles; place in a small bowl. Place onion and garlic on baking sheet; lightly coat with cooking spray. Broil 20 minutes or until browned, turning after 10 minutes. Add onion and garlic to tomatoes in bowl. Discard foil.

❸ Arrange tortilla strips in a single layer on a baking sheet; coat with cooking spray. Broil 9 minutes or until lightly browned, stirring occasionally.

❹ Place tomatoes, chiles, onion, and garlic in a food processor. Process 1 minute or until blended. Spoon tomato mixture into a large saucepan; cook over medium heat 2 minutes, stirring constantly. Reduce heat to low; cook 6 minutes, stirring occasionally. Stir in cilantro and next 5 ingredients; bring to a boil. Cover, reduce heat, and simmer 15 minutes. Ladle 1 cup soup into each of 8 bowls; top each serving with about 6 tortilla strips, 1 tablespoon avocado, 1 tablespoon queso fresco, and 1 cilantro sprig. Yield: 8 servings.

CALORIES 149; FAT 6.8g (sat 2.1g, mono 2.9g, poly 0.8g); PROTEIN 5.8g; CARB 17.5g; FIBER 4.6g; CHOL 9mg; IRON 0.9mg; SODIUM 490mg; CALC 96mg

Simple Additions

QUICK & EASY ▪ KID FRIENDLY
Pesto Sliders

Mixing salt and pepper into the beef seasons it more thoroughly than sprinkling the surface of the patties. Serve with baked chips. A full tablespoon of curry paste makes this a boldly spicy dish. Use 2 teaspoons if you prefer milder flavor.

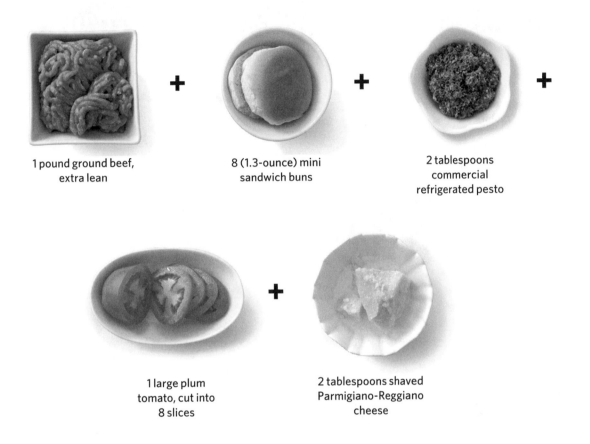

1 pound ground beef, extra lean

8 (1.3-ounce) mini sandwich buns

2 tablespoons commercial refrigerated pesto

1 large plum tomato, cut into 8 slices

2 tablespoons shaved Parmigiano-Reggiano cheese

Directions: Gently combine ground beef, ¼ teaspoon salt, and ¼ teaspoon freshly ground black pepper in a bowl. Divide beef mixture into 8 equal portions, shaping each into a ¼-inch-thick patty. Heat a grill pan over medium-high heat. Coat pan with cooking spray. Add patties to pan; cook 3 minutes on each side or until desired degree of doneness. Spread bottom half of each bun with ¾ teaspoon pesto, and top each with 1 tomato slice and 1 patty. Top each patty with ¾ teaspoon shaved Parmigiano-Reggiano cheese and the top half of bun. Yield: 4 servings (serving size: 2 sliders).

CALORIES 416; FAT 16.5g (sat 6.2g, mono 6.9g, poly 2.3g); PROTEIN 29.7g; CARB 38.8g; FIBER 2.3g; CHOL 65mg; IRON 4.4mg; SODIUM 754mg; CALC 149mg

Penne with Sausage, Garlic, and Broccoli Rabe

Use hot turkey Italian sausage to add a little kick to this hearty, quick pasta meal. For a less bitter flavor than broccoli rabe, substitute Broccolini.

1 pound broccoli rabe
(rapini), trimmed

8 ounces penne
(tube-shaped pasta)

1 tablespoon
extra-virgin
olive oil

8 ounces turkey
Italian sausage

6 garlic cloves,
thinly sliced

Directions: Cook broccoli rabe in boiling water 2 minutes. Remove with a slotted spoon and plunge into ice water; drain well. Coarsely chop. Return water to a boil. Add pasta; cook according to package directions, omitting salt and fat. Drain pasta in a colander over a bowl, reserving ¼ cup cooking liquid. Heat oil in a large nonstick skillet over medium-high heat. Remove casings from sausage. Add sausage to pan; cook 4 minutes or until browned, stirring to crumble. Add garlic; sauté 1 minute. Stir in broccoli rabe; cook 1 minute, stirring frequently. Stir in pasta, reserved cooking liquid, ½ teaspoon salt, and ¼ teaspoon freshly ground black pepper; cook 1 minute or until thoroughly heated. Serve immediately. Yield: 4 servings (serving size: 1½ cups).

CALORIES 367; FAT 9.6g (sat 2.3g, mono 4.5g, poly 2.1g); PROTEIN 22.1g; CARB 49.1g; FIBER 1.9g; CHOL 48mg; IRON 3.4mg; SODIUM 730mg; CALC 72mg

SuperFast

This month: Mediterranean. Get a taste of the region's vivid flavors with these quick and easy 20-minute dishes.

Scallop Piccata with Sautéed Spinach

1½ pounds sea scallops (about 12)
¼ teaspoon salt
¼ teaspoon freshly ground black pepper
5 teaspoons canola oil, divided
1 garlic clove, chopped
½ cup vermouth
3 tablespoons chopped fresh parsley
2 tablespoons fresh lemon juice
2 tablespoons butter
4 teaspoons capers
1 (10-ounce) package fresh baby spinach

❶ Heat a large cast-iron skillet over high heat. Pat scallops dry with paper towels. Sprinkle salt and pepper over scallops. Add 1 tablespoon oil to pan, swirling to coat. Add scallops; cook 2 minutes on each side or until browned and done. Remove from pan; keep warm.
❷ Reduce heat to medium. Add garlic to pan; cook 10 seconds. Add vermouth, scraping pan to loosen browned bits; cook 2 minutes or until liquid is reduced by half. Remove from heat. Add parsley and next 3 ingredients, stirring until butter melts. Pour sauce in a bowl.
❸ Heat remaining 2 teaspoons oil in pan over medium-high heat. Add spinach; sauté 30 seconds or until spinach almost wilts. Drizzle sauce over scallops; serve with spinach. Yield: 4 servings (serving size: ⅓ cup spinach, 3 scallops, and 1½ tablespoons sauce).

CALORIES 275; FAT 13.1g (sat 4.2g, mono 5g, poly 2.5g); PROTEIN 30.9g; CARB 8.3g; FIBER 1.8g; CHOL 71mg; IRON 2.8mg; SODIUM 607mg; CALC 122mg

Chicken and Mushroom Panini

Cooking spray
2 cups presliced cremini mushrooms
1 teaspoon minced garlic
¼ cup canola mayonnaise
2 tablespoons chopped sun-dried tomatoes, packed without oil
1 tablespoon capers
8 (1½-ounce) slices ciabatta or sourdough bread
8 ounces chopped skinless, boneless rotisserie chicken breast
4 (1-ounce) slices reduced-fat provolone cheese

❶ Heat a large nonstick skillet over medium-high heat. Coat pan with cooking spray. Add mushrooms and garlic to pan; sauté 3 minutes or until mushrooms are tender. Remove from heat; set aside.
❷ Place mayonnaise, tomatoes, and capers in a mini food processor; pulse until well combined. Spread 1 tablespoon mayonnaise mixture over each of 4 bread slices; top each with ¼ cup mushroom mixture, 2 ounces chicken, 1 cheese slice, and 1 bread slice.
❸ Heat a large grill pan over medium heat. Coat pan with cooking spray. Add sandwiches to pan. Place a cast-iron or other heavy skillet on top of sandwiches; press gently to flatten sandwiches. Cook 2 minutes on each side or until bread is toasted (leave cast-iron skillet on sandwiches while they cook). Yield: 4 servings (serving size: 1 sandwich).

CALORIES 474; FAT 15.5g (sat 4.1g, mono 7.6g, poly 2.6g); PROTEIN 33.7g; CARB 49.9g; FIBER 2.2g; CHOL 63mg; IRON 3.7mg; SODIUM 974mg; CALC 57mg

Fennel-Sardine Spaghetti

Look for imported sardines in the Latin or Mediterranean section of your supermarket.

8 ounces uncooked spaghetti
1 medium fennel bulb (about 8 ounces)
2 tablespoons olive oil
1 cup prechopped onion
3 garlic cloves, chopped
1 cup tomato sauce
1 teaspoon dried oregano
⅛ teaspoon crushed red pepper
1 (15-ounce) can sardines in tomato sauce, undrained

❶ Cook pasta according to package directions, omitting salt and fat; drain.
❷ Trim outer leaves from fennel. Chop fronds to measure ½ cup. Discard stalks. Cut bulb in half lengthwise; discard core. Thinly slice bulb.
❸ Heat oil in a large skillet over medium-high heat. Add sliced fennel and onion; sauté 4 minutes. Add garlic; sauté 20 seconds. Stir in tomato sauce, oregano, red pepper, and sauce from sardines. Cover and reduce heat.
❹ Discard backbones from sardines. Add sardines to pan; gently break sardines into chunks. Cover and cook 6 minutes. Toss pasta with sauce; sprinkle with chopped fennel fronds. Yield: 4 servings (serving size: 1 cup pasta and 1 cup sauce).

CALORIES 520; FAT 18.9g (sat 4g, mono 10.2g, poly 3.3g); PROTEIN 31.7g; CARB 54.5g; FIBER 4.4g; CHOL 65mg; IRON 5.3mg; SODIUM 804mg; CALC 75mg

White Bean Soup with Gremolata

SOUP:

- 2 teaspoons olive oil
- ½ cup finely chopped pancetta
- 1 cup prechopped onion
- ½ cup prechopped celery
- 2 teaspoons minced garlic
- 2 cups fat-free, less-sodium chicken broth
- ½ cup water
- ¼ teaspoon black pepper
- 2 (19-ounce) cans cannellini beans, rinsed and drained
- 1 bay leaf

GREMOLATA:

- 1 tablespoon chopped fresh parsley
- 2 teaspoons grated lemon rind
- 1 teaspoon minced garlic

❶ To prepare soup, heat oil in a large saucepan over medium-high heat. Add pancetta; sauté 2 minutes. Stir in onion, celery, and 2 teaspoons garlic; sauté 3 minutes or until almost tender. Stir in broth and next 4 ingredients. Bring to a boil; reduce heat, and simmer 8 minutes, stirring occasionally.

❷ To prepare gremolata, combine parsley, rind, and 1 teaspoon garlic. Sprinkle over soup. Yield: 4 servings (serving size: 1½ cups soup and about 1½ teaspoons gremolata).

CALORIES 227; FAT 7.6g (sat 2.4g, mono 3.2g, poly 1.4g); PROTEIN 9.8g; CARB 28.7g; FIBER 7.7g; CHOL 10mg; IRON 2.6mg; SODIUM 710mg; CALC 75mg

---

Ingredients with Mediterranean Zing

Dry Sherry: For rich Spanish character

Kalamata Olives: Meaty texture, fruity flavor

Dried Oregano: Pungent and woodsy taste

Fennel: Bulb and fronds add mild anise notes

Spanish-Style Clams with Red Peppers and Sherry

It would be a shame to let any sauce go to waste, so serve over pasta or with crusty French bread.

- 2 tablespoons olive oil
- 2½ cups thinly vertically sliced onion
- 3 garlic cloves, minced
- ½ cup chopped bottled roasted red bell peppers, rinsed and drained
- ⅓ cup fat-free, less-sodium chicken broth
- 3 tablespoons dry sherry
- ½ teaspoon black pepper
- ¼ teaspoon smoked paprika
- ⅛ teaspoon salt
- 2 pounds littleneck clams, scrubbed
- ¼ cup chopped fresh parsley

❶ Heat oil in a large sauté pan over medium-high heat. Add onion to pan; sauté 5 minutes or until lightly browned, stirring frequently. Stir in garlic; cook 30 seconds. Add bell peppers and next 6 ingredients, stirring gently. Cover and cook 4 minutes or until clams open; discard any unopened shells. Sprinkle with parsley. Yield: 4 servings (serving size: about 1½ cups).

CALORIES 279; FAT 9.3g (sat 1.2g, mono 5.1g, poly 1.5g); PROTEIN 30.5g; CARB 15.4g; FIBER 1.7g; CHOL 77mg; IRON 10.3mg; SODIUM 348mg; CALC 135mg

---

Lamb Chops with Olive Couscous

- 1 tablespoon dried oregano
- 2 tablespoons extra-virgin olive oil
- ½ teaspoon black pepper
- 3 garlic cloves, minced
- 8 (4-ounce) lamb loin chops, trimmed
- ½ teaspoon salt
- Cooking spray
- 1 (14-ounce) can fat-free, less-sodium chicken broth
- 1 cup uncooked couscous
- ½ cup cherry tomatoes, halved
- ¼ cup chopped pitted kalamata olives
- 3 tablespoons crumbled feta cheese

❶ Preheat broiler.

❷ Combine first 4 ingredients. Sprinkle lamb with salt; rub with 1 tablespoon oil mixture. Place on a broiler pan coated with cooking spray. Broil 4 minutes on each side or until done.

❸ While lamb cooks, heat a medium saucepan over medium-high heat. Add remaining oil mixture; cook 20 seconds, stirring constantly. Stir in broth; bring to a boil. Stir in couscous. Remove from heat; cover and let stand 5 minutes. Fluff with a fork. Stir in tomatoes, olives, and cheese. Serve couscous mixture with lamb. Yield: 4 servings (serving size: 2 lamb chops and 1¼ cups couscous mixture).

CALORIES 480; FAT 19.8g (sat 5.6g, mono 10.8g, poly 1.7g); PROTEIN 36.2g; CARB 36.8g; FIBER 3g; CHOL 97mg; IRON 3.3mg; SODIUM 793mg; CALC 90mg

From Our Table To Your Table

Cooking Light editors and Test Kitchens professionals offer personal-favorite recipes to create a holiday feast that hits all the right notes of the season.

WORKING AT A FOOD MAGAZINE is heaven for food lovers, but it does mean we taste the equivalent of five to 10 holiday meals in a few short weeks every year, sifting through many dozens of contenders to find the recipes that are good enough to grace our pages. And each time we brace ourselves for holiday taste testings (in June, by the way), we face the same problem: How do we make Christmas dinner feel fresh while still honoring the traditions that make the holidays so important?

With this menu we offer our personal favorites and creative innovations: green beans with mushrooms but no canned soup in sight, mashed potatoes with the butter (imbued with horseradish) on the outside for more drama, and the familiar flavors of German chocolate cake, but in creamy mousse form.

It's a meal we crafted for you, and after testing and tasting it ourselves, we know it's one that will have your guests oohing and ahhing before they take the first bite.

COOKING LIGHT'S BEST HOLIDAY MENU
(Serves 8)

Winter Salad with Roasted Beets and Citrus Reduction Sauce

Crab Bisque

Brined Pork Loin with Brown Sugar-Bourbon Glaze

Cipollini and Apples with Bacon

Mashed Yukon Gold Potatoes with Horseradish Butter

Sherried Green Beans and Mushrooms

Roasted Pear Crème Brûlée Tart

German Chocolate Mousse

Winter Salad with Roasted Beets and Citrus Reduction Dressing

"My ultimate starter salad would celebrate the produce of the season and make a knockout-gorgeous addition to the table."
—Timothy Q. Cebula, Associate Food Editor

- 4   medium beets (red and golden)
- Cooking spray
- ¾   cup fresh orange juice
- ½   teaspoon sugar
- 1   tablespoon minced shallots
- 2   tablespoons white wine vinegar
- ¾   teaspoon kosher salt, divided
- ½   teaspoon black pepper, divided
- ¼   cup extra-virgin olive oil
- 4   cups torn Boston lettuce
- 2   cups trimmed watercress
- 2   cups torn radicchio
- ½   cup (2 ounces) crumbled goat cheese

1 Preheat oven to 400°.

2 Leave root and 1-inch stem on beets; scrub with a brush. Place beets on a foil-lined jelly-roll pan coated with cooking spray. Lightly coat beets with cooking spray. Bake at 400° for 1 hour and 10 minutes or until tender. Cool beets slightly. Trim off beet roots and stems; rub off skins. Cut beets into ½-inch-thick wedges.

3 Bring juice and sugar to a boil in a small saucepan; cook 10 minutes or until reduced to 2 tablespoons. Pour into a medium bowl; cool slightly. Add shallots, vinegar, ½ teaspoon salt, and ¼ teaspoon pepper, stirring with a whisk. Gradually add oil, stirring constantly with a whisk.

4 Combine lettuce, watercress, and radicchio. Sprinkle lettuce mixture with remaining ¼ teaspoon salt and ¼ teaspoon pepper; toss gently to combine. Arrange about 1 cup lettuce mixture on each of 8 salad plates. Divide beets evenly among salads. Drizzle about 1 tablespoon dressing over each salad; sprinkle each salad with 1 tablespoon cheese. Yield: 8 servings.

CALORIES 127; FAT 9.1g (sat 2.4g, mono 5.4g, poly 0.8g); PROTEIN 3.1g; CARB 8.2g; FIBER 1.7g; CHOL 6mg; IRON 1mg; SODIUM 253mg; CALC 53mg

We crafted recipes with vibrant colors, dishes that offer great pacing as you enjoy the meal: Some bites are creamy, rich, and indulgent, while others are crisp and fresh.

Crab Bisque

"I wanted to create a second course that's indulgent, rich, and pretty, too. Funny: The first time we tried this and pureed the soup in a food processor, we almost decided to start over because the texture wasn't smooth. But then we put it in the blender, and it came out perfectly creamy."

—Mary Drennen Ankar,
Test Kitchens Professional

Cooking spray
1¼ cups thinly sliced shallots (about 4 large)
1 celery stalk, finely chopped (about ½ cup)
4 garlic cloves, minced
3 tablespoons vermouth
¾ teaspoon kosher salt
¼ teaspoon freshly ground black pepper
⅛ teaspoon ground red pepper
1 pound jumbo lump crabmeat, shell pieces removed and divided
3 cups fat-free milk
1 cup clam juice
1.5 ounces all-purpose flour (about ⅓ cup)
½ cup heavy whipping cream
2 tablespoons chopped fresh chives
1½ teaspoons fresh lemon juice

❶ Heat a large Dutch oven over medium heat. Coat pan with cooking spray. Add shallots and celery to pan; cook 10 minutes or until softened, stirring occasionally. Add garlic; cook 1 minute. Stir in vermouth; cook 1 minute or until liquid evaporates. Add salt, peppers, and 8 ounces crabmeat.
❷ Combine milk and clam juice in a large bowl. Weigh or lightly spoon flour into a dry measuring cup; level with a knife. Whisk flour into milk mixture; add to pan. Bring to a boil, stirring constantly. Cook 1 minute or until slightly thickened, stirring constantly.
❸ Place half of milk mixture in a blender. Remove center piece of blender lid (to allow steam to escape); secure blender lid on blender. Place a clean towel over opening in blender lid (to avoid splatters). Blend until smooth. Pour into a large bowl. Repeat procedure with remaining milk mixture. Return pureed mixture to pan. Stir in cream; cook over medium heat 3 minutes or until thoroughly heated.
❹ Combine remaining 8 ounces crabmeat, chives, and lemon juice in a medium bowl. Top soup with crabmeat mixture. Yield: 8 servings (serving size: ¾ cup soup and about ¼ cup crabmeat mixture).

CALORIES 188; FAT 6.7g (sat 3.6g, mono 1.8g, poly 0.6g); PROTEIN 16.3g; CARB 14.1g; FIBER 0.5g; CHOL 80mg; IRON 1.3mg; SODIUM 453mg; CALC 204mg

Brined Pork Loin with Brown Sugar–Bourbon Glaze

"Brined pork is about as good as it gets. Throw some bourbon on it, and it somehow gets better."

—Mike Wilson,
former Test Kitchens Professional

1 gallon water
1 cup kosher salt
1 (5-pound) French-cut pork loin rib roast, trimmed (about 8 bones)
1 cup packed brown sugar
½ cup cider vinegar
3 tablespoons bourbon
1 teaspoon black peppercorns
1 bay leaf
¼ cup extra-virgin olive oil
2 tablespoons chopped fresh thyme
1 tablespoon freshly ground black pepper
6 garlic cloves, minced

❶ Combine 1 gallon water and salt in a large stockpot, stirring until salt dissolves. Add pork; refrigerate 24 hours.
❷ Remove pork from brine; discard brine. Pat pork dry with paper towels.
❸ Preheat oven to 375°.
❹ Combine sugar, vinegar, bourbon, peppercorns, and bay leaf in a small saucepan. Bring to a boil; cook 9 minutes or until reduced to ⅔ cup. Strain mixture through a sieve over a bowl; discard solids. Set aside.
❺ Combine oil, thyme, 1 tablespoon ground black pepper, and garlic in a small bowl; rub evenly over pork. Place pork on a large roasting pan. Bake at 375° for 1 hour and 10 minutes. Brush sugar mixture evenly over pork; bake an additional 20 minutes or until thermometer inserted into the thickest portion of pork registers 140° (slightly pink). Place pork on a platter. Cover with foil; let stand 15 minutes before slicing. Yield: 8 servings (serving size: 1 chop).

CALORIES 357; FAT 14.2g (sat 3.5g, mono 8.3g, poly 1.5g); PROTEIN 25g; CARB 28.4g; FIBER 0.3g; CHOL 62mg; IRON 1.8mg; SODIUM 628mg; CALC 40mg

Cipollini and Apples with Bacon

"The holidays are only time I feel it's worth it to fool around with these tiny onions. They become really tender and brown, which pairs well with the slight crunch from the apples. And the browned onions and blush pink fruit look just lovely together and brighten up the table."

—Tiffany Vickers,
Assistant Test Kitchens Director

1 tablespoon butter
4 medium Gala apples, cored and cut into (¼-inch-thick) wedges
2 slices applewood-smoked bacon, chopped
20 ounces small cipollini onions, peeled
⅓ cup fat-free, less-sodium chicken broth
2 tablespoons cider vinegar
1½ teaspoons fresh thyme leaves
½ teaspoon salt
¼ teaspoon freshly ground black pepper

❶ Melt butter in a large skillet over high heat. Add apples to pan; cook 6 minutes or until edges are very brown, stirring frequently. Remove apples from pan;

set aside. Reduce heat to medium. Add bacon to pan; cook 3 minutes or until crisp. Remove bacon from pan, reserving drippings; set bacon aside. Add onions to drippings in pan; cover and cook 8 minutes or until golden, stirring occasionally. Stir in broth, vinegar, and thyme; cook 7 minutes. Uncover; return apples to pan. Cook 3 minutes or until thoroughly heated. Stir in bacon, salt, and pepper. Yield: 8 servings (serving size: about ³/₄ cup).

CALORIES 117; FAT 4.1g (sat 1.8g, mono 1.5g, poly 0.4g); PROTEIN 1.7g; CARB 19.7g; FIBER 1.7g; CHOL 8mg; IRON 0.4mg; SODIUM 237mg; CALC 23mg

Mashed Yukon Gold Potatoes with Horseradish Butter

"I wanted to contribute some big flavors. Horseradish is such a pungent ingredient that a little goes a long way, and the bay leaf infuses the potatoes with no added sodium."

—Kellie Gerber Kelley, Senior Food Stylist

HORSERADISH BUTTER:
Cooking spray
1 tablespoon minced shallots
¼ cup butter, softened
1 tablespoon chopped fresh parsley
2 teaspoons prepared horseradish

POTATOES:
6½ cups cubed peeled Yukon gold potatoes (about 2½ pounds)
1 bay leaf
¼ cup 1% low-fat milk
¼ cup fat-free, less-sodium chicken broth
¼ cup reduced-fat sour cream
1 teaspoon salt
¼ teaspoon freshly ground black pepper

❶ To prepare horseradish butter, heat a small nonstick skillet over medium heat. Coat pan with cooking spray. Add shallots to pan; cook 1 minute. Remove from heat; cool.

❷ Combine shallots, butter, parsley, and horseradish in a small bowl; blend well. Transfer butter mixture to a sheet of plastic wrap. Shape butter mixture into a 3-inch-long log, using plastic wrap to help mold. Wrap log tightly in plastic wrap; refrigerate until firm.
❸ To prepare potatoes, place potatoes and bay leaf in a large saucepan; cover with water. Bring to a boil. Cover, reduce heat, and simmer 20 minutes or until tender; drain. Discard bay leaf. Press potatoes through a ricer or food mill into a large bowl. Combine milk and broth in a microwave-safe dish. Microwave at HIGH 1 minute or until warm. Add milk mixture, sour cream, salt, and pepper to potatoes, stirring until well blended. Serve with horseradish butter. Yield: 8 servings (serving size: ½ cup potatoes and 1½ teaspoons horseradish butter).

CALORIES 182; FAT 6.7g (sat 4.2g, mono 1.8g, poly 0.3g); PROTEIN 4g; CARB 26.1g; FIBER 1.8g; CHOL 18mg; IRON 1.3mg; SODIUM 369mg; CALC 21mg

Sherried Green Beans and Mushrooms

"Everybody expects to see green beans at the table, but I wanted to add some unexpected flourishes."

—Julianna Grimes, Associate Food Editor

1½ pounds haricots verts, trimmed
3 tablespoons butter, divided
⅓ cup thinly sliced shallots
¾ pound exotic mushroom blend, coarsely chopped
¼ cup dry sherry
3 tablespoons chopped fresh flat-leaf parsley
2 teaspoons chopped fresh thyme
¾ teaspoon kosher salt
½ teaspoon freshly ground black pepper

❶ Steam haricots verts 5 minutes or until crisp-tender; remove from heat.
❷ Melt 2 tablespoons butter in a large skillet over medium-high heat. Add

shallots to pan; sauté 3 minutes, stirring occasionally. Add mushrooms; sauté 5 minutes or until liquid evaporates. Stir in sherry; bring to a boil. Cook until liquid almost evaporates (about 2 minutes). Add remaining 1 tablespoon butter and haricots verts; cook 30 seconds or until thoroughly heated, tossing to coat. Remove from heat. Add parsley, thyme, salt, and pepper; toss to combine. Yield: 8 servings (serving size: about 1 cup).

CALORIES 80; FAT 4.3g (sat 2.7g, mono 1.1g, poly 0.2g); PROTEIN 2.4g; CARB 8.3g; FIBER 3.5g; CHOL 11mg; IRON 0.8mg; SODIUM 256mg; CALC 56mg

Roasted Pear Crème Brûlée Tart

"This tart contains all the elements of every good dessert—flaky crust, crunchy caramelized sugar, creamy custard, and soft roasted fruit. You can make all the components ahead of time, but brûlée the pears just before serving."

—SaBrina Bone, Test Kitchens Professional

PASTRY:
1 tablespoon granulated sugar
¼ teaspoon salt
4 ounces all-purpose flour (about ¾ cup plus 2 tablespoons)
¼ cup chilled butter, cut into small pieces
2 tablespoons ice water
Cooking spray

PASTRY CREAM:
¼ cup packed brown sugar
3 tablespoons all-purpose flour
⅛ teaspoon salt
2 cups 2% reduced-fat milk
1 (4-inch) piece vanilla bean, split lengthwise
1 large egg, lightly beaten

TOPPING:
1 teaspoon fresh lemon juice
¼ teaspoon ground cinnamon
⅛ teaspoon ground nutmeg
2 medium pears, peeled, cored, and halved
⅓ cup granulated sugar   *Continued*

❶ Preheat oven to 450°.

❷ To prepare pastry, place first 3 ingredients in a food processor; pulse to combine. Add butter; pulse 10 times or until mixture resembles coarse meal. With processor on, slowly add ice water through food chute, processing just until dough starts to come together. Turn dough out onto a piece of plastic wrap; press into a disk. Cover and chill 10 minutes in freezer. Place dough between 2 sheets of plastic wrap; roll dough into a 10-inch circle. Fit dough into a 9-inch round removable-bottom tart pan coated with cooking spray; pierce dough with a fork. Bake at 450° for 10 minutes or until lightly browned. Cool completely on a wire rack.

❸ To prepare pastry cream, combine brown sugar, 3 tablespoons flour, and ⅛ teaspoon salt in a medium, heavy saucepan. Gradually add milk, stirring with a whisk. Scrape seeds from vanilla bean; add seeds and bean to milk mixture. Cook over medium-high heat until thick and bubbly (about 5 minutes), stirring constantly. Place egg in a large bowl. Gradually stir hot milk mixture into egg. Return milk mixture to pan; cook 2 minutes or until mixture reaches 185° and coats the back of a spoon, stirring constantly. Discard vanilla bean. Spread pastry cream onto a baking sheet; cover entire surface with plastic wrap. Refrigerate 20 minutes or until chilled. Spread pastry cream evenly into tart shell; cover and chill at least 2 hours or until set.

❹ Preheat oven to 450°.

❺ To prepare topping, combine juice, cinnamon, nutmeg, and pears; toss well to coat. Place pears, cut sides down, in an 11 x 7–inch baking dish coated with cooking spray. Bake at 450° for 45 minutes or until tender. Cool completely; thinly slice. Place on paper towels; pat dry with additional paper towels. Arrange pear slices spoke-like over pastry cream. Cover and chill at least 30 minutes.

❻ Sprinkle remaining ⅓ cup granulated sugar evenly over pears, leaving a ½-inch border. Holding a kitchen blow torch about 2 inches from the top of custard, heat sugar, moving the torch back and forth, until sugar is melted and caramelized (about 3 minutes). Serve immediately. Yield: 8 servings (serving size: 1 wedge).

CALORIES 241; FAT 7.6g (sat 4.5g, mono 2.1g, poly 0.4g); PROTEIN 4.8g; CARB 39.3g; FIBER 1.8g; CHOL 42mg; IRON 1.2mg; SODIUM 194mg; CALC 92mg

German Chocolate Mousse

"I felt compelled to make a chocolate dessert option, too. It's a twist on an all-time favorite in my household, like having German chocolate cake, but in a more decadent, satisfying, and rich form."

—SaBrina Bone,
Test Kitchens Professional

1⅓ cups 1% low-fat milk
2 teaspoons unflavored gelatin
1 teaspoon vanilla extract
8 ounces dark chocolate chips
4 cups frozen light whipped topping, thawed
¼ cup flaked sweetened coconut, toasted
¼ cup chopped pecans, toasted

❶ Combine first 3 ingredients in a heavy saucepan; let stand 2 minutes. Cook over medium-high heat to 180° or until tiny bubbles form around edge (do not boil). Remove from heat and add chocolate; cover and let stand 5 minutes. Stir until chocolate melts.

❷ Pour chocolate mixture into a medium bowl; cover and chill 30 minutes or until set. Gently fold in whipped topping. Spoon about ⅔ cup mousse into each of 8 dessert bowls. Cover at least 2 hours or until set. Top each serving with 1½ teaspoons coconut and 1½ teaspoons pecans. Yield: 8 servings.

CALORIES 269; FAT 16.3g (sat 10.8g, mono 4.3g, poly 1.1g); PROTEIN 3.2g; CARB 32.7g; FIBER 2.5g; CHOL 2mg; IRON 1.5mg; SODIUM 38mg; CALC 53mg

Umami's Impact

Discover how umami, the fifth taste sensation beyond sweet, sour, salty, and bitter, brings savory heartiness to meatless dishes.

Corn and Chile Quesadillas

If you can't find fresh Anaheim chiles, substitute about ¼ cup chopped canned green chiles.

2 Anaheim chiles (about ½ pound)
2 teaspoons olive oil
1 cup thinly sliced shiitake mushroom caps (about 1¼ ounces)
1 cup frozen whole-kernel corn, thawed
¼ cup chopped green onions
⅛ teaspoon salt
⅛ teaspoon freshly ground black pepper
4 (8-inch) flour tortillas
1 cup (4 ounces) shredded aged Gouda cheese
Cooking spray
½ cup bottled salsa

❶ Preheat broiler.

❷ Cut chiles in half lengthwise; discard seeds and membranes. Place chile halves, skin sides up, on a foil-lined baking sheet; flatten with hand. Broil 8 minutes or until blackened. Place in a zip-top plastic bag; seal. Let stand 15 minutes. Peel and chop. Reduce oven temperature to 200°.

❸ Heat oil in a large nonstick skillet over medium-high heat. Add mushrooms; sauté 2 minutes or until lightly browned. Add corn and next 3 ingredients; sauté 2 minutes. Place mushroom mixture in a medium bowl; stir in chopped chiles. Wipe pan clean.

❹ Place about ¼ cup mushroom mixture and ¼ cup cheese over half of 1 tortilla. Repeat procedure with remaining 1¼ cups mushroom mixture, remaining ¾ cup cheese, and remaining 3 tortillas. Heat pan over medium heat. Coat pan with cooking spray. Place 1 tortilla in pan; cook 2 minutes or until cheese melts and bottom of tortilla is golden brown. Fold tortilla in half; place on a baking sheet. Place in 200° oven to keep warm. Repeat procedure with remaining tortillas. Cut each quesadilla into wedges; serve with salsa. Yield: 4 servings (serving size: 1 quesadilla and 2 tablespoons salsa).

CALORIES 341; FAT 15.1g (sat 6.7g, mono 6.1g, poly 1.5g); PROTEIN 13.6g; CARB 39.5g; FIBER 4.4g; CHOL 25mg; IRON 2.7mg; SODIUM 738mg; CALC 293mg

Seitan Stir-Fry with Black Bean Garlic Sauce

Look for seitan—also called wheat gluten—in Asian markets or the refrigerated sections of health food or specialty stores. Black bean garlic sauce is sold in the international section of some supermarkets and at Asian markets.

- 2 cups boiling water
- 1 ounce dried shiitake mushrooms
- 2 tablespoons Chinese rice wine or sake
- 2 tablespoons black bean garlic sauce (such as Lee Kum Kee)
- 2 teaspoons cornstarch
- 2 tablespoons canola oil, divided
- 2 cups thinly sliced drained seitan (about 8 ounces)
- 1 tablespoon finely chopped garlic
- 1 tablespoon finely chopped peeled fresh ginger
- 4 cups (2-inch) cut green beans (about 1 pound)
- 2 cups hot cooked brown rice
- ¼ teaspoon salt
  Fresh cilantro sprigs (optional)

❶ Combine 2 cups boiling water and mushrooms in a small bowl; cover and let stand 20 minutes. Drain and rinse mushrooms, reserving ½ cup soaking liquid; drain mushrooms well. Discard mushroom stems; thinly slice mushroom caps.

❷ Combine reserved liquid, rice wine, black bean sauce, and cornstarch in a small bowl; stir with a whisk. Set aside.
❸ Heat 1 tablespoon oil in a large non-stick skillet or wok over medium-high heat. Add seitan to pan; stir-fry 2 minutes or until lightly browned. Place seitan in a medium bowl. Heat remaining 1 tablespoon oil in pan over medium-high heat. Add garlic and ginger to pan; stir-fry 30 seconds. Add mushrooms and beans; cover and cook 3 minutes. Add black bean sauce mixture to pan; cook 1 minute or until sauce slightly thickens. Add seitan to pan; cook 1 minute, stirring occasionally. Combine rice and salt; serve seitan mixture over rice. Garnish with cilantro sprigs, if desired. Yield: 4 servings (serving size: about 1½ cups seitan stir-fry and ½ cup rice).

CALORIES 474; FAT 10g (sat 0.8g, mono 4.6g, poly 3.5g); PROTEIN 35.5g; CARB 60.7g; FIBER 9.9g; CHOL 0mg; IRON 5.3mg; SODIUM 818mg; CALC 57mg

Wild Mushroom and Lentil Cottage Pie

Yukon gold potatoes, mushrooms, soy sauce, and tomato paste boost umami taste in this satisfying winter entrée.

TOPPING:
- 1½ pounds cubed peeled Yukon gold potato
- 1½ teaspoons salt, divided
- ⅔ cup low-fat buttermilk
- ¼ teaspoon freshly ground black pepper
- ⅛ teaspoon ground nutmeg
  Dash of ground red pepper

FILLING:
- 1 cup dried petite green lentils
- 4 cups water
- ½ teaspoon salt
- 1 bay leaf
- 2½ cups organic vegetable broth, divided
- 3 tablespoons all-purpose flour
- 1 tablespoon olive oil
- 1½ cups finely chopped onion
- 1 cup finely chopped carrot

- ½ cup thinly sliced celery
- 4 (4-ounce) packages presliced exotic mushroom blend (such as shiitake, cremini, and oyster)
- 2 tablespoons dry sherry
- 1 tablespoon soy sauce
- 1 tablespoon tomato paste
- 1 teaspoon fresh thyme leaves
- 1 tablespoon white truffle oil
  Fresh chopped chives (optional)

❶ To prepare topping, place potato and 1 teaspoon salt in a medium saucepan; cover with water. Bring to a boil. Cook 20 minutes or until very tender; drain. Return potato to pan. Add buttermilk, ½ teaspoon salt, black pepper, nutmeg, and red pepper to potato; mash with a potato masher until smooth. Set aside.
❷ Preheat oven to 375°.
❸ To prepare filling, combine lentils, 4 cups water, ½ teaspoon salt, and bay leaf in a saucepan; bring to a boil. Reduce heat and simmer 25 minutes or until lentils are tender. Drain; set aside.
❹ Combine ½ cup vegetable broth and flour in a small bowl, stirring with a whisk until well blended. Set aside.
❺ Heat oil in a large skillet over medium heat. Add onion and next 3 ingredients; cook 7 minutes, stirring occasionally. Stir in remaining 2 cups broth. Add sherry, soy sauce, tomato paste, thyme, and lentils to mushroom mixture. Bring to a simmer over medium-high heat. Stir in flour mixture; cook until mixture thickens (about 2 minutes), stirring constantly with a whisk.
❻ Spoon lentil mixture into a 2-quart casserole; top with potato mixture, spreading evenly. Bake at 375° for 25 minutes or until potatoes are golden. Drizzle oil over potatoes. Garnish with chopped chives, if desired. Yield: 8 servings.

CALORIES 235; FAT 4.3g (sat 0.6g, mono 2.6g, poly 0.4g); PROTEIN 9.8g; CARB 39.7g; FIBER 5.8g; CHOL 1mg; IRON 2.6mg; SODIUM 734mg; CALC 54mg

Vegetarian Bolognese with Whole Wheat Penne

The Parmigiano-Reggiano rind simmers with the sauce, infusing it with deep umami taste.

- ¼ cup dried porcini mushrooms (about ¼ ounce)
- 1 tablespoon olive oil
- 1½ cups finely chopped onion
- ½ cup finely chopped carrot
- ½ cup finely chopped celery
- 1 (8-ounce) package cremini mushrooms, finely chopped
- ½ cup dry red wine
- ¼ cup warm water
- ½ teaspoon salt
- ½ teaspoon freshly ground black pepper
- 1 (28-ounce) can organic crushed tomatoes with basil, undrained
- 1 (2-inch) piece Parmigiano-Reggiano cheese rind
- 12 ounces uncooked whole wheat penne (tube-shaped pasta)
- ½ cup (2 ounces) grated Parmigiano-Reggiano cheese

1 Place dried mushrooms in a spice or coffee grinder; process until finely ground.
2 Heat oil in a large saucepan over medium-high heat. Add onion and next 3 ingredients; sauté 10 minutes. Add wine; simmer 2 minutes or until liquid almost evaporates. Add warm water and next 4 ingredients to onion mixture. Stir in ground mushrooms. Cover, reduce heat, and simmer 40 minutes. Keep warm. Remove rind; discard.
3 Cook pasta according to package directions, omitting salt and fat. Place 1 cup of pasta in each of 6 bowls. Top each portion with ¾ cup sauce and 1 tablespoon cheese. Yield: 6 servings.

CALORIES 334; FAT 7.2g (sat 2.1g, mono 2.5g, poly 1.9g); PROTEIN 14.8g; CARB 57.7g; FIBER 9.7g; CHOL 9mg; IRON 3.3mg; SODIUM 542mg; CALC 156mg

Special Occasion Recipe

Chocolate Babka

This sweet yeast cake—in the tradition of French *baba au rhum*, Italian *pannetone*, and Austrian *kugelhopf*—is a Hanukkah favorite. We adore it warm from the oven with coffee and often make it when we have company. A fresh loaf is also a welcome gift. To get a jump-start on the baking, roll out dough, fill, shape, and refrigerate overnight in pan. It will rise to the top of the pan in the refrigerator, and then the next morning you can let it come to room temperature, top it with streusel, and bake as directed.

DOUGH:
- 1 teaspoon granulated sugar
- 1 package dry yeast (about 2¼ teaspoons)
- ¾ cup warm 1% low-fat milk (105° to 110°)
- 6 tablespoons granulated sugar
- ½ teaspoon vanilla extract
- ¼ teaspoon salt
- 1 large egg yolk, lightly beaten
- 7.5 ounces all-purpose flour (about 1⅔ cups), divided
- 5.85 ounces bread flour (about 1¼ cups)
- 5 tablespoons butter, cut into pieces and softened
- Cooking spray

FILLING:
- ½ cup granulated sugar
- 3 tablespoons unsweetened cocoa
- ½ teaspoon ground cinnamon
- ¼ teaspoon salt
- 4 ounces semisweet chocolate, finely chopped

STREUSEL:
- 2 tablespoons powdered sugar
- 1 tablespoon all-purpose flour
- 1 tablespoon butter, softened

1 To prepare dough, dissolve 1 teaspoon granulated sugar and yeast in warm milk in bowl of a stand mixer; let stand 5 minutes. Stir in 6 tablespoons granulated sugar, vanilla, ¼ teaspoon salt, and egg yolk. Weigh or lightly spoon flours into dry measuring cups; level with a knife. Add 6 ounces (about 1⅓ cups) all-purpose flour and bread flour to milk mixture; beat with dough hook attachment at medium speed until well blended (about 2 minutes). Add 5 tablespoons butter, beating until well blended. Scrape dough out onto a floured surface (dough will be very sticky). Knead until smooth and elastic (about 10 minutes); add remaining 1.5 ounces (about ⅓ cup) all-purpose flour, 1 tablespoon at a time, to prevent dough from sticking to hands (dough will be very soft).
2 Place dough in a large bowl coated with cooking spray, turning to coat top. Cover and let rise in a warm place (85°), free from drafts, 1½ hours or until doubled in size. (Gently press two fingers into dough. If indentation remains, dough has risen enough.) Punch dough down; cover and let rest 5 minutes.
3 Line bottom of a 9 x 5-inch loaf pan with parchment paper; coat sides of pan with cooking spray.
4 To prepare filling, combine ½ cup granulated sugar and next 4 ingredients in a medium bowl; set aside.
5 Roll dough out onto a generously floured surface into a 16-inch square. Sprinkle filling over dough, leaving a ¼-inch border around edges. Roll up dough tightly, jelly-roll fashion; pinch seam and ends to seal. Holding dough by ends, twist dough 4 times as if wringing out a towel. Fit dough into prepared pan. Cover and let rise 45 minutes or until doubled in size.
6 Preheat oven to 350°.
7 To prepare streusel, combine powdered sugar, 1 tablespoon all-purpose flour, and 1 tablespoon butter, stirring with a fork

until mixture is crumbly; sprinkle streusel over dough. Bake at 350° for 40 minutes or until loaf is browned on bottom and sounds hollow when tapped. Cool in pan 10 minutes on a wire rack; remove from pan. Cool completely on wire rack before slicing. Yield: 16 servings (serving size: 1 slice).

CALORIES 220; FAT 7.1g (sat 4.3g, mono 2g, poly 0.5g); PROTEIN 4.1g; CARB 36g; FIBER 1.5g; CHOL 25mg; IRON 1.4mg; SODIUM 111mg; CALC 23mg

How to Shape a Perfectly Gorgeous Babka

1 Roll dough out to a large square, then sprinkle with the filling almost to the outside edge. It's OK if some of the filling leaks out as you shape the bread; that'll make it prettier.

2 Carefully twist the dough 4 times as if wringing out a towel. This creates an interior spiral that distributes the chocolate filling in a beautiful way.

3 Fit the dough roll into the prepared pan; it may be a tight squeeze, but any lumps or bumps create interest once baked. Sprinkle with the buttery streusel for added texture.

Here We Come A-Caroling

You don't need a great voice to enjoy our make-ahead menu for a casual winter dinner party, and guests will sing your praises.

NO MATTER HOW DUBIOUS the singing—and we've perpetrated our share of off-key fa-la-las over the years—a round of joyful caroling is a gift to the neighborhood and an appetite-builder to the singers. A good walkabout of caroling makes almost everyone happy and then eager to eat and drink. We find no statistics on the incidence of caroling in America, but we suspect it may be on the wane. And so we offer this caroling menu as a gift to those who would defend a sacred tradition—and eat well while doing it!

CAROLING PARTY MENU
(Serves 8)

Chili-Spiced Almonds

Warm Caramelized Onion Dip

Frisée Salad with Maple-Bacon Vinaigrette

Belgian Beef and Beer Stew

Herbed Asiago Rolls

Chocolate-Hazelnut Meringues

Brown Sugar Cheesecake with Cranberry Compote

Applejack-Spiked Hot Cider

Vanilla-Almond Steamer

Orchestrating the Party

Up to 2 weeks ahead:
• Bake and freeze rolls

Up to 2 days ahead:
• Make meringues

Up to 1 day ahead:
• Cook stew
• Caramelize onions for dip
• Make spiced almonds
• Prepare and chill salad dressing
• Bake and chill cheesecake
• Cook and chill cranberry compote

1 day ahead:
• Cook and chill milk mixture for steamer
• Prepare and chill cider

3 hours ahead:
• Cut and combine salad greens

1 hour ahead:
• Thaw rolls at room temperature

45 minutes ahead:
• Heat stew

15 minutes ahead:
• Heat onions and mix dip

5 minutes ahead:
• Reheat cider and steamer
• Heat dressing and toss salad
• Pull cheesecake and compote from refrigerator

Continued

Chili-Spiced Almonds

These flavorful nuts make a convenient, portable snack. Store at room temperature in an airtight container for up to a week.

- 1 tablespoon water
- 1 large egg white
- 1 pound raw, unblanched almonds
- ½ cup sugar
- 1 tablespoon salt
- 1 teaspoon Spanish smoked paprika
- 1 teaspoon ground cumin
- 1 teaspoon ground coriander
- ½ teaspoon chili powder
  Cooking spray

1 Preheat oven to 300°.
2 Combine water and egg white in a large bowl; stir with a whisk until foamy. Add almonds; toss well to coat. Place almonds in a colander; drain 5 minutes.
3 Combine almonds, sugar, and next 5 ingredients in a large bowl; toss to coat. Spread almond mixture in a single layer on a jelly-roll pan coated with cooking spray. Bake at 300° for 15 minutes. Stir almond mixture; reduce oven temperature to 275°. Bake an additional 40 minutes, stirring every 10 minutes. Remove from oven; cool 5 minutes. Break apart any clusters. Cool completely. Yield: 4 cups (serving size: 2 tablespoons).

CALORIES 98; FAT 7.2g (sat 0.5g, mono 4.5g, poly 1.6g); PROTEIN 3.1g; CARB 6g; FIBER 1.8g; CHOL 0mg; IRON 0mg; SODIUM 221mg; CALC 1mg

Warm Caramelized Onion Dip

Serve with hearty crackers or sliced French bread.

- 2 teaspoons olive oil
- 4 cups chopped onion (about 2 large)
- ¾ teaspoon chopped fresh thyme
- ½ cup light sour cream
- ⅓ cup (about 1½ ounces) grated Parmigiano-Reggiano cheese
- ⅓ cup (3 ounces) ⅓-less-fat cream cheese
- ⅓ cup reduced-fat mayonnaise
- ¼ teaspoon salt
- ¼ teaspoon freshly ground black pepper
- ¼ teaspoon hot pepper sauce (such as Tabasco)
- ¼ teaspoon Worcestershire sauce

1 Heat oil in a large nonstick skillet over medium-high heat. Add onion and thyme to pan; sauté 10 minutes or until golden brown. Reduce heat to low; cook 20 minutes or until onions are deep golden brown, stirring occasionally. Remove from heat. Add sour cream and remaining ingredients, stirring until blended and cheese melts. Yield: 12 servings (serving size: 3 tablespoons).

CALORIES 81; FAT 4.9g (sat 2.3g, mono 1.2g, poly 0.6g); PROTEIN 3.1g; CARB 7.7g; FIBER 0.9g; CHOL 12mg; IRON 0.2mg; SODIUM 206mg; CALC 58mg

Frisée Salad with Maple-Bacon Vinaigrette

Bitter greens like radicchio and endive provide a pleasant counterpoint to the sweet, slightly smoky dressing.

- 6 cups torn frisée leaves
- 1 cup thinly sliced radicchio
- 4 cups (¾ inch) diagonally cut Belgian endive (about 3 heads)
- 4 slices center-cut bacon
- ¼ cup chopped shallots
- 2 tablespoons Champagne vinegar
- 4 teaspoons maple syrup
- 1 teaspoon extra-virgin olive oil
- 1 teaspoon Dijon mustard
- ¼ teaspoon salt
- ⅛ teaspoon freshly ground black pepper
- 3 ounces (about ¾ cup) crumbled blue cheese

1 Combine first 3 ingredients in a large bowl. Cook bacon in a large nonstick skillet over medium heat until crisp. Remove bacon from pan, reserving drippings; crumble. Add shallots to drippings in pan; cook 30 seconds, stirring constantly. Remove from heat; stir in vinegar and next 5 ingredients. Pour dressing over salad greens; toss well to combine. Add crumbled bacon and cheese to greens; toss gently. Yield: 8 servings (serving size: about ¾ cup).

CALORIES 96; FAT 6g (sat 3g, mono 2.3g, poly 0.3g); PROTEIN 5g; CARB 6.3g; FIBER 2g; CHOL 13mg; IRON 0.7mg; SODIUM 352mg; CALC 94mg

Belgian Beef and Beer Stew

An amber Belgian beer like De Koninck is ideal in this dish, though most amber beers or brown ales—such as Newcastle—would work just fine. Garnish with fresh thyme.

- 3 slices center-cut bacon, cut into ½-inch pieces
- 2½ pounds boneless chuck roast, trimmed and cut into 1½-inch cubes
- 2 cups chopped onion (about 2 medium)
- 5 cups sliced cremini mushrooms (about 12 ounces)
- 2 garlic cloves, minced
- 3 tablespoons all-purpose flour
- 1 (12-ounce) bottle amber beer
- 2 cups (½-inch-thick) slices carrot (about ½ pound)
- 1¾ cups (½-inch-thick) slices parsnip (about ½ pound)
- 1 cup fat-free, less-sodium beef broth
- 2 tablespoons country-style Dijon mustard
- 1 teaspoon salt
- 1 teaspoon dried thyme
- ½ teaspoon caraway seeds
- ½ teaspoon freshly ground black pepper
- 1 bay leaf

1 Cook bacon in a large Dutch oven over medium-high heat until crisp. Remove bacon from pan, reserving drippings; set aside. Add half of beef to drippings in pan; cook 5 minutes, browning on all sides. Remove beef from pan. Repeat procedure with remaining beef.

② Add onion to pan; sauté 4 minutes. Stir in mushrooms and garlic; sauté 4 minutes or until half of liquid evaporates. Stir in flour; cook 2 minutes, stirring occasionally. Stir in beer, scraping pan to loosen browned bits. Add bacon, beef, carrot, and remaining ingredients to pan; bring to a boil. Cover, reduce heat, and simmer 2 hours or until beef is tender. Discard bay leaf. Yield: 8 servings (serving size: 1 cup).

CALORIES 373; FAT 12.2g (sat 5g, mono 5.2g, poly 0.9g); PROTEIN 40.4g; CARB 18.4g; FIBER 3.9g; CHOL 118mg; IRON 5.1mg; SODIUM 780mg; CALC 56mg

Herbed Asiago Rolls

 2 tablespoons honey, divided
 1 package active dry yeast (about 2¼ teaspoons)
 ¾ cup warm water (100° to 110°)
 1 large egg, lightly beaten
 11.25 ounces all-purpose flour, divided (about 2½ cups)
 ¾ cup (3 ounces) shredded Asiago cheese, divided
 ¾ teaspoon salt
 ½ teaspoon dried oregano
 ½ teaspoon dried basil
 ½ teaspoon fennel seeds
 ¼ teaspoon ground red pepper
    Cooking spray

① Dissolve 1 tablespoon honey and yeast in warm water in a large bowl; let stand 5 minutes. Stir in remaining 1 tablespoon honey and egg. Weigh or lightly spoon 9 ounces (about 2 cups) flour into dry measuring cups; level with a knife. Combine 9 ounces flour, ½ cup cheese, and next 5 ingredients in a bowl; stirring with a whisk. Add flour mixture to yeast mixture, stirring to form a soft dough. Turn dough out onto a floured surface. Knead until smooth and elastic (about 8 minutes); add enough of remaining 2.25 ounces (about ½ cup) flour, 1 tablespoon at a time, to prevent dough from sticking to hands.
② Place dough in a large bowl coated with cooking spray, turning to coat top.

Cover and let rise in a warm place (85°), free from drafts, 1 hour or until doubled in size. (Gently press two fingers into dough. If indentation remains, dough has risen enough.) Punch dough down; cover and let rise 1 hour or until doubled in size.
③ Preheat oven to 425°.
④ Punch dough down; cover and let rest 5 minutes. Divide dough into 12 equal portions. Working with one portion at a time (cover remaining dough to prevent drying), roll each portion into a ball. Place balls 2 inches apart on a baking sheet coated with cooking spray. Cover and let rise 30 minutes. Uncover balls; sprinkle remaining ¼ cup cheese over tops of balls. Bake at 425° for 18 minutes or until browned. Remove from baking sheet; cool 10 minutes on a wire rack. Yield: 1 dozen rolls (serving size: 1 roll).

CALORIES 143; FAT 3g (sat 1.4g, mono 0.8g, poly 0.2g); PROTEIN 5.3g; CARB 24.1g; FIBER 0.9g; CHOL 24mg; IRON 1.5mg; SODIUM 235mg; CALC 73mg

Brown Sugar Cheesecake with Cranberry Compote

Thick cranberry sauce lends brilliant color and sweet-tart taste to this rich cheesecake.

CHEESECAKE:

 1¾ cups gingersnap crumbs (about 30 cookies, finely crushed)
 2 tablespoons butter, melted
 1 tablespoon fat-free milk
    Cooking spray
 2 cups (1 pound) ⅓-less-fat cream cheese
 1 cup (8 ounces) fat-free cream cheese
 ½ cup packed dark brown sugar
 ¼ cup granulated sugar
 1.3 ounces cake flour (about ⅓ cup)
 2 large eggs
 ½ cup reduced-fat sour cream
 2 tablespoons maple syrup
 1 tablespoon vanilla extract

COMPOTE:

 2 cups fresh cranberries (about 8 ounces)
 1 cup shredded peeled ripe pear (1 medium)
 ½ cup packed dark brown sugar
 ¾ cup fresh orange juice (about 3 oranges)
 ¼ teaspoon ground cinnamon

① Preheat oven to 400°.
② To prepare cheesecake, combine crumbs, butter, and milk in a medium bowl; stir with a fork. Firmly press mixture into bottom of a 9-inch springform pan coated with cooking spray. Bake at 400° for 3 minutes; cool on a wire rack. Reduce oven temperature to 325°.
③ Place cheeses in a large bowl; beat with a mixer at high speed until smooth. Add sugars, beating until well combined. Weigh or lightly spoon flour (about ⅓ cup) into a dry measuring cup; level with a knife. Add flour to cheese mixture; beat well. Add eggs, 1 at a time, beating well after each addition. Add sour cream, syrup, and vanilla; beat well. Pour cheese mixture into crust. Bake at 325° for 40 minutes or until cheesecake center barely moves when pan is touched. Turn oven off. Remove cheesecake; run a knife around outside edge. Return cheesecake to oven; partially open oven door. Cool cheesecake 1 hour in oven. Remove from oven; cool completely on a wire rack. Cover and chill at least 8 hours.
④ To prepare compote, combine cranberries and remaining ingredients in a medium saucepan over medium-high heat; bring to a boil. Reduce heat and simmer 5 minutes or until cranberries pop, stirring frequently. Cool to room temperature; serve over cheesecake. Yield: 16 servings (serving size: 1 slice cheesecake and about 2 tablespoons compote).

CALORIES 272; FAT 10.6g (sat 6.2g, mono 3.1g, poly 0.5g); PROTEIN 7.4g; CARB 37.2g; FIBER 1.4g; CHOL 55mg; IRON 1.5mg; SODIUM 320mg; CALC 92mg

Applejack-Spiked Hot Cider

- 2 tablespoons butter
- 2 tablespoons dark brown sugar
- 10 black peppercorns
- 8 whole allspice berries
- 5 whole cloves
- 2 (3-inch) cinnamon sticks
- 6 cups apple cider
- 1 tablespoon honey
- ½ teaspoon vanilla extract
- 2 (2-inch) orange rind strips
- 2 (2-inch) lemon rind strips
- ¾ cup applejack brandy

❶ Melt butter in a large saucepan over medium heat. Stir in sugar and next 4 ingredients; cook 1 minute. Add cider and next 4 ingredients; bring to a simmer. Reduce heat to medium-low; simmer 15 minutes. Remove from heat; stir in applejack. Strain; discard solids. Yield: 8 servings (serving size: about ⅔ cup).

CALORIES 189; FAT 2.8g (sat 1.8g, mono 0.7g, poly 0.1g); PROTEIN 0g; CARB 28.1g; FIBER 0g; CHOL 8mg; IRON 1mg; SODIUM 41mg; CALC 4mg

Chocolate-Hazelnut Meringues

Make up to two days ahead and store in an airtight container at room temperature.

- 5 large egg whites
- ½ teaspoon cream of tartar
- ⅛ teaspoon salt
- ½ cup granulated sugar
- ½ cup packed brown sugar
- 1 teaspoon vanilla extract
- 3 ounces semisweet chocolate
- ⅓ cup blanched whole hazelnuts, toasted and finely chopped

❶ Preheat oven to 250°.
❷ Place egg whites in a large bowl; beat with a mixer at high speed until foamy. Add cream of tartar and salt, beating until soft peaks form. Gradually add sugars, 1 tablespoon at a time, beating until stiff peaks form. Add vanilla; beat 1 minute.

❸ Cover two baking sheets with parchment paper. Spoon 24 (2-inch-round) mounds onto prepared baking sheets. Place in oven; bake at 250° for 1 hour or until dry to touch, rotating pans halfway through cooking. (Meringues are done when surface is dry and meringues can be removed from paper without sticking to fingers.) Turn oven off. Cool meringues in oven 1 hour. Remove from oven; carefully remove meringues from paper.
❹ Place chocolate in a medium glass bowl. Microwave at HIGH 1 minute or until almost melted, stirring until smooth. Dip one side of each meringue in chocolate and hazelnuts. Yield: 12 servings (serving size: 2 meringues).

CALORIES 135; FAT 4.3g (sat 1.4g, mono 1.7g, poly 0.3g); PROTEIN 2.6g; CARB 22.7g; FIBER 0.4g; CHOL 0mg; IRON 0.6mg; SODIUM 51mg; CALC 13mg

Vanilla-Almond Steamer

This hot drink pairs nicely with Chocolate-Hazelnut Meringues (at left).

- 8 cups 1% low-fat milk
- ½ cup sugar
- 2 (3-inch) cinnamon sticks
- 2 teaspoons vanilla extract
- ¼ teaspoon almond extract
-    Ground cinnamon
-    Cinnamon sticks (optional)

❶ Combine milk and sugar in a medium saucepan over medium-high heat; cook until sugar dissolves, stirring frequently. Add cinnamon sticks to milk mixture; cook 5 minutes, stirring occasionally (do not boil). Remove from heat; let stand 20 minutes. Stir in extracts. Place pan over medium-high heat; cook 3 minutes or until thoroughly heated. Remove and discard cinnamon sticks. Garnish with ground cinnamon and, if desired, cinnamon sticks. Yield: 8 servings (serving size: about 1 cup).

CALORIES 154; FAT 2.6g (sat 1.6g, mono 0.8g, poly 0.1g); PROTEIN 8g; CARB 24.3g; FIBER 0g; CHOL 10mg; IRON 0.1mg; SODIUM 123mg; CALC 300mg

Red Velvet Cupcakes

"My cupcakes have such an incredibly rich chocolate flavor that friends are surprised when I tell them the recipe is light."

—Nicolette Maneschalchi, San Francisco, California

CUPCAKES:
-    Cooking spray
- 10 ounces cake flour (about 2½ cups)
- 3 tablespoons unsweetened cocoa
- 1 teaspoon baking soda
- 1 teaspoon baking powder
- 1 teaspoon kosher salt
- 1½ cups granulated sugar
- 6 tablespoons unsalted butter, softened
- 2 large eggs
- 1¼ cups nonfat buttermilk
- 1½ teaspoons white vinegar
- 1½ teaspoons vanilla extract
- 1 ounce red food coloring (about 2 tablespoons)

FROSTING:
- 5 tablespoons butter, softened
- 4 teaspoons nonfat buttermilk
- 1 (8-ounce) block cream cheese, softened
- 3½ cups powdered sugar (about 1 pound)
- 1¼ teaspoons vanilla extract

❶ Preheat oven to 350°.
❷ To prepare cupcakes, place 30 paper muffin cup liners in muffin cups; coat with cooking spray.
❸ Weigh or lightly spoon flour into dry measuring cups; level with a knife. Combine flour and next 4 ingredients in a medium bowl; set aside. Place granulated sugar and unsalted butter in a large bowl; beat with a mixer at medium speed until well blended (about 3 minutes). Add eggs, 1 at a time, beating well after each addition. Add flour

mixture and 1¼ cups buttermilk alternately to sugar mixture, beginning and ending with flour mixture. Add vinegar, 1½ teaspoons vanilla, and food coloring; beat well.

❹ Spoon batter into prepared muffin cups. Bake at 350° for 20 minutes or until a wooden pick inserted in center comes out clean. Cool in pan 10 minutes on a wire rack; remove from pan. Cool completely on wire racks.

❺ To prepare frosting, beat 5 tablespoons butter, 4 teaspoons buttermilk, and cream cheese with a mixer at high speed until fluffy. Gradually add powdered sugar; beat until smooth. Add 1¼ teaspoons vanilla; beat well. Spread frosting evenly over cupcakes. Yield: 30 cupcakes (serving size: 1 cupcake).

CALORIES 205; FAT 7.3g (sat 4.5g, mono 2g, poly 0.3g); PROTEIN 2.3g; CARB 33.5g; FIBER 0.3g; CHOL 34mg; IRON 0.9mg; SODIUM 168mg; CALC 35mg

Chicken and Wild Rice Salad with Almonds

(pictured on page 238)

"The fig vinegar makes this dressing spectacular and unique, but you can substitute white wine vinegar if you can't find it."

—Ashley Bone,
Spring Hill, Tennessee

DRESSING:
¼   cup fig vinegar or white wine vinegar
2   teaspoons sugar
1   teaspoon Dijon mustard
¼   teaspoon salt
1   garlic clove, minced
2   tablespoons canola oil

REMAINING INGREDIENTS:
2   cups fat-free, less-sodium chicken broth
1½   cups uncooked wild rice
1   tablespoon butter
     Cooking spray
1   pound skinless, boneless chicken breast
¼   teaspoon salt
⅛   teaspoon black pepper
1   cup chopped celery
½   cup shredded carrots
⅓   cup dried cranberries
¼   cup chopped almonds, toasted
2   tablespoons minced red onion

❶ To prepare dressing, combine first 5 ingredients in medium bowl. Gradually add oil, stirring with a whisk until well blended. Cover and chill.

❷ Combine broth, rice, and butter in a medium saucepan; bring to a boil. Cover, reduce heat, and simmer 45 minutes or until rice is tender and liquid is absorbed. Remove from heat; cool.

❸ Heat a grill pan over medium-high heat. Coat pan with cooking spray. Sprinkle chicken with ¼ teaspoon salt and pepper. Add chicken to pan; cook 8 minutes on each side or until done. Cool; cut into ½-inch cubes.

❹ Combine cooked rice, chicken, celery, and remaining ingredients in a large bowl. Add dressing; toss gently to coat. Cover and chill. Yield: 6 servings (serving size: about 1⅓ cups).

CALORIES 352; FAT 10.3g (sat 2g, mono 5g, poly 2.5g); PROTEIN 25g; CARB 40.6g; FIBER 4g; CHOL 49mg; IRON 1.6mg; SODIUM 455mg; CALC 42mg

Mocha Cream-Filled Meringues

"I love the contrast of textures in a recipe. This dessert has the crispness of the meringue nests, the creamy smooth filling, and crunch of the cacao nibs."

—Patrice Hurd,
Bemidji, Minnesota

MERINGUES:
2   large egg whites
¼   teaspoon cream of tartar
     Dash of salt
⅔   cup granulated sugar
2   tablespoons unsweetened cocoa
½   teaspoon instant coffee granules
½   teaspoon vanilla extract
¼   cup cacao nibs (such as Scharffen Berger)

FILLING:
3   tablespoons unsweetened cocoa
3   tablespoons boiling water
½   teaspoon instant coffee granules
½   cup powdered sugar
½   cup (4 ounces) ⅓-less-fat cream cheese
1½   cups frozen reduced-calorie whipped topping, thawed
8   teaspoons chocolate syrup
2   teaspoons cacao nibs

❶ Preheat oven to 300°.

❷ To prepare meringues, cover a baking a sheet with parchment paper. Draw 8 (4-inch) circles on paper. Turn paper over; secure with masking tape.

❸ Combine egg whites and cream of tartar in a large bowl; beat with a mixer at high speed until soft peaks form using clean, dry beaters. Add salt. Gradually add granulated sugar, 1 tablespoon at a time, beating until stiff peaks form. Add 2 tablespoons cocoa, ½ teaspoon coffee, and vanilla; beat well. Fold in ¼ cup cacao nibs. Divide batter evenly among 8 circles on prepared baking sheet; spread to fill circles using the back of a spoon.

❹ Bake at 300° for 35 minutes. Turn oven off; cool meringues in closed oven 1 hour. Carefully remove meringues from paper. Cool completely on a wire rack. (Meringues can be stored in an airtight container for up to a week.)

❺ To prepare filling, combine 3 tablespoons cocoa, water, and ½ teaspoon coffee in a small bowl, stirring with a whisk until smooth. Cool. Combine powdered sugar and cream cheese in a medium bowl; beat with a mixer until smooth. Add cocoa mixture; beat well. Fold in whipped topping. Spoon ¼ cup filling into center of each meringue; drizzle 1 teaspoon chocolate syrup over each filled meringue. Sprinkle ¼ teaspoon cacao nibs over each serving. Yield: 8 servings (serving size: 1 filled meringue).

CALORIES 233; FAT 8.3g (sat 5.9g, mono 1g, poly 0.1g); PROTEIN 3.8g; CARB 38.4g; FIBER 1.2g; CHOL 10mg; IRON 1.9mg; SODIUM 107mg; CALC 28mg

Two-Pepper Rigatoni and Cheese

"This is a great basic recipe because there are many possibilities for variations."
—Jeff Towle, Kingwood, Texas

    5   cups uncooked rigatoni (16 ounces
        uncooked pasta)
    2   tablespoons butter, divided
    1   cup chopped red bell pepper
    3   tablespoons all-purpose flour
    3   cups fat-free milk
    1   cup shredded fontina cheese
    1   cup shredded sharp Cheddar cheese
    1   tablespoon finely chopped pickled
        jalapeño pepper
    ¾   teaspoon salt
    ½   cup sliced green onions
        Cooking spray
    2   (1-ounce) slices white bread

❶ Preheat oven to 375°.
❷ Cook pasta according to package directions, omitting salt and fat. Drain well; place in a large bowl.
❸ Melt 1 tablespoon butter in a saucepan over medium-high heat. Add bell pepper; sauté 5 minutes. Add to pasta.
❹ Add flour to pan. Gradually add milk, stirring with a whisk until smooth. Bring to a boil; cook 2 minutes or until thickened, stirring constantly. Remove from heat. Add cheeses, stirring until cheeses melt and mixture is smooth. Stir in jalapeño and salt. Add cheese mixture to pasta, tossing well to coat. Stir in green onions. Spoon pasta mixture into a 13 x 9-inch baking dish coated with cooking spray.
❺ Place bread in a food processor; pulse 10 times or until coarse crumbs measure 1 cup. Melt remaining 1 tablespoon butter. Combine butter and breadcrumbs in a bowl; toss until blended. Sprinkle breadcrumb mixture over pasta mixture. Bake at 375° for 15 minutes or until browned. Yield: 8 servings (serving size: 1 cup).

CALORIES 408; FAT 12.8g (sat 7.8g, mono 3.3g, poly 0.6g); PROTEIN 19.2g; CARB 54.5g; FIBER 2.4g; CHOL 40mg; IRON 2.5mg; SODIUM 550mg; CALC 293mg

The Sacred Power of Oil

Coming at the darkest time of the year, Hanukkah offers light, inspiration, and glorious symbolic foods that honor an ancient miracle.

AFTER SUNDOWN ON DECEMBER 11, Jews throughout the world will light a candle to commemorate an ancient miracle, adding one flame each for seven more nights until an eight-candled menorah is aglow on the last.

As the candles flicker, we are reminded of the story of a handful of Jews, led by Judah Maccabee and his brothers, who overpowered the much larger tyrannical Assyrian army in Mo d'iim, a valley close to Jerusalem, in 164 B.C.E. Upon purifying and rededicating the Temple, only a single day's portion of pure, undefiled oil could be found. But that tiny bit miraculously burned and shone light for a full eight days. Hanukkah is the annual celebration of this triumph—and of the power of oil itself.

In honor of the miracle of the oil, symbolic Hanukkah foods are cooked in or prepared with oil. Olive oil was traditional, but canola or other vegetable oils are used today, too. These dishes pay homage to a story of victory over darkness, of enduring light beaming out of scarcity.

Loukomades with Honey Orange Sauce

    1   tablespoon dry yeast
    1¼ cups warm water (100° to 110°)
    1   tablespoon canola oil
    2   teaspoons grated orange rind,
        divided
    ½   teaspoon salt
    1   large egg
 13.5 ounces all-purpose flour (about
        3 cups)
    5   cups canola oil
    1   cup fresh orange juice
    1   cup honey
    1½ teaspoons ground cinnamon

❶ Dissolve yeast in warm water in the bowl of a stand mixer. Add 1 tablespoon oil, 1 teaspoon rind, salt, and egg, beating at medium speed with paddle attachment. Weigh or lightly spoon flour into dry measuring cups; level with a knife. With mixer on low speed, add flour 1 cup at a time, mixing until a spongy, soft dough begins to form (dough will be very soft and wet). Cover bowl with plastic wrap; let rise in a warm place (85°), free from drafts, 1 hour.
❷ Clip a kitchen or candy thermometer to side of a large, heavy saucepan. Add 5 cups oil to pan; heat over medium-high heat until thermometer registers 375°. Reduce heat to medium, checking frequently to maintain oil temperature. Carefully spoon 4 (1-tablespoon) dough portions into hot oil; cook 2 minutes on each side. Remove fried dough with a slotted spoon; drain on paper towels. Repeat procedure with remaining dough.
❸ Combine remaining 1 teaspoon rind, juice, honey, and cinnamon in a medium saucepan over low heat, stirring occasionally until honey dissolves. Keep warm. Serve sauce with loukomades. Yield: 24 servings (serving size: 2 loukomades and about 1½ tablespoons sauce).

CALORIES 135; FAT 3.3g (sat 0.3g, mono 1.8g, poly 1g); PROTEIN 2.2g; CARB 25g; FIBER 0.7g; CHOL 9mg; IRON 1mg; SODIUM 53mg; CALC 8mg

Israeli Cauliflower with Panko

- 6 cups cauliflower florets
- 2 tablespoons water
- 3 tablespoons olive oil, divided
- ½ cup panko (Japanese breadcrumbs)
- 1 garlic clove, minced
- 1 tablespoon chopped fresh parsley
- ½ teaspoon salt
- ¼ teaspoon freshly ground black pepper

1 Combine cauliflower and 2 tablespoons water in a microwave-safe bowl. Microwave at HIGH 6 minutes or until crisp-tender. Drain.

2 Heat 1½ tablespoons oil in a large nonstick skillet over medium-high heat. Add panko; cook 3 minutes or until toasted, stirring constantly. Remove panko from pan.

3 Heat remaining 1½ tablespoons oil and garlic in pan over medium-high heat. Add cauliflower; sauté 5 minutes or until golden, stirring occasionally. Add panko, parsley, salt, and pepper; toss to combine. Yield: 8 servings (serving size: about ⅔ cup).

CALORIES 78; FAT 5.3g (sat 0.7g, mono 3.7g, poly 0.6g); PROTEIN 2g; CARB 6.7g; FIBER 2g; CHOL 0mg; IRON 0.4mg; SODIUM 181mg; CALC 18mg

Potato-Apple Latkes

(pictured on page 240)

- 6 cups shredded peeled Yukon gold potatoes (about 2 pounds)
- 2 cups shredded Gala or Honeycrisp apples (about 2 medium)
- 1½ teaspoons salt, divided
- ½ teaspoon freshly ground black pepper
- 2.25 ounces all-purpose flour (about ½ cup)
- 6 tablespoons canola oil, divided
- 1 teaspoon granulated sugar

1 Combine potatoes, apples, and 1 teaspoon salt in a colander. Let stand

20 minutes, pressing occasionally with back of a spoon until barely moist. Combine potato mixture, remaining ½ teaspoon salt, and pepper in a large bowl. Weigh or lightly spoon flour into a dry measuring cup; level with a knife. Add flour to potato mixture; toss well to combine.

2 Heat a 12-inch nonstick skillet over medium-high heat. Add 1½ tablespoons oil to pan, swirling to coat. Add potato mixture in ⅓-cupfuls to pan to form 4 latkes; flatten slightly. Cook 6 minutes on each side or until golden brown. Remove latkes from pan; keep warm. Repeat procedure 3 more times with remaining oil and potato mixture. Sprinkle latkes evenly with sugar. Yield: 8 servings (serving size: 2 latkes).

CALORIES 235; FAT 10.6g (sat 0.8g, mono 6.2g, poly 3.2g); PROTEIN 3.6g; CARB 31.3g; FIBER 2.4g; CHOL 0mg; IRON 1.4mg; SODIUM 302mg; CALC 4mg

Greek Cod Cakes

CAKES:

- 4 cups 2% reduced-fat milk
- 2 pounds cod fillets, cut into 2-inch pieces
- 1 cup panko (Japanese breadcrumbs), divided
- ¼ cup minced fresh flat-leaf parsley
- 2 tablespoons grated onion
- 2½ teaspoons grated lemon rind
- 1½ teaspoons salt
- 1 teaspoon freshly ground black pepper
- 3 large eggs, lightly beaten
- 2 garlic cloves, minced
- ¼ cup fresh lemon juice, divided
- ¼ cup olive oil, divided

SAUCE:

- ½ cup canola mayonnaise
- 2 tablespoons chopped fresh flat-leaf parsley
- 2 teaspoons chopped fresh dill
- 2 teaspoons Dijon mustard
- 2 teaspoons fresh lemon juice
- 1 teaspoon minced fresh garlic
- ½ teaspoon freshly ground black pepper

1 To prepare cakes, bring milk to a simmer over medium heat in a large, heavy saucepan. Add fish; cover and simmer 5 minutes or until fish flakes easily when tested with a fork. Drain well. Combine fish, ½ cup panko, and next 7 ingredients; stir in 2 tablespoons juice. Divide fish mixture into 16 equal portions, shaping each into a ½-inch-thick patty. Dredge patties in remaining ½ cup panko, pressing to coat.

2 Heat 1 tablespoon oil in a large nonstick skillet over medium-high heat. Add 4 patties to pan; cook 4 minutes on each side or until golden and thoroughly heated. Remove from pan; drain on paper towels. Repeat procedure 3 more times with remaining oil and patties. Drizzle with remaining 2 tablespoons juice.

3 To prepare sauce, combine mayonnaise and remaining ingredients. Serve sauce with cakes. Yield: 8 servings (serving size: 2 cakes).

CALORIES 266; FAT 14.4g (sat 1.8g, mono 8.3g, poly 2.8g); PROTEIN 24.3g; CARB 7.7g; FIBER 0.6g; CHOL 122mg; IRON 1mg; SODIUM 679mg; CALC 43mg

Fennel, Blood Orange, and Watercress Salad

- 3 cups thinly sliced fennel bulb
- 3 cups trimmed watercress
- 1½ cups blood orange sections
- ¾ cup pomegranate seeds
- ¾ teaspoon grated lemon rind
- 2½ tablespoons fresh lemon juice
- 2½ tablespoons extra-virgin olive oil
- ½ teaspoon salt
- 1 garlic clove, minced
- ¼ teaspoon ground black pepper

1 Combine first 4 ingredients in a large bowl. Combine rind and next 4 ingredients, stirring with a whisk. Drizzle dressing over salad; toss gently to coat. Sprinkle with pepper. Yield: 8 servings (serving size: about ¾ cup).

CALORIES 116; FAT 4.4g (sat 0.6g, mono 3.1g, poly 0.5g); PROTEIN 1.7g; CARB 18.4g; FIBER 3.5g; CHOL 0mg; IRON 0.4mg; SODIUM 170mg; CALC 78mg

Food and the City: A Holiday Love Story

Food maven Molly O'Neill savors Christmastime in the Big Apple, where bright lights shine on fabulous foods as eclectic as the city itself.

UNLIKE MANY PLACES, New York City does not have a born-and-raised residency requirement. You can be born in Columbus, Ohio, as I was, but if you love New York City and you know New York City, you're a New Yorker. We're fueled by some combination of the city's pace and vigor, drive and hope. We thrive on its offerings in the arts, letters, theater, music, and sports. And we relish nothing more than the discovery of a fabulous street vendor or teeny no-name eatery, except perhaps a meal in one of the New York's world-famous restaurants.

Coney Island Skewered Shrimp

- 2 tablespoons chopped fresh parsley
- 2 tablespoons olive oil
- 1 tablespoon fresh lemon juice
- 1 teaspoon kosher salt
- ½ teaspoon grated lemon rind
- ¼ teaspoon crushed red pepper
- 2 garlic cloves, minced
- 100 large shrimp, peeled and deveined (about 4 pounds)
- Lemon halves (optional)

❶ Preheat broiler.
❷ Combine first 7 ingredients in a large bowl. Add shrimp to bowl; toss to coat. Thread 5 shrimp onto each of 20 (12-inch) wooden skewers. Arrange 10 skewers on a large baking sheet. Broil 3 minutes on one side; carefully turn and broil 2 minutes or until shrimp are done. Place skewers on a serving platter. Repeat procedure with remaining 10 skewers. Serve with lemon halves, if desired. Yield: 10 servings (serving size: 2 skewers).

CALORIES 218; FAT 5.9g (sat 1g, mono 2.4g, poly 1.5g); PROTEIN 36.9g; CARB 2.1g; FIBER 0.1g; CHOL 276mg; IRON 4.5mg; SODIUM 457mg; CALC 97mg

QUICK & EASY
Carrots Roasted with Smoked Paprika

Slicing the carrots lengthwise gives them a distinctive look, while smoky spice balances their natural sweetness.

- 2 tablespoons olive oil
- 1½ teaspoons Spanish smoked paprika
- 1 teaspoon kosher salt
- ½ teaspoon freshly ground black pepper
- 2½ pounds medium carrots, peeled and halved lengthwise
- 2 tablespoons finely chopped fresh cilantro

❶ Place a jelly-roll pan on bottom oven rack. Preheat oven to 450°.
❷ Combine first 5 ingredients in a large bowl; toss well. Arrange carrot mixture in a single layer on preheated pan. Bake at 450° for 25 minutes, stirring after 12 minutes. Sprinkle with cilantro. Yield: 10 servings (serving size: about ⅓ cup).

CALORIES 72; FAT 3g (sat 0.4g, mono 2g, poly 0.4g); PROTEIN 1.1g; CARB 11.1g; FIBER 3.3g; CHOL 0mg; IRON 0.4mg; SODIUM 267mg; CALC 39mg

Persian Street Vendor Kebabs

- 1 cup grated onion (about 2 medium)
- 10 tablespoons dry breadcrumbs
- 1½ teaspoons kosher salt
- 1 teaspoon ground turmeric
- 1 teaspoon freshly ground black pepper
- ½ teaspoon paprika
- 3 garlic cloves, minced
- 2 large eggs, lightly beaten
- 1½ pounds ground turkey breast
- 1½ pounds ground lamb
- ⅛ teaspoon saffron threads
- 2 tablespoons extra-virgin olive oil
- Cooking spray
- ¼ teaspoon ground sumac
- ½ cup plain fat-free Greek-style yogurt
- 2 teaspoons chopped fresh cilantro
- 1 teaspoon fresh lemon juice
- 1 teaspoon honey
- ⅛ teaspoon ground red pepper

❶ Place onion in a sieve over a large bowl 30 minutes, pressing occasionally to squeeze out excess liquid. Discard liquid.
❷ Prepare grill to medium-high heat.
❸ Combine onion, breadcrumbs, and next 8 ingredients in a large bowl; stir until well blended. Divide meat mixture into 40 equal portions, shaping each into a 3 x 1–inch rectangle. Thread 4 pieces onto each of 10 (12-inch) skewers.
❹ Heat a small skillet over medium heat. Add saffron to pan; cook 30 seconds or until fragrant, stirring constantly. Crush saffron in a small bowl; stir in oil.
❺ Place kebabs on a grill rack coated with cooking spray; grill 8 minutes or until done, turning after 5 minutes. Brush oil mixture evenly over kebabs. Sprinkle kebabs evenly with sumac. Combine yogurt and remaining ingredients in a small bowl; stir until well blended. Serve kebabs with yogurt sauce. Yield: 10 servings (serving size: 1 kebab and about 1 tablespoon sauce).

CALORIES 303; FAT 15g (sat 5.2g, mono 6.7g, poly 1.4g); PROTEIN 31.9g; CARB 9g; FIBER 0.8g; CHOL 113mg; IRON 2.1mg; SODIUM 441mg; CALC 45mg

Duck and Sausage Cassoulet

1½ pounds dried cannellini beans
1 (1-pound) boneless pork shoulder
   (Boston butt), trimmed and cut into
   1½-inch pieces
½ teaspoon kosher salt, divided
½ teaspoon freshly ground black
   pepper, divided
1 tablespoon canola oil
2½ cups finely chopped onion (about
   2 medium)
1 cup thinly sliced carrot (about
   ½ pound)
4 garlic cloves, minced
1 (14-ounce) can whole tomatoes,
   drained and chopped
2 fresh flat-leaf parsley sprigs
1 celery stalk
1 fresh thyme sprig
1 bay leaf
8 cups fat-free, less-sodium chicken
   broth, divided
2 cups water
5 duck confit legs (about 2½ pounds)
Cooking spray
¾ pound chicken sausage
1 (1-ounce) slice white bread

❶ Sort and wash beans; place in a bowl. Cover with water to 2 inches above beans; cover and let stand 8 hours. Drain beans.
❷ Sprinkle pork with ¼ teaspoon salt and ¼ teaspoon pepper. Heat oil in a large Dutch oven over medium-high heat. Add pork to pan; cook 6 minutes or until browned, turning occasionally. Remove pork from pan; reduce heat to medium. Add onion and carrot to pan; cook 8 minutes or until lightly browned, stirring occasionally. Add garlic and tomatoes; cook 2 minutes, stirring occasionally. Tie twine around parsley, celery, thyme, and bay leaf to secure. Add beans, pork, 4 cups broth, 2 cups water, and herb bundle to pan. Bring to a simmer; cook, covered, 2 hours or until beans are tender. Stir in remaining ¼ teaspoon salt and ¼ teaspoon pepper. Cool bean mixture to room temperature; cover and chill overnight.

❸ Preheat oven to 400°.
❹ Arrange duck confit legs in a 13 x 9-inch baking dish. Bake at 400° for 15 minutes or until thoroughly heated. Remove skin and meat from bones; shred meat into large pieces. Discard skin and bones.
❺ Reduce oven temperature to 325°.
❻ Bring bean mixture to a simmer over medium-low heat. Spoon half of bean mixture into a large Dutch oven; stir in duck. Spoon remaining half of bean mixture on top of duck mixture. Bring remaining 4 cups broth to a simmer in a medium saucepan; pour evenly over bean mixture. Bake at 325° for 2 hours. Reduce oven to temperature to 275°.
❼ Heat a large skillet over medium-high heat. Coat pan with cooking spray. Add sausage to pan; cook 6 minutes or until browned, turning occasionally. Cool slightly; cut into 1-inch pieces. Stir bean mixture; add sausage pieces. Place bread in a food processor; pulse 10 times or until coarse crumbs measure ½ cup. Sprinkle breadcrumbs evenly over cassoulet. Bake at 275° for 1½ hours. Let stand 20 minutes before serving. Yield: 10 servings (serving size: about 1½ cups).

CALORIES 474; FAT 11.5g (sat 3.6g, mono 4.6g, poly 2.3g); PROTEIN 41.9g; CARB 49.9g; FIBER 12.9g; CHOL 100mg; IRON 11.7mg; SODIUM 853mg; CALC 180mg

QUICK & EASY
Brussels Sprouts with Pancetta

2½ pounds Brussels sprouts, trimmed
1 tablespoon kosher salt
½ cup chopped pancetta (about
   4 ounces)
¼ teaspoon kosher salt
¼ teaspoon freshly ground black
   pepper
1 tablespoon cider vinegar

❶ Preheat oven to 450°.
❷ Cook Brussels sprouts and 1 tablespoon salt in boiling water 6 minutes or until almost tender. Drain and plunge into ice water; drain well.
❸ Cook pancetta in a large skillet over

medium-low heat until crisp, stirring occasionally. Remove pancetta from pan, reserving drippings.
❹ Place Brussels sprouts on a baking sheet. Add reserved drippings, ¼ teaspoon salt, and pepper; toss to coat. Bake at 450° for 15 minutes or until browned, stirring after 10 minutes. Combine Brussels sprouts, pancetta, and vinegar in a large bowl; toss well. Yield: 10 servings (serving size: about ⅔ cup).

CALORIES 90; FAT 4g (sat 1.7g, mono 1.8g, poly 0.6g); PROTEIN 5.5g; CARB 10.2g; FIBER 4.3g; CHOL 8mg; IRON 1.6mg; SODIUM 318mg; CALC 48mg

Viennese Almond Crescents

Look for almond meal—also known as almond flour—in health food and specialty stores. Bake the cookies ahead and store up to six months frozen in an airtight container, with wax paper between layers. Thaw 30 minutes and dust the cookies with powdered sugar just before serving.

7.5 ounces all-purpose flour (about
   1⅔ cups)
⅔ cup almond meal
¼ teaspoon kosher salt
1 cup butter, softened
⅓ cup granulated sugar
1 cup powdered sugar

❶ Preheat oven to 350°.
❷ Cover 2 large baking sheets with parchment paper. Weigh or lightly spoon flour into dry measuring cups; level with a knife. Combine flour, almond meal, and salt in a small bowl; stir well with a whisk. Combine butter and granulated sugar in a large bowl; beat with a mixer at medium speed until light and fluffy (about 4 minutes). Gradually add flour mixture to butter mixture; beat until combined. Chill 10 minutes.
❸ Shape dough into 40 (2-inch) logs; bend logs to form crescent shape. Arrange crescents 2 inches apart on prepared baking sheets. Bake at 350° for 12 minutes or until edges are slightly

Continued

golden. Remove from baking sheets; cool on a wire rack. Sprinkle cookies evenly with powdered sugar. Yield: 40 cookies (serving size: 1 cookie).

CALORIES 113; FAT 5.5g (sat 3g, mono 1.7g, poly 0.4g); PROTEIN 1.7g; CARB 14.5g; FIBER 0.5g; CHOL 12mg; IRON 0.7mg; SODIUM 44mg; CALC 7mg

QUICK & EASY
Fennel Slaw with Orange Vinaigrette

    ¼   cup extra-virgin olive oil
    1   tablespoon sherry vinegar
    1   teaspoon grated orange rind
  1½   tablespoons fresh orange juice
    1   teaspoon kosher salt
    ¼   teaspoon freshly ground black pepper
    ¼   teaspoon crushed red pepper
    3   medium fennel bulbs with stalks (about 4 pounds)
    2   cups orange sections (about 2 large oranges)
    ½   cup coarsely chopped pitted green olives

❶ Combine first 7 ingredients in a large bowl.
❷ Trim tough outer leaves from fennel; mince feathery fronds to measure 1 cup. Remove and discard stalks. Cut fennel bulb in half lengthwise; discard core. Thinly slice bulbs. Add fronds, fennel slices, and orange sections to bowl; toss gently to combine. Sprinkle with olives. Yield: 16 servings (serving size: ¾ cup).

CALORIES 64; FAT 4.4g (sat 0.5g, mono 3.1g, poly 0.7g); PROTEIN 0.8g; CARB 6.5g; FIBER 1.9g; CHOL 0mg; IRON 0.4mg; SODIUM 230mg; CALC 31mg

12 Days of Sweetness and Light

A dozen classic *Cooking Light* treats that celebrate the sweetest season of giving.

Coconut-Almond Macaroons

    3   tablespoons almond paste
    1   teaspoon vanilla extract
    4   large egg whites, divided
  1⅓   cups powdered sugar
  1¼   teaspoons baking powder
    ¼   teaspoon salt
  3½   cups flaked sweetened coconut
    ½   cup granulated sugar

❶ Preheat oven to 350°.
❷ Combine almond paste, 1 teaspoon vanilla, and 2 egg whites in a large bowl; beat with a mixer until well blended. Combine powdered sugar, baking powder, and salt. Add powdered sugar mixture to almond paste mixture, beating until blended. Stir in coconut.
❸ Place remaining 2 egg whites in a medium bowl; beat with a mixer at high speed until soft peaks form using clean, dry beaters. Gradually add granulated sugar, 1 tablespoon at a time, beating until stiff peaks form. Gently fold egg white mixture into coconut mixture.
❹ Drop dough by level tablespoons 2 inches apart onto a baking sheet lined with parchment paper. Bake at 350° for 20 minutes or until firm. Cool on pan 2 to 3 minutes on a wire rack. Remove cookies from pan, and cool completely on wire rack. Yield: 32 macaroons (serving size: 1 macaroon).

CALORIES 80; FAT 3.2g (sat 2.5g, mono 0.4g, poly 0.1g); PROTEIN 0.9g; CARB 12.6g; FIBER 0.4g; CHOL 0mg; IRON 0.2mg; SODIUM 69mg; CALC 15mg

MAKE AHEAD
Cranberry Liqueur

Give away this jewel-toned potion in small decanters or glass bottles. Drench home-made fruitcake with the liqueur. Or drizzle it over ice cream and fruit for an instantly glamorous dessert. Or just sip it, chilled, in liqueur glasses.

    2   cups sugar
    1   cup water
    1   (12-ounce) package fresh cranberries
    3   cups vodka

❶ Combine sugar and water in a medium saucepan; cook over medium heat 5 minutes or until sugar dissolves, stirring constantly. Remove from heat, and cool completely.
❷ Place cranberries in a food processor; process 2 minutes or until finely chopped. Combine sugar mixture and cranberries in a large bowl; stir in vodka.
❸ Pour vodka mixture into clean jars; secure with lids. Let stand 3 weeks in a cool, dark place, shaking every other day.
❹ Strain cranberry mixture through a cheesecloth-lined sieve into a bowl, and discard solids. Carefully pour liqueur into clean bottles or jars. Yield: 4½ cups (serving size: ¼ cup).
NOTE: Liqueur can be stored refrigerated or at room temperature for up to a year.

CALORIES 193; FAT 0g; PROTEIN 0.1g; CARB 25g; FIBER 0.8g; CHOL 0mg; IRON 0.1mg; SODIUM 1.2mg; CALC 2mg

Lemon Curd

Fresh lemons are a must in this recipe and give it unbeatable flavor. For a lime curd variation, substitute lime rind and juice.

- 1 cup plus 2 tablespoons sugar
- 1 tablespoon cornstarch
- ⅛ teaspoon salt
- 1 cup fresh lemon juice (about 5 medium lemons)
- 3 large eggs
- 2 tablespoons butter
- 1 teaspoon grated lemon rind

❶ Combine first 3 ingredients in a medium, heavy saucepan, stirring with a whisk. Stir in juice and eggs; bring to a boil over medium heat, stirring constantly with a whisk. Reduce heat, and simmer 1 minute or until thick, stirring constantly. Remove from heat; add butter and lemon rind, stirring gently until butter melts.
❷ Spoon mixture into a medium bowl; cool. Cover and chill at least 6 hours or overnight (mixture will thicken as it cools). Yield: 2½ cups (serving size: 1 tablespoon).

CALORIES 35; FAT 1g (sat 0.5g, mono 0.3g, poly 0.1g); PROTEIN 0.5g; CARB 6.4g; FIBER 0g; CHOL 18mg; IRON 0mg; SODIUM 17mg; CALC 2mg

Sweet Challah

- 1 package dry yeast (about 2¼ teaspoons)
- 1 cup warm water (100° to 110°)
- 3 tablespoons honey
- Dash of saffron threads, crushed
- 3 tablespoons butter, melted and cooled
- 1 teaspoon salt
- 1 large egg
- 14.25 ounces bread flour (about 3 cups), divided
- Cooking spray
- 1 teaspoon cornmeal
- 1 teaspoon water
- 1 large egg yolk, lightly beaten
- ¼ teaspoon poppy seeds

❶ Dissolve yeast in 1 cup warm water in a large bowl; stir in honey and saffron threads. Let stand 5 minutes. Add melted butter, 1 teaspoon salt, and egg; stir well with a whisk.
❷ Weigh or lightly spoon flour into dry measuring cups; level with a knife. Add 13.1 ounces flour (about 2¾ cups) to yeast mixture, and stir until a soft dough forms. Cover and let stand 15 minutes.
❸ Turn dough out onto a lightly floured surface. Knead until smooth and elastic (about 8 minutes); add enough of remaining flour, 1 tablespoon at a time, to prevent dough from sticking to hands (dough will be very soft).
❹ Place dough in a large bowl coated with cooking spray, turning to coat top. Cover and let rise in a warm place (85°), free from drafts, 40 minutes or until doubled in size. (Gently press two fingers into dough. If indentation remains, dough has risen enough.)
❺ Punch dough down. Shape dough into a ball; return to bowl. Cover and let rise an additional 40 minutes or until doubled in size. Punch dough down; cover and let rest 15 minutes.
❻ Divide dough into 3 equal portions. Working with 1 portion at a time (cover remaining dough to prevent drying), on a lightly floured surface, roll each portion into a 25-inch-long rope with slightly tapered ends. Place ropes lengthwise on a large baking sheet sprinkled with cornmeal; pinch ends together at untapered ends to seal. Braid ropes; pinch loose ends to seal. Cover and let rise 20 minutes or until almost doubled in size.
❼ Preheat oven to 375°.
❽ Combine 1 teaspoon water and egg yolk, stirring with a fork until blended. Uncover loaf, and gently brush with egg yolk mixture. Sprinkle evenly with ¼ teaspoon poppy seeds. Bake at 375° for 30 minutes or until loaf sounds hollow when tapped. Cool on a wire rack. Yield: 1 loaf, 12 servings (serving size: 1 slice).

CALORIES 157; FAT 4.1g (sat 2.1g, mono 1.2g, poly 0.4g); PROTEIN 5g; CARB 26.9g; FIBER 0.9g; CHOL 42mg; IRON 1.7mg; SODIUM 202mg; CALC 7mg

STAFF FAVORITE • QUICK & EASY
Mexican Chocolate Cookies

These cookies earned our Test Kitchens' highest rating. They're lovely after dinner with a few last sips of red wine.

- 5 ounces bittersweet (60 percent cacao) chocolate, coarsely chopped
- 3.4 ounces all-purpose flour (about ¾ cup)
- ½ teaspoon ground cinnamon
- ¼ teaspoon baking powder
- ¼ teaspoon salt
- Dash of black pepper
- Dash of ground red pepper
- 1¼ cups sugar
- ¼ cup butter, softened
- 1 large egg
- 1 teaspoon vanilla extract

❶ Preheat oven to 350°.
❷ Place chocolate in a small glass bowl; microwave at HIGH 1 minute or until almost melted, stirring until smooth. Cool to room temperature.
❸ Weigh or lightly spoon flour into a dry measuring cup; level with a knife. Combine flour and next 5 ingredients; stir with whisk.
❹ Combine sugar and butter in a large bowl; beat with a mixer at medium speed until well blended (about 5 minutes). Add egg; beat well. Add cooled chocolate and vanilla; beat just until blended. Add flour mixture; beat just until blended. Drop dough by level tablespoons 2 inches apart on baking sheets lined with parchment paper. Bake at 350° for 10 minutes or until almost set. Remove from oven. Cool on pans 2 minutes or until set. Remove from pans; cool completely on a wire rack. Yield: 32 cookies (serving size: 1 cookie).

CALORIES 80; FAT 2.9g (sat 1.7g, mono 0.6g, poly 0.1g); PROTEIN 0.7g; CARB 12.8g; FIBER 0.1g; CHOL 10mg; IRON 0.2mg; SODIUM 35mg; CALC 4mg

Pecan-Date Bars

CRUST:
- 4.5 ounce all-purpose flour (about 1 cup)
- ⅓ cup packed brown sugar
- ¼ teaspoon salt
- ¼ cup chilled butter, cut into small pieces
- Cooking spray

FILLING:
- ¾ cup dark corn syrup
- ⅓ cup packed brown sugar
- ¼ cup egg substitute
- 2 tablespoons all-purpose flour
- 1 tablespoon bourbon
- 1 teaspoon vanilla extract
- ¼ teaspoon salt
- 1 large egg
- ½ cup chopped pitted dates
- ⅓ cup chopped pecans, toasted
- 2 tablespoons semisweet chocolate minichips

❶ Preheat oven to 400°.

❷ To prepare crust, weigh or lightly spoon 4.5 ounces flour (about 1 cup) into a dry measuring cup; level with a knife. Combine 4.5 ounces flour, ⅓ cup sugar, and ¼ teaspoon salt, stirring well with a whisk. Cut in butter with a pastry blender or two knives until mixture resembles coarse meal. Press mixture into bottom of an 11 x 7-inch baking dish coated with cooking spray. Bake at 400° for 12 minutes or until lightly browned. Cool completely.

❸ Reduce oven temperature to 350°.

❹ To prepare filling, combine corn syrup and next 7 ingredients in a large bowl, stirring well with a whisk. Stir in dates, pecans, and chocolate chips. Pour mixture over prepared crust. Bake at 350° for 35 minutes or until set. Cool in pan on a wire rack. Cover and chill 1 hour or until firm. Yield: 24 servings (serving size: 1 bar).

CALORIES 123; FAT 3.6g (sat 1.3g, mono 1.6g, poly 0.5g); PROTEIN 1.4g; CARB 22g; FIBER 0.7g; CHOL 14mg; IRON 0.6mg; SODIUM 89mg; CALC 13mg

Raspberry–Cream Cheese Brownies

FILLING:
- ⅓ cup sugar
- ⅓ cup (3 ounces) ⅓-less-fat cream cheese, softened
- 2 teaspoons all-purpose flour
- ½ teaspoon vanilla extract
- 1 large egg white

BROWNIES:
- Cooking spray
- 3.4 ounces all-purpose flour (about ¾ cup)
- ¼ teaspoon baking powder
- ¼ teaspoon baking soda
- ⅛ teaspoon salt
- 1 cup sugar
- ⅔ cup unsweetened cocoa
- ¼ cup butter, melted
- 1 tablespoon water
- 1 teaspoon vanilla extract
- 1 large egg
- 2 large egg whites
- 3 tablespoons raspberry preserves

❶ Preheat oven to 350°.

❷ To prepare filling, place first 5 ingredients in a bowl; beat with a mixer at medium speed until well-blended. Set aside.

❸ To prepare brownies, coat bottom of an 8-inch baking pan with cooking spray (do not coat sides of pan). Weigh or lightly spoon 3.4 ounces flour (about ¾ cup) into dry measuring cups; level with a knife. Combine flour and next 3 ingredients in a bowl. Combine 1 cup sugar and next 6 ingredients; stir well with a whisk. Add to flour mixture; stir just until moist. Spread two-thirds of batter in prepared pan. Pour filling over batter, spreading evenly. Carefully drop remaining batter and preserves by spoonfuls over filling; swirl together using tip of a knife. Bake at 350° for 40 minutes or until a wooden pick inserted in center comes out almost clean. Cool on a wire rack. Yield: 16 servings (serving size: 1 brownie).

CALORIES 153; FAT 4.9g (sat 3g, mono 1g, poly 0.2g); PROTEIN 3g; CARB 26.2g; FIBER 1.4g; CHOL 25mg; IRON 0.9mg; SODIUM 105mg; CALC 17mg

Chocolate-Drizzled Mandelbrot

Mandelbrot are crunchy cookies similar to Italian biscotti.

- 7.75 ounces all-purpose flour (about 1¾ cups)
- 1½ teaspoons baking powder
- ¼ teaspoon salt
- ¾ cup sugar
- ¼ cup butter, softened
- 2 large eggs
- 2 teaspoons vanilla extract
- ½ cup chopped dried cherries
- ½ cup finely chopped almonds, toasted
- ¼ cup dark chocolate chips
- 1 teaspoon light-colored corn syrup
- 1 teaspoon water

❶ Preheat oven to 325°.

❷ Weigh or lightly spoon flour into dry measuring cups; level with a knife. Combine flour, baking powder, and salt, stirring with a whisk.

❸ Combine sugar and butter in a large bowl; beat with a mixer at medium speed until well blended. Beat in eggs and vanilla. Add flour mixture to sugar mixture; beat until combined. Stir in cherries and almonds.

❹ Shape dough into 2 (9-inch-long) rolls. Place rolls on a baking sheet covered with parchment paper; pat to 1-inch thickness. Bake at 325° for 30 minutes or until rolls are golden. Cool on baking sheet 10 minutes.

❺ Cut each roll diagonally into 12 (½-inch-thick) slices. Place, cut sides down, on baking sheet. Bake at 325° for 15 minutes. Turn cookies over, and bake an additional 10 minutes (cookies will be slightly soft in center but will harden as they cool). Remove from baking sheet; cool completely on a wire rack.

❻ Combine chocolate chips, corn syrup, and 1 teaspoon water in a small microwave-safe bowl. Microwave at HIGH 10 seconds at a time until nearly melted; stir until smooth. Spoon chocolate mixture into a small zip-top plastic bag; seal. Snip a tiny hole in 1 corner of bag. Drizzle chocolate over cookies. Yield: 24 cookies (serving size: 1 cookie).

CALORIES 117; FAT 4.1g (sat 1.8g, mono 1.1g, poly 0.4g); PROTEIN 2.1g; CARB 17.7g; FIBER 0.7g; CHOL 23mg; IRON 0.6mg; SODIUM 74mg; CALC 27mg

MAKE AHEAD
Popcorn Brittle

Cooking spray
5½ cups popcorn, popped without salt or fat
1½ cups sugar
6 tablespoons light-colored corn syrup
¼ cup water
3 tablespoons molasses
1 tablespoon butter
½ teaspoon baking soda
½ teaspoon vanilla extract
¼ teaspoon salt

❶ Line a baking sheet with foil; coat foil with cooking spray. Set aside.
❷ Place popcorn in a large zip-top plastic bag; seal. Crush popcorn using a meat mallet or rolling pin; set aside.
❸ Combine sugar, syrup, and ¼ cup water in a medium saucepan over medium heat. Cook 1 minute or until sugar dissolves, stirring constantly. Cook, without stirring, until candy thermometer registers 270° (about 8 minutes). Stir in molasses and butter; cook until thermometer registers 290° (about 5 minutes). Stir in baking soda, vanilla, and salt. Stir popcorn into boiling syrup mixture. Working quickly, pour popcorn mixture onto prepared pan; spread to ¼-inch thickness using a wooden spoon coated with cooking spray. Cool completely; break into large pieces. Yield: 12 servings (serving size: about 1½ ounces).
NOTE: Store brittle in an airtight container at room temperature for up to four days.

CALORIES 165; FAT 1.1g (sat 0.5g, mono 0.4g, poly 0.1g); PROTEIN 0.5g; CARB 39.9g; FIBER 0.6g; CHOL 3mg; IRON 0.4mg; SODIUM 123mg; CALC 12mg

Toasted Coconut Marshmallows

Cooking spray
2 cups flaked sweetened coconut, toasted
2½ envelopes unflavored gelatin (2 tablespoons plus 1¼ teaspoons)
¾ cup cold water, divided
2 cups granulated sugar, divided
⅔ cup light-colored corn syrup
1 tablespoon vanilla extract
¼ teaspoon salt
2 large egg whites
⅔ cup powdered sugar
3 tablespoons cornstarch

❶ Line a 13 x 9–inch baking pan with heavy-duty plastic wrap, allowing plastic wrap to extend 1 inch over sides of pan. Lightly coat plastic wrap with cooking spray. Spread coconut in an even layer in bottom of pan; set aside.
❷ Sprinkle gelatin over ½ cup cold water in a small bowl; set aside.
❸ Combine remaining ¼ cup water, 1¾ cups granulated sugar, and corn syrup in a large saucepan. Cook, without stirring, over medium-high heat until a candy thermometer registers 260° (about 15 minutes). Remove from heat; gradually stir in softened gelatin (mixture will appear foamy).
❹ While sugar mixture cooks, beat vanilla, salt, and egg whites at high speed in a heavy-duty stand mixer with whisk attachment until foamy. Gradually add remaining ¼ cup granulated sugar, 1 tablespoon at a time, until stiff peaks form. Gradually pour in gelatin mixture, beating until very thick (about 5 minutes). Gently spread marshmallow mixture over coconut in prepared pan. Coat 1 side of another sheet of plastic wrap with cooking spray. Place plastic wrap, coated side down, over marshmallow mixture. Chill 8 hours or until firm.
❺ Sprinkle powdered sugar and cornstarch over a cutting board. Remove top sheet of plastic wrap. Invert marshmallow mixture over powdered sugar mixture.

Using a dough scraper, cut mixture into about 1-inch squares. Store between sheets of wax or parchment paper in an airtight container. Yield: 8 dozen (serving size: 3 marshmallows).

CALORIES 107; FAT 1.5g (sat 1.3g, mono 0.1g, poly 0g); PROTEIN 0.9g; CARB 23.4g; FIBER 0.2g; CHOL 0mg; IRON 0.1mg; SODIUM 43mg; CALC 2mg

QUICK & EASY
Spicy Oatmeal Crisps

3.4 ounces all-purpose flour (about ¾ cup)
1 teaspoon ground cinnamon
½ teaspoon baking soda
½ teaspoon ground allspice
½ teaspoon grated whole nutmeg
¼ teaspoon salt
¼ teaspoon ground cloves
¼ teaspoon freshly ground black pepper (optional)
1 cup packed brown sugar
5 tablespoons butter, softened
1 teaspoon vanilla extract
1 large egg
½ cup old-fashioned rolled oats
Cooking spray

❶ Preheat oven to 350°.
❷ Weigh or lightly spoon flour into dry measuring cups; level with a knife. Combine flour and next 7 ingredients in a bowl. Beat sugar, butter, and vanilla in a large bowl with a mixer at medium speed until light and fluffy. Add egg; beat well. Stir in flour mixture and oats.
❸ Drop by level tablespoons 2 inches apart onto baking sheets coated with cooking spray. Bake at 350° for 12 minutes or until crisp. Cool on pan 2 to 3 minutes or until firm. Remove cookies from pan; cool on wire racks. Yield: 2 dozen (serving size: 1 cookie).

CALORIES 81; FAT 3.1g (sat 1.7g, mono 0.9g, poly 0.3g); PROTEIN 1.5g; CARB 12.2g; FIBER 0.7g; CHOL 15mg; IRON 0.6mg; SODIUM 71mg; CALC 12mg

Orange-Pecan Tea Bread

A small amount of salt in a quick bread or cake batter balances its sweetness.

7.9 ounces all-purpose flour (about 1¾ cups)
1 teaspoon baking powder
½ teaspoon baking soda
¼ teaspoon salt
¼ teaspoon ground nutmeg
¼ teaspoon ground allspice
½ cup granulated sugar
½ cup low-fat buttermilk
¼ cup chopped pecans, toasted
3 tablespoons 1% low-fat milk
3 tablespoons canola oil
3 tablespoons orange marmalade
2 teaspoons grated orange rind
2 large eggs
Cooking spray
½ cup powdered sugar
1 tablespoon fresh orange juice
1½ teaspoons chopped pecans, toasted

❶ Preheat oven to 350°.
❷ Weigh or lightly spoon flour into dry measuring cups; level with a knife. Combine flour and next 5 ingredients in a large bowl, stirring with a whisk; make a well in center of mixture. Combine granulated sugar and next 7 ingredients, stirring with a whisk; add to flour mixture, stirring just until moist.
❸ Spoon batter into an 8 x 4-inch loaf pan coated with cooking spray. Bake at 350° for 45 minutes or until a wooden pick inserted in center comes out clean. Cool 10 minutes in pan on a wire rack; remove from pan. Cool completely on a wire rack.
❹ Combine powdered sugar and juice, stirring until smooth. Drizzle glaze over bread, and sprinkle with 1½ teaspoons pecans. Yield: 14 servings (serving size: 1 slice).

CALORIES 171; FAT 5.6g (sat 0.9g, mono 2g, poly 2.4g); PROTEIN 3.2g; CARB 27.4g; FIBER 0.7g; CHOL 31mg; IRON 1mg; SODIUM 144mg; CALC 44mg

So Easy, So Elegant

A dazzling dessert doesn't have to start from scratch—a few store-bought ingredients let you spend less time in the kitchen and more time relishing the praise.

Chocolate Baklava

Layered phyllo dough and Nutella—a creamy hazelnut-chocolate spread—form the base of this nutty pastry dish that's sure to be a crowd-pleaser.

¾ cup honey
½ cup water
1 (3-inch) cinnamon stick
1 cup hazelnut-chocolate spread (such as Nutella)
½ cup toasted hazelnuts, coarsely chopped
½ cup roasted pistachios, coarsely chopped
⅓ cup blanched toasted almonds, coarsely chopped
⅓ cup toasted walnuts, coarsely chopped
½ teaspoon ground cinnamon
⅛ teaspoon salt
Cooking spray
24 (14 x 9-inch) sheets frozen phyllo dough, thawed
½ cup butter, melted

❶ Combine first 3 ingredients in a medium saucepan over low heat; stir until honey is completely dissolved (about 2 minutes). Increase heat to medium; cook, without stirring, until a candy thermometer registers 230° (about 10 minutes). Remove from heat; keep warm. Remove cinnamon stick; discard.
❷ Preheat oven to 350°.
❸ Place hazelnut-chocolate spread in a microwave-safe bowl; heat at HIGH 30 seconds or until melted. Combine hazelnuts and next 5 ingredients. Lightly coat a 13 x 9-inch baking dish with cooking spray. Working with 1 phyllo sheet at a time (cover remaining dough to prevent drying), place 1 phyllo sheet lengthwise in bottom of prepared pan, allowing end of sheet to extend over edges of dish; lightly brush with butter. Repeat procedure with 5 phyllo sheets and butter. Drizzle about ⅓ cup Nutella mixture over phyllo. Sprinkle evenly with one-third of nut mixture (about 1½ cup). Repeat procedure twice with phyllo, butter, Nutella, and nut mixture. Top last layer of nut mixture with remaining 6 sheets phyllo, each one lightly brushed with butter. Lightly brush top phyllo sheet with butter; press baklava gently into pan.
❹ Make 3 even lengthwise cuts and 5 even crosswise cuts to form 24 portions using a sharp knife. Bake at 350° for 35 minutes or until the phyllo is golden brown. Remove from oven. Drizzle honey mixture evenly over baklava. Cool in pan on a wire rack. Cover and store at room temperature. Yield: 24 servings (serving size: 1 piece).

CALORIES 238; FAT 13.4g (sat 4.3g, mono 5.6g, poly 2g); PROTEIN 4g; CARB 27.8g; FIBER 1.6g; CHOL 10mg; IRON 1.3mg; SODIUM 148mg; CALC 29mg

Mocha Affogato with Vanilla Cream

½   cup vanilla low-fat yogurt
¼   cup heavy whipping cream
1   tablespoon powdered sugar
4   cups chocolate low-fat ice cream
1   cup hot brewed espresso
½   cup Frangelico (hazelnut-flavored liqueur)
½   cup finely chopped bittersweet chocolate

1 Place colander in a medium bowl. Line colander with 4 layers of cheesecloth, allowing cheesecloth to extend over outside edges. Spoon yogurt into colander. Refrigerate, uncovered, 1 hour. Spoon drained yogurt into a bowl; discard liquid.

2 Place cream and powdered sugar in a bowl; beat with a mixer at high speed 2 minutes or until stiff peaks form. Gently fold whipped cream into yogurt. Refrigerate cream mixture until ready to serve.

3 Spoon ½ cup ice cream into each of 8 mugs; top each serving with 2 tablespoons hot espresso and 1 tablespoon liqueur. Top each serving with 2 tablespoons cream mixture; sprinkle each serving with 1 tablespoon chopped chocolate. Serve immediately. Yield: 8 servings.

CALORIES 289; FAT 6.5g (sat 3.6g, mono 2g, poly 0.3g); PROTEIN 3.2g; CARB 47.9g; FIBER 0.3g; CHOL 16mg; IRON 0.5mg; SODIUM 72mg; CALC 112mg

Apple Strudel

2   tablespoons butter
¼   cup packed brown sugar
6   medium Granny Smith apples, peeled and thinly sliced
2   tablespoons fresh lemon juice
½   teaspoon ground cinnamon
⅛   teaspoon salt
1   sheet frozen puff pastry dough, thawed
¼   cup chopped walnuts
2   tablespoons granulated sugar

1 Preheat oven to 400°.

2 Melt butter in a large skillet over medium-high heat. Stir in brown sugar; cook 1 minute or until sugar melts. Stir in apples. Sprinkle with juice, cinnamon, and salt. Reduce heat, cover, and cook 9 minutes or until apples are tender and golden, stirring occasionally. Spread apples in a single layer on a baking sheet to cool (about 10 minutes).

3 Roll puff pastry to a 15 x 12–inch rectangle on a lightly floured work surface. Spoon apple mixture along 1 long edge of pastry; roll up jelly-roll fashion. Gently press seam to seal.

4 Place nuts and granulated sugar in a food processor; pulse 10 times or until nuts are finely ground. Sprinkle strudel with nut mixture, pressing gently into dough. Place strudel on a baking sheet lined with parchment paper. Bake at 400° for 25 minutes or until golden brown and crisp. Let stand 5 minutes; slice. Yield: 8 servings (serving size: 1 slice).

CALORIES 185; FAT 7.7g (sat 2.6g, mono 2.4g, poly 2.2g); PROTEIN 1.4g; CARB 30.7g; FIBER 2.3g; CHOL 8mg; IRON 0.6mg; SODIUM 75mg; CALC 20mg

Pear Crisp with Amaretti Topping

6   peeled Anjou or Bartlett pears, cored and cut into ¼-inch-thick slices (about 2½ pounds)
½   cup packed brown sugar, divided
2.85   ounces all-purpose flour (about ½ cup plus 2 tablespoons), divided
1   tablespoon fresh lemon juice
⅛   teaspoon salt
    Cooking spray
12   amaretti cookies (Italian almond macaroons)
6   tablespoons chilled butter, cut into small pieces
⅓   cup sliced almonds, toasted
½   cup heavy whipping cream
2   tablespoons powdered sugar

1 Preheat oven to 350°.

2 Place pears in a large bowl. Sprinkle with 6 tablespoons brown sugar, 2 tablespoons flour, juice, and salt; toss well to coat. Transfer mixture to an 11 x 7–inch baking dish coated with cooking spray.

3 Place cookies in a food processor; process until finely ground. Weigh or lightly spoon remaining 2.25 ounces (about ½ cup) flour into a dry measuring cup. Combine 2.25 ounces flour, cookie crumbs, and remaining 2 tablespoons brown sugar in a medium bowl; cut in butter with a pastry blender or 2 knives until mixture resembles coarse meal. Stir in nuts. Sprinkle crumb mixture evenly over pear mixture. Bake at 350° for 50 minutes or until pears are tender. Let stand 10 minutes before serving.

4 Combine cream and powdered sugar in a medium bowl. Beat with a mixer at high speed until stiff peaks form. Spoon about 1 tablespoon whipped cream mixture onto each serving. Yield: 9 servings.

CALORIES 320; FAT 14.7g (sat 8g, mono 4.5g, poly 0.9g); PROTEIN 3.4g; CARB 46.7g; FIBER 2.3g; CHOL 38mg; IRON 0.9mg; SODIUM 114mg; CALC 47mg

Chocolate-Caramel Angel Food Cake

1   (16-ounce) box white angel food cake mix
2   ounces bittersweet chocolate, chopped
¼   cup packed brown sugar
¼   cup butter
3   tablespoons heavy cream
    Dash of salt
3   tablespoons chopped, toasted pecans

1 Bake cake according to package instructions. Cool completely.

2 Place chocolate in a microwave-safe bowl. Microwave at HIGH 30 seconds or until melted, stirring every 10 seconds. Drizzle chocolate over cake. Combine sugar and next 3 ingredients in a small, heavy saucepan over medium-high heat; bring to a boil, stirring just until sugar dissolves. Reduce heat and cook 4 minutes (do not stir). Remove from heat.

Continued

Quickly drizzle caramel over cake. Top with pecans. Yield: 12 servings (serving size: 1 slice).

CALORIES 241; FAT 8.8g (sat 4.4g, mono 2.2g, poly 0.7g); PROTEIN 4g; CARB 39.4g; FIBER 0.6g; CHOL 15mg; IRON 0.4mg; SODIUM 321mg; CALC 54mg

Cherry Tortoni

2/3 cup sugar, divided
1 tablespoon amaretto (almond-flavored liqueur)
1 (12-ounce) package frozen pitted dark sweet cherries
1 tablespoon water
2 teaspoons cornstarch
1/3 cup sliced almonds
12 vanilla wafers
1/2 teaspoon cream of tartar
Dash of salt
4 large egg whites
1 (8-ounce) container frozen reduced-calorie whipped topping, thawed

❶ Combine 1/3 cup sugar, amaretto, and cherries in a medium saucepan; bring to a boil. Reduce heat and cook 10 minutes or until sugar dissolves and cherries are soft, stirring occasionally. Combine 1 tablespoon water and cornstarch in a small bowl, stirring until smooth. Stir cornstarch mixture into cherry mixture; bring to a boil. Cook 1 minute, stirring constantly. Spoon cherry mixture into a bowl; cover and chill 1 hour. Drain mixture through a sieve over a bowl, reserving cherry mixture and juices. Set cherry mixture aside. Cover and chill juices.
❷ Place almonds and wafers in a food processor; process until coarsely ground.
❸ Combine remaining 1/3 cup sugar, cream of tartar, salt, and egg whites in top of a double broiler. Cook over simmering water until a thermometer registers 150° (about 6 minutes), stirring constantly with a whisk. Remove from heat. Beat with an electric mixer at high speed until stiff peaks form. Spoon whipped topping into a large bowl. Gently fold one-fourth of egg white mixture into

whipped topping; gently fold in remaining egg white mixture. Fold 1/2 cup almond mixture into egg white mixture; gently fold in drained cherry mixture.
❹ Line a baking sheet with parchment paper; place 10 (3-inch) ring molds on parchment paper. Spoon 1/2 cup egg white mixture into each mold; sprinkle remaining almond mixture over tops. Cover loosely with plastic wrap; freeze 4 hours or until set. Let stand 10 minutes at room temperature. Run a knife around outside edge; remove from molds. Serve with reserved cherry juice. Yield: 10 servings (serving size: 1 [3-inch] tortoni and 2½ teaspoons sauce).

CALORIES 177; FAT 5.4g (sat 2.8g, mono 1.4g, poly 0.5g); PROTEIN 3.5g; CARB 29.6g; FIBER 1.3g; CHOL 1mg; IRON 0.4mg; SODIUM 68mg; CALC 33mg

Lemon-Almond Tarts

1/2 cup blanched almonds
3 tablespoons brown sugar
20 vanilla wafers
1/4 cup butter, melted
Cooking spray
1 (10-ounce) jar lemon curd
3 large egg whites
1/8 teaspoon salt
1/2 cup granulated sugar
1/4 cup water

❶ Preheat oven to 400°.
❷ Place first 3 ingredients in a food processor; process until finely ground. With motor running, drizzle butter through food chute; process until well blended. Press mixture into bottom and up sides of each of 8 (4-inch) tart pans coated with cooking spray. Bake at 400° for 10 minutes or until toasted. Cool completely on a wire rack.
❸ Preheat broiler.
❹ Spoon curd evenly into prepared crusts. Place egg whites and salt in a large bowl; beat with a mixer at high speed until soft peaks form. Combine granulated sugar and 1/4 cup water in a saucepan; bring to a boil. Cook, without stirring, until candy thermometer registers 250°.

Pour hot sugar syrup in a thin stream over egg whites, beating at high speed until stiff peaks form. Spread egg white mixture over lemon curd. Broil 30 seconds or until lightly browned. Yield: 8 servings (serving size: 1 tart).

CALORIES 342; FAT 14.7g (sat 5.4g, mono 5.2g, poly 1.3g); PROTEIN 3.9g; CARB 52.4g; FIBER 5g; CHOL 44mg; IRON 1mg; SODIUM 182mg; CALC 37mg

Simple Additions

Lamb Shanks Braised with Tomato

Meltingly tender shanks and their simple yet rich-tasting sauce make a hearty meal for a winter night. Serve with polenta.

Cooking spray
4 (12-ounce) lamb shanks, trimmed
1/2 teaspoon salt
1/4 teaspoon freshly ground black pepper
4 garlic cloves, minced
3/4 cup dry red wine
2 (14.5-ounce) cans diced tomatoes with basil, garlic, and oregano
1/4 cup chopped fresh parsley

Directions: Heat a large Dutch oven over medium-high heat. Coat pan with cooking spray. Sprinkle lamb with 1/2 teaspoon salt and 1/4 teaspoon freshly ground black pepper. Add lamb to pan and cook 4 minutes on each side or until browned. Remove from pan. Add garlic to pan; sauté 15 seconds. Add wine; cook 2 minutes, scraping pan to loosen browned bits. Stir in tomatoes; cook 2 minutes. Return lamb to pan. Cover, reduce heat, and simmer 1 hour. Turn lamb over; simmer 1 hour or until meat is done and very tender. Place lamb on a plate; cover loosely with foil. Skim any fat from the surface of the sauce. Bring to a boil; cook 10 minutes or until sauce thickens. Return lamb to pan; cook 4 minutes or until lamb is thoroughly heated. Stir in parsley. Yield: 4 servings (serving size: 1 shank and ¾ cup sauce).

CALORIES 254; FAT 11.4g (sat 4.8g, mono 4.8g, poly 0.8g); PROTEIN 25.9g; CARB 11.7g; FIBER 3.5g; CHOL 89mg; IRON 2.9mg; SODIUM 439mg; CALC 64mg

Roasted Cornish Hens with Cherry-Port Glaze

Ginger gives the sweet-tart glaze a little bite.

  Cooking spray
  ½ cup cherry preserves
  ½ cup port
  1 tablespoon grated fresh ginger
  1 tablespoon balsamic vinegar
  ½ teaspoon salt, divided
  2 (1½-pound) Cornish hens
  ¼ teaspoon freshly ground black pepper

Directions: Preheat oven to 400°. Place a wire rack on a baking sheet; coat rack with cooking spray. Combine preserves, port, ginger, vinegar, and ¼ teaspoon salt in a small saucepan. Bring to a boil; cook 9 minutes or until slightly thickened, stirring occasionally. Remove and discard giblets and necks from hens. Rinse hens with cold water; pat dry. Remove skin; trim excess fat. Working with 1 hen at a time, tie ends of legs together with twine. Lift wing tips up and over back; tuck under hen. Sprinkle evenly with remaining ¼ teaspoon salt and ¼ teaspoon freshly ground black pepper. Set on wire rack on baking sheet. Bake at 400° for 15 minutes. Brush hens with cherry mixture; bake 40 minutes or until a thermometer inserted in meaty part of thigh registers 165°, brushing with cherry mixture every 10 minutes. Let stand 5 minutes. Remove twine; split hens in half lengthwise. Yield: 4 servings (serving size: ½ hen).

CALORIES 277; FAT 4.9g (sat 1.3g, mono 1.8g, poly 1.2g); PROTEIN 29.4g; CARB 27.5g; FIBER 0.1g; CHOL 133mg; IRON 1.3mg; SODIUM 394mg; CALC 22mg

Beer-Battered Fish and Chips

(pictured on page 239)

  1 pound cod fillets, cut into 3-inch pieces
  1 cup dark beer (such as Negro Modela), divided
  1 pound baking potatoes, cut into (¼-inch) strips
  Cooking spray
  ¼ cup canola oil, divided
  ¾ teaspoon salt, divided
  3.38 ounces all-purpose flour (about ¾ cup)
  ½ teaspoon freshly ground black pepper

Directions: Preheat oven to 450°. Combine fish and ¼ cup beer in a medium bowl. Cover and chill 1 hour. Place potatoes on a jelly-roll pan coated with cooking spray. Drizzle with 1 tablespoon oil and sprinkle with ¼ teaspoon salt; toss well. Bake at 450° for 20 minutes or until browned and crisp, stirring after 10 minutes. Drain fish; discard liquid. Sprinkle fish with ¼ teaspoon salt. Weigh or lightly spoon flour into dry measuring cups; level with a knife. Combine remaining ¾ cup beer, flour, and ½ teaspoon freshly ground black pepper in a medium bowl. Add fish to beer mixture, tossing gently to coat. Heat remaining 3 tablespoons oil in a large nonstick skillet over medium-high heat. Remove fish from bowl, shaking off excess batter. Add fish to pan; cook 3 minutes or until browned. Turn fish over, and cook 3 minutes or until done. Sprinkle fish with remaining ¼ teaspoon salt. Serve immediately with chips. Yield: 4 servings: (serving size: about 4 ounces fish and about ½ cup chips).

CALORIES 398; FAT 15g (sat 1.1g, mono 8.4g, poly 4.6g); PROTEIN 24.6g; CARB 40.7g; FIBER 2.2g; CHOL 40mg; IRON 2.4mg; SODIUM 524mg; CALC 30mg

Use Alaskan cod in Beer-Battered Fish and Chips, and serve with malt vinegar.

Our Prettiest Holiday Cookies

Because there's no such thing as too many cookie options in December, we offer you four bonus recipes that are equally delicious and beautiful.

Iced Browned Butter Sugar Cookies

With nutty, caramel notes from browned butter and a fair bit of salt to balance the flavors, these cookies will become an instant favorite. Look for pearlized sugar in gourmet markets or craft stores; the coarse crystals reflect light to give the cookies a sparkly, jewel-like appearance.

- 9 tablespoons unsalted butter
- 1 cup granulated sugar
- ½ teaspoon vanilla extract
- 3 large egg yolks
- 8 ounces all-purpose flour (about 1¾ cups)
- ½ teaspoon salt
- ¼ teaspoon baking powder
- 1 cup powdered sugar
- 1½ tablespoons half-and-half
- ¼ teaspoon vanilla extract
- ⅓ cup pearlized sugar or turbinado sugar

❶ Preheat oven to 350°.
❷ Melt butter in a large skillet over medium-low heat; cook 6 minutes or until dark brown. Pour butter into a large bowl; let stand 5 minutes. Add granulated sugar and vanilla.

Beat with a mixer at medium speed until well blended (about 2 minutes). Add egg yolks; beat at medium speed until well blended (about 1 minute).
❸ Weigh or lightly spoon flour into dry measuring cups; level with a knife. Combine flour, salt, and baking powder; stir with a whisk. Add flour mixture to butter mixture; beat at low speed just until combined. Turn dough out onto a sheet of wax paper; knead gently 7 times. Roll dough to a ¼-inch thickness. Cut with a 2½-inch star-shaped cookie cutter into 32 cookies; reroll scraps as necessary. Arrange cookies 1-inch apart on baking sheets lined with parchment paper. Bake, 1 batch at a time, at 350° for 10 minutes or until edges are lightly browned. Cool cookies completely on wire racks.
❹ Combine powdered sugar, half-and-half, and ¼ teaspoon vanilla, stirring with a whisk until smooth. Spoon about ¾ teaspoon icing onto each cookie; sprinkle with ½ teaspoon pearlized sugar. Yield: 32 cookies (serving size: 1 cookie).

CALORIES 104; FAT 3.8g (sat 2.2g, mono 1g, poly 0.2g); PROTEIN 1g; CARB 17g; FIBER 0.2g; CHOL 28mg; IRON 0.4mg; SODIUM 42mg; CALC 7mg

Chocolate-Hazelnut Thumbprints

- 4.5 ounces all-purpose flour (about 1 cup)
- 1 cup powdered sugar
- ⅓ cup unsweetened cocoa
- ¼ teaspoon salt
- ½ cup butter, softened
- 1 teaspoon instant espresso (optional)
- 2 large egg yolks
- ½ teaspoon vanilla extract
- ⅔ cup finely chopped hazelnuts, toasted
- ⅓ cup hazelnut-chocolate spread (such as Nutella)

❶ Preheat oven to 350°.
❷ Weigh or lightly spoon flour into a dry measuring cup; level with a knife. Combine flour, sugar, cocoa, and salt; stir with a whisk. Place butter in a large bowl; beat with a mixer at medium speed until light and fluffy (about 2 minutes). Combine espresso, if desired, and egg yolks; stir with a whisk. Add yolk mixture and vanilla to butter; beat well. Add flour mixture to butter mixture; beat at low speed just until combined.
❸ Turn dough out onto a sheet of wax paper; knead 6 times or until smooth and shiny. Shape dough into 28 (1-inch) balls. Roll sides of balls in nuts, pressing gently. Arrange balls 1-inch apart on baking sheets lined with parchment paper. Press thumb into center of each cookie, leaving an indentation. Bake, 1 batch at a time, at 350° for 10 minutes. Remove cookies from pans; cool completely on wire racks. Spoon a scant ½ teaspoon hazelnut-chocolate spread into center of each cookie. Yield: 28 cookies (serving size: 1 cookie).

CALORIES 104; FAT 6.5g (sat 2.7g, mono 2.3g, poly 0.4g); PROTEIN 1.6g; CARB 10.9g; FIBER 0.8g; CHOL 23mg; IRON 0.6mg; SODIUM 46mg; CALC 11mg

Ginger-Lemon Pinwheel Cookies

GINGER DOUGH:

- ¼ cup unsalted butter, softened
- ⅓ cup packed dark brown sugar
- ¼ cup molasses
- 1 large egg yolk
- 6 ounces all-purpose flour (about 1⅓ cups)
- ¾ teaspoon ground ginger
- ¾ teaspoon ground cinnamon
- ¼ teaspoon salt
- ⅛ teaspoon ground nutmeg
- Dash of ground allspice

LEMON DOUGH:

- 5 tablespoons unsalted butter, softened
- ⅔ cup granulated sugar
- 1 large egg white
- 2 teaspoons grated lemon rind
- ¾ teaspoon vanilla extract
- 6 ounces all-purpose flour (about 1⅓ cups)
- ¼ teaspoon salt

❶ To prepare ginger dough, place ¼ cup butter and brown sugar in a medium bowl; beat with a mixer at medium speed until well combined (about 3 minutes). Add molasses and egg yolk; beat at medium speed until well blended. Weigh or lightly spoon 6 ounces (about 1⅓ cups) flour into dry measuring cups; level with a knife. Combine 6 ounces flour, ginger, and next 4 ingredients, stirring with a whisk. Add flour mixture to butter mixture; beat at low speed just until combined. Wrap dough in plastic wrap; chill 30 minutes.

❷ To prepare lemon dough, place 5 tablespoons butter and granulated sugar in a medium bowl; beat with a mixer at medium speed until well combined (about 3 minutes). Add egg white; beat until well blended. Beat in rind and vanilla. Weigh or lightly spoon 6 ounces (about 1⅓ cups) flour into dry measuring cups; level with a knife. Combine 6 ounces flour and ¼ teaspoon salt, stirring with a whisk. Add flour mixture to

butter mixture; beat at low speed just until combined. Wrap dough in plastic wrap; chill 30 minutes.

❸ Unwrap ginger dough. Roll ginger dough between sheets of plastic wrap or parchment paper into a 13 x 8½–inch rectangle (³⁄₁₆-inch thick); chill 10 minutes. Unwrap lemon dough. Roll lemon dough between sheets of plastic wrap or parchment paper into a 13 x 9–inch rectangle (³⁄₁₆-inch thick); chill 10 minutes. Carefully stack ginger dough on top of lemon dough, leaving a ½-inch border along one long edge. Starting with long side without a border, roll up dough, jelly-roll fashion. Seal edges (do not seal ends of roll). Cover with plastic wrap; freeze 30 minutes.

❹ Preheat oven to 350°.

❺ Unwrap dough roll. Slice with a sharp knife into 40 slices (about ¼-inch thick). Reshape into rounds, if necessary. Arrange slices 1-inch apart on baking sheets lined with parchment paper. Bake, 1 batch at a time, at 350° for 8 to 9 minutes or until set and lightly browned. Cool on wire racks. Yield: 40 cookies (serving size: 1 cookie).

CALORIES 81; FAT 2.8g (sat 1.7g, mono 0.7g, poly 0.2g); PROTEIN 1.1g; CARB 13.1g; FIBER 0.3g; CHOL 12mg; IRON 0.6mg; SODIUM 33mg; CALC 9mg

Raspberry Linzer Cookies

Ground almonds give these cookies a hearty taste and extra crunch.

- 7.5 ounces all-purpose flour (about 1½ cups plus 2 tablespoons), divided
- 1 cup whole blanched almonds
- ½ teaspoon baking powder
- ½ teaspoon ground cinnamon
- ¼ teaspoon salt
- ⅔ cup granulated sugar
- ½ cup unsalted butter, softened
- ½ teaspoon grated lemon rind
- 4 large egg yolks
- 6 tablespoons raspberry preserves with seeds
- 2 teaspoons powdered sugar

❶ Weigh or lightly spoon 2.25 ounces (about ½ cup) flour into a dry measuring cup; level with a knife. Place 2.25 ounces flour and almonds in a food processor; process until finely ground. Weigh or lightly spoon remaining 5.25 ounces (about 1 cup plus 2 tablespoons) flour into a dry measuring cup. Combine almond mixture, remaining 5.25 ounces flour, baking powder, cinnamon, and salt, stirring well with a whisk.

❷ Place granulated sugar, butter, and rind in a large bowl; beat with a mixer at medium speed until light and fluffy (about 3 minutes). Add egg yolks; beat until well blended. Beating at low speed, gradually add flour mixture; beat just until a soft dough forms. Turn dough out onto a sheet of plastic wrap; knead lightly 3 times or until smooth. Divide dough into 2 equal portions; wrap each portion in plastic wrap. Chill 1 hour.

❸ Preheat oven to 350°.

❹ Roll each dough portion into a ⅛-inch thickness on a lightly floured surface; cut with a 2-inch rectangular cookie cutter with fluted edges to form 36 cookies. Repeat procedure with remaining dough portion; use a 1-inch rectangular fluted cutter to remove centers of 36 rectangles. Arrange cookies 1-inch apart on baking sheets lined with parchment paper. Bake, 1 batch at a time, at 350° for 10 minutes or until edges are lightly browned. Cool on pans 5 minutes. Remove from pans; cool completely on wire racks.

❺ Spread center of each whole cookie with about ½ teaspoon preserves. Sprinkle cut-out cookies with powdered sugar. Place 1 cut-out cookie on top of each whole cookie. Yield: 36 cookies (serving size: 1 cookie).

CALORIES 96; FAT 5.1g (sat 1.9g, mono 2.2g, poly 0.7g); PROTEIN 1.8g; CARB 11.4g; FIBER 0.6g; CHOL 29mg; IRON 0.5mg; SODIUM 25mg; CALC 18mg

Piecrust Basics

After years of tinkering to perfect the flavor and texture, we present our best pastry ever!

We've baked more than a few pies over the years and struggled to balance the ratio of fat to flour for optimum flavor and texture while keeping the crust healthy. Here, we share our tastiest recipe to date. Once you master the shell, you can confidently bake a pie for any occasion. If you're out to impress, make it a tart.

All-Purpose Light Piecrust

- 5 ounces all-purpose flour (about 1¼ cups)
- 1 teaspoon sugar
- ¼ teaspoon salt
- ¼ teaspoon baking powder
- ¼ cup vegetable shortening
- 4 teaspoons unsalted butter, melted
- ¼ cup boiling water

❶ Weigh or lightly spoon flour into dry measuring cups; level with a knife. Combine flour and next 3 ingredients in a medium bowl; cut in shortening with a pastry blender or 2 knives until mixture resembles coarse meal.

❷ Make a well in center of flour mixture. Combine butter and ¼ cup boiling water. Pour butter mixture into center of well. Gently draw flour mixture into butter mixture until moist clumps form. Press dough into a 4-inch circle; cover and chill 30 minutes.

❸ Slightly overlap 2 sheets of plastic wrap. Unwrap dough; place on plastic. Cover dough with 2 additional sheets of overlapping plastic wrap. Roll dough into a 13-inch circle. Yield: 1 piecrust (8 servings).

CALORIES 127; FAT 7g (sat 2.8g, mono 3.1g, poly 0.7g); PROTEIN 1.9g; CARB 14.1g; FIBER 0g; CHOL 5mg; IRON 0.8mg; SODIUM 146mg; CALC 14mg

CHIVE PIECRUST VARIATION:
Prepare All-Purpose Piecrust, omitting sugar. Add 2 tablespoons minced fresh chives to flour mixture. Yield: 1 piecrust (8 servings).

CALORIES 125; FAT 7g (sat 2.8g, mono 3.1g, poly 0.7g); PROTEIN 1.9g; CARB 13.6g; FIBER 1g; CHOL 5mg; IRON 0.9mg; SODIUM 147mg; CALC 15mg

Gingery Cranberry-Pear Pie with Oatmeal Streusel

PIE:

- 1 cup water
- ⅓ cup granulated sugar
- ½ cup dried cranberries
- 1 (1-inch) piece peeled fresh ginger, cut into ¼-inch-thick slices
- 1 teaspoon grated orange rind
- 2 teaspoons fresh lemon juice
- 6 peeled Anjou pears, cored and cut into ¼-inch-thick slices (about 3 pounds)
- 1.13 ounces all-purpose flour (about ¼ cup)
- ⅓ cup packed brown sugar
- All-Purpose Light Piecrust dough (at left)
- Cooking spray

STREUSEL:

- 1.5 ounces all-purpose flour (about ⅓ cup)
- 2 tablespoons unsalted butter, melted
- 2 tablespoons orange juice
- 1 cup old-fashioned oats
- ⅓ cup packed brown sugar
- ½ teaspoon ground ginger
- ½ teaspoon ground cinnamon
- ¼ teaspoon salt

❶ Position oven rack to lowest third of oven. Preheat oven to 400°.

❷ To prepare pie, combine 1 cup water and granulated sugar in a small saucepan over medium-high heat; bring to a boil. Add cranberries, fresh ginger slices, and rind; return to a boil, stirring until sugar dissolves. Reduce heat to low and simmer 15 minutes or until liquid is reduced to 2 tablespoons. Remove from heat; discard ginger slices. Cool.

❸ Combine lemon juice and pears in a large bowl; toss. Weigh or lightly spoon 1.13 ounces (about ¼ cup) flour into a dry measuring cup; level with a knife. Combine 1.13 ounces flour and ⅓ cup brown sugar. Add flour mixture to pear mixture; toss to coat. Stir in cranberry mixture.

❹ Remove 2 sheets plastic from All-Purpose Light Piecrust dough. Fit dough, plastic wrap side up, into a 9-inch pie plate coated with cooking spray. Remove top sheets of plastic wrap. Fold edges under; flute. Spoon pear mixture into prepared crust.

❺ To prepare streusel, weigh or lightly spoon 1.5 ounces (about ⅓ cup) flour into a dry measuring cup; level with a knife. Combine butter and orange juice in a medium bowl, stirring well. Add flour, oats, and remaining ingredients; toss. Sprinkle oat mixture evenly over pear mixture. Cover pie loosely with foil; place pie plate on a baking sheet. Bake, covered, in the lower third of oven at 400° for 1 hour. Uncover and bake an additional 15 minutes or until browned. Cool on a wire rack 1 hour. Cut into wedges. Yield: 12 servings (serving size: 1 wedge).

CALORIES 300; FAT 7.4g (sat 3.2g, mono 2.7g, poly 0.8g); PROTEIN 3.3g; CARB 58.5g; FIBER 4.7g; CHOL 8mg; IRON 1.7mg; SODIUM 154mg; CALC 38mg

Spiced Pumpkin Chiffon Pie

All-Purpose Light Piecrust dough
    (page 384)
Cooking spray
1¼   cups canned pumpkin
½   cup packed brown sugar
½   teaspoon grated lemon rind
¾   teaspoon ground cinnamon
¼   teaspoon salt
⅛   teaspoon ground nutmeg
2   large egg yolks
⅔   cup evaporated low-fat milk
1   envelope unflavored gelatin
¼   cup fresh orange juice
2   large egg whites
⅛   teaspoon cream of tartar
5   tablespoons granulated sugar,
     divided
3   tablespoons water
½   cup heavy whipping cream
½   ounce shaved bittersweet chocolate

❶ Preheat oven to 400°.
❷ Remove 2 sheets of plastic from All-Purpose Light Piecrust dough. Fit dough, plastic wrap side up, into a 9-inch pie plate coated with cooking spray. Remove top sheets of plastic wrap. Fold edges under; flute. Pierce bottom and sides of dough with a fork; freeze 10 minutes. Line bottom of dough with a piece of foil; arrange pie weights or dried beans on foil. Bake at 400° for 25 minutes or until browned. Cool on a wire rack 15 minutes; remove weights and foil. Cool completely.
❸ Combine pumpkin and next 6 ingredients in a medium saucepan, stirring with a whisk. Stir in milk; bring to a boil. Reduce heat and simmer 4 minutes or until slightly thick, stirring frequently. Remove from heat. Sprinkle gelatin over orange juice in a small microwave-safe bowl; let stand 1 minute. Microwave at HIGH 15 seconds, stirring until gelatin dissolves. Stir gelatin mixture into pumpkin mixture. Cool.
❹ Place 2 egg whites and cream of tartar in a large bowl; beat with a mixer at high speed until frothy. Gradually add 1 table-spoon granulated sugar, beating until soft peaks form. Combine remaining ¼ cup granulated sugar and water in a saucepan; bring to a boil. Cook, without stirring, until candy thermometer registers 250°. Pour hot sugar syrup in a thin stream over egg whites, beating at high speed until stiff peaks form. Gently stir one-fourth of egg white mixture into pumpkin mixture; gently fold in remaining egg white mixture. Pour into cooled crust. Refrigerate 4 hours or until set.
❺ Place cream in a medium bowl; beat with a mixer on high speed until soft peaks form. Spread evenly over pie; top with chocolate. Cut into wedges. Yield: 10 servings (serving size: 1 wedge).

CALORIES 274; FAT 13.2g (sat 5.8g, mono 3.8g, poly 1.6g); PROTEIN 5.3g; CARB 34.5g; FIBER 1.4g; CHOL 63mg; IRON 1.5mg; SODIUM 173mg; CALC 82mg

Caramelized Onion and Canadian Bacon Tart

All-Purpose Light Piecrust dough
    (page 384)
Cooking spray
1   tablespoon Dijon mustard
2   tablespoons extra-virgin olive oil,
     divided
4   cups thinly sliced Spanish onion
     (about 1¾ pounds)
2   teaspoons sugar
¾   cup water, divided
½   cup diced Canadian bacon
1   tablespoon chopped fresh flat-leaf
     parsley
1¾   teaspoons freshly ground black
     pepper, divided
1   teaspoon kosher salt
2   teaspoons fresh lemon juice
½   teaspoon dried sage leaves
⅛   teaspoon ground whole nutmeg
1   tablespoon unsalted butter
1½   cups herb-seasoned stuffing mix
     (such as Pepperidge Farm)
½   cup fat-free, less-sodium chicken
     broth
1   cup (4 ounces) shredded Jarlsberg
     cheese

❶ Preheat oven to 400°.
❷ Remove 2 sheets plastic wrap from All-Purpose Light Piecrust dough. Fit dough, plastic wrap side up, into a 9-inch round tart pan coated with cooking spray. Remove top sheets of plastic wrap. Press dough into bottom and up sides of pan; fold excess crust back in and press to reinforce sides. Pierce bottom and sides of dough lightly with a fork; freeze 10 minutes. Line bottom of dough with a piece of aluminum foil; arrange pie weights or dried beans on foil. Bake at 400° for 20 minutes or until lightly browned.
❸ Reduce oven temperature to 375°.
❹ Remove weights and foil. Brush dough evenly with mustard. Bake at 375° an additional 5 minutes or until done. Cool completely on a wire rack.
❺ Heat 1 tablespoon oil in a large skillet over medium heat. Add onion and sugar; reduce heat and cook 10 minutes, stirring occasionally. Stir in ½ cup water; cook 25 minutes or until onion is light brown and liquid thickens, adding remaining ¼ cup water, 1 tablespoon at a time, as necessary to moisten onion. Remove from heat; stir in bacon, parsley, 1 tea-spoon pepper, and next 4 ingredients.
❻ Place butter in a small microwave-safe bowl; microwave at HIGH for 30 seconds or until butter melts. Add remaining 1 tablespoon olive oil, stirring to combine. Combine butter mixture, remaining ¾ teaspoon pepper, stuffing mix, and broth, stirring until moist.
❼ Sprinkle cooled crust with cheese. Spoon onion mixture over cheese; top with stuffing mixture. Place tart on a baking sheet. Bake at 375° for 25 minutes or until golden brown. Cool 10 minutes on a wire rack. Cut into wedges. Yield: 8 servings (serving size: 1 wedge).

CALORIES 293; FAT 16.9g (sat 7g, mono 7.4g, poly 1.4g); PROTEIN 10g; CARB 26.7g; FIBER 1.8g; CHOL 27mg; IRON 1.5mg; SODIUM 705mg; CALC 165mg

Mushroom and Roasted Pepper Tarts

These individual tarts make a restaurant-quality presentation and taste as good as they look. You can prepare them ahead, chill, and reheat just before serving.

Chive Piecrust dough (page 384)
Cooking spray
- 1 tablespoon Dijon mustard
- 1 cup boiling water
- ½ cup dried porcini mushrooms (about ½ ounce)
- 1 tablespoon canola oil
- 2 tablespoons chopped shallots
- 4 ounces cremini mushrooms, thinly sliced
- 3½ ounces shiitake mushroom caps, thinly sliced
- 1 garlic clove, minced
- 2 tablespoons Madeira wine
- 1 teaspoon chopped fresh thyme
- 1 tablespoon chopped fresh flat-leaf parsley
- 1 teaspoon fresh lemon juice
- 1 teaspoon freshly ground black pepper
- ¾ teaspoon kosher salt
- 3 tablespoons grated fresh Parmigiano-Reggiano cheese, divided
- ½ cup 2% reduced-fat evaporated milk
- 2 tablespoons half-and-half
- 1 large egg
- 1 large egg white
- ⅓ cup chopped bottled roasted red bell pepper
- 2 tablespoons finely chopped fresh chives

1 Preheat oven to 400°.
2 Divide Chive Piecrust dough into 5 equal portions. Place each portion between two sheets of plastic wrap; roll into a 6-inch circle. Remove top sheet of plastic wrap. Place each dough circle, plastic wrap side up, into a 4-inch round tart pan coated with cooking spray. Remove remaining plastic wrap. Press dough into bottom and up sides of pan; fold excess crust back in and press to reinforce sides. Pierce bottom and sides of dough lightly with a fork; freeze 10 minutes. Line bottoms of dough with a piece of aluminum foil; arrange pie weights or dried beans on foil. Bake at 400° for 25 minutes or until lightly browned. Cool on a wire rack 15 minutes; remove weights and foil. Brush crusts with evenly with mustard.
3 Reduce oven to 375°.
4 Combine 1 cup boiling water and porcini mushrooms in a bowl; cover and let stand 20 minutes or until mushrooms are soft. Strain mixture through a sieve over a bowl, reserving mushrooms and ¼ cup liquid. Finely chop mushrooms.
5 Heat oil in a large skillet over medium heat. Add shallots; cook 1 minute, stirring occasionally. Add cremini and shiitake mushrooms; cook 8 minutes, stirring occasionally. Add garlic; cook 1 minute, stirring occasionally. Stir in porcini mushrooms, wine, and thyme; cook 1 minute. Add reserved ¼ cup soaking liquid, scraping pan to loosen browned bits. Reduce heat; cook 3 minutes. Stir in parsley, lemon juice, pepper, and salt.
6 Divide mushroom mixture evenly among prepared crusts. Combine 2 tablespoons cheese and next 4 ingredients, stirring with a whisk; divide mixture evenly among tarts. Sprinkle tops evenly with remaining 1 tablespoon cheese and bell peppers. Place tarts on a baking sheet. Bake at 375° for 35 minutes or until set. Cool on a wire rack 10 minutes. Sprinkle top evenly with chives. Yield: 5 servings (serving size: 1 tart).

CALORIES 332; FAT 17.2g (sat 6.3g, mono 7.4g, poly 2.1g); PROTEIN 10.6g; CARB 31.1g; FIBER 2.5g; CHOL 57mg; IRON 2.9mg; SODIUM 708mg; CALC 165mg

SuperFast

These Asian-inspired 20-minute entrees feature seared beef in a sweet-salty-spicy sauce, a colorful main-dish salad with oranges and toasted noodles, the easiest glazed salmon, tofu with ground pork, and more.

QUICK & EASY
Cold Peanut Noodles with Shrimp

- 1 tablespoon chopped fresh basil
- 2 tablespoons rice vinegar
- 2 tablespoons low-sodium soy sauce
- 2 tablespoons creamy peanut butter
- 1 tablespoon dark sesame oil
- 1 teaspoon bottled ground fresh ginger
- 1 teaspoon chile paste with garlic
- ¼ teaspoon salt
- 1 garlic clove, minced
- 12 ounces fresh Chinese egg noodles
- 1 cup matchstick-cut carrots
- 8 ounces peeled and deveined medium shrimp
- 1½ cups julienne-cut red bell pepper
- ½ cup thinly sliced green onions, divided
- ½ cup chopped dry-roasted peanuts

1 Combine first 9 ingredients in a large bowl; set aside.
2 Cook noodles in boiling water 1 minute. Add carrots and shrimp; cook 2 minutes or until shrimp are done. Drain in a colander over a bowl, reserving cooking liquid. Rinse noodle mixture under cold water; drain. Add noodle mixture, bell pepper, and ¼ cup onions to peanut butter mixture, tossing to combine. Add enough of reserved cooking liquid to keep sauce creamy. Sprinkle with remaining ¼ cup onions and peanuts. Yield: 4 servings (serving size: 2 cups noodle mixture, 1 tablespoon onions, and 2 tablespoons peanuts).

CALORIES 486; FAT 16.9g (sat 2.9g, mono 7g, poly 5.2g); PROTEIN 30.7g; CARB 54.7g; FIBER 5.1g; CHOL 86mg; IRON 3mg; SODIUM 933mg; CALC 80mg

Mao Pao Tofu

1 (3½-ounce) bag boil-in-bag rice
2 tablespoons low-sodium soy sauce, divided
2 tablespoons dry sherry, divided
½ pound lean ground pork
1 tablespoon peanut oil
1 (14-ounce) package extra-firm water-packed tofu, drained and cubed
3 tablespoons thinly sliced green onions
1 tablespoon minced peeled fresh ginger
1 tablespoon chile paste with garlic
2 teaspoons minced fresh garlic
¼ teaspoon salt
1 cup fat-free, less-sodium chicken broth
2 teaspoons cornstarch
1 tablespoon water

1 Cook rice according to package directions, omitting salt and fat.
2 Combine 1 tablespoon soy sauce, 1 tablespoon sherry, and pork; set aside.
3 Heat oil in a wok over high heat. Add tofu; stir-fry 3 minutes. Add pork mixture; stir-fry 3 minutes. Stir in onions and next 4 ingredients; stir-fry 30 seconds. Add 1 tablespoon soy sauce, 1 tablespoon sherry, and broth; cook 2 minutes. Combine cornstarch and water; stir with a whisk. Add to wok; cook 30 seconds or until slightly thick, stirring constantly. Serve over rice. Yield: 4 servings (serving size: 1¼ cups tofu mixture and ½ cup rice).

CALORIES 342; FAT 14.3g (sat 3.8g, mono 2.7g, poly 4.6g); PROTEIN 23.3g; CARB 27.8g; FIBER 0.3g; CHOL 43mg; IRON 2.3mg; SODIUM 562mg; CALC 78mg

Kung Pao Shrimp

1 tablespoon low-sodium soy sauce, divided
1½ teaspoons dry sherry, divided
2 teaspoons cornstarch
1 pound peeled and deveined medium shrimp
1 tablespoon peanut oil
¼ cup coarsely chopped dry-roasted peanuts
2 tablespoons thinly sliced green onions
1 tablespoon minced peeled fresh ginger
1 tablespoon minced fresh garlic
½ teaspoon crushed red pepper
1½ cups thinly sliced celery
1 cup chopped red bell pepper
¼ cup fat-free, less-sodium chicken broth
1 teaspoon rice vinegar
¼ teaspoon salt

1 Combine 1 teaspoon soy sauce, 1 teaspoon sherry, cornstarch, and shrimp, tossing well to coat; set aside.
2 Heat oil in a wok over high heat. Add peanuts and next 3 ingredients; stir-fry 30 seconds. Stir in celery and bell pepper; stir-fry 2 minutes or until crisp-tender. Add shrimp mixture; stir-fry 2 minutes. Add remaining 2 teaspoons soy sauce, ½ teaspoon sherry, and broth. Bring to a simmer; cook 1 minute or until slightly thickened. Remove from heat; stir in vinegar and salt. Top with onions. Yield: 4 servings (serving size: 1¼ cups).

CALORIES 224; FAT 9.1g (sat 1.5g, mono 3.6g, poly 3.1g); PROTEIN 25.9g; CARB 9.1g; FIBER 2.3g; CHOL 172mg; IRON 3.4mg; SODIUM 574mg; CALC 91mg

Sour Beans with Minced Pork

Achieving the correct balance of flavor in the beans depends on using two types of vinegar—white vinegar alone will make the beans too tart, while just rice vinegar will yield a taste that's too mild.

1 (3½-ounce) bag boil-in-bag long-grain rice
1 cup white vinegar
1 cup rice vinegar
1¼ pounds green beans, trimmed and cut diagonally into ½-inch pieces
4 teaspoons peanut oil
1 tablespoon minced peeled fresh ginger
1 tablespoon minced fresh garlic
1 teaspoon crushed red pepper
½ pound lean ground pork
⅓ cup fat-free, less-sodium chicken broth
3 tablespoons low-sodium soy sauce
1½ teaspoons cornstarch
⅓ cup thinly sliced green onions
¼ matchstick-cut carrots

1 Cook rice according to directions.
2 Bring vinegars to a boil in a large saucepan. Add beans; cook 2 minutes. Drain beans (do not rinse).
3 Heat oil in a large nonstick skillet over medium-high heat. Add ginger, garlic, and pepper; sauté 30 seconds. Add pork to pan; cook 2 minutes or until browned, stirring to crumble. Add beans; cook 2 minutes, stirring occasionally. Combine broth, soy sauce, and cornstarch; stir with a whisk. Stir broth mixture into pork mixture; cook 1 minute or until thickened. Divide rice among 4 plates; top evenly with pork mixture. Sprinkle with onions and carrot. Yield: 4 servings.

CALORIES 290; FAT 9.8g (sat 2.8g, mono 3.6g, poly 1.6g); PROTEIN 16.6g; CARB 34.4g; FIBER 5.5g; CHOL 43mg; IRON 2.6mg; SODIUM 483mg; CALC 66mg

Miso-Glazed Salmon with Wilted Spinach

Look for time-saving pretoasted sesame seeds on the spice aisle.

FISH:

- 1 tablespoon white miso paste
- 2 teaspoons mirin (sweet rice wine)
- 2 teaspoons rice vinegar
- 2 teaspoons low-sodium soy sauce
- ½ teaspoon sugar
- ½ teaspoon grated peeled fresh ginger
- 2 (6-ounce) skinless salmon fillets
- 1 teaspoon toasted sesame seeds

SPINACH:

- 2 teaspoons dark sesame oil
- 1 teaspoon bottled minced garlic
- 1 (10-ounce) package fresh spinach
- 2 teaspoons low-sodium soy sauce

❶ Preheat broiler.
❷ To prepare fish, combine first 6 ingredients in a bowl; brush evenly over fish. Arrange fish on a foil-lined baking sheet; broil 8 minutes or until desired degree of doneness. Sprinkle with sesame seeds.
❸ To prepare spinach, while fish broils, heat sesame oil in a large nonstick skillet over medium-high heat. Add garlic and spinach; cook 30 seconds or until spinach just begins to wilt, tossing constantly. Stir in 2 teaspoons soy sauce. Yield: 2 servings (serving size: 1 fillet and ¾ cup spinach mixture).

CALORIES 347; FAT 16.5g (sat 3.3g, mono 6.9g, poly 5.1g); PROTEIN 37.5g; CARB 12.6g; FIBER 4.9g; CHOL 80mg; IRON 5.3mg; SODIUM 805mg; CALC 175mg

Mongolian Beef

- 2 tablespoons low-sodium soy sauce
- 1 teaspoon sugar
- 1 teaspoon cornstarch
- 2 teaspoons dry sherry
- 2 teaspoons hoisin sauce
- 1 teaspoon rice vinegar
- 1 teaspoon chile paste with garlic
- ¼ teaspoon salt

- 2 teaspoons peanut oil
- 1 tablespoon minced peeled fresh ginger
- 1 tablespoon minced fresh garlic
- 1 pound sirloin steak, thinly sliced across grain
- 16 medium green onions, cut into 2-inch pieces

❶ Combine first 8 ingredients, stirring until smooth.
❷ Heat oil in a large nonstick skillet over medium-high heat. Add ginger, garlic, and beef; sauté 2 minutes or until beef is browned. Add onions; sauté 30 seconds. Add soy sauce mixture; cook 1 minute or until thickened, stirring constantly. Yield: 4 servings (serving size: 1 cup).

CALORIES 237; FAT 10.5g (sat 3.5g, mono 4.3g, poly 1.1g); PROTEIN 26g; CARB 9.1g; FIBER 1.7g; CHOL 60mg; IRON 2.7mg; SODIUM 517mg; CALC 67mg

Asian Chicken Salad

- 2 tablespoons butter
- 2 tablespoons sliced almonds
- 1 (5-ounce) package Japanese curly noodles (chucka soba), crumbled
- 2 tablespoons low-sodium soy sauce
- 1½ tablespoons rice vinegar
- 1 tablespoon dark sesame oil
- 1 tablespoon honey
- 1 teaspoon Chinese mustard
- 1 teaspoon bottled ground fresh ginger
- ½ teaspoon chile paste with garlic
- 4 cups thinly sliced napa (Chinese) cabbage
- 2 cups thinly sliced red cabbage
- 2 cups chopped skinless, boneless rotisserie chicken breast
- ½ cup chopped fresh cilantro
- 1 cup jarred fresh orange sections, drained

❶ Melt butter in a large nonstick skillet over medium-high heat. Add almonds; sauté 1 minute. Add noodles; sauté 3 minutes or until almonds and noodles are toasted. Set aside.
❷ Combine soy sauce and next 6 ingredients in a large bowl, stirring with a whisk. Add napa cabbage and next 3 ingredients; toss gently to coat. Top with oranges and almond mixture. Yield: 4 servings (serving size: about 2 cups).

CALORIES 407; FAT 13.9g (sat 5g, mono 4.7g, poly 2.6g); PROTEIN 29.2g; CARB 42.5g; FIBER 3.6g; CHOL 75mg; IRON 1.6mg; SODIUM 484mg; CALC 117mg

Our Favorite Macadamia Butter Cookies

A fresh-baked batch of these nut- and fruit-studded treats is sure to bring good cheer.

Macadamia Butter Cookies

- ⅔ cup macadamia nuts
- ½ cup granulated sugar
- ½ cup packed light brown sugar
- 1 teaspoon vanilla extract
- 1 large egg
- 5.6 ounces all-purpose flour (about 1¼ cups)
- ½ teaspoon baking soda
- ¼ teaspoon salt
- ⅛ teaspoon ground nutmeg
- ½ cup sweetened dried cranberries, chopped
- 1 tablespoon granulated sugar

❶ Preheat oven to 375°.
❷ Place nuts in a food processor; process until smooth (about 2 minutes), scraping sides of bowl once. Combine macadamia butter, ½ cup granulated sugar, and brown sugar in a large bowl; beat with a mixer at medium speed. Add vanilla and egg; beat well.

❸ Weigh or lightly spoon flour into dry measuring cups; level with a knife. Combine flour and next 3 ingredients, stirring with a whisk. Add flour mixture to sugar mixture; beat at low speed just until combined (mixture will be very thick). Stir in dried cranberries. Chill 10 minutes.

❹ Divide chilled dough into 30 equal portions; roll each portion into a ball. Place 1 tablespoon granulated sugar in a small bowl. Lightly press each ball into sugar; place each ball, sugar side up, on a baking sheet covered with parchment paper. Gently press top of each cookie with a fork. Dip fork in water; gently press top of each cookie again to make a crisscross pattern. Place 15 cookies on each of 2 baking sheets.

❺ Bake cookies, 1 baking sheet at a time, at 375° for 9 minutes or until golden. Remove cookies from pan; cool on a wire rack. Repeat procedure with remaining cookies. Yield: 30 servings (serving size: 1 cookie).

CALORIES 78; FAT 2.5g (sat 0.4g, mono 1.8g, poly 0.1g); PROTEIN 1g; CARB 13.5g; FIBER 0.5g; CHOL 7mg; IRON 0.4mg; SODIUM 44mg; CALC 7mg

Dinner Tonight

Here are five stopwatch-tested menus from the *Cooking Light* Test Kitchens.

QUICK & EASY
Herb-Roasted Beef and Potatoes with Browned Butter Brussels Sprouts
············*40 minutes*

Shoulder tender (also labeled "petite tender") is a relatively new cut of beef that's moderately lean, quick-cooking, tender, and flavorful.
Simple Sub: If you can't find beef shoulder tender, you can also use beef or pork tenderloin.

2 tablespoons chopped fresh thyme, divided
1 tablespoon chopped fresh rosemary
1 tablespoon chopped fresh parsley
2½ tablespoons olive oil, divided
1¼ teaspoons kosher salt, divided
¾ teaspoon black pepper, divided
2 garlic cloves, minced
2 (8-ounce) beef shoulder tender roasts, trimmed
Cooking spray
1 (20-ounce) package refrigerated potato wedges (such as Simply Potatoes)

❶ Preheat broiler.
❷ Combine 1 tablespoon thyme, rosemary, parsley, 1 tablespoon oil, ¾ teaspoon salt, ½ teaspoon pepper, and garlic; rub evenly over both sides of beef. Place beef on the rack of a broiler pan coated with cooking spray; place rack in pan.
❸ Combine potatoes, remaining 1½ tablespoons oil, remaining ½ teaspoon salt, and remaining ¼ teaspoon pepper; toss well to coat. Arrange potato mixture onto rack around beef. Broil 7 minutes. Turn beef over. Broil 7 minutes or until beef is desired degree of doneness. Remove pan from oven. Place beef on a cutting board; let stand 5 minutes. Stir potatoes; sprinkle with remaining 1 tablespoon thyme. Cut beef across grain into thin slices; serve with potatoes. Yield: 4 servings (serving size: about 3 ounces beef and ¾ cup potatoes).

CALORIES 318; FAT 14.6g (sat 3.6g, mono 8.7g, poly 1.3g); PROTEIN 26.1g; CARB 18.7g; FIBER 3.9g; CHOL 66mg; IRON 3.2mg; SODIUM 788mg; CALC 16mg

BROWNED BUTTER BRUSSELS SPROUTS:
Steam 1 pound trimmed, halved Brussels sprouts 5 minutes or until crisp-tender; drain well. Melt 1½ tablespoons butter in a large skillet over medium heat, and cook until butter browns. Add Brussels sprouts; cook 6 minutes or until tender, stirring frequently. Stir in 2 teaspoons lemon juice, ¼ teaspoon salt, and ¼ teaspoon black pepper.

QUICK & EASY ▪ MAKE AHEAD
Ancho Pork and Hominy Stew with Jalapeño Corn Bread
············*40 minutes*

Simple Sub: Use regular chili powder in place of ancho, and decrease cumin by half.
Prep Pointer: For great corn bread crust, heat the skillet in the oven for five minutes before adding batter.
Make-Ahead Tip: You can freeze the stew for up to two months.

2 tablespoons ancho chile powder
2 teaspoons dried oregano
1½ teaspoons smoked paprika
1 teaspoon ground cumin
½ teaspoon salt
1½ pounds pork tenderloin, trimmed and cut into ½-inch pieces
1 tablespoon olive oil, divided
2 cups chopped onion
1½ cups chopped green bell pepper
1 tablespoon minced garlic
2½ cups fat-free, less-sodium chicken broth
1 (28-ounce) can hominy, drained
1 (14.5-ounce) can fire-roasted diced tomatoes, undrained

❶ Combine first 5 ingredients in a large bowl; set 1½ teaspoons spice mixture aside. Add pork to remaining spice mixture in bowl, tossing well to coat.
❷ Heat 2 teaspoons oil in a large Dutch oven over medium-high heat. Add pork mixture to pan; cook 5 minutes or until browned, stirring occasionally. Remove pork from pan; set aside. Add remaining 1 teaspoon oil to pan. Add onion, bell pepper, and garlic; cook 5 minutes or until tender, stirring occasionally. Return pork to pan. Add reserved 1½ teaspoons spice mixture, broth, hominy, and tomatoes; bring to a boil. Partially cover, reduce heat, and simmer 25 minutes. Yield: 6 servings (serving size: 1⅓ cups).

CALORIES 300; FAT 8.3g (sat 2.1g, mono 3.7g, poly 1.4g); PROTEIN 28.9g; CARB 26.9g; FIBER 6.1g; CHOL 76mg; IRON 3.2mg; SODIUM 523mg; CALC 51mg

Continued

JALAPEÑO CORN BREAD:

Preheat oven to 450°. Combine 1 cup low-fat buttermilk, ¼ cup canola oil, 3 tablespoons sugar, ¼ teaspoon salt, and 2 large eggs in a large bowl, stirring with a whisk. Sprinkle 4 teaspoons baking powder over batter; whisk until blended. Fold in 1 cup yellow cornmeal, 4.5 ounces (about 1 cup) all-purpose flour, and 1 chopped jalapeño pepper. Spoon batter into a 10-inch cast-iron skillet coated with cooking spray. Bake at 450° for 20 minutes or until lightly browned.

QUICK & EASY
Spanish Spaghetti with Olives with Pear, Date, and Manchego Salad

······································*30 minutes*

Kid Pleaser: Sub chicken broth for sherry, and either omit the olives or change to milder black ones.
Flavor Hit: Saffron adds a welcome earthy quality to the sauce.
Prep Pointer: To prevent a sticky mess, coat your knife with cooking spray before chopping dates.

- 8 ounces thin spaghetti
- 1 tablespoon olive oil
- 2 cups chopped onion
- 2 teaspoons minced garlic
- 1 teaspoon dried oregano
- ½ teaspoon celery salt
- ¼ teaspoon crushed red pepper
- ¼ teaspoon freshly ground black pepper
- ¼ teaspoon crushed saffron threads (optional)
- 8 ounces extra-lean ground beef
- 1⅔ cups marinara sauce
- ½ cup sliced pimiento-stuffed olives
- ¼ cup dry sherry
- 1 tablespoon capers
- ¼ cup chopped fresh parsley, divided

❶ Cook pasta according to package directions, omitting salt and fat; drain.
❷ Heat oil in a large skillet over medium-high heat. Add onion to pan; sauté 4 minutes or until tender. Add garlic; sauté 1 minute. Stir in oregano, celery salt, red pepper, black pepper, and, if desired, saffron. Crumble beef into pan; cook 5 minutes or until browned, stirring to crumble. Stir in marinara, olives, sherry, capers, and 3 tablespoons parsley. Bring to a boil; reduce heat and simmer 15 minutes.
❸ Add spaghetti to sauce mixture. Cook 2 minutes or until thoroughly heated. Sprinkle with remaining 1 tablespoon parsley. Yield: 4 servings (serving size: about 1¾ cups).

CALORIES 445; FAT 12.1g (sat 3g, mono 5.9g, poly 0.8g); PROTEIN 22.3g; CARB 60.6g; FIBER 5.4g; CHOL 21mg; IRON 5.2mg; SODIUM 832mg; CALC 72mg

PEAR, DATE, AND MANCHEGO SALAD:

Arrange 1 cup gourmet salad greens on each of 4 plates. Finely chop 2 ripe Bosc pears; toss with 2 teaspoons lemon juice. Divide pears, 6 finely chopped pitted dates, and 2 tablespoons chopped walnuts evenly among salads. Combine 1½ tablespoons extra-virgin olive oil, 2 teaspoons sherry vinegar, ¼ teaspoon salt, and ⅛ teaspoon black pepper; stir with a whisk. Drizzle evenly over salads. Top each salad with ½ ounce shaved Manchego cheese.

QUICK & EASY • MAKE AHEAD
Antipasto-Style Penne with Lemon-Garlic Broccoli Rabe

······································*40 minutes*

Make-Ahead Tip: You can prepare this pasta toss up to two days ahead; cold leftovers are great.
Simple Sub: Try substituting another cured meat, like sopressata, capicola, or cotto ham, for prosciutto.
Vegetarian Swap: Omit prosciutto and add 2 ounces cubed provolone cheese for more protein.

- 1 medium red bell pepper
- ½ cup pitted kalamata olives, chopped
- ⅓ cup refrigerated pesto
- 3 ounces prosciutto, chopped
- 1 (7-ounce) jar oil-packed sun-dried tomato halves, drained and chopped
- 1 (6-ounce) jar marinated quartered artichoke hearts, drained and chopped
- 8 ounces uncooked penne pasta (about 2 cups)
- ½ cup (2 ounces) grated Parmigiano-Reggiano cheese, divided
- ¼ cup pine nuts, toasted

❶ Preheat broiler.
❷ Cut bell pepper in half lengthwise; discard seeds and membranes. Place pepper halves, skin sides up, on a foil-lined baking sheet; flatten with hand. Broil 8 minutes or until blackened. Place in a zip-top plastic bag; seal. Let stand 5 minutes. Peel and chop bell pepper; place in a large bowl. Stir in olives and next 4 ingredients.
❸ Cook pasta according to package directions, omitting salt and fat; drain. Add cooked pasta and ¼ cup cheese to bell pepper mixture; toss to combine. Spoon about 1 cup pasta mixture into each of 6 bowls; sprinkle each serving with 2 teaspoons cheese and 2 teaspoons nuts. Yield: 6 servings.

CALORIES 404; FAT 21.3g (sat 4.4g, mono 10.6g, poly 4.4g); PROTEIN 16.5g; CARB 39.9g; FIBER 4.3g; CHOL 21mg; IRON 2.9mg; SODIUM 764mg; CALC 162mg

LEMON-GARLIC BROCCOLI RABE:

Heat a large skillet over medium-high heat. Add ¼ cup water and 1¼ pounds trimmed broccoli rabe. Cover and cook 3 minutes. Add 2 tablespoons olive oil, ¼ teaspoon crushed red pepper, and 2 minced garlic cloves. Cook, uncovered, 2 minutes or until tender. Remove from heat; stir in 2 teaspoons grated lemon rind, ¼ teaspoon kosher salt, and ¼ teaspoon black pepper.

Meaty, rich, and slightly fruity kalamata olives bring big flavor to any dish. To speed up preparation, purchase pitted olives in a jar or from the olive bar of larger markets.

QUICK & EASY

Pork Chops with Pomegranate Pan Sauce with Sour Cream Mashed Potatoes and Garlic Green Beans

30 minutes

Flavor Hit: Shallots lend body and mild onion taste to the glaze.
Simple Sub: Use finely chopped green onions in place of chives for the potatoes.
Time-Saver: You can use microwave-ready bags of fresh green beans and skip the blanching step.

- ½ teaspoon garlic powder
- ½ teaspoon salt
- ½ teaspoon ground cumin
- ¼ teaspoon black pepper
- 4 (4-ounce) boneless center-cut pork loin chops
- 2 teaspoons olive oil
- ⅓ cup chopped shallots
- ¾ cup pomegranate juice
- 1 tablespoon sugar
- 1 tablespoon balsamic vinegar

1 Combine first 4 ingredients in a small bowl; sprinkle over pork chops.
2 Heat oil in a large nonstick skillet over medium-high heat. Add pork chops; cook 3 minutes on each side. Remove and keep warm. Add shallots to pan; cook 45 seconds, stirring constantly. Add juice, sugar, and vinegar; bring to a boil. Cook 5 minutes or until slightly syrupy. Return pork chops to pan; cook 1 minute, turning frequently until well coated. Spoon remaining glaze over pork chops. Yield: 4 servings (serving size: 1 pork chop).

CALORIES 232; FAT 8.8g (sat 2.7g, mono 4.6g, poly 0.8g); PROTEIN 24g; CARB 13.1g; FIBER 0.3g; CHOL 67mg; IRON 1.3mg; SODIUM 352mg; CALC 34mg

SOUR CREAM MASHED POTATOES:

Prepare 1 (20-ounce) package refrigerated mashed potatoes according to package directions. Stir in 3 tablespoons reduced-fat sour cream. Top each serving with 1 teaspoon butter and ½ teaspoon minced fresh chives.

GARLIC GREEN BEANS:

Cook ¾ pound trimmed green beans in boiling water 5 minutes or until crisp-tender. Drain and plunge into ice water; drain. Heat a large nonstick skillet over medium-high heat. Add 1 tablespoon butter to pan; swirl until butter melts. Add 3 thinly sliced garlic cloves; sauté 2 minutes or until golden brown. Add beans, ¼ teaspoon salt, and ¼ teaspoon black pepper; cook 2 minutes or until heated.

Breakfast, Lunch, and Dinner in... Miami

A modern melting pot yields delicious flavors in tropical Miami.

MIAMI IS MORE LIKE another country than just another American city. Nearly 60 percent of its residents are foreign born, and while no passport is required to visit, a Rosetta Stone immersion course would help. That diverse population—plus a near-tropical year-round growing season and a perch right on the Atlantic ocean—makes Miami one-of-a-kind.

In just one block of a sleek, swanky neighborhood like the Design District or South Beach, restaurant menu boards cover such Caribbean-cooking mainstays as fiery curries and jerk seasoning, South American arepas and empanadas, traditional matzo ball soup, or high-end steaks with duck-fat frites. At Sra. Martinez, Michelle Bernstein, a James Beard award winner who was born and raised in Miami by an Argentinean mother and a Minnesotan father, shows just how the city's many influences distill into a single dish. She riffs on the classic Cuban sandwich, using salty, creamy briny sea urchin in place of the traditional roast pork, pressed in buttered bread until hot and crispy. While much of the rest of the country is dining on cellar roots if they want to eat locally, Miamians are still yanking heirloom tomatoes off the vine, feasting on stone crabs, and tearing open fresh grapefruits—just some of what is at its peak in winter months there.

Breakfast
Breakfast Tortilla

Breakfast in Miami may happen at 4 a.m. after a night out dancing. A Cuban breakfast may be as simple as a sweet roll and *cafecito*, but an open-face omelet with potatoes offers a more satisfying start to the day. Cubans are renowned for preparing a variety of root vegetables, including the exotic yucca and boniato, and most definitely the plain white potato, which is often cubed and fried into *papas bravas*. Versailles, an earthy Cuban eatery (despite its lofty name and glitzy décor), serves up a hearty open-face omelet, called a *tortilla* in Spanish style, served with potato and a sprinkling of cheese. Our version maximizes flavor with the addition of Yukon gold potatoes, fresh tomatoes, and kicky Manchego cheese.

½ pound Yukon gold potato (about 1 medium)
4 large eggs
1 large egg white
¾ teaspoon salt, divided
½ teaspoon freshly ground black pepper
1 tablespoon minced fresh chives, divided
1 tablespoon olive oil
1 garlic clove, minced
3 tablespoons finely grated Manchego cheese
1 teaspoon extra-virgin olive oil
½ cup halved grape tomatoes

❶ Preheat oven to 350°.
❷ Place potato in a saucepan; cover with water. Bring to a boil. Reduce heat; simmer 20 minutes or until tender; drain. Cool. Peel potato and thinly slice.

❸ Combine eggs, egg white, ¼ teaspoon salt, ½ teaspoon pepper, and 2 teaspoons chives in a bowl; whisk until blended.
❹ Heat 1 tablespoon oil in an 8-inch ovenproof nonstick skillet over medium heat. Add garlic and potato slices; cook 30 seconds, gently turning potato until coated with oil. Sprinkle potato mixture with ½ teaspoon salt. Press potato mixture into a solid layer in bottom of skillet. Pour egg mixture over potato mixture. Cook 1 minute. Gently stir mixture and press potato back down in bottom of skillet. Cook 2 minutes. Remove from heat. Sprinkle with cheese.
❺ Bake at 350° for 7 minutes or until center is set. Remove from oven. Drizzle with 1 teaspoon extra-virgin olive oil. Loosen sides of tortilla from skillet and slide onto a serving platter. Top with tomato and remaining 1 teaspoon chives. Yield: 4 servings (serving size: 1 wedge).

CALORIES 190; FAT 10.7g (sat 2.8g, mono 5.5g, poly 1.2g); PROTEIN 10g; CARB 14g; FIBER 1.2g; CHOL 215mg; IRON 1.3mg; SODIUM 581mg; CALC 77mg

Lunch
Cuban Sandwich

At David's Café (davidscafe.com), a Cuban sandwich is flat-pressed *a la plancha* on a hot electric grill and eaten straight from its wax-paper package. We've switched out the usual oven-roasted pork roast for marinated and grilled pork tenderloin, which is best started a day ahead.

GARLIC-ORANGE MOJO MARINADE:
3 tablespoons extra-virgin olive oil
½ cup minced onion
6 garlic cloves, minced
½ teaspoon kosher salt
½ teaspoon dried oregano
½ teaspoon freshly ground black pepper
¾ cup fresh orange juice (about 2 oranges)
2 tablespoons fresh lime juice
1 (1-pound) pork tenderloin
Cooking spray

½ cup chopped dill pickle plus
1 teaspoon dill pickle brine

2 tablespoons yellow mustard

2 teaspoons extra-virgin olive oil

REMAINING INGREDIENTS:

4 (3-inch) pieces Cuban bread, cut lengthwise

4 ounces thinly sliced reduced-fat Swiss cheese

3 ounces thinly sliced deli less-sodium ham

1 cup baby spinach

❶ To prepare marinade, heat oil in a small skillet over medium-high heat. Add onion and next 4 ingredients; cook 3 minutes or until onions are soft. Remove from heat; stir in juices. Measure out 2 tablespoons mojo marinade; set aside. Place pork in a large zip-top plastic bag; add remaining mojo marinade, turning to coat. Refrigerate 4 hours or overnight. Cover and refrigerate 2 tablespoons reserved mojo marinade.

❷ Prepare grill.

❸ Place pork on grill rack coated with cooking spray. Discard remaining mojo marinade. Grill 26 minutes, turning occasionally, or until thermometer registers 155°. Remove from grill; cover with foil 10 minutes. Slice half of tenderloin into 16 thin slices. Reserve remaining half of tenderloin for another use.

❹ To prepare relish, combine dill pickle, brine, reserved 2 tablespoons mojo marinade, mustard, and oil in a small bowl; stir well.

❺ Hollow out top and bottom halves of bread, leaving a ½-inch-thick shell; reserve torn bread for another use. Spread 2 teaspoons relish over each half. Arrange pork, cheese, ham, and spinach evenly on bottom half of bread; replace top half.

❻ Heat a nonstick grill pan over medium-high heat. Coat pan with cooking spray. Add sandwiches to pan. Place a cast-iron or heavy skillet on top of sandwiches, and press gently to flatten. Grill 4 minutes on each side or until cheese melts and bread is toasted. Cut sandwiches in half diagonally, and serve immediately. Yield: 4 servings (serving size: 1 sandwich).

CALORIES 397; FAT 13.5g (sat 4.4g, mono 4.6g, poly 1.7g); PROTEIN 30.3g; CARB 34.8g; FIBER 1.8g; CHOL 43mg; IRON 2.9mg; SODIUM 984mg; CALC 398mg

Dinner

Grilled Mahimahi with Mango Salsa

Loads of local chefs make use of the dazzling array of tropical treasures that grow year-round here. But the mango, a true backyard gem with hundreds of local varieties, symbolizes all things good and sweet in Miami cooking. In fact, the chefs who originally brought Miami's unique cuisine to national attention in the 1980s were dubbed The Mango Gang. One of them, Chef Allen Susser of Chef Allen's, still gives away free dinners to those who bring him a hundred pounds of fruit. In South Beach, Chef Claudio Giordano of Alta Mar combines mango and pineapple in a tangy relish and serves it on that day's fresh catch—anything from tuna to mahimahi to pumpkin swordfish. Michael Schwartz, of Michael's Genuine Food & Drink in the Design District, dices papaya and mango into a scorching hot relish to serve alongside black sticky rice and local black grouper cooked in his wood-burning oven. Though this dish is inherently light, we keep flavors fresh and lively with the addition of serrano chile and ginger.

¼ cup canned light coconut milk, divided

6 tablespoons fresh lime juice (about 4 limes), divided

4 (6-ounce) mahimahi fillets

1 diced peeled ripe mango (about ½ pound)

¾ cup diced seeded peeled cucumber (about ½ medium)

⅓ cup finely diced red bell pepper

2 tablespoons minced red onion

1 serrano chile, minced

1 tablespoon chopped fresh cilantro

1 teaspoon minced peeled fresh ginger

¾ teaspoon kosher salt, divided

¼ teaspoon freshly ground black pepper

Cooking spray

4 lime wedges

4 fresh cilantro sprigs

❶ Combine 3 tablespoons coconut milk and 3 tablespoons lime juice in a shallow dish; add fish, turning to coat. Cover and marinate at room temperature 15 minutes.

❷ Combine remaining 1 tablespoon coconut milk, remaining 3 tablespoons lime juice, mango, and next 6 ingredients in a bowl. Add ¼ teaspoon salt; toss well.

❸ Remove fish from dish, and discard marinade. Sprinkle fish with remaining ½ teaspoon salt and pepper.

❹ Heat a large grill pan over medium-high heat; coat with cooking spray. Cook fish 4 minutes per side or until fish flakes easily when tested with a fork. Serve with mango salsa and lime wedge. Garnish with cilantro sprig. Yield: 4 servings.

CALORIES 198; FAT 1.7g (sat 0.6g, mono 0.3g, poly 0.3g); PROTEIN 32.2g; CARB 12g; FIBER 1.6g; CHOL 124mg; IRON 2.2mg; SODIUM 507mg; CALC 39mg

Low and Slow

Low-temperature roasting brings out the best in foods and yields tender, intensely-flavored, and evenly-cooked meats, fish, and produce.

Dijon and Herb–Crusted Standing Beef Rib Roast

- 2 (1-ounce) slices white bread
- 1 (5-pound) standing rib roast, trimmed
- 1 teaspoon salt
- ½ teaspoon ground black pepper
- Cooking spray
- ½ cup chopped fresh basil
- ½ cup chopped fresh parsley
- ¼ cup Dijon mustard
- 1 teaspoon chopped fresh thyme
- 3 garlic cloves, minced

❶ Place bread in a food processor; pulse 10 times or until fine crumbs measure ¾ cup. Heat a small skillet over medium heat. Add breadcrumbs to pan; cook 12 minutes or until toasted, stirring frequently. Cool 5 minutes.

❷ Sprinkle roast evenly with salt and pepper. Heat a large skillet over medium-high heat. Coat pan with cooking spray. Add roast to pan; cook 5 minutes, browning on all sides. Remove roast from pan. Combine basil and next 4 ingredients in a bowl; spread mustard mixture evenly over roast. Pat breadcrumbs into mustard mixture on roast. Place roast on rack of a roasting pan coated with cooking spray; place rack in pan. Let stand at room temperature 1 hour.

❸ Preheat oven to 200°.

❹ Bake roast at 200° for 4½ hours or until a thermometer registers 135° or desired degree of doneness. Let stand 20 minutes before slicing. Yield: 12 servings (serving size: about 3½ ounces beef).

CALORIES 229; FAT 13.9g (sat 5.4g, mono 5.7g, poly 0.6g); PROTEIN 22.2g; CARB 2.3g; FIBER 0.3g; CHOL 103mg; IRON 1.8mg; SODIUM 298mg; CALC 27mg

Slow-Roasted Grape and Yogurt Parfaits

The roasting process softens the grapes slightly but heightens their flavor.

- Cooking spray
- 2 cups seedless black grapes
- 2 cups seedless red grapes
- 3 tablespoons sugar
- 2 cups plain fat-free Greek-style yogurt, divided
- ¼ cup walnut halves, toasted and coarsely chopped, divided
- 8 teaspoons honey, divided
- Thinly sliced fresh mint (optional)

❶ Preheat oven to 200°. Coat a jelly-roll pan with cooking spray.

❷ Rinse grapes; drain well, leaving slightly moist. Combine grapes and sugar in a large bowl; toss to coat. Arrange grapes on prepared pan. Bake at 200° for 3 hours or until grapes soften but still hold their shape. Remove from oven; cool completely.

❸ Spoon ¼ cup yogurt into bottom of each of 4 parfait glasses. Top each serving with about ⅓ cup grapes, 1½ teaspoons walnuts, and 1 teaspoon honey. Repeat layers with remaining ingredients; garnish with sliced mint, if desired. Yield: 4 servings (serving size: 1 parfait).

CALORIES 298; FAT 5g (sat 0.5g, mono 0.7g, poly 3.5g); PROTEIN 12.2g; CARB 55.5g; FIBER 2g; CHOL 0mg; IRON 0.9mg; SODIUM 46mg; CALC 100mg

Slow-Roasted Brown Sugar and Dill Cured Salmon

- ½ cup packed light brown sugar
- ⅓ cup chopped fresh dill
- 2 tablespoons kosher salt
- 1 (3-pound) salmon fillet
- Cooking spray
- ½ cup low-fat mayonnaise
- 2 tablespoons Dijon mustard

❶ Combine first 3 ingredients in a bowl. Place fish, skin side down, in a 13 x 9–inch baking dish. Rub sugar mixture over fish. Cover and refrigerate 8 hours.

❷ Preheat oven to 175°.

❸ Wipe off remaining sugar mixture from fish with a paper towel. Coat a jelly-roll pan with cooking spray. Place fish, skin side down, in pan.

❹ Bake at 175° for 1 hour and 10 minutes or until fish flakes easily when tested with a fork.

❺ Combine mayonnaise and mustard; stir well. Serve mayonnaise mixture with fish. Yield: 8 servings (serving size: about 5 ounces salmon and about 1 tablespoon mayonnaise mixture).

CALORIES 333; FAT 19.5g (sat 3.7g, mono 6.7g, poly 7.2g); PROTEIN 33.9g; CARB 3.6g; FIBER 0g; CHOL 100mg; IRON 0.6mg; SODIUM 402mg; CALC 22mg

WATERCRESS-CUCUMBER SALAD:
Combine 6 cups watercress, 1½ cups thinly sliced English cucumber, and 1½ cups thin vertically sliced red onion in a large bowl. Combine 1 tablespoon fresh lemon juice, ½ teaspoon Dijon mustard, ¼ teaspoon freshly ground black pepper, and ⅛ teaspoon salt in a small bowl. Slowly add 2 tablespoons extra-virgin olive oil to juice mixture, stirring constantly with a whisk; drizzle over watercress mixture. Toss gently to coat. Yield: 8 servings (serving size: about 1 cup salad).

Slow-Roasted Malaysian Spiced Leg of Lamb

1 (4-pound) boneless leg of lamb, trimmed
1 tablespoon olive oil
¼ cup ketchup
3 tablespoons dark brown sugar
1 tablespoon grated peeled fresh ginger
2 tablespoons oyster sauce
1 tablespoon Sriracha (hot chile sauce, such as Huy Fong)
2 garlic cloves, minced
Cooking spray

❶ Let lamb stand at room temperature 1 hour. Roll up lamb jelly-roll fashion; secure at 1-inch intervals with twine. Heat a skillet over medium-high heat. Add oil to pan; swirl to coat. Add lamb; cook 6 minutes, browning on all sides.
❷ Combine ketchup and next 5 ingredients in a large bowl. Coat lamb evenly with ketchup mixture. Place lamb on rack of a roasting pan coated with cooking spray; place rack in pan.
❸ Preheat oven to 200°.
❹ Bake lamb at 200° for 2 hours or until a thermometer registers 135° or until desired degree of doneness. Let stand 20 minutes before slicing. Yield: 12 servings (serving size: about 3 ounces lamb).

CALORIES 246; FAT 10.3g (sat 3.9g, mono 4.6g, poly 0.6g); PROTEIN 31.1g; CARB 5.3g; FIBER 0.1g; CHOL 101mg; IRON 2.6mg; SODIUM 163mg; CALC 15mg

LEMONGRASS-MINT RICE:

Combine 1½ cups fat-free, less-sodium chicken broth, 1 tablespoon chopped peeled fresh lemongrass, ¼ teaspoon ground turmeric, and 1 (14.5-ounce) can light coconut milk in a medium saucepan; bring to a boil. Stir in 2 cups jasmine rice; cover, reduce heat. Simmer 15 minutes or until liquid is absorbed. Remove from heat; let stand 5 minutes. Stir in 3 tablespoons chopped fresh cilantro, 1 tablespoon chopped fresh mint, and ½ teaspoon salt. Yield: 8 servings (serving size: about ½ cup rice).

SPICY SUGAR SNAP PEAS:

Bring 3 quarts water to a boil in a large saucepan. Add 5 cups sugar snap peas; cook 2 minutes or until crisp-tender. Drain well. Heat 2 teaspoons sesame oil in a large skillet over medium heat. Add 2 teaspoons minced garlic to pan; cook 30 seconds, stirring frequently. Add peas, 1 tablespoon sambal oelek, and ¼ teaspoon salt; toss well. Yield: 8 servings (serving size: about ¾ cup peas).

Slow-Roasted Pulled Pork

PORK:

2 tablespoons dark brown sugar
1 tablespoon smoked paprika
1 tablespoon chili powder
1 teaspoon salt
2 teaspoons ground cumin
1 teaspoon freshly ground black pepper
½ teaspoon dry mustard
½ teaspoon ground chipotle chile pepper
1 (5-pound) boneless pork shoulder (Boston butt), trimmed
Cooking spray
2 cups water, divided
½ cup apple cider vinegar
⅓ cup ketchup

SAUCE:

¾ cup apple cider vinegar
½ cup ketchup
3 tablespoons dark brown sugar
2 teaspoons smoked paprika
1 teaspoon chili powder

REMAINING INGREDIENTS:

Hamburger buns (optional)
Sandwich-cut bread-and-butter pickles (optional)

❶ To prepare pork, combine first 8 ingredients in a small bowl. Rub sugar mixture evenly over pork. Let pork stand at room temperature 1 hour.
❷ Preheat oven to 225°.
❸ Place pork on rack of a roasting pan coated with cooking spray; place rack in pan. Pour 1 cup water in bottom of roasting pan. Bake at 225° for 1 hour.
❹ Combine ½ cup vinegar and ketchup in a medium bowl; brush pork with ketchup mixture (do not remove from oven). Bake an additional 3 hours, basting every hour with ketchup mixture.
❺ Pour remaining 1 cup water in bottom of roasting pan. Cover pork and pan tightly with foil. Bake an additional 3¾ hours or until a thermometer registers 190°. Remove from oven; let stand, covered, 45 minutes.
❻ To prepare sauce, combine ¾ cup vinegar and next 4 ingredients in a small saucepan. Bring to a boil over medium-high heat, stirring occasionally with a whisk. Boil 5 minutes or until slightly thick. Shred pork with 2 forks. Serve with sauce. Serve shredded pork on hamburger buns with pickle chips, if desired. Yield: 16 servings (serving size: about 3 ounces pork and about 1 tablespoon sauce).

CALORIES 283; FAT 15.4g (sat 5.5g, mono 6.8g, poly 1.5g); PROTEIN 26.2g; CARB 8.1g; FIBER 0.4g; CHOL 90mg; IRON 2.1mg; SODIUM 402mg; CALC 40mg

Aromatic Slow-Roasted Tomatoes

1 tablespoon sugar
1 tablespoon extra-virgin olive oil
½ teaspoon salt
½ teaspoon dried basil
½ teaspoon dried oregano
¼ teaspoon freshly ground black pepper
4 pounds plum tomatoes, halved lengthwise (about 16 medium)
Cooking spray

❶ Preheat oven to 200°.
❷ Combine first 7 ingredients in a large bowl, tossing gently to coat. Arrange tomatoes, cut sides up, on a baking sheet coated with cooking spray. Roast at 200° for 7½ hours. Yield: 8 servings (serving size: 2 tomato halves).

CALORIES 63; FAT 2.2g (sat 0.3g, mono 1.3g, poly 0.4g); PROTEIN 2g; CARB 10.6g; FIBER 2.8g; CHOL 0mg; IRON 0.7mg; SODIUM 157mg; CALC 26mg

Continued

TOMATO SAUCE:

Process slow-roasted tomatoes until smooth; put through a food mill. Heat 2 teaspoons olive oil in a saucepan over medium heat. Add 1 large sliced garlic clove; cook 2 minutes. Stir in tomato puree. Increase heat to medium-high; simmer 1 hour or until sauce yield equals 1¾ cups.

Garlic and Rosemary Slow-Roasted Turkey

- 1 (12-pound) fresh or frozen turkey, thawed
- 9 garlic cloves, divided
- 1 tablespoon chopped fresh rosemary
- 8 teaspoons butter, softened
- 1 tablespoon paprika
- 1½ teaspoons salt
- 1½ teaspoons ground black pepper
- 3 sprigs fresh rosemary
- Cooking spray

❶ Remove and discard giblets and neck from turkey. Trim excess fat. Starting at neck cavity, loosen skin from breast and drumsticks by inserting fingers, gently pushing between skin and meat. Mince 3 garlic cloves; combine minced garlic, chopped rosemary, and next 4 ingredients in a bowl. Rub butter mixture under loosened skin and over breast and drumsticks. Lift wing tips up and over back; tuck under turkey. Place remaining 6 garlic cloves and rosemary sprigs in body cavity. Tie legs together with kitchen string. Let turkey stand 1 hour at room temperature.
❷ Preheat oven to 500°.
❸ Place turkey, breast side up, on rack of a roasting pan coated with cooking spray. Place rack in oven. Bake at 500° for 30 minutes. Reduce oven temperature to 250°. Bake 2 hours or until a thermometer inserted into meaty part of thigh registers 165°. Remove from oven; cover loosely with foil. Let stand 30 minutes. Discard skin. Yield: 12 servings (serving size: about 6 ounces turkey).

CALORIES 366; FAT 8.6g (sat 3.6g, mono 1.9g, poly 1.8g); PROTEIN 67g; CARB 0.7g; FIBER 0.3g; CHOL 229mg; IRON 4.6mg; SODIUM 461mg; CALC 50mg

The Power of Positive Drinking

A cocktail (or beer or wine) can be as good for your body as it is for your frame of mind.

TRUE STORY: The National Institutes of Health blocked publication of a 1972 study showing that moderate drinking lowered rates of heart disease deaths, worrying that Americans couldn't be trusted not to drive to the nearest bar and start guzzling. Fortunately, we're getting the message about moderation. Today, we drink about a third less than our martinis-with-lunch 1950's forebears, according to data from the long-running Framingham Heart Study. And evidence about the many health benefits of alcohol is so strong it can no longer be censored—or ignored.

A recent study of the Mediterranean diet listed moderate alcohol consumption ahead of diet and exercise as the lifestyle factor most solidly connected to the diet's vaunted health benefits. Looking at the medical literature, a rational person might conclude that alcohol is the new aspirin—take one drink a day. But of course, alcohol comes with social costs that lab studies can't always factor, like addiction, driving under the influence, or risk of serious injury. We're not suggesting that everyone start drinking, but if you do and do so responsibly, then this one's for you. Cheers!

QUICK & EASY
Hot Buttered Vanilla Rum

- 1½ cups water
- 2 tablespoons sugar
- 1 vanilla bean
- 1 (2-inch) piece lemon rind
- 1 cup dark rum
- 1 tablespoon butter

❶ Bring first 4 ingredients to a boil in a small saucepan. Remove from heat; cover and let stand 15 minutes. Strain mixture through a fine sieve over a bowl, reserving liquid; discard solids. Return water mixture to pan. Add rum and butter to pan; bring to a simmer over medium heat, stirring until butter melts. Serve immediately. Yield: 4 servings (serving size: ½ cup).

CALORIES 178; FAT 2.8g (sat 1.8g, mono 0.7g, poly 0.1g); PROTEIN 0g; CARB 6g; FIBER 0g; CHOL 8mg; IRON 0.1mg; SODIUM 21mg; CALC 1mg

QUICK & EASY
Newfangled Old-Fashioned

- 1 cup premium bourbon or rye whiskey
- ¼ cup 100% cherry juice (not sour)
- 2 teaspoons Angostura bitters
- Ice
- 4 (2-inch) orange rind strips (optional)
- 4 maraschino cherries (optional)

❶ Combine first 3 ingredients in a cocktail shaker; shake to combine. Divide bourbon mixture evenly among 4 tumblers filled with ice. Garnish each serving with 1 rind strip and 1 cherry, if desired. Yield: 4 servings (serving size: about ½ cup).

CALORIES 167; FAT 0g; PROTEIN 0g; CARB 4.1g; FIBER 0g; CHOL 0mg; IRON 0.1mg; SODIUM 2mg; CALC 3mg

Sparkling Pomegranate Cocktail

1½ cups pomegranate juice
¼ cup grenadine
1 (750-milliliter) bottle Prosecco or dry sparkling wine, chilled
6 lime slices (optional)
Pomegranate seeds (optional)

❶ Combine juice and grenadine in a 2-cup glass measure. Divide juice mixture evenly among 6 champagne flutes or wine glasses. Top each serving evenly with wine; garnish each serving with lime slices and seeds, if desired. Yield: 6 servings (serving size: about ¾ cup).

CALORIES 178; FAT 0g; PROTEIN 0.3g; CARB 22.1g; FIBER 0.3g; CHOL 0mg; IRON 0.4mg; SODIUM 17mg; CALC 22mg

Rosemary Lemon Drop

1 cup plus 2 tablespoons sugar
¾ cup water
2 teaspoons chopped fresh rosemary
1 cup vodka
¾ cup fresh lemon juice (about 5 lemons)
Crushed ice
Fresh rosemary sprigs (optional)

❶ Bring first 3 ingredients to a boil in a small saucepan, stirring just until sugar dissolves. Cover and remove from heat; let stand 20 minutes. Strain through a fine sieve over a bowl, reserving liquid; discard solids. Cover and chill.
❷ Combine chilled syrup, vodka, and juice. Pour over crushed ice in a cocktail shaker; shake to combine. Strain mixture evenly into 6 martini glasses; garnish with rosemary, if desired. Yield: 6 servings (serving size: about ½ cup).

CALORIES 238; FAT 0g; PROTEIN 0.1g; CARB 40.1g; FIBER 0.1g; CHOL 0mg; IRON 0mg; SODIUM 1mg; CALC 3mg

The *Cooking Light* Way to Cook

Enjoy a sneak peek into our best cookbook ever, full of tips and photos to guide you through all the steps that lead to recipe success.

Fruit and Walnut–Stuffed Pork Loin

Dried fruits are rehydrated in a blend of orange-flavored liqueur and red wine. Use a combination of orange juice and chicken broth for a nonalcoholic alternative. The pork loin is coated in a breadcrumb mixture to form a crisp crust.

½ cup dry red wine
¼ cup dried sour cherries
¼ cup chopped dried apricots
¼ cup chopped dried plums
2 tablespoons Triple Sec (orange-flavored liqueur)
⅓ cup finely chopped walnuts
2 tablespoons chopped shallots
1¼ teaspoons salt, divided
½ teaspoon grated lemon rind
2 (1-ounce) slices French bread
1 teaspoon chopped fresh thyme
¼ teaspoon freshly ground black pepper
2 garlic cloves, minced
1 (2½-pound) boneless center-cut pork loin roast, trimmed
2 tablespoons Dijon mustard
Cooking spray
Fresh parsley sprigs (optional)

❶ Preheat oven to 400°.
❷ Combine first 5 ingredients in a medium microwave-safe bowl; microwave at HIGH 2 minutes. Let stand 10 minutes or until fruit is plump. Drain mixture through a sieve, reserving fruit mixture. Combine fruit mixture, walnuts, shallots, ¼ teaspoon salt, and rind.
❸ Place ¾ teaspoon salt, French bread, and next 3 ingredients in a food processor; process until fine crumbs form.
❹ Cut pork in half lengthwise, cutting to, but not through, other side; open halves, laying the pork flat. Starting from center, cut each half lengthwise, cutting to, but not through, other side; open halves, laying pork flat. Cover with plastic wrap; pound to an even thickness. Discard plastic wrap. Spread fruit mixture over pork, leaving a ½-inch border. Roll up pork, jelly-roll fashion, starting with one long side. Secure with wooden picks. Sprinkle outside of pork evenly with remaining ¼ teaspoon salt; brush evenly with mustard. Sprinkle breadcrumb mixture over pork; press gently to adhere. Place pork on a broiler pan coated with cooking spray. Bake at 400° for 55 minutes or until a meat thermometer inserted in the thickest part registers 155°. Let pork stand 10 minutes. Remove wooden picks. Cut into 16 (½-inch-thick) slices. Garnish with parsley sprigs, if desired. Yield: 8 servings (serving size: 2 slices).

CALORIES 323; FAT 12.4g (sat 3.7g, mono 4.5g, poly 3.1g); PROTEIN 29.7g; CARB 18.9g; FIBER 1.4g; CHOL 79mg; IRON 1.9mg; SODIUM 573mg; CALC 41mg

Classic Crème Caramel

4 cups 2% reduced-fat milk
1 vanilla bean, split lengthwise
Cooking spray
1²/₃ sugar, divided
¼ water
¼ teaspoon kosher salt
6 large eggs
3 tablespoons heavy whipping cream

❶ Preheat oven to 225°.
❷ Heat milk and vanilla bean over medium-high heat in a medium, heavy saucepan to 180° or until tiny bubbles form around edge (do not boil); remove pan from heat. Cover and set aside.
❸ Coat 10 (6-ounce) custard cups with cooking spray, and arrange cups on a jelly-roll pan.
❹ Combine 1 cup sugar and ¼ cup water in a small, heavy saucepan; cook over medium-high heat until sugar dissolves, stirring frequently. Continue cooking 7 minutes or until golden (do not stir). Immediately pour into prepared custard cups, tipping quickly until caramelized sugar coats bottom of cups.
❺ Combine remaining ²/₃ cup sugar, salt, and eggs in a large bowl, stirring with a whisk. Remove vanilla bean from milk mixture; reserve bean for another use. Gradually pour warm milk mixture into egg mixture, stirring constantly with a whisk; stir in cream. Strain egg mixture through a sieve into a large bowl; pour about ½ cup egg mixture over caramelized sugar in each custard cup. Bake at 225° for 2 hours or until custards are just set. Remove from oven; cool to room temperature. Place plastic wrap on surface of custards; chill overnight.
❻ Loosen edges of custards with a knife or rubber spatula. Place a dessert plate on top of each cup; invert onto plate. Drizzle any remaining caramelized syrup over custards. Yield: 10 servings (serving size: 1 custard).

CALORIES 236; FAT 6.5g (sat 3.1g, mono 2.2g, poly 0.5g); PROTEIN 7.1g; CARB 38.4g; FIBER 0g; CHOL 140mg; IRON 0.6mg; SODIUM 139mg; CALC 138mg

Dinner Rolls, Five Ways

One dough recipe yields five roll variations. To freeze rolls, bake, cool completely, wrap in heavy-duty foil, and freeze. Thaw and re-heat (still wrapped) at 400° for 12 minutes or until warm.

2 teaspoons sugar
1 package dry yeast (about 2¼ teaspoons)
1 (12-ounce) can evaporated fat-free milk, warmed (100° to 110°)
18 ounces all-purpose flour (about 4 cups), divided
1 large egg, lightly beaten
1 teaspoon salt
Cooking spray
1 teaspoon cornmeal
2 tablespoons butter, melted and cooled
Poppy seeds (optional)

❶ Dissolve sugar and yeast in warm milk in a large bowl; let stand 5 minutes.
❷ Lightly spoon flour into dry measuring cups; level with a knife. Add 3 cups flour and egg to milk mixture, stirring until smooth; cover and let stand 15 minutes.
❸ Add ¾ cup flour and salt; stir until a soft dough forms. Turn dough out onto a floured surface. Knead until smooth and elastic (about 8 minutes); add enough of remaining flour, 1 tablespoon at a time, to prevent dough from sticking to hands (dough will feel tacky).
❹ Place the dough in a large bowl coated with cooking spray, turning to coat top. Cover and let rise in a warm place (85°), free from drafts, 40 minutes or until doubled in size. (Press two fingers into dough. If an indentation remains, dough has risen enough.) Punch dough down; cover and let rest 5 minutes.
❺ Divide dough into 16 equal portions. Working with one portion at a time (cover remaining dough to prevent drying), shape each portion into desired form (see Kitchen How-to: Shape Dough, at right). Place shaped dough portions on each of 2 baking sheets lightly sprinkled with ½ teaspoon cornmeal. Lightly coat shaped dough portions with cooking spray; cover with plastic wrap. Let rise in a warm place (85°), free from drafts, 20 minutes or until doubled in size.
❻ Preheat oven to 400°.
❼ Gently brush dough portions with butter; sprinkle with poppy seeds, if desired. Place 1 baking sheet on bottom oven rack and 1 baking sheet on middle oven rack. Bake at 400° for 10 minutes; rotate baking sheets. Bake an additional 10 minutes or until lightly browned on top and hollow-sounding when tapped on bottom. Place on wire racks. Serve warm, or cool completely on wire racks. Yield: 16 servings (serving size: 1 roll).

CALORIES 151; FAT 2.1g (sat 1.1g, mono 0.5g, poly 0.2g); PROTEIN 5.4g; CARB 27g; FIBER 0.9g; CHOL 18mg; IRON 1.7mg; SODIUM 187mg; CALC 69mg

Kitchen How-to: Shape Dough

Use one simple dough to yield five rich, tender dinner roll variations.

Roll: Divide the dough into 16 equal portions; shape each portion into a ball.
Knot: Divide the dough into 16 equal portions; shape each portion into an 8-inch rope. Tie each rope into a single knot; tuck the top end of the rope under the bottom edge of the roll.
Snail: Divide the dough into 16 equal portions; shape each portion into a 20-inch rope. Working on a flat surface, coil each rope in a spiral pattern.
Cloverleaf: Divide the dough into 16 equal portions; divide each portion into three balls. Working with three balls at a time, arrange the balls in a triangle pattern on baking sheet (be sure the balls are touching each other).
Twist: Divide the dough into 16 equal portions; shape each portion into an 18-inch rope. Fold each rope in half so that both ends meet. Working with one folded rope at a time, hold the ends of the rope in one hand and the folded end in the other hand; gently twist.

The *Cooking Light*
Produce & Organics Buying Guide

How to Buy the Best Fresh Produce

When you arrive at the produce section, remember this: whether you choose conventional or organic, imported or domestic, the key is to eat produce in abundance and variety. Here, we'll show you how to buy the best, keeping in mind budget and good nutrition, all while maintaining an appetizingly delicious, healthful diet.

Fruits and Vegetables

Nutrition and Health

Fruits and vegetables are among the most nutritious foods you can eat. They're inherently low in calories and rich in a multitude of vitamins and minerals, as well as fiber. Eating a diet rich in vegetables and fruits may help reduce your risk for stroke, coronary heart disease, type 2 diabetes, and certain cancers.

• **Calcium:** Essential for healthy bones and teeth, necessary for function of muscles, nerves, and glands. Top sources: Collards, turnip greens, edamame (green soybeans)

• **Fiber:** Soluble fiber helps balance cholesterol levels, lowering risk of heart disease. Insoluble fiber aids digestion and can help provide a feeling of fullness with fewer calories. Top sources: Beans, artichokes, pears

• **Folic acid:** Helps form red blood cells and is important during pregnancy. Top sources: Dark leafy greens, broccoli, edamame

• **Iron:** Aids in healthy blood and normal functioning of cells. Top sources: Edamame, lentils, lima beans

• **Potassium:** Helps regulate fluid retention and influences kidney function. Top sources: Potatoes, dark leafy greens, bananas

• **Vitamin A:** Keeps eyes and skin healthy and helps protect against infections. Top sources: Orange vegetables (winter squash, sweet potatoes, carrots), orange fruits (mango, cantaloupe, apricots), and dark leafy greens

• **Vitamin E:** Helps protect vitamin A and essential fatty acids from oxidation. Top sources: Dark leafy greens, red bell pepper, papaya

• **Vitamin C:** Helps heal cuts and wounds, keeps teeth and gums healthy, and aids in iron absorption. Top sources: Citrus fruits, bell pepper, mango

Choose Colorful Produce

Plants produce phytonutrients to protect them from disease. In humans, phytonutrients work as antioxidants, immune boosters, and anti-inflammatories. These compounds have only recently been documented, so exact levels in produce are often unknown. What's more, different varieties of fruits or vegetables may have varying levels. Until scientists learn more about phytonutrients, the best way to obtain them is to aim for variety based on color. Blueberries derive their color from an antioxidant called anthocyanin, so the deeper the color, the more of it they contain. The deepest orange carrots are highest in beta-carotene. The reddest tomatoes and watermelon are highest in lycopene.

Continued

What One Serving Looks Like

1 medium fruit · 1 cup chopped raw fruits or vegetables · 1 cup whole small items, like berries or grapes · 2 cups leafy greens

Genetically Modified (GMO) Items

Molecular biologists genetically engineer some seeds to enhance traits such as resistance to herbicides, instead of using traditional breeding methods. The Food and Drug Administration has approved more than 50 bioengineered foods, including papayas, potatoes, squash, sweet corn, tomatoes, and soybeans. Produce that is going to be labeled "organic" cannot be genetically modified.

At the Market

Although produce comes in many shapes and sizes, there are a few general rules you can use to select the best.

• **Pick it up.** See how the item feels in your hand. Most fruits and vegetables should feel heavy for their size. Pick up a few comparable items and judge them against each other.
• **Use your eyes.** Avoid soft spots, browning, or wilting. These may be caused by damage during transit or an indication that the produce is past its prime.

• **Dig through displays.** Often the freshest items are stocked in the back of a row or the bottom of a bin, while the ripest items are displayed first.
• **Ask.** If you're still uncertain, ask the purveyor. He or she should be able to guide you to the freshest items.

Ways to Save

With careful buying, you can meet the recommended servings for less than $2.50 per day, according to the U.S. Department of Agriculture.

• **Buy in season.** Buy fresh produce when it is in season (and therefore more abundant and less expensive). The produce will be more flavorful, too. To learn more about which produce items will come into season during the summer months, turn to our Summer Cookbook (page 135).
• **Mix it up.** To avoid waste, use items most likely to spoil—like highly perishable berries or delicate leafy greens—within a day or two of purchase. Save sturdier items, such as root vegetables like carrots or beets, for later in the week.

Herbs

Using both fresh and dried herbs is an easy way to add lots of flavor without adding significant amounts of fat, calories, or sodium. You can find fresh herbs in the produce section at your local market.

Herb Glossary

Basil: Basil, a member of the mint family, is one of the most important culinary herbs. Sweet basil, the most common type, tastes like a cross between licorice and cloves.

Cilantro: Also called coriander or Chinese parsley, cilantro has a pungent flavor. The leaves are often mistaken for flat-leaf parsley, so read the tag to verify that you're buying the correct herb. Cilantro is susceptible to heat, so add it at the end of the cooking process.

Mint: This herb can be used in both sweet and savory dishes. Mint comes in many varieties, but spearmint is the preferred choice for cooking. Its bright green leaves are fuzzy, making them very different

basil · cilantro · mint · oregano · parsley · rosemary

from the darker-stemmed, rounded leaves of peppermint.

Oregano: Oregano has an aromatic, warm flavor. It's commonly used in Greek and Italian cooking.

Parsley: Parsley can go in just about every dish you cook because its mild, grassy flavor allows the flavors of other ingredients to come through. Curly parsley is less assertive than its brother, flat-leaf parsley (often called Italian parsley).

Rosemary: Rosemary is one of the most aromatic and pungent of all herbs. Its needlelike leaves have a strong and pronounced lemon-pine flavor.

Sage: Sage's long, narrow leaves have a distinctively fuzzy texture and a musty flavor redolent of eucalyptus, cedar, lemon, and mint. Use it with discretion; it can overwhelm a dish.

Thyme: Thyme pairs well with many other herbs—especially rosemary, parsley, sage, savory, and oregano. Because the leaves are so small, they often don't require chopping. Add thyme during cooking; its powerful taste develops best at high temperatures.

sage

thyme

What to Store Where

REFRIGERATOR

Keep these items in perforated plastic bags in the refrigerator's produce drawers, where moisture levels are higher.

Artichokes	Carrots	Grapes
Asparagus	Cauliflower	Green onions
Beans	Celery	Leafy greens
Beets	Cherries	Leeks
Berries	Corn	Peas
Broccoli	Cucumbers	Radishes
Cabbage	Figs	Summer squashes

COUNTERTOP

Choose a spot that's away from direct sunlight. Choose a container that allows for air circulation, like a vented bowl or perforated bag.

Apples**	Peaches*
Apricots	Pears*
Avocados*	Peppers
Bananas	Pineapple
Citrus fruits	Plums*
Eggplant	Pomegranates
Kiwifruit*	Pumpkins
Mangoes	Tomatoes
Nectarines*	Watermelon
Papayas	Winter squashes

*Refrigerate after ripening
**After 7 days move to refrigerater

PANTRY

The following items should be stored away from light in a well-ventilated area in the pantry or a cupboard.

Garlic
Onions
Potatoes

How to Buy the Best Organics

Once relegated to a small section, organic food can now be found in just about every corner of the grocery store. If you've never purchased organic items, perhaps you have questions about whether or not these products are worth their premium price tag. Here, we'll give you plenty of reasons to try them.

Organic Labeling Terms

"100% organic" ▶
Such foods are organic down to the very last crumb, so they carry the USDA green and white "certified organic" seal. Most often, these are whole foods—apples, oranges, grains, or those with only one or two ingredients, like pasta.

USDA ORGANIC

◀ **"Organic"**
At least 95 percent of the ingredients are organic. The rest comes from a list of allowable ingredients. These foods also carry the USDA seal and are generally composed mostly of whole-food ingredients—canned soups or frozen foods.

"Made with organic ingredients" ▶
At least 70 percent of the ingredients are organic. However, these foods, which may be any type of processed or packaged food, cannot carry the USDA seal.

Organic Certification

In 2002, the U.S. Department of Agriculture implemented uniform standards for American organic farmers and manufacturers. Organic foods must be grown or produced without chemical pesticides or fertilizers, and, in livestock, without the use of antibiotics or growth hormones. Organic foods cannot be genetically modified, irradiated, or cloned. Further guidelines govern specific foods. For instance, organic chickens must be raised with outdoor access.

Pesticide Problems

Pesticide residues are much lower in organic foods than conventionally grown ones. Chemicals used in agriculture that may find their way into the food supply are monitored by the Environmental Protection Agency, which sets limits on how much pesticide residue foods can contain. According to the Food and Drug Administration's Pesticide Residue Monitoring Program, which collects and tests random samples of domestic and imported foods, fruits and vegetables have the highest levels of trace pesticides—54.9 percent of fruit and 23.8 percent of vegetables. Studies have shown certain types of produce are consistently high in pesticide levels, which may make organic varieties a suitable alternative.

At the Market

Environmental concerns, your health goals, and the amount of your food budget determine which organic products make sense for you. But these shopping strategies can help:

• **Prioritize your purchases.** Invest your organic dollars in traditionally pesticide-heavy produce instead of low-pesticide foods. (See page 403 for purchasing tips.)

• **Think local and seasonal.** Locally grown, seasonal produce may have a lower environmental cost than organic items that use fossil fuels and energy to travel long distances in shipping. If possible, consider local and organic produce.

• **Keep good nutrition in mind.** When buying meats, dairy, or processed foods, factor the item's whole nutritional package first, then consider the method by which it was produced. Minimizing sodium and saturated fat has proven health benefits, such as helping to reduce risk of cardiovascular disease.

• **Don't worry about organic seafood.** At the moment, there are no government standards for what makes fish or shellfish organic.

Ways to Save

• **Ramp up.** If you want to work organics into your budget gradually, start with one or two key foods you eat frequently—like milk or eggs.

• **Shop the source.** Go directly to a farm or a local farmers' market for the best deals on organic produce, milk, eggs, and meats. Prices there for organic goods are often cheaper than in supermarkets, and products are usually fresher. Check-localharvest.org to find local purveyors in your area. Another reason to buy local: You can ask the farmer about how he or she raises food. For example, smaller organic operations may allow cattle more room to graze.

• **Buy private label.** Supermarkets and specialty stores like Safeway, Stop & Shop, Kroger, Publix, Wal-Mart, and Whole Foods all offer their own private-label organic food lines. Because there is no middleman, you can save as much as 20 percent, sometimes more. For example, Safeway's O organics brand large brown eggs sell for $4 per dozen—that's $2 less than a comparable national organic brand.

Best Produce to Buy Organic

The fruits and vegetables below are among those most likely to contain trace levels of pesticides, so consider buying organic when possible.

Apples · Potatoes · Lettuce · Cherries · Bell Peppers · Strawberries · Celery · Spinach · Carrots · Nectarines · Peaches

Skip Organics and Save Money

These are the top five fruits and top five vegetables least likely to contain trace levels of pesticides, so feel free to buy conventional.

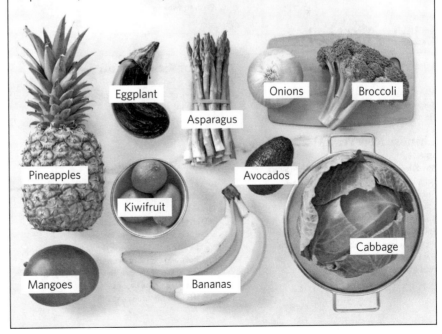

Eggplant · Asparagus · Onions · Broccoli · Pineapples · Kiwifruit · Avocados · Cabbage · Mangoes · Bananas

Menu Index

A topical guide to all the menus that appear in Cooking Light Annual Recipes 2009.
See page 419 for the General Recipe Index.

Simple Suppers

Meal Makeover Menu 1 *(page 19)*
serves 4
Smothered Steak Burgers
Shoestring Fries with Garlicky Dijon Mayo
Beer or iced tea

Meal Makeover Menu 2 *(page 20)*
serves 5
Romaine salad with shredded carrots
Cajun Red Beans and Rice
Garlic breadsticks

Meal Makeover Menu 3 *(page 21)*
serves 4
Mixed greens salad with toasted pine nuts
Double-Mushroom Pizza
Red grapes

Meal Makeover Menu 4 *(page 21)*
serves 6
Chili Pasta with Beans
Steamed broccoli
Corn bread muffins

Meal Makeover Menu 5 *(page 22)*
serves 4
Green tea
Shrimp and Broccoli Fried Rice with Toasted Almonds
Sliced mango and kiwi

Meal Makeover Menu 6 *(page 22)*
serves 4
Hummus with carrot sticks
Falafel Pitas
Greek yogurt with honey and toasted walnuts

Meal Makeover Menu 7 *(page 23)*
serves 4
Buttermilk Oven-Fried Chicken with Coleslaw
Dinner rolls

Soup and Sandwich Menu *(page 44)*
serves 8
Moroccan Pumpkin Soup
Warm pear and cheese sandwiches
Orange segments

Hearty Weeknight Supper Menu
(page 55)
serves 4
Balsamic Pork with Shallots
Roasted Brussels sprouts
Brown rice
Pinot noir
Vanilla low-fat ice cream with caramel sauce and
    toasted slivered almonds

Season's Bounty Menu *(page 86)*
serves 4
Shrimp Salad with Blood Oranges and Slivered Fennel
Minted pea soup
Sparkling water
Fresh strawberries with crème fraîche

Soup and Salad Menu *(page 130)*
serves 6
Summer Caesar Salad
Asparagus soup
Sauvignon blanc
Raspberries topped with whipped cream

Family Fare Menu *(page 164)*
serves 4
Grilled Spice-Rubbed Whole Chicken
Tomato-basil pasta salad
Grilled zucchini slices
Iced mint tea
Greek yogurt with blueberries

Casual Mexican Meal Menu *(page 183)*
serves 6
Grilled Fiesta Shrimp
Glazed grilled pineapple
Corn tortillas
Margaritas
Mango sorbet

Simple Steak Supper Menu *(page 204)*
serves 4
Beef Tenderloin Steaks with **Lemon-Rosemary Salt**
Mashed potatoes sprinkled with cracked black pepper
Steamed haricots verts or green beans
Zinfandel
Pound cake with fresh berries

Global Kitchen

Indian Inspiration Menu *(page 27)*
serves 7
Mixed Vegetable and Rice Pilaf
Yogurt-marinated chicken
Naan bread

Chinese New Year Menu *(page 35)*
serves 8
Stir-Fried Shrimp with Garlic and Chile Sauce
Long Life Noodles
Stir-Fried Bok Choy and Lettuce with Mushrooms
Chinese Potstickers
Spicy Sweet-and-Sour Chicken
Salt-Baked Chicken
Pickled Spiced Cucumber, Carrots, and Daikon
Double Mango Pudding
Green tea
Assorted beers and wines

Flavor Fiesta Menu *(page 114)*
serves 4
Grilled Flank Steak with Avocado Relish
Black beans and rice
Mango wedges
Mexican beer
Flan

Meze Menu *(page 192)*
serves 8
Eggplant with Capers and Red Peppers
Tzatziki
Bulgur, Mint, and Parsley Salad
Bread Salad with Mint and Tomatoes
Beet and Arugula Salad with Kefalotyri
Artichoke and Eggplant Skewers
Spiced Chicken Skewers with Lemon Vinaigrette
Lamb-Stuffed Grape Leaves
Mussels with Tomatoes and Dill

New Twist on Chicken Menu
(page 203)
serves 4
Egyptian-Spiced Chicken
Currant couscous
Wilted fresh spinach
Iced mint tea
Seasonal figs with crème fraîche

Mediterranean Plate Menu *(page 247)*
serves 3
Panzanella Salad
Simple seared scallops
Fettuccine tossed with olive oil
Sauvignon blanc
Lemon sorbet

Casual Entertaining

Special Occasion

Recipe Title Index

An alphabetical listing of every recipe title that appeared in the magazine in 2009.
See page 419 for the General Recipe Index.

Month-by-Month Index

A month-by-month listing of every food story with recipe titles that appeared in the magazine in 2008. See page 419 for the General Recipe Index.

General Recipe Index

A listing by major ingredient and food category for every recipe that appeared in the magazine in 2009.

HOW TO USE IT AND WHY Glance at the end of any *Cooking Light* recipe, and you'll see how committed we are to helping you make the best of today's light cooking. With chefs, registered dietitians, home economists, and a computer system that analyzes every ingredient we use, *Cooking Light* gives you authoritative dietary detail like no other magazine. We go to such lengths so you can see how our recipes fit into your healthful eating plan. If you're trying to lose weight, the calorie and fat figures will probably help most. But if you're keeping a close eye on the sodium, cholesterol, and saturated fat in your diet, we provide those numbers, too. And because many women don't get enough iron or calcium, we can also help there, as well. Finally, there's a fiber analysis for those of us who don't get enough roughage.

Here's a helpful guide to put our nutrition analysis numbers into perspective. Remember, one size doesn't fit all, so take your lifestyle, age, and circumstances into consideration when determining your nutrition needs. For example, pregnant or breast-feeding women need more protein, calories, and calcium. And men older than 50 need 1,200mg of calcium daily, 200mg more than the amount recommended for younger men.

IN OUR NUTRITIONAL ANALYSIS, WE USE THESE ABBREVIATIONS:

sat	saturated fat	**CHOL**	cholesterol
mono	monounsaturated fat	**CALC**	calcium
poly	polyunsaturated fat	**g**	gram
CARB	carbohydrates	**mg**	milligram

Daily Nutrition Guide

	WOMEN AGES 25 TO 50	WOMEN OVER 50	MEN OVER 24
Calories	2,000	2,000 or less	2,700
Protein	50g	50g or less	63g
Fat	65g or less	65g or less	88g or less
Saturated Fat	20g or less	20g or less	27g or less
Carbohydrates	304g	304g	410g
Fiber	25g to 35g	25g to 35g	25g to 35g
Cholesterol	300mg or less	300mg or less	300mg or less
Iron	18mg	8mg	8mg
Sodium	2,300mg or less	1,500mg or less	2,300mg or less
Calcium	1,000mg	1,200mg	1,000mg

The nutritional values used in our calculations either come from The Food Processor, Version 7.5 (ESHA Research), or are provided by food manufacturers.

Credits

Karen Ansel, MS, RD
John Ash
Melanie Barnard
Heather Bauer, RD
Lisa Bell
Alison Bing
Cassandra Blohowiak
David Bonom
Elisa Bosley
Toni Brogan
Barbara Seelig Brown
Dan Buettner
Jaime Harder Caldwell, MA, RD
Maureen Callahan, RD
Viviana Carballo
Melanie J. Clarke
Martha Condra
Kathryn Conrad

Adam Cooke
Lorrie Hulston Corvin
Greg Drescher
Jim Eber
Victoria Pesce Elliott
Maria Everly
Efisio Farris
Josh Feathers
Charlotte Fekete
Roy Finnamore
Nathan Fong
Caroline Ford
Laurent Gras
Anissa Helou
Clif Holt
Jill Silverman Hough
Lia Huber
Nancy Hughes
Raghavan Iyer
Bill Jamison

Cheryl Jamison
Elizabeth Jardina
David Joachim
Barbara Kafka
Emily Kaple
Holly V. Kapherr
Kathleen Kanen
Elizabeth Karmel
Jeanne Kelley
John Kessler
Jamie Kimm
Viana La Place
Sissy Lamerton
Barbara Lauterbach
Joseph Lenn
Karen Levin
Alison Lewis
Jeffery Lindenmuth
Susan Herrmann Loomis
Becky Luigart-Stayner
Karen MacNeil

Deborah Madison
Donata Maggipinto
Tasia Malakasis
Ivy Manning
Jennifer Martinkus
Debby Maugans
James McNair
Tory McPhail
Kate Merker
Jackie Mills, MS, RD
Diane Morgan
Eunice Mun
Joan Nathan
Marion Nestle, PhD, MPH
Liz Neumark
Rose Nguyen
Cynthia Nims
Kana Okada
Molly O'Neill
Jean Patterson
Laraine Perri
Marge Perry

James Peterson
Michelle Powers
Sara Quessenberry
Amy Riolo
Eric Ripert
Anthony Rosenfeld
Michael Ruhlman
Brett Ryder
Amelia Saltsman
Suvir Saran
Mark Scarbrough
Sara Schneider
Robert Schueller
Lauri Short
Martha Rose Shulman
Ellen Silverman
Marie Simmons
Marcia Whyte Smart
Kim Sunée
Elizabeth J. Taliaferro

Corinne Trang
Julie Upton, MS, RD
Gary Vaynerchuck
Sara Vigneri
Carole Walter
Robyn Webb
Mary-Ellen Weinrib
Bruce Weinstein
Joanne Weir
Anne Willan
Walter Willett, MD, PhD
Anna Williams
Debra Williams
Faith Willinger
Mike Wilson
Laura Zapalowski